国家社科基金
GUOJIA SHEKE JIJIN HOUQI ZIZHU XIANGMU
后期资助项目

袁同礼年谱长编

Yuan Tongli: A Chronicle

四

雷　强　撰

中华书局
ZHONGHUA BOOK COMPANY

一九五〇年　五十六岁

一月六日

李芳馥覆函先生,谈平馆上海办事处、个人前途等事。

守公尊鉴:

十二月四日手示转到,祗悉一是。公远在海外犹时时以馆事为念,想一生心血所在,无时不欲发扬而光大之。但现时国内一切维新,出版工作亦不能例外,所编一九四九年英文《季刊》一部分稿件皆成废纸,一九四八年英文《季刊》在上海解放前印好未能邮寄,解放后由军管会全部封存。虽公及子明兄处又海外预约各家皆无法照寄,来函亦未能复,将来究应如何办理,想总馆必有以善其后。此后,无论编印何种刊物皆须适合国策,现时中央人民政府下设教育部、文化部,图书馆属文化部文物局,将来想必计划出版新书刊目录等类刊物,目前尚非其时。闻政府深盼我公归国继续主持国立北京图书馆,公若归不独为本馆贺,亦为中国全国图书馆事业贺也。办事处存书业已北运一节系传闻之误,但现正在清理装箱北运中,限本月内办理完毕。办事处正式撤销,宝庆路房屋及傢具等大约由森老主持之古物管理委员会接收。关于办事处被接管经过,前曾上一函报告一切,接管后经费由上海市高等教育处担负,馆务尚能部分进行。去岁七八月间,王有三兄曾来函促王育伊兄及馨北上工作,因此间事前曾接北方来信,有守公归来定有刘老老进大观园之感之语(王子访、王念伦已被斗争出馆)。故提出若干具体问题,如职位、薪津、住房、馆中新组织等,复函请答,但无一字回音,约一月后又来信再嘱北上,同人再申前请亦未得复。去年十月间,郑西谛(现任文物局局长)决定偕赵斐云同中央其他人员来华东接收中央所属各机关,同时撤销办事处。此一关系同人切身问题事件,馆方竟无一字通知,郑、赵二位于上月到沪,郑君热忱说服同人北上,盛意可感。颂声兄一切简单,去京可无问题;育伊兄因家事,坚不欲北上;馨则因北京房荒严重,住屋无着,全家路费、添装冬衣及重新组织家庭须巨额现款,无力担负,现时北上实不可能。但若馆中不准给假,失业后在现状下再就业,万分不易,然此亦无可奈何之事。处大时代,个人原不足轻重也。据郑西谛云,国际出版品交换处将由北京图书馆接收,移京继续办理,若果成事实,则将来定感上海有特设一办事处之必要。他日再起炉灶,重觅房屋,必大不易。馆方此举来日当悔,我公若在国内,一切当另成一局面也。中央大学已改名为南京大学,中央图书馆名称尚未更改,将来是否仍为国立或改属地方,亦未决定。蒋慰堂现在香港,来函叫苦,托人疏通,俾能返国。据人云,纵能归来,欲复员中央图书馆,不可能也。肃此,敬请双安。弟妹统此问好。

后学李馨吾上

一九五零年一月六日

〔University of Chicago Library, Yuan T'ung-li Papers, Box 2〕

按:翌年,李芳馥调任上海市文物管理委员会,曾任图书整理处主任,1952 年 7 月,担任上海图书馆首任馆长。

一月十日

熊式一覆函先生,请与国会图书馆、加州大学(洛杉矶分校)联系汇寄书款细节,并告年幼子女已来英团圆。

守和吾兄:

大示敬悉。国会图书馆之款八十元,尚未寄到,望代一询。如尚未寄出,即请改寄费君收,附函乞代交。如已寄出,望示弟何时寄出?加州大学之百十元,已来函接洽,□已覆书,想下月可汇来,弟已请勿汇英镑。唐笙女士顷来函谓已迁居 17 Prospect street, Great Neck, N. Y.,不知前承代寄衣服可转到否,念念。弟之四小女及五小儿均于年内来英,在赣湘粤展转半年,果可出险,至为庆幸。知注顺闻,尚请俪福。

弟式顿首

一月十日

内子率小儿女各叩。

〔University of Chicago Library, Yuan T'ung-li Papers, Box 4〕

按:"费君"应指费成武(1914—2001),江苏吴江人,1930 年入中央大学艺术系,从徐悲鸿学习绘画,1946 年与张倩英(1914—
2003)、张安治、陈晓南等四人赴英深造,后与张倩英结为伉俪。
唐笙(1922—2016),上海人,1942 年上海圣约翰大学经济系毕
业,1944 年赴英国留学,时应在联合国总部任同声传译员,1951
年回国。

一月十九日

王重民致函先生,请速归国并告知新增重要馆藏。

> 守和吾师道鉴:

> 去冬曾作一长禀,请师即作归计,并称最好能由欧洲经苏联返国。
久未奉来谕,不知决计如何? 如不能由苏联归来,则最好能将善本带
回,但此事在未与美国恢复邦交以前,似亦难办。因生不知那边情况,
请一切酌量,总之,回国之期,愈早愈好!

> 刻馆中正在讨论组织法,因今年要把馆中组织弄好负责人及职工
聘定。现有职工 158 人,1950 年已批准再增 104 人。现只恨房舍不够
用耳。

> 西谛、斐云往宁、沪接收各个国立文教机关,乘机买了瞿氏铁琴铜
剑楼藏书三〇二种,赠送五十二种。又购顾千里批校金石拓片 1200
种,宋元本十余种。其余,适园、旧山楼诸名名家,各有所获。嘉业堂
剩余,不久也可归吾馆。朱桂老东西已都归吾馆。(故宫殿本书及方
志亦可挑一份来,只恨无处可容,又怕叔平先生不痛快,尚未动手。)

> L. C.所欠三百十一元,最好仍由美领馆转拨,否则请子明兄领了,
存在 Riggs 银行生名下,但汇来北京更好。因生正在买一处房子,尚
欠四五百元,愈快愈好,请代催。专此,即请钧安!

> > 生重民顿首

> > 1950 一月十九日

> 吾师所作善本书目补编稿,请速速寄来。又及。

> > 〔袁同礼家人提供〕

按:"适园"即南浔张均衡(1872—1927)旧藏;"旧山楼"即常熟赵
宗建(1825—1900)旧藏。

一月

先生致信金问泗。〔《金问泗日记》下册,页 990〕

　　按：此信于 2 月 1 日送达。

二月二日

王重民致函先生，请代向国会图书馆催款以便在京购房。

　　守和吾师道鉴：

　　　　半月前上一信，称买定一所房子，亟需款。三年前售与 L. C. 书款，尚未领到，请代催。领出后，一可代存华府 Nat. Riggs Bank 生名下，则可在此间用支票支取。（每次只能支五十元）二请一直汇来北京。购房定钱已付，三月底非有钱不可，请千万代催为感。专此，即请旅安！

　　　　　　　　　　　　　　　　　　　　　　　　生重民顿首
　　　　　　　　　　　　　　　　　　　　　　　　二月二日

〔University of Chicago Library, Yuan T'ung-li Papers, Box 3〕

二月四日

先生撰写一份备忘录，向中基会申请拨付平馆购买英美期刊购书款。

Memo Re Grant to the National Library of Peiping

　　At the annual meeting of the Board of Trustees of the China Foundation held in the fall of 1949, a grant of ＄5,000 was made to the National Library of Peiping.

　　It appeared that only the first installment of ＄1,250 had been made in the spring of 1949. According to Mr. C. M. Wang, the Acting Director, our subscriptions to American and British periodicals for 1949 have not yet been paid. Nor has he placed periodical subscriptions for 1950. A number of complaints have been received from the publishers.

　　It is hoped that the China Foundation will arrange to pay the other three installments of the grant of ＄5,000 made in 1949, so that a minimum number of periodical subscriptions can be continued by the Library without causing any serious break of its valuable file of scientific journals.

　　Respectfully submitted,

　　　　　　　　　　　　　　　　　　　　　　　　T. L. Yuan
　　　　　　　　　　　　　　　　　　　　　　　　Director

February 4, 1950

〔台北"中央研究院"近代史研究所档案馆,〈中华教育文化基金董事会〉,馆藏号 502-01-03-010,页 15〕

按:此件为打字稿,落款处为先生签名,此份备忘录附于翌日致胡适信中。

二月五日

先生致信胡适,询问中基会上年资助平馆款项拨付情况,并请考虑资助编辑计划。

适之先生:

近闻中基会不日举行年会,未识孟麟、咏霓诸先生已到纽约否?为念。关于补助平馆之款,上年似仅拨付 1250 元,如良才先生已抵纽约,务请向其一询,附上说明一纸,即希交其一阅是荷。同礼前向罗氏基金申请补助,候两月之久仍未通过。兹奉上简单编辑计划三份,未识中基会对于困在美国之学者能否赐予补助如有三千五百元即可敷用。如承赞助,尤为心感。近接有三来信,仍嘱早日返平,但观目前局势,如能在美可以维持,仍拟在此暂留也。尊处如有《人民日报》,并盼赐寄一阅,至盼。专此,敬候著祺。

同礼谨启
二月五日

〔台北"中央研究院"近代史研究所档案馆,〈中华教育文化基金董事会〉,馆藏号 502-01-03-010,页 14 〕

按:"良才先生"即叶良才,广东梅县人,1925 年岭南大学毕业,获商学士学位[1],后长期在中基会工作,时负责会中财务。胡适在落款处标注" $3,600.00 HS."

二月八日

Joseph F. Ford 覆函先生,感谢帮助校阅凤凌日记译稿,并约晚饭。

8th February 1950

Dear Dr Yuan,

Thank you very much for your letter clearing up many points about

---

[1]《私立岭南大一览》,1932 年 3 月,页 299。

my translation which had been obscure to me. You must wonder why I have not replied earlier. As a matter of fact, my office work has been rather heavy in the last month, but I have now taken up the translation again and am making progress little by little. In quite a short time I hope to be able to put the whole work in your hands. I do appreciate very much indeed your kind offer to read it through for me, as I am conscious that apart from the names which I have not identified there are also weaknesses in many passages of the translation. It is sometimes hard to grasp the meaning of the Chinese text.

If you have had any difficulty about consulting the English periodicals at the B.I.S. reading room, please let me know. I understand that the library has been transferred to the Embassy Annexe at 3100 Massachusetts Ave.

If you need an introduction there, I shall be glad to arrange to take you in at almost any time. It would be quite convenient for me since the Annexe is only a stone's throw from my office.

I have just read an article by Dr. Needham on scientific exchanges between Asia and the West and he has much to say in it about China. In case you have not read it I am sending you separately a copy of the number of "Asian Horizon" which contains the article.

If you should be free on Friday evening, 10th February, I shall appreciate it very much if you would have supper with me, possibly at the Peking restaurant, or any other place which would be more convenient to you. This would give me an opportunity to ask you about some difficult points in connection with Fung Ling's diary.

Yours sincerely

J. F. Ford

〔University of Chicago Library, Yuan T'ung-li Papers, Box 2〕

按：Joseph Francis Ford（1912－1993），英国外交官，本谱中译作"福特"，曾任英国驻华大使馆一等秘书，后将蒙古巴禹特氏凤凌日记（《游余仅志》）译成英文，题为 *An Account of England 1895—*

1896, by Fung Ling, Naval Attaché at the Imperial Chinese Legation in London, China Society Occasional Papers, No. 22 (London, 1983)。在序言中,福特提及先生对他的鼓励与帮助,尤其就日记中涉及清、英人士姓名多予辨识。该函为福特亲笔。

二月九日

胡适覆函先生,告知1949年中基会拨付平馆经费情况,并言暂无可能补助先生个人研究。

Feb. 9, 1950

守和兄:

一月五日信悉。

孟邻与咏霓都没有能赶到,故昨日(八日)的会已延至三月七日,但不知那时能足法定人数否(孟邻电告 JCRR 的公务使他须留到二月十五日左右)。

现叶良才兄已来纽约。尊函已与他看了。他说,平馆去年第二期之 $1,250 已拨付平馆留京沪办事处同人,似是为"应变"之用?我检中基会 Executive Committee 六月三日会议录,果有纪录,云平馆连修理费共 $5,400,已支付 $2,900,尚保留 $2,500。

尊函所提补助事,此时无人有权讨论,想能蒙原谅。我当留意此事,但现有机构只能 administer the investment of the Endowment Fund,而无动用款项之权也。

匆匆,敬祝大安。

弟胡适

"人民日报"九月以后未借得。

〔University of Chicago Library, Yuan T'ung-li Papers, Box 7〕

按:一月五日信,应为"二月五日信"。"尊函所提补助事",应指《西文汉学书目》(考狄书目续编)计划。

二月二十二日

金问泗致函先生。〔《金问泗日记》下册,页992〕

三月三日

罗光(罗马)覆函先生,赠诗集并询问先生有无徐光启的史料。

同礼先生惠鉴:

昨奉手示,浅薄拙作,谬索奖誉,徒增汗颜。然欣老乃我国现代之明哲,拙作之被见重或非无由矣。兹谨遵谕,付邮寄上,兼呈拙作《罗马晨钟》一册,以博一粲。惜近出版之第二诗集《海滨夕唱》尚未到罗马,他日收到后,亦将奉赠,以求教于先达也。《拜访兴老日记》固未刊印,《益世周刊》所刊者仅两篇,《拜访兴老记》此两文大俱转抄于传内,故无寄阅之价值。方豪神父留在台湾,惟久无信来,不悉近状若何? □□先生已康复,近已到馆办公矣。光欲作《徐文定公传》,惜史料不易得,不知尊处藏有方豪神父所著《徐光启》否? 如有,千祈借读一次,不宣。谨祝旅安。

末铎罗光谨复

一九五〇年三月三日

因不知尊号,恕直称名。

按:罗光(1911—2004),湖南衡阳人,神父,早年赴罗马,在梵蒂冈传信大学学习,获多个博士学位,长期担任“国民政府驻梵蒂冈使馆”教务顾问。“兴老”指陆征祥,“拙作”应指其所著《陆征祥传》,1949 年香港真理学会初版,《罗马晨钟》(圣保禄会印书馆)、《海滨夕唱》(新生出版社,1950 年)均为其诗集。1953 年,罗光所著《徐光启传》由香港公教真理学会出版。

三月四日

胡适致函先生,告中基会会期并请代查光绪朝历任浙江学政。

守和兄:

孟邻兄已到,咏霓兄未到,故中基会董事仅到七人,故须改在美京开会,以便全体到司徒大使病室内开会几分钟,以足法定人数。我与叶良才兄拟三月六日下午到京,住 Dupont Plaza(在 Dupont Circle)。甚盼能与兄一谈。兄向罗氏基金之请求,最近有结果否? 望兄留一字在 Dupont Plaza(Hotel)见告,或打电话见告。至感至感! 兄的原说帖及致我信,已交叶良才兄了。

匆匆,敬问双安。

弟适之

一九五十,三,四夜

倘兄去图书馆,乞代查光绪初年至十三年的浙江学政是何人。十三年是瞿鸿禨。十四年是潘衍桐。至感！

〔University of Chicago Library, Yuan T'ung-li Papers, Box 7〕

按：先生收到此函后即致信瞿同祖，询问光绪朝历任浙江学政事。王重民致函先生，谈馆内所购英文期刊，并请代催恒慕义将此前国会图书馆所欠购书款尽早汇华。

守和吾师道鉴：

三月三日电报奉悉。1949 年欠 Faxon 款已还清，1950 年的正在去订。但数月以来，接到美国期刊极少，1950 年份几于还没有接到，至于接不到原因，尚不大明白，已向 Faxon 去信询问。

毓铨夫妇已抵京，藉吾师已决定返国，极为欣慰，起程愈早愈好。寄 L. C. 善本书一百箱，若能带回，不知方便不方便。又前要美国官书、地图之类，想积压已不少？可否转运来，或带来？闻现在运费极贵，如能运回，共约需用运费若干？如能估计，请告知。虽说现在不一定能有这项运费，但我们可以试试看！

前连去两信，请师询问恒先生，将生二三年前让与该馆之图书欠费三百十二多元寄来。刻因需款甚急，请再代催为祷！专此，即请旅安！

生重民顿首
三月四日

帝俄旧档译稿，已登记，不能寄出，前已由子刚兄奉告矣。又及。

〔袁同礼家人提供〕

三月十日

先生致信胡适，谈《西文汉学书目》（考狄书目续编）及胡适西文著作目录编辑等事，并附抄录《潘衍桐列传》。

适之先生：

编辑书目事，诸承赞助，感何可言。兹已着手内中关于我国学者之著作，希望搜集全目。关于先生之著作，前有 Delafield 先生编一简目，如渠仍住在楼下，盼托其寄下一阅，三五日后即奉还也。关于补助费之发给，似可援中基会前例，每季拨发一次，即希尊酌。关于浙江学政，仅查出《潘衍桐列传》一文，其《拙余堂诗文集》及《缉雅堂诗话》，遍查国内各图书馆书目，似均未入藏，浙江书局书目亦未列入，余容觅到,再行奉闻。专此,敬候著祺。

同礼叩

三月十日

附《潘氏列传》,又致叶良才先生一函,请面交。

〔台北胡适纪念馆,档案编号 HS-US01-061-024〕

按:Eugene L. Delafield(1907—2001),美国善本书商,20 世纪 40 年代曾与胡适同住纽约 81 街 104 号公寓,自此开始收集胡适在美国发表的文章、讲演稿,时住纽约 82 街 1790 号公寓 704 室,后与先生一同汇编《胡适先生西文著作目录》。该信附《潘衍桐列传》抄件两页,为先生亲笔。①

先生致信叶良才,此前收到王重民电报并与胡适商谈决定依其请求向平馆大通银行账户付款。

March 10, 1950

Dear Mr. Yip:

I have had two letters from Mr. C. M. Wang asking me to cable him as soon as the balance of ＄2,500 from the Foundation is credited to the account of the Library in the Chase National Bank.

I have had a talk a with Dr. Hu about this matter. He thought that the Treasurers can be authorized to issue the check. May I therefore request you to let me know after you have sent the check to the Chase National Bank, Park Avenue Branch, for the credit of the Library, so that I can cable to Mr. Wang to this effect.

When you come down to Washington again, please give me a ring (TR-1638), as we want to entertain you here.

Yours sincerely

T. L. Yuan

〔台北"中央研究院"近代史研究所档案馆,〈中华教育文化基金董事会〉,馆藏号 502-01-03-009,页 62〕

熊式一致函先生,告知尚未收到加州大学书款并略谈北京师范大学近况。

---

① 台北胡适纪念馆,档案编号 HS-US01-006-001。

守和吾兄有道：

　　月前收到手教及支票时，此即以航空小简作覆，至今尚未达到，致劳悬念，甚歉甚怅。加州大学圕亦有月余未回弟之信，故日前又曾去函询问寄款之事，现在只盼此简及日前寄加州之函可递到也。傅仲嘉兄自政府改变后即被推为师大教务会主席，小女德兰不时有简禀寄英，但北平及各大学之新气象则得诸他人，然亦仅闻一二，实难窥全豹也。前闻梅月涵兄云适之先生及在美之同仁拟组织"自由中国"，不审其近况如何。今者国联将拒蒋而纳北平新政府之代表团，则台湾之命运即将完毕矣。余再叙，即颂俪福。

弟熊式一顿首
三月十日

〔University of Chicago Library, Yuan T'ung-li Papers, Box 3〕

　　按："加州大学圕"应指莫余敏卿所在之洛杉矶分校图书馆，该所似购入了熊式一所藏明活字本《锦绣万花谷》。"傅仲嘉"即傅种孙（1898—1962），字仲嘉，江西高安人，数学家、教育家，1920年毕业于北京高等师范学校并留校任教，1945年曾赴英考察，1947年回国担任北平师范学院数学系教授。熊德兰（1924—2009）为熊式一长女，1948年8月由牛津回国，时在北京师范大学任教。该函以航空信方式寄送，熊式一在信封背面注"牛津　海伏山房熊简"，其中"海伏山房"即Heyford Hill House。

三月十三日

瞿同祖覆函先生，告知清光绪年间浙江学政情况。

守和先生左右：

　　别来时深倾企。昨奉大札，经查先文慎自订年谱（见长沙瞿氏家乘，哥大中文圕有此书），任浙江学政系光绪十一年至十四年。因前任学政病故出缺，故于乙酉六月即行到任。据年谱"三月十五日奉命简放浙江学政。是年更换学政，本在八月朔。因浙学刘廷枚病故出缺，蒙恩特简……六月到任，七月录科。"前任学政刘廷枚，经查民国杭州府志，其履历如下：江苏元和人，同治戊辰进士，光绪十年以国子监祭酒任（卷一八公署——学政题名碑）。至于后任潘衍桐则为：广东南海人，同治乙丑进士，光绪十四年以左春坊右庶子任（仝上）。

以上各条想皆先生所欲详知者,故一一摘录,以供参考。专此奉复,敬请道安。

后学瞿同祖拜启

三月十三日

〔台北胡适纪念馆,档案编号 HS-MS01-006-001〕

按:瞿同祖(1910—2008),湖南长沙人,历史学家,时在哈佛大学中国政治经济研究室从事研究,其祖父为晚清大学士瞿鸿禨(1850—1918),谥文慎。"七月录科"有批注——(即科试?);信尾部标注有光绪元年(1875)至光绪十四年冬(1888)历任浙江学政,自胡瑞澜至潘衍桐,此两处皆为胡适亲笔。该函于 3 月 15 日送达先生处。

三月十五日

谭卓垣覆函先生,就合作编纂 A Comprehensive Bibliography on China for the Last 50 Years 的范围、体例、时间跨度以及已完成期刊篇目情况、财力支持等方面给予意见和陈述。

University of Hawaii

Honolulu, T. H.

March 15, 1950

Dear Dr. Yuan:

Many thanks for your letter of March the 9th. It was read with great interest and enthusiasm. I am greatly impressed by what you have been doing. It seems like an excellent project. Perhaps if we put our heads together, we may produce something very useful. In the following lines I am trying to tell you my plan for the Bibliography and what I have been doing these years.

General plan: A COMPREHENSIVE BIBLIOGRAPHY ON CHINA FOR THE LAST 50 YEARS. This includes books and periodical literature on China in all languages (Chinese and Japanese). But since Chinese and Japanese books are not fully available in this country, it seems logical to begin with Western materials first (At least we Chinese want to find out what other people have done in Chinese studies). This Bibliography will be arranged according to subject (I have worked out a definite scheme) with a general index of authors and sub-subject matter. Under each subject will be listed all books and important articles in chronological order with special emphasis on scholarly items indicated by book-review excerpts and annotations.

Period covered: The year 1921 was thought to be a good starting point for the reason that it could be a continuation of Cordier's *Bibliotheca Sinica*. But the arrangement in Cordier is so inconvenient that most of users prefer to have it revised. At the suggestion of William Hung, the years 1895 – 1945 was adopted (The ending of the first Sino-Japanese War to the ending of the Second Sino-Japanese War). However, there is sufficient good argument for the period starting with 1901 and ending in 1950. In fact, this seems to be a better choice for the reason that we can bring the material up-to-date.

What has been done: I started working on this Bibliography in 1947. Due to the fact that I have been tied up with both teaching and library work (with no full-time assistant), the progress is rather slow. So far, I have finished indexing 36 sets of periodicals in about 8,000 cards. There are quite a number of periodicals which I want to include but unfortunately the U. H. library does not have them. In addition to the above more than 2,500 titles of books have been listed with book-review excerpts on. This kind of work takes a lot of time. Averagely only 10 to 15 book reviews are read per day including copying. With the exception of reviews in German, I think I have covered 70 percent of the important book reviews. What remains to be done is the listing of titles, which is comparatively easy.

Financial Support: Personally, I don't think we have to worry about publisher. William Hung told me that Harvard-Yenching Institute would be willing to publish such bibliography. Or else we can approach either the American Council of Learned Societies or the Rockefeller Foundation. But our urgent need at present is financial backing for clerical help and typists. It would be an excellent idea to present our project to the International Conference on Bibliography and ask for appropriation of subsidies for this work.

Proposition: A Comprehensive Bibliography on China in all languages (1901–1950). This Bibliography will be comprised in 4 parts: (1) In English, French and German languages; (2) In other European and Central Asian languages; (3) in Chinese languages with English translations; (4) In Japanese with English translations. If financial support is assured, the first two parts will be ready for publication by the end of 1951. Then we can proceed with parts 3 & 4. This is only my personal view about this project and I should like to hear your opinion and plan. I know occidental scholars are greatly interested in Part 3, but you and I would like to make a complete bibliography. If both of us agree on general principles, we can discuss details later.

Mr. Ho To-yuan is still in Canton and seems to be doing well. In his letter to me recently he did not say much for the fear of censorship. I am trying to ask him to do some buying for the U. H. library.

I am sure you have seen Skachkov's *Bibliography of Russian Books and Articles on China 1730–1930*. Fairbank's work which I have examined in mimeographed form deals with materials concerning modern China for the Harvard Program of Regional Studies. His work will be included in ours. Sometime in the future I am going to ask him for permission to quote his annotations. The Harvard University press has announced that this bibliography will be out sometime in March. We have already ordered a copy.

With best regards to you and your family.

Yours very sincerely,

C. W. Taam

〔University of Chicago Library, Yuan T'ung-li Papers, Box 1〕

按：A Comprehensive Bibliography on China for the Last 50 Years 即*China in Western Literature*（《西文汉学书目》）之最早题名，可

惜谭卓垣1956年病故,未能完成计划中的期刊部分。Mr. Ho To-yuan 即何多源;*Bibliography of Russian Books and Articles on China 1730-1930* 即俄苏汉学家 П. Е. Скачков(Petr E. Skachkov,1892-1964),本谱译作"斯卡奇科夫",编著的*Bibliografiia Kitaia; sistematicheskyi ukazatel' knig i zhurnal' nykh statei o Kitaie na russkom yazyke, 1730-1930*,1932年列宁格勒国家社会经济出版社初版,1948年美国学术团体理事会刊行影本。Fairbank's work 即费正清与刘广京合编的*Modern China：a bibliographical guide to Chinese works, 1898-1937*,1950年初版。

三月十六日

先生致信胡适,告其清光绪年间浙江学政情况。

　　适之先生:

　　　　前以《瞿文慎年谱》此间尚未入藏,曾函瞿同祖君,昨得其复函,特为奉上。又托友人将哥大所藏《搢绅全书》详细检查,附上清单,并乞尊阅是盼。如有其他资料,至希随时见示,当为搜集也。匆匆,敬候著祺。

　　　　　　　　　　　　　　　　同礼拜上

　　　　　　　　　　　　　　　　　三,十六

　　　　潘衍桐以后之学政

　　　　　　陈　彝　光绪十七年

　　　　　　徐致祥　光绪二十年

　　　　　　陈学芬　光绪二十三年

　　　　　　唐景崇　光绪二十四年

　　　　　　文　治　光绪二十五年

　　　　　　　　　〔台北胡适纪念馆,档案编号 HS-MS01-006-001〕

　　按:"陈学芬"即陈学棻(1837—1901),字桂生,安陆城关人,同治元年钦点翰林院庶吉士,后历任国史馆纂修、文渊阁校理等职,光绪二十三年调任浙江学政,主持该省乡试。

三月二十三日

先生致信德礼贤神父,感谢其寄赠《基督教入华史》第二、三卷,并请协助收集意大利文有关中国的文献,另已函请平馆寄送《图书季刊》中陈垣、向达的文章。

March 23, 1950

Dear Professor D. Elia:

I am most grateful to you for your letter of March 3rd and for your kindness in sending vol 2 & 3 of Ricci's works to the National Library at Peiping.

After looking over these volumes, I must once more express my great admiration and respect for your scholastic achievements. You have said the last word on the life and times of Ricci.

I want to thank you in particular for the extracts which you had sent to me. They are extremely useful to me, as I have been compiling a bibliography of books and periodical articles on China, to supplement Cordier's. In my efforts to include Italian titles, I have to ask your help and assistance. May I ask you to give me a list of the names of authors of works in Italian on China? With such a list, I can check up the title in Italian Catalogues.

The greatest difficulty is to obtain information about articles in periodicals and scientific journals. Is there any periodical index in Italy?

For your own articles, I hope you will give me a list indicating where they are published. If you have copies of the extracts to spare, please send me the same.

I am asking our Office in Peiping to send you the *Bulletin* containing Chen's article and the work by Hsiang Ta. Since Siberian railways have been running regularly, I presume that it would take less time to correspond with friends in China. If you need further information concerning Ricci, you may write to Mr. Wang Chung-min, the Acting Director, who will be glad to help you in any way he can.

With many thanks and best wishes for your success,

Yours sincerely,

T. L. Yuan

Kindly forward the enclosed letter to Prof. Tucci.

〔袁同礼家人提供〕

按：vol 2 & 3 应指 *Storia dell'introduzione del cristianesimo in Cina*
（《基督教入华史》），该件为录副。
先生致信 Giuseppe Tucci，告知将编纂有关中国研究的书目，请其寄送著述
清单尤其是期刊文章。

March 23, 1950

Dear Professor Tucci:

I have been on leave from my work in China and I have been
engaged in compiling a bibliography on China. In this bibliography, I
hope to include books and periodicals published since 1900.

For Italian titles and especially for your own writings to be included
in the bibliography, I have to rely on your help. I shall be much obliged to
you if you could give your advice and suggestions.

American libraries do not have a complete set of your writings. I
enclose a list of them taken from the card catalogues of various libraries.
Will you kindly add other titles, especially periodical articles, which are
not listed there? I am most anxious to list as complete information as
possible, and in this undertaking, I must ask for your assistance.

May I also trouble you to ask your publisher to send a complete
prospectus concerning your monumental work *Indo-Tibetica*. How many
volumes are there in the complete set? Are other volumes to appear in the
future?

With sincere thanks for your assistance,

Yours sincerely,

T. L. Yuan

〔袁同礼家人提供〕

按：Giuseppe Tucci（1894-1984），通译为朱塞佩·图齐，意大利藏
学家，1925 年至 1930 年以意大利驻印度外交使团成员身份，在印
度国家大学和加尔各答大学教授意大利文、中文，1929 年当选意
大利皇家学院院士，1930 年被聘为那不勒斯东方大学中国语言
文学首席教授，1932 年起担任罗马大学文学与哲学系印度和远
东宗教哲学教授。*Indo-Tibetica* 今译作《梵天佛地》，分为 4 卷，

分别于 1932 年、1933 年、1935 - 36 年和 1941 年出版。此件为录副。

三月二十四日

先生致信顾立雅,告正在编纂《西文汉学书目》(考狄书目续编),请教其发表期刊文章的篇目,并请在巴黎时代为探询《通报》的索引是否已经编制完成,代为留意欧洲年轻汉学家和他们的著述。

March 24, 1950

Dear Dr. Creel:

Mr. Tsien wrote me recently that you expect to spend your furlough in Europe. I hope that on your way to New York, you will stop at Washington in order to let me have the pleasure of seeing you.

I have recently been engaged in compiling a bibliography on China to serve as supplement to Cordier's. I enclose herewith a list of your writings and if there are any omissions, please give me the additional titles. For periodical articles, I have to reply on your help. May I ask you to be good enough to send me a list of these articles, indicating where they were published.

I used to read your articles in the *T'oung Pao* and I have been wondering whether any index to the *T'oung Pao* has ever been published. As far as I know, there are at least three indexes being prepared.

When you go to Paris, may I ask you to find out from the Société Asiatique whether the index to the *T'oung Pao* is now completed? I met the lady who did the indexing in 1945, but I have not had any further news.

If you could make notes on young sinological scholars in Europe as well as their publications and let me look over them after your return, I shall be most grateful.

With best wishes for your continued success,

Yours sincerely,

T. L. Yuan

〔袁同礼家人提供〕

按:此件为录副。

三四月间

先生汇美金拾元与何多源(广州),请其协助购买书报。

四月四日

顾立雅教授助理 June Work 覆函先生,前信到时顾立雅已远赴欧洲,但已通过航空信联系,根据本人意愿请略过 1934 年以前的出版书籍,另外就期刊文章可根据实际需求拣选,并将在巴黎代先生询问《通报》索引是否完成。

April 4, 1950

Dear Dr. Yuan:

Your letter of March twenty-fourth to Dr. Creel, enclosed with one to Mr. Tsien, arrived after Dr. Creel left for Europe; so, since I am taking care of Dr. Creel's correspondence during his absence, Mr. Tsien gave it to me. I transmitted your requests to Dr. Creel by air mail and have now received his answer.

I have made for you a list of his publications, beginning with the year 1934, because he has said in his letter: "As for my publications, nothing earlier than 1934 is any good. I'd prefer to have the earlier ones omitted." I suspect that some of the periodical articles included in my list may be useless for your purpose. You can probably tell from the titles if this is so. The two published in 1949 in People and United Nations World consist only of extracts from the book Confucius, the Man and the Myth.

Dr. Creel also says in his letter: "Please write Dr. Yuan that I'll do the best I can to get the information he wants in Paris."

I hope that you are well, and wish you every success. It is good to know that you are engaged in compiling a work so much needed in Chinese bibliography, and I certainly hope that your work is going well.

Sincerely yours,

June Work

〔袁同礼家人提供〕

按:顾立雅 1934 年之前出版的书籍似只有一种,名为 *Sinism: a*

study of the evolution of the Chinese world-view ,1929 年芝加哥出版。June Work,钱存训教授在其回忆录中将此位女士记作琼华,言其为人和善,对钱存训一家甚为照顾。①

四月八日

王重民覆函先生,退回先生前所汇美金二百元,并商洽平馆在美善本书运回等事。

守和吾师道鉴:

三月九日手谕,已由香港世圻兄转来,以前一信附有致斐云、稼轩信者则尚未接到。吾师所汇两百元,子明兄所汇一百元,均收到。唯该两佰元汇到上海,应先换成人民券,方能汇来北京。又因十一姊亦寄来伍百元,买房之费已有富余,因将吾师之两百元退回,请收到后代存Riggs 银行,写 C. M. Wang, Nat. Library, Peking, China 即可。现存折上只剩几毛钱,再加入两佰元,如有在美零用之处亦方便也。俄文译稿迄未寄上者,实因现在出版书籍,以观点为重,对于帝俄旧史料,更要善于批评,方为有用著作。否则不但无益,而且有害。即于吾师个人方面,亦是如此,即是发表材料有不正确处,于将来亦不好也。生窃念吾师研究工作,颇有兴趣,但研究时应特别注重观点,最好将材料带回,到北京后再继续研究,将来由科学院出版,较在美国出版更好也。现在出版事业极发达,较国民党统治时代,其数量已超过数十倍。国学季刊、燕京学报以及科学院各种专门刊物,已由新华书店承印,即均将恢刊。吾师著述完成后,一定极易出版也。在美寄存善本书,将来再运固好,但如果现在能运,便早日起运更好。即便不能直运天津,不知是否可运抵香港? 台湾解放,总在今年之内,惟不知在何月耳。当然,如早早解放,则搬运更容易也。为照顾台湾古物,可能有人与军队同时登陆,而且现在已有人在保护,一定没有损失。故寄美之书,若先期运到香港,更是一件大好事! 南京上海两办事处均已撤消,全部图书运回,颂声兄已来馆。馨吾、育伊转在上海古委会作事。但徐森老已被任为文物局文物处处长,日内北上,则李、王二君,或将仍来馆作事也。Faxon 去年欠费已开支票,想早已收到。如基金会真补了去年两季的,则 1950 年份即可继续订阅。唯美国重要杂志，久未收到，殆美政府有意扣留之故欤？若果如此，则订了亦收不到，不知可否在美找一代收处？英国杂志，即可续订（现已请到英镑八百镑外汇）。苏联方面，已订妥期刊 220 种，月报十几种，因太便宜，故均订双份。其他学术机关，已正式成立交换方式。唯蒙古、新疆等史料之在亚洲苏联者，尚未作正式交换耳。闻子明兄言，L. C.正在印卡片，吾馆新书卡片，现在需用八份，清写太难，在未能正式印卡片之前，在一二年内过渡时代，也想油印。请师调查一下，L. C.该印刷机是否在我国适用，所用底版成本如何？吾师如认为可用，归国时请带来一套。又吾师究竟与 L. C. 条约何时可满，何时可以回国？请先告知。L. C.善本书目，已印九卷，末一卷及附录俟吾师稿到后，即再付印。又恒先生来信，亦言及此事。北大出版组估单，前未寄出，日内可由李续祖寄去，请先告恒先生。即请旅安！

师母等统此问候。

生重民顿首

四月八日

请先答复：

1.吾师何时能回国？

2.印刷机（油印卡片）要多少钱？

3.基金会补去年两季补助费已存入银行否？

〔袁同礼家人提供〕

按：李续祖（1890—？），字晓宇，河北宛平人，历任北京大学预科教员、化学系讲师[1]，与程瀛章合著《化学小史》（商务印书馆《百科小丛书》），后曾长期负责北京大学出版部。

四月十日

McReid 致函先生，告知已将平馆购买的缩微阅片机运往天津大沽港。

April 10, 1950

Dear Mr. Yuan:

We enclose a copy of our ticket No. 57196 covering a Kodagraph Film Reader Model C which was shipped by freight via the steamship, S.

---

[1]《国立北京大学一览》，1934 年，页 363。

E. Pacific Transport Lines, to the National Library of Peiping, via Taku Bar and Tientsin.

If any further correspondence becomes necessary for the next shipment, please refer to me about the number.

Yours very truly,

Eastman Kodak Company

McReid

Export Sales Department

〔Rockefeller Foundation. Series 601: China; Subseries 601.R: China-
Humanities and Arts. Vol. Box 47. Folder 393〕

按:此为抄件。

谭卓垣覆函先生,认同前信合著书目的分工建议,并谈费正清与刘广京所编书目的侧重和起始时间。

University of Hawaii

Honolulu, T. H.

April 10, 1950

Dear Dr. Yuan:

Many thanks for your letter of March the 30th. It is perfectly agreeable to me that you will concentrate on titles in less known languages while I do those in English, French and German. It is very good of you to index those journals that are not found in the University of Hawaii library. This saves me a trip to the States.

Fairbank's Bibliography has two parts: one in European languages and the other in Chinese with English annotations. They deal chiefly with political, social, economic and intellectual aspects of modern China since 1898.

With best warm regards,

Yours cordially,

C. W. Taam

〔袁同礼家人提供〕

按:此件为打字稿,落款处为其签名。

四月十二日

福特致函先生,邀请十八日赴宴。

(Hobart 1340 extension 27)

12th April

Dear Professor Yuan,

  I wonder if you could have supper with me one evening next week at the 北京楼. Any evening would suit me, but I suggest Tuesday at 7 p. m. I have got a copy of 薛福成's diary and am finding it quite interesting.

Yours sincerely

J. F. Ford.

〔University of Chicago Library, Yuan T'ung-li Papers, Box 2〕

  按:薛福成(1838—1894),字叔耘,号庸庵,江苏无锡人,清后期外交家、洋务运动的主要领导者之一,其出访欧洲的日记,今通称作《出使英法义比四国日记》。该函为其亲笔。

四月十四日

先生致信法斯,告知接到运货通知并感谢洛克菲勒基金会对平馆的赞助。

April 14, 1950

Dear Dr. Fahs:

  With reference to my previous correspondence regarding the order for a Film Reader out of the balance of your grant, I have just received a letter dated April 10, 1950, from Eastman Kodak Company, copy of which is herewith enclosed.

  As you will note, the Reader has been shipped to China via the S. E. Pacific Transport Lines.

  May I avail myself of this opportunity to thank your Foundation once more for the great assistance which has been extended to us. We greatly appreciate your valuable help in various ways.

Yours very sincerely,

T. L. Yuan

Director

〔Rockefeller Foundation. Series 601: China; Subseries 601.R: China-Humanities and Arts. Vol. Box 47. Folder 393〕

　　　　　　按：此件为打字稿，落款处为先生签名。

先生致信谭卓垣，告知已开始为夏威夷大学缺藏期刊的文章做索引，请其寄送书目分类法，并转告 Davidson 夫人来信谈其中文著作译作目录的进展。

　　　　　　　　　　　　　　　　　　　123 B Street, S. E.

　　　　　　　　　　　　　　　　　　　Washington, D. C.

　　　　　　　　　　　　　　　　　　　April 14, 1950

Dear Dr. Taam:

　　Thank you so much for your letter of April 10th. I shall start indexing these journals that are not found in the University of Hawaii library. The lists which you kindly checked have been most useful.

　　If it would be convenient to you, I shall appreciate it if you could send me a copy of your classification scheme. I shall also send you new titles in English, French and German that come to my attention.

　　With regard to English translations of Chinese works, I have had the following reply from Mrs. Davidson:

　　"The work goes on and seems endless. I am now in the process of completing one phase which is in the proof-reading state.

　　The List is happily confined to translations from the Chinese into French, English and German. It includes all translations of approximately one hundred characters (including all poetry) and is thus extensive in scope. We have followed a subject classification, with some exceptions. The sections now in typescript are Classics, and Language and Literature.

　　Your friend who is contemplating a Japanese list has my admiration. Tell him courage and persistence, time and funds, are the essential ingredients for that dish. He will also need a good working staff, well mixed. The task of checking through the periodical literature is in itself a vast, time-consuming undertaking."

　　Her address is: 6 Glenbrook Avenue, Hamden, Conn. You may write to her for further information. I understand that her work is being supported by the American Council of Learned Societies.

　　With kindest regards,

Yours sincerely,

〔袁同礼家人提供〕

按：Mrs. Davidson 应指 1947 年曾与王重民合作尝试重编 *Encyclopedia Sinica* 的女士。[①] 该件为录副。

四月十七日

Chadbourne Gilpatric 致函先生，代法斯表示收到前信。

April 17, 1950

Dear Dr. Yuan:

　　As Mr. Fahs has just left for an extended trip in the Far East, I will acknowledge your letter of April 14. We are glad to know that the Film Reader has been shipped to China and your report of the fact brings to an end our formal interest in the transaction.

　　Although the present situation is a little discouraging for immediate expectations, I certainly hope the Reader will be put to good use and serve the important microfilm purposes which you have had in mind.

Sincerely yours,

Chadbourne Gilpatric

〔Rockefeller Foundation. Series 601: China; Subseries 601.R: China-Humanities and Arts. Vol. Box 47. Folder 393〕

四月十九日

何多源致函先生，告平馆人事、隶属情况及北京物价。

　　守和先生尊鉴：

　　广州解放后以事忙，迄未修函致候兴居，至以为歉。敝校学生人数由三千人减至五百人，经费困难。下学期能否维持，尚在未可知之数。有三兄函邀赴北京圖担任编纂参考书工作，待遇有小米六百斤，源现在考虑中。据京圖同人来函谓，王祖彝、王子访二人已去职，其余仍旧，代馆长为重民兄。现京圖隶属文化部文物局，部长沈雁冰，局长

---

① 雷强《普林斯顿大学图书馆藏王重民、孙念礼往来书札》，《精一文献》（微信公众号），2020 年 10 月 27 日。

郑振铎,局长之下有图书处长(未定人选)及博物处长(裴文中)。现京圖工作人员待遇由三担半小米至八担,办公费、事业费每月有小米二万二千斤。北京物价,小米每斤人民券一千一百元,猪肉每斤五千元,面粉每袋九万五千元,普通人家每人每月生活费约需小米一百五十斤。此间每日有北京《人民日报》阅读,故所知北京情形颇详。月前先生寄下美金拾元,现尚余陆元,应代购何物,敬乞示知为感。此请钧安。

后学何多源上

一九五〇四月十九日

〔University of Chicago Library, Yuan T'ung-li Papers, Box 2〕

按:该函实由香港寄出。

四月二十日

谭卓垣覆函先生,就合编书目的分类法、范围给予意见,希望与先生讨论并得出最终决定。

April 20, 1950

Dear Dr. Yuan:

Your letter of April the 14th was duly received and immediately I went through the Classification scheme again and have just finished typing it this morning. I hope you will run through it carefully and make suggestions and improvement. Its formulation has been based on all the materials on hand. As we go along, we may have some alterations and additional items. As a whole I must admit that the main divisions are rather arbitrary.

When you wrote me saying that Mrs. Davidson has been working on the English translations of Chinese and Japanese titles, I thought that Parts 3 & 4 of our proposed project has been covered by her party. From your last letter, I note that she only confines to translations from the Chinese into French, English and German. I am wondering whether or not she will include in her List much more than that.

What I propose to do in Parts 3 & 4 of our project is as follows: We want to compile a bibliography of Chinese and Japanese titles (books and periodical articles) which deal with Chinese studies. It will be work similar to that attempted by the *QUARTERLY BULLETIN OF CHINESE BIBLIOGRAPHY* but different from it in the respect that we only list items that have direct bearing on China. For example, we don't include all Chinese books dealing with history but only those having connection with Chinese history. The Harvard-Yenching Institute published two indices called *A BIBLIOGRAPHY OF ORIENTALOGICAL CONTRIBUTIONS IN……JAPANESE PERIODICALS*（①日本期刊三十八种中东方学论文篇目,②一百七十五种日本期刊中东方学论文篇目）. In our project we want to include also Japanese books on China or Chinese studies and have the authors romanized and the titles translated into English. I am sorry that I did not make it clear to you in my first letter. Such a project is a tremendous job which will need large appropriation of fund and quite large working staff. I wish you will take this up in the coming International Conference on Bibliography.

Enclosed I am sending you my drafted Classification for a Bibliography on China and also some samples for recording books and periodical articles which we have been using for our purpose. I sincerely invite your criticism.

With best regards,

Yours sincerely,

C. W. Taam

〔袁同礼家人提供〕

按:此件为打字稿,信中汉字及落款为谭卓垣亲笔。

德礼贤致函先生,告将方豪索取的《基督教入华史》第二、三卷暂寄先生处,请在台湾局势平稳时代为转投,并提供个人著述简表及意大利汉学家人名。

Roma, April 20th 1950

Dear doct. Yüan:

Fr. Fang Hao is writing to me from Formosa ("National" Taiwan University, Taiwan:台湾台北"国立"台湾大学) asking very earnestly to send him a copy of Vol. II and III of my Fonti Ricciane.

I was fortunate enough to have those copies be sent to him by my

Editor. But since things are not quiet in the neighboring of Formosa and might get worse in the near future, I thought it better to send them to your own address with the joining prayer to think of the best way of having them shipped to him when you will have an occasion of doing so. I trust you for this and in the mean-time I will write to Fang Hao to let him know. When the two books will reach you, please let me know it.

Your letter of March 23rd announced me that you had received the copies which I had sent you for yourself and the Peiping Central Library, and I am glad you were pleased with them. A great amount of work was requested for the achievement of them, and I hope they may be useful to future historians.

As for the names of authors of works in Italian on China, they are not so many. At random I give you some: Vacca Giovanni, Rosso, Allegra, Cracco, Bortone, Bertuccioli, Musso, Vannicelli. A full list of all my articles from 1912 to 1947 will be given in the coming ANNUARIO per l'anno accademico 1946-1947 of the University of Rome which is not out yet and which I do not know exactly when it will come out. When it comes, I will try to get a copy for you. You will find there even the periodicals where they were published. I do not know whether in Italy there is any periodical Index.

I must thank you very much for your generosity for my further information concerning Ricci. I will surely avail myself of it, since now I should work on Ricci's Correspondence, where may other questions come up. I thank you also for the *Bulletin* containing Chen's article and the work by Hsiang Ta, which you have asked for me and which I hope will receive in the near future.

I forwarded your letter to Prof. Tucci.

With my best regards.

Yours sincerely

P. D' Elia

〔袁同礼家人提供〕

按：方豪(1910—1980)，字杰人，浙江省杭县人，1922年入杭州天主教修道院攻读拉丁文，后入宁波圣保罗神学院升司铎，1935年晋升为神父，曾任浙江大学、复旦大学教授兼系主任、院长。

四月二十七日

先生致信王重民，请其为美国国会图书馆、英国图书馆协会周年纪念典礼分别准备赠品。

有三吾弟：

美国国会图书馆将举行一百五十周年纪念典礼，本馆应送一小中堂或其他赠品。前已函告，谅在办理之中。兹英国图书馆协会今夏将举行壹百周年纪念，已邀请丁濬君代表本馆出席。敝意本馆或图书馆协会应送一赠品，即希尊酌，径寄丁君转交是荷。(丁君住址：c/o Y. M. C. A., Glasgow. Scotland)。目下西伯利亚铁路想已畅通，寄欧包裹当可于三星期内寄到也。此颂，时祉。

同礼顿首

四月廿七日

〔谢欢副教授提供〕

按：1800年4月24日，美国国会图书馆成立。"英国图书馆协会今夏将举行壹百周年纪念"所指之事似应为1850年8月14日英格兰及威尔士通过《公共图书馆法》(Public Libraries Act)，规定以地方税收支持公共图书馆服务，并非指英国图书馆协会成立一百周年。Y. M. C. A.即基督教青年会(Young Men's Christian Association)。

五月四日

先生访胡适，晤谈。〔University of Chicago Library, Yuan T'ung-li Papers, Box 7〕

五月六日

胡适致函先生，请就胡适《书目与著作目》作凡例，并告知中基会批准资助先生个人的研究计划，另请代查光绪朝《鄞县志》。

守和兄：

前天晤谈，甚快慰。

关于我自己的"书目与著作目"，上次你说的范围——Sinology——使我感觉兴趣。我盼望你抄示 Cordier 原目的一二个例子，并请你自已拟一个条格,例如你的"新目"里"胡适"名下,你要列些什么著作,如何排列,——使我可以试作我上次提议的"胡适学术著作选目"。

又中基会通过的你的研究费三千六百元,原案是从七月一日起。如你需要早日开始支付,乞即通知我或叶良才兄。

内人上月大概已得护照签证,但搭伴或需一短时期。

匆匆,敬问双安。

弟胡适
五,六午

又有一事乞代查。国会圕有光绪三年的鄞县志刻成在光绪三年冬月,总修为陈恕、陈劢、徐时栋、董沛,乞代查原序例中说此次修志始于何时,共需多少年月,主持的鄞县知县是何姓名,学官(教官)是何姓名。

〔University of Chicago Library, Yuan T'ung-li Papers, Box 7〕

五月七日

颜复礼覆函先生,告知其尚未收到身处东柏林的小海尼士覆信,故先生此前属意的书籍暂时无法获取,并附上佛尔克、福兰阁著作目录。

7th May 1950

Dear Prof. Yuan:

In reply to your letter of the 4th April, I am sorry to have to inform you that my attempts to contact Dr. Haenisch-Berlin with a view to obtaining through him the publication required by you ("*Die internationalen Beziehungen im Zeitalter des Imperialismus*") have been unsuccessful, since my several letters directed to him have been left unanswered, presumably because as director of the Public Scientific Library, situated in the Russian sector of Berlin, he is not free in his correspondence. I will now try to obtain a copy of this publication by advertising for it in a special periodical and shall inform you of the result as soon as possible.

As to the bibliography, compiled by you, of books and articles on China, I shall be very glad to assist you in the field of German sinology. To begin with I am sending you to-day as printed matter two lists of the writings of German sinologues A. Forke and O. Franke; a photostat-copy of the first part of the bibliography of Franke's writings will soon follow, accompanied by a list of my own articles. The most prolific of all German sinologues is undoubtedly Wolfram Eberhard, residing in America since 1948; his address is now: University of California, Department of Social Researches, Berkeley. You can also write to my old friend Prof. Ferdinand Lessing, attached to the same University of California, Department of Oriental Languages, Berkeley 4; Lessing is originally a German born, but has become an American citizen in 1936. There is a third German sinologue residing now in America: Prof. Helmut Wilhelm at the university of Seattle, who is probably known to you from China.

In regard to the "Combined Indices to Shih Chi" I am much obliged to you that you have written to your office at Peiping to secure a copy of this work which is indispensable for my further research work and to mail it to me direct.

With many thanks for your assistance and kind regards,

Fr. Jäger

〔University of Chicago Library, Yuan T'ung-li Papers, Box 2〕

按：*Die internationalen Beziehungen im Zeitalter des Imperialismus* 通译作《帝国主义时代国际关系》，由苏联历史学家 Михаил Николаевич Покровский（Mikhail N. Pokrovsky，1868－1932）主编，涉及大量沙俄对清朝的外交档案，20 世纪 30 年代在柏林出版德文译本。A. Forke 即 Alfred Froke（1867－1944），德国汉学家，通译作"佛尔克"，1890 年至 1893 年担任德国驻华使馆翻译生，后长期执教于汉堡大学。Wolfram Eberhard（1909－1989），德国汉学家。*Combined Indices to Shih Chi* 即《史记及注释综合引得》（引得第四十号），1947 年 12 月哈佛燕京学社引得编纂处初版。

五月九日

先生致信胡适，略述胡适《书目与著作目》范围及体例。

适之先生：

奉到赐书，至感至谢！兹将尊处著作简目打好一份，随函附上，以时间匆促,遗漏之处,当必甚多,而在英国发表之论文,尚未加入,容日内再为搜集。散处所编之书目,以西文发表关于中国者为限已买 L.C.印行之卡片一全套,共费四百余元,先生大部分著作,均将收入,其体裁系一种分类书目 Classified Bibliography,书末另附著者索引。此函所附之件,即索引之初稿,以发表年月前后为次序,惟一年以内发表之论文,熟先熟后,拟请赐予指示为感! 又大著散在各处,检阅诸多不便,往往有极重要之论文,发表于不常见期刊之内,如 *Harvard Divinity School Bulletin*。兹拟代辑为专集第一集属于思想方面者,第二集属于政治方面者。此间有照像设备,搜集成帙毫无困难。如荷同意,当先拟一草目奉上,再请尊酌指示为幸! 匆复,敬颂著祺。

同礼谨上

五月九日晚

关于《鄞县志》之编纂经过,附原序二篇,一并奉上。

〔台北胡适纪念馆,档案编号 HS-US01-061-004、HS-US01-005-028〕

金问泗致函先生。〔《金问泗日记》,页 996〕

五月十日

先生在九日信上又补写一段,收到中基会补助款,略述研究计划,并告自己对普林斯顿大学葛斯德图书馆选聘馆长一事颇有兴趣。

又前奉四月十五日公函,通知会中补助费系由四月起至明年三月止,并附来支票壹千捌百元,已如数收讫,至谢至谢。目前工作,拟先将苏联、东欧及北欧、拉丁国家出版之文献编一简目,其数量已甚可观;至于英德法文发表者,则随时搜集,较易着手;最费时间者,即搜集期刊及专集中之论文,而按其性质予以分类,亦不易也,预计二年以后,方能完成。近闻 Swann 女士有退休之意,普仁斯敦大学图书馆副馆长 Heyl 近以继任人选征求 Hummel 之意见,闻渠已复函推荐同礼前往,但晤面时,渠并未提起,故亦不便询问一切。窃意此事如能实现,则在美可留二三年编辑上项目录,可在公余之暇为之。如该馆待遇尚好,则中基会之补助费,届时拟即退还。便中如晤 Heyl,或渠提到 Hummel 之推荐时,似可声明此人可以胜任,如何措辞,即希钧裁为荷!

同礼又上

　　　　　　　　　　　　　　　　　　五月十日

〔台北胡适纪念馆，档案编号 HS-US01-061-004、HS-US01-
005-028〕

五月十五日

先生致信顾子刚，告已在美为平馆续订由 Faxon 经售的期刊，并建议向该
公司预支壹仟美金，另外建议为来年订购英美期刊做好准备，尤其是向人
民政府申请外汇，此外询问宋琳等人近况。

　　　　　　　　　　　　　　　　　May 15, 1950

Dear Mr. Koo:

　　In his letter of March 4, Mr. Wang complained about the non-receipt
of American Periodicals for 1950. I wrote to Faxon and found that
subscriptions for 1950 were not received. I now enclose copies of our
correspondence.

　　As the Post Office here accepts printed China for all of China and as
the earlier number of certain journals may not be available if we do not
place the order now, I have taken the liberty of placing the subscriptions
for Mr. Wang. I have also cancelled a number of them as they are already
in P. U. M. C.

　　When I was in New York, I called on the Chase Bank at the Park
Ave. at 60th St. They told me that they have been holding the statement,
and they have not even sent you the credit note for ＄2,500 from the
C. F.

　　Faxon has complained in his earlier letters that Chinese libraries do
not pay for their subscriptions and they owe him over ＄20,000. I would
therefore suggest that you send Faxon a deposit of ＄1,000, in view of
the ＄2,500 already in the Bank.

　　It is time for Mr. Wang to arrange with the authorities to have more
exchange foreign in order to be prepared for the subscriptions for 1951
including those of British journals. In one of his letters, he said that
＄20,000 have been promised, but I wonder whether it has been actually
received by the Library.

Have you received the invoices of books which I bought for the Library under your check of ＄100? They were sent to Mr. Wang from Hong Kong and the books were sent in 7 parcels. There are two books which should not be displayed to the public.

I have a copy of the People's Yearbook published in Hong Kong. Could you send me similar titles, including a recent telephone directory of your city? Have you sent me the scroll for L. C.?

In your next letter, please tell me something about Mr. Sung Lin and the two Wangs who were dismissed last year. Have they joined the Ministry of Education and left our dormitory?

With kind regards,

Yours truly,

〔袁同礼家人提供〕

按:此时,宋琳已离馆,1951 年 7 月被聘为中央文史研究馆馆 员①;two Wangs 应指王祖彝、王访渔,亦已离馆。此件为底稿。 胡适覆函先生,对编辑《书目与著作目》提出意见并告知可搜集的来源,另 谈其已接受普林斯顿大学聘请出任该校图书馆葛斯德专藏负责人。

May 15, 1950

守和兄:

谢谢你五月十日的信。

鄞县志二序,可补我的笔记的不足。谢谢。

关于我的书目,尚不及细校,只记出数点:——

① *Royal Asiatic Society Journal*——North China Branch——有我 几篇文字:

(1)Wang Mang(王莽)—长文,似在 1929。

(2)The Establishment of Confucianism as State Religion of the Han Empire(长文)似在 1929 或 1930。

(3)Review of John Ferguson's book on "Chinese Painting"(Signed "H. S."—似在 1928. vol.)

---

① 《中央文史研究馆馆员传略》(增订版),北京:中华书局,2014 年,页 20。

②*Royal Asiatic Society Journal*—London 有我最早的一篇"Notes on Lionel Giles's translation of the 敦煌录",似在 1915 or 1916——其时我署名"Suh Hu"。

③Demiéville 评我的书的文字都在河内出的 *Bulletin*,其中似有不少资料?

④你此目的最后一类"Articles about Dr. Hu",其中有几篇是我自己的文字,如 Asia 所收"A Historian Looks at Chinese Painting"是我的一篇 Lecture,如 *China Review* 收的"Hu—Marobushi Letters"即是我"告日本国民"二函的译文。以后如有所见,当再奉告。(此时的 first impression 是:此目所收,应删者多,很少是有关学术的文字。)

又记得我的"说儒"有 Franke(儿子)的全译本,在德国发表。四十自述有 Hoffmann 的全译本,也在德国发表。我的丧礼改革一文,有 Werner 的英译文。我的短剧"终身大事"英文本全文收在 A. E. Zucker's *Chinese Drama* 书里。

承兄提议"代辑为专集",此意弟愿意仔细考虑,但拟限于几篇有勉两的学术文字。日内拟先草一目寄上,请你指示。

你信上说起 Princeton 的事,昨日星期 New York *Times* & N. Y. *Herald Tribune* 都有 Princeton U. 校长 Dodds 发表请我作"Fellow of the Univ. Library and Curator of Gest Oriental Library with rank of professor"的消息。

此事的经过是这样的。

去年年底,Princeton 有信来,说有人 nominated 我为"Alfred Hodder Fellow",是一种 post doctorate fellowship。当时因为我要谋改换 status 以便接太太来,故曾覆信允考虑。后来校长知道了,来信提议改请我为"Library Fellow",并要我作 Gest 的 Curator。当时我曾托人去说,"中国学人在此的,有人比我更胜任此事。"我的意思是预备推荐你(Miss Swann 已退休了)。但此人来说,校长特别要请我,如果我为了护照的身份(status)问题,他愿意声明这是一个 full professor 的 rank,虽然我不须教书上课。

我后来想想,我可以先去 Princeton 打开文史的一条路(Humanities),然后请守和兄来专力整理 Gest。我在 1943-4,Princeton 曾请我去看

Gest Collection，要我替他们想想"政策"（policy）。那时 Swann 在那儿把持不放，一切都谈不到。此时他们自动请我，我有打开门户的机会，故暂时接受了。将来我去 Princeton 时，一定要使他们明白请专家学者的必要，一定要请老兄来计画商量这一大批中国书如何能发生作用。此意我想老兄定能相信，定能了解。（我的 Fellowship stipend 是全年＄4,500，每月为＄375。我可以专作我的研究著作。Curator 别无薪俸。因为他们并不期望我每日办公。）

鄞县志自光绪二年三年（1876-77）以后，曾有续修本否？乞便中赐示。

匆匆，敬问双安。

适之

内人四月底已得 visa，大约此时已搭伴去香港暂住，候伴来美。

〔University of Chicago Library, Yuan T'ung-li Papers, Box 7〕

按：A. E. Zucker's *Chinese Drama* 应指 A. E. Zucker, *The Chinese Theater*，1925 年波士顿 Little, Brown, and Company 初版；"Franke（儿子）"即傅吾康，福兰阁之子，1935 年《中国学刊》（*Sinica-Sonderausgabe*）上刊有傅吾康所译《说"儒"》。Werner 即 Edward Theodore Chalmers Werner（1864-1954），英国外交官、汉学家，他对《丧礼改制》的翻译收录在 *Autumn Leaves*，1928 年上海别发洋行初版。"校长 Dodds"即 Harold W. Dodds（1889-1980），美国学者，1933 年至 1957 年担任普林斯顿大学校长。5 月 14 日，普林斯顿大学公布聘请胡适出任葛斯德专藏负责人的决定。

五月十七日

图齐覆函先生，应前请寄上其著述清单，并已联系书商询问可否寄送《梵天佛地》的存卷。

Rome

17th May, 1950

Dear Mr. Yuan:

Thank you very much for your kind letter of March 23rd and for all you say.

I am glad to hear that you are compiling a bibliography on China and that you think I may be of use to you. Herewith enclosed you will find a complete bibliography of my writings.

As regards my *Indo-Tibetica*, the book is now out of print and only the 4th volumes (3 tomes) is on sale. However, I will ask the publishers whether they can send you a prospectus of the work. The complete set amounts to volumes in 7 tomes.

If there is anything else I can do for you, please let me know and I shall be only too pleased to help you.

With kind regards.

Yours sincerely

Giuseppe Tucci

Piazza Vescovio 21, Rome.

P. S. I am also enclosing a prospectus of *Indo-Tibetica*.

〔University of Chicago Library, Yuan T'ung-li Papers, Box 3〕

按：该信附 6 页著述清单，共计 148 种；另有一页《梵天佛地》介绍。

五月二十日

先生致信胡适，寄上近日搜集的西文论文简目。

适之先生：

日前奉到十五日赐书，诸承指示，至为心感。此间所藏英国皇家学会 N. C. B.学报，适有数期为他人借去，无法检阅。又 Zucker 及 Franke 所译之文尚未觅到，俟日后查明再行补入。兹先将近日搜集之论文简目随函奉上，即乞钧阅。至于 Hoffmann 所译之《四十自述》系分期刊载，似未全译，而该期刊亦在第二次大战时停刊，一俟查明其住址，当与之通讯一询也。关于编辑专集事，先生未免谦虚，敝意仍主张印甲乙两集，仍祈考虑。检阅各方志目录，光绪三年《鄞县志》系最后所编印，以后并无续修之本。普仁斯敦事是一极大荣誉，将来如能打开一条路，亦一大收获，于中美文化促进贡献极大。内人闻尊夫人已抵香港，甚为欣慰，盼不久可以觅到妥便。昨史语所何君（北大毕业）见告，孟麟先生不久可以来美，如能同船来美，实一好伴也。专此，敬颂著祺。

同礼拜启

五月二十日

〔台北胡适纪念馆，档案编号 HS-US01-005-027〕

按："英国皇家学会 N. C. B.学报"应指 *Journal of the North China Branch of the Royal Asiatic Society*（《皇家亚洲文会北华支会会刊》）。Hoffmann 即 Alfred Hoffmann(1911–1997)，德国汉学家，中文名霍福民，曾向龙榆生学词，1935 年《东方舆论》(*Ostasiatische Rundschau*)连载了其翻译《四十自述》中的一节"'逼上梁山'——文学革命的开始"(Das Werden der literarischen Revolution)。"何君"，待考。

五月二十七日

卫德明覆函先生，对未能在华盛顿晤面表示歉意，并告傅吾康、霍福民等德国汉学家的联系方式。

5. 27, 50

Dear Mr. Yuan,

Thanks for your letter. Unfortunately, I was in Washington only for one day and was not able to follow up my first round of unsuccessful calls. I hope I will have more luck next time.

The last I heard from Wolfgang Franke is that he is still in Peking. His bargaining with Hamburg University had not reached any finality. His translations of Hu Shih's 说儒 was published in *Sinica-Sonderausgabe* 1934 and 1935. (This was a special issue of the Sinica in which more scholarly articles were printed. Only four issues appeared altogether).

Dr. Alfred Hoffmann's address is:

　　Bergrather strasse 70

　　(22c) Eschweiler, Kr. Aachen, British Zone

and Fuchs might be reached through

　　Sinologisches Seminar

　　Universität Hamburg

where he was substituting for Franke when I heard about him.

Unfortunately, I have no contacts in the Russian zone of Germany. But I suppose letters will be forwarded directly.

Our □□□ you will find rather meager. But it costs a lot of money to build up a library and unfortunately, we have completely run out of it.

Yours truly

Hellmut Wilhelm

〔袁同礼家人提供〕

按:Fuchs 即 Walter Fuchs(1902-1979),德国汉学家,中文名福克司或福华德,师从福兰阁,博士论文以唐末吐鲁番地区政局为研究对象,1938 年来华,长期在辅仁大学任教,1947 年回国,时应在汉堡大学执教。该函为其亲笔。

六月十一日

田清波致函先生,告将寄送中文书籍,介绍其在蒙古地区传教的情况。

Arlington, le 11 juin 1950

Cher Monsieur Yuan,

Je regrette beaucoup ne pouvoir rien dire concernant ce taiji de Junghar tué par □□□□□. Je ne sais rien de particulier à ce sujet. Je regrette aussi que je n'aie pas de photos de Mongols. J'en ai eu autrefois, mais je les ai distribuées par ci par là à mes amis quand j'étais encore à Pékin.

Je vous envoie par poste un petit livre écrit en chinois sur nos missions en Mongolie. Vous y trouverez les informations que vous demandez.

Autrefois nos missions de Mongolie ont parfois été l'objet de critiques de la part de certaines gens qui ignoraient les conditions propres aux pays situés au nord de la grande muraille. On nous a accusés d'être des impérialistes, etc. Vous me feriez plaisir si, après avoir lu ce petit livre, vous voudriez bien m'écrire en quelques mots votre opinion sur l'œuvre des missionnaires en Mongolie.

Quant à la question que vous me posez sur la manière dont les Mongols regardent les missions, je dois dire que les Mongols se convertissent très difficilement au christianisme, parce qu'ils sont très attachés au lamaïsme, mais en général les relations entre missionnaires et

Mongols et entre Mongols catholiques et Mongols non catholiques sont cordiales.

Agréez, cher Monsieur Yuan, l'assurance de ma profonde considération.

Antoine Mostaert

〔袁同礼家人提供〕

按：该函为其亲笔。

六月十二日

怀特致函先生，告知他本人愿意支持先生的研究计划，但并不适合作为项目管理人。

June 12, 1950

Dear Dr. Yuan:

I take pleasure in sending you a letter to Dr. Fisher supporting the project about which you wrote me. I am enclosing a copy for your personal file. We are much interested in what you are doing and will expect to help you in any way we can if you call on us to do it. I am probably not the best person to be the supervisor of your research though there is no reason why you could not give my name as a reference to the Department of State if you would like to do it. You know how these administrative responsibilities eat up a man's time, so I have been obliged to delegate responsibility for supervising research to my colleagues. In addition to the resources of our own Faculty on which we can draw informally, we have, of course, Professor Goodrich's department. It strikes me that this is an area in which you may wish to take counsel with people in both of these departments.

In the paragraph above, I spoke of drawing upon Columbia resources informally. There is some kind of regulation about tuition payment which we wish to avoid in this case. I am not clear just what that regulation says as I write, but I am sure the simple consultation you have in mind will present no problem whatsoever.

Good wishes for the success of this application which I am pleased you let me write to support.

Sincerely yours,

Carl M. White

〔袁同礼家人提供〕

按：本年早些时候，美国国务院宣布对在美滞留的中国学生、教授和学者提供一项总额为六百万美金的紧急援助计划，提供用以购买开展研究所需要的材料以及在美参加学术活动的经费。此件为打字稿，落款处为其签名，附怀特致 Thomas R. Fisher（Division of International Exchange of Persons, U. S. Department of State）信一封。

六月十八日

颜复礼致函先生，告知其在某旧书店找到十六卷本的《帝国主义时代国际关系》，如欲购买请速覆电，并已与小海尼士取得联系。

18th June, 1950

Dear Mr. Yuan,

I am very glad to inform you that through an advertisement an antiquarian of this place has succeeded in finding a complete copy of the German edition of the Russian publication concerning the international relations, ……The edition consists of 16 volumes, the price is 280 DM, which must be considered very moderate. Please let me know as soon as possible (perhaps by cable) if you want me to buy this copy for you. Recently I received a letter from Dr. Haenisch with certain wishes directed to your address. In my next letter I shall inform you about the details.

Hoping that you will kindly reply at your earliest convenience,

Yours sincerely,

Fr. Jäger

〔University of Chicago Library, Yuan T'ung-li Papers, Box 2〕

按：an antiquarian of this place 应指名为 Doerling 的旧书店。

七月七日

王重民致函先生，略述国内友人境况。大意如下：

寿萱很好，思杜即毕业。……生已搬入新房，很舒适。……毓铨夫妇已在东四七条买一所大房，因愈大愈便宜，不过房税较重一点，但平均也仅每年每间十斤小米而已。

……张约园抄本邮书,已与张芝联通信说明,有妥便人即带往上海。……

〔《胡适日记全集》第 8 册,页 520〕

按:9 月 25 日(前),先生将此信转示与胡适,极有可能是因其提到胡思杜。张芝联(1918—2008),历史学家,"张约园抄本邮书"即胡适从张芝联处所借抄本《全氏七校水经注》,此书似由他人代管,正欲送还上海张芝联处。

七月十六日

先生致信颜复礼,期待其寄来佛尔克、福兰阁及其本人的著作清单,并请联系海尼士父子、福克司以获取他们的著作清单,另请转寄致霍福民信。

July 16, 1950

Dear Professor Jager:

I am most grateful to you for sending me the bibliography of Professors Forke and Franke. I hope to receive from you soon a photostat copy of the first part of the bibliography of Professor Franke together with a list of your own writings. I shall get in touch with the other three gentlemen you mentioned in your recent letter.

I would like to have a list of the writing of Professor Haenisch now at Munich and of Dr. Haenisch at Berlin. If you have occasion to write to them, will you kindly convey my wishes. I understand that Dr. Fuchs is now at Hamburg. If you see him, will you also ask him to send me a list of his writings and give him my present address? I hope he has resumed his scientific work.

Dr. Haenisch compiled for me a list of German sinological literature covering the years 1939–1944, which was published in our *Quarterly Bulletin of Chinese Bibliography* for December 1947. If you are able to communicated with Dr. Haenisch, would you be good enough to request him to compile a second list covering the years 1945–1950? I think it would be an extremely useful list and I shall see to it that it is published in China or in the United States. If you write him on my behalf, your letter will not receive much attention from the censors as one from the United States. The firm Otto Harrassowitz at Leipzig is in close touch with him and you may write him in care of that firm which is, of course, also situated in the Russian zone.

I enclose a letter to Dr. Hoffmann and I shall appreciate it if you could forward it for me. I would like to obtain a copy of the *Sinica-Sonderausgabe* for 1934 and 1935 which contain Wolfgang Franke's translation of Hu Shih's 　　　　I understand that it is a special edition of the Sinica in which more scholarly works were printed, and only four issues appeared. May I trouble you to buy a copy for me and let me know the cost?

With sincere appreciation for your assistance,

Yours sincerely,

I just received your letter of June 18th and I do wish to thank you for obtaining a copy of the German edition of the Russian documents. I have sent you a cable, asking you to buy the set. Please ask the antiquarian to mail these volumes to Washington and let me know the cost of postage, so that a draft will be sent to you.

〔University of Chicago Library, Yuan T'ung-li Papers, Box 2〕

按：Haenisch now at Munich 即海尼士，Dr. Haenisch at Berlin 则应指其子 Wolf Haenisch。a list of German sinological literature covering the years 1939-1944 正式题名为 Sinological Literature in German, 1939-1944: a selected bibliography，刊于《图书季刊》英文本 New Series Vol. 7 No. 1-4，并未标注编者姓名。Hu Shih's 后的空格应填入"说儒"。此件为底稿，右上时间错写为 June，笔者自行订正。

七月十八日

先生致信胡适，代袁慧熙向江冬秀问好，并请胡适为霍福民新书题写书名。

适之先生尊鉴：

前函计达座右，入暑以来，想起居胜常，尊夫人到纽以后，生活尚习惯否？内人时以为念，嘱笔致候。近接 Hoffmann 自德来信，谓所译李煜之词业已付印，前曾有函致尊处由"大使馆"转寄者恳写"李煜"二字，以便印于封面之内。兹以该书亟待装订,特嘱从旁一催,盼从速写就寄德。如尊处未备中国笔墨,想领事馆可以借到也。朝鲜战事似非最近期内所能解决,惟台湾紧张局面似可稍苏。关于台湾 Stalin 想不致成大问题也。匆上,敬候俪祺。

同礼谨上

七月十八

Alfred Hoffmann 地址:

22c Eschweiler B/Aachen, Bergrather-str. 70, British Germany

〔台北胡适纪念馆,档案编号 HS-US01-006-020〕

按:霍福民之书题名 *Die Lieder des Li Yü 937-978*(《李煜》),1950 年初版,确由胡适题写书名。撰写此信时,先生的通信地址已变更为 108 6th Street N. E., Washington D. C.

七月二十四日

先生致信 Thomas R. Fisher,正式提交就中国图书馆史研究的资助申请,并附上自己的学术经历和工作履历及怀特的推荐函。

July 24, 1950

Dr. Thomas R. Fisher

Division of International Exchange of Persons

U. S. Department of State

1778 Pennsylvania Avenue, N. W.

Washington 25, D. C.

Dear Dr. Fisher:

I understand that Chinese research scholars are eligible for aid under the new program of emergency aid authorized by Congress.

If policies and procedures governing the program have been decided upon, may I take this opportunity to submit my application for your consideration? Enclosed herewith please find a statement of my academic and professional career and a letter of recommendation from Dr. Carl M. White, Dean, School of Library Service, Columbia University, who has consented to serve as my supervisor.

I am now engaged in writing the history of libraries in China. It deals with one important aspect of the cultural history of China which has not yet received adequate attention from Western scholars. In view of the vast field, the gathering of scattered material and the work of interpretation will take at least two years.

If financial assistance can be given under your program of emergency aid, I propose to continue the work at Washington, making full use of the resources of the Library of Congress, but to go to New York occasionally for consultation and advice from Dr. White as well as other faculty members at Columbia. I shall be grateful to you if due consideration could be given to this application.

Very sincerely yours,

Tung-li, Yuan

〔袁同礼家人提供〕

按：该件为录副。

陈荣捷覆函先生，寄上其著述目录，并请先生代向胡适、韩权华问候。

July 24, 1950

Dear Dr. Yuan:

When I returned from an extensive trip to the West Coast and the University of Chicago, I found your kind letter of June 6 waiting for me. I am indeed sorry to have missed you in Washington. I hope you will visit Dartmouth again someday.

Enclosed please find a list of my publications in English. It does not include book reviews, of which I have published about fifty.

When you see Dr. Hu Shih and when you write Madame Wei Li-huang, kindly give them my kindest regards.

Sincerely yours,

Wing-tsit Chan

〔袁同礼家人提供〕

按：陈荣捷（1901—1994），广东人，岭南大学毕业，后赴美留学，获哈佛大学博士学位，归国后曾任岭南大学教务长，1936年再次赴美，后长期在美执教，研究朱子。此件为打字稿，落款处为其签名并钤印。随函附一页目录。

八月十四日

程绥楚致函先生,告知大陆情况。〔袁同礼家人提供〕

　　　按:此函中附有致袁澄短信一封。

八月十七日

福特致函先生,请送回凤凌日记译稿并告知其将暂回英国。

> British Embassy
>
> Washington
>
> August 17th

Dear Dr. Yuan,

　　As I am leaving for England on the 24th I should be glad if you would return to me any of the manuscript on Feng Lin's diary which you may happen to have. It would also be a great service to me if you could get back from the Library of Congress the Chinese text, which I think you lent to one of the staff. I have received news from Pin Hsi in Peking, together with 2 photographs of his father. I hope that we may meet before I leave, and I would show you the photos. If I had had your telephone number I would have telephoned, instead of writing, and if you will let me have the number, I may still be able to propose a time for a meeting, as I should very much like to see you.

　　I have continued with Hsueh Fu-ch'eng's diary, but today had to return the book to the Congressional Library. I hope to take it up again (or something of the kind) when I get to Peking.

　　As I have 3½ months leave due to me in England, I shall not get to Peking till late in the year.

> Kindest regards,
>
> J. F. Ford

P. S.　Did Dr. Needham come, and did you see him?

> 〔袁同礼家人提供〕

　　　按:Pin Hsi 待考。该函为其亲笔。

八月二十二日

Chen Yu-sheng 致函先生,请协助询问国会图书馆有无购入宝礼堂旧藏善本。

August 22, 1950

Dear Mr. Yuan,

First of all, I must ask you to pardon me for my intrusion. I have something which need help and President Fu-Ssu-nien told to write to you. I hope you will render me your kind assistance in the matter.

My relative, the Pan's family (广东南海宝礼堂潘) has the famous collection of antique books. This collection consists of about two thousand volumes of 经史子集, all engraved and printed in Sung Dynasty. The late Mr. 潘宗周 started collection sixty years ago and the family had, for the past two generations, spent almost all they had on the collection. All these volumes had been studied and sorted by the most eminent authorities on Chinese literature and history, as well as confirmed by noted authorities on antique printing and engraving. By their combined efforts a catalog in four volumes was drawn up as key to these volumes. It is now considered as one of the best and most complete collections in China.

When Shanghai was in danger in the spring of last year, the British Council authorities in Shanghai approached Mr. Pan and talked about the safety of the books. They also asked about the price. It was hard for Mr. Pan to name it. The family has spent not less than US $ 500,000.- on the collection and asked this sum as compensation. Mr. Pan was glad to place his books in safety and be made use of by the British sinologists. The British authorities then proposed to loan the collection to Bodleian Library for two years and after that buy the collection. This, Mr. Pan declined to accept as the family would like ready payment. Meanwhile situation in Shanghai turned from bad to worse the British authorities helped most kindly in packing and shipping the collection free to Hongkong where it is now under safe-keeping.

As Mr. Pan does not think Hongkong a nice place to keep his books now, he asked me to write the Congress Library to inquire if they would buy the collection. President Fu said you will be able to help us in some way. He had seen the books once himself and claimed they are of priceless value.

Will you please help us to sell the collection to the Congress Library or any other institution in the United States? The Pan's family will accept a price as low as US $ 400,00 - against cash payment. They also offer a commission of 5%. I am sure you will be glad to see the books in safety too. I shall send you the four volumes of catalog if you wish.

Thanking you in anticipation and awaiting your reply.

Yours sincerely,

Chen Yu-sheng, Miss

Secretary,

Taiwan University

〔University of Chicago Library, Yuan T'ung-li Papers, Box 2〕

八月三十日

先生致信赵元任,问其西归前的行程并望来华盛顿一晤。

> 元任先生惠鉴:
>
> 　　近闻大驾携眷东来,想仍在纽约。下月前往西岸之时,想必路过华京,亟愿一聚。务希到此后先行电告,以免相左,至盼至盼。三、四两小姐想均同来,不识如兰夫妇能同来一游否? 统俟面述,顺颂俪安。尊夫人同此不另。

弟同礼顿首

八,三十

> 　　通讯处 108 6th street, N. E., Near East Capital to A Sts. N. E., Washington, D. C. 电话 Li-4-1638

〔University of California, Berkeley, The Bancroft Library, Yuen Ren Chao papers, carton 10, folder 39, Yuan, Tongli and Yuan, Huixi〕

> 按:"如兰夫妇"即赵如兰(1922—2013)和卞学鐄(1919—2009),后者天津人,航空航天专家,其父为卞肇新。8 月 21 日,赵元任先生一家驾车两辆,抵达纽约看望梅贻琦和张彭春等人,8 月底西行,似并未路过华盛顿。

九月二日

田清波致函先生,前信请寄圣母圣心会在华传教史无法满足,但其将寄上蒙古传教史料,并告不用急于归还。

Arlington, le 2 septembre 1950.

4651 North 25th St.

Cher Monsieur Yuan,

　　Dans votre dernière lettre vous me demandiez de vous procurer une *Histoire des Missions de Scheut en Chine*. Comme cette histoire n'a pas été écrite, je n'ai pu vous satisfaire. Mais je viens de mettre la main sur un livre qui traite de l'histoire des missions modernes chez les Mongols. Je viens de vous l'envoyer par poste.

　　Je ne suis nullement pressé de revoir le livre. Lisez-le tout à votre aise. J'espère que vous êtes en bonne santé.

　　Vous souhaitant tout le succès désirable, je vous prie, Cher Monsieur, d'agréer l'assurance de ma profonde considération.

Antoine Mostaert

〔袁同礼家人提供〕

　　按:该函为其亲笔。

九月十七日

何多源覆函先生,谈代订图书杂志、广州地区高校近况、国内学习俄文的趋势及北大图书馆学毕业生情况。

　　守和先生尊鉴:

　　　　八月三日手书敬悉。《郑樵校雠略研究》及《人民中国》经于日前挂号上,至在香港出版之周刊则托香港广大中学代订,因香港出版品如未经此间登记者不能进口也。最近政府颁布禁止珍贵文物图书出口,凡寄出图书杂志均须送市政府新闻出版处审查,核准后方能将书送邮局查验放行。L. C.之书报俟审核后方能寄出,《东方杂志》已停刊,但中华书局出版之《新中华》月刊内容颇佳。

　　　　源本学期原已接中山大学之聘任代主任职,但广大校长许崇清先生极力慰留,不便离去。广大本学期经济情形好转(学生约有千人),待遇可增一倍,较中大为高。岭大方面亦趋好转,教授月薪约有港币二百余元,并供给住屋。现白米每市担约值港币二十余元,每人每月伙食约港币三十元(美金一元值港币六元)。岭大校长仍为陈序经先生,王力为文学院长,现有学生约千三百人,每人收费每学期学什费约四百元港币,比燕京大学高两倍半,为全国学费之最昂者,但其学生来源多为华侨子弟及香港富商之子女,对于学费不在乎也。

现国内学校课程列俄文为第一外国语,源已开始学习四个月。本市电台早晚播送俄语教授,颇便学习。坊间俄文书籍、杂志颇多,但精通俄语者,全国统计只有千人,而英文人才则有十三万之多。先生早年在北京圕创办苏联研究室,足具远见。先生在北大创办之图书馆学专修科,今年第一届毕业,均由政府分配工作。台驾何时返国,便乞示知。此请大安。

后学何多源上
一九五〇九月十七日

〔University of Chicago Library, Yuan T'ung-li Papers, Box 2〕

按:《郑樵校雠略研究》,钱亚新著,1948 年 12 月商务印书馆印行。广大中学即私立广州大学的附属中学。《东方杂志》1904 年 3 月 11 日由商务印书馆创刊,1948 年 12 月终刊,后曾在台湾地区复刊;《新中华》月刊应指《新中华》半月刊,1933 年 1 月由中华书局创刊。许崇清(1888—1969),字志澄、芷澄,广东番禺人,教育家,曾多次出任中山大学校长,时任私立广州大学校长。该信以航空信方式寄送。

九月二十五日

朱士嘉覆函先生,谈国内情况并请先生归国。

守和先生:

收到你最近的信,知道尊况为慰。现在敬答问题如下:

(一)武大教员名录尚未印发。(二)关于科学(用英文写的)杂志,此间没有听到,北京方面或许有。有三一定知道。(三)归国后的观感。归国后到过武昌、汉口、北京、上海。归纳起来,政府上下廉洁、苦干,检讨自己工作。各机关极力免避浪费,力求简省。所以解放一年半以后,财政方面,出入平衡,物价稳定。北京、汉口市面日渐繁荣。上海方面春季生气凋落,但从八月起渐见起色。政府提倡生产,学生都参加。今年各地丰收。承灾区域大大的缩小,政府对此曾设法救济,没有借用外国人一分钱。政府对于以前的反动分子非常宽容。如果他们能反省合作,尽量请他们帮忙。并且用感化的方法而不用高压的手段。我现在这里一方面学习(自己多看新的著作),一方面开一门中美关系史。带回来许多中文档案,不久望利用。有三除在北京图书馆以外,还兼北大的图书馆专修科的工作。寿萱当北大博物馆馆长。毓铨在北京历史博物馆做事。先晋与寿萱仝事。国内需要专家,尤其前辈如先生者出来指导。现在作何归计否。告诉你的消息望专告其他的朋友。祝好!

　　　　　　　　　　　　　　　　　　　后学士嘉

　　　　　　　　　　　　　　　　　　　九,廿五

叔平长故宫博物院,曾邀武昌文献馆讲档案。

　　　　　　　　　　　　　　　　　〔袁同礼家人提供〕

　　按:专告,似当作"转告"。1950 年春,朱士嘉在美结识记者路易·斯特朗(Anna Louise Strong,1885-1970),受其影响,并在周鲠生、陈翰笙等人的劝告下决定回国,同年 9 月在武汉大学历史系任教,兼任该校图书馆馆长。该函由香港蔚林图书公司转投,以航空信方式寄送。

九月
先生外出休假。
十月二日
田清波致函先生,告知闵玉清手稿应在比利时保存但很难识别,其将会联系贺歌南以获取先生感兴趣的资料。

　　　　　　　　　　　　　　　Arlington, le 2 octobre 1950

Cher Monsieur Yuan,

　　Les lettres de Mgr Bermyn n'ont été préservées qu'en petit nombre. Je suppose qu'une partie en doit être en Belgique, mais il serait assez difficile de trouver quelqu'un qui veuille faire des recherches dans cette correspondance, surtout parce que l'écriture de Mgr Bermyn est très difficile à lire. Je sais que vous vous intéressez à l'histoire de la mort de ce □□ du "□□ Banner". Je ferai comme ceci. J'écrirai encore aujourd'hui au J. Van Hecken, l'auteur du livre "Les Missions chez les Mongols", qui est à présent à 宁夏. Il s'est occupé beaucoup de l'histoire des Ordres et il pourra peut-être nous donner des informations. Il pourra aussi nous indiquer la voie de trouver cette lettre du 7 mars 1907.

Je vous communiquerai sa réponse.

Veuillez agréer, Cher Monsieur Yuan, l'assurance de ma profonde considération.

Mostaert

〔University of Chicago Library, Yuan T'ung-li Papers, Box 2〕

按:Mgr Bermyn 应指闵玉清(Alfonso Bermyn, 1853-1915),圣母圣心会会士,比利时人,1901 年 4 月,教廷任命其为蒙古西南代牧区宗座代牧。J. Van Hecken 即贺歌南神父(Jos Van Hecken, 1905-1988),圣母圣心会会士,比利时人,1931 来华传教,1952 年赴日本后经美国辗转返回比利时。*Les Missions chez les Mongols*,1949 年北京北堂印书馆印行。该函为其亲笔。

十月三日

先生致信颜复礼,请其联系小海尼士补寄 1946 年出版的德国汉学家著述目录,此外请寄本人及福克司著述目录,并告知已收到书店寄来十六册《帝国主义时代国际关系》德译本。

October 3, 1950

Dear Prof. Jaeger:

I am most grateful to you for your Chinese letter which you sent to me in August. It was so beautifully written that I showed it to some American sinologues, they feel very much ashamed that they cannot have that accomplishment. I congratulate you for having written in such literary style and beautiful calligraphy.

I was away for the whole month of September and knowing that you also had a nice vacation, I did not try to bother you with further requests. All I want to say is to thank you most sincerely for the bibliographies of Prof. Franke and Prof. Forke which you so kindly sent to me. They are very useful to my work.

Will you also kindly thank Dr. Haenisch for me for sending me a list of books on China since 1947? I have asked our office at Peiping to send similar lists to him at Berlin, as it is very quick for them to write to him via Siberia.

Dr. Haenisch sent me a list of books on China in 1946 in which he included all German sinological works published up to the end of 1945. Now, this list starts with 1947, it does not have titles published in 1946. When writing to him, could you ask him to compile a list for German sinological works published in 1946 and have it sent to me?

I only need a bibliography of your own writings as well as Dr. W. Fuchs. If he is in Hamburg, will you ask him to send me his own list and extend to him my best wishes and kind regards?

If it is not too much trouble to you, could you send me a list of German sinologues and the institutions with which they are connected? There are probably many young scholars whom I have not met and whose writings I have not seen.

I am glad to get the Indexes to *Shih-Chi* which I ask the Harvard University Press to send to you. If you need other books, please let me know. I shall be most happy to send them to you.

I have received all the volumes of the German translation of Russian documents for which I am most indebted to you. I wrote to Doerling about the safe arrival of the 16 volumes and asked him to inform you about it.

With renewed thanks for your kindness and assistance,

　　　　　　　　　　　　　　　　　　　　　　Yours sincerely,

P. S. I hope you will kindly send me the bibliography of Prof. Haenisch's writings. Is it easy to compile a bibliography of the writings of Dr. Arthur von Rosthorn, the Austrian professor of Chinese at Vienna?

〔University of Chicago Library, Yuan T'ung-li Papers, Box 2〕

按：Arthur von Rosthorn（1862－1945），奥地利外交官、汉学家，通译作"讷色恩"。此件为底稿，实发时间似乎应为 10 月 4 日。

十月二十四日

西门华德覆函先生，欣悉《西文汉学书目》（考狄书目续编）计划，并谈在英为程绥楚谋事无望,另伦敦现有七册《永乐大典》售卖,国会图书馆是否有能力购入。

　　　　　　　　　　　　　　　　　　　　24th October, 1950.

My dear Director Yuan,

　　I was very glad to have your letter of 23rd September which I also showed to Professor Edwards. I was glad to have your news and was very interested to hear that you are preparing a supplement to the *Bibliotheca Sinica*. Is there any hope that this supplement will include an index to the whole work? I am enclosing a new list of Professor Edwards' writings and my own list will follow as soon as ready.

　　We are all very glad to have Harry back and you are right in supposing that he was far less enthusiastic than Mr. van der Sprenkel. But there are special reasons why I would like you to keep this information confidential. Experience must vary according to the place one happened to be and as you know Harry was in Chengtu.

　　Re *Asia Major*, We are just preparing the first number of Volume II. Volume I is complete with two issues which are out.

　　Thank you for enquiring about Mrs. Liu whose work is indeed very satisfactory. I am afraid, however, that we can do nothing for Mr. Cheng of whom I saw a good deal while in Hongkong. We have no vacancy here at present nor is there any to my knowledge at the B. B. C. You are of course aware of the many Chinese, particularly of diplomatic staffs in Europe, who do not wish to return to China and there are therefore so many applicants for the few posts in existence that frankly speaking it would be unkind to raise Mr. Cheng's hope for a post in this country.

　　You may be interested to know that a short time ago the School was offered the following 7 volumes of the *Yeongleh-dahdean:*

　　　　807/8, 1036/7, 5244/5245, 13872/3,

　　　　13874/5, 15713-15715,16217/8.

The School of course is not in a position to buy them but do you think the Congress Library or alternatively the Peking Library would? If so, I shall let the owner know. As you will see, none of the volumes concerned is included in your list.

　　With kindest regards,

Yours very sincerely,

W. Simon

〔University of Chicago Library, Yuan T'ung-li Papers, Box 2〕

　　按：Professor Edwards 应指 Evangeline Edwards（1888－1957），伦敦大学亚非学院教授，主讲中国文学。Harry、Mrs. Liu 待考。*Asia Major*，1949 年在英国复刊；Yeongleh-dahdean 即《永乐大典》，下同。此件为打字稿，落款处为其签名。

十月二十五日

先生致信怀特，因美国国务院疏忽导致必须重新提交中国图书馆史研究的资助申请，请其在新表格中签字并寄出。

October 25, 1950

Dear Dr. White:

　　You are very kind last June to write to the Department of State in support of my application for a grant-in-aid. As I have not heard from the Department for so long, I called at Dr. Fisher's Office the other day and found that my application had been misplaced, so it has not had the attention of the Department.

　　I was told that I have to make a new application and to fill a form which has to be endorsed by the official supervisor. I am sending it to you and hope you will put your signature on application. Please note various items listed in the announcement, a copy of which is enclosed for your information.

　　I also enclose a tentative outline which has to be approved by the supervisor. If you find it satisfactory, please mail my application and the various documents direct to Dr. Thomas R. Fisher, Division of Exchange of Persons, Room 534, Department of State, Washington 25, D. C.

　　Thanking you once more for your interest and assistance,

Yours sincerely,

T. L. Yuan

〔袁同礼家人提供〕

按：该件为录副，并附 Tentative Outline for the History of Books
and Libraries in China 两页。

先生致信 Thomas R. Fisher，告知已联系怀特请其在新的申请书中签字并
寄送国务院审查。

October 25, 1950

Dear Dr. Fisher:

On July 24, 1950, I submitted an application for a research grant
under your program of emergency aid to Chinese student and Scholars. As
I have not heard from you, I made inquiry at your office and found that
my application had been misplaced.

Since you have issued new forms to be filled out by every applicant,
I am asking Dean White of the School of Library Service, Columbia
University, to put his signature on my application. I also enclose a
tentative outline and a vita.

The book which I propose to write deals with one important aspect
of the cultural history of China which has not received adequate attention
from Western scholars. I shall be grateful to you if due consideration
could be given to this application, so that the work will be initiated at an
early date.

Very sincerely yours,

Tung-li, Yuan

〔袁同礼家人提供〕

按：该件为录副。

孟治致函先生，告知 *Thesis and Dissertations by Chinese Students in America*
早已绝版，如实在需用可以短期借用，并谈因印刷成本高涨，华美协进社早
已无力刊印公告。

October 25th, 1950

Dear Dr. Yuan:

The booklets "*Thesis and Dissertations by Chinese Students in*

America" have been out of print for some time. We do have our reference copies in the Library in case you would want to make use of them for a short while.

Because of the present high cost of printing the Institute has been unable to do much in the way of putting out printed material. The China Institute Bulletin and the Journal were also discontinued a couple of years ago.

Your letter was given to Dr. Y. C. Mei who comes to this office several times each week.

With kind regards,

Sincerely yours,

Chih Meng

〔华美协进社英文信纸。袁同礼家人提供〕

十月二十七日

费正清致函先生，应前请寄上其本人著述目录。

October 27, 1950

Dear Mr. Yuan:

It is very good to hear from you and I am happy to send separately copies of our China Papers, Vol. IV, and of a draft volume of Western Bibliography with annotations for our students.

Your list of my articles arrived just at time when I had to compile such a list and I am happy to return two copies of the final product. You will note that many items are of course of little scholarly value for your purposes.

With best regards in which Mrs. Fairbank joins,

John K. Fairbank

〔袁同礼家人提供〕

按：此件为打字稿，落款处为其签名，并附三页 List of Publications。

十月三十日

怀特覆函先生，表示申请资助有两种渠道，因先生非居住在纽约，建议向居住地所在机构提交此项申请。

October 30, 1950

Dear Dr. Yuan:

I make prompt acknowledgment of your letter of October 25 in order that you may tell me how I may best assist the discussions you are having with the officers of the State Department. According to the instructions which reached Columbia this fall, this might take either of two forms. One would be for you to submit a project to Columbia. Such an application could be sent to me, but all applications of this kind are approved by a single officer in the University. Some officer in the School of Library Service or in the Libraries would undoubtedly be called upon to supervise any Columbia project in your field. So far as I am aware, the University has had only a few applications, and the applicant has in every case planned to do his work in residence. Non residence would pose a new problem, and I doubt whether the University would undertake to supervise a project unless it were in a position to give effective supervision. The reason for supposing that this might be so lies in the fact that the University must give a report of progress, I understand, from time to time on how the work is progressing. I have to date not talked with my colleagues in the School about this kind of undertaking. Knowing how hard-pressed everyone feels he is, this would be another problem which would have to come up for consideration. I think it would depend a good deal on what the proposal was in detail.

The other way I might be of some help would be for you to apply to some other institution of your own choice and, in so doing, list my name as a reference. I should be pleased to list my name if I may assist best in that way.

With kind personal regards, I am,

Yours sincerely,

Carl M. White

〔袁同礼家人提供〕

按:此件为打字稿,落款处为其签名。

十一月二日

先生致两怀特信。其一，仍然希望哥伦比亚大学作为隶属机构申请国务院对华人学者、学生的紧急资助，但可以将监督人改为恒慕义。

November 2, 1950

Dear Dr. White:

Thank you so much for your letter of October 30.

Since I consider the School of Library Service as my Alma Mater, I prefer very much to have the School sponsoring my project in writing a book on the history of books and libraries in China. I enclose therefore a formal application which you may like to have for transmission to the officer in charge of these applications at Columbia.

If non-residence would pose a new problem, I wonder whether this problem could not be solved by delegating a part of supervision to some scholar here in Washington. Dr. Arthur W. Hummel, Chief, Division of Orientalia, Library of Congress, would be glad to supervise a research project of this kind if you would write to him officially. In talking with him the other day, he gave me to understand that he strongly endorsed this project.

The Library of Congress would be ready to sponsor such projects as bibliographical compilations and the making of indexes. As to the writing of a monograph on the history of Chinese books and libraries, they feel that it should more logically be sponsored by a library school.

If you do not find it possible to sponsor this project because of non-residence limitations, I shall fully understand your position. In any case, I shall be glad to hear your decision at your convenience.

With sincere thanks,

Yours sincerely,
T. L. Yuan

〔袁同礼家人提供〕

按：该件为录副。

其二，寄送先生研究计划，请哥伦比亚大学图书馆学系作为"中国典籍史、图书馆史"项目的支持方并向学校递交申请计划并将其递交国务院。

November 2, 1950

Dear Dr. White:

In connection with my application for a research grant from the Division of Exchange of Persons, Department of State, I beg to submit the following project for your consideration and approval.

I have been gathering material for a book to be published in English and entitled: History of Books and Libraries in China. The purpose of this study is to survey the history of books and libraries in the growth of Chinese civilization. It will include the evolution of Chinese characters, writing materials, the manuscripts, paper-making, invention and spread of printing, famous presses and the traditional method of book production. It will also deal with the history of ancient, mediaeval and modern libraries and the role of books and libraries in the development of Chinese scholarship. Emphasis will be placed on the relationship between the successive stages of book and library development to the social and cultural conditions of the various periods. A tentative outline is herewith enclosed.

It is my desire that the School of Library Service will sponsor and endorse this project. I shall come to New York occasionally for consultation and advice and I shall keep in close touch with the supervisor or supervisors whom you may appoint to supervise the work.

If this application is approved by the University, will you write to the State Department (Dr. Thomas R. Fisher) enclosing my application and various documents in accordance with regulations as noted in the Announcement, copy of which was sent to you in my recent letter.

Yours sincerely,

T. L. Yuan

〔袁同礼家人提供〕

按:该件为录副。

十一月四日

杭立武致函先生，商洽平馆运台图书开箱检查事。

守和吾兄惠鉴：

久疏函候，甚以为歉。近况奚若，时在念中。关于北平图书馆三十七年十二月由南京随故宫等机关文物运台十八箱图书，因箱件系用杉木薄板所制，沿途舟车转运，其中少数表面略有微伤。抵台后，经"行政院"会议议决，设置"中央博物图书院馆联合管理处"，此批十八箱交由本处"中央博物组"代为保管，与古物存放一处。今春为防空袭，并已一同移置郊外仓库，以策安全。惟据保管方面陈述，此批箱件，在京起运时，未经当事人办理委托保管等手续，内容清册既未带来，箱上锁钥亦未移交。移台迄今，将近二载，未能擅自启封，箱内纸质图书，是否有检视、加置防虫药物及晒晾必要，以免有虫蛀潮霉之虞。为保护文物起见，用敢肃函奉商。如何处理之处，敬请赐示，以便遵办。崑此，敬请旅安。

弟杭立武拜启

十一月四日

〔University of Chicago Library, Yuan T'ung-li Papers, Box 2〕

按：此函皆为代笔，落款处钤"杭立武"印。先生收到后，于 15 日覆信。

十一月六日

怀特覆函先生，告知已将先生申请书递交校方，正在等待就非居住地一项的审批意见。

November 6, 1950

Dear Dr. Yuan:

I have received your letter of November 2, have placed the application and the supporting documents in the hands of the Assistant Provost in order to secure a ruling on the question of non-residence and will await word from that quarter before taking the next step. I know you would like to have our decision as soon as possible, and we are working to that end.

With kind personal regards, I am

Yours sincerely,

Carl M. White

〔袁同礼家人提供〕

按:此件为打字稿,落款处为其签名。

十一月二十日

Dorothea Scott 夫人覆函先生,告前请留意澳门出版书籍已由葡萄牙驻香港领事馆在澳门搜集,而战后香港报刊、公报相关目录则由一位避难在此的女教授负责,并代丈夫询问在北平时提及的京剧图谱类书籍的题名。

20th November, 1950

Dear Dr. Yuan:

I have delayed a little in answering your second letter of October 30th because it has taken me some time to find out about the books published in Macao. However, the Portuguese Consulate-General here in Hongkong have promised to get the required information from Macao for me. They have not mentioned anything about a search fee and I hope they will simply supply a copy of the list issued by the Imprensa Nacional. If this has to be purchased, I will let you know.

While I have been finding out about the Macao publications, I have had a search made through the post-war Hongkong Gazettes for you and now enclose a list of the relevant publications. The headings are self-explanatory and as the number of books in category (1) is so small only one list has been made. I think there will be no difficulty in sorting out the titles for the bibliographical headings you require.

The work was done by a refugee Chinese professor who was very glad of the opportunity to do a small temporary job as she has no permanent job here and very little money.

She spent five hours searching here in the University and another hour in typing and arranging the list. I don't really like being a financial "go between" and can only suggest that the more or less standard rate for private teaching here in Hongkong be applied, i. e., HK $ 12 an hour, making a total of HK $ 72 or US $ 12. I think she would be very satisfied with that.

I haven't met Mr. Fitzgerald yet but Mr. Scott has met him casually several times. I hope he will dine with us this week.

Mr. Scott is spending all his spare time doing a series of oil paintings from his existing drawings and notes of Chinese drama characters, and completing his graphic records whenever opportunity offers. Until now these have been few in Hongkong but 张君秋 is now giving a season every Saturday afternoon at a big theatre in Kowloon, so once a week at least "China proper" comes to Hongkong!

My husband has also always regretted that he did not ask you for the Chinese titles of the illustrated books on the Drama you mentioned were in the library in Peking. If it is possible for you to remember any of them, I know he would be very grateful to have a note of them in Chinese and English.

Yours sincerely,

Mrs. Dorothea Scott

Librarian.

〔University of Chicago Library, Yuan T'ung-li Papers, Box 2〕

按:Mrs. Dorothea Scott(1890-1960),英国人,1950 年 8 月出任香港大学第二任图书馆馆长,1958 年 4 月 3 日,她推动成立了香港图书馆协会,并被选为该协会主席。Mr. Scott 即其丈夫 Adolphe C. Scott(1909-1985),戏剧学家,对京剧及日本传统戏剧有较为深入的研究。Mr. Fitzgerald 即 Charles P. Fitzgerald (1902-1992),英国历史学家,中文名费知乐,伦敦大学毕业,1923 年来华,1950 年受澳大利亚公使 Douglas Copland 邀请,前往堪培拉澳大利亚国立大学任教。张君秋(1920—1997),原名滕家鸣,字玉隐,祖籍江苏丹徒,出生于北京,京剧演员。

十一月二十一日

罗文达覆函先生,寄上其著述简目并就德语汉学期刊情况略作介绍。

November 21, 1950

Dear Dr. Yuan:

Your kind note of Nov. 20 reached me today. By the same mail I am sending you a copy of my bibliography from FEQ. 1937/47. A supplement for the Oriental countries (outside of the Far East & Central Asia) was submitted two years ago to the <u>Bull</u>. Of the New York Public Lib., but they have as yet not published it. A suppl. to the bibliography in FEQ, but for the years 1931/36 was publ. in mimeographed form by the Russian Research Center, Harvard. Unfortunately, I have no spare copies left. But you could get a copy through Prof. John K. Fairbank, 127 Littauer Ceutes, Cambridge, Mass., whose auspices it was published.

Regarding German Sinological journals, there is *Oriens*, publ. by Brill in Leiden; *Artibus Asiæ*, Ascona (Switzerland); *Sinologica*, Basel; *Archiv für Ostasien*, Düsseldorf (diseon-Aimred after the first issue); *Zeitschrift der Deutschen Morgenländischen Ges*, has resumed publication in Wiesbaden; *Saeculum*, a new quarterly, started publication this year, it contains a number of good articles in the Far Eastern field, esp. China.

A note on German sinology 1949/50 is going to appear in the next issue of FEQ. I hope that this information may be of use to you.

Kindest regards,

　　　　　　　　　　　　　　　　Yours Sincerely,

　　　　　　　　　　　　　　　　Rudolf Löewenthal

　　　　　　　　　　　〔袁同礼家人提供〕

按：罗文达通讯地址为 310 Stewart Avenue, Ithaca, New York。该函为其亲笔。

十一月二十四日

西门华德覆函先生,寄上其著述目录,并告牛津大学博得利图书馆新购得《永乐大典》。

　　　　　　　　　　　　　　　　24th November, 1950.

My dear Director Yuan,

Thank you for your letter of 3rd November and for your kind enquiry about my health. I am in fact almost all right and hope that my illness will have 'fizzled out' by the end of the year. Enclosed please find the list of my writings. I shall also be writing to Haloun about your request.

Re the *Yeongleh-dahdean*, I understand that the owner has meanwhile offered the 7 volumes to the Bodleian Library but he has also been told about your interest in this matter.

A copy of the *Quarterly Bulletin of Chinese Bibliography*, English edition 1947 will follow as soon as I can get hold of it.

Meanwhile, I remain, with very kind regards,

Yours sincerely,

W. Simon

〔伦敦大学亚非学院（School of Oriental and African Studies, University of London）信纸。University of Chicago Library, Yuan T'ung-li Papers, Box 2〕

按：Haloun 应指 Gustav Haloun（1898-1951），捷克汉学家，曾长期执掌剑桥大学中国语言和历史教席。此件为打字稿，落款处为其签名。

十一月二十五日

先生致信怀特，根据国务院 Thomas R. Fisher 建议，请将此前申请退回以便改由国会图书馆作为支持方再次提交。

November 25, 1950

Dear Dr. White:

Dr. Fisher of the State Department sent me a copy of his letter to Provost Gentzler dated November 17th. From that communication I was given to understand that I should do the writing at the Library of Congress under the sponsorship of Dr. Hummel.

May I request you to return to me the application forms, so that I can take up the matter here?

May I avail myself of this opportunity to express to you and also to Mr. Gentzler my sincere appreciation for your interest and assistance. I am sure that I can count upon your further aid whenever necessary.

With warmest personal regards,

Yours sincerely,

T. L. Yuan

〔Columbia University Library, New York State Library School Collection, Series 2 Student Records, Box 65, Folder Yuan, T. L.〕

按:此件为打字稿,落款处为先生签名,于11月28日送达。

十一月二十六日

李芳馥致函先生,谈个人情况及沪上、国内情形,并附中华医学会书目。

守公赐鉴:

前上一函,谅能先此达览。顷复承手示,对贱恙屡致惓惓,垂眷愈殷,铭感愈切。本年四月大病,幸告好,但病后调养未善,致气体虚弱。现在文管会任图书处主任之职,每日晨七时出,晚六时归,有不胜繁剧之感。此间接收图书达二十五万册,尚待接收者有六十余万册,现拟租赁雷士德研究所房屋,筹备一大规模之图书馆,但工作人手缺乏,内部人士问题极难处理,专门人才只有王育伊兄一人。本月起又被调往中国科学院图书馆,故筹备工作几无法进行。目前国内抗美援朝运动各处风起,平馆报名参加志愿军者闻有多人,保家卫国有争先恐后之象。英文《季刊》于本年一月全部运回北京,沪上无存书。曾屡函子刚兄照寄,竟未寄上,不知是否有所不便,当再函询之。中国科学院方面由育伊兄查得,另纸所开各刊物随函附上,但物理化学著作书目,则尚未查出。海关、亚洲文会、震旦博物院(前有请求公家接收之讯)、广学会等处出版西文书业务,皆已停顿。兹附上中华医学会书目一纸,如续有所得当再奉上。至于国人用俄文撰述者,至今尚未之闻。南京图书馆现由贺昌群□任馆长,顾斗南在该馆供职,其他南北同人一切如常。此差堪告慰者也。肃此,敬请道安。

后学李馨吾谨上

一九五〇年十一月廿六日

〔袁同礼家人提供〕

按:"雷士德研究所"全称应为"雷士德医学研究院"(Henry Lester Institute for Medical Research),以英国旅沪著名建筑师、地产商和慈善家亨利·雷士德(Henry Lester)命名,1932年在上海建成,位于爱文义路(今北京西路)。

十一月二十七日

王重民覆函先生,告国内局势、平馆情况,劝先生早日归国并谈及注意事项。

守和吾师道鉴:

奉到手谕后,即和郑西谛、王冶秋商议,他们都非常欢迎吾师早早回国,继续发展我图书馆事业,多多为人民大众服务。

新的中央人民政府内主持文教的是"文化教育委员会",主管文化、教育等部,新闻、出版等署和科学院。部署院下面各设若干局,文化部内有文物局,是主管图书馆、博物馆和考古发掘等事。文教委员长是郭沫若,文化部部长是沈雁冰,文物局局长是郑振铎,副局长是王冶秋。文物局内又设三处:图书馆处处长大约是向达,博物馆处处长是裴文中,副处长是王振铎;考古处处长大约是夏鼐,副处长是苏炳琦。觉明事情颇忙,不大愿就。西谛原有请吾师之意,因不在京,所以大家劝觉明,直到现在,觉明可允维持过渡,俟吾师到后再转让。裴文中亦表示愿办一个"自然博物馆",西谛答应他馆长兼处长,所以吾师到后,西谛亦拟请师以馆长兼处长,如此则一切可极得手矣。

觉明现充北大校务委员兼图书馆馆长,韩寿萱除北大外,兼历史博物馆馆长,该馆已有职员四十余人,收入各方捐赠珍品数万件,大非昔比矣。曾昭燏即可发表中央博物院院长,徐森老则将发表中央图书馆馆长。蒋慰堂各方面托人来说,要来京作事,但因他和反动派有较长的历史,如回来,亦需要先给予较长时期的训练和改造。在最近将来,不能负任何行政责任。西谛已明白表示。

至于馆中情形,从一九五〇年可开始发展,计划书已呈上去。现有职工一百六十七人,(宁沪不在内)明年可再增一百人上下。今年收赠及购买之书有十二万多册,明年国内出版者又都可得一份或两份赠送本,更可能有两万美元买外国书。办公费以外还有事业费,所以作书套,订洋装都有很充足的款子。静生房子不一定能收回,所以明春要在大书库后另盖一个同样大的书库,楼下不留办公室,共有七层,书架稍加密,可容两百万册书。在未盖其他大楼以前,先在东边树林内多盖一些平房。又上海所存报纸,已卖与出版总署,即可用以买一处宿舍。出版事业,以后统由出版总署办理,明年吾馆除年报及四十周年纪念刊外,要出一份"新书月报"和"全国新书总目"。

吾师回国问题,要加赶并提前实现,但有二事,要特别注意,并且应该立即行动:

一、给郑西谛、王冶秋写一信,表明立即回国,并且愿为人民大众服务。寄美善本书,可把提单带回,一俟航运畅通,一定可提回。

二、回国路线,最好取道欧洲。不论签赴英或赴法护照,并不难办理,到法国如不易,签赴苏护照,可去另一小民主国家,赴苏俄一行。此事最重要。因为一则苏联东方学者方面,对吾师感情素好,而由苏回国,最为国人所崇拜也。师兄姊等能维持,最好不要回国,师母暂留亦可,则吾师单人旅行,虽经行数国,亦不到有若何困苦也。

以上两点,请师详慎考虑,但生所见,则极为正确也。至于行政一节,现在不像以往那样困难。以往把一切责任集于馆长一人,许多地方是劳而无功;现在作长官,是只管计划大政,不管人事,故能垂拱而治,想吾师一登祖国土地,立时能看清楚是进步多多了!

北大代 L. C.所印善本书目,恒先生好像没有看明白我那封中文信,说所以长钱的原故,不是因为别的,是因为篇数增多了! 最好找出那封信,向他解释一下,增加的篇幅,我那信上都写明白了!

现已印完九卷,我想都寄去,请恒先生依印成卷数、页数作引得,大概不久就可接到。

吴光清兄想不回国,不知钱存训兄是否赶即回来。孙云铸有一弟弟,在美国学图书馆学,闻已毕业,明年回国。北大图书馆专科自成立以后,专任缺人,能有一位副教授或讲师来帮忙最好,不知钱存训兄肯作否?

专此,即请旅安!

师母统此问候。

生重民顿首
十一月廿七日
〔袁同礼家人提供〕

按:王振铎(1911—1992),字天木,河北保定人,燕京大学毕业,曾在北平研究院等处任职。"苏炳琦"应为苏秉琦(1909—1997),河北高阳人,考古学家,1934 年北平师范大学历史系毕业,后任

北平研究院史学研究所副研究员。孙云铸(1895—1979)，江苏高
邮人，古生物学家、地质学家，该函中谈及其弟应指孙云畴
(1917—2014)，后确归国并任北京大学图书专修科教员。

十一月二十八日

怀特覆函先生，告知已将申请文件寄还至先生在华盛顿的住址。

November 28, 1950

Dear Dr. Yuan:

The assistant Provost wrote Mr. Fisher in regard to your application. His reply of November 17 indicates the procedure required by the legislation governing the fund appropriated for the program. The letter clarified matters for us here at Columbia. The purpose of my writing is to be sure that a copy reached you. The letter states that a copy of it was mailed to you at your Washington address, which I take to mean your residence.

With kind personal regards, I am,

Very sincerely yours,

Carl M. White

P. S. Your kind letter has just came. We have telephoned the Ass. Provost office regarding the application and assumed it will be returned.

〔袁同礼家人提供〕

按：此件为打字稿，落款和补语皆为其亲笔。

十二月六日

何多源致函先生，告在广州、香港购买书刊的情况。

守和先生尊鉴：

十一月廿六日挂号寄上下列各种期刊，想不久可以到达座右。

一、《人民中国》二卷三——七期及第九期(今日寄上八、十两期)；

二、《中国科学》一卷一期；

三、《燕京社会科学》五卷一期(英文本)一九五〇年；

四、《新建设》第二期(赠阅本)；《科学通报》，中国科学院印行。

又前托友人在港代定《天地新闻》半年，需港币三十元，值美金五
元，未知有收到此刊否？如未收到，请即示知，以便向出版者交涉。由

十月三日起寄往韩慕义先生处之书刊,已值美金壹百四十九元八角三分,未悉已收到一部份否? 便请一查示知,然后再寄。因此间最近虽收挂号寄往国外之邮件,但声明不负安全到达之责也。又因邮件须由香港转寄,故邮资比由美国寄此间约高一倍。例如由美寄航空信来广州不过美金二角五分,但由此寄美国则要美金五角。嘱代购英文刊物,已函京沪搜购。一俟购得,当即寄奉不误。此请钧安。

后学何多源上
一九五〇十二月六日

〔University of Chicago Library, Yuan T'ung-li Papers, Box 2〕

按:"韩慕义"即恒慕义。落款处左侧注有"中国新地图,寄十元"、"十二,廿二"字样。该函非何多源亲笔,且由香港广大中学Dr. W. H. Tam 转寄先生,W. H. Tam 待考,似为此函誊缮之人。

十二月二十三日

杭立武覆函先生,告知平馆运台图书目录前由傅斯年寄到,并谈开箱检查预算。

守和吾兄左右:

十一月十五日惠书敬悉。北平图书馆所藏内阁大库之目录,业经故孟真兄检寄,民国廿一年《北平图书馆馆刊》第六卷第四期中刊载王庸君所编者备用。该批箱件拟于短期内开始检查,所需费用由保管处估计约新台币七四〇〇元(附奉预算表),折美金七百元。本处经费拮据,承贵馆慨予负担,至为感慰。如汇款,希寄台中市振兴路四十四号"中央文管处"。庄尚严、梁廷炜两君仍在本处故宫组任职,承嘱各节,自当转知照办。专此奉复,并颂旅祺!

弟杭立武敬启
十二月廿三日

附概算表一纸

检查北平图书馆存本处文物十八箱用费概算

做箱费:每个新台币叁佰元,十八个共计伍仟肆佰元(内加铁皮防潮)。

包装费及樟脑费:纸张,新台币贰佰元;樟脑,新台币捌佰元。

酬劳缮写及工人工资费:新台币壹仟元。

以上合计新台币柒仟肆佰元正。

〔University of Chicago Library, Yuan T'ung-li Papers, Box 2〕

按：全函皆为代笔，落款处钤"杭立武"印。先生在结尾处标注"一月四日复，仅有一百八十元"。

十二月三十一日

颜复礼覆函先生，寄上前请书目、行述，并告傅吾康将接替自己出任汉堡大学汉学教授。

同礼先生阁下：

岁云暮矣。弟尚思将本年书信债务为之束清。十月四日大札尚未奉覆，此乃最紧急之债务。阁下十二月廿日来函道及此，诚有因也。久未奉覆之原因乃最近三月中，弟为其他无法延搁之工作所羁绊，虽全衷欲将阁下所需要之各种书目完成，终无暇及此，怅何如之。弟于前函中已道及弟固甚愿支持阁下之书目工作也。目下弟尚须作一长篇批评论文，约一月十日左右可完毕，然后必开始书目工作以答尊愿。今暂寄上以下各种：

1.拙着 Forke 书目一份。

2.拙着 Otto Franke 行述一份。

3.中国建筑学研究之首创人 Ernst Boerschmann 之着作书目一份。

No. 1 and 2 will be sent by ordinary post。Erich Haenisch 之完备着作书目，容觅得寄上。Fuchs 曾在汉堡充当代理教授二学期，弟早已将尊愿转达。渠现在明兴充当代理教授，如渠尚未寄上彼之着作书目，则弟将代为收集寄呈。

阁下果能再与弟二月时间，则感激甚矣。汉堡方面，弟之后继任乃 Otto Franke 之子 Wolfgang Franke，曾居中国十三年，在北京中德文化学院任务，并充北京大学、成都大学教授，其夫人为中国女士。关于寄上德国最近出版汉学研究书籍之事，弟当向 Doerling 书局接洽不误。

值此桃符换旧，弟谨以至诚祝阁下百吉，尤望政治局面之转变不致对阁下有何影响也，想一时阁下亦难有可能返国。最后，弟尚不能不声明，弟之前信及此信乃请此间一中国太太翻成中文，由弟抄呈。阁下之美誉，弟何敢当之哉。

专此奉覆，即颂台社，并贺年禧。

弟颜复礼 Fritz Jäger 顿首

一九五〇年十二月卅一日

〔University of Chicago Library, Yuan T'ung-li Papers, Box 2〕

按："拙着"当作"拙著"，"着作"当作"著作"。Ernst Boerschmann（1873-1949），德国建筑师，二十世纪初来华，行程数万里，对中国各省古建筑均有考察，拍摄了大量照片，回国后出版了一系列有关中国的专著。Doerling 似为古旧书店，待考。

是年

先生加入美国远东学会（Far Eastern Association），成为正式会员。

一九五一年　五十七岁

一月二日

程绥楚函覆函先生，请写推荐信与费知乐，为其谋取澳大利亚国立大学研究职位。

守和先生、夫人尊鉴：

前收到嘱寄各件，当日即照办。北京圖馆一函则添了一香港地名，以免麻烦。费知乐先生见过，后又在英文化会听他讲演，已于年终卅日去澳。买书工作，由此间蔚林公司代办，贵不可言。他说东方学院刚有一点点开始，要待他去澳后始知如何组织，此公对中国学问进度不太深，不及西门远甚。尊示所云甚是，但其购书工作，当时似另有经纪包围，晚不便多参加。澳洲大学（Prof. C. P. Fitzgerald, The Australian National University, Canberra, Australia）之东方学院将来不招学生，只作研究，校长为前澳驻华大使（尊处可能有此人名字）。关于用人，照他说到澳后才开始组织，故在港无法答应，这一点是事实，费为长者，一望便知。晚送他一本此间新出之《神武天皇新考》，要约他吃饭因时间不定而未果。现在看情形他一定要用晚这类研究员帮忙，但一时晚亦无法表现区区所知，和他谈了一小时余，后来在文化会与他只寒暄了几句，告诉了他一声，如果要用袁先生正式向澳大校长介绍或详细推荐，我可以再寄信请在美国的袁先生写。他已知绥为寅恪先生的学生，晚曾从刘文典师习《庄子》、《文选》及晚唐温李诗（当时约四十余人，晚以史系选习，分数最高），去南开是寅恪先生派助教来问的，时在《北方日报》主社评，南开教中国近代史、民国外交史及西洋通史（此科冯柳漪先生考虑狠久，结果许晚教文学院，另一杨先生燕大留美者教法学院，成绩则晚较杨受欢迎，澄弟曾习过），晚意仍恳劳神赐一函与其校长，详为介绍，另请附一函与 Fitz.先生，其校长函亦可请费代为面交，只求能去安心研究几年，照情形看，对费先生是有帮助的。此间彼所见者（或者马鉴等另有介绍，则不得而知），恐不一定内行，港大中文系便等于虚设也。费近日已到澳（可能航空去，书另交运输公司），尊函能直接寄澳更好。*Newsdom* 即《新闻天地》英文板，只能自第九期起，前者已无存，平寄不要邮费，不知已收到否？订单存此备查询，自 No.9－No.12 作一次寄。冬来望多多珍重，至念至念。余续上，敬请双安，弟妹均此问好。

　　　　　　　　　　　　　　　　　　　　　　晚绥楚敬上

　　　　　　　　　　　　　　　　　　　　　　一月二日

背面另抄点简历以为参考。

　　　　　　　　　　　　　　　　　　　　〔袁同礼家人提供〕

　　按：*Newsdom*，1950 年在香港复刊，半月刊。该函后附个人介绍百余字。

一月五日

费正清覆函先生，赞同此前先生提出在广州购买中文出版物的计划并寄上一百美金备用，并期待面谈用以解决细节问题。

　　　　　　　　　　　　　　　　　　　　5 January 1951

Dear Mr. Yuan:

　　Your letter of December 19 concerning the possibility of procuring Chinese publications from Canton deserves immediate action, and without waiting further I enclose a check for ＄100.00 in the hope that you can use it to begin a flow of current materials from the Canton area and the back files of appropriate publications. Naturally this must be a bit experimental. We will try to make desires more specific when we know more of the possibilities and also as our efforts here to develop a project for translation develop.

　　I look forward to seeing you about the middle of January in Washington to further about this.

　　We will eventually meet the problem of bringing these materials into the Harvard collection in such a way as not to create overhead and un-balance in the collection. But I think we should probably begin as though this were a special project on an emergency basis. The object of your agent in Canton should be to get materials which are of interest concerning the current situation and the recent past. You can suggest the type of thing we need quite as well as any of us could. We would be interested in all aspects and in ephemeral publications, posters and the like, quite as much as in regular periodicals. On the other hand, we want to avoid mere junk which is repetitious and duplicative. I suppose this is a utopian concept and will therefore leave it in your hands at your discretion.

Our next move should be to work out a more effective plan for the flow of these publications so as to get it regularly financed.

I am looking forward to seeing you.

With best regards,

John K. Fairbank

Dr. Chiu says items dated 1949 or 1950 are not likely to be duplicated of what we have.

〔University of Chicago Library, Yuan T'ung-li Papers, Box 2〕

按:此件为打字稿,落款及补语均为其亲笔。

一月中旬

先生与费正清会面,商讨编制在香港、台湾和欧洲等地从事研究工作的中国学者通信录,并将这些信息编成非正式出版物寄送美国的中国学研究者。〔University of Chicago Library, Yuan T'ung-li Papers, Box 2〕

一月十九日

晚七时,曾琦招宴,先生、夫人袁慧熙和袁清、刘大钧夫妇及其子、郑友揆夫妇及其子、杨雪伦夫人及其二子、童夫人等与席。席间,曾琦与先生等讨论时局。〔《曾琦先生文集》(下),台北:"中央研究院"近代史研究所,1993 年,页1511〕①

> 按:郑友揆(1909—1999),浙江镇海人,经济学家,先后在沪江大学、燕京大学学习,在北平社会调查所从事研究工作,后赴美留学,时应在布鲁金斯学会(Brookings Institution)供职。杨雪伦,时应在国会图书馆东方部(日文)服务。"童夫人"似指童季龄夫

① 《曾琦先生文集》此处排印有误,原文为"七时宴李守和夫妇及其幼子"。

人,待考。杨云竹夫妇本亦受邀,但因故未到。

一月中下旬

梅贻琦、韩咏华及子女在先生处小住。〔袁同礼家人提供〕

一月二十二日

先生致信美国中华医学基金会秘书 Agnes M. Pearce,询问北京协和医学院科研人员名单。

January 22, 1951

Dr. Agnes M. Pearce, Secretary

China Medical Board

New York 22, N. Y.

Dear Dr. Pearce:

　　As I am engaged in compiling a scientific bibliography of China, I am in need of a list of scientific staff of the Peking Union Medical College at the present time. If your office happens to have such a list, may I borrow it for a few days?

　　If you have any information from Dr. Lee, perhaps you will let me know. Dr. Lee is an old friend of mine and I have great admiration for his ability to handle situations in times of emergency.

Yours sincerely,

T. L. Yuan

〔Rockefeller Foundation, "China Medical Board, Inc. records." Box 160 Folder 1167〕

　　按:此件为打字稿,落款处为先生签名,于翌日送达。

费慰梅致函先生,请先生为《远东季刊》撰写有关在美中国学者的信息类短文。

Jan. 22, 51

Dear Dr. Yuan:

　　John tells me that you would be willing to furnish me with a list of Chinese scholars in America for the next issue of the *Far Eastern Quarterly* with their present positions and addresses. I should certainly much appreciate having such a list for the "News of the Profession" and am sure that it would interest our readers.

The copy for the May issue has just gone to press, unfortunately-for I should like to have had it for this issue. The next is the August 1951 issue for which the deadline for my receiving material is April 10th. I realize that it may be more difficult for you to provide current addresses for persons in a summer issue when people are eager to be changing jobs. But I hope you will consent to undertake it.

You will understand that the Chinese scholars of greatest interest to Far Eastern Associations members and *FEQ* readers are those who are specialists or some experts of Far Eastern affairs & cultures (rather than natural scientists, etc.).

I was glad to find news of you from China. My kind regards to your family too.

Sincerely yours,

Wilma Fairbank

Of course, I always want news of special researches going forward here or in China.

〔University of Chicago Library, Yuan T'ung-li Papers, Box 2〕

按:John 即费正清。查《远东季刊》,似未刊登过此类文章。该函
为费慰梅亲笔。

一月二十三日

程绥楚致函先生,告知陈寅恪嘱寄《元白诗笺证稿》,并请先生鼎力支持其
赴澳大利亚谋教职。

守和先生、夫人双前:

前寄一书报告费知乐先生去澳,计已先此达览。昨接寅恪师函
云,寄来一本《元白诗笺证稿》,嘱即速寄上,但已数日未见到,正写信
去问,岭大财产近因故被封,此书亦在内,将来解冻再□寄,先将手边
一本寄来,其意似要此本速到先生手中也,俟到即为寄上不误。香港
同美禁运,各货涨价至一二倍到十倍不等,如一旦有事,教员阶级便要
饿毙,故去澳之意极殷,仍有待鼎力,直函与费知乐先生一商。晚已另
写好一英文函并一诗笺及寅恪师前为绥签好之 To whom it may

concern 一件，证明所习过之国史及国学科目。拟明日直航寄坎培拉，现在可不问报酬，因家慈在长沙，每月只要七八十元港币生活费，合澳币才十五元也。澄弟有函嘱转寄天津信，已代办不误，恐已放寒假，故先不写信寄 Colgate。昨吟就一诗，寄怀尊驾，先书此，容日另用好纸寄，尚祈正韵是祷。余再上，敬叩年禧。弟妹仝此问好。

晚绥楚敬上

一月二十三投邮

〔袁同礼家人提供〕

按：1950 年 11 月，《元白诗笺证稿》作为《岭南学报丛书》第一种由该校中国文化研究室初版。Colgate 即 Colgate University，袁澄在此就读并获得学士学位。该信后附《敬怀袁守和馆长》、《送费知乐先生行》两短诗。

一月二十四日

裘开明致函先生，已按前请寄送留美学生名录七册，华美协进社刊行的同学名录则请联系该所，此前寄平馆存在哈佛燕京图书馆的缩微相机请早日取走，并告其将联系顾子刚今后涉及平馆在美财产事宜请直接联系先生而非代管人。

January 24, 1951

Dear Dr. Yuan:

In answer to your inquiry of January 5, I am sending to you under separate cover a lot of seven directories of Chinese students in the U. S. A. from 1934 to 1943 which belong to the Library, and also a folder of Tsinghua, Yenching, and Nankai alumni in the U. S. A. which belongs to me personally.

As no doubt you have access to the Directories of Chinese students in America published by the China Institute, we are not sending those to you.

As to the microfilm camera which belongs to your Library, please take it away at your earliest convenience. (I can send it to you charges collect by the Railway Express.) Since your Library still has many rare books deposited in the Library of Congress, you can surely also deposit the camera over there too.

After the camera leaves Cambridge, I shall write to Mr. Koo, telling him that in the eyes of the American government you are still the Librarian of the National Library of Peiping and that you still have the custody of its funds and its property (e. g., rare books) in America. Regarding the property of the National Library, he should write to you and not to me as a private citizen of China. We three are all friends, but we must get the legal points straight in our minds, so as not to hurt our personal friendship.

With all good wishes,

Very sincerely yours,

A. Kaiming Chiu

〔University of Chicago Library, Yuan T'ung-li Papers, Box 2〕

按:microfilm camera 似于 1953 年秋移存至斯坦福大学胡佛研究院和图书馆①,但最终去向不明。

一月二十六日

费正清致函先生,此前建议编印在台、港地区及欧洲的中国学者通讯录,应以私下印制而非对公发行的形式进行。

January 26 1951

Dear Mr. Yuan:

It was a great pleasure to see you in Washington and make up schemes for the promotion of good works as we used to do some time ago. In this connection, I am wondering if I should put on record our hope that you will be able to prepare privately a list of Chinese scholars in Formosa, Hongkong and Europe, giving their names, addresses, fields and some synopses of their careers with a view to having this information privately distributed to individual specialists in Far Eastern studies in this country, not for purposes of publication in any formal way or to the general public, but merely for the information of the leading scholars in the United States.

① University of Chicago Library, Yuan T'ung-li Papers, Box 3.

I wonder, on second thought, if you still agree that this would be a good idea, as it seems to me. If so, I wonder how this might best be done? I should think that any list you might prepare could be duplicated by the office of Mr. Graves and sent out through it. Or, alternatively, I should be glad to do so here in my capacity as secretary of the ACLS committee.

In either case, I should be very glad to hear from you as to this project. I hope that we may separately be able to follow up on the project for a digest and will let you know about it in due course.

Sincerely yours,

John

〔University of Chicago Library, Yuan T'ung-li Papers, Box 2〕

按:ACLS 即 American Council of Learned Societies。此件为打字稿,落款处为其签名。

一月二十七日

胡适覆函先生,告知中基会拟在三月下旬开大会,拟在会上讨论是否补助先生编撰《西文汉学书目》。

守和兄:

两信均悉,谢谢。

中基会的资产,因会章有"总办事处设在首都"等条文,故已被冻结。现已去交涉解冻,大概无大问题。

一月十五日开过中基会执行委员会与财务委员会联席会,因时局动荡,有新董事主张三月底召开大会。现已发出通告会期为三月廿九日,但未必能开成。如人数不够,则改开执委会。

尊意决定不就"Digest of Current Chinese Publications",而愿意继续由中基会补助,使老兄能"以全力从事中国书目志之编纂"。鄙意原拟不必开大会,但现既召开大会,只好暂候大会中决定老兄补助的开题。倘蒙先期拟一英文说帖,继续报告已成工作,并说明继续请补助之意,则于我们最为方便。匆匆,敬祝双安。

弟胡适敬上

一九五一,一月廿七

〔袁同礼家人提供〕

一月三十一日

胡适致函先生,请在国会图书馆影照《中国新文学大系·建设理论集》中的两篇文字。

> 守和兄:
>
> 　　昨上短信,想已达览。
>
> 　　今有一事奉恳:
>
> 　　国会馆似有赵家璧主编的"中国新文学大系"(良友公司出版)十册。其首册"建设理论集"有我的"导言"一篇(pp. 1-32),又有我的"逼上梁山"一篇(pp. 3-27)。这两篇后来都没有收在"文存"或"论学近著"里。昨天在哥大见此书,其纸每页都破碎了,故我想请你替我把这两篇做一副 Photostat 影本。共有五十六页之多,费钱若干乞示知,当即寄奉。匆匆,敬祝双安。
>
> 　　　　　　　　　　　　　　　　　　　　弟适之
>
> 　　　　　　　　　　　　　　　一九五一,一,卅一夜
>
> 　　"逼上梁山"一篇本是"四十自述"的一部分,因中间留学一段没写,故没收入。

〔袁同礼家人提供〕

二月二日

Agnes M. Pearce 覆函先生,寄上职员名单并告知北京协和医学院已经被国有化。

February 2, 1951

Dear Dr. Yuan:

　　I am sorry to have delayed so long in sending you a staff list of the P. U. M. C. We have had no list later than that of September, 1949, but we have revised it as best we can, so that I think it is reasonably accurate. Dr. Loucks, who left Peking last June, has been able to bring it up to date at least to that point. I enclose the list we have prepared.

　　I regret to have to tell you we received a cable from Dr. C. U. Lee last week reporting that the P. U. M. C. had been nationalized on January 20. We hope that it will be possible for Dr. Lee to send us written details in due time, but of course are not sure that he will be able to do so or that he will be able to say very much. Like you, we have great admiration for Dr. Lee. He has brought the College through many emergencies during the past few years and successfully handled many difficult situations. We know that the recent development was beyond his control.

Sincerely yours,

Agnes M. Pearce

〔Rockefeller Foundation, "China Medical Board, Inc. records." Box 160 Folder 1167〕

按：Dr. Loucks 即 Harold H. Loucks(1894－1982)，美国医生，中文名娄克思[1]，1922 年加入北京协和医学院，后任外科系主任教授、美国中华医学基金会(China Medical Board)职员。

二月十四日

萧瑜覆函先生，告知日内瓦"中国国际图书馆"已陆续搬运迁往乌拉圭，并就所询留法学生姓名告其所知者。

> 守和先生大鉴：
>
> 昨奉惠书，敬承一一。敝馆迁移已经开始，第一、二批图书已经运出，第三批以后不日继续起运，惟工作异常繁重，非短期所能藏事。前言移馆比诸移山，实则运全馆于南美，诚所谓挟泰山以超北海，较移山为尤难也。弟离欧赴新馆时，当在三数月此间工作完全结束之后矣。承示大著《中国学者西文著述目录》，极为必要。弟十年前在巴黎曾率领一高材生作《中国学者法文著作目录》，并作提要与短评，已得百余种。惜因战事忽起，此生竟惨死于德军之手，稿件亦不知遗存何处，前功尽弃，万分可惜，否则今日定可供大著参考矣。示询论文名单之中文名姓有十分确凿者，兹另纸列附后，其他有不易查处者，有须待弟回巴时搜查十年前旧通信住址始能对照记出者，均当期诸他日也。统俟续及，即颂旅祺。
>
> 弟萧瑜顿首
>
> 四十，二，十四
>
> 又，示询黄君在美地址，未知系指小女婿黄益否？彼之住址为 Mr.

---

① 《私立北平协和医学院简章》，1936 年 9 月，页 38。

Yi Huang, 319 West, 108th Street, New York City 25，并以覆闻，又及。

又，再阅所寄留法学生论文名单，殊不完备，无里昂中法大学前后廿年中论文数百本，多未列入，尤大缺点。

又，拙著法文自由诗小剧本名*Pan-keou*（蚌壳）曾先后奏唱于巴黎Opera 及 Thêatre des Champs Elysées 及卢森堡京城等处，或亦可羼入聊充数也。

又，弟十二年来用全力以法文写著中国学典（中国百科全书）Encyclopédie Chinoise, Premièr Essai，已得一万五千余则，约合一千一百页，已大体脱稿，正在交涉待印，如得早日出版，当亦欲自荐占去大著一行。

又，执事所开留法学生论文名单，倘能将论文名目全题开示，将于考查著者中文名字大有助益，如何，乞酌。馆中装箱正忙乱中，临楮草草，至诸乞谅之。

　　　　　　　　　　　　　　　　　弟又及

〔袁同礼家人提供〕

　　按：该函附留法学生姓名中西文对照名单，即信中所言之"十分确凿者"，分为巴黎、卡昂、里尔、里昂、南锡五地。

二月十六日

晚八时半，先生和夫人访曾琦，祝贺其迁居，并赠礼物。先生建议曾琦之子曾宪斌应及早准备暑假毕业后申请研究院，如顺利则可由学校出面向美政府申领补助。〔《曾琦先生文集》（下），页1517-1518〕

　　按：2月12日，曾琦一家自Madison街1318号搬出，迁往新址3rd floor 2412, Pennsylvania Ave，新址原为陈松樵租赁的寓所，他已迁往纽约。袁慧熙拟为曾琦夫人周若南介绍打字工作，以贴补家用。曾琦对先生的提议甚为感激，在其日记中写下"其友谊殊可感也"。

二月二十七日

杨步伟致信先生、夫人，回寄年节礼物并述梅贻琦夫妇行踪，并告赵元任近况。

　　守和兄嫂：

　　久未通信，甚念。节前承赐棹毯还未道谢，真是该打。我总想等中国的火腿来了寄东西再写信,且知一直到今天才到。西边各物皆不及东边好,食物罐头等想托人带,而近来□先生太太们都是飞来飞去的,谁也不能带东西,腐乳等又不便寄,□□只得还是送你们点老东西吃吧。梅先生□□住了一个星期,也是匆匆促促的,本希望他们再来,但是梅太太急要看大彦了,大约目前也不再来了。你们小孩们都入学校了,何日贤夫妇再来西边住些时? 我们今年不能往去东方,因语言学学院今夏在加大,元任没有机会离开此地了。此地现在已百花怒放了,东边想还很冷。王文伯不幸遭此意外,希望他早日复元出院,否则身体和经济皆不得了。匆此不尽,并祝近好。

赵杨步伟上

元任嘱候

二月二十七日

另包寄上食物祈查收。

〔University of Chicago Library, Yuan T'ung-li Papers, Box 2〕

按:王徵(1887—1963),字文伯,吉林宁安(今属黑龙江省)人,胡适好友,杜威来华讲学期间曾担任翻译。1950 年 12 月 23 日晚,王徵在纽约旅馆中被烧伤,送 Roosevelt Hospital,被诊为三级烧伤。

徐家璧覆函先生,就所托之事一一答复。

守和馆长钧鉴:

敬肃者,前奉二月十六日手谕,嘱代查代办数事,只以琐务繁冗,不克即时完成。曾于二十日奉覆,请为酌予展缓期以便进行。兹以又逾一周,特将代办情形报告如左:

1.刘显卫先生地址,经亲自往稚晖学院调查,得悉刘公通讯处即在院内,其地址系85(非84)Riverside Drive。又刘公自拼姓名作 Sien-wei Liu,而稚晖学院作 Woochefee Institute,特录出以供参考。

2.哥大博士名单二十五人,已查出者仅为五人,其余各人虽经请求王际真先生、房兆楹兄协助,仍无所补益。王公尚能记忆 Konrad Hsu,但其中文姓名并不详悉,因此无由补充。此外,璧亦曾向 Columbiana 特藏探求过去中国学生名录或出版刊物,惜均无所获。馆内搜藏,除有少数《留美中国学生季报》外(均已逐期检查),并无同学名录之类之书,是以访查无由,深为歉仄。

3.哥大近两年来,中国同学姓名录看似简易,实亦无从着手。盖此间同学为数向多,但组织散漫,晤聚时稀。前年在此主办学生会事务诸同学多已纷纷离校,或回国内,此后继起无人,会务已陷于停顿状态一年余矣。加之过去(目前仍不免)学生份子复杂,颇惹移民局及FBI注意,曾零星传讯学生多人,彼等认为哥大中国学生会屡有非法活动,使彼等有对本校中国学生组织加以监视之必要,此亦近一年来学生会销沉之一重大原因。根据此种现状,同学名册遂无人搜集、无人编造,及迫尊处需用亦无法可依应命。又编制此种姓名录,事虽具有价值,但际此目前世事动乱之时,每易招人忌讳,疑为"特务",故人多讳莫如深不愿合作。此亦璧在此感觉辣手无法推进,苦衷所在耳。截至目前,璧已就本馆阅者登记片中之华人一一抄录名单一份,其余个人熟识,确在校中肄业者,亦为之加以补充,结果共得壹百余人,大抵约当全体百分之五十弱。至于详细明确名单,似可由尊处直接来函与本校外国学生顾问商洽,托为抄副备用,未悉以为若何。兹将顾问二人姓名录后,以便通讯。

Mr. Troup Matthews, Foreign Student Adviser(Teachers College 除外), University Hall Annex, Columbia University, New York 27, N. Y.

Professor Clarence Linton, Student Adviser, 108 Teachers College Main Building, Teachers, College, Columbia University, New York 27, N. Y.

4.东亚研究所章程一册,随函寄奉,乞为检览。

5.哥大华人教员姓名曾遵嘱予以查访,且并面询王际真先生,其结果仅如另单所列,其间容有遗漏,不过亦难知其实况。所云物理系教授一名,现尚在访查中,如得结果当续奉闻。

胡兄绍声回国以后,未曾来函,惟据闻渠在北京人民革命大学圕任编目事(并非圕主任),待遇则为供给制,似此渠或已入党为干部矣。

沈校长方面消息未有所闻,学校改为国立或较易于办理,但不知人事牵动将至如何地步。

　　孙兄云畴近有函来谓在北大图书专修科任专任教员,担任圖学概论暨中文编目二课,情况似尚不恶,该专修科由王有三君主持一切,当为所悉。

　　又顾兄家杰去秋返国,现已就任中国科学院(即前中央研究院)图书管理处副处长之职,据云待遇合人民币七十万元,亦极清苦。处内尚有毛兄宗荫任编目事。如此,图书管理人才现下又集中首都矣。

　　此间馆务如常。匆匆,不尽欲言。嘱办诸事,歉未能如愿周至,统乞鉴原是幸。专此,敬颂道安。

后学徐家璧谨上
二月二十七日

阖府统此问候。

〔袁同礼家人提供〕

　　按:“刘显卫”即“刘先伟”,早年赴法留学入里昂中法大学,后在里昂财政及保险学院深造[1],著有 *Les problèmes monétaires et financiers de la Chine* ,1940 年巴黎出版,先生应查此书作者,故托徐家璧探询。Konrad Hsu 应指徐章(Konrad Chang, Hsu),1924 年获哥伦比亚大学博士学位。“物理系教授一名”即吴健雄,先生在此有标注。顾家杰(1913—1979),字忍吾,江苏苏州人,1936 年毕业于武昌文华图书专科学校,1947 年赴美深造,1950 年 9 月归国。该函可能影响了先生编纂《中国留美同学博士论文目录》的进程,并推迟了其出版时间。

二月二十八日

梅贻琦、韩咏华致函先生,告知其一家行踪。

　　守和吾兄惠鉴:

　　月前在华府小聚,甚快。琦来西部,忽忽竟已一月矣。郁文携二小孩于二月一日到 S. F.,一路稍有风浪,尚不太辛苦,下船手续都尚顺利,在赵宅住三日即来 L. A.。毛家房子不大,忽加老小四口,但早晚变化,竟亦可住下。小孩管理渐次移交彬彬,遂于今日辞职负担家事,所幸文德新就之事,每月收入可有二百余元,可以勉强维持。琦等定

---

[1]《大美晚报》(上海),1933 年 5 月 18 日,第 14 版。

于星期日(三月四日)离此东去费城,稍停,九、十号返纽约。原拟来华府小住二、三日,藉与诸戚友晤叙,惟因 UN 有一 Social Commission 三月中在日内瓦开会,蒋、张诸公坚欲琦出席参加,故须早些到纽约准备一切。此去约四月下旬方得归来。最近琦等到纽约,仍暂住缪云台兄处,待琦归后,再作找房打算。嫂夫人衣服数件,拟日内先付邮寄上。月前曾接 St. Louis-Oak Hill Cemetery 管理人来信,关于鸿年坟墓似甚注意照顾,兹抄副张寄尊处分存,另以一张寄与惠年处,俾转告北平可以安心矣。

　　行前在港匆匆,只做得皋如黑绸衫一件、静侄所要长衫一件。尚有去年带港之两件衣样尚存敝处,容到纽约即当寄上。所存之款付清各项,尚余十四元四角,又买物清单当一并寄上,即祝阖府均吉。

贻琦、咏华

二月廿八

〔袁同礼家人提供〕

　　按:S. F. 即旧金山,赵宅即赵元任家,L. A. 即洛杉矶,毛家应指女婿毛文德的房子。彬彬即梅祖彬(1920—2012),梅贻琦、韩咏华夫妇的长女,西南联大外语系毕业,其丈夫即毛文德。缪云台(1894—1988),原名缪嘉铭,字云台,云南昆明人,1913 年留学美国,1920 年回国从事开发锡矿,曾任个旧锡务公司总经理、云南省政府委员兼农矿厅厅长等职。

是年春

先生致信布朗,告知自己不会提交有关中国图书馆现状的报告。〔Harvard-Yenching Institute Archives, Letter of Charles H. Brown to Alfred K'aiming Ch'iu, March 13, 1951〕

　　按:3 月 27 日至 29 日,美国图书馆协会东方馆藏联合委员会会议在费城举行,先生受邀参加,依照规定须提交论文。这一变化似为先生想"保持沉默",即不愿对中国大陆和台湾地区情况有倾向性的评述。

三月四日

程绥楚致函先生,告已寄出《元白诗笺证稿》,并请向何艾龄推荐其担任高级夜校教员。

守和先生、夫人前辈双安：

前所寄函,谅邀清览。上月二十寅恪师自穗寄来其所著之《元白诗笺证稿》一部,于二十三日挂号寄上,计程此信到时或到后一周可以收到。此书与岭南之其他美国财产同时被封,是册系寅师手边者,存图书馆亦是纪念品也。近书物已解冻,晚所购此书亦已于前日寄到。(此书印价甚贵,合港币逾12元,在港可购一本 *Concise Oxford Dic*.有余。)

费知乐先生至今一去无信,寄去的挂号函亦未见覆,昨又寄去一册寅师著《元白诗》作为赠送其新中文图书馆。香港方面,大家都以为去澳较英为好,因颇难入境也。又此间港府近办一汉文高级夜校(Evening School of Higher Chinese Studies),应征教员者凡二百八十余人,而只要十一人。事前闻不必托人介绍,故绝对未托人情,恐反而误事。不意显中者多为何艾龄等所荐,友人中有傅尚霖先生(曾在清华及中央教过,前夏在岭英夜校授课)亲告晚详情。该校用港大中文系房子上课,分中文、商业、新闻三系,每小时25元,一年上七个月课。如一学程为三小时,则可有300一月,不上课(公假亦算不上课,即实实在在上课之时数)不计,平均如得六小时,可以年入四千二百元。晚曾 apply 中国通史、隋唐史、唐诗、中国近代史(无史系,但新闻系及中文系皆有社会科学门)。港例秋季始业,此校因系明天开课,拟自目前起赶到明秋,教完前二年,明秋第一班者入第三年级。今秋尚要招生,因 apply 之人太多,教育司事实上不得不注意专家之推荐。何艾龄女士知晚在岭英为孚众望之教员,但彼实不知晚能授汉文学校,且每次来视察,皆是公事,看看上课情形。晚希望今秋前能将此夜校授课事办好,马鉴先生说最好是有两人推荐,彼允尽力(但已退休,因系旧人,渠如进言,多少有用)。何艾龄系教育司长以外,教司之第一有力者,不知我师能否打数行字为晚介绍一下,作为今夏 apply 之基础。马季明先生云,隋唐史及近代史皆非一年级课,而新闻系之一年级与他系同,故今秋应高班课程之征求较易入手。此说甚是,因一年级之课只有国文通史二□,通史已为罗香林先生弄到,渠与广东关系深,晚实不能与之抗也。费知乐先生处不知可否请再赐一函,其详细地址,此间澳使馆曾告晚。兹抄录如下：

Prof. C. P. Fitzgerald, The Australian National University, Box 4,

G. P. O., Canberra, A. C. T., Australia.

又前订之*Newsdom*已收到否？订单存此，如有询问亦请便中示及，以便去查询。本期除高一三班英文（18 小时）外，又加高三每班三小时西史，共 24 小时，月薪另加 90 元，但忙得不亦乐乎。匆匆，不尽欲言。专肃，敬请双安。弟妹均此问好。

晚绥楚敬拜上

三月四夜

〔袁同礼家人提供〕

按：何艾龄（1904—2007），何东爵士之女，生于日本长崎，香港拔萃女书院毕业，后考入香港大学英文系，1925 年毕业，旋赴英国伦敦大学留学，1929 年归国在岭南大学任教，1940 年与林则徐外玄孙郑湘先成婚，1947 年出任培侨中学校董会主席，时供职于香港教育司署。

三月十日

晚，先生设宴，杨云竹、杨雪伦、童夫人、曾琦、周若南、曾宪斌受邀与席。

〔《曾琦先生文集》（下），页 1524〕

陈受颐致函先生，谈其近况并拟请先生协助搜集与中国文学史相关的插画素材。

守和尊兄道席：

违教多时，渴想无似。客岁曾肃贺简，又以误书尊址，未登清览，最以为歉。日前晤适之、月涵两公，籍谂我兄殚心著述，不胜钦慕。弟本岁幸得罗氏基金会资助，试写《中国文学史》小册，惟学殖既已荒落，心绪又复凌乱，杀青无期，徒增惆怅，深愿吾兄有片教督之也。

月杪美国远东学会在费城举行年会，弟拟观光。散会后并拟趋承教益，冀望在兄指导之下，征集文学史略插画十一二幅。车在马前之诮，所不敢辞也。

孟真兄天年竟夭，曷胜怨怆！弟至今心境未曾复旧，想兄亦有同感。匆匆走笔，敬颂旅祺，并祝嫂夫人俪祉。世兄姊均好。

弟受颐顿首

三月十日

〔University of Chicago Library, Yuan T'ung-li Papers, Box 7〕

　　按：1950 年，洛克菲勒基金会赞助陈受颐 4000 美金，用以完成中国文学史的写作[1]，其最终成果为 *Chinese Literature: A historical introduction*，中文题名为《中国文学史略》，1961 年 Ronald Press 初版。1950 年 12 月 20 日，傅斯年因脑溢血突然去世。

三月十二日

程绥楚致函先生，告费知乐尚未开始筹建研究机构故无法邀请其赴澳，并请将信转交袁澄。

　　守和先生、夫人长者双前：

　　　　前寄出寅恪师之《元白诗笺证稿》后，上周寄一航纸，计已先此达尊览。前日接到费知乐先生自澳京来函，云所购之书至今尚在途中，一切竟无法开始，只在讨论组织之开端而已，故尚不能对晚事作任何建议，末云"I will, of course, keep your papers and let you know if any possibility exists."，是则此老尚在留意中也。渠地址如前函所告。其函系用航空包随同其他文件寄此间澳商务代办公署，再转来者，虽航空亦走了半月。台湾所出之《大陆杂志》，颇有学术性，为董作宾先生编，不知已见到否？下半页如有便，敬乞转寄澄弟为感。余容再肃，敬请双安。弟妹均此祝好。

　　　　　　　　　　　　　　　　　　　　晚程绥楚敬上
　　　　　　　　　　　　　　　　　　　　三月十二日夜
　　　　　　　　　　　　　　　　　　〔袁同礼家人提供〕

Owen Lattimore 致函先生，谈蒙古研究近况，并邀先生参加十九日喀尔喀蒙古的专题研讨会。

　　　　　　　　　　　　　　　　　　　　March 12, 1951

　　Dear Dr. Yuan：

　　　　How has your work been going this winter? Have you been able to assemble any further material in Mongolia? This spring I am hoping to get the time to settle down to draw up a draft report on the whole subject, using your material, Mongol material that we have translated here, and my own material.

---

[1] *The Rockefeller Foundation Annual Report 1950*, New York, p. 268.

For egotistical reasons, I should also be very much interested to hear whether you have been able to add to your "Lattimore bibliography".

You know you are always welcome at any of our seminars over here. Would you like to receive regular notification of them? On Monday next, March 19, we are planning to have a seminar on Khalkha Mongolia, given by Mr. Vreeland. We are also expecting Nathaniel Peffer that day, as a visitor from Columbia, and possibly Mr. Sundaram of the Indian Embassy. If you should care to come over and join us for lunch at twelve o'clock noon, we should all be delighted to see you.

Yours very sincerely,

Owen Lattimore

〔University of Chicago Library, Yuan T'ung-li Papers, Box 2〕

按：Owen Lattimore(1900-1989)，美国汉学家、蒙古学家，通译作拉铁摩尔。Mr. Vreeland 应指 Herbert Harold Vreeland III，蒙古学家。Nathaniel Peffer(1890-1964)，美国远东问题专家，毕业于芝加哥大学，作为记者在华生活 25 年，归国后长期执教于哥伦比亚大学。Mr. Sunclaram, 待考。此件为打字稿，落款处为其签名。

三月十五日

庄尚严致函先生，略谈来台后同人情形并告日常工作，请协助物色照相机以便开展字画印章、签名研究。

守和先生道鉴：

来台两载，疏候为歉。去冬读致杭先生大札，敬悉旅况清顺为慰。前代北平图书馆运来之地图十八箱，到台后杭先生命交"中央博物院"代管，亦经一载。最近会同开箱检视，见内部大致完好，有一箱微见霉痕虽无大碍，显系到台后所生，详情及新编装箱目录（由南京动身时，顾斗南未交装箱目录，亦未交钥匙），想不久院馆联合处当径寄上，不赘。故宫文物自 37 年十二月前后分三批运台，当时张柱中、欧阳邦华、励德人从中作梗，煞费苦心，今完好保存在台。严等在此经常开箱整理，凡原箱破坏者，一一换以新箱（大半均书籍箱）并加放樟脑，字画等一一加以布包袱，此均在故宫多年来所未办到之事也。竞业守护，使无险越，庶不负此责，再度流亡之痛苦。同人之在台者有那志良

原古物馆人、梁伯华原图书馆老人、吴玉璋原古物馆老人、张德恒原照相人四位老
同人，及刘奉璋、黄居祥、吴凤培（均抗战时在黔蜀新加入职员）及内
人申若侠，共为九人，知关锦注，特略陈之。惟自来台后，北平、南京两
院消息渺不可得，所念念不忘者亦即未运出之大批文物，不知将来究
竟如何乎？兹有请者，严等在此每日经常工作为开箱晾晒书籍与字
画，别无他事，欲于开箱之便摄照字画上作家印章及其签名，积少成
多，将来可成专书。此事早亦有人为之。昔严在北平曾从事此项工
作，因文物南迁而中辍。后德国孔达女士继续为之，虽已印专书，由商
务出板，然根据材料太少，只不过上海三四收藏之物。故宫之物因装
在箱内，未能尽量运用。今在台无事，正可继续此业，亦难得之良好机
会。昔日所用之照相机为警察专照指纹之照相机，机械简单，每幅一
按即可，科学日益进步，想美国若照此类物品之照像机，想必有新式
者，先生能否代为物色、选择，如不甚贵，俟杭先生到美晤面后，商酌办
理之。你虽在流亡仍能编印一二专门书籍，以作他日纪念，均出之先
生之惠助也。附上概况一本，此间情形略具其内，伏乞查收是幸。专
此，敬请道安。

　　　　　　　　　　　　　　　　　　　　庄严顿首呈
　　　　　　　　　　　　　　　　　　　　　　三，十五
　　　　　　　　　　　　　　　　　　梁廷炜附笔问安

〔University of Chicago Library, Yuan T'ung-li Papers, Box 2〕

按："你虽在流亡"当作"我虽在流亡"。那志良，字心如，河北宛
平人，古物馆第二科科员；梁伯华即梁廷纬，字伯华，河北大城人，
图书馆第二科科员；吴玉璋，字爽秋，河北大兴人，古物馆第二科
科员；张德恒，字隶修，北平人，摄影室助手。申若侠（1906—
2006），吉林人。孔达女士即 Victoria Contag（1906-1973），德国
美术史专家，"专书"即《明清画家印鉴》（*Maler-und Sammler-
Stempel aus der Ming-und Ch'ing-Zeit*），由王季铨、孔达合编，1940
年商务印书馆初版。

三月二十六日

张歆海访先生，告王徵住院医治情况。〔University of California, Berkeley, The
Bancroft Library, Yuen Ren Chao papers, carton 10, folder 39, Yuan, Tongli and Yuan, Huixi〕

三月二十七日

先生致信赵元任、杨步伟夫妇,告拟为傅斯年撰写英文讣告,并请其补充著作信息。

> 元任先生、夫人惠鉴:

> 前奉赐书并承赐赠火腿等物近日邮件甚慢,日前始寄到,厚意隆情,至为感谢。火腿远道寄来,实不敢领,当俟月涵夫妇来此共享此珍品也。孟真作古,曷胜悲怆,拟写一 Obituary 登入 *HJAS*,不识已有他人写过否?拟俟写成再请教正。近编我国学者西文著作目录,已完成大半,关于大著,兹编一简目,拟请赐予补充,并祈将内中四种之页数予以填注,想尊处藏有原书,当无困难也。费神之处,至为感谢。日昨张歆海君自纽约来此谈及文伯病状已无危险,惟仍须住院一个多月方能出院,两手受伤最重,迄今仍在包缠之中,经济损失更无论矣。加大中国教授及研究生名单,如有油印者盼代索一份,寄下为感。专此申谢,敬候俪祺。

> 寅恪近寄来近著《元白诗笺证稿》,可称佳品。

弟同礼顿首

内人嘱笔致谢

三月廿七日

〔University of California, Berkeley, The Bancroft Library, Yuen Ren Chao papers, carton 10, folder 39, Yuan, Tongli and Yuan, Huixi〕

按:HJAS 即 *Harvard Journal of Asiatic Studies*,该刊并未登载有关傅斯年(Fu Ssu-nien)的讣告。

张常信覆函先生,略述其赴美留学并在加州大学洛杉矶分校中止学业改赴英国的经过。

March 27, 1951

Dear Prof. Yuan:

Thank you very much for your kind letter March 22, 1951. Though the information does not seem to have been encouraging enough, yet I feel very grateful for your deep concern.

I will follow your kind advice by talking the matter over with my tutor and see what he could do.

　　As there is an emergency program for Chinese students who have come to the States before June 1950, I wonder if you could kindly make some enquiry whether I could be benefited by that scheme. I went to the States to study in the University of California at Los Angeles, 1948‑1949. It was your brother, Dr. T. L. Yuan, who sent me abroad as a faculty member on leave. By Christmas, 1948, I was stuck financially. However, I pulled myself through by working at odd jobs. Before I went to the States your brother recommended me to the British Council as one of the candidates for B. C. Scholarship. But as the result of which could not be known until 2/3 of a year later, Dr. suggested I had better go to the UCLA first since there was an opening at the time. All unexpectedly I got a letter from the British Council by April 1949 saying I had been granted the B. C. Scholarship. As I was financially stuck and as I was told I could study Shakespeare under Prof. A. Nicoll, I decided to leave UCLA in the middle of my work. Here I am working at the moment for M. A. on translation and production of Shakespeare. If I can get a chance, I will resume my work in UCLA or Yale for Ph. D. if you think the possibility is there, I will get a letter of readmission from UCLA at once.

　　I have talked with the British Council authority about your enquiry. Because of a drastic financial measure, the staff members of the British Council itself are to be cut. As for the possibilities of considering applications from Chinese now studying in the States or anywhere else it is entirely out of the question at least for the moment. One even hinted they wouldn't do that even they were in a position to for reasons beyond their control.

　　With thanks and regards, I am

Yours respectfully,

C. H. Chang

〔University of Chicago Library, Yuan T'ung-li Papers, Box 7〕

　　按:Prof. A. Nicoll 即 Allardyce Nicoll(1894-1976),英国文学评论家,时在伯明翰大学任英文系主任,张常信在该校攻读文学硕士,其论文题目应为 Shakespeare in China (莎士比亚在中国)。"your brother, Dr. T. L. Yuan"应指先生堂弟袁敦礼(Thomas L. Yuan)。

四月二日

赵元任覆函先生,附上已发表论文目录并谈伯克利分校华人教师情况。

守和吾兄:

手示敬悉。兹遵嘱将论文目录补充抄奉,其中 Continuity 论文未列入,因未出版也。*HJAS* 上为孟真写一 obituary 甚善,似尚无他人在写。加大教员除弟尚有 Prof. Choh Hao Li, biochem; (Assoc.) Prof. Tung Yen Lin, engine.; (Assoc.) Prof. Wing N. Mah, pol. sci.; Dr. Ting K Pan, lectr. in math; Mr. Peter Dah, lectr. in pharmacy, School of Pharmacy, San Francisco(加大之一院); 李——lectr. in physics。研究生名单未详,查出再奉告! 此上,即颂近祉,并颂潭福。

赵元任上

内人附笔问安

〔University of Chicago Library, Yuan T'ung-li Papers, Box 7〕

按:此信无落款时间,右下角有"Apr 2 1951"印记,应为赵元任所盖。

四月二十六日

胡适致片先生,感谢赠王徵医药费,并告中基会将于五月开执委会。

April 26, 1951

守和兄:

王文伯兄承兄惠助医药费 $40.00,十分感谢。

中基会本改在 April 月底开会,但仍没有够 Quorum,故现决定不开大会了。(P. H. Ho 已回国;Li Ming 已去西岸养病。)执委会大概可以在五月中开一次。

匆匆,開双安。

适之

〔袁同礼家人提供〕

按:"開双安"当作"问双安"。Quorum 即法定人数。P. H. Ho 应指霍宝树(1895—1963),字亚民,广东新会人,生于上海,1946 年10 月任行政院善后救济总署署长,翌年升任中国银行代理副总经理;Li Ming 即李铭(1887—1966),字馥孙,浙江绍兴人,银行家,1933 至 1937 年任国民政府全国经济委员会委员。此时,霍宝树、李铭均任中基会董事。

五月八日

陈受颐致函先生,感谢盛情款待,并略述离开华府后的行踪。

May 8, 1951

My dear T. L.:

This is a much belated expression of gratitude to you and Mrs. Yuan for the wonderful hospitality you both extended to me while I was in Washington last month. The many pleasant moments spent with you have meant a lot more to me than the sessions of the Philadelphia Conference.

From Washington, I went on to New York, where I stayed until April 17th. calling on old friends, seeing prospective publishers, book-hunting, etc. And to pay for my extended truancy, I have had to meet class many evenings for extra make-up sessions, which have kept me busy ever since my return. Hence my failure to write and thank you and Mrs. Yuan sooner, for which I trust you will forgive me.

I wish also to thank you for taking all the trouble to order the cards for me. The package arrived in good order quite a few days ago but still remains unopened! My conscience feels guilty every time I look at it on my desk top. Hence this hasty note to tell you I am not ungrateful. I shall write you again at greater length as soon as I have a breathing spell.

Meanwhile warmest regards to you both and to the children.

Yours as ever.

S. Y.

〔University of Chicago Library, Yuan T'ung-li Papers, Box 2〕

按:此函为陈受颐亲笔。

五月十八日

先生致信 Agnes Pearce 女士,请该会考虑资助编纂中国近现代医学及生理学文献目录。

May 18, 1951

Dear Madam:

You were very kind to send me, at my request a list of the scientific staff of P. U. M. C. for which I was deeply grateful. It helped me a great deal in checking the published writings of the leading professors of that College.

For several months I have been engaged in compiling a bibliography of the writings of Chinese medical doctors and physiologists. The purpose of this project is to have a complete record of medical literature written in Western languages by Chinese authors during the last forty years.

In view of the large amount of editorial work, I have felt the need for clerical assistance, although I am doing it entirely as labor of love. For this reason, I wonder if the project would fall in any way within the present or potential activities of your Board. I would like to explore the possibilities of obtaining a modest grant (about ＄1,500), in order to bring it to a successful conclusion. A statement regarding the project is herewith submitted.

If your available funds for this year have already been allocated, may I suggest that you hold my application for consideration next year, as my bibliography would not in any way be completed until the summer of 1952. When the manuscripts are typed ready for the printer, the China Institute in America will be glad to publish it in book form.

If Dr. Harold Loucks is still in New York, please convey to him my greetings. You may like to ask his advice in regard to my project.

Yours sincerely,

T. L. Yuan

〔袁同礼家人提供〕

李政道覆函先生，答复所询两事并附上著作清单。

同礼先生尊鉴：

敬悉来书。Dr. Liu 之中文名字，可惜我亦不知道应如何写法，甚为抱歉。关于吾国留美之天文学者，Yerkes 天文台黄授书君（S. S. Huang）所知较详，先生或可去信问他。所需拙作之名单附上，不知先生现所编写之 Bibliography 将来拟何处出版，尚乞告知。专此，敬请学安。

晚李政道上

五，十八

〔袁同礼家人提供〕

按：笔者依袁清前辈的意见，将该函暂系于此。

五月二十二日

娄克思覆函先生，告知其已将资助编写华人所著西方医学及生理学文献目录的申请提交美国中华医学基金会董事会，并询问近况及平馆情形。

May 22, 1951

Dear Mr. Yuan:

　　Miss Agnes Pearce has turned over to me, for information and reply, your letter of May 18th containing a request for financial assistance by the China Medical Board in your project of compiling a bibliography of Western medical and physiological literature by Chinese authors. I will be glad to place this request before the Board, which is now in the process of formulating its future program. It may, however, be some months before sufficient progress is made for specific requests of this kind to be given consideration. Also, it is not yet clear just what limitations the Board will set up for the type of project which it is willing to consider. I am very much interested in the work you are carrying out, however, and shall see that you receive further information concerning your request as soon as it is possible to supply such data.

　　I have wondered a good many times in the past months as to where you were and what you were doing, and I am very glad to learn about you from your letter. I wonder what is happening at the National Library in Peking these days and whether you still receive information from there. As you doubtless know, the PUMC was nationalized on January 20th, and the China Medical Board no longer maintains any contact with the institution. We hear indirectly that its time and attention is being devoted pretty largely to the care of casualties from Korea.

Most sincerely,

Harold H. Loucks

Representative

〔袁同礼家人提供〕

五月二十五日

加州(洛杉矶)大学图书馆 Robert Vosper 致函先生,表示该校无法从大同书店获得所购中文书刊,希望先生能给予意见。

May 25, 1951

Mr. T. L. Yuan

11 Eight Street, S. E.

Washington 3, D. C.

Dear Sir:

I enclose a copy of a letter received here from our agent and your acquaintance, T. K. Koo, about the problem of releasing to us books he has acquired in our interests. I'd like very much to have any advice or suggestions you could give me as to procedure in this case. It occurred to me and to Mrs. Man-Hing Yue Mok that yours would be the most useful advice we can call on.

Naturally I'm very anxious to secure these books and feel that it would be in the cultural interests of all concerned if it could be arranged. Naturally however I do not wish to involve the University in any unethical or embarrassing agreements. I understand that normal trade arrangements are difficult both between the mainland and Hong Kong and out of Hong Kong to the U. S. You are acquainted with all of these matters and will know best what I should do.

I might say that the Bank of China has officially expressed regret that it cannot be of any service in this particular circumstance. You then are our only hope and I look forward with much interest to your response.

Your very sincerely,

Robert Vosper

Acting Librarian

〔University of Chicago Library, Yuan T'ung-li Papers, Box 7〕

五月二十六日

先生致信娄克思，略述平馆和故宫博物院近况，并表示如其来华府极愿晤谈。

May 26, 1951

Dear Dr. Loucks:

Thank you so much for your letter of May 22 and for the information you gave me. I am deeply grateful to you for your interest in my work. The project I am carrying on involves so much drudgery that very few people would like to do. I only hope that my devoted service may be of some help to the medical profession at large.

I have had reports regarding the recent developments in the National Library and in the Palace Museum. Both institutions seem to be doing very well. Because of poverty, collectors have been offering their private collections to the state and these two institutions have been busy in receiving gifts of great value. I only regret that the scientific collections which I built up in Peiping have not been kept up-to-date, as no subscriptions have been placed for American and British scientific and learned journals for the last two years.

For this reason, I hope your Board will continue to subscribe the journals for P. U. M. C. and to store them here for the duration of the present emergency. You might see fit to add a few additional journals of general scientific interest which had not been subscribed before. When the time comes for forwarding them to Peiping, I am sure they will be greatly appreciated there.

When you do come to Washington, please give me an opportunity to see you. I can usually be found in the reading room of the Army Medical Library. My telephone is: Li-4-1638.

With kindest regards,

Yours sincerely,

T. L. Yuan

〔袁同礼家人提供〕

五六月间

先生患眼疾,读书、写信皆有困难。〔袁同礼家人提供〕

六月六日

Mary C. Wright 致函先生,请推荐合适的图书馆员为斯坦福研究中心就现代中国社会科学方面开展的研究提供文献服务。

June 6, 1951

Dear Dr. Yuan:

I am venturing to ask you, on behalf of the Stanford Research Institute, whether you know of any competent persons who might be available for cataloguing and bibliographic work on modern Chinese materials. The Stanford Research Institute, as you may perhaps know, is not a part of the University and is not, therefore, subject to all the limitations of the University salary scale. In general, it has been prepared to pay a realistic and competitive salary for work which it needed.

At the present time the SRI is undertaking a series of social science studies concerning modern China, with particular attention to the field of economics. Since their research people will be relying mainly on materials in the Hoover Library, the Stanford Research Institute is prepared to employ and place at the disposal of the Library an appropriate number of qualified persons. We at the Library will have no concern with the research aspects of this undertaking. Our responsibilities end with making all of our materials readily available. There is, of course, in this a very great and lasting benefit to the research in the modern Chinese field which we and others will undertake, since the results of the bibliographic and cataloguing work will be made generally available. I believe that the SRI contemplates initial appointments for a period of one year, with the hope of renewal. If you have anyone who you can suggest, I shall be grateful for an immediate reply. We shall probably have to move rather quickly, since of course bibliographic work must at least be well advanced before the research itself can begin.

Arthur joins me in greetings and all good wishes,

Sincerely,

Mary C. Wright

Curator, Chinese Collection

〔袁同礼家人提供〕

按：Mary C. Wright(1917-1970)，美国汉学家，中文名芮玛丽，费正清的学生，专攻中国近现代史；SRI 即 Stanford Research Institute；Arthur 即 Arthur F. Wright(1913-1976)，美国汉学家，中文名芮沃寿，芮玛丽的丈夫。该函寄送国会图书馆。

六月十三日

先生覆信芮玛丽，建议其聘请有经验的图书馆员参与胡佛图书馆中文馆藏建设而非图书馆专业毕业生，可联系莫余敏卿询问有无合适人选。

June 13, 1951

Dear Mrs. Wright:

It was a pleasure to hear from you and to learn the progress you have made in building up the Chinese collection at the Hoover Library.

In view of the huge collection of source material which you have accumulated, I would suggest that you try to obtain the services of a trained and experienced librarian to assist you in the undertaking. New graduates would not be competent enough to handle the situation.

I have asked several people in the East to consider your offer, but they seem to have been tied up with other work and would not be immediately available. I wonder if you have written Mrs. P. K. Mok of the UCLA at Los Angeles. She might know of someone in the West coast who would be qualified for the job.

I shall certainly bear your needs in mind. If I know some competent people, I shall not fail to let you know.

With warmest regards to you and Dr. Wright,

Sincerely,

〔袁同礼家人提供〕

按：此件为底稿。

六月十四日

许烺光致函先生,已请西北大学中国学生会会长寄送该校中国学生名录,并附上自己的著述清单,另谈自己正在撰写的两部专著。

Dept of Anthropology

June 14, 1951

Dear Mr. Yuan,

I have asked Dr. Y. Y. Yu, President of the Chinese Students Club here to send you a list of names and research of Chinese students and others here. I enclose a list of my publications here. At present I am editing one book on *Anthropology and Psychiatry* and writing a second book on *The Chinese in Hawaii: their Culture and Personality*. Both of these I hope to finish within the year. If you come to the Midwest, please look me up.

Sincerely yours,

Francis L. K. Hsu

〔袁同礼家人提供〕

按:Y. Y. Yu 应指俞益元(Yu, Yi-yuan),1951 年获西北大学(Northwestern University)力学博士学位,国民党政要吴国桢的大女婿。此函为许烺光亲笔。

六月十六日

钱存训覆函先生,谈硕士课程及论文情况,并询问平馆及北京大学图书馆学专修科近况。

守和先生尊鉴:

前奉手片,敬悉——。芝校图书系章程尚未印出,闻周内可以出版,已嘱办事室径行寄奉,不日当可收到。本周为春季最后一星期,功课甚忙,图书史一课已结束,惟无 Syllabus,参考书仅于讲及某题时随时提及介绍,并无印就书单,俟将笔记整理后,另为择录抄奉。Butler 年事已高,耳聋,口齿已不甚清,大约不久即将退休矣。最近在该班写一 Term paper,题为 China as illustrates in European Books of the 17th & 18th centuries; a cultural interpretation,底本已寄光清兄处一阅,拟嘱其阅毕送呈尊处加以指正。又 Master 论文拟写关于中国译书之影响,已经教授会议通过核准,兹将大纲一份奉呈一阅,并恳就组织及材料方面加以指示,俾得充实,大纲一份仍乞掷还为祷。北平方面想常有信报告,平馆是否隶属文化部抑属教育部,北大圖学专修科仍继续否?现有何人执教,前托华罗庚所带 shellac 应早收到,未知来信提及否?专此,即请近安,并候阖府均吉。

后学存训顿首

六,十六

〔University of Chicago Library, Yuan T'ung-li Papers, Box 2〕

按:Butler 应指 Lee P. Butler(1884-1953),美国图书馆学家,长期担任芝加哥大学图书馆学院教授。钱存训硕士论文题为 Western Impact on China through Translation: a bibliographical study(《近代译书对中国现代化的影响》①)。

杨振宁覆函先生,寄上论著目录并告行踪。

同礼老伯:

示悉。家父信已转去。侄工作已发表之诸篇目录,兹寄上一份。暑期侄在 Univ. of Ill.工作,九月中回 Princeton。此颂暑安。

侄振宁谨上

六,十六

〔袁同礼家人提供〕

按:笔者依袁清前辈的意见,将该函暂系于此。

六月十八日

先生致信芮玛丽,如该馆尚未物色合适的中文编目馆员,则推荐平馆在英学习的丁瀿前往,但须考虑贴补其来美费用。

June 18, 1951

Dear Mrs. Wright:

Referring to your letter of June 6 and my reply of June 13, I have given the matter further consideration. It has occurred to me that an experienced librarian may be available and I would like to recommend him to you very highly. His name is Joseph C. Ting who was in charge of

---

① 此处翻译据《钱存训文集》第 3 卷,页 338。

our reference work and reading room service for many years in Peking. Both you and Prof. Wright must have met him during these years while you were there.

He is a most conscientious and hard-working librarian and has rendered very valuable services to the library development in China. He has been for the last two years pursuing advanced courses in bibliography and cataloguing at the University of London and will be completing his studies in August. He has never been in the United States which he is most eager to visit and if he could be urged to join your Library, he would be an invaluable asset.

Before writing to him, I would like to know if you have got someone already in the meantime. If not, are you prepared to give him travel expenses from London to Stanford? How much would be the annual salary?

Mr. Ting won great admiration from the authorities of the School of Librarianship both at Liverpool and at London. I think the School would write you most favorably if you would write to the Director direct.

I am suffering from eye trouble and could not write as fully as I would like. Please excuse me the poor typing as I could not go out to buy a new ribbon.

Yours truly,

T. L. Yuan

〔袁同礼家人提供〕

按:此件为录副。

六月二十日

娄克思覆函先生,告知美国中华医学基金会对先生编纂医学目录的计划不予赞助。

June 20, 1951

Dear Dr. Yuan:

In further answer to your request of May 18th, I now am in a position to inform you that, unfortunately, it will not be possible for the

China Medical Board to consider your request.

In proceeding with the matter of future program, the Board recently has received the ruling, by its legal counsel, that grants can be made only to medical schools in the Far East and the United States of America. This ruling has at once eliminated many worthy projects which were being contemplated, including your own, and I am very sorry, indeed, to need to send you this information. Personally, however, I should like to send my encouragement and hope for your success.

I shall look forward to an opportunity to see you at some time when I am in Washington.

Most sincerely,

Harold H. Loucks

Representative

〔袁同礼家人提供〕

六月二十二日

先生致信胡适，请寄下李宗侗托售书单副本，并问中基会会议何时可以召开、申请补助有无结果。

> 适之先生：
>
> 玄伯托购书单，曾寄莫泮芹夫人，嘱其在西美进行，不意该单竟致遗失，顷接莫夫人来信，仍未查明下落。似记得尊处尚存有复本，兹值下学年度开始，哈佛燕京社或有款可以购置。拟请将该单寄下，或径寄裘开明君处，请其设法，想荷同意。一月以来，因患眼疾，未能读书、写信，近日已无危险，但下月应付之医药费不赀，未识中基会方面对于申请补助一案能否早予决定，执委会会议能否开成，颇以为念。文伯先生已出院否？根据近日之经验，吾人在美治病开销之大，非有大力者莫办，亦无可为何也。专此，敬候俪安。

同礼拜上

六月廿二日

> 尊夫人同此问安，内人嘱笔问候。

〔袁同礼家人提供〕

按：此件为底稿。"玄伯托购书单"，根据上下相关信函可知，应是李宗侗托先生在美出售自己的藏书,非购书单。此时,王徵尚未出院。[①] 6 月 14 日,中基会第 148 次执委会在纽约召开,会上批准资助先生 3600 美金。[②]

六月二十五日

先生致信芮玛丽,进一步提供丁瀜的信息并纠正前信中的错误,建议联系其现在的院系以了解其学习情况。

June 25, 1951

Dear Mrs. Wright:

With further reference to my letter of June 18, I now find that Mr. Joseph C. Ting did not study at Liverpool but at Glasgow in 1949－50 and at London in 1950－51. His present address is 69 Cornwall Gardens, London, S. W. 7.

As I wrote to you before, Mr. Ting is a most competent person for the work you have in mind. As a reference librarian, he assisted many readers in the use of modern Chinese material. Having had sufficient experience in bibliographic and cataloguing work, he would be able to make all of your materials readily available.

He has an amiable personality and gets along with people very well. Because of his previous record in China, he was awarded a British Council scholarship. If you are interested in him, you may write for particulars to the following:

1.Director, School of Librarianship, University of London, Gower Street, London, W. 1

2.Prof. Otto B. van der Sprenkel, Department of Oriental History, School of Oriental and African Studies, Malet Street, London, W. C. 1

Prof. Sprenkel is a specialist in the modern Chinese field, and I think it was on his recommendation that Mr. Ting was awarded a British

---

① 《胡适日记全集》第 8 册,页 613。

② 台北"中央研究院"近代史研究所档案馆,〈中华教育文化基金董事会〉,馆藏号 502－01－09－001,页 89。

Council scholarship.

I have much pleasure in recommending Mr. Ting to you, as I am sure he would be the most suitable person you are looking for.

Sincerely yours,

P. S. In case your Institute decides to have Mr. Ting for a year, I would like to suggest that you facilitate his coming either by paying his travel or advancing one month's salary depending on your own financial situation. I know Mr. Ting is a poor student and has no dollars to pay for the trip.

In order to get the necessary visa from the American consul, he would probably need a formal letter of appointment from your Institute. In this letter you may like to emphasize that he will handle the cataloguing of Chinese material, so that there will be no difficulty for him with the immigration authorities.

〔袁同礼家人提供〕

按：此件为底稿。

毕树棠致函先生，谈国内近况并劝早日回国。

守和先生：

久违雅教，曷胜系念！屡自希渊先生处藉悉尊况，而终难自慰，盖翘望大驾早日归来之殷思未尝一日去怀也！现在国内情形很好，虽然朝鲜有战事，台湾作牵掣，而生活十分安定，国家建设可谓百废皆开始俱举，展望前途，无不乐观，诚可称我国有史以来无前例也。而唯一缺乏即普遍建设之人才是！在此情况之下，有志者必可有为，有为者必当团结共进，中共之统一战线实一最伟大之建国政策，不可不从者也。仅就图书馆博物馆工作言之，现在急需一基本建设之统筹规划，而此项人材之荒凉与废落已至不堪言状，推其原因，即此方面无一真正之领袖故。中共人材济济，多是政治的，技术人才大有赖于党外时贤与一般青年。北京图书馆馆长一席，迄今虚悬，在设计中之中央文库（仿苏联制）用人亦难其选，据传说都有待于钧座之归来。实际言之，苟欲将全国圕圕计划建立起来，从旧基础上改造伟大新业，今日舍先生其谁欤？此不仅朋辈应如此拥护，即先生自思之，亦属责无旁贷而居之不移者矣！故深望先生及时倦游，早作归计，盖情势日变，过迟亦不相宜。暑假已届,最好先由美而欧,畅游东欧诸新国家,嗣到苏联作一详细考察,将归后之通盘设计在旅途上即准备完全,至时必驾至辙随,左右逢源,不识长者以为然否?树仍在清华,庸碌无所表现,盖以复校时馆务丛脞,人事挫折,胃症剧发,前后动手术两次,幸免于死,而康健几尽失矣。自解放后,馆政依然废弛,学习改革亦不易上轨道,实则整个图书馆界亦犹是也。思维及此,而每动意出国遨游一番,以快心胸,而不知应所往为是。先生回国,至时当有以惠教及我,谨仰望以俟! 言不尽意,诸乞谅察,藉烦台绥。

晚毕树棠再拜

一九五一年六月廿五日

在苏联所存之《永乐大典》,现已完璧而还,想先生当已于报端阅悉矣。又及。

〔University of Chicago Library, Yuan T'ung-li Papers, Box 2〕

芮玛丽覆函先生,告 Bonnar Brown 将联系先生讨论聘用丁潵的细节问题。

June 25, 1951

Dear Dr. Yuan:

Thank you so much for your letters of June 13th and June 18th.

Mr. Joseph C. Ting would appear to have excellent qualifications for our purpose. As I think I mentioned to you, in this particular instance the Hoover Library is not the employer; this present project in modern Chinese studies is being undertaken by the Stanford Research Institute, with which we have no formal connection at all. However, since the Stanford Research Institute expects to use our materials, they are prepared to add to their staff enough persons competent in library work and bibliography to see that their research people are adequately provided for. The problem is, therefore, a little different from what it would be if we were proceeding to make an appointment ourselves in the usual way. It may be that in a few more months we ourselves will have the funds to do this. The present opening is in the hands of the Stanford Research Institute. I am, therefore, transferring your letter to Dr. Bonnar Brown of the Stanford Research Institute. He will doubtless write you concerning the salary range contemplated, special qualifications, and the problem raised by the fact that Mr. Ting is now in London.

Arthur joins me in all good wishes.

Sincerely

Mary C. Wright

Curator, Chinese Collection

〔袁同礼家人提供〕

许烺光致函先生,告知其新书的正式题名。

Dept. of Anthropology

June 25, 1951

Dear Dr. Yuan

In the bibliography which I sent you the other day please make one correction. The book of mine, which is coming off the press this fall in London, will be entitled *Religion, Science and Human Crises* instead of the original *The Twain Shall Meet*. There will be no subtitles for this book.

Sincerely yours,

Francis L. K. Hsu

〔袁同礼家人提供〕

按:其新书全称为*Religion, Science and Human Crises: a study of China in transition and its implication for the West*,1952 年伦敦初版。该函为其亲笔。

六月二十八日

程绥楚致函先生,请为其在美国高校图书馆谋取职位。

守和先生双前:

敬启者,前覆之函计早达览,挂号所寄寅恪师之《元白诗笺证》并附小书目一本,未悉已经收到否? 平寄虽慢,但已经三四个月,或不致延误遗失也,念甚念甚。前奉手示,嘱购 1951《大公报》手册,至今不见再版,书款尚存在此,是否留作购他书之用,并乞示知为祷。澳洲久无消息,闻马季明先生云其所购许地山先生藏书,前三月始点齐运走,可能新学院至今尚未有成立。此间报载,美国近来较易获职,夏济安兄之弟志清在耶鲁已获 Ph. D.学位，来信云已得职作研究工作，并告晚云只要能设法到美，到后工作谋生较前为易云云。晚甚盼能得美方大学有中文圖者之工作，只求够生活便足，家母月需港币百元至百廿元，等于美元廿元以内。如到美工作，香港有人可以转汇。关于此类工作，甚盼先生能代为留意，栽植之恩自当图报，情势日非，香港已岌岌不易维持矣。百业萧条，生活日高，在本岛图发展已不可能矣。尊府想皆清吉，念念。余俟续上。专肃，敬请双安。

晚程绥楚敬上
六月廿八夜
〔袁同礼家人提供〕

七月初①

先生前往哈佛燕京图书馆，与裘开明晤谈，后者告知斯坦福研究所与胡佛图书馆合作，有意雇用高级编目人员，先生对此颇感兴趣。〔Harvard-Yenching Institute Archives, Letter of Alfred K'aiming Ch'iu to Mary Clabaugh Wright, July 6, 1951〕

> 按:6 月 8 日芮玛丽致信裘开明，请求推荐合适的编目人员。7 月 6 日裘开明覆信芮玛丽，请其直接与先生联系，或由先生推荐合适的人选。

七月三日

方豪(台北)致函先生，告知赴台后研究兴趣，并请先生代为寻找赴美访学机会。

> 守和先生大鉴:
>
> 奉别以来，倏逾二载，回首故都，恍同隔世! 比维旅祉安和，为颂无量。顷承转到德礼贤神父大作二册，感激莫名! 豪伏处岛上，已一年有半，以有关中西交通史之书籍不多，乃转而研究台湾史，颇有所获，奉上近作数篇，阅后请随尊意送赠任何图书馆。惟研究台湾史仅为一时兴到之举，且历史甚短，不能作长久计划。屡欲作美国之行，或在图书馆工作，或协助美国汉学家，未知有此类机缘否? 不必顾及豪之神父身份，豪亦向不喜倚赖教会，先生如能代为设法，以满足其希

---

① 裘开明给芮玛丽的信中称:7 月 5 日(周一)袁同礼访问了哈佛燕京图书馆。查本年日历，该日实为周四，周一为 7 月 2 日，两个时间孰为正确，笔者并不能确认，只能将访问时间定在 7 月初。7 月 27 日，芮玛丽信中标注裘开明的来函为 7 月 6 日，特此注明。

望,实所大愿,惟切不可与(未成功前)于野声主教或适之先生辈述及,以免影响此间工作。

豪幼攻拉丁文,长而自习法文与意文,最后始学英文,故英语不甚流畅,且带法音,自思到美数月,必能改进。读英文书则毫无困难也。

如有机会,则聘书与每月薪水之证明书,最为重要,否则,不能办护照。两年以来,首次通函,即作不情之请,亦将爱安言耳。幸勿见笑。赐书请寄台湾台北罗斯福路四段 32 巷 2 号。因暑假不到大学,故以不寄大学为宜。专此奉谢,敬请旅安。

晚方豪拜上
七月三日

〔University of Chicago Library, Yuan T'ung-li Papers, Box 2〕

按:"德礼贤神父大作二册",参见 1950 年 4 月 20 日德礼贤之函。1949 年 2 月 7 日,方豪自上海启程赴台,10 日抵高雄,14 日至台北,翌日赴台湾大学拜见傅斯年,并就任该校历史系教授。[1]

七月上旬

芮玛丽致函先生,邀请前往胡佛图书馆工作。

按:芮玛丽对延聘先生并未抱太大希望,但坦言先生如能加入,对该馆中文馆藏的发展将是极宝贵的(invaluable),参见 7 月 27 日芮玛丽致裘开明函。[2]

七月十日

Bonnar Brown 致函先生,代表斯坦福研究中心提出聘任的初步要约,并告知项目将持续数年,但只能先聘任一年。

July 10, 1951

Dear Dr. Yuan:

　　Mrs. Wright has written you previously about the research project on China which we are undertaking. This will utilize a large mass of materials at the Hoover Library which are practically untouched since

---

[1] 李东华撰《方杰人(豪)先生年谱稿》,《文史哲学报》,第 34 期,1985 年,页 25。

[2] Harvard-Yenching Institute Archives, Letter of Mary Clabaugh Wright to Alfred K'aiming Ch'iu, July 27, 1951.

having been received. One of the first and very extensive jobs will be to catalog them and prepare bibliographic information on selected subjects.

It has occurred to us, without knowing anything of your plans, that it just might be possible that you would be interested in coming out to take charge of a group of cataloguers and bibliographers that will carry out this work.

As Mrs. Wright stated in her letter, the program is planned to continue for several years. We are able to make an appointment for only one year, but there would be hope of renewal.

We could pay $ 5, 000 for the year period, which would include a three weeks' vacation. We could also undertake to pay the way of yourself and your wife out here and back.

If you are interested, I should like you to advise me at your earliest convenience, so we can prepare the formal appointment. Naturally we would like to have you as soon as possible, but the program is sufficiently flexible so we can probably conform with your schedule. Accordingly, please indicate when you would be available.

I appreciate your information about Joseph C. Ting, although I am afraid, he is too far away for it to be possible to work anything out with him.

Yours sincerely,

Bonnar Brown

Assistant Chairman,

Department of Business and Industrial Economics

〔袁同礼家人提供〕

七月十五日

颜复礼致函先生,寄上其本人、海尼士、福兰阁、佛尔克著述清单,告小海尼士近况,请先生在国会图书馆查找有无《四书翼注论文》,并请复制其中《孟子》部分的结尾及《国风》杂志的篇目。

Hamburg 6, July 15, 1951

Schäferkampsallee 43

Dear Mr. Yuan,

　　Enclosed you receive:

1)The Bibliography of the writings of Prof. E. Haenisch

2)A list of the papers written by me

3)Two Supplements to the bibliographies of O. Franke and A. Forke

　　In your letter of 20th Dec. 1950, you asked me for another copy of the bibliography of the writings of A. Forke; I hope that you received the copy sent off by me immediately after the receipt of your letter. I hope also that the copy of the obituary written by me in memory of Prof. O. Franke has reached you in due time. I am very sorry I could not send you the bibliography of the writings of Prof. Haenisch before. This delay was called forth by several reasons, but it would lead me too far if I should go here into details. Please, be assured that for the future I shall readily assist you in your bibliographical work. As to Dr. Fuchs, I beg to inform you that he left Hamburg a year ago and went to Munich where he is very likely to get the sinological chair of Prof. Haenisch who has resigned recently owing to age. I informed Dr. Fuchs by letter that you would like to get a list of his writings, but I do not know whether he has complied with your request. If you are still interested in this matter, I shall try to compile such a list. Do you know that Dr. Wolfgang Haenisch, the son of Prof. E. Haenisch, resides no longer at Berlin? He has been recently appointed director of the Library of the University in Marburg.

　　Finally, may I ask you a favour? I should be much obliged to you if you would kindly inform me whether the Library of Congress has a copy of the following work:

　　　　四书翼注论文 by 张甄陶 hao:惕庵

Should that be the case, please let me have a photostat of the different commentaries concerning the <u>last sentences of the Mong-tse</u> = text, included in that work. As to this sentence, J. Legge in his *Chinese Classics* Vol. II p. 502 says: "The concluding sentences here wonderfully vex commentators. In the 'Supplemental Commentary' (四书翼注论文) are found five different interpretations of them. But all agree that Mencius somehow takes upon himself the duty and responsibility of handing down the doctrines of the sage." Unfortunately, Legge does not cite the texts of these five commentators.

In this moment one thing more comes into my mind: I need urgently the following articles by 李源澄:评胡适说儒, published in Kuo-feng 国风 Vol.VI, Nr. 3/4 (Nanking 1935), pp. 24-35. Please, can you help me in getting a copy of this article?

Thanking you very heartily for your assistance,

Yours sincerely,

Fritz Jäger

〔University of Chicago Library, Yuan T'ung-li Papers, Box 4〕

按:国会图书馆似未存有《四书翼注论文》,先生收到后请钱存训在芝加哥大学图书馆代为抄录。

七月二十三日

先生致信钱存训,询问其暑假行程并请代问芝加哥大学图书馆有无可能收购李宗侗藏书。

存训吾兄:

前闻暑假中大驾拟偕眷来华京一游,不识下月内能否实现,至盼驾临,俾能一聚。芝大用 quarter system,尊处何日休假,为念。兹有适之先生寄来李玄伯先生售书书单书价过昂,如拟购可商减,此间大半业已入藏,不识芝大有采购之可能否? 即希代为询明示复为荷。专此,顺颂暑安。

袁同礼顿首

七,廿三

新地址:11 8th Street, S. E. Washington 3, D. C.

〔钱孝文藏札〕

七月二十五日

钱存训覆函先生,告知芝加哥大学图书馆此时无力购买李宗侗藏书,先生此前所询人名亦无法查实。

守和先生:

顷奉廿三日手示,敬悉一一。书单已收阅,此间书款无多,不能购善本,且大部亦已入藏,故仍将原单附还,至乞检收。所询人名亦无法查询,因现在校之中国人均系 1940 以后来芝,以前旧人,大都不识。P. T. Cheng 现亦不在该处工作,前寄一函闻送至徐贤修君处,伊不识其人也。徐家璧君月初来芝休假,顺道参加 ALA 大会,训亦前往数次。九月间本拟去东部休假,但因赶写论文未毕,届时恐尚须留芝耳。闻 Stanford 有请我公前往之意,未悉确实否?匆匆,顺颂暑安。

后学存训顿首

七,廿五

〔University of Chicago Library, Yuan T'ung-li Papers, Box 2〕

按:李宗侗所藏善本似在 20 世纪 70 年代归于芝加哥大学,《钱存训文集》第 3 卷页 348"其他有李玄伯教授旧藏明刊本、稿本及写本多种约 200 余册,系 1960 年代过世后,由家属转让",此说时间并不准确,因李宗侗应在 1974 年去世。徐贤修(1912—2001),温州鹿城人,数学家,1935 年毕业于清华大学数学系,1946 年赴美留学就读于布朗大学数学系,后任新竹清华大学校长。

七月二十八日

朱家骅致函先生,请在美为联合国中国同志会谋取书籍。

守和吾兄大鉴:

自离大陆以来,音闻阻隔,言念之劳,无时或释。虽知兄在美国,但以不知通讯处所,无从修候。月前谢次彭兄来函,得审兄已参加美国国会图书馆工作,及阅附来致彼之函,更知其详,深慰怀□,并稔兄愿在国会图书馆内为联合国中国同志会挑选复本书籍,尤为感淑。本会前身为国联同志会,远于民国八年在北平成立,想为兄所深知。民廿五年起,即由弟主持,中因一再播迁关系□□民二十八年在渝会所被炸,卅五年复员时迁京途中船沉长江□段,图书文卷大部遗失,至为可惜。此一有数十年历史之社会团体,过去并无多大成就,更滋惭愧。前年年底随同政府由蓉迁至台北后,深感国际情势之重要,当即恢复工作。去年六月廿五日韩战发生后,联合国渐趋积极,因此本会工作开展之顺利亦为过去所未有,且有堂皇之会舍甚多,各方所重视。惟注意国际问题之人士在此最感困难者,则为外国书报缺乏,常感苦闷不堪。此间美国新闻处虽常轮流借给图书,为数有限,终非久远之计,欲向国外添购新书,则因经费与外汇关系,更谈不到。因此拟向美国国会图书馆请求赠送复本书籍,更有吾兄在彼帮同挑选,最为理想,必要时亦可出资购买。现由会正式备函,兹特随函附上,请亲送转致,并请鼎力协助成全,至深感祷。至寄递邮费一节,因"中研院"尚有余款存在赵元任兄处,当函赵兄垫付,将来由会与院在此转账,不审兄意以为如何。崇此奉托,顺颂台祺。

弟朱家○顿首
廿八

按:此函附致赵元任信,内容如下,

元任吾兄大鉴:

联合国中国同志会现向美国国会图书馆请求赠送复本书籍,正托由袁守和兄就近代为进行中,倘获允准,则邮递费用请兄即在院中存款内代为垫付,将来由会与院在此转账可也。崇此奉达,顺颂台祺。

弟朱家○顿首
廿八

〔台北"中央研究院"近代史研究所档案馆,〈朱家骅〉,馆藏号301-01-23-535〕

按:此两件均为底稿,标注抄送"同志会"。

芮玛丽覆函先生,非常高兴先生接受聘请,告知吴文津已担任该校图书馆中文编目员,并向斯坦福研究中心强调编目工作的重要,虽然该中心意识到这一问题但似乎并无意聘请远在伦敦的丁潘。

July 28, 1951

Dear Dr. Yuan:

I am delighted to have your letter of July 21st and your own direct confirmation of the news that you will be able to join us. We are much in need of your advice concerning the future direction of our program of acquisitions concerning modern China as well as concerning the effective organization materials at this end.

Naturally the great bottleneck is cataloging. We have been fortunate in obtaining the services of a very competent young man who has recently finished his training at the University of Washington, Mr. Wen-chin Wu. He seems to me to be doing an excellent job. However, with one clerical assistant he can scarcely be expected to keep up with the requirements of a large group of researchers. I am still receiving an occasional application, which I am forwarding to the SRI, but nothing very promising is turning up. As usual, it is much easier to find people to use materials than those who are willing and competent to make them ready for use. Fortunately, Dr. Rowe knows the picture well enough to realize that the present SRI staff for this project is unbalanced, and I believe that he is sympathetic to the idea of correcting that imbalance by appointing more people to the library side of the project.

When you first suggested Mr. Joseph Ting, I wrote at once to the Director of the Library School at the University of London and to Professor van der Sprenkel; however, I have not yet had their reply. I also turned over copies of all the correspondence to the SRI people and expressed the hope that they might find it possible to bring Mr. Ting here. I gathered the impression that they were very reluctant to look so far afield as London and that they have so far taken no action. However, they can now see as well as I can the difficulty which is likely to develop in the course of the coming year unless the situation is remedied. I am therefore venturing to repeat to them my earlier suggestion that they seriously consider an immediate appointment for Mr. Ting, with a provision of a salary advance for travel expenses. In all this I am assuming that Mr. Ting as a professional librarian will be quite prepared to "slug it out". There is always one difficulty in appointing a person of his experience to a routine post of this kind. Such a person often may himself wish to proceed with research and with consideration of the more general bibliographic problems in the expectation that "someone else" will handle the troublesome details. As it happens, we are relatively well supplied or soon will be with people concerned with the broader aspects, and it is just these troublesome details that may throw the whole project into jeopardy.

It would be most helpful to me and also to the SRI people if we could have your assurance that Mr. Ting would be prepared to devote himself to library chores.

Looking forward to seeing you in September,

Sincerely,

Mary C. Wright

Curator, Chinese Collection

P. S. Your letter of July 26 has just arrived. The enclosed recommendation of Mr. Ting is certainly impressive. I will return the original as soon as it has been copied.

It looks a little as if Mr. Ting may be too competent a person for the routine work of cataloging here, but I should like to have your opinion on this point.

〔袁同礼家人提供〕

按：Dr. Rowe 应指 David N. Rowe(1905-1985)，美国汉学家，生于南京，通译作"饶大卫"，时应任斯坦福研究所顾问。此件为打字稿，落款和补语皆为其亲笔。

七月三十一日

先生致信芮玛丽，就斯坦福研究中心积累现代中国史料提出两点意见，并建议其继续联系在伦敦的丁瀗。

July 31, 1951

Dear Mrs. Wright:

Thank you ever so much for your letter of July 28. I am particularly happy to hear that Dr. Rowe is at present connected with SRI. Kindly extend to him my greetings.

Concerning your program of acquisitions of current material, I shall be delighted to assist you in making the Hoover Library an important center of documentation concerning modern China. I trust that you already have good agents in Hong Kong and Formosa and you can count on them for the regular supply of current material. I would like to suggest that you try every means to build up:

1.A complete collection of telephone directories of all cities both in Communist and China; from which a great deal of information can be obtained.

2.A collection of photographs of all sorts showing the life in modern China, to be supplemented by the cuttings of illustrations from newspapers and magazines. Three copies of illustrated news should be subscribed for this purpose. Such a collection of pictorial material would be of immense value to research scholars.

Concerning Mr. Ting, I really feel that it would be a great pity if we lose him. He is a good cataloguer in every way and is a devoted and hard-working librarian. In other words, he takes more pleasure in serving others than in engaging research himself. I can assure you that he would be the right person you are looking for. The reason why you have not heard from the people in London is probably due to the fact they are now on vacation during the summer.

Under separate cover, I am mailing you a number of Chinese current periodicals. I am sure that you may have them already, but it is always useful to have extra copies especially when you want to cut down the illustrations for the purposes set forth above.

With best wishes for your continued success,

Yours sincerely,

〔袁同礼家人提供〕

　　按:此件为底稿。

七八月间

先生致信金问泗(比利时)。〔《金问泗日记》下册,页 1035〕

　　按:此信于 8 月 8 日送达。

八月五日

胡适覆函先生,告知其所撰书评两篇皆出于愤慨,并祝贺先生出任斯坦福研究中心胡佛研究所中文编纂主任。

　　守和兄:

　　谢谢你八月二日的信。

我评 Payne 一文（Payne's *Mao Tse-tung* was one of 40 "most outstanding books of 1950" selected by the American Library Association. What will old Dr. Brown of the ALA think of it!），是有意用气力写的，意在惩罚这种轻薄妄人。此文我有许多副本，若老兄愿留一份或几份，我当寄上。已寄上两份，乞送一份给恒先生。

我评 De Francis 一文，已在 *American Historical Review* 的七月号登出，此文我没有副本，故不能寄呈。七月号刚出版，馆中必易得也。此文用意亦是惩罚妄人。岂有不能辨别"胡适"与"胡愈之"的人而配高谈"中国文字改革"的！

老兄得 Stanford 大学之函约，我听了十分高兴。是否特别注重 Hoover Library 的东方书报的整理？我听说 Hoover Library 收到近年中国抗战及中国共产党的材料甚多，而无法整理，故外人不易利用。若能得老兄领导指示整理的途径，一定可以发现许好资料。关于中基会补助金停止下半年（十月至三月）一层，我甚赞同尊意，请你写一英文短信，当即照办。匆匆，敬问双安。

> 弟胡适
>
> 八，五
>
> 〔袁同礼家人提供〕

按："许好资料"当作"许多资料"。胡适所作书评刊于 7 月 2 日 *Freeman*（页 636－639）。"DeFrancis 一文"实指 John DeFrancis, *Nationalism and Language Reform in China* 一书，1950 年普林斯顿大学出版，胡适所作书评刊于 *American Historical Review* 第 56 卷第 4 期（页 897－899）。

八月八日

Weldon B. Gibson 致函先生，告知拟聘用丁瓒担任斯坦福研究中心高级编目员，但无法负担其离英赴美的旅费。

August 8, 1951

Dear Dr. Yuan:

Mrs. Wright has turned over to us the correspondence on your ex-colleague, Mr. Joseph C. Ting, who is now at the University of London. It is our understanding that Mr. Ting might be available for employment at the end of September. We wonder if you could give us some help in regard to the possible employment of Mr. Ting at Stanford Research Institute. We are therefore furnishing you with answers to some of the questions in your letter of June 18 to Mrs. Wright. We would appreciate your reactions to our proposals, and ask that you do not, as yet, contact Mr. Ting until we have had an opportunity to weigh your answers.

We are prepared to offer Mr. Ting a position of "Senior Bibliographer-Chinese Literature". The salary for this classification would start at $ 300.00 per month, subject to the usual deductions for Social Security and income taxes. Work week, vacation allowances, sick leave and holidays are as described in our letter to you dated July 16, 1951.

We cannot, under our contract, provide Mr. Ting with transportation from London to Palo Alto. We are prepared to furnish him with transportation funds equal to the cost of a one-way air fare from New York to San Francisco, plus incidental travel expenses and funds for transportation of personal effect amounting to $ 300.00. This amount may be spent at his discretion (expecting of course that he would arrive at Palo Alto at a date we would agree upon) and would pay the greater portion of his travel expense, assuming a tourist class ship passage and rail transportation from New York to Palo Alto.

We would like very much to have Mr. Ting with us, and I imagine that you would enjoy working with him again. Please let us know how you feel about these proposals as quickly as possible, since, if your reaction is favorable, we will have many details to work out if we are to get Mr. Ting here this fall.

Very truly yours,

Weldon B. Gibson

Chairman-Department of Business and Industrial Economics

〔University of Chicago Library, Yuan T'ung-li Papers, Box 3〕

按:Weldon B. Gibson(1917-2001),美国经济学家,1947 年在斯坦福研究中心担任全职研究工作。此件为打字稿,落款处为其签

　　　名。收到此函后,先生应在 13 日覆信。

八月九日

金问泗致函先生。〔《金问泗日记》下册,页 1035、1037〕

　　　按:先生收到后即覆,并于 8 月 22 号送达。

八月十日

叶良才覆函先生,告知已转交先生致胡适的信,并欢迎下周来纽约晤谈。

August 10, 1951

Dear Dr. Yuan:

　　I thank you for your letter of August 8, 1951, enclosing one letter for our Acting Director, Dr. Hu Shih. I have duly forwarded your letter to Dr. Hu.

　　We are so glad to hear that you will be going to Stanford next term. We shall look forward to seeing you in New York next week. Emma hoped that you will be able to come to our house this time.

　　I do not know Dr. Tung Ta-cheng referred to in your letter. The names of the Taiwan University fellows are given in the two lists herewith enclosed.

Yours sincerely,
L. T. Yip

〔袁同礼家人提供〕

　　　按:Emma 即叶良才夫人;Tung Ta-cheng 应指董大成(1916—2008),高雄人,1949 年赴美深造,是台湾大学医学院第一批赴美进修的教授,后担任台湾大学医学院生化学科主任。

八月中旬

先生赴纽约,曾与胡适晤谈,所涉及诸事之一为推荐方豪来美访学。

八月十五日

芮玛丽覆函先生,感谢此前的建议并告收到寄赠刊物。

August 15, 1951

Dear Dr. Yuan:

　　Thank you very much for your letter of July 31st and for your useful suggestions concerning our future acquisitions program.

Thank you particularly for the parcels of current Chinese periodicals which you were kind enough to donate to the Library. These have now reached us safely.

I believe that the SRI is making an effort to engage Mr. Ting, and I certainly hope that things can be worked out.

Looking forward to seeing you shortly,

Sincerely,

Mary C. Wright

Curator, Chinese Collection

〔袁同礼家人提供〕

按：此件为打字稿，落款处为其签名。

八月十七日

陈受颐覆函先生，就所寄文章略施修改，并告该校图书馆所藏《殷虚文字乙编》情况。

守和尊兄著席：

大示及明信片均已拜读，大著体大思精，佩服无似。厚承赐阅，感激之极。承命注意文字上之斟酌，愧不敢当，籀读之际，偶有疑点，辄用铅笔注示，以作芹献，统希卓夺。僭越学陋之处，并盼海涵。

《殷虚文字乙编》此间图书馆查已入藏第一册，弟回平时所代买续出一册，前月亦已由台北寄到矣。

文从下旬东徙，闻之怃然，弟本意北行侍坐，畅聆教益。日来肠胃又复作祟，不敢多动，此愿之偿，只好俟诸来年矣。匆匆奉复，敬颂夏安。

弟受颐顿首

八月十七日

顷由电话匣知 David W. Davies 图书馆欠兄之数，如十日后始完手续，应将支票径寄新地址，知注并以奉闻。

〔University of Chicago Library, Yuan T'ung-li Papers, Box 2〕

按：《殷虚文字乙编》由董作宾编著，分为上、中、下三辑，依次于1948 年、1949 年、1953 年出版，收录殷墟第十三次至第十五次考古挖掘所获的刻辞甲骨文字。1948 年 3 月 6 日，陈受颐由美抵达香港,后又在广州、南京、上海等地盘桓,5 月 31 日抵平,8 月上旬由香港乘船返美。①

八月二十一日

方豪覆函先生,抄寄台湾"立法委员"名单并谈德礼贤著作翻译、台湾地区出版的英文期刊及杂志等事。

守和先生大鉴:

七月十八日尊翰奉读已久,因学校在暑假中,人事颇有更动,故教授名单不易录寄,现亦仅能先寄文学院一份,余续寄。"立法委员"名单等候更久,因有"附逆"者,有在港澳而未表明态度者,甚至有已处死者,最近始托人抄得一份。仅附奉,乞检收。

关于德神父书,一部份可译,一部份乃将中文译为意文,若再译为中文,则无意义;其最重要部份,当为尚未出版之利氏外文遗牍,故弟拟俟全集完全出版后,再加摘译,想先生亦必以为然也。先作介绍,当然可办,惜台北无适当刊物可发表。

台湾之英文刊物仅有博物馆出版 *Quarterly Journal of the Taiwan Museum* , Published by the Taiwan Museum, Taipei, Taiwan 颇有价值,各国交换甚多;又新出 *Newsdom* 半月刊,则报道内幕消息。其他有一小型英文日报。拙编台大文史哲学报及拙著若干种,另邮寄奉。弟事承留心并示多点,谢谢。专复,敬请撰安。

弟方豪谨复

八,廿一

〔袁同礼家人提供〕

按:*Quarterly Journal of the Taiwan Museum*(《台湾博物馆季刊》),1948 年创刊。

八月二十三日

先生致信钱存训,请其协助抄录《四书翼注论文》章节并告国内消息。

公垂吾兄:

奉到十六日手书,欣悉近况。承寄章程,至谢。日内当可寄到。

兹将德国 Jaeger 教授托钞之件另纸录出，即希费神一查示复为荷。如需影照，并乞径寄德国汉堡该教授手收，所垫费用并望示知。近接清华图书馆毕树棠君来信谓"虽然朝鲜有战事，台湾作牵掣，而生活十分安定，国家建设百废俱举，展望前途无不乐观，诚可称我国有史以来无前例也"。又嘱到苏联作详细考察，大约返国时必须如此方能左右逢源。馆中近举行《永乐大典》展览会，包括苏联退回之十一册及涵芬楼献诸政府之二十余册及馆中所藏者九十余册，颇扬扬大观也。又尊处购中文书除顾子刚外，尚委托其他商店否，亦希示及。顺颂秋安。

同礼顿首

廿三

又汉堡大学经弟交涉亦退回《永乐大典》二册，现存国会图书馆。

德国 Jager 教授托钞之件：

《四书翼注论文》，张甄陶著，字惕庵，内孟子最末一句之五种注解，该句为"由孔子而来至于今……然而无有乎尔，则亦无有乎尔"。参见 J. Legge: *Chinese Classics* Vol. Ⅱ, p. 502

"in the 四书翼注论文, there are found five different interpretations of them. But all agree that Mencius somehow takes upon himself that duty and responsibility of handing down the doctrines of the sage."

Jager 教授需要者即是 text of these five commentators。如字句太多则用 Photostat 复印，其费用若干，示知后照奉。

Jager 教授地址列下：Prof. Fritz Jager, Hamburg 6, Schäferkampsallee 43, Germany (British Zone)

〔钱孝文藏札〕

按："章程"应为前信所言"芝大史学系及图书馆系新章程"。1951 年 7 月，苏联列宁格勒大学东方学系归还中国《永乐大典》11 册，由文化部拨交平馆；同月，商务印书馆即涵芬楼捐献 21 册；8 月，平馆特举办《永乐大典》展览。"汉堡大学经弟交涉亦退回《永乐大典》二册"应指卷 975-976、10483-10484，今存台北故宫博物院。

八月二十八日

George Boas 致函先生，请先生以航空信方式寄送对拉铁摩尔学术能力的评价并告知此项表述可能用作证言对外公开。

August 28, 1951

Dear Dr. Yuan:

The recent charges against our colleague, Owen Lattimore, include that of not being a reputable scholar. It is admitted that he is a clever and able journalist, but since he has no university degree and no title of "Professor", he is accused of occupying a position on the Faculty under false pretenses.

As a friend of Lattimore's, I believe that it is important to vindicate his reputation and that vindication can come only from those of his colleagues who occupy chairs of Far Eastern thought, language, culture, history, and the like. Would you be kind enough to send me by air-mail your opinion of Lattimore's professional ability, with permission to quote your opinion over your signature? My purpose is to gather such opinion in one memorandum for him to use in any way he sees fit. If you do not wish certain parts of your reply to be quoted, kindly indicate such parts. It is understood that Lattimore will, if he uses your statement, present it either to the investigating committee of Congress or to the press or to both.

May I add that this invitation was initiated by me personally and that I have not been prompted to issue it by anyone in the administration of the Johns Hopkins University.

Yours sincerely,

George Boas

Professor of the History of Philosophy

〔University of Chicago Library, Yuan T'ung-li Papers, Box 2〕

按：George Boas(1891-1980)，美国学者，专攻哲学史，时任约翰霍普金斯大学哲学系教授，时美国参议院内部安全委员会（Senate Internal Security Subcommittee）指控拉铁摩尔涉嫌伪证罪，George Boas 组织人员、财力协助拉铁摩尔展开法律辩护。该函寄送华盛顿。

八月下旬

先生前往斯坦福研究中心,任胡佛研究所中文编纂主任(Chief Bibliographer)。

> 按:先生主持编纂《中国手册》,历时两年,参加此项工作者还有吴元黎(后任旧金山大学经济学教授)、许芥煜(后任旧金山州立大学中国文学教授)、侯服五(后任麻省大学政治学教授)等。在此期间,先生与该校图书馆中文编目吴文津颇多往来。[1]

九月一日

先生与斯坦福研究中心签订聘用合同。〔袁同礼家人提供〕

> 按:该份合同约定先生月薪为420美金,但没有注明服务年限。

九月十二日

先生致信钱存训,告知到斯坦福大学后的情况并请其查询古籍。

公垂吾兄惠鉴:

> 日前途经芝城,诸承款待,心感无似,又见尊夫人恢复健康,尤为欢慰。抵此后即开始办公除弟外尚有助手四人,书籍并不如想像之多,且质的方面亦太差,今后如能作系统之收藏,自可加以改善。王君到此后对于工作颇形不满,且思虑过多,神经时有过敏之处,已竭力劝其安心工作,一切不必介意。日内当约其共看电影,以解其烦闷也。前托查张甄陶《四书翼注论文》,芝大曾入藏否?此书曾在何处著录,亦乞一查。此间工具书不多,故赖台端一检旧籍也。专此申谢,顺颂俪安。

同礼顿首

九,十二

尊夫人同此致谢。

> 通讯处:2055 Williams Street, Palo Alto, Calif.

〔钱孝文藏札〕

> 按:信中《四书翼注论文》处用黑色笔标注有"856,1317,三八卷,乾隆五二年(1787)刊本,六册□",应为钱存训标记。信的背面则有"嘉庆十五年刊本"字样,"庆"字避讳,写作"广",此处则应为先生笔记。

---

[1] 吴文津《美国东亚图书馆发展史及其他》,台北:联经出版事业公司,2016年,页279-280。

九月二十八日

先生覆信朱家骅,告知已应斯坦福研究中心之聘,原请实有不便,但已在加州各大学代为拣选复本寄送联合国同志会,并可与"国立编译馆"馆际互借相关图书。

　　骝先先生尊鉴:

　　　　近奉七月廿八日赐书,藉悉道履绥和,至为欢慰,并悉联合国同志会正在征集图书,嘱为协助,自当效劳。惟尊函寄到之时,同礼已来西岸,故国会图书馆复本无法挑选,惟闻所存者为数无多,已由该馆径函贵会矣。兹在加利福尼亚各大学中挑选若干种,由各校径寄会中,大约月半以后可以寄到。此外,又请研究国际关系之团体以其刊物捐赠贵会,谅可陆续收到。同礼近为"国立编译馆"采购关于国际关系之书刊,皆系最近出版,是资研究。如能与馆中商洽借阅较为便利,至少会中应索一书目,以供参考,谅尊意亦为然也。同礼近应司丹佛大学之聘来此工作,嗣后通讯请用新地址为荷。专此,敬候道祺。

后学袁同礼拜上
九月廿八日

　　奉赠 Utley: *The China Story* 一书,由平邮寄上,似可嘱人译成中文也。附致"余部长"一函,亦盼转寄为感。

　　新地址:2055 Williams Street, Palo Alto, Calif. U. S. A.

　　　　〔台北"中央研究院"近代史研究所档案馆,〈朱家骅〉,馆藏号
　　　　301-01-23-535〕

　　按:Utley 即 Freda Utley(1898-1978),英国学者、政治活动家、畅销书作家,*The China Story*,1951 年芝加哥初版。"余部长"即余井塘(1896—1985),原名榆,字景棠,后改字井塘,以字行,江苏兴化人,政治人物,时应任"内政部部长"。该档未存先生致余井塘信。

十一月二日

先生致信钱存训,询问 Midwest Inter-Library Center 地址并请查阅古籍。

　　公垂吾兄:

　　　　近闻报载芝加哥成立 Mid-west Interlibrary Center,借芝加哥大学之地而建筑,想距校不远。兹有一信,请查明地址加封寄出为荷。所

询德文所译"赤档",芝大想已入藏,请查共有若干册,示知为荷。又弟需用《汉晋书影》一册罗振玉影印本,加大及此间均未入藏,请查尊处是否有此书,如能由兄名义借出寄下最好,否则将号码示知,以便委托此间当局以馆际借书办法借阅也。匆匆,顺颂俪安。

弟同礼顿首
十一月二日

弟下月返华京,如在芝城停留,拟到 Inter-library Center 参观,并须到 Newberry Library 查询西班牙文之书籍也。芝大史学系及图书馆系新章程,请俟出版后各寄下一份是盼。

〔钱孝文藏札〕

按:1951 年 10 月 5 日,Midwest Inter-Library Center 落成开馆,该中心于 1949 年筹设,其启动资金来自卡内基基金会。1918 年,罗振玉辑《汉晋书影》并印行。

十一月十二日

李石曾覆函先生,告日内瓦"中国国际图书馆"已迁移乌拉圭首都。

守和吾兄大鉴:

上月廿七日手书奉悉。知有游孟都之意,尤表欢迎。"中国国际研究院"与图书馆正在移设此间,图书等已到四百箱左右,尚有同等之数仍在迁移中。自本年双十节已开始办公,并时常举行各项会议,如兄能参加,至为欣盼。在大驾未到孟都之前,可否先由兄指定令亲彭望邺先生 前驻美使馆秘书 代表出席,如此情形兄以何项关系 北平国立图馆长或中国图协会主持人 参加,同乞示知为祷。此颂公绥。

弟李煜瀛启
十一月十二日

〔University of Chicago Library, Yuan T'ung-li Papers, Box 6〕

按:时,该馆位于乌拉圭国家图书馆二楼特辟的中国厅内,但书籍多放置于地下室。另,所有移运图书箱数似不及函中所述规模。①

彭望邺(蒙得维的亚)致函先生,告知已随魏道明移居乌拉圭。

---

① 黄渊泉《"中国国际图书馆"六十年简史》,《"国立中央图书馆"馆刊》第 16 卷第 3 期,1994 年,页 17。

守和表弟台惠鉴：

　　久未通候，良深怀想。近在石曾先生处，聆悉旅祉佳胜，至以为慰。邺自卅八年随魏前大使出国由法辗转来此，亦已数月。"中国国际图书馆"书籍已由瑞士迁来，宣扬中国文化，此其权舆，邺亦以得有参加之机会为幸。兹悉台驾有游孟都之意，极为欣忭。谨附小笺，奉候起居，不一。此颂公祺。

愚表兄彭望邺敬启
十一月十二日

〔University of Chicago Library, Yuan T'ung-li Papers, Box 6〕

按：彭望邺，字仰侯，江苏苏州人，1913 年北京大学法科政治学门毕业。1951 年 9 月，魏道明由巴黎前往乌拉圭。

十一月二十一日

查良钊覆函先生，告知中华人民共和国文化访问团赴印经过，并谈华侨在印情况。

守和先生惠鉴：

　　前奉十月十四日手书，藉悉一是。承询所谓文化访问团来印情况，因该团系受政府招待，代表官派，一切旅程集会皆有规定，并无与外人自由会叙之可能，除丁西林团长及其他指定代表在集会作宣传演讲外，在德里居留约一星期（十月廿九至十一月六日）参加形式招待会，并无自由接谈之可能。虽然德里大学曾以名誉博士学位给丁西林与冯友兰，亦无机会与人谈话。

　　十一月一日是西南联大第十五周年纪念日，那天下午可巧该团团员三人被邀来参观此间中央教育学院，院长邀我参加招待他们的茶会，因为有冯友兰在内，我想联大八年同事，借此机会见一见面亦可稍为知道一些老同事的情况。没想到三人之外还有一位同来，当我同副院长及其他两位印度朋友走进茶会场所的时候，已经在开始后约十分钟，当我在进门时看见冯友兰坐在院长之旁，我走过去的刹那间，冯等已先起立，未与其他招待的十几位教员打招呼就走出去了。

　　宏章原在 UNESCO Sci. Office，住学校附近，我常到他家中吃中国饭，去年中共派大使来德里，他也全家赴站欢迎并时常接近。在今年九月廿三，他携眷返国内大陆休假，夫妇携一男三女飞港，闻其原拟留两女一男在国内上医科大学,夫妇二人携最幼一女于十一月杪返德里。现假期将满,尚无归来消息,昨闻其公子已有函致此间友人,谓全家留国内,似此则或留学习,能否再回 UNESCO 现尚无从揣测。

印度对于中国虽有友情,但很少了解。关于印度有关中国之著作出版无多,近托此间学院图书馆主任代拟目录,寥若晨星,原条附奉,恕未另抄。

前年十二月于无意中来印度参加 UNESCO Seminar on Rural Adult Education,遂留国外在德里大学任教,同事相处颇洽,明年四月暑假即满期,届时是否继续留印,现尚无从预计。匆此布复,不尽欲言。即颂旅祺。

　　　　　　　　　　　　　　　　　　弟良钊拜启

　　　　　　　　　　　　　　　　　　十一月廿一日

内子及子女三人皆在国内,偶有数行信,亦无从知环境真况。只好想想:"No news is good news."

　　　　　　〔University of Chicago Library, Yuan T'ung-li Papers, Box 2〕

按:查良钊时任德里大学中央教育研究院客座教授。1951 年 6 月,中华人民共和国决定派文化代表团出访印度、缅甸,团长为时任文化部副部长的物理学家、戏剧家丁西林,副团长为李一氓,团员除冯友兰以外还有陈翰笙、郑振铎、刘白羽、钱伟长、吴作人、季羡林、常书鸿、狄超白、张骏祥、丁昌、倪裴君、周小燕等。9 月 20 日下午 6 时许,代表团乘火车离京,取道广州、香港、新加坡,在缅甸驻留 5 天后,10 月 28 日到达印度。"宏章"即殷宏章(1908—1992),祖籍贵州贵阳,生于山东兖州,植物生理和生物化学家,1944 年至 1945 年赴剑桥大学访问,1948 年至 1951 年在印度任联合国教科文组织南亚科学合作馆科学馆员,后归国。

十一月二十四日　伯克利市

美国东方学会西部分会(American Oriental Society, Western Branch)在加州大学伯克利分校 Forestry Building 召开会议,先生参会,并在下午四时许发言,题目为 The Beginnings of Library Technique in China。〔袁同礼家人提供〕

　　按:参会的其他中国学者有陈世骧、李方桂、赵元任等人。

十一月二十六日

先生致信钱存训,告知《汉晋书影》已用毕奉还及年底行程计划。

公垂吾兄著席:

　　日前奉手书并承借阅《汉晋书影》,至谢。该书曾在东方学会西部分会开年会时予以传观,俾明了汉简之形式。兹已用毕,仍交Hoover 图书馆交邮寄还,即希点收为荷。弟大约于下月廿日左右返华京度岁,明年一月十日左右拟在芝城稍留数小时,当再趋教。报载冯友兰、郑西谛诸人在印考查,想尊处亦知之矣。匆匆,顺颂俪安。

　　　　　　　　　　　　　　　　弟袁同礼顿首

　　　　　　　　　　　　　　　　　十一,廿六

　　附东方学会秩序单一纸。

〔钱孝文藏札〕

十一月二十七日

朱家骅覆函先生,告知尚未收到美国各图书馆赠送复本书籍,并谢先生赠书一册。

守和吾兄大鉴:

　　前奉手书,备荷存注,并审文□业已转赴司丹佛大学任教,诸尚安盛,忭慰何量。关于国会图书馆及各大学赠送本会书籍,迄今尚未寄到,得便仍希惠予帮忙催寄,至深企感。尊赠 *The China Story* 一书,尤所感谢,至本会与大陆社寄上书刊未知已否察入,为念。附致余井塘兄一函,早已代为转致矣,知注并及。复颂台祺。

　　　　　　　　　　　　　　　　弟朱家○顿首

　　　　　　　　　　　　　　　　　　廿七

〔台北"中央研究院"近代史研究所档案馆,〈朱家骅〉,馆藏号
301-01-23-535〕

　　按:此件为底稿,标有"十一,廿八,航"字样。

十一月二十八日

程绥楚致函先生,转赠夏济安主编的刊物,并谈撰写申请哈佛燕京学社奖学金的论文主旨。

守和先生、夫人双前:

　　敬启者,在十一月十六日挂号寄上英文 *Free China Review*,系夏

济安先生(代总编辑)自台湾寄来嘱奉上请赐指正者。夏君在九月份有文一篇(以前各期多有彼之文字),系讨论中国文化之前途者,彼深盼能得到尊驾之指示与批评。夏曾到过尊府,但晚已不记得曾拜见过否。渠原任北大外语讲师,现在台大教英文及西洋小说,彼英文造诣甚具苦心。该刊将为"中央党部"接收,因经费关系,于是以后将多刊要人言论。此实为宣传之最蠢技术,不若津贴给教授办,外人反重视所刊言论也。夏与刘崇鋐师皆为编委。夏君之弟志清,为 K. C. Li 基金自北大送耶鲁研究外文学者,已得博士学位,尚留在耶大。夏君在前年即领有出国护照,但因经济关系,不能成行,渠亦盼到美再多读书。晚自接到尊示后,即着手准备论文,与表兄劳榦通信讨论,然非有书而又有半年时间不能作成,彼不得已指导晚就已有材料中排编二题,任选一个,一为"东汉初年的经济发展";二为"商君的思想及秦代社会"。前者太简单,后者则参考书易得(在香港),故已选定第二题译成英文,盖以为秦之声威,决非始皇短期达到西方,至少在始皇前一百年树立。穆公用孟明图霸西戎起——围郑之次年(629 B. C.)已早于始皇三四百年,而商君入秦在 361B. C.,变法得到成功。前之管子甚短,桓公图霸只一时,宋王荆公则失败,以言"土改",恐只有商君成功,晚乘此意与之商讨,劳以为然,故作此题,以证明强秦后垂一百余年而始皇得以西垂偏国统一七雄,使中国进入统一之帝国时期。近又与宾四师讨论过二次,拟稿成,先奉上请教。蔚林公司已告晚,手册及科学刊皆已缺,另尚有人完觅也。另外大公书店(与《大公报》无关,商营)出有一剪贴而成之一九五〇手册,系报章集成,甚厚,内容亦有点用,拟日内购寄。

哈佛燕京社之 Fellowship,不识系作研究工作抑能入校读书?论文成后,请求手续是否有表格要填?均乞一并便中示知。崇基学院,颇有前途,美基督教大学基金联合及伦敦皆有资助,将在九龙沙田建校,此间 Bishop Hall 助力甚大,岭南美国蓝教授明年将来此教课,李应林先生在教会颇孚人望,渠亦盼晚能去美一行。杂志约二十余日到,恐尚要十天也。余俟再上,敬祝双安。

晚绥楚敬上

十一,廿八日

下次赐示,乞暂照信底之崇基校址。

〔袁同礼家人提供〕

按:Bishop Hall 应指 Ronald Owen Hall(1895-1975),中文名何明华,1951 年至 1967 年任圣公会港澳教区会督。李应林(1892—1954),字笑庵,广东南海人,曾任广州岭南大学校长,后来在香港参与创办崇基学院,并担任首任校长。

十二月四日

胡适覆函先生,请不要东来,告知其最近行程安排,并询问先生推荐方豪前往哈佛燕京学社的进展。

> 守和兄:
>
> 十一月九日的信,至今未覆,罪过罪过! 千万请恕罪。
>
> 先人日记,日内即寄给你,乞转赠。是否赠 Hoover Library or Stanford Univ. Library? 便中倘蒙示知,以便决定寄一部或两部。有二事奉告:
>
> ①十七日我的生日,我不能在纽约,因事势如此,实无颜做生日,故借讲演之事,十二夜即去 Univ. of Notre Dame,十五日事毕后赴 The Natural Law Institute,即去中部小休,"躲避生日"也! 千万请你不要为此事东来。敬谢谢吾兄的盛意!
>
> ②方豪(杰人)先生来信,说起吾兄拟推荐他去哈佛燕京作研究工作,他很高兴,信上说吾兄曾拟约我推动此事。此事是否已在进行中? 有需要我助力之处否? 均乞示知。
>
> 匆匆,敬祝双安。
>
> 弟适
>
> 十二月四日

〔University of Chicago Library, Yuan T'ung-li Papers, Box 7〕

按:1948 年底,方豪本拟前往成都就四川大学教职,后胡适劝其"应该去台湾"。①

十二月五日

先生覆信胡适,谈捐赠胡传日记事并请协助推荐方豪至哈佛燕京学社访学。

①《方杰人(豪)先生年谱稿》,页 24。

适之先生：

　　奉到四日手教，欣悉种切。本拟于十七日以前赶到纽约参加祝寿。今既外出旅行，拟俟新年时补祝并拜年也。尊人日记如赠Hoover Library 壹部，实已敷用，如有多份可赠下列诸处，近均参观，知其需要。关于方杰人拟来美研究一节，曾告其向该社径行申请，如有填写留美 Reference 之必要，可写先生大名，此事于八月间曾经面陈，谅尚记忆。如哈佛燕京社不来信询问其成绩大约在明年三月以前，或以申请人多，暂无希望，如来信征求尊意，则再推动玉成其事，至所感荷。该社向来侧重耶稣教会人士，至于对天主教学者有无歧视则不知也。匆匆，敬颂俪安。

同礼敬上
十二，五日

尊夫人同此问安。

　　1.Far Eastern Library

　　University of Washington

　　Seattle, Washington

　　2.East Asiatic Library

　　University of California

　　Berkeley, Calif.

　　3.Claremont Colleges Library

　　Harper Hall

　　Claremont, Calif.

　　4.East Asiatic Library

　　University of California at Los Angeles

　　Log Angeles 24, Calif.

〔台北胡适纪念馆，档案编号 HS-US01-091-003〕

十二月七日

拉铁摩尔覆函先生，感谢寄来有关外蒙古史料，并回寄张之毅所编蒙古书籍、期刊目录。

December 7, 1951

Dear Dr. Yuan:

Thank you very much for your letter of November 27, together with the material in Mongolia, which has arrived safely. We are starting to work on it here.

Of course, I shall respect your confidence. I appreciate very much the valuable work you have done in gathering this material.

Under separate cover, I am sending you a copy of the Chang Chih-yi bibliography on Mongolia. Unfortunately, this work was completed when I was under very heavy pressure, so that I could not give it a final editing, with the result that there are a good many misprints and mistakes in Romanization.

With all good wishes.

Yours very sincerely,

Owen Lattimore

Director

〔University of Chicago Library, Yuan T'ung-li Papers, Box 2〕

按：张之毅（1911—2003），江苏泰州人，1947 年在斯坦福大学获得硕士学位，论文题为 The Oasis Economy of Sinkiang，bibliography on Mongolia，后改题为 A Bibliography of Books and Articles on Mongolia，载于 *Journal of the Royal Central Asian Society*（Vol. XXXVII）。

十二月十四日

李石曾覆函先生，告致彭望邺信已转交，并劝其暂缓回国。〔University of Chicago Library, Yuan T'ung-li Papers, Box 6〕

十二月十五日

彭望邺覆函先生，告通讯地址，并表明年愿前往北美另谋生计。

守和表弟台惠鉴：

昨石曾先生交下手书，敬悉一一。承委代表出席此间国际图书馆各项会议，至所欣愿。李公见告来函于尊衔上冠"前"字以示区别，具

见苦心,惟渠意则尚不无稍异耳。客里残年将经三度,天涯沦落能不
怅然。明春拟作北美之行,颇有另谋生计之想,倘能于华府或纽约间
重图良晤,曷胜盼幸。临笺神往,不尽所怀。专复,顺颂旅安,并祝
年釐。

愚表兄彭望邺拜启

十二月十五日

　　通讯处:W. Y. Peng, Calle Juan Paullier 1110, Apt. 13, Montevideo,
Uruguay

〔University of Chicago Library, Yuan T'ung-li Papers, Box 6〕

十二月十八日

先生致信陈受颐,告知将回华盛顿并请寄赠国会图书馆《元白诗笺证稿》
一部。

　　受颐吾兄著席:

　　　　日前承款待,至以为谢。行色匆匆,未能畅谭。目下相距匪遥,至
　　盼得暇来此小住,至表欢迎。寅恪之书闻尊处业已购到,拟请将渠赠
　　L. C.之书壹部交邮,径寄该馆 Dr. A. W. Hummel, Library of Congress,
　　Wash. D. C.,或寄舍下均可。弟明日东归,明年一月十日左右方返此
　　间。专此申谢,顺颂年釐。

弟同礼顿首

十二,十八

　　嫂夫人同此致谢。

　　　　承代订购之件,尚未寄到,谢谢。

　　　　华京住址:11-8th street, S. E. Washington 3, D. C.

〔台北"中央研究院"台湾史研究所,陈受颐文书(副本)〕

十二月

先生遇夏志清,并收到夏济安从台北辗转寄来的刊物。〔《夏志清夏济安书信
集》卷2,页141〕

一九五二年　五十八岁

一月十四日

克莱普致函先生,感谢赠予平馆照片。

January 14, 1952

Dear Dr. Yuan:

Very many thanks for the picture of the National Library of Peiping which you left at my office last Friday. I am very grateful. It is still-no matter what-the most beautiful library I have seen.

Sincerely yours,

Verner W. Clapp

Chief Assistant Librarian

〔袁同礼家人提供〕

按:该函寄送胡佛图书馆,此件为录副。

一月十八日

熊式一致函先生,劝说竞争剑桥大学中文文学及语言讲座教授席位。

守和吾兄:

剑桥大学中文文学及语言讲座夏伦教授于十二月廿日逝世,继任人选未定,我辈国人之在此者热盼吾兄来此。盖投票人大多知吾兄,如(1)Prof. Walter Simon,(2)Prof. Eve Edwards 皆在伦敦大学,(3)Arthur Waley 居伦敦 50 Gordon Square, London, W. C. 1,(4)Prof. Homer H. Dubs 在牛津大学,(5)Prof. E. R. Dodds, Christ Church Oxford。在剑桥者三人,为(6)Prof. H. W. Bailey 梵文教授,一为(7)Prof. N. B. □□□□□语言学教授,此外,尚有一人,弟不记其姓名,(8)为埃及学教授 Prof. S. R. K. Glanville。夏殁后,各派均欲得此席,但多资望不足,故彼此反对,恐皆难得此八人之通过。Joseph Needham 与吾兄亦有旧,吾兄亦可与之商酌,若能速速来此一游,顺便与此八人之中五六人见面谈之,更易成功也;若通信则只好与颇有交情之人商酌,且书信来往亦易误事,如能速来,则此八人之中虽有不熟悉者亦可介绍见面倾谈,至投票时当可生效,此乃为国家争地位,想吾兄不怪弟之多事也。按剑大之中文教授一席,自夏伦来后极力扩充图书,现已略有基础,若吾兄继任,则定可冠全欧矣。前数年,陈寅恪兄不就牛津,以至今日如此。若陈寅恪今日在牛津,则只须牛津一提吾兄,定可获选也,惜哉惜哉。故尤望吾兄能来此,将来国人皆全赖吾兄也。此外,剑大图书馆长 H. R. Creswick 想吾兄与之有交谊,彼当与剑大之三投票人熟悉,可为吾兄介绍也。匆此,顺颂俪福。令郎来牛津事如何?

弟式顿首
一月十八日

〔University of Chicago Library, Yuan T'ung-li Papers, Box 2〕

按:"夏伦教授"即 Gustav Haloun,研究诸子百家、大月氏、管子等,1939 年担任剑桥大学汉学讲席教授。Prof. Eve Edwards 即 Evangeline Edwards,1937 年担任远东学院院长。Prof. Homer H. Dubs(1892-1969),美国汉学家,中文名德效骞,1947 年赴牛津大学担任汉学讲席教授。Prof. E. R. Dodds 即 Eric R. Dodds(1893-1979),英国古典学家,专攻希腊文化,1942 年曾访华,与先生有往来。Prof. H. W. Bailey 即 Harold W. Bailey(1900-1996),1936 年至 1967 年任剑桥大学梵文教授,通译作"贝利"。Prof. N. B. □□□□□,熊式一此处有涂抹,待考。Prof. S. R. K. Glanville(1900-1956),英国东方学家,专攻埃及文化研究。H. R. Creswick(1902-1988),1949 年至 1967 年担任剑桥大学图书馆馆长。

一月二十二日

先生致信陈受颐,告知剑桥大学汉学讲座教授席位暂虚并拟推荐。

受颐吾兄著席:

弟于日前携眷来此,以途中遇雪,由盐湖而南经 Las Vegas, Bakersfield 等地而达金山,虽多留二日,尚属幸运也。寅恪之书如尚未寄华京,请寄此间为盼。顷闻剑桥大学汉文讲座 Prof. Haloun 突然作古,继任人选正在考虑之中,英人虽主张聘用英人,但资望不足难得其选,势须延聘华人。敝意以吾兄担任最为理想,未识有意前往否?
弟及适之均可推荐也。闻剑桥方面组织一小委员会,考虑继任人选,
以 Waley, Dubs, Dodds, Simon, Edward, Bailey 诸人组织之,如投票时
能得大多数之票,即可获选。因此职为国家争地位,故愿奉告,即希赐
予考虑是幸。如 Claremont 方面不易摆脱,未识心目中有无适当之人,
并乞便中示及为幸。匆匆,顺颂教祺。

弟同礼顿首

一月廿二日

通讯处:730 College Ave., Palo Alto, Calif.

〔台北"中央研究院"台湾史研究所,陈受颐文书(副本)〕

一月二十三日

莫余敏卿致函先生,感谢赠与玉器及告知书目信息,并谈其购买股票想法。

January 23, 1952

Dear Mr. Yuan:

I trust that you must have had a very wonderful time back East with your family. How is Mrs. Yuan and other members of your family? Has Mrs. Yuan come West with you? I hope she does.

Mr. Mok & I want to thank you very much for the most beautiful piece of jade you sent us. It arrived in good condition.

Thank you also very much for the reference you so kindly gave me regarding the words Mr. Rudolph asked me. He said he found them in 容媛's 金石书录目 under 金类 on p. 2: 考古图-北平图书馆藏明刻黑字本. Do you think the words 黑字 should be 墨子?

As we are unable to buy books from China for some time, I feel more free now. I think I can do some research work in my house. Will you advise me what I should do? Any Chinese books about literatures, printing, books etc. worthwhile translating?

Following your advice on buying stocks, I have bought some last December and I am beginning to receive some dividends now. But I think the prices are too high now. I might buy some more when they come down a little.

Regarding two books you asked me to get for you, I have not heard from the girl yet. As soon as she comes to the Library, I will ask her again.

With kindest regards to you & your family.

Sincerely,

Man-hing Yue Mok

〔University of Chicago Library, Yuan T'ung-li Papers, Box 2〕

按:该函为其亲笔。

一月二十五日

先生致信福特(北京),请其协助联系王重民并获得其签署的法律授权书,用以提取他在美的银行存款。

January 25, 1952

Mr. J. F. Ford

British Embassy

Peking

Dear Mr. Ford:

In spite of my silence, I have been thinking of you and your work quite often. I trust that you are enjoying your stay and that Mrs. Ford and children are doing well. I hear that Professor Emperson has left for England and I hope you may give me his address, if you know it.

I am writing to ask for a favor. Mr. Wang Chung-min, the Acting Director of the National Peiping Library, asked me some time ago to collect some money from the Library of Congress for him. In doing so, he should sign a statement (Power of Attorney) before the British Counsel in Peking who will put his signature and seal.

Since I have difficulties in communicating with Mr. Wang, may I request you to get in touch with him and request him to appear before the British Counsel? If he does not want to come to the Consulate, could you or Mr. Bryan call on him, or arrange with him to meet at a certain place, in order to have him sign the power of attorney. Please explain to him that if he does not sign, this account will be closed on June 30, 1952. After that date it would be extremely difficult to claim this amount.

I shall greatly appreciate your assistance in this matter and I hope you could send me the power of attorney after it has been signed and properly sealed. Please ask your friend in Hong Kong to mail it to me by air-mail, if possible.

I have been wondering whether your translation of the Fung Ling's diary will soon be published. Have you got time to work on Hsueh Fu Cheng's travels to Europe?

We have been living at Palo Alto, Calif. And we enjoy our stay here very much. We shall spend some time in England before we return to China.

With sincere thanks and kindest regards,

Yours sincerely,

T. L. Yuan

〔University of Chicago Library, Yuan T'ung-li Papers, Box 2〕

按：Professor Emperson 应指 William Empson（1906－1984），英国文学评论家、诗人，中文名燕卜孙，先后执教于西南联合大学、北京大学，1952 年返回英国。Hsueh Fu Cheng 即薛福成。该信另附一份"Power of Attorney by Individual for the Collection of Checks Drawn on the Treasurer of the United States"。

二月五日

克莱普覆函先生，将应前请寄送 *Information Bulletin*，而所需的书目除两本已经绝版外均将寄出。

February 5, 1952

Dear Dr. Yuan:

I shall be glad to arrange, in accordance with your request of January 23, 1952, to send you copies of the Information Bulletin.

As for the bibliographies which you require: two of these, the one on the Mongolias and the Western languages bibliography of Korea, are already out of print. Will send the others, the out-of-print publications should, however, be available in the Sandford libraries.

Sincerely yours,

Verner W. Clapp

Chief Assistant Librarian

〔袁同礼家人提供〕

按：该函寄送胡佛图书馆，此件为录副。

二月二十八日

刘国蓁覆函先生，告知已将寄送平馆之书籍转递，并告知代购报刊的情况。

守和先生阁下：

叠奉来示，敬悉种切。转寄北平图书馆之书包共七包，经已收齐，即改地址交邮付去，想不日当可到达也。该费另列后，最近付下美钞五元，亦已妥收。代购女内衣背心共四件（最大号者）由包裹邮付上，并代定香港《大公报》三个月，自本月廿一号起寄发也。补购《新华月报》及《人民手册》，经代搜集无从购得，即告知蔚林公司，而其回覆则谓该刊不准出口，搜求亦不易得等语。《新华月报》自去年四月起，已不发海外矣；《人民手册》1951 亦售罄，1952 未出版，如有消息定当代购付上。截至现在止，尊账告一段落，尚余港银一元二角在晚处，计算如下：第一次美钞五元找得港银三十三.六元，第二次美钞五元找得港银三十三.一元，即共来港银六十六.七元，支数为十一月十七日邮票一元，十二月十五日航邮二元，十八日食经二元，廿二日航邮二元，廿四日邮票一元，一月十五日《中国史地词典》九元，二月十八日寄北平图书籍七包邮费共十五.四元、车银八毛，订《大公报》三个月连邮费每月十七元，共银十八.六元，女内背心四件十二元，寄费十七元，共支银六十五.五元是也，特此奉闻。赐还各剪报已收到二次，《北游纪实》由十月十四日至十一月廿六日，至十月二十日《文汇报》港闻一则及《救援难胞的话》一则、《陈君葆的坏人观》一则，尚未见赐还，乞请示知为盼。敝馆所藏各大陆之杂志有《人民文学》、《人民周报》、《人民音乐》、《人民诗歌》、《人民教育》、《人民戏剧》、《文学学习》、《文艺新地》、《文艺报》、《天风》、《中国青年》、《世界知识》、《自然科学》、《科学通报》、《现代妇女》、《华南文艺》、《华南青年》、《新中华》、《新儿童教育》、《新建设》、《新观察》、《时事手册》、《新教育》、《电世界》、《说说唱唱》、《广东教育与文化》、《语文学习》、《学习》、《学习知识》、《翻译通报》共三十种而已。至国内各大学教授名单，陈馆长亦无有，而一时记不得许多姓名也,待迟日有刊物纪载时当付上也。前代寄发大陆各信件,时至今日并无收有回件,亦以为念,倘有得收定当转呈也。港中各样如常,乏善可陈。专此,敬请著安。

愚晚国蓁谨上

一九五二年二月廿八晚灯下

〔University of Chicago Library, Yuan T'ung-li Papers, Box 2〕

按:刘国蓁(K. C. Lau)时任香港大学冯平山图书馆馆员,与陈君葆馆长颇为熟悉,1953 年 11 月离职。

三月二日

钱存训覆函先生,告知硕士论文已提交并拟继续攻读博士学位,请赐中国古代印刷的史料。

守和先生尊鉴:

前奉手示,藉悉月前过芝,途中为大雪所阻,绕道方抵金山,谅多辛苦。久拟作书奉候,奈以学期又将结束,论文不能再延,故周前始将全稿打毕缴卷,因篇幅过长,所费不赀约化百余元,幸校方批评尚佳,堪以告慰。兹附奉大纲一份,并乞指示。现因 Creel 及图书馆学校之怂恿,故又决定继续读 Ph.d 学位,或可得一免费奖学金,即可免缴学费。因每学期只能选读一班,中文系又要加教"现代文选"两班,故不知时间能否分配,希望两三年内可告一段落也。论文题目尚未决定,拟将中国古籍之时代及作者做一系统的研究,不知值得做博士论文否?(Creel 现拟译《战国策》,嘱共同研究其时代及作者,故想兼及他书,可作论文之一部材料。)惟个人兴趣仍在现代,不知尚有其他值得研究之题目否,乞先生多加指示,并建议一二题目以资参考,是所至幸。

又先生前在旧金山宣读论文《中国古代图书馆之发展》,如有副本,不知能赐借一读否?又四月间此间有一系列之公开演讲,训担任之题目为"中国书与印刷",同时并拟举办一中国印刷展览,倘有相同材料,并乞指示为祷。

新居已定,想有一番忙碌,西部天气宜人,当可稍享安居读书之福也。匆匆,顺颂双绥,并问尊府均吉。

后学存训顿首

三月二日

〔University of Chicago Library, Yuan T'ung-li Papers, Box 2〕

三月八日

先生致信陈受颐,告陈寅恪之书径寄斯坦福住址并谈陈序经近况。

受颐吾兄:

上月曾上一书,计达座右。大著想已杀青,亟愿先睹为快。寅恪之书,前奉手教,拟寄内人转交图书馆,想仍未寄出,渠已来此,即希将该书径寄敝处为荷。报载序经被当局扣留,当系事实,尊处如有其他消息,并盼示及。下月远东年会,拟参加否? 专此,顺颂教祺。

弟同礼顿首

三,八

〔台北"中央研究院"台湾史研究所,陈受颐文书(副本)〕

三月十四日

先生致信钱存训,就寄来硕士论文及博士论文题目给予意见。

公垂吾兄惠鉴:

奉到手教并论文大纲,欣悉种切。论文内容及体裁均佳,以之充作博士论文,足可应选。兹拟再选题目另作博士论文,足征好学不倦,至为钦佩。《古籍之时代及作者》一文,亦一极大贡献,似可先参考荷兰华侨某君所作之《白虎通》Leiden 大学出版,戴文达教授指导,再作决定。此人于 1949 年夏间来美,曾到芝加哥,不识晤面否? 近日杂务相缠,未及详为考虑,一俟稍暇,当选择一二,以供参考。前在加大宣读之论文仅限十分钟,故内容欠佳,刻拟稍事稍改,送 Library Sci. Quart.,不识该刊收此项稿件否? 一俟打好再行奉上。适之先生近在普仁斯敦举行中国印刷展览,恐无展览目录,前已函询,俟得复音再行函达。吴子明兄在 L. C.常常陈列此类图籍,再参考渠所写各文,足供参考。在德国 Mainz 地方 Gutenberg 学会年鉴中亦有关于中国印刷之论文,不识已见及否? 匆复,顺颂著祺。

弟同礼顿首

三月十四日

〔钱孝文藏札〕

按:"荷兰华侨"即曾珠森(Tjan Tjoe Som,1903—1969),印度尼西

亚梭罗出生,所作之《白虎通》即 *Po Hu T'ung: the comprehensive discussion in the White Tiger Hall*, Leiden: Brill, 1952 年出版。Library Sci. Quart 应指 *The Library Quarterly*,上世纪五十年代该刊并未发表过署名为 T. L. Yuan 的文章,1952 年 10 月刊行的第 22 卷第 4 期有钱存训的文章 A History of Bibliographic Classification in China(《中国书目分类的历史》)。1952 年 2 月 20 日至 4 月 20 日,胡适在普林斯顿大学图书馆主持举办"中国书展览"并撰写了展览序言,题为 Eleven Centuries of Chinese Printing: an exhibition of books from the Gest Oriental Library。Gutenberg 学会年鉴应为 *Gutenberg-Jahrbuch*,1926 年创刊,刊登印刷史研究论文,尤其针对早期印刷术、摇篮本。

四月中旬

先生寄两本大陆出版的新书书目与裘开明。〔《裘开明年谱》,页 505〕

四月二十二日

先生致信洪业,请代询方豪有无可能赴哈佛燕京学社访学,并告知燕京大学各院多被合并。

April 22, 1952

Dear Prof. Hung:

I have read with much interest your article on the *Secret History of the Yuan Dynasty*. If you should have reprints of this as well as those of other articles, may I request you to spare a copy for my use? I am looking forward to your forthcoming book on Tu Fu. Will it be published by the Harvard University Press?

Sometime ago Prof. Fang Hao 方豪 applied for a fellowship from the Harvard-Yenching Institute. I trust that by this time your Trustees may have reached a decision in regard to his application. Could you inform me whether he has had any chance in this regard?

There was a UP report from H. K. to the effect that various colleges of Yenching have been amalgamated with Tsing Hua and the Peking University. If you happen to have further information from Yenching, I hope you will drop me a note.

My daughter will be studying chemistry at the Graduate School at Harvard in the fall. I shall ask her to call on you and Mrs. Hung when she gets there.

With kindest regards,

Yours sincerely,

T. L. Yuan

〔Harvard-Yenching Library, Papers of William Hung (1893-1980)

1915-1996, From Yuan Tung-li to William Hung, Apr. 22, 1952〕

按:此件为打字稿,落款处为先生签名。

四月二十五日

洪业覆函先生,寄送关于蒙古秘史的论文,并告知《杜甫:中国最伟大的诗人》即将于五月问世,另方豪的申请尚未有决议。

April 25, 1952

Dear Dr. Yuan:

Under separate covers, a reprint of my humble paper on "The transmission of the book known as *The Secret History of the Mongols*" was mailed to your address yesterday.

The publisher, Harvard University Press, will distribute my book *Tu Fu: China's greatest poet*, early in May.

The trustees of the Harvard-Yenching Institute will not meet until next week. I have not heard of Professor Fang's application.

I have not heard from friends in Peiping since Christmas. The news of the closure of Yenching University is indeed sad though not unexpected.

My wife and I will be pleased to meet your daughter when she comes to Cambridge for her graduate studies.

With kindest regards,

Very Sincerely yours,

〔Harvard-Yenching Library, Papers of William Hung (1893-1980)

1915-1996, From William Hung to Yuan Tung-li, Apr. 25, 1952〕

按:此件为底稿。

四月二十八日

先生致信裘开明,推荐方豪赴美访学及其他事。大意如下:

> 上星期我寄给你 2 本大陆出版的新书书目。你核查完这些书目后,请回寄给我。台湾大学的方豪(Fang Hao)教授提交了哈佛燕京学社资助申请。他是一名很有才华的学者,我希望他能获得资助。如果董事会过一段时间开会的话,你能否为他争取这个机会? 如有消息,烦请你告知我。获悉有关燕京大学方面的坏消息,我感到很悲伤。希望你不久后可以完成你的报告,届时能否告诉我一些相关的消息? 裘太太和你们的孩子都一切可好? 我女儿秋天的时候继续在哈佛读化学,全托你和裘太太照顾她了。

〔《裘开明年谱》,页 505〕

按:原信应为英文。

五月七日

Bonnar Brown 致函先生,告知斯坦福研究中心希望就先生的聘期展至 1953 年 6 月 30 日。〔袁同礼家人提供〕

五月十二日

先生覆信 Bonnar Brown,将认真考虑聘期延长之请,但就合约的细节希望可以当面商洽。

May 12th, 1952

Dear Dr. Brown:

　　Your letter of contract extension for my employment dated May 7, 1952 reached me this morning. Please permit me to thank you for it. I have fully noted the terms contained therein.

　　Since there are some minor points that I should like to take up with you personally upon your return to office Thursday, May 17, I find it difficult to comply with your request of furnishing your office a written acceptance by May 15. However, I hope this letter of acknowledgment will let you know that I am taking the terms of your extension of my employment under advisement, until I have discussed the above-mentioned minor points with you. Thereupon I shall notify your office in writing of my decision.

Faithfully yours,

T. L. Yuan

〔袁同礼家人提供〕

按：该件为录副。

五月十六日

上午，先生与 Bonnar Brown 晤谈，商洽斯坦福研究中心聘任细节和待遇问题。〔袁同礼家人提供〕

五月十七日

先生致信 Bonnar Brown，接受该所延长聘期的请求，但请其认真考虑该项目所有人员加薪的问题，希望在七月正式合同中有所体现。

May 17, 1952

Dear Dr. Brown:

With reference to your letter of May 7 and my reply of May 12, I write to inform you that I accept the proposal and conditions as stated in your letter.

My acceptance is based on the conversation we had together yesterday morning in the course of which you kindly assured me that the question in connection with the raise of salaries to the whole staff would be duly considered and that I might expect to receive fair treatment, as the Analysts have already received, when the new contract comes into effect in July.

Sincerely yours,

T. L. Yuan

〔袁同礼家人提供〕

按：此件为录副。

五月下旬

先生致信杨联陞，袁澄因签证问题无法赴英国读书，请为其询问去哈佛大学读研究生的可能。〔《杨联陞日记》(稿本)〕

按：1951 年底，牛津大学接收袁澄为本科生。[1] 1952 年 5 月 28 日，

---

① 《思忆录》，中文部分页 139。

杨联陞收悉此信,并立刻为其询问,了解到申请至 8 月 15 日截止。

六月九日

先生致信裘开明,介绍从香港蔚林图书公司购书,并告《四部要籍序跋》购买途径。大意如下:

> 兹奉上两本由香港 Willing Book Co.寄给我的 1950 年和 1951 年的《全国新书目》。如果你对其中的图书有兴趣,可以把帐单寄给 Willing 图书公司,并在发票上注明编号"No. TLY 011"。我想贵馆应该已经订购了《四部要籍序跋》,该书包括了重要的中文著作的序言和跋文。因此书仅限售 209 本,所以非常值得购买。你可以向台北商务印书馆订购(每册 35 美元)。烦请告诉我最近获得贵社基金资助的人员名单。

〔《裘开明年谱》,页 508〕

　　按:原信应为英文。

六月十五日

赵元任致函先生,告将寄上《三国演义》,并询问何校可购《小屯殷虚文字》,另告暑期行踪。

June 15, 1952

守和我兄:——

　　另封附上《三国演义》八册,是世兄要读,答应了好久到现在才寄上,对不住得很!

　　杨梅史语所杨时逢来信说有《小屯殷虚文字甲编》一册、《乙编》二册,400 pp. each., 8 vo, US＄80,邮费约加＄10.00。吾兄对于各校图情形熟悉,不知有无学校或机关要买此书的,加大已经有了。

　　我们下星期三开车到 Indiana(1216E Hunter Ave, Bloomington, Indiana)。本来是我先坐火车到剑桥开会去,别人随后来。上星期忽然发了几天眼帘炎,只得把剑桥之行取消,直接到 Indiana 去了。咱们大概秋天见了,此颂近祉。

嫂夫人均此。

赵元任

韵卿附笔问候

〔University of Chicago Library, Yuan T'ung-li Papers, Box 2〕

按:杨时逢(1903—1989),安徽石埭人,其姑母即杨步伟,1926 年
南京金陵大学毕业,时应任历史语言研究所研究员。《殷虚文字
甲编》,董作宾编著,1948 年 4 月出版,收录殷墟第一次至第九次
发掘所获的刻辞甲骨 3942 号;《殷虚文字乙编》,董作宾主编,
1948 年 10 月出版,收录殷墟第十三次至第十五次发掘所采获的
甲骨文字。本年 6 月 18 日,赵元任驾车东行,22 日抵印第安纳州
Bloomington 参加暑期语言讲习班,至 8 月 15 日结束。①

六月十六日

方豪致函先生,告知在欧行踪。

> 守和先生大鉴:

> 敬启者,弟已到马德里,曾往国立图书馆、王家图书馆(Escorial)
及 Toledo 教堂图书馆访书,略有所获,非短函所能详。后日赴 Sevilla,
然后再往 Salamanca,转葡萄牙,访 Coimbra 及 Lisboa。最后经法、比、
意返台。十日内若有指示,请寄 c/o the Mr. Edward Wu, Ponzano 85,
Madrid;十日后则寄"巴黎大使馆"卫青心先生留交。

> 先生在 California 之地址,竟未记录在通讯册上,不得已只好寄老
地址一试。旅中草草,乞恕为幸。敬请暑安。

> > 弟方豪叩上

> > 六,十六

> 〔University of Chicago Library, Yuan T'ung-li Papers, Box 2〕

按:托莱多大教堂(Cathedral de Toledo)是西班牙著名的教堂,位
于马德里城南托莱多城内。Sevilla、Salamanca、Coimbra、Lisboa
分指塞维利亚、萨拉曼卡、科英布拉、里斯本。

六月十八日

先生致信赵元任,就出版方式和营销方式谈两点建议。

> 元任先生:

> 奉到赐书 Linguistics Institute 所印之暑校章程盼寄一份,欣悉不日东行,敬祝
一路顺风。Indiana 天气较热,仍希格外珍摄为祷。《小屯殷虚文字》
容易出售,兹将图书博物两馆名单奉上,即请转寄,并请转告下列

---

① 《赵元任年谱》,页 324-325。

两事：

（一）用 Limited Edition 办法，每部编一号数（否则书价太高，不易销售）；

（二）由台北寄出一英文说明愈简单愈好，附一空白订单，说明收款地点（check or money order 均可），并说明仅印五十部或百部，购者从速。

承寄《三国演义》，谢谢，得暇时弟亦拟再读一遍也。专复，敬候暑祺。

尊夫人同此问安。

弟同礼顿首

六，十八

慧熙嘱笔致候

〔University of California, Berkeley, The Bancroft Library, Yuen Ren Chao papers, carton 10, folder 39, Yuan, Tongli and Yuan, Huixi〕

按：信中先生似并未理解 15 日赵元任来函中的意思，以为询问《小屯殷虚文字》出版后在美营销方法。该信附美国图书馆、博物馆名单一页。

六月三十日

Bonnar Brown 致函先生，告知斯坦福研究中心正式延长先生聘期至 1953 年 6 月 30 日，月薪 450 美金。〔袁同礼家人提供〕

按：该薪金待遇为扣除社保和个人所得税后数额。

七月二日

先生致信方恩，感谢帮助查找中国学者姓名，并表示有意将旧作扩充并加入亚洲基督教高等教育联合董事会计划出版的美国对华及东南亚国家政策书系。

July 2, 1952

Dr. William P. Fenn

United Boards for Christian Colleges in China

150 Fifth Avenue

New York, N. Y.

Dear Dr. Fenn:

I greatly appreciate your courtesy in finding out the Chinese names of several scholars whose scientific writings I was particularly interested. For similar matters I had written to my old friend Mr. Li Siao-yuan at Nanking. But in view of the situation prevailing there, I thought it best not to write to him at least for the time being.

Dr. Martin Yang told me recently that you are making plans to bring out a series of books relating to American policy toward China and Southeast Asia. This program interests me very much, as there has been so much misunderstanding on the part of these peoples concerning American motives and ideals.

As you may recall, I wrote a short article (in Chinese) during the war on Sino-American cultural relations. It was published by the Institute of Chinese-American Cultural Relations at Chungking, but I have no copies at hand. It could be enlarged and new materials should be added. If you are interested in bringing out booklets of this and similar kind, I shall be glad to assist you in this undertaking.

My bibliographical work here is not pressing, so I have plenty of time for writing monographs of this kind.

With sincere greetings and kind regards.

Yours sincerely,

T. L. Yuan

〔Yale University Divinity School Library, United Board for Christian Higher Education in Asia Records, RG 11 Series Ⅱ, Box 79, Folder 2146〕

按：Martin Yang 即杨懋春(1904—1988)，字勉斋，山东胶州人，曾在齐鲁大学学习社会学，后考入燕京大学社会学研究所，1939 年赴美留学，入康乃尔大学并获得哲学博士学位，博士论文为 Market Town and Rural Life in China(《中国的集镇制度和乡村生活》)，抗战胜利后回国任农林部督察、东北行辕经济委员会副处长等职，1947 年夏任齐鲁大学社会学教授，1949 年赴美讲学。a short article (in Chinese)即《战后中美文化之关系》，收录于《战后中美文化关系论丛》(《中美文化协会丛书》四)。该信于 9 日送达。

七月四日

童季龄覆函先生,谈其返台计划。

守和兄:

由季陶兄转缄敬悉。返台港研究经济问题,乃万不得已之计划,如能来美,则研究对象或将改写,但来美之事,困难重重。迄今为止,尚觉无把握,弟已坐候两年零七个月,耐心几乎销磨罄静,惟以吾兄及诸老友,仍不断多方翊助,如有万分之一之希望,自仍当努力进行。实在绝望,即当遄返台港,另寻出路。南美生活虽低,而文化环境太劣,即普通读物(英文)亦多陈旧缺略,欲从事研究绝不可能。闻孙恭度兄云,日本英文旧籍甚多,而对东方问题资料大为丰富,劝弟于返台港后,设法赴日,此亦是一种计划,须东返后乃能决定。顺颂俪祺。不具。

弟季龄敬上
四十一,七,四

〔University of Chicago Library, Yuan T'ung-li Papers, Box 2〕

按:"罄静"似当作"罄净"。"季陶兄"即刘大钧。孙拯,字恭度,安徽寿县人,经济学家,早年赴日留学,毕业于东京帝国大学经济科,曾任资源委员会经济研究室主任。

七月八日

拉铁摩尔覆函先生,谈其外蒙古著述的进展。

July 8th 1952

Dear Dr. Yuan,

Many thanks for your note of July 3rd. I am delighted to hear that you have been keeping up your interest in Outer Mongolia.

The book on which Peter Onon and I have been working is not an autobiography, but a biography of SukeBatur. Peter is not in this morning, and I do not have the manuscript at hand, but my recollection is that the Revolutionary Mongolian People's Party was created not in 1918, but in 1919 and 20, and not in Moscow but in a series of meetings, first in Urga, and then in Kyakhta and Verkhny Udisk. After this, a group of delegates of the new party did proceed to Moscow, but neither SukeBatur nor

Choibalsang was in the party.

I think you will find the essential facts confirmed in a recent Chinese translation of the "official" biography of the late Choibalsang by Tsedenbal. Hoover Library has this, and Mary Wright knows about it, because she drew it to my attention. It contains numerous quotations from Choibalsng's "Short History of the Revolution."

We are still hoping to get out to California for a few weeks in August and September.

If we can do so, it will be a great pleasure to see you again.

Very sincerely,

Owen Lattimore

〔University of Chicago Library, Yuan T'ung-li Papers, Box 2〕

按:信中所谈之书应为 *Nationalism and Revolution in Mongolia with a Translation from the Mongol of Sh. Nachukdorji's "Life of Sukebatur"*,1955 年牛津大学出版社初版。Peter Onon 应为彼·乌尔贡格·鄂嫩(Urgunge Onon P.),SukeBatur 即达木丁·苏赫巴托尔(1893—1923),蒙古人民党的创始人之一,外蒙古独立过程中最重要的人物之一。Urga 即库伦(今乌兰巴托),Kyakhta 即恰克图,Choibalsang 即霍尔洛·乔巴山(1895—1952),蒙古人民共和国早期领袖,Tsedenbal 即尤睦佳·泽登巴尔(1916—1991),蒙古政治家。此件为打字稿,落款处为其签名。

七月九日

方恩覆函先生,告知此前杨懋春转述的书系主题有误,而且以汇编报纸和杂志文章为主。

July 9, 1952

Dear Dr. Yuan:

It was a pleasure to hear of you and to learn of your interest in our literature program.

I fear that Dr. Yang gave you a not entirely correct impression of the plans we have in mind. There is no thought of books on American policy or on cultural relations. Rather we are concerned with providing for

Chinese in Southeast Asia effective statements of important democratic and Christian values and ideals. Most of these will be in the form of newspaper or magazine articles.

We appreciate your offer of help and, if it turns out that we need anything of the sort you suggest, we shall be only too happy to turn to you.

With warm regards and best wishes, I am,

Cordially yours,

William P. Fenn

Executive Secretary

〔Yale University Divinity School Library, United Board for Christian Higher Education in Asia Records, RG 11 Series Ⅱ, Box 79, Folder 2146〕

七月十七日

董作宾致函先生,告琐事缠身,欲赴美讲学。

……弟近来被拉抱任事务太多,弄到绝对不能工作。兄知弟非好事者,半辈子不作主管人,不做官,为的专心把一门学问弄好,现在一天到晚,为杂事纠缠,愈来愈多。(弟血压高,有随时找孟真兄去的危险!)弟年近六十(实57),尚能作工之时日已不多矣,如此下去,这一世就完了。现在惟一的希望,是换一环境,做一点结束的工作。弟自芝大返国,许多书稿未带回,为的是再去一趟。前两年有带家眷的问题,现在弟可以只身前往了。如果能在美讲学一两年,多少可以续几文养家,并自己写出一点东西,私愿已足,并非贪图大名大利。

此间旧友如济之,现在工作极努力,安阳发掘总报告,不久可以付印一部分了。史语所出来的人有一半,多在台大兼课。史语所无基础,打算造一点房子,现仍无把握。孟真去世后,研究所由弟负责维持,贫困家弱,为一病夫,较之北平、南京,不胜今昔之感! 望吾兄有以接教护助之! 专颂旅安!

弟董作宾拜上

七月十七日

〔University of Chicago Library, Yuan T'ung-li Papers, Box 2〕

按：1951 年 1 月至 1955 年 8 月，董作宾担任历史语言研究所所长。该函仅存最后一页。

七月二十三日

方豪覆函先生，感谢协助申请哈佛燕京学社访学，并告其在西班牙、葡萄牙访查档案文献之收获。

守和先生大鉴：

昨（廿二日）自马德里来此，欣奉大教。哈佛之事，多承鼎力推介，成与不成同深感激。赴美旅费弟可自筹，惟此事只好俟诸明年，因此次来欧旅费之一部分系预支《中西交通史》第一册及《华侨史》稿费，故必须赶回台湾完成。明年如能写《中西交通史》第二、三册及《台湾史》，则赴美旅费亦不成问题矣。但东京大学有约弟赴日之议，西班牙方面拟邀弟在该国工作一二年，协助纂辑中班字典，一切均在未定之天。

此次在 Sevilla 之 Archivo General de Indias 获见马尼拉古地图多帧，颇可见华侨□兴衰之迹及有关郑成功史料，均已摄影或抄录。在里斯本国会档案室更得读澳门中文资料，凡四大包，约计一千数百件。馆长坚约弟编目，时不我许，只编至四百七十二号（工作时间仅限上午十一时至下午四时，极不合理，弟往往不用午饭，忍饥为之），皆为清代最盛时代及初衰时代之中西交通史料，举凡英美势力之初渐、鸦片之取缔、俄国第一艘船之东驶澳门、租银之催交与缴付、中国官吏之视察，以及越界造屋等无不齐备。中葡势力之消长极为明显。馆长任事已三十余年，谓从无一人加以利用，现在未编目之文件亦已经弟详为检阅、择要摄影。此次在葡京时又适遇 Boxer、Braga 等学人，同聚一处，至为愉快。某司铎发明桌上读 Microfilm 机，弟购得全世界第二部，现仍在改进中，但已为人定去六、七架，价位在一千葡币，至为方便。久无适之先生消息，便中祈代致意。时值溽暑，海外羁旅，更宜为学珍卫。不一一。

弟方豪拜复

七，廿三

在葡国共留十八日，不日赴法，惜意、法圃及文献馆暑期多不开放，实为憾事。又及。

〔University of Chicago Library, Yuan T'ung-li Papers, Box 2〕

按：Archivo General de Indias 即西印度群岛综合档案馆，位于西班牙南部塞维利亚（Sevilla）。"里斯本国会档案室更得读澳门中文资料"应指葡萄牙东波塔档案馆（Arquivo Nacional da Torre do Tombo）藏清代澳门中文档案，确为方豪首次发现并编目、利用。Boxer、Braga 所指学人待考。

八月十二日

裘开明覆函先生。大意如下：

> 很抱歉我们还没有核对完 1950 年和 1951 年的新书目录，遵照你的建议，我们向香港 Willing Book Co.购买了这两部书。事实上，我们还没有完成对 Wayne Altree 先生所购的全部新书的编目工作，这些书是 Altree 先生在香港为胡佛图书馆买书时顺便帮我们买的。但是草编目录纸片已经排入公共检索四角号码目录。因此对于我们来说查找馆藏新书并不难。另外，如果你想知道你需要的书我馆是否有藏，我们将很乐意帮你检索任何专门的文献或简目。关于获得学社资助的人选名单，秘书处说名单尚不完整，入选名单要等到 11 月份以后才能确定，届时将会在哈佛大学名录上公布。但是我知道台湾大学的方豪教授不在入选名单上。我们已经购买了一套《四部要籍序跋》。非常感谢你的建议。

〔《裘开明年谱》，页 512〕

按：原函应为英文。

八月十三日

先生致信恒慕义，请其协助董作宾来美从事研究工作，希望可以留意有关基金会资助项目及其他学术资源。

Dear Dr. Hummel:

On the eve of your departure for the Far East, I hate to bother you with matters of no immediate concern to your mission. There is, however, one project which I have always been greatly interested, viz, the publication of the studies on Oracle Bones by Professor Tung Tso-Pin. In view of its importance to Sinology, I trust you would also take a similar interest.

While much has been published on the subject from the finds of An Yang excavations, there are still many more significant materials in the collection of "Academia Sinica" which have not been systematically studied. As Professor Tung is the only person capable of doing this kind of work, support should be given to him in order to enable him to devote his entire time to this work.

Letters received from Professor Tung indicate that he is now so heavily burdened with administrative work that he simply cannot find the time to do any scientific research. But since he had made rubbings of these bones with which he can work equally well, he wishes to come to the United States to continue the work on this project. This would be an ideal arrangement, if some institution in the United States would sponsor his visit. I know that both Chicago and Berkeley are very keen on this project, but financial difficulties have prevented its early realization.

It has occurred to me that the collection of oracle bones in the possession of Mr. Menzies deserves further study. If Professor Tung can come over, he and Mr. Menzies may find it desirable to collaborate together toward the early publication of the results. As both are not enjoying good health, it is of utmost importance that immediate support should be extended to them.

I feel that if it is not easy to arrange a visit from Professor Tung at this time, one of the Foundations should be approached with a view to obtaining a special grant for this project, so that Professor Tung may be relieved from administrative duties and may devote his entire time to research.

When you arrive at Taipeh, I hope you will get in touch with Professor Tung and see some of his work. On your return you may discuss further with Professor Creel, Dr. Graves and others, so that some concrete plan may be worked out at that time.

With best wishes for a most pleasant journey,

Sincerely yours,

T. L. Yuan

〔University of California, Berkeley, The Bancroft Library, Yuen Ren Chao papers, carton 10, folder 39, Yuan, Tongli and Yuan, Huixi〕

按:此为抄件,附于 8 月 25 日致赵元任信中。

八月十四日

戴志骞致函先生,告其近况并预祝大作早日问世。

August 14, 1952.

Dear Mr. Yuan,

It has been several months since our last correspondence. I am happy to know that two of your children are entering the graduate school. Time certainly flies rapidly. I always visualize that from Tsing Hua days to the present it is just a vivid wink of a colorful dream.

Mrs. Tai has been offered a position as the librarian of Lincoln Community School. She goes to her school library at 7.45 every morning from Mondays to Fridays and returns home at 5. p. m. From our flat to the school, it requires an hour in travel by train and bus. I stay at home to look after the flat, to shop some of our daily necessities and to study Spanish at my leisure.

I am very happy to know that you are given the opportunity to compile a Bibliography on China as a supplement to Cordier's. Your work will be much appreciated by scholars in future.

Mrs. Tai joins me in sending our kindest regards to Mrs. Yuan and yourself.

Yours sincerely,

T. C. Tai

〔University of Chicago Library, Yuan T'ung-li Papers, Box 2〕

按:时,戴志骞的联系地址为 2527 Estrada, Martinez, Buenos Aires, Argentina。此件为打字稿,落款处为其签名。

八月二十四日

颜复礼(汉堡)覆函先生,收到国会图书馆寄来的书籍照片,但因为规定无法向东德的莱比锡汇款,只得请在美友人偿还垫款并补拍正确的页码,另告将寄送从东德获得的第一本有关中国的书籍。

Hamburg, 24th August, 1952

Dear Mr. Yuan,

I have still to acknowledge receipt of your letter dated 18th June for which I thank you most sincerely. In the meantime, I received the seven photostats from the Library of Congress which I urgently need for my research work about Wang Cheng, I should like to express my heartfelt gratitude for your assistance in this matter. I understand the amount of Dollars 3.15 has been debited to your account by the Library of Congress for which I would like to reimburse yourself. I regret to inform you that I was unable to follow your request and pay DM 10.80 to Messrs. Harrassowitz & Co., as under the prevailing foreign exchange laws the payment in German currency of amounts due by a foreigner is not permitted. I, therefore, requested Mrs. von Winterfeldt who is at present in the United States and whom you will probably know from China, to remit to you for my account US Dollars 7.--. As the Photoduplication Service of the Congress Library had copied some wrong pages by mistake, I have directly requested the Service to copy the right pages. I should be obliged if you would kindly also bear the costs for these photostats using the balance of the afore-mentioned amount.

When in future you are interested in buying books from Germany, I would recommend to you to let me know the title of the book so that I may order them at Harrassowitz and pay for same.

As to German literature concerning Communist China, I should like to draw your attention to the following facts:

There are practically no books published in Western Germany on the new China.

Books on China printed in Eastern Germany are mostly translation from Russian and English versions and I suppose you are not interested in such publications.

As I had previously informed you the local booksellers cannot obtain books from the Russian zone for different reasons.

In the meantime, I requested my relatives residing in the Eastern Zone to send me some books on China and I am pleased to inform that I have just received the first book which contains the memoirs of an

Austrian surgeon about his experiences in China since 1939/40. He is a close follower of Communism. I am sending you the book by order mail as a printed matter and trust it will reach you safely.

With many thanks and kind regards,

Yours faithfully,

Fritz Jäger

〔University of Chicago Library, Yuan T'ung-li Papers, Box 2〕

按：此件为打字稿，落款处为其签名。

八月二十五日

先生致信赵元任，告董作宾有意来美从事研究，请为其留意合适的机会。

元任先生：

光阴过的甚快，暑校工作想已结束，不识已到康桥否？希望下月中旬可以西返。上月接彦堂来信仍愿来美研究，目前入境既感不易，似可在美为之先筹一笔补助费，俾能摆脱杂事专作研究，将来遇有适当机会，再行来美亦无不可。两周前 Hummel 赴台北、香港各地购书。弟曾致彼一函，托其访晤彦堂，与之拟一研究计划，筹出数千元之研究费似尚不难。信稿附上，不识尊意以为如何？加大下年度经费均已核定，似亦不易聘请也。余俟面谈。顺颂旅安。

弟同礼顿首

八，廿五

尊夫人同此问安。

〔University of California, Berkeley, The Bancroft Library, Yuen Ren Chao papers, carton 10, folder 39, Yuan, Tongli and Yuan, Huixi〕

按：8 月 19 日，赵元任抵达麻省剑桥。加州大学亦无多余经费可供申请，参见翌年 3 月 13 日与钱存训信。

九月十日

毕乃德致函先生，请教陆征祥入京师同文馆的史料，并请留意广方言馆中法文教席记载。

September 10, 1952

Dear Dr. Yuan:

Thank you for returning my copy of the 1893 T'ung-wen Kuan

Calendar. I trust that you were able to find some useful material therein.

In going through the material, I have collected on the Kuang-fang yen-kuan, I have discovered that Lou Tseng-Tsiang was one of four graduates of the French Department of that school who were recommended in 1890 to be sent to Peking for examination by the Tsungli Yamen to enter the T'ung-wen Kuan. His name is the only one of the four which appears nowhere in the 1893 T'ung-wen Kuan Calendar. I have no explanation of this and wonder if you have one. Of course, he may have gone to Peking, been examined, and assigned somewhere else without entering the T'ung-wen Kuan at all; I know of other cases of this kind. Yet in Mr. Lou's biography in *Who's Who in China* he states that he was one time a student in the T'ung-wen Kuan. I would appreciate any light that you can throw on this matter as it might help to explain some similar cases-for example, one in which four graduates of the Mathematics Department were sent to Peking and none of their names appears in the 1893 Calendar.

An earlier letter of yours raises another question about the Kuang-fan yen-kuan. You mentioned a French professor in the school whom I presume was a friend of Mr. Lou. According to the Kuang-fan yen-kuan materials that I have, French was being taught there in 1881 by a Chinese, although the document which mentions this fact also states that he was not entirely satisfactory and that the Chinese Minister to France had been asked to look for a competent French teacher. I know from another document that French was being taught in 1894 by a Chinese. It is quite possible that the Frenchman you inquired about taught in school some time in the interim and I would appreciate your sending me any evidence that you may have of that fact. As you can see, the material that I am having to depend upon for the description of this Shanghai school is very spotty indeed. As you no doubt have discovered, the Kiangnan Arsenal 记 hardly mentions the school.

Sincerely yours,

Knight Biggerstaff, Chairman

Department of Far Eastern Studies

〔University of Chicago Library, Yuan T'ung-li Papers, Box 2〕

按：four graduates of the French Department of that school 应指刘镜人（1868—?）、刘式训（1868—1929）、陆征祥（1871—1949）、翟青松（1870—1940），a French professor in the school 应指 Alphonse Bottu，陆征祥记作"玻杜先生"。①

九月十三日

李书田（纽约）覆函先生，恳请协助李书华申请来美。

守和先生道右：

八、廿九示敬悉。国务院主管救济中国学生教授之人复兄原函，前寄巴黎，俟索回后当寄上。该人为 John G. Byers, Chief, Chinese Assistance Section, Special Service Branch, Educational Exchange Service, United States International Information Administration, Department of State, Washington 25, D. C.

照国务院所宣布之新办法字义，在欧之中国教授学者，当然可以申请，请依此字义转托詹森大使，润章之申请案，一由加州大学物理系主任转国务院，一曾由美国驻法大使馆自愿协助转国务院，詹森在内设法后，可有希望，即望恳切奉托詹森大使为祷！

弟已返纽约住，地址如上，仍在原顾问工程师事务所之纽约事务所从事规划 Ohio Turnpike 之 Continuous Bridges。专复，并请道安。

弟李制书田敬上

九，十三

〔University of Chicago Library, Yuan T'ung-li Papers, Box 2〕

按：李书田所在工程师事务所为"Civil & Hydraulic Engineering Consultant"，其联系地址为 Rm, 6W2, 504 W, 112th St. New York 25, N. Y.

十月十四日

先生致信赵元任，恳请协助申请项目以利李书华来美。

① 罗光《陆征祥传》，香港真理学会出版，1949 年，页 19。

元任先生：

　　近接李书田君_{在纽约}来函，谓润章在法经济颇窘，国人在欧谋事尤感不易，而渠又不愿托人为之说项。曾于一九五一年与加大物理系主任通讯，旋即接到加大校长署名之聘书，其时本拟申请 ECA 之津贴，不意留欧之中国学者未承列入补助之列，以致迟迟未能来美。现入境似无问题，而抵美后之生活尚待筹划，闻加大偶有接受政府或工业界之委托研究专题之机会，如能准予参加此项研究，由校方酌予待遇，则于个人经济不无小补。尚希遇机与物理系主任一谈，促其随时留意。不胜感荷，余俟面谈。顺颂俪安。

弟袁同礼顿首
十，十四

附润章致物理系主任函稿，以备参考。

〔University of California, Berkeley, The Bancroft Library, Yuen Ren Chao papers, carton 10, folder 39, Yuan, Tongli and Yuan, Huixi〕

　　按：1953 年 3 月，李书华由欧洲赴美，在纽约定居。

十一月十六日

胡适致片先生，告知赴台行程。

　　今早(十六)从纽约起飞，搭的是西北线，故不经金山。十八下午到东京，十九早到台北。大示收到，甚感谢。毅生文未见到。有三事亦未有刊闻。近读中共出的思想改造文选四集，中有金岳霖一文，说他经过了两年多的"学习"，已认识辩证唯物论"硬是真理"！祝双安。

适之

　　内人在纽约，颇多朋友照料，乞告嫂夫人。

适之

〔袁同礼家人提供〕

　　按：《思想改造文选》(第 4 集)，1952 年 5 月由光明日报社发行，收录陈垣、周培源、金岳霖、梁思成、钱伟长等人文章，其中金岳霖文题为《批判我的唯心论的资产阶级教学思想》。该片无落款日期，但由邮戳可知此片于 1952 年 11 月 17 日由西雅图寄出。

十一月二十八日

西门华德覆函先生，询问先生近况及工作，建议重新加入 China Society。

28th November, 1952

My dear Director Yuan,

I was so glad to have your news the other day. The letter reached me in an envelope stamped 'Oxford' and so I do not know whether the California address means that you have left the Congress Library and are doing something else. Please let me know because I need hardly say that I am very much interested in your personal well-being, and that of your family.

I have written to Miss Yates, who is the Secretary of the China Society (of which I am a member of Council). I enclose the list of publications still available with prices. At the same time, she raised the question whether you wish to consider re-joining the Society. The annual contribution is still only 1 guinea and if you or your Institute were to join the Society you would receive future publication free of charge. I add the name and address of the Secretary in case you wish to correspond with her.-Miss Joan Yates, the China Society, 133 Fellows Road, London, N. W. 3.

I shall be sending an offprint of my latest article on 'erl' in a few days, as soon as I have received my offprints which should be the case in a day or two. I suppose you received the preceding part some time ago?

With all good wishes for you and your family,

Yours very sincerely,

W. Simon

〔University of Chicago Library, Yuan T'ung-li Papers, Box 2〕

按：此件为打字稿，落款处为其签名。

十二月三日

徐亮（华盛顿）覆函先生，谈在武汉家属近况，并告知国会图书馆华人馆员去留情况。

守和先生钧鉴：

前奉读手教，敬悉覃第迎釐、兴居集福。令郎留英在牛津大学研读，深为庆幸。文华专校被接收以后，闻沈校长早被迫让位，由"政府"委派王某接任,至于王君之履历,弟一无所知。据最近来自丹佛之教授云,沈宝环尚在丹佛图书馆服务,明春可能返台湾,确否仍待证明。去夏曾驱车游芝加哥,沿途风景甚优美,不幸返华京后足部湿气大发,寸步难移,颇为所苦。先后告假在家诊治休息达三星期之久,始克痊愈,承垂问,至感至感。前接武汉来信始悉岳丈已于九月初旬逝世,小孩等现由岳母代管,姊妹屡次来信催促弟等从速返国照料子女。前已去函询问以后信件及款项应交何人收管,现尚未得回信,承告知汇款方法,至为感激。来示云已学会开车,并已行驶七千余里,驾驶技术定必熟练,以后旅行更觉便利也。国会图书馆因征兵关系,书库排架员甚为缺乏,又以待遇相当菲薄,不易聘请美国人,故年青之中国学生被雇佣者有贺白石、罗孝山及荣正,此三人将来可能变为正式职员。得国务院补助金在国会图书馆服务者大都因助金先后终止,而离馆如李丙昆、荆磐石、马在天夫人、曹耀琛、陈创、张齐、李兴贤、刘永仁、戴清旭(与尤桐结婚,现返布林司登)及赵在田(已返台湾)。现仍继续在馆工作者有杨雪伦(仍在日文部)、郑宝华(日文部)、陶维勋(中文部)、袁孟晋(中文部)、王隐三(中文部)、马在天(中文部);在法律图书馆者有杨泉德、梁耀炳、陈英竞、张一峰;在欧洲部者有张纯朋(彼现至联合国充当中国代表团顾问,以后或再返馆工作);在采购部者有张发舜;在科学部者有曾培光(曾琦之侄);属中文部非作中文部工作者有刘大钧。耑此,即请钧安。

袁太太安好。

弟徐亮上

十二月三日

内人附笔问安

又廖天任在 South Asia Section 工作。闻房兆楹夫妇均在士丹佛图书馆工作,想常与之见面,请代问候。

〔University of Chicago Library, Yuan T'ung-li Papers, Box 2〕

按:徐亮,湖南人,武昌文华图书馆学专科学校毕业,曾任上海东方图书馆主任。[1] 1951年8月,中南军政委员会教育部接办文华

---

① 《私立武昌文华图书馆学专科学校一览》,1935年,页97。

图专。1955年沈宝环返台,在东海大学图书馆服务。

十二月三十日

先生致信法斯,请洛克菲勒基金会考虑资助编纂《西文汉学书目》。

December 30, 1952

Dear Dr. Fahs:

For the past three years I have been working on a comprehensive bibliography of China in Western languages. In undertaking this task, I have had financial assistance from the China Foundation.

Owing to its limited income and its commitments elsewhere, no further support from that Foundation would be forthcoming. Since it is a specific, short-term piece of bibliographical research, I wonder whether your Foundation would be interested in lending your support, so that the present work may be brought to early completion.

After having gone through the important collections in the East, I am making a survey of the major collections along the Pacific coast. I expect to spend a year here and the Mid-West before returning to Washington.

In view of the uncertainty of obtaining assistance in the future, I am hoping to turn all of my manuscripts to the Library of Congress after the completion of Part 1, Section 1. I am therefore particularly anxious to complete it on which I have already devoted much of my time. I am sure that with your support, it could be successfully concluded. May I therefore apply for a grant-in-aid from your Foundation for the academic year July 1953–June 1954?

For your further information, a brief statement regarding the project is herewith submitted. In view of the scholarly nature of the undertaking, I hope the application may receive due consideration from you and your colleagues.

Sincerely yours,

T. L. Yuan

〔Rockefeller Foundation. "Rockefeller Foundation Records, Projects, Rg 1.2." Series 200: United States; Subseries 200.R: United States-Humanities and Arts. Box 362. Folder 3274〕

按:此件为打字稿,落款处为先生签名,随信附上 2 页关于 Supplement to Cordier's Bibliotheca Sinica (1921–51)补充说明,翌年 1 月 19 日送达法斯手中。

一九五三年　五十九岁

三月五日

先生致信胡适，告知将寄上《明代农民革命史料》《傀儡戏考原》二书，另提及中国科学院印行书三种、清华大学理学院与北京大学合并等事。

> 适之先生：
>
> 大驾返美后，亟盼在金山晤谭，嗣闻改乘西北飞机，未得聆教，至为怅怅。返纽约后想可略事休息，不识近日有何著作，在台讲演闻将印成言论集，出版后并盼赐寄为感。前函所述毅生所编之《明代农民革命史料》已在香港购到，一俟收到当即奉赠。孙子书近著《傀儡戏考原》业已函购，到后亦拟寄上。近见郭沫若报告，谓科学院印行（一）《小屯殷虚文字乙编》、（二）《居延汉简考》、（三）《郭象庄子注校记》，不识何人所作，或系史语所北平部分遗下之稿，顷已函告董彦堂矣。大陆方面迄无信来，昨见上海《解放日报》内载去秋北大招生，以投考数学系者为最多，清华理学院各系业与北大合并。又该报载上海市人民代表会议主席团，列有王芸生、沈尹默、陆阿狗及其他"先进生产者"，亦一趣闻。王芸生被调赴津，上海《大公报》与天津《大公报》原名《进步日报》合并，前曾托友人在港订购，据云不许出国。敬候道祺。
>
> 同礼敬启
>
> 三月五日
>
> 尊夫人前同此问安，内人附笔问候。

〔台北胡适纪念馆，档案编号 HS-US01-064-001〕

按：是年 1 月 17 日，胡适离开台北至东京盘桓数日，后经阿拉斯加返美。《明代农民革命史料》应指郑天挺、孙钺等辑《明末农民起义史料》，1952 年 6 月中华书局初版。孙楷第《傀儡戏考原》，1952 年 9 月上杂出版社初版。《郭象庄子注校记》作者为王叔岷，1949 年后随史语所迁台，此处应指 1950 年 1 月《"中央研究院"历史语言研究所专刊》之三十三。

三月二十五日

Far Eastern Survey 刊登先生文章，题为 Railway Construction in China。〔Chang, Li. "Railway Construction in China." *Far Eastern Survey*, vol. 22, no. 4, 1953, pp. 37–42〕

> 按：该文虽标明作者为"Li Chang"，并介绍其"曾任中华民国铁道部的官员，现在英国大学从事经济研究"，但根据 1954 年 3 月 10 日先生致张君劢信，可知该文实为先生用笔名所写，失收于《袁同礼文集》。

四月十日

洛克菲勒基金会批准编号为 RF52201 的资助计划，给予先生（国会图书馆）九千美金，用以编纂 *Bibliotheca Sinica*，其中七千美金用作先生的薪水，其余则支付事务类费用。〔Rockefeller Foundation. "Rockefeller Foundation Records, Projects, Rg 1.2." Series 200: United States; Subseries 200.R: United States-Humanities and Arts. Box 362. Folder 3274〕

四月二十五日

李冰（台北）覆函先生，请协助在美出售齐如山旧藏小说、戏曲类古籍。

> 守和学长吾兄左右：
>
> 　　昨诵环云，恍同晤对，多年积愫，为之一舒。此间旧友除傅孟真作古外，尚有毛子水、狄福鼎、刘兆滨（毅人）、陆雪塘诸人，谭声丙未能来台。早岁同学不但星散，在大陆者且不能自由来信，回首当年曷胜感慨。前恳代为接洽之藏书，为弟之长辈世交齐如山先生之物，如老所藏戏曲、小说为数甚多，其携来台者仅十之一耳。吾兄如与哈佛谈妥，则将来大陆书如存在，如老愿径将全部让与哈佛。至于所谈书价，烦兄斟酌，唯以老人来台，资产均遗北平。现以将近耄年，虽然精神矍铄，时犹执笔倡导正义，然以境遇所迫，经济状况并不甚佳，几经考虑，愿将售价让至当年购进之数，约伍仟元，祈兄推爱迅为进行。又如老谓与兄有戚谊，并嘱代致谢忱。至其所让之价，请兄核以当地时价情形，如有必要，再事减低亦无妨也。一切祈鼎力玉成，感荷同深，便乞示复。匆此，顺颂著安。
>
> 　　　　　　　　　　　　　　　　　　弟冰顿首
> 　　　　　　　　　　　　　　　　　　四二，四，廿五

再者,书单中《律吕正义后编》一种,如老因友人请让,正接洽中。请兄与哈佛函洽时,暂将此书除外。将来倘此间不妥,如老愿将此一并加入,不另计价。

冰又及

〔袁同礼家人提供〕

按:李冰与先生为北京大学同年,参见 1916 年谭声丙致先生信按语部分。狄福鼎,字君武,江苏太仓人,1919 年北京大学文本科哲学门毕业,翌年赴法留学。刘兆滨,字毅人,北京大学毕业后曾担任安徽省财政会代表。陆雪塘,字省道,浙江海宁人,1917 年北京大学第一部英文甲班毕业。

Richard C. Rudolph(京都)致函先生,询问先生对中国考古工作近况的调查计划,是否有意刊行相关论文,此外询问顾子刚的联系方式。

Nakagawara-cho, S.

Shimogamo, Sakyo-ku

Kyoto, Japan

25 April, 1953

Dear Dr. Yuan:

It was with great interest that I read the title of your paper, "Archaeological Work in China, 1949–1952." on the AOS program. I am here in Japan on a Guggenheim Fellowship working on a history of Chinese archaeology-not an art history, but a history of the development of archaeology in China as a science-and this is just the kind of material I am interested in.

In fact, I have just been preparing such a survey myself from some reports that I knew of such as those in *Chung Kuo yen chiu*, *Min Tsu Hsueh yen chiu*, *K'o Hsueh t'ung pao*, etc. Do you plan to publish your paper? If you do, I shall not attempt to publish my survey but shall use the material in my book and will rely upon your paper for additional information. I shall be glad to hear of your plans.

The last time we met was in the Library in Peking in 1948 with Mr. Koo. I now want to write to him on behalf of our library and wonder if you will be good enough, when you answer this letter, to include his address. As you know, we have a large shipment of books tied up there, for which we have paid, and are trying to get them released.

With warm regards, I am

Sincerely yours

R. C. Rudolph

〔University of Chicago Library, Yuan T'ung-li Papers, Box 2〕

按:是年4月25日,美国东方学会西部分会在西雅图华盛顿大学召开第三次年会,先生提交论文 Archaeological Work in China, 1949-1952,实应为 Some Academic Activities in China 1949-1952 之一部,并由胡昌度代为宣读①,该篇失收于《袁同礼文集》。Chung Kuo yan chiu 音为"中国研究",但对应的刊物待考,信文中另外两种则为《民族学研究》《科学通报》。

五月七日

胡适覆函先生,告有意请美方设法以缩微胶片方式拍摄在台湾的各处善本书。

> 守和兄:
>
> 真真对不住你,这许久没有回你的信!
>
> 《农民革命史料》收到了,十分感谢你!
>
> 大概明末的"流寇"不是完全没有意识的暴动。我在一部清初小说豆棚闲话里发现一首"流寇"军中流行的"西调":
>
> 老天爷,你年纪大,
>
> 你耳又聋来眼又花,
>
> 你看不见人,你听不见话!
>
> 杀人放火的享尽荣华,
>
> 吃素看经的活活饿杀!
>
> 老天爷,你不会做天,你塌了罢!
>
> 老天爷,你不会做天,你塌了罢!!
>
> 这是很有力量的呼喊。其实任何一个时代的大动乱,多少总带一点革

---

① "Notes of the Society." *Journal of the American Oriental Society*, vol. 73, no. 4, 1953, p. 237.

命性质。罗思华的自传里说白莲教原名"百连",即"一连十,十连百"之意。可见十八世纪的"教匪"也是有组织的一种运动,不幸史料毁的太干净,我们竟不能考知十七世纪后期到十九世纪初年的"白莲教"的信史了。太平天国近在百年之内,但如果当日没有许多史料保存在外国,我们也就不容易懂得太平天国的人物与主张了。

去台湾看了台北、台中("故宫","中央圖")、杨梅(史语所)各地堆积的美术品、史料、善本书,不能不想得四大危险——火、白蚁、地震、空袭——的可怕。所以我力主张采用我在十年前(1942)主张缩照(microfilming)北平馆的善本书的办法,就建议给"故宫"、"中央博物院"的"共同理事会",各理事都赞成这个意思,推出一个小组委员会(云五,骝兄,天放,志希,雪屏,董彦堂,钱思亮和我)研究进行。小组会一月八日开会,估计"故宫"、"中央圖"、史语所、国史编纂会、台大、台省立圖各地的史料与善本书,约有一千一百五十万叶。他们决议委托我在美国设法募款,进行缩照的计画。

我同恒慕义先生谈起,他也到过台中,看了两天的书,他很赞同此议。他说,十年前的北平馆善本书二千八百多部,共照了二百五十万exposures,费时三年多,照成一千〇七十卷胶片。他把我的简明说明书交与国会馆的专家Dr. Born & Mr. Holmes考虑,他们估计,此次须用六架照相机在台中、台北同时工作,也需时三年。他们估计此次缩照经费约共美金十二万五千,至十五万之谱。国会馆允与合作,但不能担负此款。他们要我试向各基金会谈谈。我回到纽约,作了一个说明书,包括国会馆专家的估计。现在谈过的是哈佛燕京学社与Ford Foundation's Mr. Raymond T. Moyer。哈燕方面已无希望。Ford方面,尚未到正式讨论时期。据我所知,Mr. Moyer对此很热心。但请款手续颇繁重。我盼望国会馆能主持此一大事。恒君已有长信给Mr. Moyer,很恳切的赞成此事。以上是大致情形。将来有何发展,当再向老兄报告。

顷向国会馆买得北平馆藏赵一清朱墨校朱谋㙔水经注笺的microfilm一卷,细细看了,觉得缩照之法真可以保存孤本善本书。北平馆的善本二千八百多种,有了胶片分存世界各大图书馆,从此不怕毁灭了。倘在台的善本孤本书及史料也能照样缩照保存,确是一大幸事。想老兄定赞同此议。便中幸赐指示,至感,至欢迎。

　　个天月涵兄在此,我们谈及老兄今年有不在斯丹佛之说,不知现时有何计画,望便中赐告。匆匆,敬问双安。并问斯丹佛诸友人好。

适之

一九五三,五,七夜

〔University of Chicago Library, Yuan T'ung-li Papers, Box 7〕

　　按:Raymond T. Moyer(1899-1993),通译为"穆懿尔",1921年毕业于俄亥俄州欧柏林学院,1921年至1923年赴山西太谷铭贤学校(Oberlin-Shansi Memorial School)教授英文,后短暂返回美国并入康乃尔大学获农学硕士学位,20世纪30年代在山西中部推动农村改革,建立试验区;二战结束后先后受聘于联合国善后救济总署及美国联邦政府,参与远东地区战后重建,担任中国农村复兴联合委员会(Joint Commission on Rural Reconstruction)五人小组的美方首席代表。先生在斯坦福研究中心的任职确于1953年6月底终止。

五月

裘开明致函先生,告已获取齐如山(李冰)待售古籍书单,请先生居间联系。

守和吾兄英鉴:

　　前承赐书,因书单一时未寄到,故迟至今始复。昨收到光清兄由华京寄来台湾李君出售单书,此间教授如海先生Hightower等对该单所列各书均甚感兴趣,不知全部售价若干,可否请兄向李君接洽。其中,律吕正义后编、拍案惊奇及其二三种已为敝馆所藏,可以除去,否则亦请将此数种另开一价目单,若本馆购得全部,将来可另售给他馆也。……

〔袁同礼家人提供〕

　　按:该函仅存第一页。据李冰6月22日函、裘开明某日英文信函的逻辑关系,将此函系于五月。Hightower即James R. Hightower(1915-2006),美国汉学家,通译作"海陶玮",时在哈佛大学任教,专攻中国诗歌和文艺评论。

The Far Eastern Quarterly 刊登先生文章,题为 Some Academic Activities in China 1949-1952。〔*The Far Eastern Quarterly*, vol. 12, no. 3, 1953, pp. 301-310〕

按：此文以匿名形式发表，分两大部分，前一部分是台湾地区的学术研究，主要以"中央研究院"历史语言研究所为对象；后一部分则针对中国大陆地区，以中国科学院近代史所和考古所、南京博物馆、历史博物馆等学术机构为对象。该篇失收于《袁同礼文集》。

Far Eastern Survey 刊登先生和袁澄合撰文章，题为 Ceylon's Trade with Communist China。〔*Far Eastern Survey*, vol. 22, no. 6, 1953, pp. 70-72〕

按：Ceylon 即斯里兰卡（锡兰）。该文失收于《袁同礼文集》。

六月上旬

裘开明致函先生，告知经相关学者协商后，哈佛燕京学社汉和图书馆愿意出价 1000 美金购入齐如山待售古籍。

My dear Dr. Yuan:

Thank you very much for your letter of May 1st. Prof. Elisséeff, Hightower and I have had a conference on the list of Chinese drama and novels from Prof Chi-Ju-shan's library. I have been authorized by them to make an offer of one thousand dollars ($ 1000) for the whole collection with the exception of the two titles mentioned in your letter of May 1st. Will you kindly communicate our offer to the owner?

I have calculated the total number of volumes in the collection, which amounts to 332 vols. Thus, the unit price is equal to about $ 3.00 per volume which is 50% higher than the price which we have been paying for Ming and Ching editions from Bunyudo and other Chinese bookstores in Japan.

With all good wishes,

Very sincerely yours,

A. Kaiming Chiu

〔袁同礼家人提供〕

按：Bunyudo 应指文求堂，日本古旧书店。此为抄件，未注明时间。

六月十日

先生致信 Walter H. Judd，愿意接受其邀请，担任 Aid Refugee Chinese

Intellectuals 顾问。

June 10, 1953

Hon. Walter H. Judd

Chairman

Aid Refugee Chinese Intellectuals, Inc.

1790 Broadway

New York 19, N. Y.

Dear Sir:

Thank you so much for your letter of June 3 in which you were good enough to ask me to serve as a member of your Advisory Committee.

I have a very high regard for the aims and activities of your organization, and I shall consider it a great honor to associate myself with certain aspects of your important undertaking. I am, therefore, glad to serve on the Advisory Committee and to be of any service to you in the development of your new Literature Program.

With best wishes for your continued success,

Yours sincerely,

〔University of Chicago Library, Yuan T'ung-li Papers, Box 2〕

按：Walter H. Judd（1898－1994），美国医生、政治家，中文名周以德，1925 年受美国海外传道委员会（American Board of Commissioners for Foreign Missions）的委派，前往中国，先在金陵大学接受一年的语言培训，后赴福建北部邵武协助 Edward Bliss（福益华，1865－1960）医生在当地创办医院，1931 年曾短暂回国，1934 年再次来华，担任山西汾阳医院院长，1938 年 2 月归国，1943 年至 1963 年担任众议院议员。

六月二十二日

李冰覆函先生，请再为齐如山待售古籍的价格与哈佛燕京学社汉和图书馆联系。

守和学长吾兄左右：

前承惠书，适齐老先生之少君去港，近始归来，认为哈佛出价太低,并经决定两项办法如后。拟恳吾兄斟酌情形,如有可行,祈为转达。

（一）全部售价最低为两仟元。

（二）将附单各书除外,售价壹仟元。

匆此奉复,顺颂著安。

弟李冰顿首

六月廿二

〔袁同礼家人提供〕

按:附单一纸,小说类有《三国演义》(明板二十卷本)7 种,音乐戏曲类《昭代萧韵》(殿板朱墨本)8 种,共计 95 册。

六月二十三日

Leonardo Olschki 致函先生,邀请先生为马可波罗诞辰七百周年纪念活动撰写文章。

June 23, 1953

Dear Dr. Yuan,

I do not know whether you remember me, but I may recall to your mind our first meeting in Professor Chao's house years ago, when you came over from Peking with a few friends and countrymen of yours. So, I am taking the liberty of writing you after two years' stay in Italy. I feel very much honored by getting in touch with you after Professor Chao gave me your address and encouraged me to write you. I want to inform you that the University of Venice and Professor Tucci's Oriental Institute in Roma are preparing a centennial celebration of Marco Polo, in 1954. They are planning the publication of one or two volumes of scholarly contributions more or less connected with Marco Polo's book and era. Both are eager to have Chinese scholars represented in this publication of an intercontinental character.

Would you contribute to it with one or more essays devoted to some aspects of Chinese history and civilization during the Yuan era? I am sure that both the hometown of Marco Polo and Professor Tucci would very much appreciate your cooperation. Moreover, I shall be grateful to you if you could suggest some more Chinese scholars who might join you in the celebration of the Venitian traveler.

　　With kind regards,

Yours sincerely,

Leonardo Olschki

〔University of Chicago Library, Yuan T'ung-li Papers, Box 2〕

　　按：Leonardo Olschki（1885-1961），意大利的东方学者，德国犹太人后裔，1939 年移民美国，时任加州大学教授，该函为其亲笔。

六月二十五日

先生覆函 Leonardo Olschki，表示非常荣幸参与马可波罗纪念的相关学术活动，并略述编辑有关专著、期刊文章目录的困难，告即将前往华盛顿。

June 25, 1953

Dear Dr. Olschki:

　　I am so happy to hear that you have returned after two years' absence. I shall be greatly honored to collaborate with you in the forthcoming celebration of Marco Polo. Thank you so much for your remembrance.

　　For sometime past, I have compiled bibliography of writings about Marco Polo in European languages. It would be appropriate to have it included in the projected publications you have in mind.

　　The main difficulty in this undertaking lies in the fact that scholarly articles on Marco Polo are so much scattered in various journals that one is always afraid of serious omissions. For Italian titles, I hope you could lend me the necessary support.

　　I am about to leave for Washington, D. C. and as soon as I get settled there, I shall continue to gather materials for this bibliography. I have also to correspond with scholars in various countries to seek their help and collaboration.

　　With best wishes for your success in this important scholarly undertaking,

Yours sincerely

〔University of Chicago Library, Yuan T'ung-li Papers, Box 2〕

按：此件为底稿。

七月一日

裴开明覆函先生，告知哈佛燕京学社汉和图书馆将齐如山待售藏书的出价提高至 1500 美金，并说明理由。

July 1, 1953

Dear Dr. Yuan:

Thank you very much for your letter of June 26, in which you advise us that the price asked by Professor Chi Ju-shan for his collection of Chinese books on drama and novels is ＄2000.

Dr. K. T. Wu's appraisal of the collection for ＄2500 is rather high, because when Professor James R. Hightower checked over the list, he was willing to offer only ＄250－＄500 for the whole lot. My own feeling is that both of them are rather way off the mark, because Dr. Wu is probably unfamiliar with the current prices of old Chinese books on the present book markets in Japan, since L. C. has not been buying much recently, while Professor Hightower's notion of Chinese book prices was derived form his own expenditures for Chinese old books in Peiping before the war.

Both Professor Serge Elisséeff and I are rather familiar with the present-day prices for old Chinese books in Japan, since our Library has been buying such books rather heavily since 1946. One of the reasons for Professor Elisséeff's trip to Japan in the spring was to buy books for the Library. He came back in April. As I told you in a previous letter, the average price for Ming and Ch'ing editions from Japan is about two dollars (＄2.00) per pên. For Ming editions alone it is about ＄5.00 per pên. These figures are a good guide, since the averages have been based upon mass quantities from different dealers in both Tokyo and Kyoto.

Since receiving your letter of June 26, we have recalculated the total number of titles and of volumes. They are 71 titles and 328 volumes. At ＄4.50 per pên, the price of the whole collection will come to ＄1500.00, which is the figure Professor Elisséeff has asked me to communicate to you for concluding this transaction. In addition, we shall pay for the transportation of these books from Formosa or Hong Kong to Cambridge. Please communicate our new offer to Professor Chi. Thank you very much.

　　With all good wishes.

Sincerely yours,

A. Kaiming Chiu

Librarian

〔袁同礼家人提供〕

　　按:哈佛燕京学社汉和图书馆实际购入者应为 72 种,328 册,信中遗漏 1 种。

七月十五日

陈受颐覆函先生,告知来函及书均收到,并称赞先生的匿名文章。

　　守和吾兄道席:

　　昨返自 San Diego,大函两通、书籍两包均已拜读拜收,感谢之极。孙子书君近著厚承假读,尤为多谢,一两星期内细读一过,钞撮要点之后,当如令转寄适之先生也。吾兄代支买书之款二十四元七角二分,已通知学校图书馆从速径行寄奉矣。

　　《远东季刊》近载不署名之论文,弟拜读后即知为大著,今承明诏,更知眼力不差,愉快之忱,匪言可达。望兄此后时作此类益世文章,以药悬蒙。大陆变色以来,弟之孤闻寡陋益甚于前,长此以往,必成美国式之三家村学究也。惟兄时时有以教督之。

　　蔚林图书公司为何人所经营,有无经售书目可供参考,新书之流通于台港两地者,就大体说,以向何方采购较为省费,便希教示为感。

　　《大陆杂志》办得极有精彩,诚如大文所言,然微闻经费甚感支绌,如定户减少,或有停办之虞(此系据弟之学生谭维理 Laurence Thompson 在台北美国新闻署任职所言),不知确否?

　　久未看见颉刚名字,弟但知其未到台湾,而不知其流落何所,近况何如,有吃意外或例外之苦否? 闲中读孟真遗著,抚今追昔,感慨无极。匆匆走笔,敬颂夏安。

弟受颐顿首

七月十五日

寅恪北上之消息,港中友人来信曾约略说过,而未知其详,序经则甚苦闷云。

弟颐又拜

〔University of Chicago Library, Yuan T'ung-li Papers, Box 2〕

按:"孙子书君近著"即孙楷第《傀儡戏考原》。"《远东季刊》近载不署名之论文"即 Some Academic Activities in China 1949 - 1952。蔚林图书公司即 Willing Book Company,20 世纪 50 年代中前期香港较为活跃的书店。Laurence Thompson 多在台湾,郭廷以日记对该人亦提到①,曾作 American Sinology, 1830-1920: A Bibliographical Survey,刊《清华学报》1961 年第 22 卷。

七月十六日

先生致信裴开明,认为哈佛燕京图书馆就齐如山代售古籍出价太低,建议最低价为 2300 美金,否则无法成交。

July 16, 1953

Dear Dr. Chiu:

I have duly forwarded your letter of July 1 to Prof. Ch'i Ju-shan.

In his reply, Prof. Ch'i stated that he is in close touch with the second-hand book market in Japan. His son is engaged in business in Tokyo and is still buying books for him. He asks whether you have found any titles of his collection listed in the catalogues of book dealers.

Being a famous collector, he attaches great importance to his collection. As he is well to do, he is not in need of money. In view of what I wrote him about the work of the Harvard-Yenching Institute, he is willing to dispose of the various items at ＄2,300. He further promised that as soon as he is able to get the rest of his collection now stored in Peking, he will give a preference to your Institute. For the whole list, please consult the last two issues of *National Peiping Library Bulletin*.

Such being the case, will you kindly return to him the list of books which I forwarded to you through Dr. K. T. Wu, if you are not interested

---

① 郭廷以著《郭量宇先生日记残稿》,台北:"中央研究院"近代史研究所,2012 年,页 153。

in its purchase at the price of $ 2,300.

Sincerely yours,

〔袁同礼家人提供〕

按:此件为底稿。

七月二十三日

裘开明覆函先生,告知哈佛燕京图书馆接受以 2300 美金购入齐如山所藏戏曲、小说类古籍的建议。

July 23, 1953

Dear Dr. Yuan:

Thank you very much for your letter of July 16, asking a definite price of $ 2,300 for the whole collection of Professor Ch'i's books as represented on the list you sent to our Library through Dr. K. T. Wu of the Library of Congress.

We accept this offer without any exception. Payment will be made on receipt of every book on that list in Cambridge.

Sincerely yours,

A. Kaiming Chiu

Librarian

〔袁同礼家人提供〕

按:此件为打字稿,落款处为其签名。

七月二十六日

先生致信裘开明,称赞哈佛燕京学社图书馆决定购入齐如山藏戏曲、小说类古籍的决定,但《律吕正义后编》《拍案惊奇》两种善本是否在此次收购之中,请其再次确认。

July 26, 1953

Dear Dr. Chiu:

I have your letter of July 23 stating that your Library agrees to buy Professor Ch'i Ju-shan's collection of books on Chinese drama and novels at $ 2,300. I wish to congratulate you for this wise decision, as many titles in the collection are so rare that they are no longer easily available. I hope you could arrange to microfilm all the rare editions and make them available to scholars elsewhere.

Before I write to inform Professor Ch'i about your decision, I wish to make sure that it is your understanding that the following two works: *律吕正义后编*、*拍案惊奇* are not included in this lot. I raised this point because Professor Ch'i understood clearly that these two works were not included in the lot when he asked for a price of ＄2,300. He based his understanding on your two letters: (1) that of May in which you stated that you were authorized to make an offer of ＄1,000 with the exception of these two items; (2) that of July 1 in which you stated that the total number of titles and volumes in the whole collection was 71 and 328 respectively.

In your letter of July 23, you stated that you "accept this offer without exception" which seems to indicate you wish to include these two items. As I have no list of these books on hand, I have no means of checking the number of titles and volumes. But in order to avoid any possible misunderstanding between you and Professor Ch'i, will you give me another letter making clarification on this point? On hearing further from you, I shall forward all your letters to Professor Ch'i.

With kindest regards,

Yours sincerely,

〔袁同礼家人提供〕

按：此件为底稿。

是年夏

钱存训致函先生，询问何时赴华盛顿，路过芝城请下榻聚谈，另请协助找寻《东西学书录》。

守和先生尊鉴：

久疏函候，敬维兴居佳胜，阖府安吉为无量颂。前接光清兄函告，先生将于秋间去美京续编高弟爱目录，未知宝眷是否同行，均在念中。过芝时务乞见告，俾能晤教也。如能在此小留数日，舍间当可下榻，希能早日示知为幸。兹有恳者，训急需用（增广）东西学书录徐维则（相生）辑，顾燮光补，系一九〇二年增订本，曾遍询国会、哈佛、哥大及加大……

〔University of Chicago Library, Yuan T'ung-li Papers, Box 2〕

按:此函不全。

八月六日

裘开明覆函先生,表示哈佛燕京学社汉和图书馆出价是针对齐如山全部待售古籍,但可以不包括《律吕正义后编》。

August 6, 1953

Dr. T. L. Yüan:

Thank you very much for your letter of July 26 which interpreted our letter of July 23 correctly. We want the whole collection, because we feel that we are paying the maximum price for the books, since your initial price offered to the Library of Congress, as stated in your letter of June 26, is ＄2500. The reduction for our Library from your original asking price is only ＄200. Hence, we are justified in wanting the whole collection according to Professor Ch'i's list without any exception. Therefore, our July 23 letter superseded all our earlier letters, which made an exception of the two works you mentioned in your letter for a lower price. However, if Professor Ch'i wants to keep the *Lü Lü Chêng i hou pien* 律吕正义后编, he may do so, because we have the same work in the identical 1746 Palace edition, but we must have the *P'o an ching ch'i* 拍案惊奇, because our edition seems to be different from his.

With all good wishes, sincerely yours,

A. Kaiming Chiu
Librarian
〔袁同礼家人提供〕

按:齐如山所藏《拍案惊奇》三十六卷,明末凌蒙初撰,清消闲居刻本,共十二册。

八月七日

先生致信裘开明,告知将于九月份赴哈佛大学,推荐该馆购存《光明日报》,并建议其可请刘国秦在香港代购大陆出版的期刊杂志。

August 7, 1953

Dear Dr. Chiu:

When I come to Cambridge in September, I expect to consult the following three journals which, according to a list sent to me by Mr. Yui, are on file in your Library:

Meanwhile, may I request you to check up whether any issues published in 1953 have been received.

I understand that your Library has not subscribed any daily papers published in China Mainland. If so, may I recommend the *Kuang Ming jih-pao* published in Peking? It contains much information on educational and cultural activities which is not found elsewhere.

Mr. K. C. Lau, Fung Ping Shan Library, Hong Kong, has been serving as an agent for the University of Chicago to supply current publications from the mainland. According to Mr. T. H. Tsien, the files of current periodicals from China at Chicago are most complete. If your Library has difficulties in procuring publications from the mainland, you may perhaps like to give a trial order to Mr. Lau whom I recommend highly.

Sincerely,

〔袁同礼家人提供〕

按：此件为底稿，其中空格处应填写汉字——光明日报。

八月十三日

裘开明覆函先生，告知哈佛燕京学社汉和图书馆自八月十七日闭馆，并告该馆订阅了六份大陆报纸，但因为出口限制大都无法继续收到，如刘国柰可在香港代购这些报纸则愿意委托该人。

August 13, 1953

Dear Dr. Yuan:

Thank you for your letter of August 7. I am very glad to know that you are coming to Cambridge at long last. At first, we were expecting you to be here in August, but now you are coming here in September. That's fine. Beginning next Monday, August 17, the Library will be closed for four weeks for repair and cleaning. Only one or two members will be working here, and the rest of the Library staff will be away for vacation.

Professors Elisséeff, Yang and some other faculty members may be here. I intend to be away for about three weeks, and will return to Cambridge on or after Labor Day. If you come here before my return, please drive down with your daughter, who has been at our cottage in Plymouth before, to see Cape Cod.

I am a little surprised to read your statement: "I understand that your Library has not subscribed any daily papers published in China mainland." As a matter of fact, we have been subscribing to six mainland Chinese daily papers right along, namely, (1) *The Jen min jih pao*, Peking, (2) *Ta Kung Pao*, Tientsin, (3) *Kuang ming jih pao*, Peking, (4) *Chieh fang jih pao*, Shanghai, (5) *Ch'ang chiang jih pao*, Hankou and (6) *Nan fang jih pao*, Canton. But due to the export restriction placed by the Peking Government last year, on export of newspapers and magazines from China, we are not getting any other paper except the *Jen min jih pao* (*The People's Daily*) from Peking, for which we have a complete file since its beginning in February of 1949.

Do you think that Mr. K. C. Lau of Hong Kong University would be able to send us all the prohibited papers and periodicals like the *Kuang ming jih pao*, *Hsin hua yueh pao*, etc.? If he could get us the forbidden goods, we would be very glad to make him our agent, otherwise his services would be of little use to us, because we already have an agent in Hong Kong. John Fairbank was there in March, and Professor Elisséeff was also in Hong Kong in February. Fairbank made special arrangements with people in Hong Kong to send new publications to Harvard. I also doubt the claim of Mr. Tsien that Chicago University Library has the most complete file of current Chinese periodicals! Since both Mr. Tsien and I could render only partial opinion about each respective library, Chicago and Harvard, please ask some third party to give you an impartial estimate of the strength of these two libraries in current Chinese publications! I was in Chicago in April and had a good talk with Mr. Tsien.

Enclosed please find your list of Chinese periodicals and papers. All those marked "H" are here.

  With all good wishes,

Very sincerely yours,

Kaiming

Librarian

  承询汪启淑:《水曹清暇录》,敝馆无此书,日本静嘉堂文库藏有此书,日本文久二年(1862)刊本,《江苏国学圕目录》载一部,同此版本,不知此书中国有何刊本,便中请示知为盼。

开明谨上

〔袁同礼家人提供〕

  按:此件为打字稿,落款处及中文补语皆为其亲笔。

八月二十二日

先生致信胡佛研究所和图书馆执行秘书 Richardson 夫人,已按商妥的结果将平馆在美的小型照相机和存书寄送该所暂存。

August 22, 1953

Dear Mrs. Richardson:

  In the course of our previous conversation, I understood from you that the Hoover Institute and Library would be glad to store, for the duration of the cold war, a small camera and a carton of books for the National Library of Peiping, Peiping, China.

  I am therefore sending them to you for safe-keeping and I wish to assure you of our sincerest appreciation for your assistance.

  May I take this opportunity to express to you my hearty thanks for the privilege of using one of the cubicles in the Hoover Library and of consulting the wonderful collection of your books. It has been an unusual privilege which I shall always treasure in the years to come.

Yours sincerely,

T. L. Yuan

〔University of Chicago Library, Yuan T'ung-li Papers, Box 3〕

  按:该件为录副。

八月二十五日

先生致信裴开明,建议哈佛燕京学社与美国新闻处(台北)或香港地区书店取得联系,以获取所需大陆新闻报纸。

August 25, 1953

Dear Mr. Chiu:

I have received the reply from Prof. Ch'i which I am enclosing herewith for your information. Under the present customs restrictions, it seems wise to solicit the assistance of USIS in Taipeh. If I remember correctly, Mr. Josiah W. Bennett has been in charge of the Information Service. May I suggest that your Institute gets in touch with Mr. Bennett who may like to be of service to you.

The Hoover Library here receives all the current issues of the mainland daily papers subscribed through the Apollo Book Shop, Hong Kong. The last issue of the *Kuang ming jih pao* received here was dated July 18. If you do not receive the prohibited papers, you may try Apollo or Mr. Lau. Under the present circumstances, it may be worthwhile to use more than one agent in Hong Kong.

Yours sincerely,

〔袁同礼家人提供〕

按:USIS 即 United States Information Service,一般译为"美国新闻处"。Josiah W. Bennett(1917-1992),中文名卞承修,时担任美国新闻处驻台负责人。Apollo Book Shop 应指智源书局,1947 年成立,香港首家以日文杂志、书籍批发及零售为特色的书店。此件为底稿,后附一简目,题为 Books in a carton deposited in the Hoover Library August 23 1953,共 9 种英法文书籍。

九月一日

刘国蓁致函先生,告知代寄各信均已发出,并转呈北京来函。

守和先生阁下:

许久未修书致候,抱歉殊深,恭维起居康乐、著述宏福为颂。八月五日手示,敬悉一一,附美钞二元,亦已收妥矣。承命代寄发北京英使馆 Ford 先生信一封,径已直接寄去,一因由港寄出不受检查,二因

Mrs. Scott 当时赴英伦去故也。令妹信亦已即寄发,想均得收也。蒙鼎力介绍四处圈函商,曷胜感铭,惟至今尚未得接来信也。美钞二元找港银十一元八角,连上数三元五角五分,共十五元三角五分,代购寄国内邮票一元及此次航邮费二元,对比尚存十二元三角五分。今日得接北京来信,兹特转呈,伏祈察收为荷。港中天气仍炎热,争秋夺暑之故也。专此,敬请著安。

　　　　　　　　　　　　　　　　　　愚晚刘国蓁顿首

　　　　　　　　　　　　　　　　　　一九五三年九月一日

〔University of Chicago Library, Yuan T'ung-li Papers, Box 2〕

　　按:该函右侧标注 Claremont UCLA、U. of Wash.、U. of Calif.等字样,应为先生代刘国蓁介绍的数家美国大学图书馆。

九月十一日

刘国蓁致函先生,告知单位地址不便收取信函,请改寄其私人地址。

　　守和先生尊鉴:

　　　　日前付上北京来信,计尘钧鉴。敝馆自本年一月时则由总馆馆长(Mrs. D. Scott)直接管理,向安无异。惟自本月一日起,以前由邮局直接投递敝馆公私信件皆要更改派至大学总馆,由总馆长审查后方发还。此事发生后,极为不方便,但未知其是何原故及用意何在,至公家之信件由渠处决则甚应该,但私人之信件亦要审查,则似乎不合道理也。兹为避免麻烦起见,以前寄馆地址更改寄至舍下(地址列后),以后倘蒙赐示,请照址掷下,必无误也。晚前拜托代介绍美国各大学图书馆代为购办书籍杂志事,现暂拟取消,敬恳先生代通知以前四处图书馆查照或通知更改地址,请不可寄敝馆代转也。令亲戚处亦请代通知为盼。匆匆。专此,敬请撰安。

　　　　　　　　　　　　　　　　　　愚晚刘国蓁顿首

　　　　　　　　　　　　　　　　　　九月十一日

(敝英文地址)K. C. Lau, 36 Lockhart Road, 3rd. fl., Wantsai, Hong Kong.

　　中文地址如下:香港湾仔洛克道卅六号四楼。

〔University of Chicago Library, Yuan T'ung-li Papers, Box 2〕

　　按:该函寄送地址为 730 College Avenue, Palo Alto, California,而

此时先生已赴麻省。

九月十二日　马萨诸塞州剑桥

晚,先生夫妇携袁静、袁清前往杨联陞处吃饭,同席者有吴宪夫妇(携吴婉莲、吴应)、裴开明夫妇等人。〔《杨联陞日记》(稿本)〕

> 按:吴宪(1893—1959),字陶民,福建侯官人,生物化学家、营养学家,清华学校毕业,后赴美入麻省理工学院,1919 年获博士学位,归国后在协和医学院执教,时已退休在波士顿定居,其夫人为严彩韵。

九月十九日

晚,先生和夫人赴陈观胜家聚会,裴开明、杨联陞、蒋彝、吴宪夫妇、先生夫妇、洪业夫妇等人亦受邀前往,约十时散。〔《杨联陞日记》(稿本)〕

> 按:陈观胜(1907—?),华裔美国佛教学者,生于夏威夷,后获哈佛大学博士学位,在夏威夷、加州、哈佛大学等校执教。

九月二十二日

下午,裴开明在家设宴欢度中秋,先生与夫人、洪业夫妇、陈观胜夫妇、吴宪夫妇、韩咏华、沈志荣、曾宪七等人受邀与席。〔《杨联陞日记》(稿本)〕
田清波覆函先生,感谢寄赠匿名文章使其得以了解中国学术界的成绩与动态。

Arlington, le 22 septembre 1953.

Cher Monsieur Yuan,

　　Merci beaucoup de m'avoir envoyé un tirage à part de votre bel article 《 Some Academic Activities in China 1949‐1952 》. J'y ai appris avec grand plaisir que les savants chinois, malgré tout, continuent avec succès leurs recherches dans tous les domaines de la science.

　　Il y a quelques mois je vous ai envoyé deux tirages à part d'articles parus dans le Harvard Journal of Asiatic Studies. Comme je ne savais pas que vous étiez à présent à Cambridge, je les ai envoyés à votre ancienne adresse. J'espère toutefois que vous les aurez reçus.

　　Encore une fois merci de votre extrêmement intéressant article.

　　Agréez, Cher Monsieur Yuan, l'assurance de ma haute considération.

A Mostaert

〔袁同礼家人提供〕

　　按:1948 年 11 月,田清波离开北平,翌年 2 月抵达美国,随即前往弗
　　吉尼亚阿灵顿郡天主教圣母圣心会福传中心(Missionhurst),1949 至
　　1953 年,他在 *Harvard Journal of Asiatic Studies* 发表了多篇文章,故
　　函中提到寄送给先生的是哪些并不能确定。该函为田清波亲笔。

十月七日

刘国蓁致函先生,告因其兼顾为他人代购书刊事务,被冯平山图书馆辞退,
请先生介绍在港谋事。

　　守和先生尊鉴:

　　　　晚命途多舛,因为别人服务代购书籍事,大学当局认为兼顾副业,
　　与服务规约有所抵触,强迫晚自动辞职,此不得已之举。由下月起,晚
　　已辞退冯平山图书馆职员职守,经已去函秉华先生报告。此后找寻职
　　业当然严重困难,因图书馆学人才在香港致用者甚少,生活问题甚难
　　解决,用是函达,恳请鼎力赞勷,介绍在港贵亲友在教育界服务或其他
　　中学图书馆任职,感荷恩慈,寔无既极。顷接奉令岳丈大人来信,谨将
　　原封奉呈,伏祈察收为幸。专此,敬请著安。

　　　　　　　　　　　　　　　　　　　　愚晚刘国蓁顿首
　　　　　　　　　　　　　　　　　　　　一九五三年十月七日
　　　　　　　　　　　　　　　　　　　　〔袁同礼家人提供〕

　　按:"秉华先生"及本谱中之"秉华东翁"皆指冯秉华(Fung Ping-
　　wah,1911—1981),冯平山三子,香港汉文中学毕业后考入香港
　　大学中文系。

十月上旬

先生独自一人前往华盛顿。〔《传记文学》第 68 卷第 1 期,页 57〕

　　按:先生卸任斯坦福研究中心编纂主任后,继续担任国会图书馆
　　中国文献顾问(Consultant in Chinese Literature)。

十月十日

图齐(罗马)致函先生,请为马可波罗诞辰七百周年大会撰写文章——有
关马可波罗的书目。

　　　　　　　　　　　　　　　　　　　　October, 10, 1953

　　Dear Dr. Yuan Tung-li,

　　　　As you probably know, we are preparing throughout the coming year to celebrate the 7th centenary of the birth of Marco Polo. We wish to solemnize this important cultural event in honour of the great traveler, by a series of lectures to be held at our Institute, and by publications edited by the same: to this purpose we wish to avail ourselves of the cooperation of the outstanding Orientalists of our time. Prof. Leonardo OLSCHKI and many other personalities are of course cooperating.

We are requesting the kind cooperation of Chinese scholars, and naturally we could not overlook your name, considering your most valuable contributions to the Polian Bibliography. I have the pleasure to inform you that among the many publications edited by our Institute, a remarkable place is given to the collection of IL NUOVO RAMUSIO, volumes dedicated to records of famous travelers and history of geography. It would be therefore most suitable to include in our collection a volume on the complete Bibliography of Marco Polo, with special regard to the Eastern part of it. If you could take charge also of the part concerning the West, it would be all to the better. Of course, such plans require careful definition, but I am only giving you a broad outline of our program, and I would be much obliged if you could assure me of your cooperation, at least on principle. You have specialized in a most unusual and valuable field, and your help would be greatly appreciated. The prestige of the man who we want to honour, and the common interest we take in his work, give me confidence that you will kindly help for the success of these celebrations.

Hoping to hear from you soon, sincerely,

Giuseppe Tucci

〔University of Chicago Library, Yuan T'ung-li Papers, Box 3〕

按：our Institute 即 Istituto Italiano per il Medio ed Estremo Oriente，意大利中东和远东研究所。Polian Bibliography 应指 Bibliography of Marco Polo。落款处为其签名。该函寄送加州 Palo Alto。

十月十二日

自本日起，先生赴国会图书馆东方部，持王重民所编该馆善本书录书稿（影

本)与馆藏文献对照,一方面校订错误,一方面重排书稿(影本)顺序。〔袁同礼家人提供〕

> 按:因为食宿费用过大,先生偶尔会回剑桥寓所(60 Orchard Street)休息,该项工作至 12 月 11 日暂时告一段落。

十月二十七日

刘国蓁覆函先生,已持介绍信拜访 Arthur W. Hummel Jr.,但因其英文不熟尚未填写申请表格,请指教。

> 守和先生尊鉴:
>
> 日前得奉十五日手示,敬悉。附令岳信一封及介绍函一封,均已收妥。令岳信经已寄发,想已到达矣。蒙鼎力赞勷介绍晚于美国新闻处图书馆工作,铭感殊深。晚已持函往谒 Hummel 先生,据回答谓现在本港美国新闻处接华盛顿训令裁减经费,人事方面由七十五人可能减至五十三人,暂时难以应付,待五六月后或有机会,并着晚填写 Application for Position 格式纸寄回与他收,听候通知也。他讲国语甚流利,而且极为有礼貌者,但该格式纸以英文为主要,而晚之英文不甚通顺,恐难适合,是以并未有填写寄回,未悉尊意以为如何? 恳请赐教为幸。得接北京来信,特为转呈,敬希察收。尊址已迁至美东,日前转上令岳信,未知可能得收否? 前付来美钞二元,前后付上航邮四次,共八元,现尚存四元三角半。谨此奉闻。专此,敬请教安。
>
> 愚晚刘国蓁顿首
> 一九五三年十月廿七日
> 〔袁同礼家人提供〕

> 按:Hummel 先生即 Arthur W. Hummel Jr.(1920-2001),恒慕义之子,美国外交官,中文名恒安石,生于山西汾阳,曾在私立辅仁大学任教,1981 年里根当选总统以后,命恒安石出任美国驻华大使。

是年秋

福特覆函先生,告其已离开北京返回英国,并述魏智夫人近况,另告翻译薛福成日记进展等事。〔袁同礼家人提供〕

十一月一日

晚,Bayard Lyon 在家设宴,先生、周策纵受邀与席。〔《传记文学》第 68 卷第 1

期,页 57-60〕

　　按:Bayard Lyon,中文名赖伯阳,曾在北洋大学教授英文,与先生
为旧识。赖伯阳的夫人通晓多种语言。席间,先生曾以法文和俄
文回答有关欧美汉学家的问题。

十一月九日

噶邦福致函先生,告知其已离开中国前往澳大利亚,并略述袁复礼等人近
况,另请联系梅贻琦以便开具清华大学履历证明。〔University of Chicago
Library, Yuan T'ung-li Papers, Box 2〕

十一月十二日

先生致信图齐(罗马),略谈撰写庆祝马可波罗诞辰七百年大会的会议论
文内容,并请其协助查找有关信息。

November 12, 1953

Dear Professor Tucci:

　　It is indeed a great pleasure to hear from you and to learn that plans
for celebrating the 7th centenary of the birth of March Polo are well under
way. I am particularly delighted that a complete bibliography of Marco
Polo may be included in your collection of IL NUOVO RAMUSIO. I am
fully confident that under your leadership and distinguished direction, the
celebration next year in honour of Marco Polo will be a great success.

　　It would indeed be a great honour to me to be able to contribute a
bibliography on Marco Polo. As I have planned, this bibliography would
include all editions of Marco Polo and all important writings about him
and his travels which are published in all Western European languages as
well as in Chinese. There are, in addition, a number of books and articles
in Japanese which you may prefer to ask the cooperation of a Japanese
scholar for their compilation, so I shall not try to include them.

　　There are a number of scholarly articles on the famous traveler
scattered in various Italian journals. Without any index to these articles, it
has not been easy to check them fully. If possible, I shall plan to take a
short trip to Italy next summer in order to examine them personally.
Meanwhile, I hope some of my Italian friends would be able to help me in

any way they can. I shall also look forward to your personal help and encouragement.

  With warmest regards and all good wishes,

Yours sincerely,

Yuan Tung-li

〔University of Chicago Library, Yuan T'ung-li Papers, Box 3〕

  按：该件为录副。

十一月二十六日

先生覆信噶邦福，告已联系梅贻琦请其出具相关履历证明，并请其再为详述离开中国的经历。

60 Orchard Street

Cambridge 40, Mass.

November 26th

Dear Prof. Gapanovich:

  I am so happy to learn from your recent letter that you and your family got out of China at last. When you have time, please write me more fully concerning the help you received in evacuating from China. I hope you obtained some support from the International Refugee Organization at Hong Kong. Do you know if the eldest son of General and Mrs. Horvath got out after all. The last news I had of him was that had been detained in prison.

  I have written to President Y. C. Mei whose address is care of the China Institute, 125 East 65th Street, New York 21, N. Y. and urged him to mail you a letter certifying you that you were a professor of History at Tsing Hua. With this letter you might be able to find better position in Canberra. I hear that Mr. Fitzgerald is now in New York, but I have not met him. Lord Lindsay is there connected with the Far Eastern Department, I hope he may be of some assistance to you.

  Thank you for conveying the news about my brother and his family. As to the piano, the one I had before 1937 had long been sold. The one I bought in 1947 was remodeled in Shanghai which my sister-in-law does not quite remember. So, when you write to her, just tell her that it is very old piano and Miss Liu whom we had entrusted her to sell would not substitute it. Sorry for this misunderstanding.

〔University of Chicago Library, Yuan T'ung-li Papers, Box 2〕

按：General 即 Dmitry L. Horvath（Дмитрий Леонидович Хорват，1858-1937），俄国陆军中将，通译作"霍尔瓦特"，1902 年至 1920 年担任中东铁路总办，后至北京担任北洋政府交通部顾问，白俄社团领袖。Mrs. Horvath 即 Camilla A. Horvath，爱好绘画。Lord Lindsay 及 Miss Liu，待考。此件为底稿。

十二月一日

图齐覆函先生，欢迎来年前往意大利，并表示会竭尽所能协助编纂有关马可波罗书目。

Rome, December 1, 1953

Dear Dr. Yuan Tung-li,

Many thanks for your very kind letter of November 12, which I have received with great pleasure. I did not doubt you would take a deep interest in our planned celebrations in honour of Marco Polo, and would kindly and willingly help us with your exceptional knowledge with regard to a bibliography on the great Traveler.

I am also glad to hear that you take into consideration coming to Italy next Summer, and I assure you it shall be a pleasure to welcome you among us. Concerning your research work on articles and scattered papers to be found in Italy, you will receive from our Institute all the help you may need. In order to facilitate this research, you had better give us some precise indications about what papers or books you need to consult, and we will do our best in this connection. The lack of an index is of course a great drawback, but you will be able to overcome it thanks to your fine scholarship.

With all good wishes, and best regards,

Yours sincerely,

Giuseppe Tucci

〔University of Chicago Library, Yuan T'ung-li Papers, Box 3〕

按：此件为打字稿，落款处为其签名。

十二月七日

慕阿德致函先生，寄上其著述目录及家人有关中国的文章篇目。

7 Dec. 1953

Dear Dr. Yuan:

It was a great pleasure to me to hear from you last week and to know that you are still well and active. In reply to your question, Marco Polo Ⅲ and Ⅳ are not yet published, but I hope to hear soon that the French government is prepared to publish them. Nothing is yet quite decided, and I do not suppose that anything can actually appear before 1955.

It is very good news that you are making a Supplement to *Bibl. Sinica*. I was very much afraid that it would never be kept up to date, and many of us suffer from the want of any complete bibliography of Far Eastern works. I hope that your Supplement will have an index from the first. I send a list of my own writings printed in 1933, and have written in the margins the papers that have been printed since then. In the last section (Miscellaneous) I have marked some items which may concern China, and my In Memoriam of my Father (G. E. M.) contains a list of his publications.

With all good wishes for your health and prosperity in the coming year.

Yours sincerely,

A. C. Moule

P. S. There are papers on the "Hang-Chow Bore"-one entitled "Tidal Bores Medieval and Before Christ"-in the "*China Journal*" and "*New China Review*" by my brother George Theodore Moule, about 30 to 20 years age; and a paper by my brother Henry William Moule "A Chinese Version of the Incarnation" [translated, I think, from 神仙传] in -. I cannot find the reference!

A. C. M.

〔袁同礼家人提供〕

按：Tidal Bores Medieval and Before Christ 刊于 *China Journal of*

Science and Arts Vol. II, September, 1924, No. 5。George Theodore
Moule(1863－1942)、Henry William Moule(1871－1953)，皆为其
兄长,亦生于宁波,并同为圣公会传教士。此函为其亲笔。

十二月十五日

齐如山致函先生,感谢代售其在台所存小说、戏曲古籍,并述卖书之原因。

　　守和兄惠鉴:

　　　数年不晤,想诸事顺适也。为书事诸蒙费神,总算多卖几百元。
按此书本不应出售,因舍下所存小说、戏曲都特编成目录,经重民、子
楷二兄改正并曾登贵图书馆季刊,如此一卖则该目录便非完璧矣,颇
觉可惜。但此书在台湾实在难于保存,必须三天一晾、五天一一曝,真
是烦不胜烦。虽如此,该书有虫者已经不少,不得已只好出手,且北平
一部份将来是否保存的住,也难断定也。再者,目下在台湾生活亦大
不易,所以弟常写点稿子,藉以补助日用。有此一笔进款,果能运用有
方,生活便可安定,弟亦可稍事休息矣。此皆我兄之所赐也。好在至
交,不必客气耳。近来与北平曾通信否?图书馆及知交均如何,殊念。
兹本地代弟出版了两本书,特奉上两本,即希指正外,《国剧概论》五
本请转赠知交可也。此上,敬颂时安。

　　　　　　　　　　　　　　　　　　　　　齐如山敬上
　　　　　　　　　　　　　　　　　　　　　十二月十五日

　　　书籍由海运印刷品寄出,但住址误书,由 Stanford Univ. Library 转
交,请关照图书馆届时转交阁下为荷。

　　　又因友空军上校王进桢君赴美之便,特托带绣花被面一件,嘱友到美
后转寄阁下,尚祈笑纳,并祈收到后见覆是幸。

　　　　　　　　　〔University of Chicago Library, Yuan T'ung-li Papers, Box 2〕
　　　按:《国剧概论》为齐如山所著,1953 年台北文艺创造出版社初
版,此书应随其旧藏一并寄往美国。先生在该信尾部注有"一月
十日函至上校"。

十二月十六日

程绥楚覆函先生,谈其教学、专栏写作的近况。

　　守和先生、夫人双前:

　　　久未问安,昨奉到九日手示,欣感之余,尤以得悉尊况胜常、贵体

纳福为慰。前表兄劳榦自波斯顿来函，云曾两次拜候，时大驾去东部未返，从其来信得知学术界情形，彼每月只百五十元，竟不能稍动，极以为苦云。澄弟今春有过一函，近极少通讯，想已快卒业矣。内地情形，除知其币制跌价外，余无所闻。征兵又起（近日之事），壮丁分配，每县极多，于生产大有妨害。湖南每月家慈须二百数十至三百港币（因外汇一港元始终为 4420 人民币）一月，初解放时，仅 60 元也，生活甚苦。出口证因晚曾在国立大学教课，已领不到，且七十之年，无人护送，亦来不成。崇基学院现有三年级，系美国 U.B.C.C.C. 出钱，此间 Bishop Hall 为董事之一，伦敦圣公会亦有帮助，然行政人员皆系外行，学生程度有的只够中学，殊难乐观。晚系专任讲师，现授通史 6 小时，大二国文 6 小时，兼圖主任。近二三年来，每日为《新生晚报》（此间中午出版，重国际新闻之报，销数大，其作风如老《大公报》）写一篇幽默散文（略似林语堂早岁在 *China Critic* 之 Little Critic），凡二年余，未断一日（千五至二千字），竟成为港之首三个受欢迎之一栏（广告公司估计者），于是各报纷纷来约，现为《香港时报》（台湾办，新闻最全，译作最好，比星岛标准高），《工商日晚报》（何世礼家办，日报为港第一销数，可入台，三倍于星岛），每日上午上课办公到午后一点，自二至下午五点半写作，夜写一篇，每日六千字，分为四篇，故极忙，晨六点半起。住"九龙诺士佛台七号"，须渡海，现月入约千八至二千，但因未成婚，须纳税，住公寓，消费大。因写得太多，弄到不能读书。此港外省人（称上海人）日久几已全完了，晚因初来即入教界，故为外帮人中仅有能维持之数人。游台者云气象甚佳，但拖延下去，愈来愈不易有为，盖已养成器矣。承转稿费，信封请寄 Mr. S. C. Cheng, Chung Chi College, Caine Rd. H. K. 即可。该杂志始终未见到，能购得一份否？或请便中示知其地址，以便直接索取。烦神甚为不安，惟有铭感。弟妹想皆已卒业，前澄弟寄来一相，有小弟，竟猜不到是谁。余再上，敬叩年禧。

晚绥楚敬上

十二，十六

〔袁同礼家人提供〕

按：*China Critic* 即《中国评论周报》，1928 年创刊，Little Critic 即

林语堂在其上登载之"小品文",1935 年 8 月曾集结出版。Chung Chi College 即崇基学院,1951 年由前广州岭南大学校长李应林、前上海圣约翰大学校董会主席欧伟国及香港圣公会领袖何明华在香港创办,代表基督教在华发展高等教育传统的延续,后为香港中文大学。

十二月中旬

先生离开华盛顿,回到马萨诸塞州剑桥,与家人团聚。〔袁同礼家人提供〕

    按:自此,先生继续校订王重民书稿,至翌年 3 月 28 日,完成大部分工作。

一九五四年　六十岁

是年初

先生建议费正清从香港购入《文汇报》，因该报经济新闻较其他日报丰富。〔《裘开明年谱》，页 562〕

按：1 月 11 日，费正清致信裘开明，认为应当积极购入该报。

一月七日

噶邦福覆函先生，告北平旧友及平馆近况。〔University of Chicago Library, Yuan T'ung-li Papers, Box 2〕

一月十一日

先生致信 Mary E. Ferguson，请告知方恩联系方式以便协助袁清申请普林斯顿大学奖学金。

January 11, 1954

Dear Miss Ferguson:

Although I have not written to you for some time, you are much in our thoughts. I trust that you and your sister are doing well. It is indeed a pleasure to learn from the Walters here that you have been helping the work at UBCC. We wish you every success and we look forward to seeing you in the not too distant future.

My youngest son is planning to go to Princeton next fall. He received the grade of A throughout the years in the high schools and he would like to apply for scholarly aid. The Director of Admissions at Princeton suggested that we get in touch with the Princeton-Yenching Foundation of which Dr. William P. Fenn is the Secretary. I wonder whether you could send us the necessary information and if possible, send us the forms of application, the closing date, etc.

After having spent two years at Stanford, we have moved to Cambridge for a temporary stay. We have suffered great financial losses and we are not able to send the young boy to College without scholarship aid.

　　With greetings and warmest regards from Mrs. Yuan and myself,

　　　　　　　　　　　　　　　　　　　　Sincerely,

　　　　　　　　　　　　　　　　　　　　T. L. Yuan

〔Yale University Divinity School Library, United Board for Christian Higher Education in Asia Records, RG 11 Series Ⅱ, Box 79, Folder 2146〕

　　按:Mary E. Ferguson(1897-1989),福开森女儿,中文名福梅龄,曾长期在北京协和医学院任职,时任亚洲基督教高等教育联合董事会助理秘书。此件为打字稿,落款处为先生签名。

一月十二日

程绥楚覆函先生,告知大陆新近出版的书籍颇为精美并寄《红楼梦新证》。

　　守和先生、夫人双前:

　　　　敬启者,手示并转汇稿费五十元,于上周收到不误,诸多费神,殊深铭谢,遥维贵体纳福定如所愿。此间今年圣诞大不如昔,购买力弱,尤以外省人更是一蹶不振。北平方面,近来大印其书,见其影印宋板《离骚》,精美异常,又作家出版社重印《程乙本红楼》,新式标点略加方言短释,精美异常,仅售十二元 H. K.,致本地出之粗版翻书,大受打击。最难得者,校对无一错字错号,似此则较前进步多矣。台湾情形想已见到,贞一兄近仍在安排选举大做文章,此间即中立报纸亦视之一笑,方寸之地所务仍在虚名,全海外侨民不胜感慨。澄弟久无信,想多平安家报,甚以为念。崇基春初可迁一新租校舍,较今日者略广,普通图书亦够用,惟学生太不肯用功读书也。余容再上。专此,敬请双安,并叩年禧,阖府清吉平安。

　　　　　　　　　　　　　　　　　晚绥楚敬上

　　　　　　　　　　　　　　　　　一月十二夜

　　　　住址:香港九龙诺士佛台七号,程靖宇。(晚用此字及笔名写文,因绥楚二字内地银行已登记,月有侨汇进去,文凭系绥楚名,故教书不得不用此,住址则但知靖宇也。)闻出有新《红楼梦新证》一书,容觅得寄上,又启。

《红楼新证》已购到,另包平寄上,恐须一月半始到。因克利夫兰明早开行,已不及矣。一,十二夜。

〔袁同礼家人提供〕

按:《红楼新证》即《红楼梦新证》,周汝昌著,1953 年 9 月棠棣出版社初版,印数 5000 册。"克利夫兰"应指在香港和美国间往来的邮轮。该函背面(即航信信封)上另有程绥楚的个人简历。

一月二十六日

梅贻琦致函先生,告知中基会资助研究侧重有所变化,并告胡适将赴台与会。

……尊嘱关于研究计划,如拟就时不妨先寄至中基会,待有适当时期,再为决定。不过近来台湾方面欲清华减少此间用费,尽量补助台湾大学及在台其他院校,故在美研究补助恐须有若干减缩,中基会情形亦大致相若,如何或须待春夏间再核之。

适之约于下月十日左右飞赴台湾开会,琦希望可不去,不知终能免却此行否? 匆颂春安,不一。

贻琦

一月廿六

郁文嘱代候,祖彤请安。

〔袁同礼家人提供〕

按:该函仅存最后一页。"适之约于下月十日左右飞赴台湾开会",似指本年 2 月胡适飞赴台湾与会。

一月二十七日

先生致信福梅龄,告知袁清因成绩优秀当可获得奖学金,无须打扰方恩,并告其王世襄、温德近况。

January 27, 1954

Dear Miss Ferguson:

Thank you very much indeed for your nice letter of January 18. When you come to Boston next time, I hope you will give us the pleasure of seeing you. Our last meeting was in Washington in 1950. Much has happened since that time.

I hear from Peking occasionally. Now Mrs. S. T. Wang is in Hong

Kong and I am sure that we shall more news about our common friends.

My son has applied for admission at Harvard and Yale. Since he has had a good record, he will have no difficulty in obtaining admission and scholarly aid. So, we shall not bother Dr. Fenn about it.

I enclose a reprint of mine which you may find useful. Mr. Wang Shih-Hsiang has been made the Chief of Exhibitions and a special Hall of Chinese Paintings has been recently opened inside the Palace Museum. I should like to write up another report if I have the time.

I am still connected with the Library of Congress with a temporary assignment in Cambridge.

With warmest regards,

　　　　　　　　　　　　　　　　　　Sincerely,

　　　　　　　　　　　　　　　　　　T. L. Yuan

I also had the following information about Prof. Winter:

"Winter was sometime suspected as an American spy, but is now treated more friendly. At first, he was avoided by all people, professors and students alike, which was the worse to a talkative man like him. Once his house took fire by accident. The firemen were slow to come. When they came, they forgot instruments. Then they could not find the water, so that poor Winter would perish in flame, not to say his house and belongings. Now people visit him and listen to him; but he is very cautious and has not much to say."

〔Yale University Divinity School Library, United Board for Christian Higher Education in Asia Records, RG 11 Series Ⅱ, Box 79, Folder 2146〕

按：Mrs. S. T. Wang 即王锡炽夫人 Lillian Bartow Towner。此件为打字稿,落款处为先生签名。

二月一日

福梅龄覆函先生,感谢寄赠期刊文章,并希望先生能够撰写一篇有关中国博物馆、图书馆的报告。

　　　　　　　　　　　　　　　　　　February 1, 1954

Dear Dr. Yuan:

Very much thanks for your letter of January 27th and for the extremely interesting and informative reprint which you sent me about academic activities in China, 1949−52. I was also interested to hear that Wang Shih-Hsiang has been made Chief Exhibitions in the Palace Museum and that a special Hall of Chinese Paintings has been recently opened.

I hope you do find the time to write another report but when I am in Boston in the spring, I look forward to hearing from you first-hand your latest news about the Museum and the Library.

What you wrote about Bob Winter is easily believed; certainly nothing would be harder on him than not have people talk with him!

With kindest regards,

Sincerely yours,

Mary E. Ferguson

Associate Secretary

〔Yale University Divinity School Library, United Board for Christian Higher Education in Asia Records, RG 11 Series Ⅱ, Box 79, Folder 2146〕

按:此件为打字稿,落款处为其签名。

二月三日

先生致信胡适,请其去台后问候王世杰,并告齐如山藏书入藏哈佛大学事。

适之先生:

近见报载,大驾于一周后将返台北,敬祝"一路福星"。不识此次可留若干日? 至盼早日返美。雪艇先生之事至为不幸,想大驾抵台后必能乘机进言,雪艇先生精神上亦可稍得安慰。同礼等深为关怀,晤面时并祈代达拳拳之意。齐如山先生所藏之戏剧小说颇多罕见之本,前由同礼介绍于哈佛,得价二千三百元,已于上月由台北寄到。内中虫蛀之处甚多,可见台北保存古籍之不易,尤盼缩小影照计划可以早日实现。不识近日 Ford 基金会方面有消息否? 本星期日先生在哥大讲演能在广播中恭听,甚为兴奋。并盼台北方面能译成中文在各报上发表也。春节以来天气较暖,长途旅行,诸乞珍重。

同礼拜上

内人附笔问安

二月三日

尊夫人同此拜年。

〔台北胡适纪念馆,档案编号 HS-US01-066-028〕

按:2 月 18 日,胡适抵达台北松山机场,3 月 10 日上午看望王世杰。

二月五日

吴光清覆函先生,告王重民辗转联系国会图书馆欲寄出北京大学印行的《美国国会图书馆藏中国善本书录》,并谈恒慕义退休等事。

守和吾兄:

手示奉悉。嘱查各书已查明注原单上,兹附还参考。上星期香港美领事馆有电致国务院转 L. C.,谓王重民曾托人通知该馆,云其 L. C. 善本书提要已出版,现正设法托人带港寄出(我意大约要相当代价),是以此间当局决定刘君缮写工作暂缓开始,想已经 General Reference & Bibliography Division(其副主任 Dubester 为出版委员会主任)或 Adkinson 另函通知。现在此间之重要事,大家均要染指作主,各人有各人之意见,决定一事手续繁多,颇费时日,最后决定又不知如何也。恒君月底退休,东方部同人决定欢宴并送礼物,馆方亦有 Luncheon 欢送。至继任何人现尚不知,新馆长亦未发表,想 Clapp 之政治方面支持仍不够。齐如山书已收到,转 Exchange & Gift Division 登记并致谢函。金大无在美同学录,James Kung Ching Lee 中文姓名为李公进,现在费城一油厂工作。余不一一。匆匆,顺颂撰安。

弟光清

二月五日

恒君之东方部历史已出版,载 *Quarterly Bulletin* 内,兹检出另封寄上。

〔University of Chicago Library, Yuan T'ung-li Papers, Box 2〕

按:"刘君"应指刘楷贤,受先生之托缮写《美国国会图书馆藏中国善本书录》书稿。Dubester 即 Henry J. Dubester(1917-2017),

1954 年 9 月 14 日起任普通参考及书目部（General Reference and Bibliography Division）主任。① Adkinson 即 Burton W. Adkinson（1909-2004），自 1949 年 11 月至 1957 年 12 月担任国会图书馆参考部主任。"齐如山书"应指《国剧概论》。

二月八日

葛邦福覆函先生，告苏联援华专家等事。〔University of Chicago Library, Yuan T'ung-li Papers, Box 2〕

二月十一日

先生赠《国剧概论》一册与杨联陞，并请其为袁清向达特茅斯学院（Dartmouth College）作推荐信。〔《杨联陞日记》（稿本）〕

　　按：袁清的中学成绩甚好，让杨联陞印象深刻。

二月中旬

先生收到杨联陞回赠的文章和书评单行本。〔《杨联陞日记》（稿本）〕

　　按：此册由袁清带来。

二月十五日

Constance M. Winchell 覆函先生，告知无法列出其馆藏有关马可波罗的书目清单。

February 15, 1954

My dear Mr. Yuan:

I am sorry that we cannot undertake to send you a list of the holdings of this library on Marco Polo. As you can imagine there are many entries under this name in our catalog and while it is true that many of them are represented by Library of Congress printed cards there are some twenty-five or more which are not. If you have definite titles which you would like to have us check we should be glad to do that, or we could check your bibliography against our catalog. We have found that so much duplication results when lists are made up from card catalogs that we cannot undertake to do this for students in other institutions. We are

---

① *Annual Report of the Librarian of Congress, for the fiscal year ending June 30*, 1955, Washington, 1956, p. v.

sorry not to be of help.

Sincerely yours,

Constance M. Winchell

Reference Librarian

The cards could probably be photographed or microfilmed for ＄1.00 -
＄1.50, if you wished to have that done.

〔University of Chicago Library, Yuan T'ung-li Papers, Box 2〕

　　按：此件为打字稿，落款签名和补语为其亲笔。

二月十九日

先生致信 Constance M. Winchell 女士，再次申请哥伦比亚大学图书馆提供
馆藏马可波罗书目清单，并提供题名和分类信息以便查询。

February 19, 1954

Miss Constance M. Winchell

Reference Librarian

Columbia University

New York, N. Y.

Dear Miss Constance:

　　I am much obliged to you for your letter of February 15 and for your
assistance in checking your holdings on Marco Polo.

　　I am enclosing herewith a list of titles which I have gathered with
which it would be easier for you to check your holdings. In the case of L.
C. cards, I put down only the serial number of each card, instead of the
complete bibliographical information. For the rest, I only put down the
year of publication, the edition and the translator, etc.

　　When I was in New York, I was a constant reader at your Library. I
had bibliographical training under Miss Mudge when I was a student at
Columbia College during 1920 - 22. It is inspiring to me to see the
wonderful reference collection which you have built since that time.

　　Thanking you once more for your courtesy,

Yours sincerely,

T. L. Yuan

P. S. I enclose check for　$ 1.50 for possible use.

〔University of Chicago Library, Yuan T'ung-li Papers, Box 2〕

按：此件为打字稿，落款处为先生签名。

三月三日

方豪致函先生，详述中文书籍、期刊中有关马可波罗游记的文字。

守和先生撰席：

适之先生归国，知大驾已回 Cambridge，但未详居处；去年十一月间，奉上拙作《中西交通史》三册（明末以前），系寄 730 College Ave. Palo Alto, Calif.，今奉大札，知尚未收到。请去函一查。第四、五册系明末清初部分，久已交稿，迄未出版。

尊编简目，不日或可再补若干，兹先奉告二事：

一、张星烺尚有《马哥孛罗游记导言》，中国地学会发行，自称"译注"，列有"《受书堂丛书》第一种"，无出版年月日，但自序作于民国十一年双十节，柳诒（先生误作贻）徵有序，尊编简目已著录，则发表于南高史地学报，时民国十三年；又书首 Dedication，亦题民国十三年八月三十日，则断为十三年出版，当不误。

二、尊编简目已著录冯承钧之《马可波罗行纪沙海昂译注正误》，沙海昂 Charignon 之《马可波罗行纪》，亦冯氏所译，商务出版，三册，现为人借去，出版年代查出后，当再奉告。

适之先生谓已受邀赴意，参加马可孛罗诞生七百年纪念会，但恐不能成行，以马可与中国之关系而言，中国不可无人出席。若先生能立即致函 Tucci 教授，来函邀请，则豪可向"教部"申请补助费，向"外部"申请护照，向台湾银行申请官价外汇。今年为圣母年，赴罗马坐飞机有折扣，故自己所费不多。豪当备一篇论文去宣读，为我国学术界争光，此事当请先生速促成之。

赴美时在希望中。旅费无问题，可自筹，豪现有二书稿，能售数百美金。哈佛燕京大约因豪系神父，故有不便，实则豪纯为研究学术而往，与教无关，观豪始终不向教会索钱，不求教会资助，自食其力，即可知也。专复，敬请旅安。

晚豪顿首

〔University of Chicago Library, Yuan T'ung-li Papers, Box 2〕

三月四日

方豪致函先生,就前信内容略作补充。

> 守和先生道席:
>
> 昨日奉上一函,已略作补充,兹再就所知,陈述一二。
>
> 1. 中国书中最早提到《马可波罗游记》,当为同治年间刊行之《中西闻见录》。并有人访求马可波罗事迹与遗物。
>
> 2. 洪钧《元史译文证补》中已引用马可游记。
>
> 3. 张星烺译《马可孛罗游记》有两种:
>
> a 据玉尔氏英文本译,民初燕京大学刊行,导言一册,本文卷一卷
>   二共一册;
>
> b 据拜内戴拖发现新本,二十五年(非二十三年)商务出版。
>
> 4. 冯承钧译《马可波罗行纪》三册,A. J. H. Charignon 注,余手头所有者无版权页,不知何年出版,序作于民国廿四年二月,商务发行。
>
> 5. 关于论文抗战期中,杨志玖撰《关于马可波罗离华的一段汉文记载》,曾获学术奖金,为一重大发现,载《文史杂志》一卷 12 期(三十年十二月)。
>
> 6. 二十九年六月十六日,重庆《益世报·宗教与文化》第十三期有阎宗临著《马可波罗与和德理》。
>
> 7. 方豪著《中西交通史》第三册第七章《元代记述中国之欧洲人阿拉伯人及非洲人》,第三节《尼古拉波罗父子之东游》,第四节《马可波罗游记及其流传》。
>
> 如先生致函意国学界,约弟前往,当可办到。适之先生恐不能成行。谨再奉陈,敬请旅安。
>
> 　　　　　　　　　　　　　　　　　　晚方豪叩
>
> 　　　　　　　　　　　　　　　　　　三,四

〔University of Chicago Library, Yuan T'ung-li Papers, Box 2〕

按:杨志玖(1915—2002),字佩之,山东长山人,回族,历史学家,1934 年入北京大学史学系,后在西南联合大学、南开大学任教。1941 年他在《文史杂志》第 1 卷第 12 期发表《关于马可波罗离华的一段汉文记载》,获得中央研究院名誉学术奖,后被译成英文转载于欧美学术刊物上。此时,方豪的住所为台北市龙泉街 84 巷 22 号。

三月五日

克莱普致函先生,邀请参加恒慕义的荣休聚会。

March 5, 1954

Dear Dr. Yuan:

Dr. Arthur Hummel will retire as Chief of our Orientalia Division on March 31, 1954. We shall take note of his retirement at a luncheon of Division Chiefs of the Library of Congress in the Whittall Pavilion at 12:30 p. m. on March 31.

Because you are not only a professional colleague of Dr. Hummel's, but also a member of the Library of Congress staff, I should like to extend an invitation to you to join us on that occasion. I would be very happy if you could be with us.

Sincerely yours,

Verner W. Clapp

Acting Librarian of Congress

〔袁同礼家人提供〕

按:该函寄送马萨诸塞州剑桥,此件为录副。

三月十日

先生致信董作宾,告哈佛燕京学社拟邀请中方学者赴美研究计划的细节,希望其尝试申请。

彦堂吾兄:

弟于去秋来康桥,本拟乘此机会为贵所在哈佛燕京社谋一笔印刷费,以便兄等著作可以继续出版。奈我国国际地位如此,而弟又人微言轻,迄今未能实现,加以主持所务之 Elisséeff 教授对于台湾颇有成见。去年赴东京、香港,经过台北而不入其门,当有深意存焉。大驾拟来美研究一节,时时关怀,惟携眷来美费用太多美国对于移民近更严苛矣,迟迟未能报命。近哈佛燕京社略有余款,拟约我国学者三人来此研究名义大约为"Exchange Research Fellow",亦尚未定,其待遇每月二百余元。虽为数无多,但供给来往旅费,并限期一年。如吾兄能在台大或贵所休假一年,仍支国内原薪,则一人来此每月尚可略有存储,于经济上亦不无小补,不识尊意以为如何? 如愿一试,可就近请适之先生写一推荐书,径寄下列地址（Serge Eliséeff, Director, Harvard-Yenching Institute, Cambridge, Mass.）。大约旅费可汇至香港，兄到港后凭护照领取。此事尚未正式发表，对于人选侧重三、四十岁之人，惟弟对于吾兄经济状况颇为关怀，故愿从旁力促其成。此外，因去年方杰人兄曾来申请，今年渠亦有希望也弟亦推荐矣。顷闻适之先生有被软禁消息，至为关怀，希望不确也。弟因搜集资料关系，定于月杪赴欧，秋间方能返美。如大驾能来美，未能在此恭候，至以为怅。在欧住址未定，如来信寄此间地址，舍下可以转寄。匆匆，不尽欲言。顺颂著祺。

弟袁同礼顿首
三月十日

便中可询济之兄愿来此否？弟即不另作函矣。

〔西泠印社 2023 年春季拍卖中外名人手迹与影像艺术专场〕

按：后，董作宾、方豪均未能赴美哈佛燕京学社访学。该信于 3 月 15 日送达台北。

先生覆信张君劢，告知去欧洲考察计划，并谈台湾及欧洲局势。

君劢先生著席：

手示拜悉。承关怀，至感。赴欧签证之 Re-entry，业经国务院核准，此事"教部"方面早已通知"外交部"，该部迟迟未办，"大使馆"又延误半月，至上月廿五日始行办妥。闻公权先生业已来美，请代问安。去年三月曾用李君名义写《大陆铁路概况》一文，兹特奉上，盼代转呈。近一年之概况，得暇亦拟草一文，所得资料已甚多，惜无时间耳。报载适之被软禁，想系实情，台湾前途如此，真可悲也！现定月杪乘法轮赴欧。时局动荡，恐日内瓦会议以后，法、比或将承认中共也。冬间返美，再行请教。匆匆，顺颂道祺。

同礼顿首
三月十日

〔国家图书馆善本组手稿特藏〕

按：《大陆铁路概况》即 Railway Construction in China，"李君名义"即 Li Chang。是年 2 月 18 日，胡适抵达台北，因《自由中国》杂志从批判共产主义转向检讨台湾内部问题、批评国民党弊病，与蒋介石关系逐渐恶化，胡适虽被猜忌，但并未被软禁。1954 年

4月至7月,瑞士日内瓦万国宫召开了一次国际性多边会议。其议程是关于重建印度支那和朝鲜的和平的问题,史称"日内瓦会议"(La Conférence de Genève)。

三月十三日

先生致信钱存训,告知柯强所藏长沙出土文物的大致情形及协助董作宾访美等事。

公垂吾兄著席:

手教拜悉。大著即将发表,亟盼早日拜读。关于美人 Cox 所藏长沙出土帛书,此君秘不示人。杨联陞君曾见过,尊处似可致函向其索一照相影本,取到后可约劳榦字贞一共同研究。但恐此君不肯示人,或请 Creel 先生致函亦可。其通讯处列下:

Mr. John Hadley Cox, c/o Gallery of Fine Arts, Yale University, New Haven, Coun.

此人所得长沙出土之铜器及木器等,均寄存于此博物院也。关于董彦堂先生来美一节,加大及芝大均以经费关系未能进行。近哈佛燕京社略有余款,拟请学者三人来此研究,限期一年,待遇不高,但供给来往旅费。弟已推荐董彦堂并询其能否于此时来美,俟得复函再为积极进行。此事该社尚未发表,须候董事会开会后方能正式决定,故可不必先告他人也。弟定月杪离此赴欧,约冬间返美,在欧住址列后以便通讯。时念尊处工作紧张,经手之事又多,尚希随时休息,勿过劳碌为荷。匆复,顺颂俪安。

弟同礼顿首

三,十三,康桥

北平报载令亲邢老先生与他人合组经史学会,熟人中有夏仁虎等,均在七十以上之老辈也。

北平馆馆长为冯仲云,故宫博物院副院长为陈乔,科学院副院长为张稼夫,均党中人员。

在欧通讯处 c/o Mr. S. I. Hsiung, Staverton House, Oxford, England

〔钱孝文藏札〕

按:John Hadley Cox(1913—2005),美国收藏家,尤其热衷购藏中国先秦时期的陶器、青铜器,20世纪40年代蔡季襄将长沙子弹库楚帛书"转让"与其。"邢老先生"应指邢端(1883—1959)，1951年7月被聘为中央文史馆馆员。1953年4月23日，文化部任命冯仲云为北京图书馆馆长；同年1月20日，社会文化事业管理局转文化部通知，任命陈乔为故宫博物院副院长；同年1月14日，中央人民政府委员会第21次会议任命张稼夫为中国科学院副院长。

先生致信图齐(罗马)，告知胡适因故无法前往参加马可波罗诞辰七百年庆典，推荐方豪前往与会。

March 13, 1954

Dear Professor Tucci:

　　I trust that your preparation for the celebration of the VIIth centenary of the Birth of Marco Polo is well under way. Before leaving for Formosa for a temporary visit, Dr. Hu Shih told me that he will not be able to come to Rome much to his regret.

　　It has occurred to me that if you wish China represented at the Celebrations, you might like to extend an invitation to Professor Fang Hao, Department of History, Taiwan University, Taipeh, Taiwan (Formosa). Professor Fang, as you may have met his acquaintance already, is a specialist on Sino-foreign relations and has written considerably on this subject. Moreover, he speaks Italian and has lived in Rome several years ago.

　　Professor Fang will pay his own travel expenses, so it will not be a burden on your budget. He is preparing for a paper to be read in Rome if he is invited.

　　I expect to sail for the United Kingdom at the end of this month. My address after April 1 will be as follows: c/o Mr. S. I. Hsiung, Staverton House, Oxford, England.

　　With kindest regards,

Yours sincerely,

〔University of Chicago Library, Yuan T'ung-li Papers, Box 3〕

按：此为底稿。

三月十六日

吴光清覆函先生,告恒慕义对先生申请续增《国会图书馆藏中国善本书录》编纂报酬之意见,并谈恒氏荣休之庆祝计划。

　　守和吾兄大鉴:

　　　　上周患重伤风,在家卧床一星期,今日返馆始读十日手示,藉悉一切。恒君谓尊函亦已收到。关于校改工作,续增酬报 750 元,彼意原无大问题。现王称书已印出,致又生枝节,请求手续又当麻烦。彼意原定之 500 元如未寄达,望迅速来函致彼转催出版部批准交会计处已行寄发。至续加之 750 元最好候王书寄到后(截至今日毫无消息),必定计划将其影印并增加尊撰之续编及编索引等项工作,届时将此 750 元列入预算当较易办,彼并谓该时虽已退休,但可建议,谅无问题云云。嘱我将上述情形先为函达,彼随后再奉复也。东方部全人公宴于廿六晚在 China Doll 举行,拟赠恒君本人皮制手提箱、其夫人鲜花(礼物),尊份已代缴并拟在贺片上代签名,所垫为数甚微,可勿介意。昨日又奉到十三日手示,内附致恒君一信,极为得体,兹略易数字附还。馆方欢送 Luncheon 系卅一日中午举行。所需之 Bibliographical services 已托 Claytor 觅到一份,昨日寄上。吾兄赴欧计划如何、何日首途,均在念念。匆匆,顺祝撰安。

弟光清上

三,一六

　　　　弟等之医药保险系 group health assin,为美京之机关,非全国性,每人每月四元,除生产非一年以后有效外,其他似无问题。

〔袁同礼家人提供〕

三月十八日

先生致信恒慕义,对其退休表示敬意并高度评价其对国会图书馆东亚馆藏所作出的不朽贡献,尤其称赞《清代名人传略》出版和协助平馆善本书运美两个重要功绩。

March 18,1954

Dear Dr. Hummel:

　　On the eve of your retirement from active service, may I offer you my hearty congratulations on the successful conclusion of a devoted and distinguished career. Under your able direction, a great collection of Oriental literature has been built up; it constitutes an invaluable repository for the growing number of scholars who come to Washington for study and research.

In developing these resources, you have foreseen the needs of future generations of scholars. In the field of Chinese literature alone, evidence of such foresight has been the systematic acquisition of source materials, the availability of which has made Washington the principal center of research in Chinese history and civilization.

One of your notable by-products and an indispensable work of reference, *THE EMINENT CHINESE OF THE CH'ING PERIOD*, is an excellent example of cooperative research. In this undertaking, you have made full use of not only the available source materials, but also the results of modern historical research in China. This splendid work would hardly have been possible had you not systematically built up a comprehensive collection of Chinese literature.

I am particularly indebted to you for the safekeeping of the rare Chinese Books from the National Library of Peiping and for your effort in microfilming these materials, thus making them available to a wide circle of scholars. All these measures bear witness to the valuable help you have given in the promotion of learning and advancement of knowledge.

Since coming to the United States, I have often turned to you for counsel in connection with my own research. Your sympathetic understanding has inspired me to greater effort. It is therefore my earnest hope that another term of your valuable service may be extended far into the future as Chief Emeritus of Orientalia, so that students of sinology may continue to come to you for advice and guidance.

With best wishes, I remain

　　　　　　　　　　　　　　　　　　　　　　Yours sincerely,

　　　　　　　　　　　　　　　　　　　　　T. L. Yuan

　　　　　　　　　　　　　　　　　　　〔袁同礼家人提供〕

　　按:此件为录副。

三月二十四日

吴光清致函先生,告知国会图书馆出版委员会仍拟按照原定计划,由刘楷贤誊抄先生校订后的"国会图书馆藏中文善本书录"书稿,并谈恒慕义退休后东方部可能之变化。

　　守和吾兄大鉴:

　　　　昨奉廿一日手示,敬悉一切。欧行既定,自宜早去早归。关于编辑提要之 500 元,即拟请恒君致 Memo 与 Dubester,请其通知会计处寄发,希望能于月底其退休及吾兄启程前办好。惟馆中手续繁多,不知来得及否? 至印好提要,馆方现托英国书商设法购置,尚无消息。正写至此处时(礼拜三九点半),又得 Publications Committee 处消息,谓现又决定不管印好提要案来否,前定手写提要计划拟依旧进行,并悉 Dubrster 今早拟打长途电话或电报至尊处通知,按照原来计划请刘君开始缮写,不知所谈结果如何? 如定好,当将蓝格子纸寄上(已印好,计 6,000 张,在中文部)。馆事愈趋复杂,大家都要作主,而且彼此又不接头,所以作事困难。恒君去后,不知何人继任,传闻有改组可能,将参考与编目分开,一切只好听其自然演变。恒君礼物,公份代垫仅二元,寄来五元太多,兹退还三元,祈查收。Army Map 中文部份主任 Dr. Suter 对政府工作厌倦,业已辞职,拟自己研究著述,遗缺由傅安接任。惟人事复杂,亦不易应付也。匆匆,顺祝双安。

　　　　　　　　　　　　　　　　　　　　弟光清上

　　　　　　　　　　　　　　　　　　　三,二四,十时

　　　　　　　　　　　　　　　　　　　〔袁同礼家人提供〕

　　按:"印好提要,馆方现托英国书商设法购置",应指王重民委托北京大学出版组所印《国会图书馆善本书提要》,因中国与英国建交,似可托英方书商(或由香港)购到。Dr. Suter 似指 Rufus O. Suter Jr.,待考。

三月二十六日

晚,杨联陞设宴为先生及夫人赴欧饯行。〔《杨联陞日记》(稿本)〕

> 按:《杨联陞日记》中有"并请于公夫妇"之语,"于公"似指于
> 震寰。

三月二十七日

先生致信中基会,申请恢复资助《西文汉学书目》(考狄书目续编)的编写
工作。

March 27, 1954

Dear Sirs:

In order to bring to early completion my editorial work on the *Supplement to Cordier's Bibliotheca Sinica*, I am submitting a memorandum with a request for financial assistance covering a period from January 1955 to December 1956. I would greatly appreciate your assistance if this request could be put on your agenda of your annual meeting.

This project has your support from April 1950 to September 1951. The editorial work was more or less interrupted from October 1951 to June 1953 when I worked for the Stanford Research Institute.

Thanking you for your interest and support,

Yours sincerely,

T. L. Yuan

〔University of Chicago Library, Yuan T'ung-li Papers, Box 1〕

三月三十一日

先生与夫人自纽约出发前往欧洲,收集英、法、德、意等国文献资料,增补
《西文汉学书目》(考狄书目续编)。〔袁同礼家人提供〕

> 按:此前,洛克菲勒基金会人文部资助先生9000美金用以完成此
> 项研究,该项资助款经国会图书馆逐月发放。①

四月六日

噶邦福致函先生,感谢寄赠期刊论文,并谈澳大利亚大学、图书馆对俄国研
究近况及文献积累情况,另略述外国旧友在北京现状。

---

① *The Rockefeller Foundation Annual Report, 1953*, p. 293.

Canberra, Apr. 6, 1954

Dear Mr. Yuan.

I have just received a Report of Russian Research Centre and Some Academic Activities in China both sent by you and must thank you for the same. Russian Research has made much progress in America, unlike the situation in Australia. Here, for instance, at Canberra, there is a university college, where elementary Russian is taught, with a minimum of students. In the Australian National University there is no room for Russian studies even in the Far Eastern Dept. We are much behind America.

Your article is interesting not only for me, but Fitzgerald, too. I shall give over to him after reading. I think you have received a letter which I sent you in February, not very long, and another much longer, sent through President Mei in March, about Soviet advisers as you desired. I still think that their number is not so big as you say, but about 40,000. And this is enough, considering their high salaries and treatment (cars, houses). I do not say of adulation with which they are surrounded.

National Library is well supplied with Russian books, particularly scientific, presented by the Academy of Science, only readers are not so many. As a counter-part the supply of European, and especially American, books is stopped, and those available are not easily accessible. And there was a purge, of course. Even Soviet books may be dangerous, Soviet Encyclopedia, for instance becomes out of date already now.

Your place was taken by your assistant, Mr. Wang. Mr. Chang was made Secretary, not as a Communist, who he is not, but because of his knowledge of languages. He accompanied the Exhibition of Chinese Art in Europe and was absent for two years.

Of our Peking acquaintances, Bielenstein and Mulder (do you know them?) are here in A. N. U. Reclus with wife is somewhere in France and still cannot release his daughter. Mr. and Mrs. Karpinsky cannot obtain an exit permit, without any accusation produced. Mrs. Marshall was paid much money for her hotel and is still in Peking, unwillingly, I think.

Now, with regards to your family.

Sincerely yours,

J. J. Gapanovich

〔袁同礼家人提供〕

按：Mr. Chang 应指张全新。Bielenstein 应指 Hans Bielenstein（1920-2015），瑞典汉学家，专攻汉代历史，中文名毕汉思，离开北京后，1952 年担任堪培拉大学东方语言学院院长，1961 年赴美执教于哥伦比亚大学。Karpinsky 应指 S. L. Karpinsky，商人，曾在天津 Rovensk & Co., L. P.（隆业）服务，后在北平开办 Mouland Co., J. A.（毛兰），从事进出口贸易①，1954 年 6 月被捕。Mulder，待考。此函为其亲笔。

四月七日

先生和夫人抵达伦敦。〔Columbia University Libraries Archival Collections, Shuhua Li Papers, 1926-1972, Volume II: Modern Eminent Chinese Leaders〕

四月十三日

图齐覆函先生，对胡适不能前来与会表示遗憾，并表示意大利方面不便邀请方豪作为备选人前来，但可以向其邀稿并列入会议结束后的论文集中。

13 Apr. 1954

Rome

Dear Dr. Yuan:

Many thanks for your very kind letter of March 13, and for the interest you are taking in our Marco Polo celebrations. I am sorry that Dr. Hu Shih is prevented from coming to Rome, as his visit would have been most welcome indeed.

With regard to your suggestion concerning an invitation to be extended to Prof. Fang Hao, I regret to say it would not be within our possibilities, much as we should be honored by the visit of such an outstanding personality. Our programs are unfortunately so overcrowded that we find it very difficult to cope with all our engagements; we could,

---

① *The North-China Desk Hong List*, 1934, p.707; *The North-China Desk Hong List*, 1941, p. 772.

however, write to him, requesting the favor of an article of his for our forthcoming publication at the close of the celebrations. We are planning to include all lectures and writings in a special volume, wholly dedicated to Marco Polo, which in a way would be a summary of our cultural manifestations.

As to the bibliography on Marco Polo, I think it should be an exhaustive one, as you say, up to 1953, and not a supplement to Yule or others.

I shall be very glad to hear from you and meanwhile I beg to remain, with kindest regards,

Yours sincerely,

Giuseppe Tucci

〔University of Chicago Library, Yuan Tʻung-li Papers, Box 3〕

按：此件为打字稿，落款处为其签名，该函寄送熊式一处收转。

四月二十日

先生致信李书华，告知英伦生活情况并建议其服用 Dolcin。

润章先生著席：

上月途经纽约，得聆教言并荷款待，至感至谢。别后于七日安抵伦敦，天气甚冷，携来衣服全部穿上仍感不敷，各屋均无暖气，尤感不便。美人浪费太多，英人则又过于省俭矣。此间食物自取销管制后应有尽有，而尤以猪肉为多，大约来自阿根廷。Cheese 及鸡蛋则来自丹麦，故对外贸易为英主要政策也。弟等在此工作如恒，惟对于此间天气颇不喜欢，幸尚未遇到雨季也。贤伉俪工作繁忙，尚希时加诊摄、多多休息，不胜企盼。弟到此后，以天气阴阴，又患 Rheumatism，继续服用 Dolcin 极有效力，尊处似可照服也。匆匆，顺颂著祺，并询起居。尊夫人同此问安。

弟同礼顿首

内人附笔致谢

四月廿日伦敦

〔Columbia University Libraries Archival Collections, Shuhua Li Papers, 1926-1972, Volume II: Modern Eminent Chinese Leaders〕

按："诊摄"当作"珍摄"。Rheumatism 即风湿病，Dolcin 则为阿司匹林和丁二酸钙片剂。

四月二十二日

刘国蓁致函先生,告其已在《华侨日报》工作,但生活艰辛,并转发袁道冲致袁慧熙信。

> 守和先生尊鉴:
>
> 　　许久未修函敬候,抱歉殊深。敬维著述丰宏,履躬清胜为颂。昨年圣诞节时,叨蒙赐赠胶质花松布一大幅,贺简一函,乃承雅意,宠锡隆情,拜领之余,曷任心镂。惟迟迟未报,得毋深滋颜汗!知晚如先生,定当原宥,幸甚幸甚。晚自去年十月时,蒙先生不遗在远,屡函介绍谒见恒安石 Hummel、黄星辉、何义均诸先生,可惜机会难逢,事未成就而感铭盛情,殊不浅鲜耳。十一月脱离港大职务后,由敝戚荐于《华侨日报》,在资料室任事。工作颇为适合,但时间极成问题,因晚上七时至二时工作,夜夜如是,并无放假,极为辛苦,而且薪金微薄,只得港大一半而已。维持甚感困难,守株待兔仍待鼎力赞勤为幸。上月得幸秉华东翁手示,藉悉先生关怀备致,去函问及贱况,感何可言。诚然,秉华东翁自一九五二年六月时委托代抄录在港数目,每月赐给津贴费港银三百元,以资弥补家用。当时港大月薪已不足维持,因晚有子女五人,先兄嫂遗孤三人,皆在求学之年,家用浩繁故也。晚屡受秉华东翁之深恩厚德,寔无既极,惟未知何日方能图报于万一,言之寔深惭愧耳。晚除夜间工作外,日间则经营一小商店于九龙,为售面包、饼干、糖果、香烟等,藉博蝇头小利,但现仍未有进展。谋事在人,成事在天,诚哉是言也。昨日奉到令岳丈大人嘱转尊夫人信一函,晚乘便偷闲敬覆,冒渎陈词,寔有辱尊听,伏祈恕宥为幸。专此,敬请崇安。

愚晚国蓁顿首

一九五四年四月廿二日

K. C, Lau, 36 Lockhart Road, 3rd fl. Hongkong.

　　　按:何义均,时应在美国驻香港领事馆任顾问。

四月

Foreign Affairs 刊登先生和袁澄共同撰写之文章,题为 The Soviet Grip on

Sinkiang。〔*Foreign Affairs*, vol. 32, no. 3, 1954, pp. 491-503〕

　　按:袁澄负责撰写初稿,先生则负责修改定稿①,仍以 Li Chang 为笔名。

是年夏

先生和夫人赴德国马尔堡(Marburg)游览,西德图书馆(Westdeutsche Bibliothek)馆长 Martin Cremer 及其夫人在 Stadtsäle 招宴,Wolf Haenisch、Wolfgang Seuberlich 受邀作陪。〔《思忆录》,英文部分 p. 39〕

　　按:Martin Cremer(1913-1988),1948 年至 1961 年担任西德图书馆馆长。

先生由欧洲大陆回抵英国,因病在医院接受手术治疗。〔《杨联陞日记》(稿本)〕

　　按:先生所患之疾病及诊治过程,可参见本谱是年 7 月 16 日致赵元任信。此事,后由蒋彝写信告知杨联陞(记在 7 月 6 日)。

五月二十四日

国会图书馆参考部主任 Burton W. Adkinson 致函先生,询问先生校订王重民编《国会图书馆善本书录》是否已经完成,以便其考虑按此前协议支付另外 500 美金的报酬。

May 24, 1954

Dear Dr. Yuan:

　　I have just heard from Mr. Wu of the Library's Orientalia Division of your letter in which you inquired about payment for your work in editing the *Catalog of Rare Chinese Books in the Library of Congress.*

　　Before initiating the necessary procedures designed to provide payment of $500.00 for your services as per agreement it would be well if we could have confirmation that your work has been completed. In your letter of March 28, 1954, you wrote that you were taking 100 photostats with you to England to complete and then forward to Mr. Liu. May I ask if the editing of these pages has been completed and if you have now made the total manuscript available to Mr. Liu.

　　Just as soon as we hear affirmatively from you, we will take the

---

① 《传记文学》第 8 卷第 2 期,页 36。

necessary steps to secure payment to you for the very worthwhile contribution you have made to this work which we all want to see published just as soon as possible.

Sincerely,

Burton W. Adkinson

Director

〔袁同礼家人提供〕

五月三十一日

刘楷贤致函先生,告知抄录《国会图书馆藏中国善本书录》书稿进展及问题。

　　守和先生赐鉴:

　　　不聆教益,转瞬两阅月,想先生旅居多福为颂。在英伦参阅,收获当亦甚多;何时转赴巴黎,时在念中。嘱还之书已还,祈勿念。奉先生自纽约来示,附写样一纸。贤依照此样张及先生前所指示多点,业于四月一日开始缮写,迄今两月,已钞过"经部","史部(1)"一半,计原稿二百六十页,抄成一百四十九页。每晚缮写二至三小时,周末约八至十小时,费时虽多,成就有限,其原因:①原稿字小而笔画潦草,有很多名词,虽用放大镜,仍须猜想或参考证实。②原稿纸地光滑,在灯光下凝视既久,时感模糊不清。③每写毕一篇,仍须标点、校对,亦颇费时间。以事倍而进行迟缓,殊为惭愧。

　　　上月末吴光清先生代表 Mr. Henry Dubester, Secretary of the Bibliography of Publication Committee 来函询问关于书目事已否进行?已函复吴先生,业已开始抄写。上周 Mr. Barton Adkinson 又来信,询问原稿最后部分,经先生携欧者,已否寄来?此信贤尚未作覆。

　　　已钞就之书目,"页数"现仍暂用铅笔标注,尚未用墨笔填写,拟在书口"中国善本书录"下,"国会图书馆藏"上,从"国"字起空二格向上写,例如:

中国善本书录	一□□国会图书馆藏
	二八
	一三九
	一四一九

是否可以？祈先生便中示知，为祷。尚此，恭请旅安！并候袁太太安！

刘楷贤顿首

五月卅一日

贡颖附笔问安

附稿纸一页。

〔袁同礼家人提供〕

六月十三日　牛津

先生致信 Burton W. Adkinson，告知善本书录稿仍未最终完成并谈工作量，希望其考虑再给予 750 美金的报酬。

8 St. Margaret's Road

Oxford, England

June 13, 1954

Dear Dr. Adkinson:

On my return to Oxford this morning, I was glad to have your letter of May 24.

I wish to report that I am still at work on the last part of the catalogue, and I am taking very good care of the photostats. As there are many bibliographical problems, I have to solve them one by one. For a work of this kind, there is no short-cut. I trust you would agree with me that in order to do a good job, it is necessary not to overlook the details which, of course, take considerably one's time and effort.

Mr. Liu has done a very good job in transcribing the descriptive notes written by Mr. Wang. So far, the section on Classics has already been completed. He is now working on the first part of the section on History which will take him several months to complete, although he can work a great deal during the summer. The section on Philosophy is also a large one, so is the section on Belles-Lettres.

When the photostats were received at Cambridge last September, they were in a state of utmost confusion, there being no logical order in any of the groups. Moreover, a considerable number of duplicates were found among them. Evidently the prints were made twice which showed clearly the carelessness of the men handling these photostats. Under these circumstances, I found it necessary to take a special trip to Washington in order to examine the books on the spot and check up all the details. At the Division of Orientalia I worked full time from October 12 up to December 11. My expenses there amounted to more than $500.

By this time the work was far from complete. It could easily take another two months if I had chosen to remain in Washington. But as my home was then in Cambridge and as living alone in Washington proved expensive, I had to continue the work (December 13–March 28) outside of the Library, disadvantageous as it had been.

More than once Dr. Hummel assured me that should the editorial work take too much of my time, I could request for additional compensation which he would support. Accordingly, in my report to Dr. Hummel, I requested for an additional amount of $750 which I thought would be a fair honorarium for the Library to pay for a work of this kind.

There is, of course, no need at all to arrange for its payment until the whole editorial work is completed. But these facts should be submitted to you in order that there should be no misunderstanding when the final payment is made.

〔袁同礼家人提供〕

按:此件应为底稿,尾页不存。

六月十五日

陈源覆函先生,询问病情及告知赵元任及本人行程。

守和吾兄:

奉手教,欣悉大驾莅英已有多日,贵恙想已康复,何日来伦,乞示知,以便把晤。"政府"改组,兹将名单抄录奉上。刊物曾列部长名字,但未有次长。刊物尚望尧圣兄按期寄上。元任兄下周由美来,仅停留一日,即去巴黎。弟亦须去法开会,但数日即返。叔华近日忙于作画。因秋间在中美有一画展,须赶紧筹备也。草此,顺颂痊祺。

弟陈源顿首

六月十五

〔University of Chicago Library, Yuan T'ung-li Papers, Box 7〕

按："尧圣兄"即陈尧圣(1911—?)，浙江上杭人，燕京大学、英国伦敦大学毕业，历任国民党中央组织部总干事，国联同志会秘书，外交部情报司科长、驻英大使一等秘书。1950年英国与台湾"断交"后，陈尧圣继续留在英国，以私人身份创办"自由中国"新闻社，并成立"自由中国"之友协会，出版中英文周刊等，曾任英国各大学中国委员会委员、中国协会理事、伦敦华侨联谊会会长等职。6月21日，赵元任夫妇及赵来思抵达伦敦，23日即渡海至欧洲大陆旅行。

七月十日

胡适致函先生，就申请中基会恢复资助《西文汉学书目》(考狄书目续编)给予初步意见。

守和兄：

久不通问，不知你此时在何处。

三月廿七日你给中基会的信，本年十月二日的年会当可提出讨论。但此时中基会的情形，已非1950年可比。这几年来，中基会的收入，差不多全部用在台湾大学与各省立学院，此项用途都系常年的Commitments，不能中断，也不能挪移。额外的用途，必须于每年度终了时的盈余项下筹之。

老兄三月廿七日的公函没有提及每年所需的款项数额。乞斟酌最低需要，赐函示知，以便提出讨论。鄙意拟提议：即以兄1951年退还本会之＄1800，于本年(1954)度盈余项下提出，作九个月的津贴，每月贰百元。另于同项盈余下提出六百元，补足此项，作为1955年全年的津贴，总数为＄2400。其1956年的津贴，则留待明年年会时提出决定。

如此办法，较为容易筹措。乞兄考虑赐示，至感。能在八月内见覆，最好。匆匆，敬祝双安。

弟胡适敬上

一九五四，七，十

〔袁同礼家人提供〕

　　按:胡适在本函中提及补助先生的设想,确为中基会最后实施之办法。①

七月十一日

傅乐淑覆函先生,请在英照俄文书两种。

　　袁先生赐鉴:

　　敬奉手谕,谢谢! 谢谢! 知先生仍在英国,正为欣慰。按李先生推测,先生或已离英去欧陆矣。晚甚盼先生万机之暇代晚从英国照书两种:(一)即 Golovin 尼布楚条约之俄文条约,并有俄使之签字,在原书第九——廿一页,此件数页最好在英国洗出;(二)异域录之俄文翻译本,据说是从满文翻出,按现在可以看到的异域录(中文的)多从丛书中抄出,虽以何秋涛之熟于北徼掌故,也只见到一种节本,最近晚"发现"了一种"全本"(?),但苦于不知是否满文译本还是一部较迟的版本。此书有法文二、英文一、德文一、俄文二,译本之多。最流行的英文译本系从中文本译出,晚甚想找到俄文本对一对,以便搞清楚到底满文本是否有1721年以后的记载。此书两俄译本,至少有一个从俄文译出,现大英博物馆即有一部。晚也恳 film 一部(不必洗出),晚将□屋中看一下其□事至那一年为止,以便推测□书满文第一版是否与流行的汉文节本相同。一切拜托之处,容日后叩谢。晚暂奉上十元,为照像之资,不足时将如数补奉。晚不日即搬家,新居仍在 105th 街上,与陶维大住隔壁。晚有厨房,将来先生偕夫人来纽约,将晚欢迎前来,晚当道谢奉觞。又晚有旧同学陈志让君,此人据云已入英籍,与一英人结婚,现在 Boxer 处工作,晚将来若仍有需要从英照书之处,拟径函陈君代办。先生若知此人地址,将来不妨示知,如不知此人亦不必费神打听。晚已翻完实录,日内将去哈佛 work 小住。匆匆,此请双安。

晚傅乐淑叩

七月十一日

〔袁同礼家人提供〕

---

① 台北"中央研究院"近代史研究所档案馆,〈中华教育文化基金董事会〉,馆藏号 502-01-08-010,页 210-211、218。

按:傅乐淑(1917—2003),山东聊城人,傅斯年侄女,历史学家,1952年获芝加哥大学历史学博士学位,时在美执教。Golovin 即签订《尼布楚条约》俄方代表之一 Фёдор Алексеевич Головин(Feodor Alekseyevich Golovin,1650-1706),该条约中被记作"俄昆尼",《清史稿》中则称作"费岳多"。《异域录》,图理琛撰,介绍蒙、俄地理历史的专著,成书于清康熙五十四年(1715)。何秋涛(1824—1862),清代地理学家,字巨源,福建光泽人,著有《朔方备乘》《北徼汇编》等。陶维大,陶孟和之女。陈志让(Jerome Chen, 1919—2019),生于四川成都,1943年毕业于西南联大经济系,1947年获中英庚款奖学金赴英留学,授业于哈耶克(Friedrich August von Hayek,1899-1992)。

七月十五日

先生与夫人在巴斯古镇游览。〔University of California, Berkeley, The Bancroft Library, Yuen Ren Chao papers, carton 10, folder 39, Yuan, Tongli and Yuan, Huixi〕

按:巴斯是英格兰西南部的一座古老小城,属于英格兰埃文郡东部的科兹沃,古罗马人最早在这里发现了温泉,兴建了庞大的浴场,如今成为重要的历史遗迹。

七月十六日

先生致信赵元任、杨步伟夫妇,询问其腰伤并告知在英行期,邀二人前来同游牛津。

元任先生、韵卿夫人:

预计你们的行程大约是在德国,又看见报载德奥边界大水,正深怀念。顷奉赐书,欣悉已抵南德,如能抽晤,极盼你们能到维也纳一游,该处为音乐发祥之地,真令人留恋不舍,且物价均较其他城市便宜也。元任先生腰筋扭了,想已痊愈。德国温泉甚多,望去洗澡,必有帮助。南德有按摩专家,亦可就近一试。我们昨日到英国西南部 Bath 看罗马时代建筑的温泉浴室,可惜不能下浴,须经当地医生证明确有风湿症者方能入院沐浴,但德国确无此限制也。下月剑桥开会,弟拟前往参加,内人听说约他一同游玩,很愿相陪。在开会时极欢迎你们来舍下小住,地方虽小而又简陋,但内人热诚欢迎。牛津左近为莎氏比亚故里,均值得参观。弟前患小便闭塞之症,住院月余,近已完全复元,目疾亦愈。接尊处电报时正在割治之时,故未能到伦敦趋晤。来书谓致蒋仲雅 28 Southmoor Road, Oxford 明片装在信内,嘱为转交,但信封内并未发现,想忘却了。余俟面谈,顺颂旅安。

　　　　　　　　　　　　　　　　　　　同礼顿首

　　　　　　　　　　　　　　　　　　　七月十六

Lowry 同此致意,慧熙附笔问安。

〔University of California, Berkeley, The Bancroft Library, Yuen Ren Chao papers, carton 10, folder 39, Yuan, Tongli and Yuan, Huixi〕

　　按:7 月 2 日,赵元任在瑞典突发腰痛,4 日略有好转。蒋仲雅即蒋彝;Lowry 似指 Thomas P. Lowry[1],待考。

八月四日

徐亮致函先生,告知华盛顿、国会图书馆近况。

　　守和先生赐鉴:

　　　　顷接惠寄之回单两纸,均已妥收,至谢至谢。黄瑞泰先生处业已去函告知,谅不久定收到以应急需。承先生慨允相助办理各事,衷心感激。来示云将参加国际东方学会,届时当遇不少之汉学家,交换意见对于学术界裨益实深也。世界局势动荡不已,在此数月之后必有显明之发展,权且拭目以待。华京天气数日前奇热,温度达百零三度,晚间大汗奔流,不能成寐,颇为所苦。现在热度稍降,略为舒适。子明先生现正休假,已至 Atlantic City 一游。东方部主任人选尚未定妥,据云有三十余"射猎",此位置最后决定当俟新馆长 Mumford 莅任以后方能发表。小弟自有此血压高之毛病以后,不敢妄动,以免意外发生,故今夏不拟驱车远行,拟于周末休假二天,如此不操劳真能收休养之效果。专此敬覆,敬请大安。

袁太太问安,澄兄佳好。

　　　　　　　　　　　　　　　　　　　小弟徐亮上

　　　　　　　　　　　　　　　　　　　内人附笔请安

　　　　　　　　　　　　　　　　　　　八月四日

〔University of Chicago Library, Yuan T'ung-li Papers, Box 2〕

---

[1] Finding Aid to the Yuen Ren Chao papers BANC MSS 83/30 c, p. 23.

按:Mumford 即 Lawrence Q. Mumford(1903－1982),1954 年至 1974 年担任美国国会图书馆第 11 任馆长。1955 年 7 月 18 日, Horace I. Poleman(1905-1965)被任命为东亚部主任。[①]

八月六日

马如容覆函先生,告知所问人名并谈胡适近访加州大学伯克利分校。

202 South Hall

Univ. of California

Berkeley 4, Calif.

August 6, 1954

Dear Dr. Yuan:

I have your air letter of August 2 which reached my yesterday. I am glad to hear from you, and to learn that you are not in and around New York but in England.

The name of Professor Bing Chin Wong in Chinese is 黄炳泉. In order to be sure that I am not wrong, I checked up with Mrs. Wong this morning who still resides in Berkeley. I have known Dr. Wong ever since he arrived from China when he was about 17 or 18 years old, for we were attending the same school in San Francisco—in fact, we were classmates in the 7th and 8th grades. We again met when I came to California for my first year of graduate work. When I returned to California in 1919, following a year of graduate work at Illinois, he was a reader in the Dept. of Mathematics, while I had a stroke of fortune by being appointed Teaching Fellow in Political Science. He took his Ph. D. a year after I did, after which both of us were appointed to the faculty until he unfortunately passed away some years ago, while I am still living on borrowed time. His death is a great loss to our Chinese in his field. He comes from 广东台山.

Here in Berkeley we had the good fortune of visiting with Dr. Hu when he was on his way to and back from Taipeh recently. He is the

---

① *Annual Report of the Librarian of Congress, for the fiscal year eding June 30, 1956*, Washington, 1957, p. v.

greatest asset we have as far as "Free China" is concerned. This is not my opinion alone, but the general consensus everywhere as far as I know. He is in good health. My daughter, Mrs. Frank Yao, who is Reference Librarian at the School of Social Work, Columbia University, reports to us from time to time on his workaday life. We just can't get him away from there. President Sproul of California had made him the most flattering of offers, but for reasons known to himself only he prefers New York. Probably that metropolis has got into his blood. Anyhow, he's happy where he is, and that is most important.

The Y. R. Chaos' are now in Europe. I presume they had dropped in on you while they were on their way. Dr. Chao is on a year's leave.

With warmest regards and the summer's greetings, I am

Sincerely yours,

N. Wing Mah

〔袁同礼家人提供〕

按：马如容(Mah, Ngui-Wing, 1893—?)，1921 年获得加州大学博士，其论文题目为 Foreign jurisdiction in China。Bing Chin Wong 的中文名实为黄炳铨(1890—?)，数学家，1923 年获得加州大学博士学位，其论文题目为 A study and classification of ruled quartic surfaces by means of a point-to-line transformation。

Giuliano Bertuccioli 覆函先生，告知其已赴香港担任意大利驻香港副领事，并谈撰写《本草品汇精要》及相关论文的初衷。

Hongkong 6/8/54

Dear Dr. Yuan:

It has been very kind of you to write to me from Oxford. Many years have elapsed since we met in 1946 in Nanking and talked about that Chinese manuscript which is preserved in the Central Library of Rome.

Writing the article about the *Pen-ts'ao p'in-hui ching-yao*, it has been my aim to prove that it was brought to Italy in the middle of the Nineteenth Century by a missionary. In the future I would like to publish something more about its authors and about the painters who illustrated it.

About this I would appreciate your advice.

Since September 1953 I am in Hongkong as Vice Consul so that I will not be able to go to Rome in the near future. But do please call on my wife who stays with my parents in Rome at Lungotevere delle Navi 30 (Tel. 30948)

I am enclosing for you another reprint, a small article about a little known writer of the Ming Dynasty and whose work I have nearly completely translated.

Hoping to read from you again.

Yours sincerely

Giuliano Bertuccioli

〔University of Chicago Library, Yuan T'ung-li Papers, Box 3〕

按：Giuliano Bertuccioli（1923-2001），中文名白佐良，意大利汉学家。*Pen-ts'ao p'in-hui ching-yao* 即《本草品汇精要》，由明孝宗敕令编绘，we met in 1946 in Nanking and talked about that Chinese manuscript 所指应为该书的抄本，先生在 1934 年访问罗马期间曾在梵蒂冈发现此彩绘书稿。Lungotevere delle Navi 即海军河岸，罗马弗拉米尼奥区的一段台伯河岸，连接吉亚科莫·马泰奥蒂桥与美术广场。落款处为其签名。

八月七日　牛津

先生致信程其保，告此前寄上《现代中国数学研究目录》卡片，并委托其排印、出版事宜。

August 7, 1954

Dear Dr. Cheng:

The bibliographical cards on mathematical literature written by Chinese scholars were mailed to you early this month. They should be received after three weeks.

The title of the bibliography may be called: *Modern China and Mathematics: a bibliographical guide*. If you should decide to have it printed by photolithographic process, they should be typed by a well-trained typist. She should be held responsible for proof-reading. I now enclose some suggestions for her to follow.

In selecting a publisher, the Interscience Publishers, Inc., 250 Fifth Avenue, New York City, may be considered. I shall leave the matter entirely to your discretion. I only hope that the manuscript may soon be published, as I have already spent a great deal of my time in bringing it to completion.

With sincere greetings and best wishes,

Yours sincerely,

T. L. Yuan

〔袁同礼家人提供〕

八月十八日

赵元任驱车来访,先生与之一同到埃文河畔斯特拉特福(Stratford-upon-Avon)参观莎士比亚故居。〔《赵元任年谱》,页335〕

八月二十四日

钱存训致函先生,告已顺利通过博士入学考试及英国人出售《永乐大典》事。

守和先生:

前得手片,敬悉旅况佳胜,至深欣慰。久未修书致候,只因自暑季以来,即忙于准备 Ph.D.笔试,因许多课程皆系六七年前所读,教员已经数易,新出书刊,不得不多加浏览。现考试已于三周前举行,共计两天,十四小时,共分三类,(一)研究方法,(二)目录史(Specialization),(三)普通图书馆学,内包括八专门:School, Academic, Public Libraries, Library History, Bibliographic Organization, Classification, Communication, International Librarianship。上周得校中通知已经 Pass,前两类均属 A 等,后一类平均 B+,故成绩尚算不差。惟尚有法文及论文尚待完成,论文题前拟写"先秦两汉书史",现拟仍旧。我公在欧,不知能否代为留意搜集一点有关材料。闻大英博物院藏有汉纸及竹简未经印行者,乞代为觅取照相影本及说明,校中有研究费可以申请应用,如费用较多,乞示知,当先行汇奉也。(巴黎除已印行之汉简外不知有与书籍制度有关之材料否?)此间一切如常,Creel 君下年升任东方语文系之 Chairman(伊原仅主管中文部分),伊仍有意请董彦堂来此,成立古史研究中心,但款尚无着也。家兄在英甚不得意,前拟来美,亦有困难,只好暂时图一糊口之计也。令公子在英闻成绩超群,不知何时可以结束。念念,敬请旅安。

后学存训拜上

八月廿四日

　　再者,日昨得一英人来函,拟出售其家藏《永乐大典》两册,闻经大英博物院 McAleavy 鉴定,为卷 803—806"诗"及卷 10110—10112 "纸"韵两册,均未经尊著收藏表著录,我公在英或已见及。此间不拟收购(不知索价若干,来函未说明)。王有三君不知现在是否仍在馆,如他处无人收购,似可致函王兄托人接洽收归国有也。其人通讯处如下:

　　　　Beatrice Brazier (Mrs. W. R. Brazier) Spinnakers, Sevenoaks, Kent, England.

闻系 James R. Brazier 于 1901 在北京觅得。

〔University of Chicago Library, Yuan T'ung-li Papers, Box 2〕

　　按:McAleavy 即 Henry McAleavy(1912-1968),英国汉学家,曾在英国驻华使馆工作,时应在大英博物馆东方部写本部兼职。信中所言两册《永乐大典》分别为诗字、纸字(只字等)册,现均藏于爱尔兰切斯特·比蒂图书馆(Chester Beatty Library)。James R. Brazier,曾任福公司(Pekin Syndicate. Ld.)北京地区总代理。[1]

八月二十五日　剑桥

下午,先生出席东方学会议(Congress of Orientalists),并以台湾地区和中国大陆的学术研究为主题做报告,尤其以安阳考古挖掘、长沙考古挖掘的收获为介绍重点。〔*The Manchester Guardian*, Aug. 26. 1954, p. 3〕

八月二十六日

蒋彝致函先生、夫人,约三十一日聚餐。

　　守和先生、夫人有道:

　　　　日前再扰郇厨,余香在口,谢谢。兹请于八月卅一日(星期二)下午六时半,移玉至香港楼 58 Shaftesbury Avenue, London, W. 1 餐叙,约

----

① *The North-China Desk Hong List*, 1909, p. 275.

有元任先生、夫人及三小姐与通伯贤伉俪及其女公子等,祈赏光勿却是幸。尚此,敬颂俪安。

弟蒋彝顿首

八月廿六日

〔袁同礼家人提供〕

按:"三小姐"即赵来思。"女公子"即陈小滢,陈源与凌叔华的独女。

九月一日

先生与赵元任一同驱车前往苏格兰。〔《赵元任年谱》,页336〕

按:此行途经纽卡斯尔、爱丁堡及约克。

九月六日

先生与赵元任回抵伦敦。〔《赵元任年谱》,页336〕

九月十日　牛津

先生致信钱存训,就大英博物馆所藏汉简情况、大陆考古相关之新发现略作介绍,并请其考虑代为向芝加哥大学转售图书一种。

公垂吾兄:

奉八月廿四日手教,欣悉博士考试均已通过,成绩优异,闻之甚慰,特此申贺。嘱搜集有关材料,大英博物院近印之 Maspero 考释之汉简想已见及,未印行者究有若干,曾经函询,但迄无复音,想主持之人不甚内行也。俟与之晤面后再为催询。近三年长沙发掘之竹简、木简、丝绢上有文字以及战国时代之毛笔等见本年六月廿五及七月九日香港《大公报》均可加以研究。按一九五一年长沙发掘系科学院考古研究所主持,一九五二五月至一九五三年四月则由湖南文化管理委员会主持,当时发掘596坟墓,雇用一批职业盗墓人,从事于粗率的发掘,因未采用科学方法,以致历史文化遭到破坏见一九五三年二月四日《光明日报》。两机关之发掘报告迄未出版,但内中关于秦汉书史之资料甚多。吾兄可函托森玉、西谛两兄设法搜集西谛任文化部副部长。弟曾函询王有三及曾昭燏南京博物院院长、贺长群南京图书馆馆长、向达诸人,均无复音,想由大陆寄信到英亦不易也。Michael Sullivan 在本年出版 *Art Bulletin*(College Art Association)Vol. xxxvi (march, 1954)曾有一文 *Pictorial Art and the Attitude toward Nature in Ancient China* 述及长沙出土之文字,前已函告,渠引用之中文书

Fig.1 帛书采自楚民族及其艺术，Shanghai，1948，Ⅱ，pl. □-1-19，想尊处业已入藏矣（曾在莫太太处见此书）。又弟误购两部一九五二出版之《十竹斋笺谱》，兹以一部交平邮寄上，如芝大或 Art Institute of Chicago 愿购时可告其将书款径寄香港蔚林书店（地址列后），书价 135 港币外加寄费，发票附在书内，希注意。将来可请该书店另补发票及收据以完手续，否则由弟出名出售，请兄代为签字可也。下周将赴德法，住址不定，两月以后方能返英，届时当再函达。匆匆，顺颂俪安。

弟袁同礼顿首
九月十日

Willing Book Co., Room 7, 20 Ice House Street, Hong Kong

〔钱孝文藏札〕

按：Maspero 即 Henri Maspero，(1883-1945)，法国语言学家、汉学家，中文名马伯乐，"考释之汉简"即 *Les Documents chinois de la Troisieme Expedition de Sir Aurel Stein en Asie Centrale*，现通译为《斯坦因第三次中亚考古所获汉文文献》。Michael Sullivan 即苏立文(1916-2013)，加拿大汉学家、艺术史家。"楚民族及其艺术"指蒋玄佁著《长沙"楚民族及其艺术"》第二卷《图腾遗迹 绢画 雕刻》，美术考古学社专刊之一，该卷 1950 年由美术考古学社（上海）出版，非 1948 年。

九月十七日　巴黎

先生致信图齐，为自己因病无法按时完成马可波罗书目而致歉，并告知将赴威尼斯看展及在罗马停留的时间、在德通讯地址等。

c/o Chinese Embassy
Paris
17 September, 1954

Dear Professor Tucci:

My recent illness which necessitated a major operation in an English hospital has delayed much of my work. It is a great disappointment to me that I shall not be able to compile a good bibliography on Marco Polo, much against my wish. In order to do a good job, it would take considerable time and energy. I now find that I could do so after my recent illness.

Professor Elisséeff of Harvard told me that the exhibit at Venice will close on October 10. I would very much like to see this exhibition, so I shall have cut short my visit to Germany. I do hope to have a glimpse of it before it closes.

Dr. Olschki told me that I should give a talk at your Institute when I come to Rome in October. Unfortunately, I shall be in Rome only for a week, October 13－18, and I thought that your program must have been overcrowded and that you have had enough speakers this year.

In case your Institute would like to have me included, perhaps you would be good enough to drop me a note at the following address:

> Professor T. L. Yuan, c/o Dr. W. Haenisch, Universitats-Bibliothek, Marburg, Germany.

If you think the audience would be interested in the recent archaeological discoveries in China, I shall be glad to give a talk on this subject.

With best wishes for your success,

Yours sincerely,

T. L. Yuan

Please give my kindest regards to Dr. Olschki.

〔University of Chicago Library, Yuan T'ung-li Papers, Box 4〕

按:the exhibit at Venice 应为威尼斯举办的有关马可波罗的展览。此件为录副。

九月二十日

王铃致函先生,谈英国汉学研究的现状并请介绍其赴欧美大学任教。

守和先生尊鉴:

不亲诲谕忽又月余,两奉手教并杂志,关顾之忱,不敢一日而忘之。尊照由 Owen, 90 Cambridge Rd. Shelford 拍摄,已去函催促,如不获答即亲去理论。此镇不过数哩之遥,自行车半小时可达也。晚旅英几年,恒叹欧洲汉学自哈新、道问达相继谢世后,硕学君子寥若晨星,无术庸才忝居高位。于是竞立门户,植党营私,鞠养提携,助相说引,致使中国学者笃行力学,辛苦无闻,博达通人无缘自见。其势力远播异土,或印尼中文系为荷籍小儿一手把持,或澳大利亚汉学惟伦敦东方学院之命是听,乃至港大教授呀呀不能为语,印度讲师瞠目难辨诗书。至若牛津、剑桥并国学大师陈寅恪者,亦不过昙花一现。下而论之,钱锺书既不见纳于前,杨廉升又复拖延于后。忍看今日祖国文化之海外传授,几何而不为犹太人之天下也。排外之心,欧洲以英国为最,英国又以剑桥为最,生徒既寥寥无几,教席更装饰门面,课程洋洋大观,往往有教授而无学生。下学期增设中国文学科目乃一犹太小子,上车不落之徒,从而趋附钻营、冠冕沐猴,又且执圣贤之书以欺世矣。

　　此次在东方学会露丑,辱蒙诸先辈过誉,鼓舞精神不少。去岁于剑桥大学讲中国数学史一学期,听众颇多,硕学之士尚谬获好评。下学期亚基米德学会亦邀作学术讲演,凡此虚荣,殊无补生计,所可惜者,频年搜集材料若干,发表无由,长此因循惰作傢依人,终非久远之计。且喜尼德汉书成有日,固尼氏一人之力,自度甚无建树,亦从兹了却些许心愿,后此校雠补缀不为难事。虽尼公厚意挽留,晚之去留实无伤此书进展。先生望重群伦,足迹所经谅多各学术界消息,尤忆十数年前傅公孟真为说先生有提携美意,以仓促远行未遑申谢,在英一度握手,又匆匆不罄欲言。几年以来,熊式一老伯爱我最深,此去星岛或重膺求贤之命,已初步有所接洽。熊老伯称南洋规模草创,刻犹一片荒郊,度建屋招生或非一年不办。际此期间,晚颇有意去美国一行。曾于大会中结识哈佛 Elisséeff 及哥伦比亚 Goodrich,拟寄去拙作尚未发表者一二份,保持联络。他如加里复尼亚乃至欧美任何学校,但求一易环境,不计地位、薪金。晚在此与世隔绝,家庭不快,种种难以卒言,先生其何以教我耶？余不一一。肃此,敬请尊安。

晚王铃敬上
九月二十日

骆惠敏夫妇均在巴黎,已去函。

〔University of Chicago Library, Yuan T'ung-li Papers, Box 2〕

按:王铃(1917—1994),江苏南通人,历史学家,毕业于中央大学,后协助李约瑟编纂《中国科学技术史》。"尼德汉书"即《中国的

科学与文明》(*Science and Civilization in China*)。1954 年,熊式
一随林语堂到新加坡南洋大学任教,受聘文学院院长,1955 年 4
月离职。

九月二十六日

王铃致函先生,告知熊式一已离英赴新加坡。

> 守和先生尊前:
>
> 前函计达,今附上照相馆来信,如尚未寄到,晚再去追询。上星期
> 六去伦敦送熊老伯行,昔以牛津、剑桥相去不远,今更不知后会何期
> 矣。尊驾过英时,务乞赐示,俾得再亲训诲。他日云山修阻,趋教无由
> 也。余不一一。肃此,敬请旅安。
>
> > 晚王铃敬上
> >
> > 九月二十六日
>
> Prof. W. Hartner, Prof. & Mrs. W. Franke, Dr. Fuchs, Dr. Hulsewé,
> 晤面时均乞代问好。

> 〔University of Chicago Library, Yuan T'ung-li Papers, Box 9〕
>
> 按: Prof. W. Hartner 应指 Willy Hartner(1905-1981),德国科学
> 家、自然科学史学家; Prof. & Mrs. W. Franke 即傅吾康与其夫人
> 胡隽吟; Dr. Hulsewé 即 A. F. P. Hulsewé(1910-1933),荷兰汉学
> 家,中文名何四维。

九月二十八日

程其保覆函先生,此前寄送卡片业已收到并请人重打以便保存,如需补助
出版或可与梅贻琦商洽办法。

> 守和先生有道:
>
> 迭奉手示及卡片一包,至深感佩。卡片登记均代改正,并已由月涵
> 先生饬人用打字机重打一遍,以便保存。至付印一层,据月涵先生意稍
> 缓再商。至先生前云拟将关于生物著作提前收集,不知现进行至何程
> 度,万一须少数补助经费,月涵先生或可设法也。专复,并颂双安。
>
> > 弟程其保顿首
> >
> > 九,廿八日
>
> 陈通伯及熊式一诸兄晤时,请代为问候。

> 〔袁同礼家人提供〕

九月下旬

先生路过法兰克福。〔University of Chicago Library, Yuan T'ung-li Papers, Box 4〕

十月十六日

顾维钧致函先生,告知已将哥伦比亚大学欧美校友所捐款项汇寄母校,并附捐款征信录一份。

> 同礼吾兄台鉴:
>
> 今年欣逢哥仑比亚大学二百周年纪念,前校长艾森豪威将军在就任美总统前曾有函致钧,冀我哥大同学对母校有所表示。经将此意转达旅居美欧及台湾各同学,并建议筹捐,多承赞助、慷慨输将。除台湾哥大中国同学会已集款购得《四库备要》全套径运哥大外,美欧两地同学共捐美金壹仟伍佰伍拾元。一再洽询各方后,经循公意,以现金扫数赠送哥大作为购备中文或有关中国之英文绝版书籍,以供母校学生参考之用。当时备函将款汇寄哥大校长之时,胡适之兄正在华府,因照若干同学主张去函,由胡适之、郭秉文及钧三人会签发出。顷接哥大校长复函,对我同学爱护母校之热忱深引感慰。兹特将钧等与哥大校长来往函暨去函所附捐款人名单影本各一份,连同经收捐款征信录一份随函奉上,统祈台察为祷。嵩此,并颂时祺。
>
> 顾维钧拜启
> 十月十六日
> 〔袁同礼家人提供〕

> 按:"哥大校长"时为 Grayson Kirk(1903–1997),1968 年因该校学生运动被迫辞职。该函为文书代笔,落款处并钤印。后附"捐款征信录(名次以学位年份为序)"二页,其中先生捐款 25 美金。

十月二十三日

刘国篆致函先生,告新亚书院尚未设立图书馆,请其赐介绍信以便向林语堂毛遂自荐。

> 守和博士先生尊鉴:
>
> 敬启者,未修书敬候瞬经数月,兼葭秋水,倍切溯洄。敬维文祺懋集,著业延釐,至以为颂。五月时拜奉由英伦来示,敬悉种切。八月时报载先生讲学情形,欣喜无似。想台驾仍继续留英,至明春方返回美国也。来示附代致顾子刚先生信,经已即为转达,未悉有无覆音为念。

蒙介绍谒见钱宾四院长,殊深感铭,惟该院尚未有图书馆设立,是以未有机会为憾。晚仍旧在《华侨日报》任事,工作烦忙,尚未觅得日间工作,生活极感困难。近日载报南洋大学校长林语堂博士将于本月底来港一行,并准备在港搜购图书,可能延聘师资等,而南洋大学创办伊始,此举当有可能,尤其是新兴之图书馆必需人才。用是不揣冒昧,恳请鼎力赞勷,赐寄一介绍函与晚,待林校长到港时持函拜晤,藉此多拼机会。若得一枝可托南洋,离港亦不甚远也。倘蒙俯允,感荷恩慈,寔无既极。临书不胜迫切待命之至。专此,敬请崇安。

愚晚国蓁顿首

一九五四年十月廿三日

〔袁同礼家人提供〕

　　按:该函寄送牛津,后又被转递巴黎。

十月

先生赴罗马访书。〔袁同礼家人提供〕

　　按:先生在罗马停留时间不长,未能与图齐等意大利学者见面。

先生在威尼斯,遇 Bo Gyllensvärd 及 Orvar Karlbeck 夫妇。〔University of Chicago Library, Yuan T'ung-li Papers, Box 4〕

　　按:Bo Gyllensvärd(1916-2004),瑞典汉学家,时应任斯德哥尔摩东亚博物馆(Museum of Far Eastern Antiquities, Stockholm)馆长;Orvar Karlbeck(1879-1967),瑞典工程师,1906 年至 1927 年、1928 年至 1934 年在华参与铁路规划与施工,爱好铜器并广泛收集。

先生在日内瓦短暂停留,并与 Arthur Breycha-Vauthier 晤谈。〔University of Chicago Library, Yuan T'ung-li Papers, Box 4〕

　　按:Arthur Breycha-Vauthier(1903-1986),奥地利图书馆学家,时应在联合国文化机构服务。

先生赴德国马尔堡(Marburg),并访霍福民。〔University of Chicago Library, Yuan T'ung-li Papers, Box 4〕

十一月一日　巴黎

先生与夫人至郭有守家,晤赵元任等人,并一同外出访友。〔《赵元任年谱》,页 337〕

按：先生与夫人宿巴黎 15 区，Hôtel Institut, 23 Boulevard Pasteur。

十一月九日

John Simon Guggenheim Memorial Foundation 致函先生，请就陈受颐学术水平和申请计划书予以评价。

November 9, 1954

Dear Dr. Yuan:

May I have your careful judgment of Dr. Shou-Yi Ch'en's quality as a scholar, of his proposal for research, and of him with reference to that proposal? A statement of the project is attached hereto.

Anything you say will be held in the strictest confidence.

Sincerely yours,

James F. Mathias

Associate Secretary

〔University of Chicago Library, Yuan T'ung-li Papers, Box 2〕

按：此件为打字稿，落款处为其签名，该函寄送华美协进社（纽约）。

十一月中旬

先生及夫人离开巴黎前往布鲁塞尔，略作停留。〔袁同礼家人提供〕

先生及夫人前往荷兰，在莱顿大学汉学研究所（Sinological Institute, Leiden University）查阅该院图书馆资料，何四维①等人提供特别帮助和便利条件，每日到晚上十时半才休息。〔University of California, Berkeley, The Bancroft Library, Yuen Ren Chao papers, carton 10, folder 39, Yuan, Tongli and Yuan, Huixi〕

十一月十八日

傅吾康致函先生，告知王铃在前往杜伦的途中突然变卦，恐不宜聘为自己的助手，并告已代为征求所需德文书籍。

November 18, 1954

Dear Dr. Yuan:

Many thanks for your letter from Roma dated October 16. Please forgive me for answering you as late as today. Mrs. Franke and I are

---

① 11 月 23 日袁慧熙致赵元任、杨步伟的信中只提到代理院长是先生的"熟朋友"，结合前后史料可知，应该指何四维，特此说明。

feeling in fact very disappointed that you could not manage to visit Hamburg. We would have been most happy to welcome you here and to talk with you.

I am most grateful to you for having thought about the question to find a suitable Chinese scholar to assist me at Hamburg University. The matter is in fact very urgent question to me. I have approached already some people but so far without any definite result. I have met Mr. Wang Ling at Cambridge and I am convinced that he is a good and promising scholar. But there is another question. We had this summer an experience not too favourable with him. After some hesitation and after having been encouraged by some other people Mr. Wang made finally in the last minute up his mind to join the Junior Sinologues Conference at Durham. All participants departed in common including him after the closure of the Cambridge Congress by special coach to Durham. After the first stop he decided without any obvious reason that he would cancel his participation and to back to Cambridge. Several other participants-among them Mrs. Franke-tried to comfort him and to persuade him to stay, but without success. He insisted to go back to Cambridge and did so. Therefrom I have the impression that Mr. Wang is a rather unstable character. Under the guidance and under the personal influence of a personality like Dr. Needham Mr. Wang does apparently very good work. Now I must confess that I have not much ability to influence and to induce others, who are under my direction, to work if they do not have the initiatives and the diligence to work spontaneously. Among others I have particularly one case in mind. I am sure you remember Mr. Ku Hua, a very intelligent and promising young man doing probably very good work as long as he was under your personal guidance in the National Library. But when after departure from Peking he went to the Deutschland-Institut in 1939 or 1940 he became under my guidance every day more lazy and more indolent and he was spoiled in a way that after your return to Peking in 1945 (or 46?) even you could make no more use of him in the National

Library. Of course it is evident that the characters of Ku Hua and Wang Ling are very different, I do not know Mr. Wang well enough to understand if he is working spontaneously or if he needs a guidance like yours or Dr. Needham. I would be most grateful to you for giving me your opinion on this question before deciding if I should approach Mr. Wang or not.

We have listed your desideratum *"Chinas Geist und Kraft"* by Tao Pung-fei, hoping to get a copy for you.

With best wishes from my wife and myself.

Yours sincerely,

Wolfgang Franke

〔University of Chicago Library, Yuan T'ung-li Papers, Box 2〕

按：Tao Pung-fei，应为 Tao Pung-fai。陶鹏飞，辽宁凤城人，东北大学毕业后赴德国留学，在柏林大学、洪堡大学学习，后与张学良女儿张闾瑛结婚，时为布雷斯劳大学（Universität Breslau）讲师，其著作 *Chinas Geist und Kraft* 直译为《中国：精神与力量》，1935 年出版。傅吾康对打字稿略有修改，落款处为其签名。该函寄送熊式一处收转。

十一月二十三日

先生及夫人抵达牛津。〔University of California, Berkeley, The Bancroft Library, Yuen Ren Chao papers, carton 10, folder 39, Yuan, Tongli and Yuan, Huixi〕

按：夫人曾致信赵元任、杨步伟夫妇，告知巴黎别后经过。

十一月二十八日　伦敦

先生致信赵元任夫妇，告知返美计划并谈在英近况。

元任先生、夫人：

数日前曾上一书，计已达览。顷由牛津转来手教，拜悉一一。关于移民局取缔益严一节，弟等在荷兰时亦见该报，诸承关怀，感谢无似。弟等拟于 Re-entry 期满之前一月离此返美，并预将护照有效期限由"大使馆"延长一年，如此则一切无问题矣。伦敦天气甚暖，迄今并未下雾，可称幸事。日内拟赴剑桥查书。兹奉上日人仓石近著见后中国语之书名，想加大或已入藏矣。余容再陈，顺颂俪安。

弟同礼顿首

内人附笔问候

十一月廿八

仓石武四郎《中国语初级教本》,东京岩波书店发行。

子杰兄赐书拜悉,谢谢,祈代问候。

〔University of California, Berkeley, The Bancroft Library, Yuen Ren

Chao papers, carton 10, folder 39, Yuan, Tongli and Yuan, Huixi〕

按:"仓石近著"全称为《ラテン化新文字による中国语初级教
本》(依据拉丁化新文字的汉语初级教科书),1953 年岩波书店
出版。

十一月三十日　牛津

先生覆信傅吾康,就王铃情绪不稳定略作解释,并表示有可能前往剑桥与
之面谈,请协助查明中国留德博士的姓名,另询洪涛生的联系地址。

13 Portland Road

Oxford, England

30th November, 1954

Dear Dr. Franke:

Thank you very much indeed for your letter of November 18 which
has been waiting me here. I remained at Leiden and the Hague too long
which prevented me from returning England sooner.

I am interested in what you say about the Durham episode. I knew
nothing about it. All I know is that since Mr. Wang was divorced by his
wife, he has not been very happy. There is doubt that that he will work
very hard under your direction and a change of environment may do him
good. I shall probably go to Cambridge after Christmas and will find out
whether Mr. Wang is able to leave his post. Personal contact would be
better than correspondence.

While in Marburg, I had a good time with Alfred Hoffmann who
showed me the "Nachrichten" published in Hamburg. Could you be good
enough to ask the publisher to send me a copy regularly with his bill? I
should like to keep in close touch with the scientific work going on in

Germany and this journal seems to be the best one I have so far seen.

I enclose a list of Chinese students who wrote their dissertations in German. Since you have students from China who remained in Germany for many years, it is possible that they might know their Chinese names. May I ask you to find them for me? Much obliged.

I hear that Mr. Hundhausen has returned to Germany and I shall be grateful if you would inform me his address. If you happen to know sinological scholars in Denmark and Finland, will you let me know their names.

I shall be here until early in February and I hope to hear good news from time to time. With sincere regards to you and Mrs. Franke.

Yours sincerely,

〔University of Chicago Library, Yuan T'ung-li Papers, Box 2〕

按：Nachrichten 直译作"消息"，具体所指待考。此件为底稿。

十二月六日

先生致信戴密微，感谢在巴黎期间给予的帮助和招待，并寄上陈寅恪近作目录，请香港书商代为购买并寄送。

6th December, 1954

Dear Professor Demiéville:

I wish to thank you once more for your courtesy and assistance extended to me during my recent visit. I am most grateful to you for the sympathetic support you have given me in connection with my work. Although it is a labour of love, one is apt to get discouraged if other scholars do not attach any importance to his labours.

During my travels I have misplaced the slip containing the titles of recent works by Professor 　　　　who is now in Peking. I give the titles below, and I have asked a bookstore in Hong Kong to mail them to you direct, if they could obtain copies from the mainland.

Whenever you have time, I shall appreciate to have from you a bibliographical list of your writings on China including periodical articles. Such a list would help me a great deal in my work.

Under separate cover, I am sending you a copy of a recent work on patterned silk in China. I trust that you may like to have it for your own collection.

With Season's greetings and warmest regards,

Yours sincerely,

T. L. Yuan

〔University of Chicago Library, Yuan T'ung-li Papers, Box 3〕

按:该件录副,空白处付诸阙如,应填写陈寅恪。参见本年 12 月 25 日戴密微函,可推知先生此信寄出之件亦忘记在底部注明陈寅恪近作篇目。

十二月八日

先生致信德礼贤神父,请其协助编纂意大利文中有中国的书目,并建议其为《天主教入华史》第四卷向美国学术机构申请资助。

December 8, 1954

Dear Professor D' Elia:

May I thank you once more for the reprints of your scholarly articles which you have been good enough to send to me? Your courtesy and kind remembrance has been gratefully appreciated.

I have been trying to compile a list of books in Italian relating to China. I feel that no one would give me the necessary advice and assistance than your good self. I shall limit the scope to books published during the last twenty-five years (1920 – 1954). As the □□□□□ □□□□□ are so numerous, I have to do the work at a later date, although I fully realize that they are more important than books.

As Italian literature on China is very important, I would like to make the list as complete as possible. Since the collection of such literature in British and American libraries is very poor, may I seek your expert assistance in this matter?

I have already written the titles of these books on cards with as much as bibliographical information as I can gather. If you would be good enough to look over these cards and supply the missing titles, I shall be glad to send the cards to you. With them, it would save you a great deal of time.

I have great admiration for your scientific work, and I know you would be willing to help me out if you could spare some time for it. Will you kindly let me hear from you?

So far, I have not seen volume 4 of your monumental work on Ricci and I have been wondering whether it has been published. If the Libreria dello Stato is in need of financial assistance in publishing the forthcoming volumes, may I suggest that you apply for a grant from one of the American cultural institutions? It may not bring immediate results, but it is worth trying. I have in mind the Harvard-Yenching Institute which has much money but is planning to spend it in India, since China is now closed for the time being. Could you let me know how many more volumes are being planned?

I trust that you are enjoying excellent health and I wish to send my sincere greetings of the Season,

Yours sincerely,

T. L. Yuan

〔University of Chicago Library, Yuan T'ung-li Papers, Box 3〕

按：your monumental work on Ricci 应指《天主教入华史》(*Storia dell'introduzione del Cristianesimo in Cina*, Roma: Libreria dello Stato, 1942-1949)，该书的最初名称实为《利玛窦资料：有关利玛窦以及欧洲与中国早期关系的原始文件（1579-1615）》(*Fonti Ricciane: documenti originali concernenti Matteo Ricci e la storia delle prime relazioni tra l'Europa e la Cina, 1579-1615*)。[①] Libreria dello Stato 即意大利国家图书馆。此件为录副。

十二月十四日

先生致信赵元任、杨步伟夫妇，寄上礼物，并告知在英暂住地。

元任先生、夫人：

日子过的真快，眼看两位就要返美，想收拾行李一定很忙。日前

---

① 宋黎明《利玛窦研究资料汇释梳理》，《文汇报》，2017 年 12 月 29 日。

我们寄些小礼物,并有一件毛衣送给 Kanta,望携回转交。如需要任何英国物品并盼示知,以便寄至船上。我们近在此觅到一所临时 Flat13 Portland Road, Oxford,较住旅馆便宜的多,大约在离此前不致再迁移了。此间天天下雨,但天气并不太冷,想巴黎天气不致如此之坏。子杰兄在名师指导之下,成绩定必大有进步。他的小孩谅已返法,一定非常热闹。你们多位小姐,想常有信来,谅均安好为念。专此,敬候俪安。

同礼、慧熙拜上
十二,十四

〔University of California, Berkeley, The Bancroft Library, Yuen Ren Chao papers, carton 10, folder 39, Yuan, Tongli and Yuan, Huixi〕

按:"Kanta"应为 Canta,即赵元任的外孙女卞昭波,其母为赵元任大女儿赵如兰,父亲是卞学鐄。"他的小孩"应指郭成吉。

德礼贤神父覆函先生,略谈《天主教入华史》第四卷尚未完成的原因,并请协助获取国会图书馆的中文资料,表示愿意竭尽所能协助先生编撰意大利文有关中国的书籍目录。

December, 14th, 1954

Dear Dr. Yuan:

It was a great and pleasing surprise to receive your letter of December the 8th. Many thanks for it.

For a long time I had been wondering about your whereabouts, and at the end I got news from one of my friends in the United States that you were working in the Library of Congress and that you were busy in continuing the *Bibliotheca Sinica* of Cordier. I then sent you, somewhere in June or this year, some recent reprints of my articles. But as I did not hear from you, I wondered where they had finally gone. Then in September I wrote a letter to your address in Cambridge, Mass. in America. But again, no answer. This will explain why your recent letter was received, as I said, with pleasing surprise.

Volume IV of my work on Ricci has not come out. One of the main reasons is the lack of practical assistance in making researches in Chinese books, which are not available here in Rome. For the preceding volumes, you helped me very much, while you were in Peking. Since you left there, although I tried it was not possible for me to get in touch with the new men of the Central Library. Now that you are working at the Library of Congress, would it not be possible to find some help of the same kind among those who are working under your leadership? This surely would be very much appreciated by me and would make the issue of the coming volumes possible. Please let me hear from you about this special query. With the recent inventions of films, this kind of research work might be easier than formerly.

Several other volumes should come out; how many will I be able to prepare myself I don't dare to say; the more, the better.

Financial assistance also is needed, and I thank you for your suggestion. If you have practical suggestions to make, giving names and addresses, I would appreciate them very much. Chinese publications with Chinese characters in Europe are very expensive and unless some cultural Institutions helps the authors, they cannot see their works published.

As I owe so much to you, I am willing to help you, as much as I can, for the revision of your cards. Are you not coming to Rome before you go back to America? If so, we may talk about the matter, when you come here. If you come, much help might be given to you perhaps from the catalogue of the Vatican Library and other Libraries. If not, the thing might be more difficult. But as I said I will do as much as I can. The only difficulty is time, as I am alone without any assistant. Besides lectures here in the Gregorian University and in the Roman State University I have other works, especially on Ricci, by the hands. Anyhow when what has to be done will be clearly settled, we may talk again about it.

I thank you very much for your kind greetings I am glad to return you a hundredfold,

yours very sincerely

Prof. Pasquale D'Elia

〔袁同礼家人提供〕

　　　　按:此件为打字稿,落款处为其签名。

十二月十八日

先生致信钱存训,略述最近在欧洲考察经过,并请协助核对近年来发表著述之中国学者信息。

　　公垂吾兄著席:

　　　　近三月来在大陆旅行,疲倦不堪,故未能早日函达,想尊处正写论文,亦必甚忙。前年长沙发掘结果曾发现古文字,于书史颇有关系,前曾建议由尊处函徐森老索取资料,不知已有复音否? 牛津有一位 G. Bownas 近研究"竹书纪年",对此问题亦有兴趣也。九月间曾寄上书一套四册,托为代售,想已脱手。近见国内外我国学者著作多种,内中大部分之中文姓名均已查出,仅有一小部分尚待查明(芝大如有中国同学录,并望代搜集一份)。兹奉上一单,请就所知者加注中文,其不详者能否在各工具书中代为一查。日人桥川时雄所编《中国时人姓名录》及日外务部所编之《人名录》,此间均未入藏,极感不便。如尊处无法查明,即希将原单转寄吴子明兄处,托其代查。弟大约两月以内可以返美,统俟再函。最近始由荷兰返英,行装尚未整理也。顺颂近安,并贺年禧。

　　　　　　　　　　　　　　　　　　　　　　弟同礼顿首

　　　　　　　　　　　　　　　　　　　　　　十二月十八日

　　　　　　　　　　　　　　　　　　　　　　〔钱孝文藏札〕

　　　　按:G. Bownas 即 Geoffrey Bownas(1923-2011),1954 年在牛津
　　　　大学任日语讲师。

十二月二十一日

先生致信霍福民,转告中国新书出版消息,并请告 *Nachrichten* 全称以便订购。

　　　　　　　　　　　　　　　　　　　　December 21, 1954

Dear Dr. Hoffmann:

　　When I was at your house in October, you inquired about new publications on issued in China. I have just seen a notice about a scholarly publication which I wish to pass on to you. The full title is as follow:

I hope to write to Dr. Seuberlich in a day or two and I shall give more titles of recent scholarly works which you should have at Marburg. If you need any current material for your research, please do let me know. I shall be only too glad to be of some service to you.

When in Marburg, you showed me a publication "*Nachrichten*" der ⋯⋯ which is a report on the progress of Far Eastern studies in Germany. You had an extra copy of one of the issues and you were kind enough to let me have it, but in a hurry, I forgot to being it along. Will you let me know the full name and where I can send my subscription? I had the impression that it is published in Hamburg.

Have you published any additional books since I had the pleasure of seeing you? If you could keep me informed about your writings, I shall be grateful.

We expect to return to the United States in February. Mrs. Yuan joins me in sending you our very best wishes for a Merry Christmas and happy New Year,

Yours sincerely,

〔University of Chicago Library, Yuan T'ung-li Papers, Box 4〕

按：此件为底稿，空行处付诸阙如。

先生致信 Luís Gonzaga Gomes，询问 Vocabulario Português-Cantonense 出版社及其所有著作的清单，并请其协助编纂澳门 Imprensa Nacional 出版目录。

December 21, 1954

Dear Dr. Gomes:

When I lived in Hong Kong, I saw your very useful Portuguese-Cantonese dictionary. But I forgot the name of the publisher. Will you be kind enough to inform me, as this dictionary is not found in the library at Oxford.

I understand that your translation of the *Ou Mun Kei Leok* had been published. As I am compiling a list of scholarly works on Macau, I should like to include all of your writings. Will you kindly inform me the titles of your other books besides these two? I shall greatly appreciate your assistance.

May I ask you to let me know your name in Chinese? Also, the names of other scholars in Macau who have written books on Macau and the Portuguese in China. Although I have not met Mr. Braga, I know his writings and his interest in the history of Macau.

Since the Imprensa Nacional at Macau does not have a list of their publications, I wonder whether you would like to compile one which would be extremely useful for future reference.

Another matter which I like to inquire is whether there is a good library in Macau where one can find all the books on Macau published both in Macau and Lisbon. I am most anxious to get such a list and I should like to have assistance such from a scholar as yourself.

Thanking you once more for your courtesy and assistance,

Yours sincerely,

T. L. Yuan

P. S. Could you inform me how many issues of the *"Noticias de Macau"* have been published and on what date was the first issue published?

〔University of Chicago Library, Yuan T'ung-li Papers, Box 2〕

按:Luís Gonzaga Gomes(1907-1976),澳门土生葡萄牙人,汉学家,中文名高美士。Portuguese-Cantonese dictionary 应指 *Vocabulário Português-Cantonense*(《葡粤辞典》),1941 年 Imprensa Nacional 初版;*Ou Mun Kei Leok* 即其用葡萄牙文翻译的《澳门纪略》,原书由清代澳门海防军民同知印光任、张汝霖编撰,1751 年成书,葡译本于 1950 年 Imprensa Nacional 初版。Imprensa Nacional at Macau 通译作澳门官印局;*Noticias de Macau* 直译为《澳门新闻》,其出版情况待考。

吴光清覆函先生,告国会图书馆东方部尚未任命主任,并谈严文郁应林语堂之邀,计划前往新加坡协助筹办南洋大学。

守和吾兄大鉴:

接奉手示,藉悉旅况多佳,至以为慰。东方部主任至今尚未任命,仍由 Poleman 等轮流代理,据闻请求该位置者达四十余人(Poleman 为其一),因节省经费暂缓发表。关于尊处洛氏补助费留难者实非 Poleman,而系由 Dubester 作祟(彼新任 Bib. & Ref. Div. 主任及出版委员会主席,所有关于目录及出版事宜均由其主管,王重民之目录当然在内),此人小人得志,颇难谈话。过去接洽函件彼处存有一份,因而留难,曾用电话解释数次无效。所致函尊处仅由 Poleman 出名,实际上与彼无关也。Beal 已去远东现在日本,约明春方返。彼曾表示愿放弃日本部分改就中文部,将来或由彼兼两部分。馆事仍纷繁,所余 ECA 马、王二人可延至五六月底。此 Program 结束时,严文郁已应林语堂邀,在 U.N. 告假一年,至南洋筹备南洋大学图书馆,年初首途(一人前往,家眷留美)。附来书单已查过,兹附还。前寄书一包,已收到,现存敝处。美京一切如常,颇为沉寂。匆匆,顺祝年禧,并祝双安。

弟光清上

十二月廿一

〔袁同礼家人提供〕

按:Beal 即 Edwin G. Beal, Jr.(1913-2002),1933 年获卫斯理大学学士学位,后赴日教授英文,随即在朝鲜半岛和中国东北、北平等地游历,曾在燕京大学西文系任教,1938 年归国入哥伦比亚大学,1941 年获东亚系硕士学位,旋即入国会图书馆服务,太平洋战争爆发后被任命为日文部负责人,1950 年获得哥伦比亚大学博士学位[1],1955 年至 1958 年兼任中文部、日文部负责人,1974 年退休,本谱中依李霖灿等人译作"毕尔"。"马、王二人"似指马在天、王隐三。

十二月二十二日

先生致信 Robert Hans van Gulik,以未能在海牙相见表示歉意,寄上蒋彝《金宝与花熊》与其子女,并询问其在日本刊行的小说或房中术译著。

December 22, 1954

---

[1] Richard C. Howard, In Memoriam: Edwin G. Beal, Jr. (1913−2002), *Journal of East Asian Libraries*, Vol 2003, No. 130, p. 70.

Dear Dr. Gulik:

I was very sorry to have missed you and Mrs. Gulik when we were in the Hague on two Sundays. Dr. Hsu Mo told me that you were usually not home on Sundays and I regret that I did not write to you a few days earlier.

Learning that all you children read Dutch fluently, I am sending you a copy of Chiang Yee's *Chin-Pao, en de reuzenpanda's* It may be of some interest to your children.

I hear that you have published quite a bit since we met in Chungking. If the novel in Chinese published in Singapore is still available, I should like to have a copy. Besides the *Trifling tale of a Spring Dream* and the *Erotic Color Prints of the Ming Period*, both of which I saw in the Library of Congress, what other books you published in Japan?

We are here in England for a short stay and we plan to leave for the United States early in February. Mrs. Yuan joins me in sending you and Mrs. Gulik our sincere greetings for a Merry Christmas and Happy New Year.

Yours sincerely,

T. L. Yuan

〔University of Chicago Library, Yuan T'ung-li Papers, Box 3〕

按:Robert Hans van Gulik(1910-1967),荷兰汉学家、小说家、外交官,中文名高罗佩,其夫人为水世芳(1912—2005),祖籍江苏阜宁,出生于北平,父亲水钧韶是外交官,她与高罗佩共有四位子女。Dr. Hsu Mo 即徐谟,时任联合国国际法庭法官,常驻海牙。Chiang Yee's *Chin-Pao, en de reuzenpanda's* 即蒋彝绘著《金宝与花熊》荷兰文本,该书原为英文(*Chin-Pao and the Giant Pandas*),1939 年在伦敦初版,1954 年在阿姆斯特丹出版荷兰文本。*Trifling Tale of a Spring Dream* 即《春梦琐言》、*Erotic Color Prints of the Ming Period* 即《秘戏图考》,分别于 1950 年、1951 年在日本限量刊行,除此两种外,还有 *Dee Goong An, three murder cases solved by Judge Dee*(《狄公案》)也是在日本印行。此件为录副。

十二月二十五日

先生致信 Walther Heissig，告已致信北京友人询问嵩祝寺所存清雍正年间官刻汉字《大藏经》之雕版下落，并请其寄送著作目录。

December 25, 1954

Dear Dr. Heissig:

　　You may recall that at the Orientalists Congress you inquired about the wooden blocks preserved at the Sung Chu Ss'u. I wrote to my friends in Peking, but so far, no reply has been received. Eventually I hope to break through the bamboo curtain, so that definite word can be obtained.

　　I am trying to compile a list of German scholarly works in the field of sinological studies. Just the other day I saw one of your articles printed in the Serta Cantabrigiensia which would have escaped my attention if I did not see that journal. Since your articles are scattered in so many journals, I wonder if you could send me a fairly complete list of your writings. I shall also appreciate your courtesy if you could send the reprints of your articles, if you have no time to compile a list.

　　I have wanted to come to Göttingen to pay you a visit, but as my British visa expires very soon, I have to return to the United States early in February. I do hope to hear from you before I leave.

　　With best wishes for a Merry Christmas and Happy New Year,

Yours sincerely,

T. L. Yuan

〔University of Chicago Library, Yuan T'ung-li Papers, Box 4〕

按：Walther Heissig(1913-2005)，奥地利汉学家，中文名海西希，专攻蒙古学，1941 年在维也纳获得博士学位，后来华在辅仁大学任教并赴内蒙古考察，时在哥廷根大学任教，1957 年则转往波恩。Sung Chu Ss'u 即嵩祝寺，藏传佛教格鲁派寺院，清康熙五十一年(1712)敕令修建。雍正十一年(1733)，清朝惟一官刻汉字《大藏经》开刻，历时 6 年完成，其后刻板存放于该寺，该寺在庚子事变时遭受劫掠。此件为录副。

戴密微覆函先生，告因接待中国知识界女性代表团而得知陈寅恪、王重民、
顾颉刚、高名凯等人近况，并询问何处可以购得《图书季刊》英文本四十年
代的各卷期。

Christmas, 1954

Dear Dr. Yuan:

Many thanks for your letter and for the beautiful plates on patterned silk. It was a pleasure to see you in our old Paris and to hear about the great work you have undertaken. Dr. Y. R. Chao has succeeded you here; I read with much interest the autobiography of his wife with all the recollections concerning many people whom I knew or read. Tempi passata!

You forgot to list the recent works of Prof. Ch'en Yin-ch'üe at the end of your letter, but many thanks for having written about them to Hongkong. Recently we received officially a delegation of Chinese ladies from Peking belonging to university circles. They told me that Prof. Ch'en is still at Chung-shan Ta-hsüh in Canton, not in Peking. They said that my old friend Wang Chung-min is all right. Ku Chieh-kang is back in Peking, running a book-shop if I understood right. Kao Ming-k'ai the linguist, who worked with me here, is busy translating the complete works of Balzac.

Herewith a list of my publications, certainly incomplete.

Wishing you a happy New Year and all success in your great work, I remain,

Very sincerely yours,

P. Demiéville

Is there a possibility to get somewhere the numbers of your *Quarterly Bulletin of Chinese Bibliography* (Chinese edition before all) published since 1940?

〔University of Chicago Library, Yuan T'ung-li Papers, Box 3〕

按：the autobiography of his wife 应指杨步伟所作《一个女人的自传》。

十二月二十九日　牛津

先生撰写 Supplement to Cordier's Bibliotheca Sinica Progress Report, 包括 Completion of Part 1, Section 1、Scope Enlarged、Some of the Difficulties、Further Support Necessary 四部分。〔袁同礼家人提供〕

一九五五年　六十一岁

一月三日

先生致信戴密微，告将为其留意《图书季刊》中英文本，建议联系莱顿的克恩研究所，另请其协助辨识留法学生中文姓名。

January 3, 1955

Dear Professor Demiéville:

　　Thank you so much for your letter. The recent works of Professor Ch'en Yin-ch'üe are given below. Recently a Chinese bookshop was opened in London, being a part of Collets Book-shop at 48 Great Russel Street, London, W. C. 1. A new catalogue in Chinese is in the process of being reprinted and I have asked the manager to mail you a copy as soon as it is ready.

　　As to the *Quarterly Bulletin of Chinese Bibliography*, one can occasionally find them in the market abroad. I shall look for both editions for you. In Leiden, there are two sets, one at the Sinological Institute, the other at the Kern Institute. Since Kern Institute may not like to keep the Chinese edition, I wonder if they are willing to exchange with French publications.

　　I mailed you in London a copy of a recent work on a graduate of the National Peking University, who utilized the reprint of the
which we published in Peking in 1947-48. I thought it might be useful to you and to M. Wang Lien-tseng who is working on the same work under your direction.

　　When I was in Paris, I copied down the titles of these published by Chinese students who have studied in France. I have been able to ascertain the Chinese names of most of them. There are still some ninety names to be identified. It is possible that among them there are many of your students whose names you might remember. For those whose Chinese names cannot be ascertained, could you pass the list on to Messra. Wang Lien-tseng, Li Tche-houa and those students who remained in Paris for a long time. Any assistance from you and your students will be much appreciated.

Since I could not extend my visa, I have to return to the United States on the 10th February. After that date, my address will be care of my daughter, Miss Ching Yuan, Converse Laboratory, Harvard University, Cambridge, Mass. I hope to hear from you before I leave England.

With best wishes for the year 1955,

Yours sincerely,

〔University of Chicago Library, Yuan T'ung-li Papers, Box 3〕

按：Wang Lien-tseng 即王联曾,早年入中法大学,时在法国留学;Li Tche-houa 即李治华(1915—?),1937 年毕业于中法大学,后赴法留学,时在法工作,翻译《红楼梦》。此件为底稿,空白处应填写汉字——切韵。

先生致信德礼贤神父,告知自己并未在国会图书馆担任正式职员,如需查找相关中文资料请联系东方部的代理主任,并谈《西文汉学书目》(考狄书目续编)意大利文部分所需帮助,及哈佛燕京学社、洛克菲勒基金会的联系方式。

January 3, 1955

Dear Father D' Elia:

Many thanks for your letter of December 14. I am so happy to hear that everything goes so well with you. It is most important that the result of your research on Ricci should continue to be published.

The Library of Congress has a good collection of the collected works of Ming scholars who were contemporary of Ricci. If you would send your inquiries to Dr. Horace I. Poleman, Acting Chief of the Orientalia Division of that Library, he will ask his Chinese assistants to look up the information for you. At present, I am serving merely as Consultant to that Library and have no administrative duties.

Yes, I have been working on the Supplement to Cordier. It is a thankless task and I do not know how soon I can complete it. At present I am concerned only with books, not periodical articles which are so numerous but more important than books. I am grateful to you for your readiness to help me out in Italian titles. Such an aid from such a distinguished scholar means a great deal to me, and I shall acknowledge it in the preface. I have collected most of the titles of Italian contribution to sinology and I shall mail you the cards in a few days. Kindly look them over and add new titles as you could find them in the Vatican Library. If you are too busy with your own research, perhaps you could find one of your students who may like to check over these cards at his spare time. I shall be glad to offer him English books published in the United States, or offer him a little honorarium if he prefers. May I leave the matter to you?

The reprints you were kind enough to send me in June have all been received. Thank you so much for your courtesy and kindness. But I did not receive your letter mailed in September. If there is anything in that letter you wanted me to do, please let me know.

My former assistants now working in the Library of Congress would be very glad to help you in your research. Any passage or any chapter you want to be microfilmed can be done very easily. So please write direct to Dr. Poleman who will give orders to his assistants.

As to financial assistance, I think you may like to approach the Harvard-Yenching Institute, Cambridge, Massachusetts, USA, whose director is Prof. Serge Elisséeff. The Institute sometimes gives grant-in-aid to outside scholars in the field of sinology, provided an English summary is attached to your main work. The policy of the Institute however, often changes, but there is no harm to try.

The other possibility would be for the Rector of your University to apply for financial assistance from the Rockefeller Foundation, 49 West 49th Street, New York 29, N. Y. Dr. Charles B. Fahs is the Director of Humanities. The Foundation does not deal with individual scholars, but only with institutions. If your university sponsors your project, it will have better results. I would therefore suggest that you write up a memorandum and hand it to your Rector. If he could write to Dr. Fahs on your behalf, it would meet the requirements of the Foundation. In other words, the Foundation would hold the University responsible for the completion of the project.

I have to return to the United States on February 10 and I regret that I shall not be able to see you on this trip. But I am sure that we shall meet before very long. Meanwhile, may I thank you once more for your assistance and assure you that I shall always be glad to be of any service to you in connection with your research.

With sincere greetings,

Yours sincerely,

T. L. Yuan

〔University of Chicago Library, Yuan T'ung-li Papers, Box 3〕

按：此件录副。

一月四日

先生致信李书华，请其协助查明留学法国的博士生中文姓名。

润章先生著席：

前在 *Oriens Extremus* 杂志拜读大著，引证极详，至为钦佩。献岁以来，想起居胜常，定符所祝。弟在德历游名城，印象至佳，惜限于时间未能到汉堡耳。在巴黎住一月，将留法同学发表之论文编一目录，内中大多数之中文姓名均已查明，尚有九十余人询诸"大使馆"陈雄飞君，渠亦不知。因念内中必有尊处之门弟子或其他熟人，爰将名单送上，即希加注其中文姓名，其不详者能否转询其他留法同学予以查明，种种费神，感谢不尽。弟定于下月中旬返美，届时当再面谢。该名单即存尊处，无须寄回也。顺颂俪安。尊夫人同此问安。

弟同礼顿首

内人嘱笔问候

壹月四日

〔Columbia University Libraries Archival Collections, Shuhua Li Papers, 1926-1972, Volume II: Modern Eminent Chinese Leaders〕

按：*Oriens Extremus* 现通译为《远东学报》，该刊为德国汉学家傅吾康等人在 1954 年创刊；李书华的文章题名为 Première mention de l'application de la boussole à la navigation，发表于该刊第 1 卷第 1 期。陈雄飞（1911—2004），上海人，震旦大学获法学博士后留学法国，获巴黎大学国际法法学博士学位。

高罗佩覆函先生，告知其在海牙的联系地址，并寄赠近著及《秘戏图考》中文自序和其他著作。

January 4, 1955

Dear Dr. Yuan:

Thanks very much for your kind letter. I do hope that we shall have an occasion for meeting you and Mrs. Yuan here in the Hauge; our home address is Vivien Straat 14, the Hauge, and our telephone 552446. If you let us know when you are about to visit Holland again, we shall be very glad indeed to show you some of the sights here.

My two elder boys (10 and 8) were delighted with the "Reuzen-panda"; many thanks for this kind gift!

Enclosed I am sending you a copy of my Chinese novel; my aim in publishing it was to draw the attention of modern Chinese writers of fictions to the rich possibilities offered by ancient Chinese crime literature. If this material would be handled by an abler pen than mine, we might get a kind of modernized Chinese genre of detective novel preferable to the clumsy Chinese versions of American thrillers one sees now on the market in Hongkong and in the Nanyang.

I am also enclosing the text of my Chinese preface to my book on Ming colour prints; some of my Chinese friends were opposed to my publishing that book, even in a very limited edition, but I think my point is stated clearly in this preface.

With all our best wishes for the New Year I remain, dear Dr. Yuan,

Yours most sincerely,

R. H.van Gulik

I also enclose a few readings words I had published here.

〔University of Chicago Library, Yuan T'ung-li Papers, Box 3〕

按：a copy of my Chinese novel 应指《棠阴比事》英译本(*T'ang-Yin-Pi-Shih: Parallel Cases from under the Pear-Tree, a 13th century manual of jurisprudence and detection translated from the original Chinese with an introduction and notes*)，1956 年在莱顿出版。my Chinese preface to my book on Ming colour prints 即《秘戏图考》的自序,高罗佩 1951 年初夏写就。此件为打字稿,落款处及补语为其亲笔。

一月五日

先生致片赵元任夫妇,告知返美行程。

元任先生、夫人：

近日尊处收拾行李,想必忙的不堪。后日,船抵英国南岸,我们本想到码头话别,近以铁路工人即将罢工,不敢出门,希望不致扩大,否则或须影响我们的行程。我们定妥二月十号开行之"United States",十五抵纽约,澄儿亦得到入美签证,同船返美。知念并闻,统俟面谈。并祝一路顺风!

同礼、慧熙拜上

五日

〔University of California, Berkeley, The Bancroft Library, Yuen Ren Chao papers, carton 10, folder 39, Yuan, Tongli and Yuan, Huixi〕

戴密微致片先生,感谢寄赠《切韵音系》并问罗振玉旧藏书籍现状。

Dear Dr Yuan,

Many many thanks for 切韵音系. A student of mine is working on 王仁昫's 切韵 and will be delighted to see this work. With all best wishes & regards, yours sincerely P. Demiéville

If you have time once, could you tell me what became of 罗振玉's collections?

5/1/55, 234 Bd Raspail, XIV

〔University of Chicago Library, Yuan T'ung-li Papers, Box 3〕

按：《切韵音系》系"《语言学专刊》第四种",李荣著,1952 年 5 月中国科学院初版。该片为其亲笔。

一月六日

先生致信胡适,告知最近在欧访查资料的收获及归期安排。

　　适之先生:

　　　　上月廿三日寄上一书,恭贺新年并报告在欧之工作,嗣见此间邮局通告,谓廿三、廿四两日由英寄美函件,以飞机失事无法运到,想该信亦在其中。此次所得资料尚称丰富,内中英法德意荷西班牙葡萄牙文者大致完成,正在整理中,自当先予出版。近接张晓峰先生来信,谓"教部"愿为出版,嘱于六月以内将稿件寄至台北,盛意可感。惟此书包括各国文字,必须亲自校对方始放心,将来如在美印行,仍赖先生赞助,并盼赐一序文,不胜感谢! 近已定妥返美船票,二月中旬可抵纽约,届时当再面陈。叶良材兄处,已托其于发放补助费时径寄华京 Riggs 银行代收矣。专此,敬颂俪安,并贺新釐。尊夫人同此问安。

同礼敬叩

一月六日

内人附笔拜年

〔台北胡适纪念馆,档案编号 HS-US01-032-011〕

　　按:张其昀(1901—1985),字晓峰,浙江鄞县人,史学家、地学家及教育家,南京高等师范学校毕业,时任"教育部"部长。

一月十五日

先生致信赵元任夫妇,告知已向汉堡大学、马来亚大学推荐王铃出任教席。

　　元任先生、夫人:

　　　　日前奉到一月六日赐书,拜悉种切。德国汉堡大学中文讲师一席,前已推荐王铃(Needham 助手),王君正在考虑。兹马来亚大学又招聘中文讲师,待遇每年壹千四百至壹千八百镑并担任来往旅费,较汉堡尤佳,故弟又推荐王铃前往,不识能如愿否? 你们到康桥后应酬必多,谅必甚忙,我们下月中旬到纽约,或能来康桥,届时当再面谈一切。你们所乘之船,想无风浪,曾晕船否? 均在念中。专此,敬颂俪安。

弟袁同礼顿首

内人附笔问安

一月十五

〔University of California, Berkeley, The Bancroft Library, Yuen Ren Chao papers, carton 10, folder 39, Yuan, Tongli and Yuan, Huixi〕

按：无论是汉堡大学还是马来亚大学，王铃均未前往就职，而是赴澳大利亚任教。

一月十七日

海西希覆函先生，感谢代为询问嵩祝寺所藏雕版，并寄送部分文章的抽印本。

Göttingen, the 17th January 1955

Dear Doctor Yuan:

Thank you so much for your kind letter. It has been very kind of you to remember my quest concerning the whereabouts of the wooden blocks which had been formerly kept at the Sung Chu Ss'u. Attached you will find a list of my recent publications. I hope it is of a little use to you. Unfortunately I have most of them no reprints left. Only of three I am able to send you offprints.

I am awfully sorry that you could not visit Göttingen, but hope that sooner or later we might meet again. Let me return your good wishes for a happy new year.

Yours sincerely

W. Heissig

〔University of Chicago Library, Yuan T'ung-li Papers, Box 4〕

按：此件为打字稿，落款处为其签名，以航空信方式寄送牛津先生寓所。

一月十八日

杭立武致电先生，告知平馆在台所存文物将移交"中央图书馆"管理。

守和兄鉴：

"教育部"令将北平图书馆文物箱转交"中央图书馆"，前已函达，未奉复示。兹以迭奉催办，无法再延，特再电告。

弟立武。

〔University of Chicago Library, Yuan T'ung-li Papers, Box 2〕

按：此电发往纽约"使领馆"，并由此转交。先生在该件电报上标注"北平馆务弟早已摆脱，该馆存台文物自可由部会商台端统筹支配"。

吴光清覆函先生，告知所托查询各件结果，并谈国会图书馆对先生申请洛克菲勒基金会继续赞助编纂《西文汉学书目》(考狄书目续编)之初步意见。

守和吾兄大鉴：

三日手示奉悉，附件嘱查列后：

(一)李石曾先生托查吴稚晖著三书，L. C.均未然入藏。

(二)查哈佛燕京学社编之《四十七种宋代传记综合引得》，沈周之名并未列入，字号引得部分亦无性甫之名，中国画家参考书数种均查过，亦无所得。

(三)陈伯达之《近代地租概谈》系中文本，馆中无英文本。

(四)Tsin Ben-li 中文姓名查不出。

(五)Hono Ming-tse 书不在书库，中文姓名无法查。

(六)Hsiang Ying 中文名为项英。

钱存训兄附来名单，因事冗尚未查毕，俟兄到华盛顿时交卷。关于请求继续洛氏补助金，上星期 Poleman、Adkinson、Dubester 等曾开会讨论，据 Poleman 谓彼已提出，现由 Dubester 查已往案件再致函 Fahs，惟 D 不大好讲话，不知彼是否有其他花样。东方部主任据闻本月内可发表，以 Poleman 希望最大，但闻逐鹿者众，不知临时又有变动否。美京住处现觅较易。Beal 现在日本，约五月间返。余不一一。匆匆，顺祝双安。

弟光清上

一，一八

〔袁同礼家人提供〕

一月二十日

先生覆信傅吾康，婉拒其邀请自己在德教授汉语基础课程，仍推荐王铃，并寄上加入德国东亚自然与民族学会的申请表，另请代购纯银烟盒。

January 20, 1955

Dear Dr. Franke:

Thank you so much for your kind letter of 14th January and for the trouble you have taken in finding out the names of some Chinese students who have studied in Germany. Your assistance is very much appreciated.

I do not recall that Mrs. Chao mentioned to me about the work at Hamburg University. She only dropped me a card to say that she had greatly enjoyed her visit. As you know, I have been trying to complete my work on a Supplement to Cordier. There is no end of it, it seems to me. So, I plan to be working at Washington for the next two years, so that at least the first part might be published. I have collected a great deal of information during my recent trip to Germany, but I need more from time to time. I shall count upon you for further information in the future.

For your teaching work, I still feel that a younger man with scientific training like Mr. Wang would be more preferrable. Although I would like to spend several years in Germany in view of the high standard of German scholarship, I do not think I like to teach young men with the elements of the Chinese language. However, I appreciate very much your kind remembrance of an old friend and I do want to thank you for your kindness.

I enclose my application for membership in the Gesellschaft für Natur and Völkerkunde Ostasiens and I shall send my fees to the Gesellschaft as soon as I receive the bill. I am leaving for the United States after three weeks' time and my temporary address will be as follows: c/o Miss Ching Yuan, Converse Laboratory, Harvard University, Cambridge, Mass.

Many of my friends here liked the cigarette cases which I bought in Wiesbaden. Three of them costed DM 38.25. The dealer allowed some discount, so the total for the three costed DM 37. I now enclose $ 10.00 and I shall be much obliged to you if you or Mrs. Franke could ask the dealer to mail them to me, possible by air, to the following address: Dr. T. L. Yuan, Passenger, S. S. "The United States", Cabin C16, c/o United States Lines, Southampton, England.

In this way, I shall be free from paying any tax. I hate to bother you with such a trifle, but if you could arrange to have them delivered before I sail on the 10th, I shall be most grateful. These cigarette cases made of sterling silver are very nice gifts to my friends in America and I am sure they would enjoy having them.

　　With warmest regards to you and Mrs. Franke and thanking you for your courtesy,

Yours sincerely,

T. L. Yuan

〔University of Chicago Library, Yuan T'ung-li Papers, Box 4〕

　　按：Gesellschaft für Natur and Völkerkunde Ostasiens，此处 and 应为 und。

一月二十一日

刘国蓁致函先生,嘱购的鱼肝油被上海海关退回,并告钱存训已将先生购重之《十竹斋笺谱》买去,另谈罗原觉欲出售旧藏书籍,请先生代为推介。

守和先生尊鉴：

　　未修书敬候瞬已月余,梅影横窗,怀思倍切。恭维□□延鸿,文祺纳燕,至以为颂。月前拜奉手示,敬悉,附圣诞咭及美钞五元均已奉到,当即遵命将该美钞找换得港银廿八元七角五分,连上存一元三角,共三十元〇〇五分,并购买五百粒庄鱼肝油丸壹瓶,包装妥当为一小盒,用平常邮寄奉令岳丈大人收纳,另付上芜笺及该丸发票一纸,倘得收后,方再续寄。因晚闻国内海关不易放行,迨至昨日得接本港邮局通知,着往取回退件,原来真是该鱼油丸,该包封面盖有"上海海关拆验,不准进口,退回。"等字样,因此知到令岳丈大人并未收得,是以晚即致函告知,以免远望。该鱼油丸一瓶九元、寄费二元五角,共十一元半,比对尚存十八元五角半在晚处。未悉该款及鱼油丸如何处置,便中恳请示知为幸。昨日得接钱存训先生来函,谓先生自蔚林书店买重了一部《十竹斋笺谱》,共港银139元,渠已代售去,嘱晚在渠存款内拨交139元与蔚林书店,声明是先生所购,支结该数并取回收条。晚当遵嘱办理,请释锦注。敝友罗原觉君藏书甚丰,现拟出让。兹另由二等航空邮奉上其藏书影本《艺术书目》一册,其他书目八页,共贰份,《朱子大全集》说明贰页。恳请鼎力赞勷介绍与英伦各大学及其他图书馆购买,尤其是南洋大学图书馆当新兴建设之时,当搜购书籍,恳请代寄一份及书目一册与熊院长,至邮费若干定当奉还。至影本《艺术书目》一册(如再须要当可再奉),该书价银港币四万元(整部不拆散),其他书目八页可分购,价银函询即覆,倘推荐成功,定必相当酬谢。敝友罗君与陈维新先生同在饮冰室门下,伦敦大学西门博士亦曾见面,该批书籍曾寄存于冯平山图书馆也。冒渎之处,敬乞原宥,便中伏希示覆,至所厚幸。匆匆,专此,敬请崇安。

愚晚刘国蓁顿首

一九五五年一月廿一日

〔袁同礼家人提供〕

按:罗原觉(1891—1965),原名泽堂,广东南海人,曾入广东高等师范学堂,师从韩文举研习国学,并拜康有为、梁启超为师,后专门从事研究鉴别碑、帖、字画等文物和古铜器、古陶瓷、古文字等。"陈维新"似有误,或为杨维新(鼎甫)。

一月二十六日

戴密微致先生两函,其一,告已就中国留法博士名单询问李治华、王联曾、刘家槐等人,但所获不多,建议先生联系"驻法使馆"。

Paris, le 26 / I / 1955

234 Bd Raspail, XIVe

Dear Dr Yuan,

Your list went round the other Chinese residents in Paris whom I know, 李治华, 王联曾, Liou Kia-hway etc. I am very sorry that the result is exceedingly poor. I also looked up at the Institut des Hautes Études Chinoises, but there are no Chinese characters! Now Liou Kia-hway has been writing on his thesis with me for about four years, & I just realized that I don't know how he writes his name! They suggested that you must enquire from "the Chinese Embassy" (or rather Consulate) here where the Chinese names should be kept in the files, but would they undertake the research?

Your list includes, I think, only the names of the authors of theses whose Chinese characters you do not know. For there have been many more theses. Did you look up the collection on the Institut des Hautes Etudes Chinoises? I think they also have a good collection at Harvard. I have a few rare ones published in funny places. If you care to send me your complete list once, I shall add whatever you might have missed and I should happen to know.

I have ordered some books from "Collett's Chinese Bookshop". They are not too dear (except 郭沫若, 金文丛考, but I was glad to have it as the original Japanese edition is unobtainable; has there also been a reprint of 两周金文辞大系? And of 古代铭刻汇考? What a pity the great scholar abandoned paleography for politics!)

Many thanks you for 切韵音系.

When are you leaving for USA? Won't you come back here before?

Yours sincerely

P. Demiéville

〔University of Chicago Library, Yuan T'ung-li Papers, Box 3〕

按：Liou Kia-hway 即刘家槐（1908—?）。《金文丛考》《两周金文辞大系》《古代铭刻汇考》，此三种书皆由日本文求堂发行，前两种于 1932 年初版，第三种于 1933 年初版。该函为其亲笔。

其二，感谢先生寄来郑振铎著作，并询问罗振玉旧藏敦煌经卷的去向。

Paris, 26 / I / 1955

234 Bd Raspail XIVe

Dear Dr. Yuan,

My letter had just left when I received yours, together with the new edition of Cheng Chen-to's book. This book has long been a "classic" of mine, as I have been studying □□□□ the last three years the Tunhuang mss. of 俗文学. This year again I am reading some of these mss. at one of my courses at the Collège de France & I often use Cheng Chen-to's book to put a □□□□ before the hearers, as I have only my photographs of each mss. and he gives a reading of some of them in his book. So one hearer □□□□ will benefit by your very kind gift for which I thank you heartily.

It is mainly in connection with these Tunhuang mss. that I am interested in the fate of Lo Chenyu's collection. He had sometimes one half of a Tunhuang mss. the other half of which is in Paris, and as I wish to publish some of these mss. I should be glad to add the other half in my publication!

I suppose the rest of the photos of Paris Tunhuang mss. of which you give a partial list in 图书季刊 were brought to Peking by 王重民 after the war from Washington.

With all best wishes for your health & work, & hopes to see you again before long, I remain,

yours sincerely

Paul Demiéville

〔University of Chicago Library, Yuan T'ung-li Papers, Box 3〕

按:该函为其亲笔。

二月二日

先生覆信 Arnold Toynbee,告知行期已定无法应邀聚餐,期待明年来英时能与之晤谈。

13 Portland Road

Oxford

2 February, 1955

Dear Professor Toynbee:

Thank you so much for your courtesy in asking me to come to lunch on Thursday the 10th of February. It is a great disappointment to me not being able to accept your kind invitation, as I am sailing on the S. S. United States that day.

Kindly convey my hearty thanks to Mrs. Toynbee. I should like so much to meet her as I have been reading her book these days. But I shall hope to see you again when I return to England next year. I should like so much to work in the reading room of the British Museum and come back once a while to refresh myself with the vast amount of source material available in London, but the matter of obtaining entry visas and re-entry visas is so much a bother, that it makes difficult for a scholar to travel from one country to the other.

With renewed thanks for your kindness,

Yours sincerely,

T. L. Yuan

〔University of Chicago Library, Yuan T'ung-li Papers, Box 4〕

按:Arnold Toynbee(1889-1975),英国历史学家,今通译作"汤因比",1925 年被任命为皇家国际事务研究所(The Royal Institute of International Affairs)研究教授兼所长。Mrs. Toynbee 即 Rosalind Murray(1890-1967),英国作家,其知名作品有 *The Happy Tree*、*The Leading Note*。该件为录副。

二月三日

汤因比覆函先生,以未能及早约定相见而致歉,并告知本周三或周四下午有暇与先生晤谈。

February 3, 1955

Dear Mr. Yuan,

I have just had your letter of the 2nd February. I had been under the impression that you were staying in England for a considerable time. Otherwise, I would have suggested an earlier date. I should be sorry not to see you again before you go. I wonder if you are going to be in London before sailing—say on Wednesday the 9th or Tuesday the 8th (the 8th would suit me slightly better, but either date would be all right). Please don't bother about this if it is a nuisance, as I know how rushed one is, during the last day or two before sailing, with all kinds of business. But, if you happen to be free for lunch on either of those days, my wife and I would be very glad to see you for lunch at the Athenaeum Annex, 6 Carlton Gardens, at one p. m.—and your son too if he were in London with you.

Otherwise I look forward to seeing you when you are in England again next year.

With best wishes, yours sincerely,

Arnold Toynbee

〔University of Chicago Library, Yuan T'ung-li Papers, Box 3〕

　　按:此件为打字稿,落款处为其签名。

二月四日

先生覆信汤因比,告因故无法前往伦敦,并恳请赠予著作。

4th February, 1955

Dear Professor Toynbee:

　　It is very sweet of you and Mrs. Toynbee to ask us to lunch before we sail. Unfortunately, we have committed ourselves with previous engagements here at Oxford which will prevent us from going to London.

　　We are most grateful to you for your kindness and when I return to London next year, I shall certainly call on you to pay my respects. Meanwhile may I send you and Mrs. Toynbee our very best wishes for your great contribution to scholarship? I hope that if you have copies of your reprints which you could spare, will you ask your secretary to mail them to me care of the steamer? I shall be very proud to have them as my treasured possessions.

　　With sincerest greetings,

Your sincerely,

T. L. Yuan

〔University of Chicago Library, Yuan T'ung-li Papers, Box 4〕

　　按:此件为录副。

二月六日

蒋彝致函先生,告知著作出版时间并询先生回美后的通讯地址。

　　守和先生有道:

　　　　上周大小儿坚果同拜,适袁太太外出,彼深以未能候安为憾。荣行在即,离津期有定否? 弟昨日伤风,不克趋前再拜,奈何奈何。关于拙著出版年月如右:

　　　　Birds and Beasts, Country Life, 1939

　　　　Lo Cheng, the boy who wouldn't keep still, Penguin, 1941

　　　　Chinpao at the Zoo, Methuen, 1941

The Story of Ming, Penguin, 1943

Dabbitse, Transatlantic Arts, 1944

YEBBIN, Methuen, 1947

至于 *The Chinese Eye* 德译本,弟处允许六本,始终未收到。盖将出版时欧战发生,为一 Leipzig 书局经印,但书局名已忘记,因弟处来往信件,均随 1940 炸弹消失,大著中最好不提此译本。其他中国作者姓名,已函各方代询,复音恐须时日,一俟有获,即当函达。可否请赐下美国通讯处。匆颂俪安。

弟蒋彝顿首

二月六日

〔袁同礼家人提供〕

按:信中所提各书之中文名依次为《鸟与兽》《罗成》《金宝游万牲园记》《明》《大鼻子》《野宾》《中国画》。先生在离开牛津前,曾携袁澄拜会蒋彝,并告袁澄"蒋先生真给中国及中国人争光,总是每年有一本新的著作"①。

二月七日

费成武覆函先生,感谢赠书。

同礼先生道席:

拜奉大示,复蒙赐赠《印度艺术》一册,不胜愧感。此书编述精美,所集图片又丰,爱不释手,当为珍藏。如此厚赐,何以言谢。怅悉尊驾将径行上船,而未能在伦敦稍留一叙,为憾。谨祝旅程风顺,一路平安,并祈时赐教言。下次来英,盼早惠音。在英如有可效劳之处,请随时示之。专此道谢,并请旅绥。

尊夫人前候安。

小弟费成武拜

蒨英附笔叩谢并候安

二月七日

〔袁同礼家人提供〕

按:张蒨英(1913—2004),毕业于中央大学艺术系,1946 年赴英

---

① 《思忆录》,中文部分页 138。

留学，后旅居伦敦。

汤因比致函先生，期待未来再见并将寄赠一些著作。

February 7, 1955

Dear Mr. Yuan,

My wife and I are sorry that we shan't have the chance of seeing you again before you sail, but I rather feared that you would be full up with engagements during these last days.

Well, I look forward to your visit to London next year, when I hope to be able to see more of you—that is, if you will be coming before the spring, when we shall be setting out on a long journey.

Meanwhile, I am sending you some small works of mine to the Steamer, under separate cover. They are a miscellaneous lot, but probably characteristic.

Looking forward to seeing you again.

Yours very sincerely,
Arnold Toynbee
〔University of Chicago Library, Yuan T'ung-li Papers, Box 3〕

按：此件为打字稿，落款处为其签名。该函寄送先生所乘坐的"美利坚"号邮轮。

何四维覆函先生，告知有关暹罗的书籍信息。

7 February 1955

Dear Professor Yuan:

Thank you for your kind letter; I am sure I will be able to send you a copy of my thesis, once it has been published.

The date on the book on Siam are as follow:

Author: Likhit Hoontrakul.

Title: *THE HISTORICAL RECORDS OF THE SIAMESE-CHINESE RELATIONS* commencing from ancient times up to the time when the Siamese people formed themselves into a State called Siam with the town of Sukhotai as Capital.

Bangkok 1951; 2p. Chinese; p. A to P Introduction, Contents and List of Maps and Illustrations; p. 1-130 text, p. 131－137 indexes, 29 illustrations.

Wishing you a happy return to the States, I beg to remain.

Sincerely yours,

A. F. P. Hulsewé

〔University of Chicago Library, Yuan T'ung-li Papers, Box 3〕

按：Likhit Hoontrakul 生平待考；第一种书 1953 年曼谷初版，第二种书信息待考。此件为打字稿，落款处为其签名，通讯地址应为 Sinologisch Instituut, Binnenvestgracht 33, Leiden, Holland。该函寄送袁静，由其转交给先生。

二月十日

先生、夫人、袁澄一同登“美利坚”号邮轮（S. S. United States）返回美国。
〔袁同礼家人提供〕

二月十五日

先生、夫人、袁澄抵达纽约。〔袁同礼家人提供〕

先生致信杜乃扬，询问在考狄《中国学书目》外，巴黎是否出版过其他有关中国的书目，并询问某些书的信息。

February 15, 1955

Dear Madame Guignard:

I was so sorry that my little time spent at Paris did not permit me to look up all the information I need in regard to French works relating to China. I now enclose a list and I shall be indebted to you if you or any of your colleagues could check up the information for me. I know that you are extremely busy with your work, but I hope you could ask other friends to help me. Any assistance you could extend to me, I shall be most grateful.

Please inform me whether there is any bibliography on China published in Paris since Cordier. I run through the *T'oung Pao* but failed to find one. If you know of any, please give me the title and the publisher.

I am rather anxious to know whether from your card catalogue you could find the titles of the these of the following:

We have safely arrived in the United States and will stay at Washington for some time. We hope to hear from you often and to know the progress of the important work you are doing.

　　With warmest regards to you and M. Guignard,

Yours sincerely,

〔University of Chicago Library, Yuan T'ung-li Papers, Box 3〕

　　按:此件为底稿,空行处付诸阙如。

二月十八日

蒋复璁致函先生,请其来台任事并寄上聘书。

　　守和先生道席:

　　　巴黎一别,忽已六载,海天遥望,时切葵思。迩维旅祺迪吉,定符私颂。去秋以张晓峰兄出长"教部",恢复"中馆"工作,公谊私交,弟均责无旁贷,勉任艰钜。只以停顿多年,事事皆须从头做起。老年体弱,时惧陨越。图书馆事业研究委员会虽载于"中馆"组织条例,因无事可做,故迄未设置。近"教部"对图书馆事业亟思发展促进,因令敝馆依法组织且有规程之颁布。先生斯学先进,敢以奉屈,谨将聘书、规程及首次会议录等寄奉,敬祈察收并予指正为祷。际兹国难方殷,人人有责,朝野各界缅怀贤硕。先生去国多年,企望弥深,敢乞早日命驾回国,共襄盛业,则不仅图书馆界之厚幸也。肃此布臆,祗请撰安。

弟蒋复璁拜启

二月十八日

〔University of Chicago Library, Yuan T'ung-li Papers, Box 2〕

　　按:该函附"国立中央图书馆"聘书一份,聘先生为该馆"图书馆事业研究委员会"委员,1955 年 1 月 14 日签发。此函为文书代笔,落款处为蒋复璁签名。

二月二十日

先生致信赵元任、杨步伟夫妇,告知返美后拜访胡适的经过并为其筹备发起祝寿纪念刊。

元任先生、夫人著席：

我们十五日返美，曾在适之处谈了二小时，知道北平方面刻正清算他的思想，动员全国文史界举行座谈会，其规模之大几与"三反""五反"时相同。因念适之在文史方面贡献最大，亟应有所表示。为求有永久性起见，敝意此时可先筹备印行其六十五岁纪念刊，分中西两种，中文本弟已函台大各教授由台北主持办理，西文本即由尊处主持，函请留美文史学者及欧美汉学家其名单弟可供给供给论文，如能于清华专款内拨一小款津贴印刷费，则进行更易。弟曾致函月涵，顷接复函表示赞同，想不久必与尊处商量进行方针。如能实现，则于适之精神方面亦可略得安慰，想两位必愿分出一部分时间办理此事也。我们此次返美乘美国船，其 novelty shop 共有三家，所售之货定价奇昂，远不如英船之廉，虽然走的很快四天半，但风浪甚大，晕船药竟不能生效。敝寓距国会图书馆甚近，闻下月大驾或能来此，亟愿晤谈，届时务乞先行示知，以免相左。弟亦拟再到哈佛查书，但尚不能预定前来日期也。通伯夫人艺展成绩如何？颇以为念。匆匆，敬颂俪安。

弟袁同礼顿首

慧熙附笔问安

二月廿日

学璜、如兰同此问候。

通讯处：11 Eighth Street, S. E. Washington 3, D. C.

〔University of California, Berkeley, The Bancroft Library, Yuen Ren Chao papers, carton 10, folder 39, Yuan, Tongli and Yuan, Huixi〕

按："六十五岁纪念刊"最终刊印时题为《庆祝胡适先生六十五论文集》(*Studies Presented to Hu Shih on his Sixty-fifth Birthday*)，分上下两册，于1956年12月、1957年5月在台北由"中央研究院"历史语言研究所出版。

二月二十三日

张其昀致函先生，告知汇寄美金三千元。

守和吾兄大鉴：

附函希察收。印刷费及购书费共三千美元，即汇寄。专此，即颂近安。

弟张其昀敬上

二,廿三

附奉拙著《革命教育》及《中国教育学术与文化》各一册（另寄）。

按:《革命教育》和《中国教育学术与文化》,1955 年台北教育与文化社出版。该件另附一英文信,内容如下,

February 23, 1955

To whom it may concern:

This is to certify that Dr. Tung-Li Yuan is an accredited official of "the Ministry of Education" sent to the United States of America for compiling a "Comprehensive Bibliography of China" and a "Bibliography of the Writings of Chinese Scholars in Western Languages".

Since they are important works of reference to scholarship any assistance extended to him in the pursuance of these projects will be much appreciated.

Dr. Yuan has also been appointed liaison officer with the U. S. National Commission for UNESCO. He is charged with the duty of keeping in touch with the important work which the Commission is doing in the United States.

Chang Chi-yun

Minister of Education

〔University of Chicago Library, Yuan T'ung-li Papers, Box 2〕

二月二十四日

费成武覆函先生,请来信说明代存英镑之缘由,以便转存。

同礼先生大鉴:

二月廿一日晨拜奉手教并附十五镑,嘱代存入贵行,拜收并悉尊驾已安抵华盛顿,甚慰。弟即于廿一日开支票十五镑并贵函径寄贵行,廿二日得贵行经理来信并退回支票,谓须弟向 Bank of England 请准外汇转划手续,始能存入该支票云,其意疑弟以英金向贵处汇划美金。故弟即往弟之银行解释,理由如下:为尊驾离英时留下剩余英金,匆匆不及亲自存入贵行,故托弟代办(弟不可说金镑自美由邮寄来,恐

引起私汇之嫌），已将支票交敝行，嘱其代办，必要时由敝行代弟申请
外汇许可。此等规定及种种限制殊为复杂。顷敝行来电话，嘱弟出示
尊函作证明，但此将引起更大误会，故祈即来函说明此款为离英前交
弟代为存入贵行者，至要至要。专此，恭请大安。

尊夫人前叩安。

弟成武拜上

二月廿四日

〔袁同礼家人提供〕

图齐致函先生，告知其从尼泊尔归来，希望先生能够如约提交有关马可波
罗书目的文章。

24 FEB. 1955

My dear Prof. Yuan,

I have come back some time ago from my expedition to Nepal, which has proved very satisfactory, and my foremost care has been that of enquiring about the progress of all our cultural initiatives, especially about the commemoration volume on Marco Polo.

I must first say how sorry I have been to have missed meeting you in Rome in October last; your stay has unfortunately been extremely short, barring the possibility of organizing a lecture, which would have been our eager wish. This, however, should not make you postpone the fulfillment of your kind promise concerning the complete Polian Bibliography, which is so essential to our volume. We are very eagerly awaiting your contribution, and hoping that your severe illness may have been completely overcome, with full resuming of your precious scholarly activities. Please be so good as to reassure us on this point, as the other articles and contributions are being actually sent to press.

I beg to renew the expression of my deep indebtedness for your aid in this connection, to which I add my warmest wishes for your health. With all my best regards, I remain,

Sincerely yours,

Giuseppe Tucci

〔University of Chicago Library, Yuan T'ung-li Papers, Box 3〕

按:severe illness 应指 1954 年夏先生在欧洲生病。此件为打字稿,落款处为其签名。

二月二十五日

先生致信福梅龄,告知已回到华盛顿,建议其在即将出版的天主教学校毕业同学录中加入各人之中文姓名,并询问杨懋春的地址。

February 25, 1955

Dear Miss Ferguson:

We have just returned from a year's travel and research in Europe. We hope now that we may be able to settle down a little bit in our beloved Washington. If you happen to come here, we hope you will give us a ring and let us have the pleasure of seeing you.

I hear that a united directory of the alumni of Christian colleges is ready for the press. It would greatly enhance its reference value if Chinese names could be inserted after their English names. May I request you to suggest it to the compiler?

Kindly put me on your mailing list to receive all of your publications including the *CHINA COLLEGES* and the *NEWSLETTER* .

If you happen to know the present address of Dr. Martin Yang, may I ask you to mail the enclosed card after filling out his address?

With kindest regards to you and Dr. Fenn,

Yours sincerely,

T. L. Yuan

〔Yale University Divinity School Library, United Board for Christian Higher Education in Asia Records, RG 11 Series Ⅱ, Box 79, Folder 2146〕

按:此件为打字稿,落款处为先生签名,于 28 日送达。

Josephine Leighton 覆函先生,告知申请 John Simon Guggenheim Memorial Foundation 基金会资助的基本事项。

February 25, 1955

Dear Mr. Yuan:

In response to your request of February 24, we send you herewith information concerning the Fellowships of this Foundation; and under another cover we send you copies of our latest Reports. You will receive application forms for 1956 as soon as they are ready for distribution-sometime this summer.

The due-date for the receipt of applications each year is October 15; and awards are made early in the following April.

Sincerely yours,

(Mrs.) Josephine Leighton

Administrative Assistant

〔University of Chicago Library, Yuan T'ung-li Papers, Box 2〕

按：John Simon Guggenheim Memorial Foundation，1925 年由奥尔加·古根海姆（Olga Guggenheim）和西蒙·古根海姆（Simon Guggenheim）夫妇创立，主要资助自然科学、社会科学、人文科学等领域的研究，即本谱中陈受颐所称"古根涵基金会"。

三月一日

先生撰写 Supplement to Cordier's Bibliotheca Sinica 报告，包括 Scope 和 Printing of Part 1, Section 1 两部分。〔袁同礼家人提供〕

李书华覆函先生，就申请研究补助给出建议并谈其最近发表的几篇中国科学技术史文章。

守和吾兄大鉴：

二月廿六日手书敬悉。下次大驾来纽，务请到敝寓便饭，藉以畅谈一切。第一时尚不去华府，将来去时，定当走访。留法同学名单，随信附上，祈查收。清华补助研究费，每人每月有一五〇元、二〇〇元，或三〇〇元等。因此项费用减少，一九五五—五六所补新人为每月一五〇元。闻中基会下年度给兄补助费每月二〇〇元，不知是否可在中基会以外其他方面再找到每月一〇〇元，凑成三〇〇之数？著作《纸的起源》，董雁堂兄来信谓已在《大陆杂志》刊完，现还印单行本，大约寄到尚需时日。俟寄到时当寄上一册，请指正。弟文中亦有一段谈到造纸法入印度，系回教徒所输入者，惟该段甚短。兄处所得《中国纸入印度》一文，由英寄到时，祈寄下一阅为感。《指南针的起源》曾用法文写出，载哈佛出版之 *ISIS*（科学史季刊），分两期登载，兹寄上单行本一份,祈指正。法文稿与中文稿稍有不同。东京国立科学博物馆已根据《大陆杂志》中文稿节译成日文,分别登载于该馆出版之《自然科学与博物馆》21 卷第 5-6 号及第 7-8 号。匆此,敬请大安。

弟李书华敬启

三月一日

〔袁同礼家人提供〕

按:ISIS 即 *The History of Science Society* 的季刊,李书华所撰写的法文文章题为 Origine de la Boussole,连载于该刊第 45 卷第 1 期(1954 年 5 月)、第 2 期(7 月)。"自然科学与博物馆"即 *Natural Science and Museums*,该刊 1954 年 6 月、8 月确实连载了李书华的文章。

三月二日

先生致信周以德,以此前因故未能为其主持的援助项目服务而致歉,并告知已经回到华盛顿,如有所需可联系。

March 2, 1955

Hon. Walter H. Judd

House of Representatives

Washington, D. C.

Dear Hon. Judd:

When I was doing bibliographical research at the Hoover Library in 1953, you very kindly asked me to serve as a member of an Advisory Committee for the Literatures Program of the Aid Refugee Chinese Intellectuals, Inc. I was sorry that I was not of much help, as I left for Europe early in 1954 to continue my research there.

I have only recently returned to the United States and shall remain in Washington for several years. Although your Literature Program is not being continued, I shall be glad to be of service to you any time you should need me. I was the Director of the National Library at Peiping 1926 to 1948 and I had the pleasure of meeting you in Peiping.

I have always regarded you as a great friend of the Chinese people. Whatever you have done for China has earned the gratitude of my fellow-countrymen. When you are so fully occupied, I hate to bother you. But if you have time, I hope to call on you from time to time in order to talk over matters of common interest.

With sincere greetings,

Yours sincerely,

T. L. Yuan

〔University of Chicago Library, Yuan T'ung-li Papers, Box 2〕

徐家璧覆函先生,告前询博士论文的作者信息、哥伦比亚大学并无校级中国留学组织等事。

守和先生尊鉴:

敬肃者,昨奉二月廿六日手谕,藉审先生业已在欧公毕返美,收获鸿钜,曷胜敬佩。惜驾过纽时,事前未能得悉,致失晋谒之机,怅憾奚似。本年远东学会年会虽正逢盛樱季节,只以未便告假,恐难如愿列席。去年该会年会在纽举行,因哥大负责筹备,曾略从旁襄助,亦曾亲聆各学者鸿论,认为获益匪浅也。关于承询各节,兹就所知谨答如左:

一、公所见之哥大博士论文作者系郭舜平君,籍隶福建,出身清华大学,曾在陈立夫"部长"任内担任"教育部"职业辅导委员会主任之职。只因家属在闽,照顾无人,业经于去岁二月回国,闻现在"教育部"留学生招待所服务(一说担任中学教员)。

二、哥大中国同学迄今仍无中心组织,惟师范学院似有肄业之中国同学教育学会,负责人名不详,亦不悉是否(油)印有会员名单。目前市内留学生服务机构有三,除孟治先生领导之华美协进社外,尚有(天主教同学)中美联谊会(86 Riverside Drive)及(United Board)主办之中国留学同学服务协会(Chinese Student and Alumni Services, 130 Morningside Drive)。现下主持中国留美同学服务协会者,系 1952TC 毕业同学耿忠之君(Dr. George Geng 原系沪江毕业)。渠经常与 TC 同学及其他学员接触,如需现下肄业同学名单(或部分名单),请径函接洽,当可获得结果。又据所知者,耿君正进行编印留美十三所教会大学毕业生暨教职员人名联合总录,大抵于本年内可以编竣出版,想来对于尊处事功辅助必多,用特尽先报导。

三、书单壹张附还,六种书中哥大仅有其二,已将所询各点注明。

又查 LC 印本目录,亦无此等书之著录,至歉。

余俟续奉,敬请道安。

晚徐家璧鞠躬
三月二日

尊夫人福安不另笺候。

〔袁同礼家人提供〕

按:郭舜平(Kuo Shun-p'ing)的博士论文题名为 Chinese reaction to foreign encroachment, with special reference to the first Sino-Japanese war and its immediate aftermath, 1953 年获得博士学位。

三月三日

杨懋春覆函先生,告知其工作现状并表示正在积极谋职,预计三月底前往华盛顿,届时愿登门拜访。

袁先生大鉴:

今早接奉手书,欣悉先生赴欧洲研究一年,今又回来美国,不胜钦羡。弟仍在 Hartford 作原来工作,顾先生亦尚在此,吴德耀君在台湾任东海大学文学院长职,洪绂先生现执教于欧海欧洲一 Western College。此间工作,决定于今夏结束,顾先生将去东海。弟因舍家在此,孩子尚年幼,故决定暂不返台。现正多方接洽将来工作,开始时甚不乐观,近则稍有眉目,惟究竟能否获得一职,尚在考虑中。先生近作何事? 定有大作问世,如蒙不弃,尚祈示知,当为祝贺也。本月末在华京有 Far Eastern Association 开会,研究东方乡村组织等题目,弟亦承邀参加,已决定前往。届时如兄仍在华京,甚望□趋府拜谒,藉聆教益。肃此敬覆,顺颂春祺。

弟杨懋春拜启
三月三日

〔University of Chicago Library, Yuan T'ung-li Papers, Box 2〕

按:"弟仍在 Hartford 作原来工作",即 1952 年 8 月杨懋春偕家眷前往 Harford Theological Seminary,参与中国基督教大学联合董事会(Associated Boards for Christian Colleges in China)"中国文字工作计画"。"顾先生"应指顾敦鍒(1898—?),字雍如,江苏吴县人,1922 年之江大学毕业,后入燕京大学执教,抗战胜利后就

任之江大学文学院院长,1948 年赴美;洪绂(1906—1988),福建
闽侯人,少入福州英华书院学习,1921 年考入福建协和大学物理
系,1925 年毕业,1928 年赴法入里昂大学,获地理学博士学位,并
转巴黎大学继续深造,1933 年归国任中山大学地理系教授,旋即
改任清华大学地理系教授,1949 年赴台,1951 年受邀赴美讲学。
1955 年 6 月,"中国文字工作计画"结束,8 月,杨懋春偕眷前往西
雅图受华盛顿大学聘请,加入中国与俄国历史研究所(Institute of
Chinese and Russian Histories Research)"中国历史与文化"研究项
目,其具体研究方向为中国社会制度的演变。[①]

福梅龄覆函先生,告知杨懋春联系地址并谈东海大学筹建进展。

March 3, 1955

Dear Dr. Yuan:

I was delighted to learn from your letter of February 25th that you
and Mrs. Yuan are back in Washington after your year of travel and
research in Europe. I have not visited Washington for a number of months
but now that you are there I hope it will not be too long before I can go
down for a few days to catch up with you and other old friends.

The united directory of the alumni of Christian colleges is in the first
stages of preparation but I am glad to assure you that one of its most
useful features will be the insertion of the Chinese characters after the
names in English.

Dr. Martin Yang's present address is 139 Girard Avenue, Hartford 5,
Conn. I forwarded your card to him at that address.

I will see that you are put on our mailing list for all publications and
I enclose herewith a copy of the December issue of *New Horizons* which
takes the place of our former publication *China Colleges*, in which I think
you will find a good deal of interest about the plans for Tunghai
University. We are busy with the first construction on the campus at this

① 杨懋春《八十自述》(下),《山东文献》第 4 卷第 1 期,页 46-47;谢莺兴《顾敦鍒教授著述年表》,《东海大学图书馆馆刊》第 39 期,页 80。"中国文字工作计画"似又称作"中国海外文教服务社"。

moment and our expectation is that entrance examinations will be held this summer with an opening in September. A president has not yet been appointed but we are hoping that this important post will be filled in the not too distant future. Other members of the faculty and administrative staff are being assembled and we hope that by a year from now the institution will be very much of a going concern.

Dr. Fenn has been spending the past six months or so in the Far East with frequent visits to Taiwan as well as other places where the United Board has interests. He will be returning in April for a month and then going back again to complete a survey he has been making of Silliman University in the Philippines.

If you ever have occasion to come to New York, I hope you will be sure to let me know. It would be a great pleasure to see you again.

With kindest regards,

Sincerely yours,

Mary E. Ferguson

Associate Executive Secretary

〔Yale University Divinity School Library, United Board for Christian Higher Education in Asia Records, RG 11 Series Ⅱ, Box 79, Folder 2146〕

按：*China Colleges* 由中国基督教大学校董联合会编辑出版，1934年在纽约创办，季刊；*New Horizons* 全称应为 *New Horizons for the China Colleges*，约在 1953 年改为此名。

三月四日

先生致信赵元任、杨步伟夫妇，欢迎来华盛顿相聚晤谈。

元任先生、夫人：

顷接手书，欣悉大驾不久可来华京，听了高兴万分！到此时想在下午，届时望赐一电话，并来此便餐。十五日或十六日，望保留一晚，如愿与任何朋友见面，当即约其来聚，可以省些两位的时间。可惜我们住处实在太小，恐怕住的不舒服，否则十分欢迎在此下榻。又我们的饭碗、碟子等，现存在康桥于震寰处（纸盒二个左右），你们汽车上

如有空的位置,不识能否略带少许。望通知小女,以便送上。先此谢
谢,顺颂俪安!

弟同礼顿首

内人附笔问安

三月四日

弟电话为 Li－3－6209,住处在国会图书馆之后由 East Captial
Street 到八街,住处为:11－8th St. S. E., Wash., 3, D. C.

〔University of California, Berkeley, The Bancroft Library, Yuen Ren

Chao papers, carton 10, folder 39, Yuan, Tongli and Yuan, Huixi〕

按:3 月 14 日,赵元任夫妇抵达华盛顿。
先生致信裘开明,告知已回到美国,请代费成武、张蒨英夫妇向其妹夫问
好,并寄上罗原觉影本《艺术书目》请其估价,另请其于本月底来华盛顿参
加远东学会年会时携带存放于震寰处之旧物。

March 4, 1955

Dear Dr. Chiu:

We have recently returned from an extensive trip in Europe. It has
been very profitable, as I have seen many books not found in American
collections. We tried to see so many things in such a short time that we
were quite exhausted on our return.

In London, we saw a great deal of Mr. & Mrs. Fei Cheng Wu, both
of them are good artists who know Hsien-Chi very well. I like particularly
the paintings and calligraphy of Mrs. Fei who is better know as　　　. If
you see your brother-in-law, tell him that the Feis wish to send their
hearty greetings.

While we were travelling in the Low countries, a friend of mine sent
me a catalogue of Chinese art books and rubbings which another of his
wished to dispose of. They are of special nature and I doubt if any
American library would be interested in their acquisition. However, I am
sending the catalogue to you and I should like to hear your views
concerning it. Could you make an estimate of their worth?

I trust that you would be coming to Washington for the FEA

Conference. If you come by train, could you bring over some of our things stored in Mr. Yui's basement? I enclose my letter to Mr. Yui and am asking him to consult you what you could check at the station if you buy ticket direct to Washington. But if you come by car, please do not let me bother you with these matters.

　　I trust that Mrs. Chiu and your children are doing well these days. Mrs. Yuan and I often had occasion to recall our pleasant visit to Cambridge last year and the kindness you have shown to us. She joins me in sending you and Mrs. Chiu our warmest regards,

Yours sincerely,

T. L. Yuan

〔袁同礼家人提供〕

　　按:your brother-in-law 似指曾宪三,待考。FEA Conference 即本年3月底举办的远东学会年会,其中4月1日至2日召开编目规则审订委员会,裘开明参加了此次会议①。Mr. Yui 应指于震寰,但拼写有误,应为 Yue。该件为录副,空白处付诸阙如。

三月五日

费成武覆函先生,前款已转入指定银行账户,并告暂未能购得绣花女袍。

同礼先生道鉴:

　　二月廿八日惠书及所附伍镑拜收。本月四日接弟之银行来信,尊款已存入贵行矣,甚慰。是日下午弟往所示旧古玩铺,欲代购绣花女袍,店妇谓一主顾取去,如不成交下周内将退回。询其有无其他类似衣服,则谓仅此一件。故拟下周内再访,希能购得,则即邮寄所示使馆地址,否则容后物色于他处,暂请不必寄款,以后算还可也,诸祈勿念。此间半月来大寒,近维起居安吉为颂。内人深感垂赏其书法,但觉草书不佳,拟作楷以求教正云,容后寄奉。专此,恭请大安。

尊夫人前叩安。

弟成武谨启

蒨英附笔致意

---

① 《裘开明年谱》,页614—615。

三月五日

〔袁同礼家人提供〕

吴文津覆函先生,告知胡佛研究所人事、刊物近况。

同礼先生大鉴:

来示敬悉,所嘱各节,兹已查就如左,

(一)本馆参考部代理主任为 Mrs. Allan Paul,前任主管 Mrs. Perry 尚在南菲研究,想在暑假后始能返美也。

(二)胡佛前出之 *Tower Talk* 现已停刊,尚无复刊之说。

(三)沈宗濂先生现寓 Mountain View,仍时来馆阅读,据称 SHEN-CHI LIU 之中文姓名为柳陞祺。

胡佛一切如常,Mrs. Wright 去年自京都返美后,已于十一月初返校工作。房兆楹夫妇仍在 Palo Alto,未任正式职务,惟作私人之研究耳。

本月终,津拟来华京远东学会之图书馆小组会议,惟不谙地方情形,不知在国会圖附近有较好之旅馆介绍否? 专此,即颂俪安。

后学吴文津拜

三,五日

〔University of Chicago Library, Yuan T'ung-li Papers, Box 7〕

按:沈宗濂(1898—1978),浙江吴兴人,清华学校毕业,后赴美留学,获哈佛大学经济学硕士学位,归国后入国民政府外交部,曾任总务司司长、蒙藏委员会驻藏办事处处长,为维护中国领土完整做出相当贡献,1953 年斯坦福大学出版社出版其与柳陞祺合著的 *Tibet and the Tibetans*。柳陞祺(1908—2003),浙江兰溪人,藏学家,1930 年光华大学毕业,1944 年前往拉萨,在蒙藏委员会驻藏办事处工作,后赴印度,1952 年底归国。

三月八日

先生致信圣言会神父顾若愚,询问兖州府保禄印书馆出版品情况,并问《华裔学志》是否于最近复刊。

March 8, 1955

Father Hermann Koster, SVD

Research Institute of Oriental Culture

No. 1, No. 4, 5 chome, Kochjimachi,

Chiyoda-ku

Tokyo, Japan

Dear Father Koster:

Father Dominik Schroder, an old friend of mine in Peking, suggested that I should write to you in regard to the publications of the Yenchoufu Mission. So far I have only seen those noted in the enclosed list, but when I visited your Mission before the war, I had the impression that you had published quite a number of books. I shall be most indebted to you if you could send me a list with full bibliographical information.

I shall also be obliged if you could advise me whether your Institute has published any journal or books during recent years. Is the *Monumenta Serica* being issued soon? Are the issues of the Mitteilungen der Deutschen Gesellschaft für Natur-und Völkerkunde Ostasiens being published regularly? Any information you could give me will be much appreciated.

I served as Director of the National Library of Peiping for many years and have had the collaboration of many German scholars. It was a great pleasure to have met Father Schroder at Leiden, Netherlands, when both of us paid a visit to the Sinological Institute there.

With sincere thanks,

Yours sincerely,

T. L. Yuan

〔University of Chicago Library, Yuan T'ung-li Papers, Box 3〕

按：Dominik Schröder(1910－1974)，德国圣言会神父、人类学家，1938 年至 1949 年在华，1945 年在辅仁大学获硕士学位。your Institute 应指 Research Institute of Oriental Culture，1955 年《华裔学志》第 14 卷由该机构复刊出版；*Mitteilungen der Deutschen Gesellschaft für Natur-und Völkerkunde Ostasiens* 通常译作《德国东亚研究会刊》。此件为录副。

三月九日

先生致信裘开明,请在哈佛燕京学社汉和图书馆查找三种书的信息,并询问该社有无可能资助《西文汉学书目》的出版或预订100部以交换其他出版品。〔袁同礼家人提供〕

　　按:该件为底稿,并未注明三种书的名字。

三月十一日

杨联陞覆函先生,告长沙绢画现存情况及相关文章,并谈将于月底前往华府参加远东学会及为胡适祝寿论文集编纂等事。

　　守和先生、夫人:

　　三月九日手示敬悉。哑行者托带香菇、榨菜,蒙从纽约寄来,已于周前收到,至感至感!在剑桥时,蒙寄东方学者大会刊物三册,尤为感激。其俄国汉学报道一篇,最为有用,已转向学生介绍矣。

　　长沙绢画出土时,曾由蒋玄怡在报端略报。继之蔡季襄有小书考释(不记其名),附五彩摹本(Cox 有此书),考证并不甚精。后来蒋玄怡印行《长沙:楚民族及其艺术》(一九四九),其第二册亦有摹本,无考证。陈槃《先秦两汉帛书考》(《史语所季刊》24本)附有小考,亦不甚精。最近饶宗颐《长沙楚墓时占神物图卷考释》(《东方文化》即 *Journal of Oriental Studies* vol. 1, no. 1, 1954 香港大学出版),始大体得通其读。内容与楚之先世及早期神话发生关联,亦由饶氏首为畅发,厥功甚伟。此绢闻仍在纽约 Metropolitan Museum,以索价过昂,不得收买,亦不欲示人,故对外人但称 technically lost。去年以友人之介,得观原物,见卷上印有反文朱字数字,恐是由另一绢图粘下者,然则传说当时发现不止一块者,信而有征矣。大陆考古学者,后亦在长沙发现彩色绢画,惟无文字耳。

　　远东学会华府年会,已决定前往参加,并于卅日午后读短文一篇,题为 Official Holidays and Office Hours in Imperial China。陈观胜兄大约不去,劳贞一兄多半亦不前往。

　　内子亦准备带小儿 Tom 同来华府观光,并拟借寓任之恭先生、夫人处,在 Silver Spring, Maryland,距华府约有一小时路程。惟近数周来,康桥小孩出疹子者甚多,Tom 每日上幼稚园,万一被传染,则携眷前往之计只可作罢。若能成行,必当到府拜访。

　　来华府以坐火车为原则,故尊处在于寓所存行李,或可交行李车代运一两件,因自己随身行李不至太多,行李票权利,不用白不用也。此情得便即将告知袁清,以便稍作准备。因是否携眷及启行日期均未全定(多半乘星期二廿九日 day coach),车票亦只可于前二三日购买,以便利用 family rate,好在大家相去甚近,常通声气,总不至措手不及也。闻裘闿辉先生似亦准备前往,详情不悉。

　　为适之先生出颂寿论丛,意思极好。由台大出头办理,亦甚合宜。若照《蔡先生颂寿纪念论文集》之盛况预测,当亦可得两巨册也。

　　专覆,敬请双安。

晚学杨联陞敬上
一九五五年三月十一日
〔袁同礼家人提供〕

　　按:"蒋玄怡"即蒋玄伯(1903—1977),字挺生,浙江富阳人,画家,早年入杭州国立艺专学习油画,后赴日留学,入东京帝国大学学习雕塑,抗战时受聘于湘湖师范学校,1949 年任同济大学建筑美术系教授。Official Holidays and Office Hours in Imperial China 后改为 Schedules of Work and Rest in Imperial China,发表在 *Harvard Journal of Asiatic Studies*（ vol. 18, no. 3/4, Harvard-Yenching Institute, 1955, pp. 301-25）。任之恭(1906—1995),山西沁源人,物理学家,1926 年毕业于清华学校高等科,后赴美国麻省理工大学学习,不久转宾夕法尼亚大学、哈佛大学,1937 年归国,执教于西南联合大学,1946 年出国,先后在哈佛大学、约翰·霍普金斯大学从事微波光谱学方面的研究工作。

三月十二日

先生致信孟治,询问华美协进社有无可能资助继续编纂《西文汉学书目》,并请寄赠该所出版物。

March 12, 1955

Dear Dr. Meng:

　　I have recently returned from one year's research in Europe, I was sorry to have missed you both in Paris and Rome, as I was then travelling in the Low countries.

I shall be much obliged to you if you would give me some information as to the possibilities of obtaining a grant from the which Dr. Y. P. Mei received last year. Is the grant made every year?

The first volume of comprehensive bibliography on China is ready for publication, but it would take three more years for the completion of other four volumes. As the grant from the Rockefeller Foundation already expired, I am exploring possibilities for further support. Any assistance from you will be most gratefully appreciated.

Since I have been entirely out of touch with the activities of your Institute, will you kindly send me the following publications and put my name on your mailing list to receive future issues.

When I come to New York in April, I shall look forward to the pleasure of seeing you.

With warmest regards to you and Mrs. Meng,

Yours sincerely,

〔袁同礼家人提供〕

按：此件为底稿，空白处付诸阙如。

先生致信芒太尔，告因故无法前往瑞典，请其寄下著述清单，并询问是否出版有关中国、蒙古和西藏地区的艺术目录。

March 12, 1955

Dear Dr. Montell:

Last October in Venice, I had the pleasure of meeting Mr. Bo Gyllensvard and Mr. & Mrs. Orvar Karlbeck who informed me rapid development of Chinese art collections in Sweden. I told that I would arrange to tome to Stockholm in the spring, but now I find I have to return to the United States, as my " re-entry permit" expired at the end of last month. I do hope, however, that I may come again to see you in the not too distant future.

In my file of Swedish publications on China, I have only the following three titles written by you. They were sent to me by your Royal Library. But I am sure that you have written more in Swedish. Could you send me a list of your writings in Swedish as well as in other languages?

I am requesting Mr. Bo Gyllensvard to buy some catalogues of Chinese art for "the Ministry of Education" at Taipeh, Taiwan (Formosa). If your Museum has published any catalogues, will you kindly send them to him, so that he could include them in the parcel. A list of these catalogues will be appreciated as I shall include those catalogues on Chinese, Mongol and Tibetan art in my bibliography on China.

Perhaps you would be good enough where can I find a complete bibliography of the writings of Sven Hedin? Is there any memorial volume published recently?

Thanking you for your assistance,

Yours sincerely,

T. L. Yuan

〔University of Chicago Library, Yuan T'ung-li Papers, Box 4〕

按:芒太尔时任瑞典民族学博物馆(Statens Etnografiska Museum)亚洲部主任。

三月十三日

劳榦覆函先生,告尚未决定是否赴华盛顿参加远东学会年会,并表示愿意为编辑庆祝胡适先生六十五岁论文集尽力。

> 守和先生赐鉴:
>
> 　　奉到惠函,承嘱于远东学会开会时期前来华府,盛意殷拳,至深铭感。华府在去年春季曾来过一次,彼时来去匆匆,仅留二日,且其时樱花已过,故每欲有机会再游,远东学会方面亦曾函约,惟榦今年暑假决定返台,不得不稍事樽节,尚未能决定耳。若乘火车或 Greyhound Bus,当即先期函知尊府。董同和及全汉昇两兄均决定暂时不到华府,并告。编印适之先生六十五岁纪念册一事,确十分有意义。榦返台后,若有可以为力之处,当尽力为之。专此,敬颂俪安。
>
>

后学劳榦谨上

三月十三日

〔袁同礼家人提供〕

按:"董同和"即董同龢(1911—1963),江苏如皋人,音韵学家,

1932 年入清华大学，毕业后进入史语所从事研究，李方桂指导其从事音韵研究。Greyhound Bus 即灰狗巴士，美国跨城市的长途商营巴士。

三月十四日

宋晞（纽约）致函先生，寄上在纽约为"教育部"代购之中国历史文物图谱目录，以求避免重复购置。

> 守和先生道席：
>
> 　　顷奉张部长晓峰先生来示，嘱将在纽约业已购取之中国历史文物图谱目录寄奉参考。兹呈上目录一份，敬请察收。后学在此将陆续搜购此类图书，如先生能将已购各书之目录赐示，庶免重购，更所企感。肃此，祗颂铎安。

后学宋晞谨上

三月十四日

〔袁同礼家人提供〕

> 按：宋晞（1920—2007），字旭轩，浙江丽水人，史学家，毕业于浙江大学史地系，1954 年冬奉派赴美任台湾在美"教育文化事业顾问委员会"秘书，同时入哥伦比亚大学研究院史学所研究欧美近代史，获硕士学位。1958 年返台，协助张其昀在台北市阳明山华岗创办中国文化学院（后改为中国文化大学）。

三月十五日

先生访瞿季刚，在其家遇赵元任。〔《赵元任年谱》，页 340〕

> 按：瞿季刚（1891—?），江苏崇明人，曾任国华银行董事。

先生致信 Henry McAleavy，索取《淞隐漫录·媚丽小传》的英译本，并请其向翟林奈预祝《大英博物馆藏敦煌汉文写本注记目录》顺利出版。

March 15, 1955

H. McAleavy, Esq.

Department of Oriental Books and Manuscripts

British Museum

London, W. C. 1

Dear Mr. McAleavy:

　　It has been some years since I had the pleasure of meeting you. I hear that your work on Wang T'ao has been published. If you have a copy of it as well as copies of your reprints which you could spare for my use, I shall be most grateful.

It was a pleasure to learn that Dr. Giles's work on the Tunhuang Catalogue is practically completed. If you see him, will you kindly convey my hearty thanks and congratulations? It is a painstaking enterprise which is not appreciated by most ordinary people, but all scholars in the field of sinology would be deeply grateful.

I had a flying visit to the United Kingdom last year, but was pressed for time that I did not try to call on you. I know that you have been doing splendid work for the Museum.

Yours sincerely,

T. L. Yuan

〔袁同礼家人提供〕

按：your work on Wang T'ao 即 *Wang T'ao: the life and writings of a displaced person, with a translation of "Mei-Li Hsiao Chuan", a short story by Wang T'ao*，即王韬传记和其小说《淞隐漫录·媚丽小传》英译，1953 年 China Society 出版。Dr. Giles's work on the Tunhuang Catalogue 即 *Descriptive Catalogue of the Chinese Manuscripts from Tun-huang in the British Museum*（《大英博物馆藏敦煌汉文写本注记目录》），1957 年大英博物馆董事会出版。

先生致信钱存训，告知有关博士论文的各种参考资料，并请其寄送芝加哥大学新刊册页。

公垂吾兄：

承寄芝大同学录，甚感。在 *Journal of Oriental Studies* 一卷一期（港大出版）见饶宗颐《长沙楚墓时占神物图卷考释》，考证精详，可供尊处参考；又蒋玄怡印行之《长沙楚民族及其艺术》，其第二册亦有摹本，无考证；陈槃《先秦两汉帛书考》（《史语所集刊》24 本）附有小考，亦不甚精，不识均已见到否？本月秒远东学会华府年会，已决定来此参加否？盼甚。Kracke 教授仍在芝大否？如有关于东方学新印之 Catalogue，望告注册部寄下一份。又 Law School 章程亦盼检寄。匆匆,顺颂俪安。

弟袁同礼顿首
三月十五

尊夫人所写之字极佳,佩服佩服。

又蔡季襄关于长沙绢画有一小书,予以考释,附五彩摹本^{考证不精},但已不记其书名。Cox 旧藏之长沙绢画,闻在 The Metropolitan Museum of Art,以索价过昂,不得收买,亦不欲示人,故对外人但称"现已遗失",特此奉闻。

〔钱孝文藏札〕

按:"远东学会"华府年会在本年 3 月 28 日至 31 日召开。Kracke 即 Edward A. Kracke Jr.(1908-1976),美国汉学家,中文名柯睿格,专攻宋史,1946 年起执教芝加哥大学,曾任美国东方学会主席。

陈受颐覆函先生,支持"胡先生祝寿论文集"之议,并谈向古根涵基金会申请事,另告拟赴台北及港澳。

守和老兄著席:

奉接本月五日惠函,知兄、嫂已遄返美京,不胜忻慰。客岁厚承赐寄典籍,广我见闻,五中铭感。特以吾兄游踪靡定,未曾修函致谢,疏狂之罪,谅邀原宥。适公六十五岁纪念汇刊之议,弟热烈赞成,如有可供奔走之处,自当从命。至西文方面编辑事宜,则深恐学殖荒落,无以副盛情耳。集稿手续费时颇多,最好能及早通知中外友好,乃不至愆期过甚。兄斫轮老手,必善筹谋也。Guggenheim 基金会处厚获吹嘘,不论事成与否同样感谢。Fulbright 补助金,弟亦曾忘形尝试,前星期得 Conference Board 官样复信,则已名落孙山矣。Guggenheim 研究计划本以 Fulbright 方案为重心,今重心已无形消失,则两败亦意中事也。学校方面业已批准例假,有如矢在弦上不得不发,而历岁砚田所入仅足糊口,战后旅行费用数倍于前,为贯彻初衷惟有举债而已(此时似不容退缩致滋物议)。以兄多年过爱,故敢聒聒,只身处此,固无可与语之人也。孟邻、惠畴两兄近有来信,嘱弟回台小住,殷勤可感,然弟此时舍台北外亦无读书之所矣,其详当于美京把晤时亲缕陈之。远东学会之出席只是题目,所冀望者吾兄之教益而已。承示粤人著作字一纸,其中但识韦荣乐之名字,已将该纸转寄舍弟受荣签注,恐彼亦不能多所增益。惟 Pardee Lowe 生长旧金山,又曾肄业士丹福,或知其中文姓名耳。Grousset 逝世消息曾于《远东季刊》看过,而写请求书时却又茫然似无所忆,此亦未老先衰之一兆欤,未可知也。又莫天一两年前仍在澳门整理著述,关于此君老兄近有所闻否? 如仍健在,弟拟路过香港之际,绕道一访也。专此,敬颂撰祺,并祝嫂夫人俪祉。

弟陈受颐顿首

三月十五日

〔袁同礼家人提供〕

按:"惠畴"即钱思亮。Pardee Lowe 即刘裔昌(1904—1996),华裔,生于旧金山,1930 年毕业于斯坦福大学,1932 年获哈佛商学院工商管理硕士,1947 年至 1949 年曾在美国驻华使馆工作,负责美国教育基金在华事务(United States Educational Foundation in China),时应在伯克利分校攻读博士学位,著有 *Father and Glorious Descendant*(《父亲及其光荣年代》,1943)等。Grousset 应指 René Grousset(1885-1952),法国历史学家,以研究中亚和远东著名,其代表作为 *L'Empire des Steppes*(《草原帝国》)。"莫天一"即莫伯骥(1877—1958),字天一,广东东莞人,藏书家,自称"五十万卷藏书楼主"。

莫余敏卿覆函先生,附赠加州大学洛杉矶分校中国学生名录,并告前询人名所获无多。

March 15, 1955

Dear Dr. Yuan:

Thank you very much for your kind letter of March 6, we are happy to learn that you have returned from a year of successful travel in Europe.

I am sending you herewith a list of Chinese students in UCLA compiled a few years ago. I understand that this is the latest one.

I am also returning to you herewith, the list of Chinese names which you sent me. I am sorry to say that I was not able to identify them. I have asked several Chinese in China Town and also have consulted the "Los Angeles Chinese Business Directory" lent to me by one of my students. I was trying to buy a copy for you but it is not for sale.

My work in UCLA is getting along. Not very many books have been acquired. The annual meeting of the Far Eastern Association at Washington, D. C. should be a very interesting one but we are not planning to go.

With best regards to you and your family,

Yours sincerely,

Man-Hing Mok

〔袁同礼家人提供〕

三月十八日

钱存训覆函先生,告知赴华盛顿行期,并请代为寻找可举办画展的场所。

守和先生:

奉到三、十五手教,敬悉种种。承示各种资料,尤为感幸。所要校中章程两种,已告注册部寄上各一份,关于东方学课程列入 Oriental Language & Literatures 及 Committee on Far Eastern Civilizations,即希查阅。顷因校方之嘱,决定前来华京参加远东学会年会及四月一、二日之编目规则审订委员会。兹拟廿八日下午 B&O 五时许之火车离芝,约廿九早八时四十五分到华京,已函托光清兄代为预定一住处,希望不久可以晤教也。昨日寄呈郭大维君齐白石学生画册一份,伊颇想到华京三月底或四月七日以前举行一次短期画展及表演,不知有无相识处所可以介绍否? 闻 Institute of Chinese Culture 常举行画展,不知可否代为一询。如该社有意,可嘱其径函郭君接洽。地址如下: Mr. David Kwok, 541 W. 113th St. (Apt. 6E), New York 25, N. Y. 郭君之画现在此间美术馆展览,四月中方毕,但伊在纽约尚有存画可用,为另一展览也。专此,顺请公安,并候阖府均吉。

后学存训拜上

三,十八

〔University of Chicago Library, Yuan T'ung-li Papers, Box 2〕

按:B&O 似指巴尔的摩(Baltimore)与俄亥俄州(Ohio)之间的火车线路,待考。郭大维,北京人,齐白石弟子,后经台湾赴美,1955年在芝加哥美术馆筹办个人画展,3 月 1 日钱存训为展览画册《大维画集》(*Modern Chinese Paintings by David Kwok*, Chicago:

Art Institute of Chicago, 1955）撰写导言"An Introduction to David Kwok and His Paintings"。

三月中旬

先生覆信宋晞,商洽购书办法,尤其是欧洲刊行书籍建议"教育部"联系相关出版社直接购入。

> 宋先生惠鉴:
>
> 顷奉三月十四日大札,并承寄下所购《中国历史文物图谱目录》一份,至为感谢。弟前此代部所购之书,仅限于欧洲出版者,与尊处业已购到者毫无重复。欧洲书价较美为廉,今后如在纽约书店中搜购欧洲出版之书似不合算,可否向部中建议尊处采购范围暂以美国出版者为限。弟对欧洲汉学界及出版界情形较为熟悉,拟将欧洲印行重要者由出版机构径行寄部,如此办法既省经费又不致重复,如荷同意,当即函告张部长备查,即希示复为荷。弟月余以后或能来纽,当再趋……
>
> 〔袁同礼家人提供〕

> 按:该件为底稿,仅存首页。

三月二十二日

吴文津覆函先生,告知抵达华府的时间,并谈已从 De Bottore 处购买画作,但因携带不便,拟将画布抽出带来。

Mar. 22, 1955

Dear Dr. Yuan:

Thank you very much for your letter. I expect to arrive in Washington on March 29. The Public Relations Office of the American Council of Learned Societies has reserved a room for me at the Hotel Washington since some of the more inexpensive hotels in the vicinity of the Capitol Grounds are booked up solid for the next few weeks. Thanks just the same for your generous offer to help, I appreciate it very much.

I have got the painting from Mr. De Bottore today and signed a receipt for it. Since the library has asked me to bring along some 25 copies of the Mote Bibliography for Mrs. Wright to distribute at the Far Eastern Association Meeting and plus my brief case and a handbag which I intend to bring with me on the plane, I find it a little difficult to bring the painting with the frame. I hesitate to check it with my baggage because the glass top is very easily broken, perhaps it can't stand the rough handling in loading and unloading of the baggage. So I am writing to find out if it would be all right for me to bring just the painting itself alone without the frame. If this doesn't meet your approval, please write back by special delivery; I will be here through Monday (March 28) afternoon, my plane takes off around 11 o'clock that night. If I don't hear from you, I'll bring you the painting, and will try to take good care of it on the way.

Nadine joins me in sending to you and Mrs. Yuan our best regards,

Sincerely yours,

Eugene Wu

P. S. – If you write, please address it to the library. The Stanford Village mail is always one-day behind whereas there are two delivers-a-day at the library.

〔袁同礼家人提供〕

按：Mote Bibliography,应指*Japanese-Sponsored Governments in China, 1937–1945: an annotated bibliography compiled from materials in the Chinese collection of the Hoover Library*,1954 年斯坦福大学初版。Nadine 即吴文津夫人雷颂平。落款及补语皆为吴文津亲笔。

三月二十七日

下午,先生接到杨联陞自车站打来的电话,遂前往车站取其帮忙带来的行李。〔《杨联陞日记》(稿本)〕

按：此次,杨联陞来华盛顿,应是参加远东学会年会,陈受颐亦出席,并与先生聚谈。

三月二十八日

上午九时许,先生在 40 Street car 上遇杨联陞,后者来先生家午餐。〔《杨联陞日记》(稿本)〕

先生致信顾子仁,询问其著作丹麦语、瑞典语译本的信息,以及一些上海作者的信息,并询问是否与顾子刚保持通信。

March 28, 1955

Dear Mr. Koo:

I have been hoping to meet you, but when I went to Iowa, you happened to be touring in the Far East. I have recently returned from a year's research in Europe. And I hope to have the pleasure of seeing you before very long.

Two of your books have been translated into Danish and I am very anxious to know the name of the publisher and the size of each book. Similarly, I should like to know the publisher and size of your work in Swedish. If you have them in your private library, will you kindly be good enough to let me know?

I also enclose a list of authors whose Chinese names I should like to know. Since you lived in Shanghai for so many years, you might know some of them. I shall be grateful if you could enlighten me.

Have you by any chance heard from T. K. who worked with me in the National Library for many years. He is a very correspondent, but since the outbreak of the Korean War, he has not written any letters. I heard indirectly that his health is improving.

Thanking you for your assistance,

Yours sincerely,

T. L. Yuan

〔袁同礼家人提供〕

按：该件为录副。

三月三十日

刘大钧覆函先生,告南洋大学聘请林语堂的风波,并谈最近研究成果,感谢供给参考书目,另请校阅初稿。

守和我兄惠鉴：

　　奉廿五日手书,藉悉已返美为慰。通信地址即在信笺上,仍拟在华府久居,弟如到美京,定当奉访也。名单中诸君只知其四,他则不知,兹将所知之中文姓名注于原单上附奉。南洋大学事殊出意料之外。语堂兄未允校长前,该处华侨曾多次以函件并托在纽友人敦聘,主要条件皆经谈妥,否则语堂亦不致贸然携眷前往,及聘约教职员。不意在其到新之后,华侨方面对于校长职权问题、预算与教职员薪级问题、校舍建筑问题等,皆行翻案,且在报端攻击语堂,闻其中有政治背景。观于最近发展,恐其即将辞职回美也。在其初约弟时,弟本颇踌躇,但因老友关系,一再考虑后,始允担任。弟在美已获得永居权,原拟个人赴新,两年内回美。南大本定于今年十二月开学,故至后年暑假,不超过两年之限制。胡博渊兄原亦在申请永居权,未及俟其批准,即赴南洋,此时真有进退维谷之势矣。恭度兄本定三月间携全眷前往(因在联合国以年龄关系,已退休),幸尚未成行,及时中止。弟为清华研究中国工业化问题,感觉报告中虽不提目前大陆状况,但自己不能不知,否则如说到工业化之可能发展(此为清华所需要者 potentialities of development),而与目前事实情形冲突,不免受人批评。颇多人以为中共经济无法获悉其实况,以不提为妙。但弟采用一种方式,从各主要工业各个单位入手,颇有所得,已写成一尚题论文,另转寄今甫印成祈指教为荷。进行研究中,承供给 Bibliography 及指示其他来源,获益甚多,并此致谢。拙作冗长,但如只阅序文及序中所指出论中共材料之四页,亦可得其大要也。尚复,顺颂俪安。

弟大钧鞠躬

三,卅

〔袁同礼家人提供〕

三月三十一日

先生赴远东学会年会会场,旁听与会人员发言,但因有约提前离开。〔University of Chicago Library, Yuan T'ung-li Papers, Box 2〕

先生致信詹森夫人,对詹森大使的去世表示哀悼。〔University of Chicago Library, Yuan T'ung-li Papers, Box 2〕

> 按:1954 年 12 月 3 日,詹森大使去世。先生与其最后一次见面,
> 应在 1953 年某日在北京楼的聚会上。

四月一日

先生设宴款待来华盛顿参加远东学会的中国学人。〔University of Chicago Library, Yuan T'ung-li Papers, Box 2〕

顾子仁覆函先生,告知与其弟顾子刚久无联系,并就所知填写著者中文姓名,关于丹麦、瑞典文译本则因未曾见过,故无法提供信息。

April 1, 1955

Dear Dr. Yuan:

I am very glad to hear from you & indirectly about my brother T. K. He kept in touch with me for some time after the liberation. But for the last 3 years & more, he has stopped writing to me. Not knowing his situation in Peking, I have also refrained from writing to him, lest I might without intention embarrass him.

I am afraid I am unable to be of much help to you on your list of Chinese authors. I have jotted down for you those Chinese names which I happen to know.

As to the books appearing under my name, I am sorry to say I have never seen them myself. As far as I can remember, they were collections of the addresses I made in Denmark on one of my visits there in the early 20's. Since I do not speak Danish, they did not send me the book at the time it was printed.

Best wishes to you.

Sincerely yours,

T. Z. Koo

〔袁同礼家人提供〕

按:该函为其亲笔。

四月二日

Mario Bussagli 覆函先生,确认先生负责马可波罗书目的收录范围,并询问何时可以寄来书目稿件。

Rome 2, Apr. 1955

My dear Dr. Yuan:

In the absence of Prof. Tucci, I am answering your kind letter of March 17, which requires a prompt reply. First of all, however, I must say that Prof. Tucci wants me to thank you very heartily for your kind wishes and congratulations. His Nepalese expedition has been very successful, numberless valuable inscriptions have been discovered, and traces of Bon-po religion.

Concerning your much expected Polian bibliography, we would

kindly request you to take charge of all titles included in American collections, and all the others it is possible to gather; you can of course except all the Italian part of it, of which we shall take care ourselves. Will you kindly let us know when we may expect to receive your mss. on cards? I hope you may carry on all your work without too much trouble, or overfatigue, considering its exceptional range.

　　With best regards, and kind wishes, I remain,

Yours sincerely,

Prof. Mario Bussagli

〔University of Chicago Library, Yuan T'ung-li Papers, Box 4〕

　　按：Mario Bussagli(1917－1988)，意大利中亚美术史家。Bon-po即藏区在佛教传入前的古老宗教，以自然崇拜为基础，今通称"苯波"。

四月五日

杨联陞覆函先生，感谢款待并另赠《哈佛亚洲研究》新作一册。

　　守和先生、夫人：

　　　　到华府次日即蒙盛设午宴，甚为不安！

　　　　开会数日中，内子及小儿均在银泉，周末由刘子健兄及任之恭先生先后开车到各处游览，名胜大抵均已点到，可算此行不虚。惟国会图书馆只是过门不入，盖恐书呆子见书故病复发，反误春游也。馆内诸公，想能见谅！

　　　　袁静、袁清姊弟，在康桥对小女恕立两次招邀晚餐，真是感激。伊初次单独看家，多得友人照拂，甚幸甚幸。

　　　　《哈佛亚洲报》新印拙稿一篇（大旨曾在去年远东学会年会报告），另包寄呈乞政！

　　　　专此布谢，敬请双安。

晚学杨联陞敬上

一九五五年四月五日

〔袁同礼家人提供〕

　　按：刘子健(1919—1993)，生于上海，历史学家，专攻宋史，初入清华大学，后转入燕京大学，抗战中曾身陷囹圄，胜利后作为中方法

律代表团成员赴东京国际军事法庭工作,1950 年获匹兹堡大学
博士学位,后在该校及斯坦福、普林斯顿大学任教。"新印拙稿"
即 Toward a Study of Dynastic Configurations in Chinese History,刊
于 Vol. 17, No. 3/4 (Dec., 1954), pp. 329−345。

四月六日

先生致信陈荣捷,感谢寄赠书评并祝贺其在远东学会宣讲论文,请其与夫
人一起查看所附名单并标注中文姓名。

April 6, 1955

Dear Professor Chan:

Thank you so much for sending me your scholarly review of Fung
Yu-lan's work. I am reading it with much interest and profit. I am
especially delighted that your critical review should have been published
by the Philosophy East and West which has a wide circulation among
scholars.

Your visit to Washington was too short and I tried to get you to a
party last Friday, but I was told that you had to leave Thursday. Owing to
a previous engagement, I was not able to attend the whole meeting on
Thursday, but I had to leave immediately after your scholarly paper and
hence had no opportunity to greet you. You certainly contributed a most
scholarly paper for which I wish to extend to you my hearty
congratulations.

Could you check up with Mrs. Chan as to the Chinese names of the
following who collaborated with her in her book published in the interest
of Chinese aid in 1940? Kindly let me know at your convenience, as you
are the only person who could advise me.

With warm regards,

Yours sincerely,

T. L. Yuan

〔University of Chicago Library, Yuan T'ung-li Papers, Box 2〕

按:your scholarly review of Fung Yu-lan's work 刊于 *Philosophy
East and West*, vol. 4, no. 1, 1954, pp. 73−79. Mrs. Chan 即李蕙馨,

1924 年与陈荣捷一同赴美,在波士顿新英格兰音乐学院学习音乐,1928 年结婚。该件为录副。

孟治覆函先生,告知已将先生列入出版品邮寄名单上。

6 April 1955

Dear Mr. Yuan:

I am very sorry not to have answered your letter before this, but illness has kept me away from the office for the past several weeks.

I am unable to give you any information concerning a grant from the Continental Development Foundation. I would like to suggest that you write directly to Mr. C. T. Shen of the Foundation at 37 Wall Street, New York, N. Y.

Your name has been put on our mailing list so that you will receive material you requested from now on. Right now we will send you a Directory of Chinese members on American College and University Faculties for the last three years, and the latest Bulletin in Chinese along with the Annual Report for 1954.

With warm regards,

Sincerely yours,
晚治

〔袁同礼家人提供〕

按:Continental Development Foundation,20 世纪 50 年代初由在美中国工程师、商业人士筹设,后与华美协进社有过较为密切的合作。C. T. Shen 待考。落款处为其签名。

四月九日

刘国蓁致函先生,谈谋事未有实质进展,并谈罗原觉待售书籍等事。

守和博士先生阁下:

敬启者,许久未修书敬候,抱歉殊深。月前拜奉由美来手示,敬悉种切。不遗在远,幸何如之,并蒙惠赠鱼油丸,曷胜感谢。南洋大学林校长已正式辞职,惟校务仍继续进行中,熊院长嘱晚径寄一履历书,定当遵命。至严先生处,晚当考虑进行也。晚近因生活问题东奔西走,仍未得温饱安定,十分惭愧,用是迟迟未报。仄歉奚似,伏希原宥,幸

甚幸甚。日昨得奉令岳丈大人来信,另附致尊夫人信一封,嘱代为转,兹特奉呈,敬希察收为幸。来示关于罗君书籍事,蒙鼎力赞勷,介绍各文化机构,殊深感铭。晚经已对罗君说及,据其答覆,谓艺术书籍非但不能减价,反而有增加可能,因该批书籍为华南所藏,无别家有如此完备者。至其他书目八页现已取消。改呈"蕴石斋书目"一份及其他藏家书目一份,将由钱存训先生代转到,希鉴察为幸(该书目因重量关系,晚径寄至钱君,请其再转呈)。晚经已与田兴智君通讯,关于阁下购置人民手册事,想渠已直接答覆矣。至日本手卷皮纸,集大庄不允先货后钱,但晚已购得三卷(每卷四元),用包裹邮奉上(不能用印刷邮),到希察收。该纸银共十二元,邮费二元半,日前用平邮奉上香港邮柬十张,想不日将可到达,该费共四元四角,连此次邮费二元,共代支二十元○九角,前存十八元八角,比对支长二元一角也。数目是如此,请勿介怀,幸甚幸甚。匆匆,余俟后陈。专此,敬请崇安。

愚晚刘国蓁顿首

一九五五年四月九日

〔袁同礼家人提供〕

按:"林校长"即林语堂,是年3月因办校方针与创办人不合辞职;"熊院长"即熊式一,曾任该校文学院院长,是年10月离开新加坡前往香港。

毛准覆函先生,告知前询留德同学中文姓名的进展,并谈代购图书的办法。

守和我兄尊鉴:

二月廿四日覆示,早已寄到。所附五元,亦已收得,乞勿念。关于以亨兄事,兄所见极对,已以转达。

询及留德同学中文姓名事,曩得第一信时,曾与从吾兄商量。惟两人所知的俱很少,所以未即作覆。弟现已将兄这次来信中所附的名单,打字钞录数份,分询卅年左右在欧的同学。一有成绩当即奉告当然不能全数查出。李玄伯先生处,弟亦曾向之提及。他的办法,亦和弟相同,但只怕成绩不会十分大。

兄所要的书关于新疆的,因不在书肆流通,所以书店无从购买。后由弟向广禄先生询及,广禄先生当慨赠一册,兹另邮奉寄。兄款五元,弟以交此间启明书店之友人郁君合台币一百七十五元,为兄购买在台出版关于边疆的书籍书单系托芮逸夫兄代开的。

兄以后需用此间的书籍,请随时通知。弟当托书店代办。书款二三十元以下的,万不必寄来,弟可代垫。俟积有成数,再由为弟在美购书。专此,顺颂平安。

在美友好,希为代候。

弟毛子水敬上。

四,九,

台湾省台北市温州街 16 巷 11 号

〔袁同礼家人提供〕

按:"广禄"即孔古尔·广禄(1900—1973),号季高,满族,察布查尔锡伯营正蓝旗人,1919 年入外交部俄文法政专门学校,后曾任驻苏联斋桑领事,因与盛世才不合被囚禁,直至吴忠信主持新疆政务始获释放,1949 年去台。

四月十四日

蒋彝覆函先生,告知在英困境并欲赴美谋生。

守和先生有道:

四月十日手教,敬奉悉。久拟修候,终因赶写《巴黎画记》日夜不停,加之各事多不顺手,心情极恶!目下居英非易易,并不是衣食住问题,只是精神及思想在无形压抑下实在受不了。世昌妄、通伯顽,而其余则勾心以图苟延耳。弟离群索居本无多求,但迎拒乏策、左右为难,生存之方又日见缩减,环境逼人之甚,实非血性方刚而意志未全定者所能忍受。前在美闻大公子来英深造,未便有言,二月初得悉同返新陆,私心深慰。今谂其业精进,可贺可贺。如今后有欲来英求学或漫游者,请婉劝三思之,若东向者自当别论。南大事在意料中,但总为林公损失慨叹。熊公闻可继续,尚无返息,若彼真归来,则有不可思议之结局也。弟欲赴美另图生路,船期已定九月九日,但护照问题尚无确实着落,如真能到达彼岸,必趋拜焉。尊嘱代查人名,早经去信各方,回复者现仅陈华全君,正为阁下所欲知之 Chen, Edward Wing-shing, author of "A Practical Encyclopedia of Chinese Cookery"。此君想系奥洲生长,祖籍广东,来信谓其名"华全"乃由其父名"陈得胜" round about 而来,弟乃熟读《封神》之徒(此典联陞知之),亦不能明也。此复,敬颂□安。令郎、令媛等统此问好。

弟蒋彝顿首

四月十四日

〔袁同礼家人提供〕

　　按:"南大事"即南洋大学筹建之事。该函左上残破。

四月十五日

柳无忌致函先生,寄赠图书一册。

　　守和先生道鉴:

　　　　旬前游华府,诸承款待,至为感铭。忌于十一号返校,照常工作。顷接英国寄来拙著《孔学小史》一册,另附上,谨请批评指正。大驾何日有新港之行,祈早示知。如在周末,或可返舍欢迎也。余后述,即请教安。

柳无忌谨上

四月十五日

〔袁同礼家人提供〕

　　按:《孔学小史》即 *A Short History of Confucian Philosophy*,1955年企鹅书局出版。

四月十七日

晚,先生设宴款待谭伯羽。

　　按:谭伯羽(1900—1982),原名谭翊,湖南茶陵人,国民党元老谭延闿长子,赴德国留学,1929年回国后历任上海兵工厂工程师、同济大学秘书长,1949年赴台,后移居美国。

四月十八日

谭伯羽致函先生,寄上两件书法作品。

　　守和先生大鉴:

　　　　昨夜宠召,谢谢。今日裁纸有不匀之处如后,初写一纸,临先五叔诗太长,未能落款,再录先上诗,写一横幅,两并奉寄,遂以塞责,皆未能佳也。乞恕为幸,不一一。

弟谭伯羽再拜

四月十八日

〔袁同礼家人提供〕

按:"先五叔"应指谭泽闿(1889—1948),谭延闿之弟,近代书法家。

四月二十四日

陈受颐致函先生,略谈"胡先生祝寿论文集"事宜及外出访学计划。

守和尊兄有道:

美京侍教,厚承赏饭,感荷莫名。关于适公六十五岁论文集事,当时以在座多人,未敢卤莽请益。兹欲奉教者数事,委员会已组成否(如无正式之组织,办事有时反觉方便)? 征文通知约略何时发出? 邀约人选如何订定? 印刷及其他费用如何筹措? 凡此问题想兄必已成竹在胸,便希赐教,最为感盼。

古根涵基金会对弟请求,业已允许(四千元),明年旅费稍有着落,此皆吾兄吹嘘之力也,万分感谢。弟拟取道东京,先返台北小住,再往马尼拉、香港、澳门、西贡、南旺、星加坡、所加达,然后转飞罗马、巴黎、伦敦、马得里地与里斯本。如时间允许,并拟赴英之前先到莱顿小住数日,瑞典、德国则无须安排,只得暂时割爱矣。此种走马看花之办法,恐于学问无大补益,但求略广见闻而已。弟在东南亚旧友尚多,欧陆则无几人,甚盼吾兄介绍及多方指导也。又钞胥费用全无办法,现正寻购摄影机,不知何种最为适用而上算,是否东洋制品较为便宜,凡此种切,均伫明教。弟以家庭负担太重,无法全年休假,只好六月中旬起飞,明年二月返校销假,因此旅程实感短促,然亦无可奈何也。专此申谢,并颂著祺。敬候嫂夫人俪祉。

弟受颐顿首

一九五五年四月二十四夜

再者,论文集事,劳贞一、全汉昇两君均极关注,并拟取得"中研院"史言所及台大诸友联络,征集文章似尚不太难也。

弟颐又行

〔University of Chicago Library, Yuan T'ung-li Papers, Box 7〕

四月二十五日

先生致信孟治,请填写华美协进社寄送名录中所知者的中文姓名并寄回,建议下一份名录尽可能收录文化和科学机构从业的华人,并予定价以收回印刷成本。

April 25, 1955

Dear Dr. Meng:

Thank you so much for your letter and the various publications of your Institute which you have so kindly sent to me. I wish to congratulate you for the great success you have achieved in all of your activities.

As the last Directory did not contain Chinese names, I have inserted them after those whom I happen to know. I am returning to you this copy and hope that you will ask your staff to do the same after those who are known to you. Please return it to me after you have done so.

For the next Directory which you are preparing for publication, I hope you would ask your staff to insert Chinese names after each person. While it would involve much correspondence and inquiry, it would be of greater reference value.

May I suggest that you would make the Directory as complete as possible by including those who are employed in cultural institutions and government departments of scientific nature such as the Bureau of Standards and the U. S. Geological Survey. Perhaps you would like to have it printed and put on sale at $ 1.00 a copy. In this way the printing cost could easily be covered.

With renewed thanks for your courtesy,

Yours sincerely,

T. L. Yuan

〔袁同礼家人提供〕

按：last Directory 应指 *Directory of Chinese Members on American College and University Faculties*。

戴密微覆函先生，感谢寄赠胡适文章的抽印本，请代向胡适表示敬意，并询问先生《西文汉学书目》书稿撰写情况。

25/4, 1955

234 Boulevard Raspail, XIV

Dear Dr. Yuan:

Many thanks for the offprints from Dr. Hu Shih. I particularly enjoyed his paper against Dr. Suzuki whose work I never appreciated. He rekindled the old zest of Dr. Hu Shih whose paper is great fun. Please convey my best thanks to Dr. Hu Shih; I do not know his address. If I knew it I would bother him with a few papers of mine.

How are you getting on with your monster undertaking? I hope you will not mind that I mentioned it at the end of the enclosed review.

With all wishes and best regards to Mrs. Yuan and yourself, I remain,

Yours sincerely,

P. Demiéville

〔University of Chicago Library, Yuan T'ung-li Papers, Box 3〕

按：Dr. Suzuki 应指铃木大拙（1870–1966），本名贞太郎，日本佛教学者，1934 年访问中国，与胡适有佛学禅宗的论战，时在哥伦比亚大学任教，his paper against Dr. Suzuki 应指 Ch'an (Zen) Buddhism in China: its history and method，刊 *Philosophy East and West* 第 3 卷第 1 期。

四月二十七日

先生致信胡适，告知钱穆发表《驳胡适之说儒》，请胡适酌情考虑代为向中基会提出增加补助。

适之先生：

香港大学出版之 *Journal of Oriental Studies* 第二期载钱宾四《驳胡适之说儒》一文，不识先生曾见到否？如有需要，当钞录寄上。近闻尊处有学术讲演两次，其讲演稿印就时并盼赐寄一份。同礼所编之书目，近又重行增补第一册，三月以后可以完成（约一千页），所收我国人士之著作约二千种，每种均须注明著者之中文姓名，迄今仍有少数尚未查明。下列三人高、张、王，先生如能记忆，盼便中示知。此项编纂工作又承会中补助，至为铭感，惟近来订购国会图书馆印行之卡片，每张一分，共购一万余张，已逾千元，因之生活颇感拮据。如会中经费稍裕，未识能否商诸各董事将补助费略予增加，或将所购之卡片改由会中购置，将来书目印成，即由会转赠台大亦是一法。兹奉上工作报告及戴密微教授来函，盼交各董事审阅，俾明年继续资助，不胜感祷。专此，敬候著祺。

同礼拜启

　　　　　　　　　　　　　　　　　　　四月廿六日

　　　　　　　　　　　　　　　　　　　〔袁同礼家人提供〕

　　按："同礼所编之书目"即 *China in Western Literature: a continuation of Cordier's Bibliotheca Sinica*。此件为底稿,由胡适 4 月 30 日之函可知该信应于 27 日誊抄后发出。

四月二十八日

梅贻琦致函先生,邀请出任《清华学报》编辑委会委员。

　　守和先生惠鉴:

　　　　敬启者,兹为吾国人士关于人文学科论著发表之便利,并藉以与国外文教机关交换、联系起见,拟于本年内将《清华学报》恢复出版。其范围,凡文史、哲学及社会、经济诸科门皆可包列;其名称,以沿用《清华学报》旧名,似在国内外便于销行;其内容,则凡吾国各界学者之研究论著皆所欢迎。惟举办之始,除编印用费另行筹备外,其征稿编辑诸事最为重要,须赖诸先生热心赞助,俾克有成。爰拟即组织《清华学报》编辑委员会,该会主席已商得何廉先生慨允担任。兹拟聘台端为《清华学报》编辑委员会顾问编辑(编辑委员会暂订名单请见附页),除关于编辑事宜另由何廉先生函洽外,谨函奉约,至希惠允,无任感幸之至。专此,敬颂著祺。

　　　　　　　　　　　　　　　　　　　梅贻琦谨启

　　　　　　　　　　　　　　　　　　　四月廿八日

　　　　　　　　　　　　　　　　　　　〔袁同礼家人提供〕

四月二十九日

全汉昇致函先生,告知数年来的大致经历,并商"胡先生祝寿论文集"初步计划。

　　守和先生钧鉴:

　　　　别后想必安吉,为慰!晚于一九四七返国,仍在"中研院"服务。一九四九初赴台,除仍在"中研院"任职外,并在台湾大学任教,近年并担任经济系主任职务。本年度美国国务院给予台大 Research Grant 之名额中,晚因忝在其列,故正月中自台北抵此研究。日前陈受颐先生自西部经华府抵此,云在萧府曾自先生处获悉编撰胡适之先生祝寿论文集事。晚曾以此事告知朱骝先先生,顷接覆示,内云:"胡先生祝寿论文集所收之文章范围较广,故决用院刊出名,仍请兄等费神为之征求文稿,早日寄下,为盼。"不知先生关于该文集之撰稿者,已拟有名单,向之征求文稿否?便中乞示及,俾晚遇见熟友时,亦就近催促,可也。晚拟于六月中左右离此赴欧一游,然后返台。离美前,甚愿能赴华府一行,藉聆教益。关于胡先生论文集事,如先生须晚在此或在台效劳,乞赐示,为荷!专此敬祝钧安。

晚全汉昇敬上

一九五五,四,廿九

〔袁同礼家人提供〕

按:"萧府"应指萧公权。

四月三十日

胡适覆函先生,就申请中基会资助的额度予以说明,并对书目收录的内容范围和时间跨度给予建议。

April 30, 1955

守和兄:

谢谢你的四月廿七日信。

卡片两张,先奉还。先答来函要点:

①China Foundation 年会,已定本年十月一日开会。吾兄的请求"明年继续资助"事,当提出讨论。

②前次暂定"每月二百元",是因为那时年会预算已决定,故我们用老兄从前退还的 $1,800,作为九个月的费用,居然得通过。此次老兄说,"能否将补助费略予增加"?我看 1955 年的月费,两次都是勉强挤入预算的(前一次九个月,今年执行委员会追加三个月),后一次是支配去年度的余款,其数已支配了,恐不能追加。今年年会时,拟提出老兄"明年继续资助"问题,或可提每月贰百五十元,每年为三千元。但年会提案大概也只能以 1956 年为度,不能预定一年以上。此点想能蒙兄谅解。

③来信提及国会图书馆卡片事,尚未及与会中商谈。但来信说"每片一分,共购到一万片",又说"已逾千元",此中当有误字?每片一分,则千元应可购十万片了。

④老兄这个工作是很大的工作,诚如 Demiéville 说的,需要

"financial help—clerical help for a work which exceeds the limits of individual effort, time, and a good health."

我细看老兄此次的 General plan,有点小意见。我想,老兄的精力与中基会的财力都有限,恐不能遍及"other European languages",尤以苏联的各共产国家,因文物交换上的困难,恐难搜罗完备。鄙见以为,现今似宜以 Part I, Section 1, 及 Part II, Section 1(尊稿误作 Section 2)为限,即以英、法、德三国为限。否则规模太大了,要吓倒本会的几位不关心文史的董事,反增加困难。此事似值得老兄从容考虑吧? 关于年代,似也应有个限制。老兄原定 1921—1955,似宜明白规定某年以后(例如 1954)绝对不收。

匆匆问安,并祝府上好。

弟适之

钱宾四的说儒驳文已见了,乞不必钞寄。

适之

〔University of Chicago Library, Yuan T'ung-li Papers, Box 1〕

《清华学报》编辑委员会何廉致函先生,向先生邀稿。

同礼先生赐鉴:

敬启者,关于《清华学报》复刊事,已由梅月涵校长于致台端之聘函中说明,兹不再赘。今后在稿件之评阅方面,尚望多加帮助,以匡不逮。如有编辑事宜,需要特别请教者,亦当随时奉闻,俾有所遵循,而免疏漏。再者,学报复刊伊始,人文学科及社会科学诸部门,在在需稿,先生学界权威,举世钦仰,如承首先倡导,赐寄鸿文,以光篇幅,则学报幸甚矣。另附上征稿简章一份,敬希赐阅为感。专此,并颂撰安。

何廉及编辑委员会仝人谨启

一九五五年四月三十日

第一期稿件定于八月一日以前收齐。又及。

〔袁同礼家人提供〕

按:后附学报编辑委员会、顾问名单一纸。1956 年 6 月,《清华学报》复刊。

五月二日

卫德明覆函先生,希望先生推荐更好的社会学者参加编纂手册的研究项目。

May 2, 1955

Dear Mr. Yuan:

Thank you very much for your letter of April 20th and your recommendation of Mr. Tung. As things stand, the economic sections of our handbooks are pretty well taken care of, but I would still be in need of a good sociologist should you have anybody to recommend.

It made me very happy to hear about the progress of your Cordier supplement. Unfortunately I cannot give you any help regarding your two requests about my old catalogs. I had accumulated a trunk full of them, all of which remained in Peking. However, I might be in a position to add some information about individual books if this might appear helpful.

As ever yours,

Hellmut Wilhelm

〔袁同礼家人提供〕

按：Mr. Tung 即童季龄。落款处为其签名。

五月五日

先生致信卫德明，力荐童季龄前往西雅图华盛顿大学协助开展研究，并请教留德学生中文姓名。

May 5, 1955

Dear Dr. Wilhelm:

Thank you for your letter of May 2.

Mr. C. L. Tung whom I recommended to you is a student of sociology. He studied it at the University of Chicago from 1920 to 1924 when I studied at Columbia. He has a thorough knowledge of social and economic conditions of China, and I am fully confident that he would be highly qualified for the work at Seattle.

I have obtained the catalogues of the Commercial Press, but I am now to identify several Chinese students who wrote their dissertations in German. Herewith is a list and if you happen to know any of them, will you put down their Chinese names? I asked Dr. W. Franke and it happened that he did not know them.

With kind regards,

Yours sincerely,

T. L. Yuan

〔袁同礼家人提供〕

按:该件为录副。

五月七日

杨联陞覆函先生,略谈胡适在哈佛大学演讲经过,并拟"胡先生祝寿论文集"征稿人员名单,请先生考察。

守和先生道鉴:

华府春游,盛蒙款待,至为感谢。近维起居清胜为慰。昨晚胡适之先生在此间为哈佛区域研究学生讲一九一七至一九三七间中国思潮,甚受欢迎。席上遇全汉昇兄,云新得朱骝先院长来信,明年"中研院"将为胡先生出颂寿论文集,嘱令晚学与先生商拟名单,以便征集欧美与我国在国外学人文字。闻人数不欲太多,并以文史方面为限。晚学大略筹计,西人中如 Karlgren、Demiéville、Dubs、Waley、Goodrich、Cleaves 似皆可请,而且可能允为撰稿。中国学者,有赵元任、李方桂、萧公权、洪业、陈受颐、陈荣捷、陈世骧、陈观胜、房兆楹、杜联喆、邓嗣禹、李田意、梅贻宝、柳无忌、王际真等,而蒋廷黻、林语堂诸先生或者亦应邀请,此仅初步拟议,敬请先生斟酌增减,并附加各人通讯地址函告全兄,以便转呈朱先生,再由"中研院"正式具函邀请。西人方面,或有须请先生另外具函坚约者,如何办理,悉凭朱先生决定可也。专此,敬请双安。

晚学杨联陞敬上

一九五五年五月七日

〔袁同礼家人提供〕

按:陈世骧(Chen Shih-hsiang, 1912—1971),字子龙,号石湘,祖籍河北滦县,1932 年毕业于北京大学,获文学学士学位,1941 年赴哥伦比亚大学留学,1945 年起执教于加州大学伯克利分校东方语文学系,协助该校筹建比较文学系。先生在此信上空白处标注"Tucci, Erich Haenisch, Herbert Franke, F. Lessing, Fitz Jäger,

Boodberg, Hummel, Elisséeff"，"李书华、瞿同祖、何炳棣、何廉、杨联陞、邓嗣禹、裴开明、李济、许烺光、张歆海、吴光清、蒋廷黻、蒋彝、熊式一、陈通伯、张仲述"，并在原信"洪业"旁标注"煨莲"。

五月九日

先生致信张君劢，因国会图书馆约定无法寄送《重印聚珍仿宋版五开大本四部备要》中《阳明全书》。

君劢先生著席；

顷奉七日手教及大稿，拜悉一一。当即到书库检查，此间有大本（259 种，1934–35）影印聚珍本及小本零种（50 种，1927 年聚珍本，但无《阳明全书》）。本拟按照大本将所注页数、卷数与译文一一核对，但在第四页原稿上见谭君朱笔，谓"His passage is the same text as on p. 2–3. Should not use different translation"，按其意见则译文似须酌改，俾与上段取得一致，因之进行上不无踌躇。爰与吴光清君商议将大本交邮寄上，但渠谓既系丛书之一部分，馆中定章不允出借，似可由尊处向哈佛借阅云云。敝意大稿既无时间性，似可先函 Moore 君，改在下期付印，同时另向哈佛、加大或华大借阅大本。如尊处另改译文，似以自行斟酌较为放心，想公亦以为然。敝意大本在美较为易得，吾人引用自较小本为便，Moore 来信亦未坚持改用小本，但谓"using his (Taam's) corrected list as the basis, but finding the imcomplete or missing words in the edition which you might have"，似未明了两本之版本大不相同，故敝意今后仍用大本，将谭君名卓垣，前岭南大学图书主任所打者作废可也。如何之处，仍祈斟酌是感。Stanford 交通不便，等候 bus 时间过长，如能搭友人之车，自较方便。同礼到西部后始学会开车，殊不得已也。匆复，敬颂旅祺。

同礼顿首

五月九日晚

〔国家图书馆善本组手稿特藏〕

按："大本（259 种，1934–35）影印聚珍本"即 20 世纪 30 年代中华书局刊行的《重印聚珍仿宋版五开大本四部备要》；Moore 应指 Charles A. Moore（1901–1967），美国哲学家、历史学家，1936 年起在夏威夷大学哲学系任教，创办学术期刊 *Philosophy East and West* 并任主编；Taam 即谭卓垣。是年 5 月，张君劢离开华盛顿，

前往斯坦福大学从事"研究中共政治问题"。① 信中所涉及文章
应指② Chang, Carsun. "Wang Yang-Ming's Philosophy." *Philosophy
East and West*, vol. 5, no. 1, 1955, pp. 3-18。

五月十九日

先生致信赵元任夫妇,请留意加州大学方面何人可为"胡先生祝寿论文
集"贡献论文。

> 元任先生、夫人:
>
> 　光阴过的真快,想你们不久又将西行,恐须再到康乃尔接小中同
> 住,又有一番热闹! 关于适之颂寿论文集事,现由骝先主持办理,大约
> 在台北编印,加大方面 Boodberg、Lessing 及世骧外,尚有何人可以邀
> 请? 能开示一单否? 至盼至盼。专此,顺颂旅安。
>
> 同礼顿首
> 五月十九
>
> 又,郑 mao-yün 中文名字,请示知。
>
> 〔University of California, Berkeley, The Bancroft Library, Yuen Ren
> Chao papers, carton 10, folder 39, Yuan, Tongli and Yuan, Huixi〕

按:"小中"即赵小中,赵元任四女儿,时在康乃尔大学学习物理。
3 月 22 日,赵元任夫妇确曾抵该校,后则继续东行,至纽约、纽黑
文、波士顿等处。Boodberg 即 Peter A. Boodberg(Пётр Алексеевич
Будберг,1903-1972),俄裔美籍汉学家,中文名卜弼德,生于海参
崴,1920 年随家人赴美,后获得加州大学博士学位,长期执教于
伯克利分校。雷兴确为《庆祝胡适先生六十五岁论文集》撰稿一
篇,题为 Wu-Liang-Shou(无量寿): a comparative study of Tibetan
and Chinese longevity rites。郑 mao-yün 实指程懋筠③(1900—
1957),江西新建人,音乐家,早年赴日留学,在东京音乐学院主修
声乐,后兼修作曲,返国后在南昌、杭州等地执教。

---

① 李贵忠著《张君劢年谱长编》,北京:中国社会科学出版社,2016 年,页 277。
② 该期所标注册出版时间为 1955 年 4 月,似乎并非真正刊行时间,具体原因待考。
③ Yuan Tung-li, *China in Western Literature*, New Haven: Far Eastern Publications, Yale University,
　1958, p. 519.

五月二十日

先生致信蒋复璁，请其协助抄录何炳棣所需文献资料。

　　慰堂吾兄著席：

　　　　前奉手教，欣悉复馆盛况，至为钦仰。适有欧洲之游，未及作复。此次所获资料为美国未入藏者为数颇多，堪以告慰。友人何炳棣先生执教于 British Columbia 大学，需用下列资料由贵馆善本目录抄出，拟请雇人抄写。兹先付上美钞拾元，深盼先抄第一种，径行寄交何先生，不胜感谢！其余各种抄费约需若干，务请预为估计径告何君，以便将钞费分期奉上。如该书等尚在台中，可否开箱提出，至盼至盼。专此奉恳，顺颂道祺。

　　　　　　　　　　　　　　　　　　弟袁同礼顿首
　　　　　　　　　　　　　　　　　　五月二十日

　　　　附上美钞十元，何君通讯处如下：

Dr. Ping-ti Ho, 2029 Wesbrook Place, Vancouver 8, B. C., Canada
拟钞登科录书单一纸。

　　　　　　　〔台北"中央图书馆"档案，档案编号 299-0091 至 299-0092〕

　　按：1954 年 8 月，"教育部"令蒋复璁筹备恢复"国立中央图书馆"。9 月，奉令恢复设置，该馆自此由设在台中县雾峰乡北沟的院馆联合管理处抽出，并完成接收联合管理处中图组所保管之图书文物。10 月，蒋复璁复职"馆长"，先假台大医学院大礼堂内办公。1948 年，何炳棣即在加拿大英属哥伦比亚大学历史系任教。所附书单未存。

五月二十三日

杨联陞覆函先生，就"胡先生祝寿论文集"先生拟增的西方撰稿人表示赞成，另告知白乐日寄送先生的宋代名人年谱目录、北宋地图，已由哈佛大学图书馆代收。

　　守和先生：

　　　　今晨奉到五月十九日手示，拟加 Tucci、Haenisch、Franke、Lessing、Jäger、Boodberg 及 Hightower、Creel、Fairbank、Gardner、Bodde 各位，晚学俱甚赞同。虽然征未必得，在得信人看来总是一种荣誉，然则以宁失之广为善耳。

图书馆日前收到 Sung Project 寄交先生宋代名人年谱目录一份，北宋地图(由日本人著作放大)一纸，尚在敝处，恐一时尚无用处，拟俟袁清到华府时带上。如果急须即乞赐示，当交邮寄呈也。先生通讯处改为国会图书馆，则已径函白乐日(Balazs)矣。

全汉昇兄游华府想已晤及，何炳棣兄住 94 Prescott St.，与劳贞一同楼昨晚来康桥搜集资料，大约可住两星期也。敬请双安。

晚学杨联陞敬上

五月廿三日

〔袁同礼家人提供〕

按：Haenisch 应指海尼士，非其子 Wolf Haenisch。白乐日(Étienne Balazs，1905-1963)，匈牙利裔法国汉学家，1923 年师从柏林洪堡大学福兰阁教授，1925 年到 1926 年由法国汉学家马伯乐指导。1949 年曾计划对宋朝进行系统研究，但因为人力、物力、财力均不允许而中辍，1954 年在充足资金保证下，将 1949 年的想法付诸实施，发起 Sung Project，邀请欧洲、美国、日本的学者尤其是年轻学人[1]，系统、协同研究宋代历史，1954 年旅欧期间先生极有可能受邀参与，给予意见并提供文献支持，因居所不定，或将杨联陞作为回美后的联系人。

五月二十五日

先生致信胡适，抄录清代方志文献中所见赵载元之相关记载。

……

翻阅馆中及其他方志目录，江苏一省并无通志，前此竟未曾注意！光绪十年之《淮安府志》仅载赵载元于乾隆五十五年署淮扬道，此外尚有方炜及永龄二人，想与先生所见的是同一版本五十九年实授的是谢启昆，《扬州府志》此间有嘉庆十五年及同治十三年两种，亦无赵载元之名，而《仁和县志》康熙以后未修，故不易查到其仕履。顷在乾隆庚戌春季《大清搢绅全书》第二本四十一页查到下列一条，或可供参考，可惜此间无乾隆五十九的年。专此，敬候道祺！

---

① 1957 年，方豪出席第十届国际青年汉学家会议，得知此研究计划的宗旨和目的，回台后曾积极倡导，并呼吁在台学人成立宋史研究会，以求相互切磋。参见李东华著《方豪先生年谱》，台北："国史馆"，2001 年，页 16。

同礼拜上

五月廿五日

〔台北胡适纪念馆，档案编号 HS-US01-004-008〕

按：该信未存起始页。赵载元，清代学者赵一清之子，其父于乾隆十九年（1754）撰写完成《水经注释》，该书稿于乾隆五十一年（1786）由其刊行问世。谢启昆（1737—1802），字蕴山，一字良璧，号苏潭，江西南康人，清代诗人。方炜、永龄，管理江南河库道道员，约在乾隆五十五年（1790）左右。

五月二十七日

杨联陞覆函先生，认为似不宜邀请田清波为胡适六十五岁祝寿论文集撰稿，日方学人中能撰写中、英文者，吉川幸次郎则是首选。

守和先生：

今晨奉到廿五日手示，加入 Elisséeff、Kennedy、Bagchi 俱甚相宜。Mostaert 神父现在美国，住 Arlington, Va. HJAS 明年或后年可能为出一期祝寿，由柯立夫主持。日前适之先生到此时，柯曾面询与 M.神父是否熟识，胡先生云不识或不记得了，柯本有意为 M 征文，闻此遂未启齿。既然不甚熟悉，而蒙古学又非胡先生所特重，则略去似亦无妨。向日本汉学家征稿而限用英文或汉文，似属不情（如向德国人征稿，自不能禁止用德文也），又老辈多已凋谢，而中年学者奇多，若只选三数人，则去取之际，甚为不易（又年辈高者，未必真好，如宇野哲人八十岁）。日本京东研究所几年论文集中似无华人著作，则中国人出论文集，不向日本征求，似亦不足为奇矣。（如真要征求，则吉川幸次郎必当在内，不但中文好，又曾译胡先生《四十自述》，大有关系也。）

王启无，现在 Univ. of Florida, Gainesville, Fla 任教，尊函已代发。

匆覆，即请双安。

晚学联陞敬上

五月廿七日

〔袁同礼家人提供〕

按：王启无（1913—1987），生于天津，1933 年毕业于清华大学，1946 年赴美入耶鲁大学，翌年获硕士学位，1951 年获哈佛大学博士学位，时在佛罗里达大学任教。

五月三十日

全汉昇致函先生,告知其最近行迹,并询问"胡先生祝寿论文集"征求投稿者名单。

> 守和先生钧鉴:
>
> 前抵华府时,获聆教益,至感至慰!晚因住在 Virginia 友人 Dr. Raper 家,出入均乘其自开汽车,故再无机会踵府叩谒,至以为憾!晚住至五月廿七日止,即乘车赴 Baltimore 一游,然后经纽约返此。
>
> 胡先生祝寿论文集征求投稿者之名单,不知先生已拟订妥当否?如已拟好,请早日赐下(连同各人通讯地址),以便由晚寄返台北,再由朱骝先生发出征稿公函,并请先生等以私人友谊关系催稿,为荷!
>
> 晚将于六月廿一日离此赴纽约,而于廿四日离美,又及。专此,敬祝钧安。
>
> 袁太太均此问好。
>
> 晚全汉昇敬上。
> 五月卅日。
> 〔袁同礼家人提供〕

六月六日

李济覆函先生,告知寄书三种,并谈其对申请哈佛燕京学社资助以支持台湾大学和历史语言所研究计划的态度。

> 守和吾兄赐鉴:
>
> 五月十六、廿七两函均前后收到,敬悉一一。昨日已邮寄出下书三种:
>
> (一)台湾大学出版纪念孟真论文专刊一本
>
> (二)吴稚老九十生辰纪念集
>
> (三)历史图谱一卷
>
> (一)、(二)两种,为弟处所获复本,奉赠吾兄者,第(三)由出版公司直寄,书价已由尊处存款拨付(共有台币四百廿元,已送来弟处,当遵嘱代为保管作购书之用)。此外各书弟已托人打听,尚无下落,关于新疆之书报经由芮逸夫兄多方托人探询,尚未得到一切实之答覆,俟有着落,当即代购邮寄华盛顿地址。承惠寄所印目录,已收到,谢谢。此书研究所有两本,弟在南京时已参考过,现拟由弟私人购买,价目何如,

祈示知，以便归入尊存款项下。今年春，由梦麟先生热心，台大与史言所曾联合拟一计划，送请哈佛燕京社考虑，至今没有下文。尊函所云"如能继续出版新书一二种，则明年向哈佛燕京社请款补助当无困难！"盛意极感，当转告史言所与台大同仁。弟个人对此，却不存任何大希望，新书自然是应该出的（这是我们的职业），但出新书，是要出版费的。现在的台湾读书人，每月的收入，照黑市计算，不到美金廿元。各文化机关的豫算，也有出版费，但真正有文化价值的，只有优后权。一年多前，故宫博物院的理事长正式提议出卖国家的收藏古物，为一些不怕饿死的人反对掉了，因此却得罪了一个有权有势的老板。至今——啊，只看他们吧！这些事，自然是原子社会的美国文化人所不能想像的，对不起，说了这些话，因兄关怀文化事业，特以奉达。即颂旅安。

弟李济拜覆

六月六日

〔袁同礼家人提供〕

按："纪念孟真论文专刊"即《傅故校长斯年先生纪念论文集》，1952年12月台北刊行。"吴稚老九十生辰纪念集"似指《吴稚晖先生纪念集》，1954年台北"中央文物"出版。"历史图谱"，待考。

Mark Tennien 覆函先生，告知订阅 *Mission Bulletin* 事宜，并建议联系 British Information Service 和 United States Information Service 获取相关书目信息。

June 6, 1955

Dear Mr. Yuan,

　　Your letter of May 3 just came in. You say that you would like to subscribe to the *Mission Bulletin*. I would suggest that you get the copies for the last year if you are interested in the events of China. It gives you a pretty good commentary which should be helpful to you.

　　I don't know exactly where to look to help you find a comprehensive list for your bibliography. I would suggest that you write a note to the British Information Service and to the USIS here in Hongkong. They both have libraries here and I presume they could give you a helpful list.

　　If I can help you out in any other way, please feel free to call on me.

With best wishes, I am,

Sincerely yours,

Rev. Mark Tennien

Editor

Mission Bulletin subscription is ＄5 U. S. per yr.

〔University of Chicago Library, Yuan T'ung-li Papers, Box 2〕

　　按：Mark A. Tennien（1900 – 1983），美国传教士，时任 *Mission Bulletin*（香港）主编，后赴日。该信所寄地址无误，但极有可能被先生漏看，参见翌年 1 月 27 日函。落款和补语皆为其亲笔。

六月十日　波士顿

上午十一时,先生至哈佛大学,遇杨联陞。晚,先生访杨联陞,谈至十一时方去。〔《杨联陞日记》(稿本)〕

六月二十日

蒋彝致函先生,寄上向洛克菲勒基金会请求资助用以研究明清画的申请书,请先生提出意见。

　　守和先生有道：

　　　　五月中旬曾上一书,并附寄 Kegan Paul 及 Bodley Head 关于两位中国作家之复信,想早登记室,未能将该作家等中名找出,深以为憾为歉。旋因继续赶画《巴黎游记》插图,致少修候,尚乞亮之。敬维贤优俪兴居清吉是颂是祝。前承盛意,嘱拟计划设法申请罗氏基金会资助事,牵延甚久,无暇着手,近将巴黎画件勉强告一结束弟着重在明清之画,因喜龙仁之书很少提及此点,且其书简略不详又无个人意见,乃即从事草就奉上,敬祈公余得便详加改定,是否有当及如何增减之处,务恳费神指示。至于申请方式及应由何处代为申请,或直接申请,均乞赐知。弟与哥大中日文部尚未发生直接关系,似有难于请求代为请款之处也。关于哥大拟译《文献通考》事,承辱函王际真兄加上弟名,极感,但王兄迄今未复弟信已数通矣,奈何奈何! 耑此,顺颂俪安。

　　　　　　　　　　　　　　　　　　　　　弟蒋彝顿首

　　　　　　　　　　　　　　　　　　　　　六月二十日

〔University of Chicago Library, Yuan T'ung-li Papers, Box 2〕

　　按：先生收到此函后即覆信。

六月二十七日

蒋彝覆函先生,已按照建议修订申请书,并谈与文礼、史克门二人的交往。

守和先生:

今晨奉到手教并指正拙拟计划各节,先生相助之诚挚,今鲜其例,为之感激涕零。弟对此种计划书未曾拟过,至于如何可再具体些,一时脑笨无法想出。兹将尊改各节打出并加上一简单书目,已遵嘱寄往 Methuen 总经理一阅,请即作书为证,书到即寄上三份不误。但如何申请,方法仍仰先生力助,只是先生事忙,烦扰殊不安也。Dr. Wenley 及 Mr. Laurence Sickman 均与弟相识,一九五三年特往 Kansas City 一拜 Sickman,承其盛意赐食。彼之母亲曾住北京很久,想先生当识之,如把晤,烦致意焉。如先生觉弟有私人去函请求之必要,俟先生收到打好计划书后再为之,谅不迟也。匆此复谢,余再陈。敬颂俪安。

弟蒋彝顿首

六月廿七日

〔University of Chicago Library, Yuan T'ung-li Papers, Box 2〕

按:Methuen 即伦敦 Methuen 出版社,自 1941 年起,蒋彝作品均在此社发行,1956 年 *The Silent Traveller in Paris* 亦由此初版。

六月二十九日

刘国羡致函先生,告知罗原觉藏书多已售予香港大学,并回复此前询问的两人信息。

守和先生尊鉴:

敬启者,许久未修函敬候,抱歉殊深。辰维撰祉延鸿,文祺纳燕,至以为颂。四月四日手示敬悉,晚因贱务羁身,无时或已,迟迟未报,歉仄奚似,伏祈原宥为幸。令岳信及蔚林书局函均已即为代转,日昨又得奉令岳来信,嘱代转尊夫人信一函,特为奉呈,敬希察收。敝友罗君之艺术书籍经已脱售与港大,为价三万五千港元,至其余版本书籍将开列书单另呈,而宋版《朱子》系与宋版《方舆纪胜》一并脱售,并要在港交易,亦即交货收银办法,想此举不易行。前蒙推荐哈佛,感激奚似,谨此致谢。代查澳门 Luís G. Gomes 通讯处为 Escola Primária Municipal, MACAU,至 Kwong, Chan Yeung 之中文姓名可能为"邝赞扬",因该书遍找各书店皆无得购买,是以该名亦未十分肯定,为憾。

晚处境尚感困难,仍未见好转,秉华东翁亦未加以援手故也。匆匆,专此,敬请崇安。

愚晚国蓁顿首

一九五五年六月廿九日

〔袁同礼家人提供〕

按:Kwong, Chan Yeung,中文名待考,"该书"应指*Everybody's Cantonese*,直译为《广东话入门》,1951 年初版,1955 年时已是第 4 版。

杜乃扬覆函先生,告知找到两册博士论文,并鼓励先生编纂《西文汉学书目》。

Paris, le 29 juin 1955

Cabinet des Manuscrits

Cher Monsieur,

Excusez-moi de n'avoir pu vous renvoyer plus tôt votre travail complété comme vous le désiriez. Les recherches ont été longues et viennent seulement d'être menées à bien.

Pour les thèses chinoises, je n'ai pu retrouver que deux mémoires. La transcription des noms est parfois si fantaisiste qu'on ne peut l'imaginer et qu'on risque de passer à côté!

Aucune bibliographie publiée en France ne prend la suite de Cordier et votre travail sera certainement des plus utiles.

Je joins à ma lettre votre feuille de demandes complétée et une feuille portant les renseignements complémentaires.

Veuillez recevoir, cher Monsieur, et partager avec Madame Yuan, nos souvenirs les meilleurs.

Mme M. R. GUIGNARD

Conservateur au Cabinet des Manuscrits

〔University of Chicago Library, Yuan T'ung-li Papers, Box 3〕

六月三十日

先生致信史克门,请协助蒋彝申请洛克菲勒基金资助。

June 30, 1955

Dear Mr. Sickman:

I have recently returned from a year's research in Europe. While in Oxford, I often saw Mr. Chiang Yee who, as you know, have been studying Chinese paintings in the British Museum. As he had made a study of Chinese paintings in America before, he is quite anxious to continue that study. I now enclose a draft memo which is self-explanatory.

Knowing that you are keen in the promotion of Chinese art studies, I promised him that I would first solicit your advice. Perhaps you could suggest the possible sources of support to enable Mr. Chiang to complete this difficult task.

I feel that if a Foundation-such as the Rockefeller Foundation-is to be approached, the project has to be submitted by a museum, not by an individual scholar. The grant will be made to a sponsoring institution and the Foundation will hold it responsible for the completion of the project.

As far as I know, the Rockefeller Foundation is not very keen to support Chinese studies generally. But if it is strongly backed up by a museum or a group of museums, it may give favorable consideration.

Since you are always so helpful to foreign scholars, I trust that you would be willing to obtain the sponsorship for Mr. Chiang's project. Would the Nelson gallery, or, in collaboration with another institution, be willing to do so? What other sources of support you would suggest that could be explored? I shall be grateful if you could advise me or Mr. Chiang with your valuable suggestion.

With kindest regards,

Yours sincerely,

T. L. Yuan

〔University of Chicago Library, Yuan T'ung-li Papers, Box 2〕

按:此件为录副。

七月一日

蒋彝致函先生,呈研究计划书三份并请转寄。

守和先生有道:

前书计达,兹寄上计划书三份,并书局总经理信三通(一信径书文雷先生,其余如有指定人名,可另书)。一切务恳鼎力费神、向机相助,则不胜感祷之至。如有指示,请即赐知,以便遵办。尚此,敬颂双安。

弟蒋彝顿首

七月一日

〔University of Chicago Library, Yuan T'ung-li Papers, Box 2〕

按:"向机相助"当作"相机相助"。"书局"应指伦敦 Methuen 出版社。

七月三日

先生致信莫余敏卿,转寄罗原觉待售古籍书目,并询问其所知在美西岸高校图书馆的华人馆员。

July 3, 1955

Dear Mrs. Mok:

Mr. K. C. Lau, formerly a staff member of the Fung Ping Shan Library, has sent me a list of books belonging to Mr. Lo, a friend of his. I am passing on the list to you for your and Dr. Rudolph's examination. If you are interested in any of the items, you may communicate with Mr. Lau at the following address:

Mr. K. C. Lau

36 Lockhart Road

Third Floor

Wantsai, Hong Kong

Some of us here are preparing a directory of Chinese librarians who are now working in libraries in this country. As far as I know there are over 70 trained men and women. Will you send me a list of those whom you happen to know? Is there a librarian at Pomona for Chinese books? If you could include those in California, I shall greatly appreciate your courtesy.

I have asked Mr. Eugene Wu at Stanford to send me a list of those working at Seattle and Palo Alto.

I hope you and Mr. Mok will have a most pleasant vacation and a good rest. We have very warm weather here and we have to go to the L.

C. even in the evenings because of its air-conditioned equipment.

Yours sincerely,

If you could find out whether Prof. Rudolph's book of Chinese Printing is still available, I should like to order a copy.

〔袁同礼家人提供〕

按:此件为底稿。

七月五日

先生致信文礼,转交蒋彝的研究备忘录,并告知其将于本年秋在哥伦比亚大学讲授中国艺术课程,请协助他继续在美开展对中国传统绘画研究的计划并获取相关资助。

July 5, 1955

Dear Mr. Wenley:

Referring to our previous conversation regarding Mr. Chiang Yee's project in a survey of Chinese paintings in American collections, I beg to send you herewith a short memo (in duplicate) which Mr. Chiang sent to me.

In the fall Mr. Chiang will give lectures on Chinese art at Columbia for three months and he has obtained the entry visa. If he could obtain the support for the continuation of his project for the survey, he would prolong his stay in this country.

Knowing that you would be in a better position to assist him in the realization of the project, may I leave the matter in your hands? I know Mr. Chiang would be extremely grateful to you if you could explore the possibilities for him and help him to complete this difficult task.

Among the possible sources of support, someone has suggested the Rockefeller Foundation. But if it is to be approached, the project has to be submitted by a museum. The grant will have to be made to, and administered by, the sponsoring institution and the Foundation will hold it morally responsible for the completion of the project.

From the annual report of the Foundation, I note that the Foundation has made large grants to Japan and Japanese studies generally. But as this is a small grant, the Foundation will give favorable consideration if it is backed up by a museum.

The only scholar whom I have written is Mr. Lawrence Sickman. I have asked his advice and suggestions regarding this project and I hope to hear from him before very long.

Yours sincerely,

T. L. Yuan

〔University of Chicago Library, Yuan T'ung-li Papers, Box 2〕

按：此件为录副。

七月十日

Jane Beck Johnson 覆函先生，就先生对詹森去世致哀表示感谢。

July 10, 1955

Dear Doctor and Mrs. Yuan：

I want you to know, even at this late date, how much we appreciated your very kind letter about Nelson. We have felt deeply the love of our friends surrounding these difficult days and it had comforted us greatly. Thank you very much for thinking of us. I do hope you will come to see us. Nelson was very fond of you and appreciated the happy associations during his years in China.

With kindest regards and all best wishes to you & yours in which Nelson Jr. & Betty Jane join me.

Sincerely,

Jane Beck Johnson

〔University of Chicago Library, Yuan T'ung-li Papers, Box 2〕

按：Jane Beck Johnson(1900-1991)，生于北京，1931 年和詹森在北京结婚。该信为其亲笔。

七月十一日

蒋彝致函先生，告知收到文礼信件，并就申请资助金额请先生给予意见。

守和先生有道：

今晨奉到文雷先生来信，敬谂前上计划书已蒙盛意转去，无任感激。文雷对之颇多友情，并嘱弟预算所需费用，弟简以叁仟美元壹年答之,其太多乎? 望有以教我,并就近顺便一商。彼之信中提到 Mr. Waite,弟不相识,暇盼赐知。弟复文雷书中提到往哥大教书及壹仟元薪水不敷应用处,想先生前次见面时已提及,故尔云云。总之,此事如能有成,皆先生之赐也。因行期已近,故多琐细,乞恕不能多述,容再陈。此颂俪安。

弟蒋彝顿首

七月十一日

（一九四八年弟有同样计划,曾托美国友人与 Langdon Warner 商量进行,但 Warner 氏不大赞成,故作罢。此次有先生相助,成功希望甚多,谢谢。）

〔University of Chicago Library, Yuan T'ung-li Papers, Box 2〕

按:Langdon Warner(1881-1955),美国考古学家及艺术史学家,通译作兰登·华纳,主要研究东亚艺术。

七月十四日

先生致信罗文达,询问一本法文著作的作者信息。

July 14, 1955

Dear Mr. Loewenthal:

I wonder if you would be good enough to ask Mr. Pickens if he happens to know the Chinese name of the following author:

Ma, Ko-tsay:*Pri ères des musulmans chinois*, tr. sur l'original en arabe et en persan Da'aouât el Moslemim. Paris E. Leroux, 1878.

As it is not mentioned in his bibliography, I wonder he has included it in the new edition which he is preparing. I shall be grateful if you could obtain the information for me.

Yours sincerely,

〔袁同礼家人提供〕

按:*Prieres des musulmans chinois* 直译应为《中国穆斯林的祈祷》,Ma, Ko-tsay 的中文名待考。此件为底稿。

七月十八日

先生向国会图书馆递交应聘申请,其属意的部门为 Library Services Division of the Legislative Reference Service,岗位为书志编纂员(Bibliographer)。〔袁

同礼家人提供〕

按：当日，该馆雇佣部门主管 Robert B. Reed 覆信先生，表示会妥善考虑。

七月二十一日

王铃覆函先生，告在英无法骤然离去，并谈近况。

> 守和老师尊鉴：
>
> 奉手教，惭汗满面。晚前函中英友协嘱径寄尊址，迄无回音。月前于友人处收集一二纸，又不知误放何处，下月初去伦敦亲访该会秘书，全部奉寄不误。此间全无前途希望，惟最近准备论文，各项费用由尼德汉私人负担，去年学费亦由尼公支拨，既受人之恩，一时便无法遽然离去。美国方面自申请 Rockefeller Foundation 失败后，意趣淡然。哈佛燕京既属临时性质，又补助无几，拟暂作罢论。台湾更无发展，惟有在此苦忍。晚自离婚后迁居独处，生活渐入轨道，愿继续努力写成《中国算学史》，虽毕生潦倒，死亦无憾矣。汉昇兄在此游览一日，他乡异国得晤故人，益增归思之念。在外蒙吾师关爱种种，不敢一日而忘之。晚生不逢时，客地飘零忽忽十载，自恨一无建树，更无面目见江东父老，犹苟且偷生亦不知所为何事。然年事虽增，壮心未死，此恨此情，罄纸难书也。
>
> 生王铃敬上

〔袁同礼家人提供〕

按：该信并未标注落款时间，暂依邮戳系于 1955 年 7 月 21 日，另王铃的通讯地址为 48 Eden Street, Cambridge。

八月二日

费成武覆函先生，尚未在英觅得合适绣服，并询可否购买荣宝斋木刻笺谱及册页等件。

> 同礼先生道席：
>
> 久未奉候，时深驰念。拜诵大示，欣悉起居安吉为慰。前承嘱代购绣服，原店之原服已售出，曾往 Liberty Co. 等处看过，索价过高，古玩铺等极少见有适当衣服，乃致迁延，未能早日报命。近见有荣宝斋木刻精印《十竹斋笺谱》及沈石田及任百年册页等，如有意，即可购后拜托仲雅先生带上。或请示知艺术品类别，若小件古玩可否，当即遵

办。闻式一先生尚在香港。蒨英之画展尚称不恶,其草书虽曾写数张,均不甚满意,当再习写,择选寄上求教也。专此,恭请俪安。

尊夫人前叩安。

弟成武顿首

蒨英附笔候安

八月二日

〔袁同礼家人提供〕

按:费成武的通讯地址为 17 De Vere Gardens, London W. 8。

八月五日

吴文津覆函先生,告知所询馆员中文姓氏,并建议联系华社以获取华盛顿大学中国留学生名册。

Aug. 5, 1955

Dear Dr. Yuan:

Your letter of August 1 arrived here day before yesterday. Here are the names of my assistants at the Hoover Library:

Mrs. Jolien Lou 娄, Miss Victoria Chiu 邱肖云, Mr. Lee Hun 李弘.

Mr. and Mrs. Leslie Tsou's address is 1249 Alder St., Eugene, Oregon.

Best wishes to both you and Mrs. Yuan.

Sincerely yours,

Eugene Wu

P. S.—I do not have a copy of the Chinese students' roster at the University of Washington. The old one is out of date. I think you write to Austin Chang, President of Hwa Sheh（华社）c/o Foreign Students' Adviser's office, Husky Union Building, University of Washington, he will send you a copy when it comes out in the fall.

〔University of Chicago Library, Yuan T'ung-li Papers, Box 3〕

八月六日

蒋彝覆函先生,告在英代购药品结果,并谈赴美计划。

守和先生:

七月廿六日手教奉悉多日,前天上午曾往 Messrs. F. L. K. Loxley 药店一询,药方事店主不能立时作答,谓如系 Private Patient 药方,很有找出可能性,若系 National Health,则该方已送往公家结账,即无从问津也。今晨再往该店,结果无法配制。弟意如先生设法函询 Dr. Smyth,也许再开原方,如赐下即设法配制带来。关于弟此次赴美事,尚未向各方提及,因办理护照及其他各项手续方面,不得不小心谨慎。费成武夫妇亦不知弟行动,行前当往取书画带上不误。弟此行有破斧沉舟之意,等到美后再设法延留至少三四年,或终老该乡亦未可知。究竟如何,此时难以决定,亦不能使英方知道耳。关于"在美国画之检讨"计划,承大力相助,希望有成。不过此等事,成功与否,有许多不能预料之处,求其在我而已,成可喜,败亦无忧。Mr. Sickman 与弟不甚相熟,彼往日本或休假很可能,或有难于作复之处。弟意最好不必函催,终久会有复信,如不复亦无可如何也。

先生处尚有第三份计划书,如未寄出,请暂勿寄出,弟处原稿散乱不知何所,将来许要借用也。弟离英期为九月九日,但请勿向英方友人说明,至祷。匆复,敬颂俪安。

弟蒋彝顿首
八月六日
〔袁同礼家人提供〕

　　按:"斧"当作"釜"。

八月十五日

先生致信赵元任,告知李霖灿来美计划并请教授其语言学,另请转达致意与陈世骧。

　　元任先生:

近日出外旅行,返华京后奉读手教,藉悉返西部后忙碌一番。惟闻尊夫人曾患血压,大家均极惦念,现在虽已低下来,仍盼随时注意一切,听其自然,无须着急。近在普仁斯敦看见尤桐,他去年曾患血压,现已完全复元矣。近接李霖灿君"中央博物院"职员函,谓有来美研究之可能,颇愿来华京整理此间所藏之 Moso 文写本。弟已劝其先到尊处研究半年,获到语言学基本训练以后,再来华京,想荷同意。渠至多在美一年,不得不事先筹划一种程序也。世骧想常晤面,近在《远东季刊》见其批评洪煨莲之"子"字长篇,写的极好,晤面时望代致钦佩之意。又前请张充和女士赐一墨迹,久未寄来,两位晤面时并望从旁一催,如能写一横批(草书),最所盼望。专此,敬颂俪安。

尊夫人同此问安。

同礼顿首

内人附笔叩安

八,十五

〔University of California, Berkeley, The Bancroft Library, Yuen Ren Chao papers, carton 10, folder 39, Yuan, Tongli and Yuan, Huixi〕

按:是年 1 月 7 日,赵元任夫妇由法国瑟堡(Cherbourg)乘船返回美国,12 日抵达纽约,自此在美国东部各大学、机构访问,6 月 11 日在纽约告别胡适、梅贻琦等人后开车返回西部,18 日回到加州。5 月,杨步伟血压升高,遵医嘱休息。李霖灿(1913—1999),生于河南辉县,美术史家,1941 年进入迁移至李庄的故宫博物院担任助理研究员,后将自丽江采集而来的文字编辑成《么些字典》,1949 年赴台,任职于台北故宫博物院。"洪煨莲之'子'字长篇"指 Harvard-Yenching Institute Chinese-English Dictionary Project, Fascicle 39.0.1: Preliminary Print,该篇评论刊于《远东季刊》(*The Far Eastern Quarterly*)第 14 卷第 3 期,页 395-402。张充和(1914—2015),时在加州大学图书馆工作。

八月二十二日

蒋彝覆函先生,感谢从旁协助申请美方赞助以开展在美中国画调查计划。

守和先生:

八月十九日手教及 Sickman 复书,均于今晨奉悉,至感赞助弟事之热忱! Sickman 复书各节,在弟意料中,因其所见与最近去世之 Langdon Warner 相同,向人要钱,总非易易,尤其目下流落海外华人之工作与言行,不为人重视。文雷屡次来信,确真有意相助,只要他力可能,或可有成。但彼仍居于第三者地位,未能直接有所决定,究竟做到如何地步,颇难预测。总之弟对此事,当喜其有成,但预备失败。要是文雷不以弟是做此 Survey 之适当者,即必落入 Warner 与 Sickman 同样思想,盖彼等以为各博物馆对中华绘画均已雇人译载编目了事矣! Siren 所写仅平铺直叙,不敢加议论,弟若能写,则必多附己见,但我见为是为非,则又大问题了。好在文雷已答应帮助,弟意听其得便图之。

这种事需要时日,成与不成,弟对先生赞助热忱,永感不忘耳。上星期四得到 Dr. Smyth 寄下药方,比即往 Loxley 配制,交下一小瓶,二英寸高,二英寸余直径,因非 National Health Insu.,故取价三先令六便士。如先生欲购一瓶,弟可往其他药房配之,此点请即示知。费成武夫妇最近晤到一次,但未提到尊件,如不大又非瓷制品(恐易破),当设法带来不误。匆复,敬颂俪安。

弟蒋彝顿首

八月廿二日

〔袁同礼家人提供〕

按:National Health Insu.应指英国国家医疗保险。

八月二十七日

刘国蓁覆函先生,告知持介绍函往新亚书院求职未果。

守和先生尊鉴:

日前拜奉八月五日手示,敬悉一一,并即将致令岳丈大人函代转去,想已到达。昨日得奉令岳手示,并附代转尊夫人信一函,兹特附呈,敬悉察收为幸。前函内附美钞贰元,经已妥收。惟棉线类之织造品皆不能寄至美国,因美禁运入口,是以嘱代购女背心一事,不敢代购寄上,因此处邮局严厉执行检查寄美包裹故也。该款尚存晚处,以待后命。晚之生活仍在困苦颠连中,尚未有其他辅助。此次蒙向钱院长推荐,感铭殊深。晚经已持函晋谒,据其答覆谓新亚书院学生只得百余人,图书亦不过二万册,是以现尚未有若何发展,而新校舍尚未兴工等,但渠将直接回信与先生关于此事也。渠将新印之新亚书院概况一册着晚寄呈,经已用印刷邮奉上,迟日当可到达。兹先将该院教授名单抄录如下:钱穆、牟润孙、唐君毅、张丕介、杨汝梅、余协中、孙祁寿、曾克耑、赵冰、王书林、胡家健、陈伯庄、伍镇雄、卓宜来、何格恩、郎家恒(美籍)、张葆恒、嵇哲、潘绍华、陆锡麟、郎兰豀、爱德信、卢维贞(上三人皆女性并美籍)等。匆匆,专此,敬请崇安。

愚晚刘国蓁顿首

一九五五年八月廿七日

〔袁同礼家人提供〕

按:胡家健(1903—2001),字建人,安徽绩溪人,东南大学教育学系毕业,曾任浙江大学教授兼学校总务长、教育部中等教育司司长等职务。唐君毅(1909—1978),字毅伯,四川宜宾人,哲学家,毕业于中央大学,历任四川、华西、中央诸大学教授,1949年赴香港,后与钱穆、张丕介等创办新亚书院。

八月二十九日

全汉昇致函先生,告知为"胡先生祝寿论文集"组稿情况并请协助。

守和先生钧鉴:

别后想必安吉,为慰! 晚于六月下旬离美,乘机赴英、法、德、意等国旅行,于最近始返抵台北。关于胡先生祝寿论文集筹备事,晚路过香港时,曾与陈受颐先生面谈,返台北后又与李济之先生(自董先生赴香港大学后,史言所由李先生负责)商讨。陈、李两先生之意,认为征稿信对中国学人不始先发,对外国学人则最好先征求其同意,然后由"中研院"正式去函征稿。因数年前史言所为傅先生论文集征稿事,曾去函高本汉,结果毫无,故此次征稿似宜特别审慎,以免有损胡先生清誉也。晚已托陈受颐先生于将来访欧遇见有关外国汉学家(如 Paul Demiéville 等)时,先口头征求同意,然后由陈先生函知史言所(或"中研院")仝人,以便将征稿函寄出。在美东方面,如 Derk Bodde,H. G. Creel,Kracke,L. C. Goodrich,A. W. Hummel,G. A. Kennedy 等教授,如先生最近有机会见面,或与之通讯,乞就近先行非正式征求其同意,并请将结果示知,以便由此间正式发出征稿函,为感! 至于哈佛方面,晚已另行去函杨联陞兄先行非正式征求同意;加州大学方面,晚亦另函赵元任先生先行口头征求 F. Lessing 教授等同意,俟有结果,然后由"中研院"去函征稿。此外如先生遇见其他较熟之汉学家,已口头征得其愿投稿之允诺,亦请速示知,以便正式发出征稿函,为荷! 在台湾方面,胡先生祝寿论文集征稿之负责人,除李济之先生总其成外,劳贞一、高去寻诸兄亦允效力。故在国外方面,请先生多加费神,并时时赐教,为感!

专此,敬祝俪安。

晚全汉昇敬上

八月廿九日

〔University of Chicago Library, Yuan T'ung-li Papers, Box 2〕

八月三十日

先生致片李书华,略述《尚书大传》版本。

> 润章吾兄:
>
> 　　《尚书大传》除雅雨堂本外,尚有《四部丛刊·左海文集》本,《青照堂丛书》本(第三七册),《古经解汇函》本(十一、十二册),侯官《陈氏遗书》本(二五、二六册),《榕园丛书》本(第二册),似可再向哥大方面一查,想总可觅到《洪范五行传》也。藕舫有一文致台湾科学人士函最近《华侨日报》,已见到否? 顺颂大安。
>
> 弟同礼顿首
> 八,三十

〔Columbia University Libraries Archival Collections, Shuhua Li Papers, 1926-1972, Volume II: Modern Eminent Chinese Leaders〕

　　按:"藕舫有一文致台湾科学人士函"应指是年 6 月 15 日竺可桢在中央广播电台的讲话,题为"对台湾科学界朋友们讲几句话"。①

八月三十一日

费成武覆函先生,告知所托购买之物皆有所获,并已请蒋彝带上。

> 守和先生道席:
>
> 　　前奉手教并支票伍镑一纸(附函当时即付邮矣),所嘱代觅物件今晨已挂号邮寄仲雅先生,拜恳带奉。昨日彼曾来舍,因尚有他约,未便携去,故今日寄去,两周必动身云。前曾数次往原店托觅绣衣,并往数处询购,极难得较满意者。现得一件长披肩,无袖但绣工尚佳,花式大方且非新货,价五镑五先令。另代购玉器两小件,亦尚可爱。因瓷瓶及木雕两件仲雅先生不易携带,故另觅此两件,一圆形雕两鱼(三镑三),另一鸟形(三镑十五),未知能否合尊意也。蒨英正楷东坡词一纸,亦一并托仲雅兄奉上,祈赐教也。专此,恭请大安。
>
> 尊夫人前叩安。
>
> 小弟成武拜上
> 蒨英附笔候安

---

① 《竺可桢全集》第 3 卷,页 223-224。

八月卅一日

〔袁同礼家人提供〕

九月二日

先生致信钱存训,请其在芝加哥大学为"胡先生祝寿论文集"征稿。

公垂吾兄:

前奉手书,承寄芝城图书馆界人名,至以为谢！嗣后陆续搜集,共得一百三十人,已托于振寰君油印后径寄尊处矣。明年十二月为适之先生六十五岁寿辰,弟即发起由台北编印颂寿纪念论文集,征集中西人士投稿,芝大方面拟请 Creel 及 Kracke 各担任一篇,便中可否先行征求同意,如允寄稿,当由台北朱骝先先生或李济之先生正式函约也。芝大今夏所设语言学,学院想已结束,如章程尚有存者,亦盼转告负责人径寄一份是荷。又文史系章程亦请寄下一份,至谢。匆匆,顺颂暑祺。

弟同礼顿首

九,二

〔钱孝文藏札〕

按:《庆祝胡适先生六十五岁论文集》并未收录 Creel(顾立雅)及 Kracke(柯睿格)的论文。

九月八日

胡适致函先生,请准备《西文汉学书目》相关材料,以便在中基会第二十六次年会上讨论是否资助。

Sept. 8, 1955

守和兄:

中基会的 26th 年会,将于十月一日在"大使馆"举行。我想请你替我预备这些资料:

①请将 Cordier 的 *Bibliotheca Sinica* 原书借出一份,我可以带到会场,给我们的董事们看看。会毕即奉还。

②请将老兄已编成的 Supplement 的一部分借给本会董事们看看,何如?

③关于 Far Eastern Association 提议代印的事,如有新发展,乞示知。倘能有新函件见示,更好。

④老兄若愿意写一叶或两叶的报告,极所欢迎。

　　我与叶良才兄大概九月廿九日或卅日到 Hotel Dupont Plaza。此次孟邻与思亮都能来,甚可喜。相见有期,敬问双安。

适之

〔袁同礼家人提供〕

九月二十八日

蒋彝覆函先生,略述入职哥伦比亚大学后的情况。

　　守和先生:

　　　　大片敬奉悉。哥大本周注册,选弟课者尚不知有多少学生,恐怕仅一二人,则课程是否能开班,还是问题。总之,此来哥大,乃借题入境,只是美金缺少,生活稍感困难。若文雷方面能有相当结果,方可稍安,但该事非人力所可强成,听之而已。文雷已有信来说明一切,屡蒙先生力助,无任感拜。目下问题很多,一时难来华府。尊物容来时再带来,否则可托便人带上。心情不定,乞许后述。此颂俪安。

弟彝顿首

九月廿八日

〔袁同礼家人提供〕

十月三日

费成武覆函先生,支票已拜收,所寄函件已付邮代转。

　　守和先生大鉴:

　　　　自康瓦尔渡假归来,奉读大示,无任欣感,惟稽覆尚祈原宥。所附支票,深谢,希代购各物尚能合尊意。函一件,已代付邮,请勿念。仲雅兄离英匆匆,未克送行,已安抵纽约,甚慰。初到必甚忙碌也,谅现或已前来相晤矣。式一先生除家书外,别无消息,闻已自港赴新加坡云。据 B. B. C.友人谓黎明先生在英,或将参加中国科工作,故略闻南大过去情形云。专此,恭请道安。

　　尊夫人前叩安。

弟成武拜

蒨英附笔候安

十月三日

　　附函恳转致仲雅兄,至感。因不知确址。

〔袁同礼家人提供〕

按：康瓦尔应指 Cornwall，位于英格兰岛西南端的半岛，泰马河的
西岸。黎明（Lai Ming, Richard, 1920-2011），祖籍广东梅县，生于
毛里求斯，早年返国就读于上海圣约翰大学附属中学，后入中山
大学获学士学位，旋赴美留学，妻子为林太乙，即林语堂次女，
1954 年随岳父前往新加坡，任南洋大学行政秘书。

十月五日

徐家璧覆函先生，转告鲁光恒婉拒此前推荐，并告纽约公共图书馆、哥伦比
亚大学图书馆中文馆员信息。

> 守和先生尊鉴：
>
> 　　敬肃者，顷奉月之三日手示，敬悉一切。嘱转致鲁君光恒（字公
> 望）一函，业已遵办。据渠表示，对于先生推荐德意，至觉感戴，惟彼因
> 申请在美长期居留之事，尚未办妥，恐一旦离美，即无法返来，是以暂
> 时颇无意他去，详细情形彼将另函尊处，兹不多赘。再者，璧于上月尾
> 曾去纽约公立圖，查得目前司编该馆中文图书者系 Virginia Wang 女
> 士，现与某张君结婚，伊之中文全名系张王朝岚。兹悉先生前曾函达
> 该馆探询此事，谅与璧所探得者相同乎？哥大圖近亦加聘国人办事，
> 兹就所知者列举二人于后：
>
> 　　叶惟宏（Yeh Wei-hung），东亚圖 "page"
>
> 　　丘万镇太太（Mrs. Margaret Ch'iu [Liu]）Cherk-typist at the
> Photographic Service Dept.
>
> 　　余俟续奉，敬请道安。
>
> 晚徐家璧鞠躬
> 十月五日
>
> 尊夫人前并请叱名叩安为感。

〔袁同礼家人提供〕

按：鲁光恒，字公望，湖南长沙人，南开大学历史系毕业，后留校任
教，并曾在中基会编译委员会任职，1936 年 8 月入清华大学文学
院任助教。[1] "先生推荐"，应指举荐其赴台湾大学图书馆任职。

---

[1]《国立清华大学教职员录（民国二十五年十月）》，1936 年，页 10。

十月十日

刘楷贤致先生两函,告知抄录《国会图书馆藏中国善本书录》经过及用时和页数,请与国会图书馆沟通为此项工作增加报酬。其一,

> 守和先生赐鉴:
>
> 　　目录钞写已告完成。对于国会图书馆方面,除函告邮寄手续外,实无再写报告之必要,盖详细情形已于五月初信中陈述,信去之后迄今已逾六个月,未得 Dr. Adkinson 一字回覆!继续再写,措词实感困难,故此另具专函寄奉先生。如蒙体念抄写艰钜,请根据信中意见,赐予馆方再事磋商,酌加抄费,则不胜感谢也。外附上函稿两张,敬乞指正是幸!并希即赐回音,以便将信及善本书录付邮。专此,敬请大安!并候袁太太安!
>
> 　　　　　　　　　　　　　　　　　　　　刘楷贤顿首
>
> 　　　　　　　　　　　　　　　　　　　一九五五年十月十日
>
> 　　贡颖附笔问安。

其二,

> 守和先生赐鉴:
>
> 　　贤蒙推荐从事钞写目录,工作已整整一年有半。在此一年半中,抽尽公余时间,每周平均工作廿小时以上者,无非遵守契约之签定,并报答先生之雅意也。兹将经过情形,详陈如次:馆方 Dr. Adkinson 第一次来信,约谓云 "According to Dr. Yuan, your fee for the completed work would be ＄1,500.00"(Jan. 19, 1954),所谓全部抄工者,当时实为估计耳。且先生曾口头告贤说:大抵每天须抄写三小时,预期十个月内可以抄完,并嘱将所耗时间据实记载云云。经贤计算,抄成每张计需 $1\frac{1}{4}$ 小时(抄写一小时,标点、校对、标页数十五分),共钞成一千二百零三页,合计需时一千五百零三小时,若以抄写工资一千五百元折合,则每小时所得,实际不及一元。此时间方面与当时预计,有所出入也。至于页数方面,除当时自府上领来者外,收到先生由英寄来者约二百余页,补遗又一百余页。凡此种种情形,敬祈俯察,并请向馆方分别提商,酌予改善抄工是幸!专此,敬请公绥!
>
> 　　　　　　　　　　　　　　　　　　　　刘楷贤顿首
>
> 　　　　　　　　　　　　　　　　　　　一九五五年十月十日
>
> 　　　　　　　　　　　　　　　　　　〔袁同礼家人提供〕

十月十一日

蒋彝覆函先生,告申请 Guggenheim Foundation 资助应静观其变不可强求,并告新居地址。

> 守和先生:
>
> 　　大示及转下成武兄函,敬奉悉。弟事承关注,极感! 文雷处最好听其自然变化,欲速恐不达。弟波城友人谓与 Guggenheim Foundation 秘书友善,将去信探询。弟哥大班今日添加二学生,孟治先生坚约弟往华美协进社作六次讲演 Appreciation of Chinese Art,汪亚尘先生所教为直接绘画技能,与弟不同,不能比也。弟来此哥大,一切接头均非妥善,所授之课并不直属于中日文部,故情形比较复杂,颇伤脑力。加之住处太小而又属旅馆式,有种种不方便之点,一切自动,很费时间,较之在牛津时相差太远,颇怀返英意。日前打油一首:纽约高高那易居,到此方知气喘嘘,端的人生为什么,不贪熊掌也无鱼。录陈一笑,此复,敬颂俪安。
>
> 　　　　　　　　　　　　　　　　　　弟彝顿首
> 　　　　　　　　　　　　　　　　　　十月十一日
>
> 　　日来承徐家璧兄导观图书馆各部,及指示在纽约生活各点诸多紧要,至深感激。此君诚朴浑厚,交谈甚相得,闻随先生极久,可佩识人之深也。弟不日将迁居,以后赐教请寄 Apt. 3D, 165 West 91st. Street, New York City, N. Y.
>
> 　　　　　　　　　　　　　　　　　　〔袁同礼家人提供〕

　　按:汪亚尘(1894—1983),原名汪松年,字云隐,浙江杭州人,1916年赴日留学,毕业于东京美术学校,归国后任上海美术专科学校教授,1928 年赴法学习,1931 年归国,曾任新华艺术专科学校教务长,时在美教授中国画。

十月十六日

胡适致函先生,请代为在国会图书馆翻检《振绮堂书录》对《水经注释》的记录。

> 守和兄:
>
> 　　在华府时,蒙大嫂亲做饺子,饱餐后至今不忘,多谢多谢。
>
> 　　老兄便中,乞查国会馆中有无振绮堂书录。如有书录,乞代检其

中对于赵一清的水经注释三部写本的记录,倘蒙抄示,无任感激！此三部是:

　　(1)水经注释底稿七册(不全)
　　(2)水经注释并刊误二十册　}改为三十六册
　　　　　　　　　　　　　　　汪曾唯书目在"西学"第三格

　　(3)水经注释并刊误二十二册　书目在"墨"字第三格

此中两部后来转入丁氏善本书室,其记录我已抄了。后来似三部都归南京蟠龙里的国学图书馆,倘蒙并检国学图书馆书目的著录见示,更所感激。(手头的南京 notes 似蟠龙里有三部,又似只有两部,故欲一释此疑。)

　　此中第一部"底稿"七册,在丁氏时已用刻本配补,故丁丙不知其为振绮堂书目著录的"底稿"了。

　　国会馆中的一部水经注释确是小山堂雕本,而印刷则在嘉庆年间。已写一跋,改定后当寄与光清兄。又吴琯本的 microfilm 已寄到,明日当一校之。乞代谢馆中诸友的帮忙。匆匆,敬问双安。

弟,适之

十,十六早

〔University of Chicago Library, Yuan T'ung-li Papers, Box 7〕

十月二十二日

先生覆信胡适,告国会图书馆并无《振绮堂书录》,但已尝试联系平馆亲属代为查询,另告江苏省立国学图书馆所藏赵一清《水经注释》版本及两种提要。

　　适之先生:

　　　　赐书拜悉。振绮堂书录为朱文藻所辑,各书目均未著录。前在北平时,曾为平馆购到艺风旧藏汪璐的藏书题识旧钞本,该题识内或有关于赵书的提要或题跋。拟致函舍妹,嘱其到馆一查姑且试试,已久未通讯。

　　　　国学图书馆的目录,共翻检四种,每种记载相同,均著录下列赵书两种:(一)抄刊配合本三十六册、(二)旧钞本二十册,均得自丁氏善本书室者见另纸,并无第三种二十二册在"墨"字第三格者。该馆另有水经注乾隆刊本,八册,有双韭山房、董秉纯、抑儒字小纯三印,又小韭山房一印,即所谓天都黄晟刊本,亦得自丁氏。赵书的提要,仅觅到两则,载在(一)耿文光山西灵石人万卷精华楼藏书记书未散,提要附奉,(二)浙江采进遗书

<u>总录</u>即四库底本,其提要因今日书库封闭,未及抄录,至于刻本究存若干部,尚待考证<u>见另纸</u>。

近日<u>孟邻</u>、<u>月涵</u>两先生已返台否? 尊夫人前患腿疾,不识已大愈否? 内人颇为系念。渠近患胃溃疡,在医院住了九天,幸未开刀,而所费已甚可观,在此真不能患病也!

专此,敬候俪安。

同礼叩上

十月廿二

〔台北胡适纪念馆,档案编号 HS-US01-044-002〕

按:"舍妹"应指袁荣礼。随信附上多页抄录古籍信息。

十月二十四日

胡适覆函先生,请勿在国会图书馆代抄《水经注释》提要,并告因先生之助得以厘清此前关于该书的误记。

守和兄:

谢谢你十月廿二日的信和抄件,<u>振绮堂</u>的<u>书录</u>及<u>藏书题识</u>都未有刻本,又没有全本保存的抄本,是很可惜的。我竟不知书录及题识的传本如此之稀有! 因此累你老兄费力检查,十分不安。但尊函益我良多,多谢,多谢! (<u>浙江进书录</u>,Gest 有一部,已抄其<u>赵书提要</u>,请不必抄了。)以此看来,<u>振绮堂</u>所藏三部赵书,仅有两部流入<u>丁氏善本书室</u>。所存两部是"底稿"本七册,配合刻本及"振绮堂抄本"为一部;另一部"版心上有'小山堂'三字",完整的保存,<u>丁氏</u>不云出自<u>汪氏</u>,似亦出自<u>汪氏</u>?

我的 notes 不完全,事隔多年,仔细翻检,始知"<u>振绮堂抄本</u>"尚残存第一,第二,第十六,第十七,第廿一,第廿六,廿七,卅五,共八册。"底稿"本似存第一(一部分),第二,第三,第四,第六,第七,第十,共七册。第五册也是抄本,版心有"东潜赵氏定本"六字,似是用刻本钞的。余皆用刻本配补的。

我因为 notes 所记<u>蟠龙里</u>所藏,有"赵氏原本"、"振绮堂抄本"、"小山堂抄本"三目,故自己疑所记实有三部抄本。现在才弄明白了。此是吾兄的助力。

<u>蟠龙里</u>的书,有四种目,承代遍翻,至感。

此目依据<u>丁目</u>,但<u>丁目</u>实有许多错误。例如吾兄指出之"<u>天都黄晟</u>刻本",实是<u>项絪</u>刻本,首册四卷缺,用<u>黄晟</u>本配补,故编目者以为<u>黄</u>刻了。是一小误。此书<u>丁目</u>疑为<u>董秉纯</u>节录<u>全谢山</u>手校本,<u>江苏四目</u>因之。是一大错。其实是<u>赵东潜</u>早年手校本,<u>赵</u>书的一切原料都在此。我后来用<u>东潜</u>手稿去比勘,才断定此为<u>东潜</u>校本,绝无可疑。手头尚藏有此本的照片多叶,他日当请老兄看看。(此书被<u>谢山</u>借去,终身不还,故有<u>双韭山房</u>印章。其"<u>小韭山房</u>"印,是<u>谢山</u>殇儿<u>昭德</u>之印,<u>昭德</u>死后,<u>谢山</u>又死了,故书归<u>董秉纯</u>。)<u>小山堂</u>刻本,我初以为现存世间的不过十几部。今承老兄开示见于著录的十二部,与我所见的八部,已共有二十部了。(<u>日本</u>的两本或是<u>吴氏</u>、<u>甘氏</u>旧藏。也有十八部。)我所藏的四部,其中一部是<u>海源阁</u>的书,其上过录<u>季沧华</u>本及<u>沈大成</u>校<u>何焯</u>、<u>戴震</u>(早年校)本,即<u>楹书隅录</u>所记之本。四部只带出一部,及个思之,尚恋恋不忘!

适之
十,廿四

<u>孟邻</u>廿日上午走了,<u>月涵</u>廿夜走了。

内人腿痛,经医生诊治,取出膝盖下水分,现已大好。

嫂夫人有恙,幸未开刀,想已安好,甚念。我盼老兄能利用 Blue Cross or Blue Shield 的医药保险法,千万不可不访询之。

适之

〔University of Chicago Library, Yuan T'ung-li Papers, Box 7〕

按:"蟠龙里"即指国学图书馆。补语为胡适用红笔所书,写在此函第一页右下角处。

十月二十七日

先生致信蒋复璁,请其考虑编纂台北新书目录,将各书店书单、各留学名录一并寄美。

慰堂先生惠鉴:

奉到手书,欣悉贵馆已迁入植物园办公,明春即可开放阅览,引企新猷,无任钦佩。台北出版新书为数极多,拟请编一选目,与国外交换均无困难,并请将各书店出版书目代弟搜集一份,自当随时通知此间友人继续订购。又台北出版之英文刊物共有若干种,亦请开示一单。

此间对于英文书之需要较中文书尤为迫切,惟著作人往往不注中文姓名,稽考不易,可否通知有关人士,以后如印英文刊物,似以加入中文姓名较为便利。台北留德、留法、留英同学会闻已先后成立,如有同学录,亦盼费神代索壹份寄下,至感。附上一单,其中著作人之中文姓名,敢祈查明示知是荷。专此,顺颂秋祺。

袁同礼顿首
十月廿七日

奉上留美图书馆学同人名单,人数虽多,但研究学问,精于目录版本之学者,则廖若晨星也。

Hsin Kwan-chue　著有中国艺术英文小册,台北"教育部"出版?

Wang, Eugene HHC.⎫
Tang, Chalmers T.　⎬ 大约在台北资委会办事
　　　　　　　　　　⎭

Lu, Wellington T. Y.: *Current Chinese Industrial & Commercial Tax Laws Taipei*, 1952　"财政部"办事?

Li, Kolu: *Die Seidenindustrie in China*. Berlin, 1927

Liang, Chiang: *Die chinesische Wirtschafts-und Sozialverfassung zwischen Freiheit und Bindung: ein Uberblick bis zum Jahre 1937*. Wurzburg, 1938

Yen Yu Tschang: *Soziale Frage und Ständische Sozialpolitik im Westen und in China*······ Weidlingau Wien, 1935 (Dissertation-Wien)

〔台北"中央图书馆"档案,299-0100 至 299-0102〕

按:是年9月19日,"中央图书馆"迁入南海路29号植物园内台湾省国语推行委员会旧址,即日治时期之建功神社旧址,翌年3月1日,正式提供阅览服务。

十月二十八日

胡适致函先生,告中基会准予再资助美金三千元用以编纂《西文汉学书目》。

October 28, 1955

Dear Mr. Yuan:

I have the pleasure to inform you that at the 26th Annual Meeting of the China Foundation held on October 1, 1955, it was decided to grant you a special research fellowship of ＄3,000, in order to enable you to complete the work on a supplement to Cordier's *Bibliotheca Sinica*.

The grant will be paid in 2 equal installments at the end of March and September in 1956.

Yours sincerely,

Hu Shih

Acting Director

〔台北"中央研究院"近代史研究所档案馆,〈中华教育文化基金董事会〉,馆藏号 502-01-08-026,页 69〕

按:此件为录副。

十一月八日

芮玛丽致函先生,拟将先生之名列入斯坦福大学访学的名单中,用以证明该校图书馆中文馆藏的质量。

November 8, 1955.

Dear Dr. Yuan:

I wonder whether we may use your name as that of a non-Stanford scholar who has done research here and at other American libraries, and who can therefore comment on the character and quality of our Chinese collection in its special fields of modern history and the social sciences. We have been making good headway on cataloging, under the terms of a Ford Foundation grant, and are well over our quotas. Now the Foundation wishes to assemble a dossier which will indicate the value of this collection to studies of modern and contemporary China.

This of course can be done only by visitors who have recently spent a considerable period of time here. Otherwise, I should not trouble you with this request.

Sincerely yours,

Mary Wright

Associate Professor and Curator, Chinese Collection

〔University of Chicago Library, Yuan T'ung-li Papers, Box 2〕

按:落款处为其签名。

十一月十五日

香港蔚林图书公司（Willing Book Company）致函先生，告知自即日起停止图书购买服务。〔University of Chicago Library, Yuan T'ung-li Papers, Box 2〕

十一月十九日

卫挺生（菲律宾）覆函先生，已按前信建议修改书稿。

Nov. 19, 1955

Dear Mr. Yuan:

Thank you for your letter of some time ago, suggesting what to do with my book to get publication. I have followed your suggestions. The pictures are nevertheless too many, though I tried to reduce the number to a minimum. It is because that the emphasis of the book was laid on the identification of the □□□□ type of culture with pre-Chin Chinese culture, and the pictures will silence all the arguments. The book is a little over 300 pages, including about 50 pages of pictures. I have already sent two copies of the manuscript, one to Mr. C. L. Tung in Washington D. C., the other to a friend in New York to help to negotiate for the publication. I hope, something may recent from the negotiation.

With best regards to you and your family,

Yours sincerely,

Tingsheng S. Wei

〔University of Chicago Library, Yuan T'ung-li Papers, Box 2〕

按：时，卫挺生的联系地址为 113 L. A. University of the Philippines, Quezon City, P. L.。

十一月二十四日

徐家璧覆函先生，婉拒翻译工作，并就所托查询各节予以答复。

守和先生尊鉴：

敬肃者，昨奉月之二十日手谕，敬悉一是。承为介绍柳无忌教授领导之翻译计划，心感无既。惟此事自始迄今，璧已在非正式形式下参加中。盖此间有一同学，经申请参加此种翻译，后曾屡以渠稿央璧参加意见或予以订正，近因承接之译稿过多，更以一半交璧代译，于是工作较前更重而加积极，惟璧均"屈"居幕后人而已。为此璧觉实无力再行承担一份应用本人名义之工作,故而只得将试译稿二纸璧还,以便先生另请他人合作,苦衷所在,伏乞格外鉴原为祷。又,本月初璧曾随蒋仲雅先生去康桥一行,在杨莲生先生府中曾晤令媛袁静女士,谈及夫人前患胃溃疡病,殊深怀念,但庆业已康复,为之不胜雀跃。惟仍希随时调摄护持,庶免复发为要。此外,璧于公余亦按时前往华美协进社聆闻蒋先生主讲之中国书画演讲(共六次,现已讲过两次),裨益良多耳。余俟续奉,敬请道安。

晚徐家璧鞠躬
十一月廿四日夜

尊夫人前并请叱名叩安为感。

再者,嘱查数事,兹已查讫,谨列结果如下:

1.哥大研究生 Chester Tang(非 Chen)所著之《庚子事变》,近已印行,其中文名写法,系"谭春霖"三字。

2.华籍印民曾珠森先生所译之《白虎通》一书,本馆卡片作:*Po hu t'ung: the comprehensive discussions in the White Tiger Hall……a contributions to the history of classical studies in the Han period*, by Dr. Tjan Tjoe Som, Leiden, E. J. Brill, 1949. V. 1-2 (Sinica Leidensia, v. 6) 编号系:East Asiatic, D899.63, Si65, v. 6

3.Henri Maspero 所编之 *Documents chinois*,经在下列目录中查寻,均未查得:本馆目录、总馆目录、L. C. Printed catalog、British Museum: Catalogue of printed books、法国国立圖书本目录。不知其著录,究应如何? 甚觉愧歉!

先生既曾在哈佛得见是书,何不央请哈佛仝人一查?

晚家璧又呈
十一月二十五日
〔袁同礼家人提供〕

按:Chester Tang 当作 Chester C. Tan,其书为 *The Boxer Catastrophe*,1955 年哥伦比亚大学出版社初版;*Documents chinois* 即 *Les Documents chinois de la Troisième Expédition de Sir Aurel Stein en Asie Centrale*,1953 年 Trustees of the British Museum 发行。

十一月二十七日

全汉昇致函先生,请先生编辑胡适英文著作目录,并在美就近征辑祝寿论文集稿件。

> 守和先生钧鉴:
>
> 　　十月九日来示,早已收阅,谢谢! 胡先生祝寿论文集之征稿函(对外国学者用英文,对本国学者用中文),此间已于日前由朱骝先、李济之两先生签名发出。先生处当已收到。关于胡先生著作详细目录,中文著作方面,此间正指定史言所三仝人共仝负责编辑。至于胡先生之西文著作,李济之先生甚赞同由先生就近利用美国国会图书馆所藏资料负责编辑。今日晚遇见李先生时,李先生嘱函达先生费神赐助,早日进行,请勿却为感!
>
> 　　由朱、李先生签署之征稿函,凡来示提及业已同意撰稿之美国学者,及赵元任、杨联陞两先生函述已允撰稿之加大与哈佛教授已分别向之寄发。如最近先生在美征得其他学者仝意,亦请示知,以便由此间发征稿函,为荷! 专此,恭祝圣诞快乐!
>
> 晚全汉昇上
十一月廿七日

〔袁同礼家人提供〕

十二月一日

先生致信 Meuvret 夫人,请其根据巴黎东方语言学院图书馆藏标注附录清单中期刊创刊、终刊时间,并请寄送巴黎东方语言学院概览及课程情况,询问该校图书馆是否有纳西文献。

December 1, 1955

Dear Madame Meuvret:

　　I presume that you must have been very busy since the reopening of your School last month. I really hate to bother you again for bibliographical information. But as a number of journals are only to be found in your Library, I hope you could spare some time to check these journals for me. Your expert assistance will be gratefully appreciated.

　　I now enclose a list of journals. Kindly supply information concerning the date of commencement and the date of suspension of each, basing on the file in your collection.

As I am anxious to know the curriculum offered in your School, will you kindly ask the Aminstrateur to send me a copy of your prospectus with the names of instructors in each course.

When you write to me, will you also inform me whether you have in your collection any Moso manuscripts from S. W. China?

I am sending you, under separate cover, two books on Buddhism in China and on Chinese Moslems which you may like to have for your own private collection. If you desire any book or any kind of assistance in the USA, please drop me a note. I shall be delighted to be of service to you at all times.

Hoping to hear from you soon and with my kindest regards,

Yours sincerely,

T. L. Yuan

〔University of Chicago Library, Yuan T'ung-li Papers, Box 3〕

按:此件为录副。

十二月二日

萧瑜覆函先生,告知中国国际图书馆迁南美近况,并拟协助辨识留法博士学生姓名。

守和先生文几:

奉惠书,忻□□晤。散处书箱大部份尚未开启因新建馆舍尚未完工,《中法大学月刊》等均无从参考查阅,此次所示名单因译音关系多有□□不能辨认十分真确,幸有谭显楫君完全证实,否则交白卷矣。此间文教事业日在进展中。石曾先生尚在台湾,最近来书甚健旺,返南美当在明年矣。大驾前有南游意,未知何时可成行也,企予望之。专覆,并颂大安。

弟萧瑜顿首

十二,二

又倘承钞示作者姓名后各附论文题目全文,弟拟试寄久留法国之一最老学生代为一问,或可查得一部分,未可知也。又及。

〔University of Chicago Library, Yuan T'ung-li Papers, Box 6〕

按:谭显楫,湖南湘乡人,1919 年 5 月毕业于留法高等工艺预备第二班。[①] 该函有折痕,扫描件未展平。

十二月十一日

蒋彝致函先生,告知其受邀将赴佛利尔艺术馆演讲。

> 守和先生有道:
>
> 久疏候问,至以兴居清吉,为颂为念。关于"中画在美检讨"一事,想已从文雷先生得知前后,兹不赘。文雷先生约弟于三月中在 Freer Gallery 讲演一次,届时当可聆教。二月前赴康桥,得晤令媛袁静博士,敬谂先生抱恙痊疴,深为慰颂。昨日曾宪七兄过纽约,比托其将由英带来各件带往康桥转请静博士带上,想不日伊即前来重叙天伦之乐也。匆此奉闻,余容后续。敬颂俪安。
>
> 弟蒋彝顿首
> 十二月十一日
> 〔袁同礼家人提供〕

按:1956 年,袁静在哈佛大学化学系获得博士学位。

十二月二十一日

刘国蓁致函先生,告已遵嘱购买各物并随圣诞礼物寄出,另告先生岳丈袁道冲现在所居地址。

> 守和博士先生尊鉴:
>
> 敬启者,顷奉令岳丈大人来示,嘱代转致尊夫人函,兹夹附呈,敬希察及为幸。时乎不再,又届圣诞佳节,晚于上月中旬包裹邮奉上英国饼干一盒,贺简一函,恭祝圣诞快乐,敬希哂纳,区区微意,聊表寸心而已,想当可及时到达。该包裹内并附前嘱代购女装背心(最细号)四件,共银六元,及杭州小剪一把,银三元。将美钞二元找得十一元五角,比对存二元半,连尚存二元半,共存五元;此次邮费二元,即存三元也。晚仍故我,仍然乏善可陈,惟望时赐教言,以匡不逮,寔深感幸。令岳丈大人已迁居,地址为松江县城中山西路一三四二号。专此,敬请崇安。
>
> 愚晚国蓁顿首
> 一九五五年十二月廿一日

---

① 《育德同学录》,1930 年 7 月,页 160。

恭贺圣诞快乐暨新年进步。

〔袁同礼家人提供〕

是年

先生编*Directory of Chinese Librarians in the United States of America*,并由于震寰油印。

　　按:该目共统计一百三十余人,参见 1955 年 9 月 2 日先生致钱存训信。

一九五六年　六十二岁

一月十二日

先生致信钱存训,感谢寄送芝加哥大学图书馆新书目录,并指出卡片中的错误,另询问人名。

公垂吾兄:

近承惠寄贵馆新书目录,至以为谢,尚缺第一、第二两期,可否赐予补寄。尊处新购之书在港、在台系由何人代为订购?近接 Willing 来信,宣告停业,想周转不灵也。又芝大收藏文史哲书籍较多,请查欧阳竟无及马一浮两先生之书已入藏者各有若干?示知为盼。顺颂大安。

弟袁同礼顿首

一,十二

又尊处所编卡片,郑叔问《南献遗征笺》应改为郑文焯撰,郑字俊臣,又字书问,别号大鹤山人。交大西文图书目录由 Wolfe S. Hwang 一九二八出版,知其中文姓名否?亦盼示知。

〔钱孝文藏札〕

按:Wolfe S. Hwang 即黄惠孚,他受时任图书馆馆长蔡亚白的委托编纂西文书目,题名为 *First Chiao-tung University Library Catalogue: Foreign Books Department* 。

一月十四日

西门华德覆函先生,祝贺《西文汉学书目》即将完成,并告 Edwin G. Pulleyblank、Katharine Po Kan Whitaker 二人生年。

14th January, 1956

My dear Mr. Yuan,

Thank you so much for your letter of 20th December, and for your and Mrs. Yuan's Christmas greetings, which my wife and I very sincerely reciprocate. I am sending you by surface mail a copy of our Calendar, and of the last Departmental report. I shall certainly let you know as soon as I have an opportunity to visit Peking, but I do not think it likely that this visit will materialize in the near future. I do not think that a report of the Trade Mission to China has been published. But I shall make enquiries and send a copy on to you if it has been published.

I am so glad to hear that your work on Cordier's supplement is about to be completed. It is a pity that articles will not be included; I hope that there may be an opportunity of including them at a later stage.

The years of birth of Professor E. G. Pulleyblank and Dr. Katharine Po Kan Whitaker (nee Lai) are 1922 in the first case and 1912 in the second.

I was glad to see Ch'en Shou-yi, whom I had not seen since my stay in Peking in 1932. He came through London, and we talked of the good old days, and of course also of you and your work.

With very kind regards, also to Mrs. Yuan.

Yours sincerely,

W. Simon

P. S. I was phoned by Mme. Mozere just after Christmas; she had been seeing friends at a place near Oxford, I called on her in Paris when I was there last September. She told me that unfortunately you missed each other during your visit to Paris. I had the impression that she was definitely on the way to recover after all the hardship she has gone through.

〔University of Chicago Library, Yuan T'ung-li Papers, Box 2〕

按:Edwin G. Pulleyblank(1922-2013),加拿大汉学家,中文名蒲立本;Katherine Po Kan Whitaker(1912-2003)即赖宝勤,女,生于香港,后毕业于香港大学英文系,1936年以公费赴英留学,此二人均在伦敦大学亚非学院学习。

一月十五日

刘国蓁覆函先生,往来信函均已转投,请先生鼎力协助谋取孟氏图书馆中文部主任职务。

守和博士先生尊鉴:

敬启者,上月廿一日拜奉十六日手示,敬悉,并附代转令岳丈大人信及美元贰元，均已拜收，即将该函另封付邮，想已到达多时矣。上月中旬得接令岳丈大人来书，嘱代转尊夫人信，量邀尊览。日昨得接美国图书馆黄星辉先生来信，谓"九龙孟氏图书馆需中文部主任一人，职责为中文图书编目及负责编辑该馆一中文期刊，待遇在四五百元左右，不知先生有意进行否？可向孟氏基金会董事会函洽（孟氏图书馆同一地址，或珠海学院院长唐惜分先生代转亦可）"等语。晚接信后则趋谒星辉先生详谈此事，随后再由渠介绍晚往访唐惜分先生商谈，据渠谓现任孟氏图书馆中文部主任将往南洋大学任职，是以要物色一人继任，渠已将晚之略历写下，并谓此事要由图书馆小组委员会讨论研究后，交由孟氏基金董事会决定云云。该馆办公时间颇长，由上午九时至下午五时，复由七时至九时，月薪约四百余元。晚现尚未提出夜间在《华侨日报》任职，如将成事，寔则提出商量也。兹有恳者，请先生鼎力赞勷，推荐晚于孟氏基金董事会及唐惜分先生，感荷恩慈，寔无既极。闻黄先生谈及该会主持人为 Rev. Charles Long, Yale Representative in HK. Mencius Foundation Committee，想先生熟识其人，而唐先生亦谓与先生相熟也。Asia Foundation 之主持人为 James Ivy，可能孟氏会是隶属该会者。现时香港美国新闻处处长为 Richard M. McCarthy，何义均先生处造访二次，未遇，至今尚无消息也。集大庄有宣纸八行信纸发售，日间买就定当奉上。匆匆，容当续禀。专此，敬请崇安。

愚晚国蓁顿首
一九五六年一月十五日

黄星辉先生嘱笔敬候钧安。

〔袁同礼家人提供〕

按："孟氏图书馆"由孟氏教育基金会[①]（Mencius Educational Foundation）主办，唐惜分时应任香港珠海学院校长，并兼孟氏图书馆馆长[②]。Rev. Charles Long 即 Charles Henry Long（1923 - 2000），美国传教士，生于费城，1943 年毕业于耶鲁学院，后又入

① 王梅香《冷战时期非政府组织的中介与介入：自由亚洲协会、亚洲基金会的东南亚文化宣传（1951—1959）》，《人文及社会科学集刊》第 32 卷第 1 期，2020 年，页 133。
② 李帆、黄兆强、区志坚《重访钱穆》（下册），独立作家-秀威出版，2021 年，页 158。

弗吉尼亚神学院进修,1954 年至 1958 年在香港服务。James Ivy
即 James T. Ivy,曾协助余英时以"无国籍之人"获取签证赴美留
学。Richard M. McCarthy,美国外交官,1947 年赴北平服务,1950
年被派往香港使领馆。

一月二十二日

刘世芳覆函先生,已应前请将姓名填注在翻译列表中,并略述其近况。

January 22, 1955

Dear Mr. Yuan,

I have yours of Dec. 30 forwarded from New Haven.

I have put down the names of my co-translators on the separate
sheet. I am sorry that these translations were all I did in English.

I shall be glad to see you in Chicago should you ever come west.

I have been working in the editorial department of a low report
publishing company since October 1952, and I have not been in the east
ever since.

With best regards,

Sincerely,

S. Francis Liu

〔University of Chicago Library, Yuan T'ung-li Papers, Box 2〕

按:刘世芳(Liu, S. Francis,1901—?),浙江宁波人,早年赴美留
学,获得耶鲁大学法学士学位,又赴德深造,归国后执教于光华大
学、东吴大学、暨南大学,曾出任上海高等法院庭长,1946 年担任
审判日本战犯的上海军事审判庭庭长。该函为其亲笔,由信文可
知先生去信应自纽黑文市发出,故 1955 年有误,暂系于 1956 年,
其联系地址为 6430 Kimbark Ave. Chicago 37, Illinois。

一月二十五日

刘国蓁覆函先生,收到先生撰写的推荐信并已遵嘱代订报刊,另谈在港索
求书画之意见。

守和博士先生尊鉴:

敬覆者,廿三日上午拜奉十六日手教,附美钞五元并代转马季明
信,下午拜奉二十日手示并致唐惜分先生及 Rev. Long 推荐信各一封,

感荷恩慈,寔无既极。日昨得奉令岳丈大人来示,嘱代转尊夫人信一函,特为奉呈,敬希察收为幸。马季明信要查得其地址方能转去,因他最近迁居故也。两推荐函日内当分别拜谒,结果如何,定当另禀。闻该缺可能在三月时方能用人,因现任该职之人三月方赴南洋大学也。嘱代订《新闻天地》(周刊杂志式),现先订三个月,共十三期,由四一四起至四二六止,到时当续订,连平常邮共十二元。至《天文台》及《自由人》(二日刊及三日刊报纸式)未悉有无直接由报馆代办,若不能代办则要每期购买,汇齐一周后寄发,则邮费可悭多少。《天文台》每份一毛半,半年约十一元七毛;《自由人》每份一毛半,半年约五元二毛,两种邮费约六元五毛,合计约廿三元四毛。此次付下美钞五元,可找廿九元一毛,尚不敷支也。宣纸八行信纸,日间当买就奉上,至代购横批等,待搜集后当另禀。本港画人如赵少昂、鲍少游等润例颇昂,如小中堂或镜屏一幅,动辄四五百元。书家佘雪曼(擅长瘦金体)已往南洋大学当教授,老前辈太史公岑光樾(北碑),晚与其熟识,润例则不成问题也。又未悉横批尺寸是否连裱装好计算,便中乞示知为幸。匆匆,余俟续禀。专此,敬请崇安。

愚晚国蓁顿首

一九五六年一月廿五日

再启者,港大教授返港后,有 Kerby 教授演讲,英文《南华早报》登载详尽,但重量问题未能付呈(改用平常邮递)。兹奉上《香港时报》译本,俾得先睹为快。阅后恩请代转与秉华先生,至所厚幸。其他教授亦有发表,待搜集后方能奉呈。

〔袁同礼家人提供〕

按:赵少昂(1905—1998),本名垣,字叔仪,广东番禺人,画家,与黎雄才、关山月、杨善深并称为第二代岭南画派四大家。鲍少游(1892—1985),名绍显,字丕文,祖籍广东珠海人,生于日本,画家。佘雪曼(1908—1993),字莲裔,重庆巴县人,毕业于中央大学艺术系,1949 年移居香港。岑光樾(1876—1960),原名孝宪,字敏仲,广东顺德人,清光绪二十七年(1901)举人,光绪三十二年(1906)赴日本留学,三十四年(1908)毕业于日本法政大学,回国授翰林院编修,赏侍读衔,后历任国史馆编修、实录馆协修等职。

"Kerby 教授"应指 Edward S. Kirby(1909–1998),时在香港大学任教,主讲政治经济学,此前受邀赴内地访问。

一月二十六日

王铃致函先生,代转之信已寄送中国大陆,所需册页等物亦在购取之中,请先生代为留意赴美学习、工作机会。

> 守和师：
>
> 　　两函均已在此付邮,嘱代转信大陆事当然照办。李公与我国学术界通讯,国内覆信亦欠迅速,生前寄家书时隔数月,迄无回音,度或事忙有以致之。面刷已向附近一家订货,约三数日可到,再奉寄不误。
>
> 　　国际调查委员会报告书,如更需要一二,中英友好协会或尚有存货数册,乞赐示,俾得前往购取。拙文辱过誉,此后当加倍努力,不敢有负吾师期望之心。已另写四篇,惜失之冗长,拟寄美发表,不知有无杂志接受也。前蒙关注,建议申请哈佛燕京社奖学金,当时以钞数不易维持在美生活,迟疑不决,今艰苦自持,到此已无愧于心。李公虽遇我甚厚,而作嫁依人终非久计。前陈受颐先生过此,又重申来美决心。如有机缘,乞吾师代为留意,他日有成,不敢一日而忘大恩也。肃此,敬请道安。
>
> 师母前乞叱名请安。

生王铃敬上

一月廿六日

〔袁同礼家人提供〕

　　按："拙文"似指其在巴黎社会科学高等学院所办 *Revue Bibliographique de Sinologie*(《汉学书评》)[1]所撰写的书评,该文以李俨《中算史论丛》为对象。

一月二十七日

先生致信 Mark Tennien(香港),询问有无全套的 *Mission Bulletin*,表示极愿购买,并询裴化行的联系地址。

January 27, 1956

---

① Ling, Wang. *Revue Bibliographique de Sinologie*, vol. 1, 1955, p. 164.

Dear Rev. Tennien:

May I thank you for your kind letter of June 6 which arrived while I was out of the country. I am happy to hear that you have been continuing the *China Mission Bulletin* regularly.

If the back issues of the new *Mission Bulletin* are still available, I should like to have a complete file of the most informative *Bulletin*. Will you kindly make up a set and mail it to me here? As soon as your invoice is received, I shall send you a check. I presume that you and your organization maintain a US Dollar account in this country and in Hong Kong. I can't send the money by the Riggs Bank here, as I have to know your identification number and have to fill out all sorts of questionnaires. The Government is, of course, afraid that remittances to Hong Kong may be re-remitted to mainland China.

I have included your two books in my bibliography on China. In addition to a Chinese translation, have your second book—No secret is safe in the bamboo curtain—has been translated into French or German? Kindly inform me the year of your birth in order to make the bibliographical information complete.

Do you know whether Pere Henri Bernard is back in Paris or still in Tokyo? I wanted to keep up my correspondence with him as he is an old friend of mine.

Thanking you in advance for your help,

Yours sincerely,

T. L. Yuan

〔University of Chicago Library, Yuan T'ung-li Papers, Box 2〕

按：此件为录副。

二月一日

张琨覆函先生，答复所询诸事。

袁先生：

1.吴金鼎先生系一九四八年九月十八日逝世，享年四十九。（1901—48）。

2.Franz Michael(1907,March 10th-)。

3.Joseph Rock 旧藏之麽些文写本尚未出售。

4.琨之论文为 Kathinavastu, a vinaya text-a comparative study of Sanskrit, Pali, Tibetan and Chinese text,尚未出版,type-written 有三百页。

5.林藜光遗著两卷,敝校圖未购置。

6.方桂先生夫妇六月底返美。

匆此,敬叩研安。

晚张琨敬叩

二月一日,一九五六年

〔University of Chicago Library, Yuan T'ung-li Papers, Box 2〕

按:张琨(1917—2017),字次瑶,生于河南开封,语言学家,其研究领域为汉藏语言学、汉语方言学,1934 年起在清华大学中文系学习,后在史语所担任助理研究员,1955 年获耶鲁大学博士,时亦在华盛顿大学(西雅图)远东语言系任教,其博士论文于 1957 年在海牙出版,正式题名为 A Comparative Study of the Kathinavastu,Indo-Iranian Monographs 第一种。1948 年 9 月 20 日,吴金鼎因病在济南去世。[①] "林藜光遗著两卷"似指《诸法集要经》(第 1 至 5 章)、《正法念处经研考》,待考。

二月三日

Anthony Maloney 覆函先生,告知 Mark Tennien 已离开编辑部,*Mission Bulletin* 只存 1953 至 1955 年各卷期,并告裴化行联系地址。

106A Kwok Man House

8A Des Voeux Road, C.

Hongkong

February 3, 1956

Dear Mr. Yuan,

Father Tennien gave me your letter of January 27, to be answered. Apparently, you did not know that Father Tennien left *Mission Bulletin* in

---

① 《齐鲁大学校刊》第 68-69 期,1948 年 10 月,页 6。

August 1955.

The only volumes of *Mission Bulletin* that are available are the years 1953, 1954 and 1955. These are priced at U. S. $ 10 per bound volume. In case you wish to have these would you please let me know.

As regards payment, a personal check made out to: *Mission Bulletin* , can be cashed without difficulty as we send these checks back to San Francisco for deposit.

Father Tennien said to inform you that the book, "No Secret is Safe" is published in Germany by Otto Muller Publishing House, Vienna, Austria.

I am not sure about the whereabouts of Pere Henri Bernard. I have a hazy recollection of having seen a letter from him, coming from Paris, recently. You could reach him at: 35 Rue de Sevres, Paris 6, France.

Sincerely yours,

Rev. Anthony Maloney, C. P.

Editor

〔University of Chicago Library, Yuan T'ung-li Papers, Box 2〕

按:Anthony Maloney(1900-1982),美国传教士,曾来华在湖南省传教。落款处为其签名。先生在该函右下角注有"Feb. 11, 函复,由刘国蓁转"。

二月十五日

刘国蓁致函先生,告知其谋求孟氏图书馆职务事正在进行,惟此前与陈君葆共事恐有消极影响。

守和博士先生尊鉴:

敬启者,昨日得奉令岳丈大人来示,嘱将致尊夫人信一函转递,兹随函附呈,敬希察收为幸。孟氏图书馆事经已继续进行,先生致 REV. LONG 函经已面交,并谈及一切。他是孟氏基金会委员之一而已,但他与《华侨日报》敝主任张荣岳牧师是好友,晚亦有托渠商谈,而答覆是因晚前与陈君葆先生共事,是以有思想问题一项云。惟致唐惜分先生信,因他往台湾考察,尚未回港,迟日当能见他呈递,演变如何,容当续禀。孟氏基金会主席是黄兆栋先生,未悉先生有认识否? 宣纸八行信笺,纸质甚劣而价又贵,是以仍未购得,甚以为歉。《新闻天地》已订妥,惟《天文台》与《自由人》无订阅,是以要每期零售,汇齐约十日则奉上一次,未悉尊意以为如何? 匆匆,专此,敬请崇安。敬贺春祺百福。

愚晚国蓁顿首

一九五六年二月十五日

〔袁同礼家人提供〕

按:张荣岳(1916—1979),广东中山人,生于香港,1933年入香港大学,1937年获得文学士学位,1945年晋升为牧师,后赴新西兰,1951年归港,任崇基学院校牧职并兼《华侨日报》主笔。黄兆栋,广东台山人,曾留学美国,后在中山大学、广州大学执教,抗战胜利后曾任广州市参议员。

二月十六日

张印堂覆函先生,告其生年及近作出版情况。

守和先生道鉴:

顷奉二月十一日手教,藉悉阁下现又转回华府,在国会图书馆任职,想工作趁心、近况安适,是所祷颂。承询印之生年,弟以生于旧历时代,年数究为一九〇二抑一九〇三,从来推考按印系生于兔年正月初七日,但自来美填报出生年月以来,均系照一九〇二,二月七日填报,只好从此,以便计算,以求划一纪录是荷。

再关印所研究之《中缅未定界地》一文,于去秋来华大前除应附地图尚未绘制,初稿业已完成,全稿单行打字近五百页,共约廿五万字。原抑草成即进行出版,后以困于经费,加以又恐深及国际纠纷,只好暂待,以免语今。匆此即达,并祝时祺。

弟印堂敬覆

一九五六,二,十六

前闻月涵校长去台并拟□□□□□□。

〔University of Chicago Library, Yuan T'ung-li Papers, Box 2〕

按:"兔年正月初七日"应为1903年2月4日。张印堂任教西南联大教授时,开始注意云南边疆问题。1943年春,他曾与方国瑜等人赴"茶里地区"(片马、江心坡)等地进行勘察。

二月二十日

郑德坤覆函先生，告知个人著述及"一民"字号原委。

> 守和先生道席：
>
> 　　顷奉二月十六日手教，藉悉先生从事编纂中国文献总目，想定洋洋大观，其有功于学术，当可想像，未知何时出版，可先睹为快。承询拙作目录，因图书均留成都，无法应命，至为抱歉。离蓉后所出小册三种如下：
>
> 　　　　*Szechwan Pottery*, pp. 16. London, 1948
>
> 　　　　*An Introduction to Chinese Civilization*, pp. 102. Hongkong, 1950
>
> 　　　　*The Story of Shui-Hu Chuan*, pp. 18, 1951
>
> 内容均甚简单，实不足以入大雅之堂者也。家兄成坤生于 1906，弟1907。Liang Chao-t'ao 中文作梁钊韬，前中山大学人类学讲师，不知其生年。"一民"系北平一藏家字号，流落香港，出让旧舊，其现代宜家一册，转归木扉，非弟号"一民"也，谨此一闻。
>
> 　　年来得文徵明、文伯仁及高克恭三件，虽非钜著，但用笔布局均极清雅，颇可一赏。何时兄临，供赏为快。专此奉覆，顺颂著祺。
>
> 弟德坤再拜
> 二月廿日
> 〔University of Chicago Library, Yuan T'ung-li Papers, Box 2〕

　　按："旧舊"疑当作"旧籍"或"旧藏"。郑德坤（Cheng Te-k'un，1907—2001），福建厦门人，考古学家，其兄为郑成坤。"木扉堂"为其室名，因其在剑桥大学任教时家中的一扇木门而得名。梁钊韬（1916—1987），广东顺德人，人类学家、教育家。

二月二十三日

先生致信张君劢，告知国会图书馆所藏有关玄奘的西文书籍信息。

> 君劢先生著席：
>
> 　　前复一片，计达座右。关于玄奘之西文书籍，兹检卡片七种，均系一九二一年以后出版者，即希惠存。此外，北平图书馆在吐鲁番购到回纥文《玄奘传》残本，曾托 von Gabain 女士现在汉堡大学执教写一论文，此间无单行本，或为他人借去，亦未可知。匆复，顺颂春祺。
>
> 同礼拜上

二月廿三日

〔国家图书馆善本组手稿特藏〕

按：信稿后附国会图书馆印刷目录卡片八张，分别是 *The Vaisesika Philosophy, According to the Dasapadartha-Sastra: Chinese Text with Translation* (1917); *La somme du Grand Véhicule d'Asanga* (1938-39); *Le Voyage d'un pèlerin chinois dans l'Inde des Bouddhas, précédé d'un exposé des doctrines de l'Inde antique sur la vie et la mort* (1932); *The Real Tripitaka: And Other Pieces* (1952); *Vijñaptimatratasiddhi: la siddhi de Hiuan-Tsang* (1928-29); *Popular Buddhism in China* (1939); *Briefe der uigurischen Hüen-tsang Biographie* (1938); *Wei shih er shih lun; or, The treatise in twenty stanzas on representation-only* (1938)。von Gabain 即安娜玛丽·冯·加班（Annemarie von Gabain, 1901-1993），德国突厥学家。1931 年在北京研究了袁复礼 1930 年从新疆携归的、保存在平馆的回鹘文《玄奘传》，1933 年又研究了保存在巴黎吉美博物馆的另一部分《玄奘传》，于 1935 年发表了《回鹘文〈玄奘传〉第五卷研究》（Annemarie von 1935: Die uigurische Übersetzung der Biographie Hüentsangs. I. Bruchstücke des 5. Kapitels. Berlin）。张君劢的地址为：Dr. Carsun Chang, 2295 Hanover Street, Palo Alto, Calif。

二月二十九日

李霖灿致函先生，告拟于三月底前往华盛顿，请先生在国会图书馆附近代为留意住所以便安心看书。

　　同礼长者赐鉴：

　　　　美国务院事多承提携，得以实现，感激不□量，现此间一切已有端绪，我国护照已在"外交部"办理中，约两周内可以办妥。晚之计画，拟于三月下旬到达华府，庶可不误四月之樱花也。前呈一函并寄草席、信纸等，想已收到矣，尚有余款七十元在此，长者拟购何物，望即示知，当遵示于台北代购带来也。前日接国会图书馆来信，云已得国务院通知，并已代为筹画一切节目，盛意可感。并云可代订住屋等情，晚意此事长者更能为后辈筹措，晚意国会圕（北平圕亦然）及书呆子之天堂,我国学人得此机会不易,自当朝夕于斯,期能有所成就。此外只须一榻安身睡眠而已,若能于圖之附近(步行可达者)得一最简单之房间即可,如是省得钱来可作购书之用,长者当悉此意,亦能为晚觅得合乎此项条件之经济住屋乎? 感激之至。若有其他更完善之方法,亦望长者航函示知,计算时间,尚有充分日月可使函件一再往复也。企盼之至。

国务院之合同为期五个月,三个月指定在国会圖研究麽些语文,两个月旅行。晚意以参观各大博物馆为中心,以两月时间,察看各大博物馆之建筑、陈列、保管、研究之各项,长者以为可否? 非抵华府后当面聆教益再做决定也。行期有定,当再函呈,若无意外,三月底之前必可到达,聆诲有期,欣喜无量。谨肃,叩春安。

晚李霖灿鞠躬
二月二十九日,台中

〔University of Chicago Library, Yuan T'ung-li Papers, Box 2〕

按:该函右下有折角,遮住一字,以□表示,此件应于 3 月 3 日送达。

三月二日

蒋彝致片先生,告知即将来华盛顿小住,并在佛利尔艺术馆演讲。

守和先生、夫人道鉴:

久疏候问,维迩来兴居清吉,是颂是念。弟因应 Freer Gallery 讲演之约,将于三月九日来华盛顿小住四日,容设法趋前拜教也。尚此,敬颂俪安。

弟蒋彝敬上
三月二日

〔University of Chicago Library, Yuan T'ung-li Papers, Box 2〕

全汉昇(台北)覆函先生,告知胡先生祝寿论文集征稿截止日期,并请就近催促北美地区学人按时寄送稿件。

守和先生赐鉴:

月前接阅来示,嘱在此将胡先生中文著作目录先行整理,晚已与李济之先生相商,躬命办理,不日当可告成,勿念! 胡先生祝寿论文集征稿截止日期,预定为 1956 年五月底。李先生深恐已接征稿函之国外学者忘记截稿日期,故拟请先生在美就近代为费神催促其早日将文稿写好寄下。除居住于加州大学、哈佛大学等处之学者,另函请赵元任先生、杨联陞先生就近代为婉转催稿外,下列各人,敬恳先生代为费神,请早日将稿寄下:(1)陈荣捷(不知已返美否?);(2)何廉(220 Everit St., New Haven Conn.);(3)李书华(Apt. 3BR, 317W. 98th St., New York 25, N. Y.);(4)李田意(不知已返美否?);(5)柳无忌(3 Woodbine St. Hamden, Conn.);(6)梅贻宝(State University of Iowa, Iowa City, Iowa);(7)蒋廷黻(Chinese Delegation to the United Nations, Empire State Building, New York, N. Y.);(8)王际真(Dept. of Chinese & Japanese, Columbia University, New York, N. Y.);(9)Prof. L. G. Goodrich, Columbia University;(10)Prof. G. A. Kennedy(Yale University, New Haven, Conn.);(11)Prof. E. A. Kracke(University of Chicago, Chicago, Ill.)。以上诸人,去年十一月均已由朱、李两先生(院中及所中)签名送出征稿函,因不便再直接去函催促,但又恐其忘记截稿日期,故拟恳请先生就近在美从旁代为婉转催促,俾能如时集稿,为感!"中研院"自南港新址落成后,史言所书籍均已一一陈列利用,中外学者来此参观者,观感为之一新。关于胡先生祝寿论文集事,先生如有高见,乞不吝赐教,为荷!专此,敬祝钧安。

晚全汉昇敬上

1956,3,2

又,先生大作,请勿忘记截稿日期为感。

〔袁同礼家人提供〕

三月四日

徐高阮覆函先生,告知所询欧阳竟无、马一浮生平及在台所藏著作情况,另将史语所职员情况抄录附上。

守和先生道鉴:

前奉尊示,承询欧阳竟无、马浮二氏生年著作等,稽迟函覆,罪甚,祈谅。欧阳生同治十年十月初八日,卒民国三十二年二月二十三日,其著作此间仅藏有《词品甲》一种。马浮生年未详,其著作藏有《复性书院讲录》、《泰和宜山会语合刻》、《尔雅台答问正续编》三种,马氏生平台湾东海大学徐佛观教授知之当颇详。吴禹铭先生系民国三十七年逝世。回文诗此间藏有者仅《回文类聚》(桑世昌编)十卷。至敝所职员名录仅写于后,尚请尊查。前者蒙寄赐廿三届国际东方学会苏联代表团论文三册,至可珍贵。因大驾当时在旅中,未及函谢,良用耿耿。关于外国东方学之发展及新著出版状况,倘荷时得赐教,受益自深,不胜企盼。专覆,敬请道安。

后学徐高阮敬上

三月四日

〔袁同礼家人提供〕

按:徐高阮(1911—1969),字芸书,浙江杭州人,毕业于清华大学,时在台北"中研院"从事研究工作。所附"历史语言研究所职员"未录,特此说明。

三月五日

罗光覆函先生,告知所询人名信息,并就其最近所著各书略为介绍。

同礼先生台鉴:

前奉手教,迄未作覆,不胜惶愧。所问之上海王神父,为献县之"王哲"神父,曾留学罗玛额我略大学,于一九四九年卒业回上海。光最近所印之拙作,中文者有《公教教义》香港一九五五年(一九五四年曾印《圣母传》《圣庇护第十传》),义文者有《论语》《大学》《中庸》译文 *Confucius, -La grande scienza-Il giusto mezzo-Il libro dei dialoghi*, Milano 1955。前数年(一九五二)曾印一《中国宗教简史》*Storia delle Religioni in Cina*, Torino 1952。留罗玛之中国神父修士尚无一完全之名章,似编就后,当必奉上。爽斋先生已于一九五四年十二月七日去世,朱夫人留住意国。嵩此敬覆,谨颂著安。

铎末罗光顿首

一九五六,三,五日

〔University of Chicago Library, Yuan T'ung-li Papers, Box 2〕

按:"似"当作"俟"。"爽斋先生",待考。

三月九日

叶理绥覆函先生,告知哈佛燕京学社愿意破例提前给予三千五百美金的出版资助。

17 Boylston Hall

Cambridge, Massachusetts

March 9, 1956

Dear Mr. Yuan:

Thank you for your letters of February 26 and March 3.

I was very glad to learn that your Supplement to Cordier's *Bibliotheca Sinica* would soon be ready for publication. We are indeed aware of the importance of this work and shall be glad to furnish a subsidy in the amount of ＄3,500. It is the usual policy of our Comptroller to withhold payment until a work is published, but in your case an exception will be made, and the money will be forthcoming as soon as the first set of proofs has been submitted to the Harvard-Yenching Institute.

With kind regards,

Sincerely yours,

Serge Elisséeff

〔Library of Congress, Council on Library and Information Resources Records, Box 95〕

按:此件为录副。

三月十一日

胡适致函先生,感谢寄来书籍两种,并请代为访求书籍,另告因最近撰写《丁文江的传记》,故未能及时覆函。

守和兄:

承寄《远山堂曲品剧品校录》及《大典》本《水经注》,多谢多谢。

我想留三十元在尊处,请代为访求大陆上出的刊物,为此等书,我不愿老兄自己花钱,此意想能蒙鉴原。

大陆上"批判胡适反动思想"汇辑,我所已得的,共有一、二、三、五、六、七辑,但第四辑未得。倘蒙老兄代为访得,至感。又《红楼梦问题讨论集》,我只有第二集,其一、三及以后诸集(if any)均乞托人代访求,至感。(此十大册,足足有二百五十万字!)

昨日翻开尊寄《水经注》,其"出版说明"云:

《水经注》是五世纪末期中国一个伟大的历史家郦道元的作

品。此书从明清以来的刻本,就把经文和注文混搅不清,以致引起一些无味的纷争。现在我们根据《永乐大典》本影印出来,这是比较接近于郦著的原来面貌的。

寥寥八十多字,没有一句不是瞎说! ①郦道元死于527A. D.,《水经注》成于晚年,其中多叙及六世纪的事,故不能说他是"五世纪末期"的人。②明清刻本有赵、全、戴三家以前及以后的大区别,以前是因袭宋刻的混淆经注本,以后是划分经注本。此中"经文和注文混搅不清"一句真是妄说之尤! ③《大典》本正是明抄宋本,正是"经文和注文混搅不清"的本子! 此是六世纪至十一世纪五百多年中传写者之误混,故最不接近原书面貌。

近三个多月来,写成《丁文江的传记》,凡十万字,已寄台北付印。故一切信札多不曾作覆。老兄前函说要为我作一著作系年目录,我读了十分愧感! 此目成时,我甚愿一校读。

匆匆草此道谢,乞恕其不周不备。并祝双安。

弟适之
三,十一早

〔University of Chicago Library, Yuan T'ung-li Papers, Box 7〕

按:《远山堂曲品剧品校录》校录者为黄裳,1955 年 4 月上海出版公司初版;《大典》本《水经注》,1955 年 4 月文学古籍刊行社初版。

三月十二日

晚,先生赴佛利尔艺术馆聆听蒋彝的演讲。〔University of Chicago Library, Yuan T'ung-li Papers, Box 2〕

按:该次演讲的主题应为"中画在美检讨"。

叶良才覆函先生,告知下周将寄上中基会资助款壹仟伍佰美金支票。

March 12, 1956

Dear Mr. Yuan:

Your letter of March 8 was received this morning. I am having the check of ＄1,500 prepared and should be able to send it to your next week.

With best greetings to you and all the members of your family.

Please tell Mrs. Yuan that we hope someday she will come to New York with you and pay us a visit.

Yours sincerely,

L. T. Yip

〔袁同礼家人提供〕

按:先生在该函左下标记"march 24 收"。

三月十三日

徐家璧覆函先生,告所询诸事。

> 守和先生尊鉴:
>
> 昨奉三月九日手示,敬悉一是。嘱查各人名自当尽力代为查询,何时得有结果,即当具报,惟请勿限时日为祷。王际真先生极少晤面,因渠办公暨来馆时间均无一定故也。Paul Daudin 所译之《聊斋志异》似尚未到馆,一俟编藏,当将该书各项目录著录查明奉报不误,乞毋置念。十二日晚仲雅先生之演讲谅甚成功,听众想亦踊跃,渠能事甚多且富幽默,实不愧为一多才多艺之士。严冬已逝,春和在即,公亦有意来纽小游否? 切盼命驾。敬颂道安。

晚徐家璧鞠躬

三月十三日下午

> 尊夫人前并请叱名候安为感。

〔袁同礼家人提供〕

按:Paul Daudin 似有误,实应为 Pierre Daudin,"所译之《聊斋志异》"即 *Cinquante contes chinois : extraits du Liao-Tchai-Tche-Yi*,1938 年越南西贡初版。

三月十六日

先生致信胡适,告嘱购之书已托英国书店配购,另请查看高克毅译文并请告示是否同意发表。

> 适之先生:
>
> 日前奉到赐书并支票三十元,嘱购之书已请伦敦 Collets 书店配购,书价较香港为廉,而由英寄美又不受海关之检查,代购之书以文史为限,艺术之书印刷颇精,不识需要否? 闻已写成在君先生传记,极愿早日拜读。渠有一篇《论中国陆军概况》一文,分析当时军阀割据

情形,极为详尽,不识先生仍记忆否兹列后? 高克毅君李富孙之婿曾译《四十自传》,其稿曾由其奉上,请予校正,不识仍能觅到否? 渠谓非得先生同意,不敢发表也。尚望便中示知,以便转告。专此,敬候俪安。

同礼拜上

三月十六日

〔台北胡适纪念馆,档案编号 HS-US01-066-029〕

按:信中提及丁文江的文章应指 V. K. Ting, China's Army, *China Year-Book*, 1925, Chaper 37, pp. 1124 - 1145 - 1216。高克毅(George Kao,1912-2008),作家、翻译家、记者,生于美国密歇根,祖籍江苏江宁,1915 年回国,燕京大学毕业后赴美进修,先后在密苏里大学及哥伦比亚大学取得新闻学及国际关系硕士学位,后发表文章并翻译美国经典小说,1972 年至 1975 年在香港中文大学翻译研究中心任职,创办《译丛》,其夫人为李梅卿(? —2003)。李富孙即"李铭",字馥荪。①

三月二十日

程绥楚覆函先生、夫人,告知大陆所出各精装精印古籍影本,并请先生作为推荐人协助申请香港大学教职。

守和先生、夫人双前尊鉴:

手示早收悉,嘱购小条字画,急切竟无可购之物。因前五六年解放不久,香港颇有字画展览,近年则已极少。且假者极多,动辄乱订价钱。若为平日客厅张挂用,则大陆近出之《燉煌壁画》(彩色荣宝套板极精),已出三辑,尚能寻到。此种系单叶,每辑十二帧,三辑共约百元,香港可裱册页。大陆已将庚辰本《红楼》影印(线装本一大函,四十元,报纸精装二巨册,三十元零),余如珍本《白香山集》、南宋本《楚辞》等等皆影印,然售价甚贵,有如古玩。其所出《英华大辞典》,新价已较旧价减半,仍须四十元,已售到罄尽。即 USIS 亦用作工具,确为连年以来之大作。大陆出书(纯学术者)甚多,有价值者亦多,且印得极美,无错字,前之商务中华时代,皆远不能比。适之校长处,零星由

① 《传记文学》第 43 卷第 1 期,页 120。

晚购寄过不少,如到纽约,当可见到也。承告哈佛燕京事,崇基在二月已接到通知(限期为三月一日满期),但校中秘而不宣(开校务会时宣布,凌院长要各系推荐,各系漫置之),至上周五又提起,晚始知。盖以Full Time 工作人员,年龄只晚一人合格。闻逾期无关,凌已答应为晚赶办。但仍须后日(三月廿二日)始能寄出,到 N. Y.要廿八,恐正遇Easter 假。兹有恳者,此信到后,请吾师即日去一函与该社,告知Chung Chi College 已推荐生(S. C. Cheng),因故信须迟到。同时在选定时,因为仍由哈佛作主,尚希我师特别托人关说。晚所定研究计划,为 Modern Comparative Philology 方面,该会 Prof. Edwin O. Reischauer去年冬初曾来港,到崇基同吃过一顿饭,彼亦为委员之一,大概由他决定也(闻林东海言,向例过期无关)。若审查成功,则八月(至迟)可到那边,与尊府诸位相见不远矣。

又最近港大公开征求各系教师共十名,其中有一名教育系者为:Readership or senior lectureship in Education (Chinese Studies). Applicants must posses a good degree with first-class experience in the field of vernacular education and should be able to contribute to the teaching side and to the research of a growing department.据打听系港大需一主持中文教学研究之人,以为本港中文师资训练作计划。同事朋友,皆以晚曾在港不断任中学及大学教八年,能粤语、国语,且深知香港中文教学之积弊者,如应征当有望。须三个 Referees,其应征书三份寄伦敦Secretary, Association of Universities of the British Commonwealth, 36, Gordon Square, London W. C. 1.,一份寄港大注册组。但港大英国人之事,常常心目中已有人,尚公开征求一下。晚现正办理。四月卅为S. Lectureship 截止期,五月七日为 Readership 截止期。现正赶办中。Ref.三位拟请吾师及胡校长,另一位将在本地请,可能为宾四师。俟应征书寄出,再为专函奉告。适之校长原答应过,如作为推荐人,当尽量为力。此事决定权最好在伦敦,在港则必须直接向港大推荐。因Senior Lectureship 晚正好够他们标准(因本港有八年不断高级中文教学经验而又能适合港大英文环境者,为数极少),其年薪为二千镑。看情形不是今秋任职,与去美不冲突,故拟一试。余俟再上。专此奉恳,敬请双安。

晚绥楚敬顿上

三,廿夜

〔袁同礼家人提供〕

按:《燉煌壁画》即《敦煌壁画选》,敦煌文物研究所编,荣宝斋新记出版印刷,1951 年至 1952 年陆续刊行,共三辑。Edwin O. Reischauer(1910-1990),生于东京,美国历史学家、日本问题专家,通译作"赖肖尔",后任哈佛燕京学社第二任社长。

三月二十五日

先生为 *Economic and Social Development of Modern China: a bibliographical guide* 撰写导言(Introduction)。〔*Economic and Social Development of Modern China: a bibliographical guide*〕

按:该书目只限于 1900 年至 1955 年底以前出版、美国各主要图书馆所藏的现代中国经济发展的出版品,以英、法、德三种语言为主,在导言中先生表示此书并非穷尽式的书目,只是作为研究实操中的指南。

三月二十六日

徐家璧覆函先生,告知委托查询各件的结果。

守和先生尊鉴:

敬肃者,前奉三月九日手示,业于十三日先覆一书,谅蒙垂鉴。兹以时间又逾二周,同时进行咨询之教授学者,如王际真先生、富路特先生、蒋仲雅先生、李润章先生等,均已先后拜谒,面请教益,谨将嘱查人名报告如次:

1.King Chien-kun,Yung-chun Tsai 及 Bhikshu Wai-dau 等三人之中文名,均不知晓。惟富先生云蔡君姓名,或能于华美协进社所编之留学生名单(册)中查得,而哥大并无此单,尊处或国会圕则或有也。李润章先生谓如 B. Wai-dau 系西藏人名,则有一喇嘛名 Norbu 者,似可咨询,其通讯处如下:25 West 70th St., New York, N. Y.

2.关于 Ke Han 暨 *Sun Yat-sen vs. Stalin* 两书,因系敝馆所有,详细著录,均已查出,请参见各纸片,惟 Ke Han 之中文姓名,仍不知悉。

3.Paul Daudin 所译之《聊斋志异》,尚未到馆,只有俟其将来运到时,再为查报一切。

以上诸节旷日持久，仍未得圆满解决，愧甚罪甚，诸乞谅之为祷！匆匆奉陈，敬请道安！

晚徐家璧鞠躬

三月二十六日下午

尊夫人前并请代为候安！

〔袁同礼家人提供〕

按：Yung-chun Tsai 即蔡咏春（1904—1983），福建晋江人，1930 年毕业于燕京大学，1947 赴哥伦比亚大学学习，1950 年获博士学位，其论文题目为 The philosophy of Ch'eng I: a selection of texts from the complete works, edited and translated with introduction and notes，旋即回国任教于燕京大学宗教学院；《中国留美同学博士论文目录》并未收录 King Chien-kun、Bhikshu Wai-dau 两人。Ke Han 者，参见 1957 年 2 月 8 日徐家璧函。

三月二十七日

Clarence B. Day 覆函先生，告前在之江大学授课情况并介绍其所编著各书。

Telephone:

Jackson 7-2973

"The Glenayr Apartments"

4421—4th Road, N.

Arlington 3, Va

March 27, 1956

Dear Mr. Yuan,

　　Your letter was forwarded to me here, where my wife and I have retired to be near a married son and a married daughter and their families here in Arlington. You ask for information for your bibliography, which I append herewith: —

　　CLARENCE BURTON DAY — born Sept. 1, 1889 (at American Fork, Utah)

　　CHINESE PEASANT CULTS, Shanghai Kelly & Walsh, Ltd., 243 pp., in color, illus., 1940. (A very rare book in U.S.A.)

HANGCHOW UNIVERSITY: A BRIEF HISTORY, 283 pp., illus., 1953 United Board for Christian Colleges in China, 150‒5th Ave., N.Y. 11, N.Y. ($ 3.00)

also —CURRENT ENGLISH READINGS — World Book Co., Shanghai, 1935

ENGLISH FOR ENGINEERING STUDENTS — Shanghai, Priv. pub., 1939.

The last two were textbooks compiled for my students in the English Department of Hangchow University, where I was a member of the staff from 1919 to 1951. I went to China in 1915 and came out in 1951, after working two years under the Communist régime.

I am currently engaged in completing an Introduction to Chinese Philosophy (or Book of Readings) and a full length novel (or *Student Romance in Wartime China 1939 ‒ 1945*). If you care to see my " Suggested Reading List " appended to my " China's Philosophers: Classical and Contemporary", I can send you a copy, though it may contain no titles that you do not already have. Or if we could meet somewhere, I should be happy to make or renew your acquaintance, especially if you happen to be a Hangchow alumnus (as I ought to remember!).

Please pardon my handwriting; I was just tired of using the typewriter.

Very sincerely yours,

Clarence B. Day

P.S. The Library of Congress has a copy of my Chinese Peasant Cults.(P. T. O.)

P.P.S. In New York, there are copies of Chinese Peasant Cults to be found in the following libraries (one copy in each): —

Butler Library — Columbia University (listed also in card index at Low Library Far Eastern Division)

Missionary Research Library, Union Theol. Seminary

　3041 Broadway, New York 27, N.Y.

Presbyterian Board of Foreign Missions Library

　156-5th Ave., New York 10, N.Y.

The China Society of America Library

　125 — East 65th St., New York 21, N.Y.

C. B. D.

〔University of Chicago Library, Yuan T'ung-li Papers, Box 2〕

按:Clarence B. Day(1889-1987),中文名队克勋,1911 年毕业于纽约汉密尔顿学院,获文学学士学位,1914 年获旧金山神学院神学学士学位。1915 年来华,在宁波传教。1919 年至 1943 年、1948 年至 1951 年在之江大学任教,讲授圣经、英语、哲学、宗教比较研究等课程,曾任英语系主任。1951 年离校回到美国。著有 *Hangchow University: a brief history*(《之江大学简史》)等。*CHINESE PEASANT CULTS* 全称为 *Chinese Peasant Cults: being a study of Chinese paper gods* ,1940 年别发洋行出版。an Introduction to Chinese Philosophy 即 *The Philosophers of China Classical and Contemporary* ,1962 年纽约出版。该函为队克勋亲笔。

三月二十八日

蒋彝覆函先生,告其无意参加古根海姆艺术基金会竞赛,并略述缘由。

守和先生:

手教暨转下陈祚龙君婚柬,至感谢。上次在华盛顿"更自由画院"所讲多肤浅,承盛意到会捧场,无任拜德! 至于 Guggenheim 基金会艺术竞赛事,蒙垂注,尤为感激,不过此种竞赛,多以油画品为主,我辈恐难加入,即便加入,亦难取胜! 个中情形复杂,非纸上一二词句所能说明。盛意及此,至为可感。匆复,敬颂俪安。

弟蒋彝顿首

三月廿八日夜深

〔University of Chicago Library, Yuan T'ung-li Papers, Box 2〕

按:陈祚龙(1923—?),湖北监利人,1946 年夏东方语文专科学校毕业,后赴印度、英国、法国深造,曾获印度大学文学硕士、牛津大学文学学士、法国巴黎大学文学博士,对佛教学及敦煌学研究极深。

三月二十九日

先生致信洪业,请教《孔雀东南飞》的法文译者等信息。

March 29, 1956

Dear Professor Hung:

May I solicit your assistance in identifying the Chinese names of the three translators noted on the enclosed card? I am also anxious to know the Chinese words for "paon", translated by Tchang Fong.

Since you have so many scholars at the Boylston Hall, will you ask the information from others, in case you do not happen to have remembered them?

With renewed thanks and best wishes for a happy Easter,

Yours sincerely,

T. L. Yuan

〔Harvard-Yenching Library, Papers of William Hung (1893 – 1980) 1915 – 1996, From Yuan Tung-li to William Hung, Mar. 29, 1956〕

按:paon 即长篇叙事诗《孔雀东南飞》,Tchang Fong 则应指法文译者张凤,该译本于 1924 年在巴黎出版。Boylston Hall 即哈佛大学内的博雅思通厅。此件为打字稿,落款处为先生签名。

四月二日

洪业覆函先生,就前询译者信息作出答复。

2 April 1956

Dear Dr. Yuan:

Several years ago, I attempted to identify Chi Hwang Chu without success. Mrs. Underwood's work on Tu Fu was so fantastic that I almost doubted her collaborator's being a Chinese scholar.

Likewise, I am ignorant of the identities of King Chien-kun and Bhikshu Wai-dau.

We have not here Tchang Fong, Le Paon: ancien poème chinois. To guese merely from the title, it seems that Chang Feng's translation is of the anonymous poem "k'ung-ch'üeh tung-nan fei　　　　　."

With seasonal greetings,

Sincerely yours,

〔Harvard-Yenching Library, Papers of William Hung (1893–1980)
1915–1996, From William Hung to Yuan Tung-li, Apr. 2, 1956〕

按:Chi Hwang Chu 即朱其璜,Mrs. Underwood 应指 Edna Worthley Underwood,此二人关于杜甫的作品应指 *Tu Fu: wanderer and minstrel under moons of Cathay*,1929 年波特兰出版。King Chienkun 即经乾堃①,比丘 Wai-dau 的中文名待考。此件为底稿,空白处应填汉字——孔雀东南飞。

四月四日

刘国蓁覆函先生,告孟氏图书馆职位务须专职,故失之交臂,并谈冯秉华归港行期、代索岑光樾横批、代购书报诸事。

守和博士先生尊鉴:

敬启者,许久未修书致候,抱歉殊深。辰维著述丰宏,履躬清胜,至以为颂。日昨叠奉由大陆寄来代转信两封,兹将原函奉上,敬希察收为幸。三月十二日拜奉八日手示,敬悉种切。孟氏图书馆事终成画饼,因该缺是要专席,由上午九时至下午九时,并不能兼职,是以几经接洽未能成事,况且晚不能辞去华侨之职而专就彼也。诸蒙眷注,感荷恩慈,寔无既极。至崇基学院图书馆主任程绥楚先生,晚未曾认识,惟闻全院行政权皆操诸院长凌道扬先生云。近闻秉华东翁决定本年六月返港之行又不能成行,或者可能改期十二月返港,是以晚希望其返港如大旱之望云霓也。晚之苦况依然如故,因日间尚未有兼职,不能弥补家计故也。前求岑太史墨宝,因渠年老又多病,迟迟未能应命,故亦未访何义均先生。现岑太史精神复元,横批经已书就,惟要笔金四十元,照其润例(一张附《天文台报》呈上)交付,并将其裱续为阔三英尺,高一英尺半,价银五元,待裱好后便可付上也。尊账计前来美元二元,随后付下五元,共找得港银四十元〇六角,支《新闻天地》三个月(本月底止),连邮十二元,《天文台》及《自由人》三个月(本月底止)八元四角,另邮费贰元,两次信资四元,宣纸一张一元,笔金四十元,裱工五元,共支七十贰元四角,比对代支长三十一元八角,谨此奉

---

① *T'ien Hsia Monthly*, Vol. 11, 1940, p. 119.

闻。嘱代购钱锺书《围城》一书,港中各书店皆无货,闻迟日可续到,届时当购就奉上。嘱查两中文姓名,遍查不获,因无该书故也。匆匆,余俟续禀。专此,敬请崇安。

愚晚国蓁顿首

一九五六年四月四日

再启者,KERBY教授之英文讲词已附《天文台》奉上,阅后乞代转秉华东翁为幸。敝友罗原觉君近藏有清初吕焕成仿周文矩《唐宫春晓图卷》,刷色通景屏风十二页(影印一大幅,另说明一大张)及《李卓吾批评水浒传》四十六册(图影一页,说明一册)皆制图片,日前由印刷挂号邮付上两套,想较迟到达。倘得收后,请代送一份与胡适之先生并请批评介绍,至所厚幸。去年奉上曾文正书札图片等,当时先生谓寄国民政府,未悉该件如何,未蒙示及,为念,便中乞示知为幸。

〔袁同礼家人提供〕

按:凌道扬(1888—1993),广东新安人,农林学家,时应任香港教育委员会委员,参与创建崇基学院并出任该校第二任院长。吕焕成(1630—1705),字吉文,浙江余姚人,清代画家。先生在该函右下角标注"二十日寄十二元支票,永隆银号抬头"。

四月八日

谭云山覆函先生,告知将寄上最近所出书刊及著述目录。

同礼先生道席:

上月奉二月廿五日手教,敬诵一是,毋任拜感。比来因医治臂痛,致稽奉复,又深歉罪。

尊驾旅欧期间,陈祚龙弟曾有信告。望风怀想,无限钦迟。近又编纂中国文献,询及刍荛,盛德大业,更不胜景仰。弟近年因饱经忧患,甚少写作。年前应南印太米尔文百科全书主编之请,草中国语文与文学史要,曾应印单行小册,特另邮奉上请教。客岁印度大学一教授团体庆祝大哲奥罗宾多(Sri Aurobindo)八十四圣诞大会,承邀主席略讲良知之觉醒,曾经报章发表。单行小册,正在筹印中,俟印出后,再寄乞正。其他零星应酬写作,未足挂齿。又此间中印学会现出版巴宙君箸波罗提木叉比较研究论文一种,亦并寄上一册,统希指教。觉月语师不幸于年初逝世,近无关中印著作。李本道七十纪庆特刊,尚在筹备之中,何时出版,尚未能确定。敝院同人研究著作,多散见于各处刊物。稍后,当搜编一简目寄上。附拙著名单一纸,敬祈赐察。专复,顺颂撰安无量。

　　　　　　　　　　　　　　　　　　　　弟谭云山拜启
　　　　　　　　　　　　　　　　　　　　一九五六,四,八

〔University of Chicago Library, Yuan T'ung-li Papers, Box 2〕

按:谭云山(1901—1983),湖南茶陵人,1927 年在新加坡结识印度大文豪泰戈尔,1928 年应泰戈尔邀请,到印度国际大学任教,1937 年该校中国学院成立,出任首任院长,至 1968 年退休。"奥罗宾多"即শ্রীঅরবিন্দ(Śri Aurobindo Ghose,1872-1950),生于加尔各答,印度政治家、诗人。巴宙(1918—?),字望蜀、望舒,号仙樵,原籍四川万县,二十岁赴印度留学,以研究印度文化与哲学为主,后获国际大学硕士及孟买大学哲学博士学位,博士论文为《梵巴汉藏对照波罗提木叉之比较研究》,是研究原始佛教生活及僧团制度的重要著作,1968 年受聘于美国爱渥华大学。1956 年 1月 19 日,师觉月去世。

四月十日

程绥楚致函先生、夫人,告崇基学院未能按时寄送推荐单,导致其申请哈佛燕京学社访问无望,并谈大陆最近影印出版情况。

守和先生、夫人双前:

前函计已达览。哈佛燕京研究社已于今日覆函,虽未责备过迟,然今年已无望,推到明年。本来给崇基之通知系在一月下旬到的,二月一日开教务会议,便已议决将规章传观,但校方竟置之不理。规定为三月一日截止,四月一日前覆函通知选录与否,而校方竟迟至三月七日在开会时重提出,事实上已过了期。等到决定推荐晚,已在三月中旬,寄出文件在三月廿三下午,三十日始到哈佛,哈佛回信(John C. Pelzel, acting director)为收到文件即日回答者。此事崇基甚失面子,因足证行政之荒唐与糊涂也。内地近到许多影印之书物,如《汉魏六朝墓志钞》及《画苑精英》(三巨册洋装,有英文目录与说明)等,皆为图书馆收藏之佳品,不知美国国会圕亦备购到否?又齐白石、仇英等画,亦有影印立轴,卖得颇便宜,如系家中悬挂,当即购赠寄上,但因本身甚便宜,航空太贵,只可平寄也。在此教书,毫无进步,一切无善足陈。惟老母在长沙,既不能出来(因按月有外汇回去),又不能入大陆去探看,恐成终身之痛矣。匆匆,余容再上,敬请双安,并问阖府安吉。

晚绥楚敬拜上
四月十日
〔袁同礼家人提供〕

按:John C. Pelzel,美国人类学家,以研究日本文化为专长,1964年3月担任哈佛燕京学社社长。

四月十八日

陈祚龙致函先生,告知其已成婚,并请将近况转告蒋彝。

守和先生道鉴:

别后祚龙之生活情况实在可说是变化多端,而其中最大且要者莫非是决定四月四日与法籍女友 Lucienne 举行大昏! 惠承寄赠纪念珍品,领受诚觉感惭交集! 道途修远,既不得亲携内子前往答拜先生之美意与期望,是则还祈容藉纸笔就此聊表谢忱。

计自去夏六月祚龙在牛津勉力幸把学事告一结束之后,随即转此找定工作一份,以求解决温饱问题;原拟转美继谋深造,而事实已不能不暂缓履行。曾劳先生指引申请奖学金之各种门径,衷心感德,殊非祚龙仅以三言两语即能明喻也。

蒋仲雅先生赴美之后即与祚龙中断音息矣。如说先生有机与渠晤见,未知可烦赐将祚龙念旧之心境稍予转达一番否? 耑此,敬颂府安!

愚陈祚龙拜上
四月十八日
〔University of Chicago Library, Yuan T'ung-li Papers, Box 2〕

按:1955 年,陈祚龙在牛津获得学位,"随即转此找定工作一份"应指在伦敦暂时工作,因该信寄出地址为 15 Parolles Road, Archway London, N. 19,1956 年晚些时候受戴何都(Robert des Rotours)、戴密微之邀赴法国工作。

徐家璧覆函先生,已代转先生致李铁铮信,并谈其他所托之事。

守和先生尊鉴：

　　敬肃者，昨奉四月十一日手示，诵悉一一。所嘱代转李铁铮"大使"一函，当即加封照转。十六日上午曾与彼晤面，亦曾提及尊询之事，并请彼直接函覆，谅已照办矣（按"李大使"地址为 420 Riverside Drive (Apt. 6-A), New York 25）。其他所询各人姓名因本馆并未藏有国务院油印本之 *Leaders of Communist China* 一书，是以又未能圆满答覆，深引为憾。其关于出版人及尺寸者，则于取书核对后一一注明于黄纸片之上，请为察阅是幸。*Ke Han* 一书，目前暂已为一读者借出，故虽欲重查尺寸，亦不可得。哥大西文目录片已取销尺寸项目，因之欲查尺寸，非取原书衡量不可，苦衷所在，务乞原宥为祷。其他所询各节，均已于原单上注明之。再者 *Far East Reporter* 所出有关新中国之小册尚夥，如有兴趣可按地址径函索取详目一份，以备稽考，未悉以为如何？纽约公演国剧，因场少座少，票不易得，以致交臂失之，殊属可惜耳。余容续奉，敬请道安。

　　　　　　　　　　　　　　　　晚徐家璧鞠躬

　　　　　　　　　　　　　　　　四月十八日下午

尊夫人前敬乞代为候安为感。

　　　　　　　　　　　　　　　　　　〔袁同礼家人提供〕

　　按：李铁铮（1906—1990），字炼百，湖南长沙人，中央大学毕业，国际法专家、外交官，1942 年担任国民政府外交部秘书，后出任驻伊朗、伊拉克等国大使，1953 年获哥伦比亚大学博士学位，1964年归国。

四月二十四日

先生致信康乃尔大学图书馆参考部，请代为查询四种书的书目信息。

　　　　　　　　　　　　　　　　　　　April 24, 1956

Reference Librarian

Cornell University

Ithaca, N. Y.

Dear Sir:

　　Will you kindly look up whether your Library has the following books? If so, kindly supply the names of the authors in Chinese characters.

Wong, Wilfred Sien-bing:

The Mental Autobiography of Bill Lee, Shanghai, 1945

————: *The Black Hole of Shanghai*. 194?

Shih, Kalgan: *Modern Coins of China*. Shanghai, 1949. What is the size of the book in centimeters? & the number of pages? Any illustrations?

Please supply full bibliographical information of the following book:

Abbe E. Gervais: *Un mois en Chine*. Sherbrooke, Canada. 1937.

With sincere thanks for your assistance,

Yours sincerely,

T. L. Yuan

〔Cornell University Library, Wason Collection Records, 1918-1988, Box 1, Folder Koo, T. K. Letters〕

按：Wong, Wilfred Sien-bing 即黄宣平（1910—1981），圣约翰大学校长卜舫济（Francis Lister Hawks Pott, 1864-1947）外甥，上海商人，年轻时曾留学加拿大多伦多大学，后在美国短暂工作，1932年回到上海。*The Mental Autobiography of Bill Lee* 是一本自传体小说，*The Black Hole of Shanghai* 则为其记述自己被汪伪特务绑架的回忆录。Shih, Kalgan 即施嘉干（1896—1975），又名施衍林，江苏吴县人，生于上海，近现代建筑家、实业家、钱币收藏家，*Modern coins of China* 中文名为《中国近代铸币汇考》。*Un mois en Chine* 意为《中国一月》，但该书信息似有问题。此件为打字稿，落款处为先生签名，于 4 月 26 日送达。

五月二日

汪敬熙覆函先生，告知其夫人已被护送回台北，并谈最近研究情况。

守和吾兄：

四月廿五日惠书，早已收到。因近日精神不舒，至稽奉复，罪甚罪甚。国人名单弟处无有，且不知何人系会中秘书。但即写信问梁炳䜣医生。内人已到台湾台北。伊系三月廿四日由此地飞回。弟试请国人医生护士带回，屡次失败。不得已请一美国护士送回。岂知此护士在回程中在西雅图飞机失事落水，幸得救！此护士人甚好，幸无麻烦。

冠贤太太早赴新加坡任中学教职,后又回香港。近来渠在何处,弟不知。弟之在美居留延长,恐出问题。六月后在何处尚不知也。

近日只以工作解忧,幸工作结果转好。上月赴大西洋城美国生理学会,读论文一篇,反应尚好。年已将六十,工作结束,除非异常,毫无用处!

匆此,奉候俪安。

弟敬熙敬上
六五,五,二
〔袁同礼家人提供〕

按:"内人"即何肇菁,"冠贤太太"应指何肇华。落款时间似应为"五六",绝无"六五"之可能。暂系于此。

五月三日

李霖灿赴国会图书馆,期间与该馆馆长 Lawrence Q. Mumford、副馆长 Lucile M. Morsch(女)、东方部主任 Horace I. Poleman、先生等人合影留念,并在 Whittall Pavilion 共进午餐。〔Library of Congress, The Records of the Library of Congress Photographes, Illustrations & Objects; Library of Congress, *Information Bulletin*, Vol. 15, No. 19, 1956, p. 241〕

按:李霖灿在国会图书馆主要查看麽些(Mo-so)文献,后被该馆称作 Mr. Mo-so。[1]

下午五时许,李幹将梅贻琦送至先生家,稍坐。后,先生夫妇随梅贻琦至李家。〔杨儒宾、陈华主编《梅贻琦文集》第 1 册,新竹:清华大学出版社,2006 年,页 43〕

按:李幹(1901—1999),字艺均,江苏无锡人,清华学校毕业后赴美国留学,入密苏里大学,1922 年获新闻学士学位,翌年获文学学士学位,1924 年获哈佛大学经济学硕士学位,1927 年获博士学位,归国后任国民政府财政部国定税则委员会委员,兼国立交通大学及国立中央大学商学院教授、铁道部科长、英文《中国评论报》特约编辑。1941 年任驻美国大使馆商务参赞,1945 年抗日战争胜利后返国,任国民政府最高经济委员会副秘书长,1947 年任驻美国技术代表团团员,旋代理团长,时任"中央银行"

---

① 李霖灿著《国宝赴美展览日记》,台北:台湾商务印书馆,1972 年,页 119。

副总裁。

徐家璧覆函先生,告所托代查之事仍未能圆满解决。

守和先生尊鉴:

敬肃者,捧读四月廿六日手示又已数日,只以探询夏夫人暨夏女士两人中文名氏不得要领,致稽裁覆,歉甚歉甚。按夏夫人确系夏云夫人,惟以与夏先生晤面极稀,是以一时无从代问。哈佛于镜宇兄似与夏府相当熟稔,或者能道伊名,亦未可知。先生似可径函于兄一询,否则请俟璧得机与夏先生晤值时再问亦可。至于夏女士名字,经问数人均不知悉。伊前同事王君目前正因事南行,约本月底左右可回纽约,届时如不嫌迟,当可面询一切,另函报知,未悉以为若何?

关于上海总商会刊物,本馆仅有一种,但非月报,似此核查周君著作,广告已属无可为力,但璧曾直接试查周著,则在总馆内藏有一册,经赴总馆查阅,则书中并无只字中文,故仍未能解决问题。上海《密勒氏评论报》所编之《中国名人录》亦未见此公,似此欲查其原名非另采途径不可,怅甚歉甚。

二届"中美文化关系讨论会"即将在周末举行,尊处距马利兰甚近,谅当前往出席。本市亦将有多人与会,李铁铮"大使"即为其中之一,届时谅可晤面也。

匆匆不一,敬颂道安。

晚徐家璧鞠躬

五月三日下午

尊夫人前乞叱名候安。

〔袁同礼家人提供〕

加斯基尔致函先生,就前询问之书目信息予以答复。

May 3, 1956

Dear Mr. Yuan:

Our Reference Department has turned over to me your letter of April 24 asking about certain books.

We have the two books by Wilfred Sien-bing Wong, but there are no Chinese characters in them, and I do not know what the characters for his name are.

The other two books, by Shih and Abbe E. Gervais, we do not have and I have no information on them at all.

I'm sorry we can't help you out.

With greetings and best wishes as ever,

Sincerely yours,

G. E. Gaskill

Curator

Wason Collection

〔Cornell University Library, Wason Collection Records, 1918-1988, Box 1, Folder Koo, T. K. Letters〕

按:two books 参见是年 4 月 24 日先生致康乃尔大学图书馆参考部的信。

五月四日　马里兰州公园市

"中美文化关系圆桌会议"在马里兰大学举办第二届会议,先生与席。

五月五日

中午,梅贻琦与李幹来先生家就餐。晚七时,清华大学校友在 China Doll 聚会,梅贻琦报告清华大学(台湾)筹备复校情形,郭秉文夫妇、牛惠生夫人、顾毓琇、萧庆云(在美清华同学会主席)、先生等四十人与会。〔《梅贻琦文集》第 1 册,页 44〕

> 按:萧庆云(1900—1984),江西泰和人,工程师,清华大学毕业后赴美留学,获加州理工学院学士学位、哈佛大学博士学位,时应任联合国运输交通委员会(United Nations Transportation and Communication Commission)委员。

五月十日

童世纲覆函先生,告知所询各件信息。

> 守公赐鉴:
>
> 　　本月五日手书敬悉。嘱件已为查明。兹逐条奉复如下:"戢俊"之履历未列入官绅姓名录内;(二)Gillis 系于民卅七年在平去世;(三)葛库之沿革,除胡先生及 Laufer 大作外,并无其它论文。匆此奉复,敬请双安。
>
> 晚世纲谨上

五六，五，十

〔University of Chicago Library, Yuan T'ung-li Papers, Box 2〕

按："官绅姓名录"似指《最近官绅履历汇录》(第一集)，敷文社编辑，1920 年 7 月初版，是记录北洋政府时期官吏履历的重要参考文献。义理寿去世时间应为 1948 年 9 月 1 日[1]。胡适所撰关于葛斯德专藏的文章有两篇，分别为 The Gest Oriental Library (March, 1952)、The Gest Oriental Library at Princeton University (1954)，"Laufer 大作"则应为 The Gest Chinese Research Library at McGill University, Montreal。

五月十四日

刘国蓁覆函先生，告转发信函、代订杂志及书籍、寄送岑光樾横批诸事。

守和博士先生尊鉴：

敬启者，未修书敬候转瞬月余，恭维著述宏富、起居安吉为颂。日前拜奉四月十八日手示，附十二元汇单一张、代寄发航笺二函，敬悉种切。迟迟未报，抱歉殊深，敬希原宥为幸。两航信经已加邮(现航笺信资是五角)付寄，想当可到达，惟至今尚未收回件也。汇单内写永隆银号名字，找换手续颇为困难，因晚与该银号不相熟故也。如下次有发汇票时，请直接写晚名便可找换矣。该汇单找得港币六十九元九角(五八二五算)，除代垫卅一元八角，此次再定《新闻天地》三个月(由五月至七月)银十二元，《天文台》五月份二元二角半，《自由人》五月份九角，三次寄费七角半，代购得钱锺书之《围城》一册四元九折三元六角，寄费五角半，总共代支五十一元八角半，比对尚存十八元零五分在晚处也。岑太史墨宝横批经已付邮，系附于晚寄与纽约敷戚陆印芳女士之包裹内(因该件重量太轻，亦需邮费二元五角，是以附寄)。如到达后，她即付邮转上。晚已将其用厚纸皮包扎妥善，写明收发地址，必无错误也。如蒙察收，敬希示知为幸。承命查香港华南邮票公司经理之中文姓名，因遍查不知其地址，而《大陆邮票目录》各书店皆无发售，如再有新发现，当即奉闻。聚珍书楼(Empire Printing Co.)出版之

---

[1] Sören Edgren, I. V. Gillis and the Spencer Collection, *The Gest Library Journal*, Vol. 6, No. 2, 1993, p. 22.

E. & C. Dialogues 著者 Huang Li-ch'ing,中文姓名晚亦有到该店访问,并无存书,更兼该店现为新人办理,是以无从得知也,有辱尊命为歉。专此,敬请崇安。

愚晚国蓁顿首

一九五六年五月十四日

〔袁同礼家人提供〕

　　按:聚珍书楼,清末时即活跃在香港印刷、出版界;*E.&C. Dialogues* 即 *English and Chinese Dialogues*,中文名为《英语指南》,该书自光绪年间至 20 世纪 50 年代曾数十次再版,著者为黄履卿。

五月十六日

宋晞致函先生,谈其研究宋史计划,并请先生赐示晚清留美学生史料。

　　守和先生道鉴:

　　　　月初在马利兰大学"中美文化关系会议"席上得晤道颜,并聆教言,无任感奋。日前接获 Sung Project 油印文件,披读之余,感慨无已。西方汉学家对我国历史文化之注意若此,日本研究我国历史之成就,亦早有佳评。而我国屡经战乱,在朝者无暇且无力及此,有志于学术研究之学人,复乏宁静安定之环境,不能作有计划或集群力而为之。晚年来寓此异邦,感触尤多。想先生或有同感。至宋史论文目录中文部分者,晚能加以辑录,惟体例若何,尚乞指教为感。该油印文件下月可寄还。关于一八八二年至一九〇八年,此二十六年间留美学生史料,如能赐示一二,更所企祷。肃此,祇颂道安。

晚宋晞谨上

五月十六日

〔University of Chicago Library, Yuan T'ung-li Papers, Box 2〕

五月十七日

徐家璧覆函先生,告此前所询诸事。

　　守和先生尊鉴:

　　　　敬肃者,昨奉五月十二日手示,敬悉种切。璧素性拘谨,见闻不广,与外界接触亦少,故每当运用知识之时,辄感捉襟见肘,深自愧憾。尊编《中国经济书目》,承将璧名列在申谢名单之内,实不敢当,要之璧对尊编诚无若何贡献也。

香港自由出版社纽约办事处似已结束,兹于本市新电话簿中遍查其名不得,数月以前代查之地址暨电话系由林顿先生供给(渠近已提前休假),但本馆与该社已有许久未通消息矣,为此嘱加址转寄之一函暂亦无法投邮。尊处所需之 *Reform through labor in China* 一书,经查明本馆尚未入藏,愚意以为何不将尊函直寄香港该社总社,则劳工一书暨其他事均可询明,未悉以为然否? 该社香港地址如下:香港九龙弥敦道五八○号 D 二楼(此系 1954 年底地址)。

适之先生著述目录如承寄下,自当遵嘱尽力核对、增补,希望有所发现。

此外,法国汉学家 Daudin 所译之《聊斋志异》一书,现已到馆,兹将其著录另纸抄奉,以备参考。按,该书有书名页二,本馆所购者似系第二版,未识对否?

夏云夫人中文姓名业于上周去函于镜宇兄探询,迄今未得覆音,颇深系念。

余俟续奉,敬请道安。

晚徐家璧鞠躬

五月十七日下午

尊夫人前乞为叱名叩安。

〔袁同礼家人提供〕

五月十九日

程绥楚覆函先生、夫人,请协助其申请香港大学教职。

守和先生、夫人俪鉴:

两奉手示,及所嘱转信,皆已转寄不误。关于司徒校长八十大寿寿礼,已将尊件交与此间联大旧友所开之海通行代为办理,昨因所谓寿星,只是用朵朵绣花拼成之"寿"字,晚过目后,觉得不好看,已请其另外设法,大约一星期内可以用航空寄出。因海通行代办甚内行,即作为生日礼,亦须问工商署领证,代办不过付点手续费,故一切委托他们,请放心,等寄出后,再将发票及寄费等单另封寄上。

兹有恳者:晚自崇基创办,至今五年,李应林逝世后,由欧伟国代理半年,即选出凌道扬。去夏予聘约时,晚仍兼图书馆主任(不兼薪,自开办起即晚兼任,唯照规定每周上课十二小时,酌减三小时,另用一职员而已），但开学时因副校长 James Pott（上海约翰 Pott 之子）反对凌之私人秘书关某，凌已下聘，而托人与晚商量让此位与关某，晚乃以全部时间教书。李应林初办时，一切从简，由学教育学之钟鲁斋任中文主任，沿袭至今未易。钟所编大学国文，错到不成话，又因系客家人（凌亦客家），客人重同乡，虽说粤语者亦视为外人。晚不合将所授之一班先修班用了港大新编之"中国文选上册"（甚佳）——该书系林仰山主任编辑，由刘百闵、饶宗颐、罗香林、吴椿四位编成，为此事开罗钟先生，彼此次订下年课程，竟为晚规定两种选修，意在排挤。董事中有半数系当初选欧伟国者（凌多一票选出），对彼等甚不满，欲藉晚之故，向凌表示，现正酝酿，晚则不安于位矣。新亚下年度将加一专管文史教授，钱宾四师尚未归，已与秘长王书林谈过，大约晚会转去新亚，新亚一切较此内行，都是北方人，易于相处也。港大应征之件，伦敦已收到回信。其所征者为 Senior Lectureship or Readership，晚应征 S. L.，因 Reader 在英制甚高，晚资历不够也。闻去年即征求过，但未录取任何人。该职位系主持中文教学法，属教育系。系主任为 Prof. K. E. Priestley，现在休假去了伦敦，须十二月返港，似此则将在英伦审查，但亦不一定，因林仰山为中文主任兼本年度之 Dean of Faculty。现在欲进行此位置，照港大以往办法，对 Referee 之征询，系在大半决定以后，故胡、钱等位，不便事前多介绍，但钱答应在本月底回来，向林仰山力荐。晚想请尊驾劳神，向伦敦 Association of Universities of the British Commonwealth, 36, Gordon Square, London W. C. 1. 之友人介绍（假如不直接认识 K. E. Priestley 的话），因为港大对 A.U.B.C. 的考虑，是颇重视的。又此间 Drake 方面，前来示云当年在济南见过，但不熟，彼等现对董彦堂先生甚重视，董即在林一处工作，如果由董面说，亦多少有效力。晚与董只在南京表兄劳榦处见过一面，此次听过他演讲而已。伦大方面如有英国学者向港大介绍亦可，此事看来权在 Priestley 与林仰山二人也。他们希望找一个有不断教学经验者，同时又能粤语、国语、英语。晚自 1949 二月至今，在港已有八年，崇基在前年冬升副教授，正合其 Senior Lecturer。不过英国人的人，极重视大人物之推荐，有时已经内定才刊广告（但此次晚打听过，并未内定），如何之处，并乞尊裁，不胜感激之至。其审查期在六月初，因 Readership 截止期在五月卅也。余容寄出包裹后再陈，专此奉恳，敬祝双安。弟妹同此问好。

晚程绥楚(Cheng Sui-chu)敬上

一九五六，五月十九夜

〔袁同礼家人提供〕

按：是年，程绥楚担任新亚书院兼任讲师，负责中国通史课程。①
A.U.B.C.即 Association of Universities of the British Commonwealth
(英联邦大学委员会)。K. E. Priestley 时任香港大学教育系主
任，中文名皮理思。该航空函于 23 日送到。

五月二十八日

徐家璧致函先生，谈搜集胡适著述目录进展。

守和先生尊鉴：

敬肃者，五月二十一日所上一函，谅承尊览。刻下已将本馆、哥大
总馆、哥大师范学院圕暨纽约公立圕所藏有关适之先生之著述目录全
部查毕，其不与前寄下之卡片雷同者，或虽同而版本有差异者均为之
另行写片。此外，并曾查讫 *International index to periodicals* (H. W.
Wilson 出版)1907 至 1956 三月份止，凡有关胡先生论著亦为之一一
写片合并随函奉上，以备采择。按 Wilson 公司尚出有其他几种索引，
均值一查，想在国会圕自易于举办，如有需璧继续协助之处，请即函示
为祷。

近阅北平所出《文物参考资料》，得悉苏联已将《永乐大典》十一
册暨原藏日本满铁圕《永乐大典》五十二册先后归还我国。又东德亦
效尤归还该类书三册，事殊可喜，但不知其亦含有若干政治意味否？

先生前曾广事调查现存卷册，对此当亦甚感兴趣也。

余不多渎，敬请道安。

晚徐家璧鞠躬

五月廿八日晚

尊夫人前乞为叩安为感。

〔袁同礼家人提供〕

按：H. W. Wilson，美国出版商，提供索引服务，1898 年成立，位于

---

① 周佳荣著《钱穆在香港：人文・教育・新史学》，香港：三联书店(香港)有限公司，2020 年，页 62。

纽约。

六月一日

杨懋春覆函先生,告知其在华盛顿大学研究工作即将结束,并寄上所嘱履历,另请代为留意合适教职。

> 袁先生道鉴:
>
> 　　上周接到您的手教,至今才覆,抱愧之至。您府上都好吗? 时以为念。袁太太近况如何? 内子特别问候。弟近来真是公私均忙,忙得不开交。公的方面必须赶写未了的文章,到六月底,我的工作就结束了,不再继续,同仁等均觉丧气。弟亦在失业之列,将来有何出路,尚未线索。弟于去岁,在此间购一苗圃,现为其所绊累,不得他移,工作结束后,即拟以此为糊口之计,能否如意,尚成问题,只好尽力为之,成败归天。嘱寄个人履历,自当遵命,不过并无多少可述耳,微小成绩,先生早已知之。过去一年在此间所写为 *Chinese Society Structure*,初稿已完,颇蒙此间学人之嘉许,现正在文字上之润色中。稿颇长,打出后共计六百余页,将来或有出版希望,但不知须待多久也。三四月间 Columbia 的 Boorman 曾来此间访问,并托弟为之作一中国社会学界人名单,弟已如命作成寄去。问及能否有机会加入其工作,回信曰无,颇为失望。先生居首都,交游广,如有线索,祈加援引。别待后叙,敬颂时祺。
>
> 弟杨懋春拜启
> 六月一日

〔University of Chicago Library, Yuan T'ung-li Papers, Box 2〕

按:事实上,杨懋春并未失去华盛顿大学中国与俄国历史文化研究所的工作,后被委派研究清末云南政局,但其颇为不满,于1958 年 9 月偕眷前往台北,执教台湾大学。*Chinese Society Structure* 后修订为 *Chinese Social Structure: a historical study*,1969年在台湾由欧亚书局(Eurasia Book Co.)发行。Boorman 即Howard L. Boorman(1920-2008),美国外交官,曾派驻北京、香港,后在哥伦比亚大学任教,本谱依郭廷以称其为"包华德",曾主持 *Biographical Dictionary of Republican China*(《中华民国名人辞典》)编纂工作。

六月七日

王毓铨致函先生,谈国内情况,并劝先生归国。

守和先生:

我们回国已经六年了。五〇年三月一日到北京,先晋去北大博物馆专修科,我去北京历史博物馆,那时国家正在政治上、军事上奠定基础,学术研究工作还未开展。五二年先晋转中央民族学院研究部文物室,去年四月我转来历史研究所第二所(所长陈垣先生,副所长侯外庐和向达先生),现正从事研究我国封建社会的土地制度。我们的生活很舒服,很正常:读书、研究,此外再没有什么事。住的是自己的房子(一九五〇年七月买的),很宽敞。在纽约十几年,我们住够了楼房,现在可恰意了。

这几年中我们经常盼望先生回国,因为在纽约时先生尝谈愿意回国。那时先生说一时路费筹备无着,暂难起程。现在这个问题可以解决了,只要先生全家愿意回国,来信说明用多少路费,我们可以向政府请求寄发。如交通有困难,政府也将设法。一入国境,各地均将殷勤招待,那就更无问题了。

今日各报载有科学院郭沫若院长谈话,号召滞留国外的学者和科学工作者早日回国,非常诚恳。今剪附一纸,请读后早日决定回国,并请便中示知为感。敬请大安。

> 王毓铨
> 一九五六,六,七
> 〔袁同礼家人提供〕

按:该函寄送杨联陞,由其转交给先生。

徐家璧覆函先生,告新获胡适著述两种题名,并谈诸事。

守和先生尊鉴:

敬肃者,昨奉六月一日钧示,藉悉种切。适之先生著述书目欲求搜全,恐属匪易,但只好尽力为之,恐最后仍须加"选"目字样,以示未能完备耳。刻璧又将 Wilson 公司所出之 *Cumulative Book Index*（或作 *United States Catalog*）自一九二八年份起通统逐本查至最近,复得二目,系前所未有者,因特抄录,随函奉上备用。

关于《永乐大典》予以影印以广流传一事,尊见极是,惟不悉何日方得着手。按现下大陆翻印古典文学盛行一时，将来或者有人提倡影印《大典》，亦未可知。

王思曾君，谅刻在华府，未识其近况奚若。昨闻陶维大女士告彼似已获得在美永久居留，则于此时尚返大陆，不知有无妨碍。觅事进展若何，亦深念及。各情俟彼抵纽后，或可得机一谈。

余俟续呈，敬请道安。

晚徐家璧鞠躬

六月七日

尊夫人前乞代候安为感。

〔袁同礼家人提供〕

六月十一日

西门华德覆函先生，对未能替程绥楚在香港大学谋取教职表示歉意，将协助杨联陞获取英国签证，并提供所需学者的生年信息。

11th June, 1956

Dear Mr. Yuan,

Thank you for your letter of 23rd May. I was very glad to hear from you and I shall append the list of dates of birth as far as I have been able to get them.

I am afraid I am not on the Appointment Board for the Lectureship in Education at the University of Hong Kong, and I am not likely to be consulted about this matter.

I shall be very glad to see Professor Tung Tung-ho when he comes through London. In the case of Professor Yang Lien-sheng, I have been able to be instrumental in getting him his visa, and am very much looking forward to seeing him again.

I was so sorry that we didn't meet more frequently during your stay in this country. Do give my very kind regards also to Mrs. Yuan.

Yours ever,

W. Simon

P. S. On my visit to Paris in September last I saw Madame Mozère on two occasions. She is gradually getting over the shock of her separation, though I think she is still deeply in love with M. Mozère. She stayed at Christmas with friends in the vicinity of Oxford, and rang me from there. When we met, she told me how much she regretted that you missed each other when you came through Paris.

Dr. C. R. Bawden, born 1924, Professor S. H. Hansford, 1899, H. McAleavy, born 1912, O. van der Sprenkel, born 1906, N. J. Whymant, born, 1894

〔University of Chicago Library, Yuan T'ung-li Papers, Box 2〕

> 按：M. Mozère 夫妇生平待考。C. R. Bawden 即 Charles R. Bawden(1924-2016)，专攻蒙古语，后担任伦敦大学亚非学院教授；S. H. Hansford 即 Sidney H. Hansford(1899-1973)，伦敦大学教授，叶慈的继任者，对中国玉器有较深入的研究。N. J. Whymant 即 A. Neville J. Whymant。落款处为其签名。

六月二十六日

杨联陞致函先生，转交王毓铨劝先生归国函，并告自己赴英与会行踪。

> 守和先生：
>
> 　　昨日收到王毓铨兄来信一封，谨此转上。王重民兄等想必亦有信来矣。
>
> 　　月之三十日，将有英伦之行，参加伦敦大学召开之东方史学(史)讨论会(七月二日至六日)，已为撰就短文一篇，略论唐至明正史。会后再在英勾留两三星期，预定七月底以前返美。时间短促，不拟转访欧陆矣。
>
> 　　敬请双安，并问潭第清吉。
>
> 晚学杨联陞拜启
> 六月二十六日

〔University of Chicago Library, Yuan T'ung-li Papers, Box 2〕

> 按：该会邀请的在美学者为拉铁摩尔、杨联陞，后者亦是该会唯一的中国学者。①

六月二十八日

先生致信 Max Loehr，祝贺新书问世并询问此中两条参考文献的具体信息，

---

① 杨联陞《国史探微》自序。

另询陶德曼所藏铜器的下落。

June 28, 1956

Dear Prof. Loehr:

Hearty congratulations for your valuable work on Jennings collection of Chinese bronze weapons. It is a great contribution to our knowledge of ancient China.

In your bibliography you listed the following two works and I shall be grateful to you if you could give me full bibliographical information, such as the name of the publisher, the number of pages and the size in centimeters:

Ecke , Gustav: *Frühe chinesische Bronzen aus der Sammlung O. Trautmann* .

Erkes, E: Das Schwein im alten China.

I had a copy of the first work, but I left in in Peking. I was extremely glad to know that you were able to get out all of your library from Peking. Some of the Chinese books you listed have become very rare now.

When writing to me, kindly give me some information as to the whereabouts of the Trautmann bronzes. I heard that Trautmann passed away when I was travelling in Germany last year, but I have no news about his collection.

Thanking you for your courtesy,

Yours sincerely,

T. L. Yuan

〔University of Chicago Library, Yuan T'ung-li Papers, Box 2〕

按:Max Loehr (1903－1988),德国汉学家、艺术史学家,通译作"罗樾",1936 年毕业于慕尼黑大学,获博士学位,后前往北平,在中德学会从事研究工作,时已入美籍,在大学执教。*Frühe Chinesische Bronzen aus der Sammlung Oskar Trautmann* ,1939 年在北平初版,中文名《使华访古录》,孙壮题署,文字部分由辅仁大学印刷,Ts'ai Hua Yin-shua-chü 即彩华印刷(书)局,负责铜器珂罗版印刷。

E. Erkes即 Eduard Erkes(1891－1958)，德国汉学家，中文名何可思，Das Schwein im alten China 直译即《中国古代的猪》。1950 年12 月 10 日，陶德曼去世，先生此处记忆有误。该件为录副。

六月

Delafield 覆函先生，愿意参与编纂胡适西文著作目录的工作，并询问稿件截止日期等细节。

> 145 E. 82nd St.
> New York City NY.

Dear Mr. Yuan

　　Having been away a few days, I found your letter on my return. Yes, I would be pleased to cooperate with you on this project. I am delighted that Dr. Hu is being honored on his 65th birthday.

　　I see by your list that there are a few titles I am not familiar with. As his birthday is the 17th of December, I should like to know what would be the so called, deadline, for me to send my list to you. I can't give you a full bibliography of the Doctor's works, as it would take more time than we have, I think. But at least I can add some items in the same form as you give in your list. In other words, I can contribute a check list.

　　I am interested to hear who you will have on your list who will be contributing essays to the volume.

　　I am looking forward to this publication especially as I feel a great man has been neglected by the world in late years. I remain,

> Most sincerely
> Eugene L. Delafield

P.S. I shall give you what I have in the way of book reviews as well.

〔University of Chicago Library, Yuan T'ung-li Papers, Box 9〕

　　按：该函为其亲笔，但无时间标注，暂系于此。

七月二日

先生向中基会理事会递交报告，申请额外补助编写《西文汉学书目》。

Dear Sirs:

　　Since the last report of my work was submitted, much progress has been made toward the completion of the first part of the Supplement to Cordier's *Bibliotheca Sinica*. Limited to works in the English, French and German languages, this first part of the Supplement would be ready for publication in the latter part of the year. It is a classified bibliography on China consisting of 16,000 titles grouped under various headings. At the end of the bibliography, there is a comprehensive index of authors, compilers, editors, translators and illustrators.

Both the Far Eastern Association and the Library of Congress have expressed the desire to assist in its publication. At the present moment the Library of Congress is exploring possibilities for having it printed by the off-set process. All L. C. and non-L. C. cards are to be retyped by a group of trained typists before the manuscripts are submitted to the printer. As it involves a great deal of expense, no final decision has yet been reached. To meet a part of the printing cost, a subsidy of $ 2,500 has been made available by "the Ministry of Education". A further grant $ 3,500 has been promised by the Trustees of the Harvard-Yenching Institute.

In concluding the first part of the Supplement, the undersigned wishes to express his sincere gratitude to the Trustees of the China Foundation whose encouragement and support contributed so much toward the completion of this work.

The second part of the Supplement consists of works on China in Russian and other European languages. Much material has already been collected, but further research remains to be done. Taking advantage of the excellent facilities offered by the Library of Congress, the editorial work could be continued without too much difficulty. In view of the desirability of its continuation, the undersigned begs to apply for a grant from your Foundation covering the period from January to December 1957. It is hoped that with your continued support, my labors could be made available to a wider circle of scholars.

Yours very sincerely,

T. L. Yuan

〔台北"中央研究院"近代史研究所档案馆,〈中华教育文化基金
董事会〉,馆藏号 502-01-09-004,页 130〕

七月三日

罗樾覆函先生,回答前信所问的两个问题。

July 3, 1956

Dear Professor Yuan:

I was surprised and very happy to receive your kind letter of June 28 and I wish to thank you in particular for your gracious verdict on my book on the Bronze Age Weapons. I still remember with gratitude that you supplied me with one or the other book I was desperately looking for, as for instance F. R. Martin's L'Age du Bronze au Musée de Minoussinsk.

As to your question concerning Gustav Ecke: *Frühe chinesische Bronzen aus der Sammlung O. Trautmann*, this is a catalog containing twenty items, text printed by the Fu-jen University Press, collotypes printed by Ts'ai Hua Yin-shua-chü, and copyrighted by Mr. Trautmann. Where the Trautmann bronzes went I unfortunately do not know; when in Germany in 1949-50, I heard that the collection had fallen into Russian hands. It may well have come to Moscow with other war spoils from Eastern Germany. I shall inquire about it with Dr. Reidemeister of the Cologne Museum.

The article of E. Erkes, "Das Schwein im alten China", is contained in *Monumenta Serica*, Vol. VII, 1942.

It is true that I was able to ship most of my books home before I left Peking, yet I had to leave behind a substantial collection of Chinese literature on art such as the *Mei Shu Ts'ung Shu*, etc., etc., practically a "complete" working set.

Hoping that you are well, I remain with my best wishes,

Sincerely yours,

Max Loehr

Professor of Far Eastern Art

〔University of Chicago Library, Yuan T'ung-li Papers, Box 2〕

按:F. R. Martin 即 Fredrik R. Martin(1868-1933),瑞典外交官、收藏家,其书直译作"米努辛斯克博物馆的青铜器",1893 年斯德哥尔摩 Samson & Wallin 初版。Dr. Reidemeister 即 Leopold Reidemeister (1900-1987),德国历史学家、艺术史专家,1945 年起负责科隆博物馆的重建。*Mei Shu Ts'ung Shu* 即《美术丛书》,黄宾虹、邓实编,上海神州国光社印行。

七月十一日

胡适来致函先生,请代购书籍三种并代查清道光年间福建各府知府人名。

> 守和兄:
>
> 谢谢你寄的书。所余款乞代买
>
> 红楼梦问题讨论集第四集
>
> 梁漱冥思想批判
>
> "胡风反动集团"案的资料(题目乞查)。
>
> 尊函已交中基会。
>
> 便中乞代查福建泉州府知府道光廿年至廿三年是何人? 又道光卅年是何人?
>
> 漳州府知府道光廿三年至廿六年是何人?
>
> 福宁府知府道光廿七年至廿九年是何人?
>
> 馆中有光绪三年的漳州府志。不知民国新修之福建通志可查其他二府知府人名否?
>
> 　　　　　　　　　　　　　　　　　　　适之
>
> 　　　　　　　　　　　　　　一九五六,七,十一
>
> 〔University of Chicago Library, Yuan T'ung-li Papers, Box 7〕

按:"尊函"应指先生向中基会申请继续补助《西文汉学书目》的编纂、出版。

七月十四日

刘国蓁致函先生,转寄北京来信并为谋新亚书院职务请先生联系钱穆,另告知续订书报、杂志等事。

> 守和博士先生尊鉴:
>
> 敬启者,未修书敬候又已月余。辰维著述丰宏,履躬清胜,定符私颂。月前奉上芜笺,量邀尊览。上月初得接敝戚由纽约来函,谓包裹经

已平安收到,先生前嘱办之岑太史字幅亦已付邮转奉,想蒙察收为幸。昨日奉到由北平来信,着代转上,兹夹附呈,敬希亮察为幸。新亚书院新校址建筑将完成,决定下学期在新校上课,并闻大加扩展,未审钱院长有无与先生通讯,晚极欲日间得到工作以谋升斗,藉资弥补生活。倘蒙齿芬所及,鼎力吹嘘,则鹪鹩之栖自可操券,务恳代为留意,不胜感祷之至。《自由人》等报均已如期寄奉,想当到达。《新闻天地》杂志到本月末便告期满,未悉尚须续定否?便中伏祈示知为幸。上次存款十八元〇五分,此次支六七月份报费六元三角,寄费一元五角,本次邮费二元,共九元八角,比对尚存八元二角五分也。谨此奉闻,专此,敬请著安。

愚晚刘国蓁顿首

一九五六年七月十四日

〔袁同礼家人提供〕

七月十六日

蒋彝致函先生,告其申请 Bollingen 基金会资助事落空并谈最近行踪。

守和先生有道:

不曾修候又久矣,维兴居清吉是颂是祝。兹奉上 Bollingen 复信,请阅,可见向人要钱总不易如愿耳。最近在哈佛讲演一次,令媛或已先闻也。今晚飞往西部一游,将住陈世骧处。顺候俪安。

蒋彝顿首

七月十六日

〔University of Chicago Library, Yuan T'ung-li Papers, Box 2〕

按:"Bollingen 复信"可参见本年 6 月 27 日杨联陞致蒋彝信。[1]

七月十七日

宋晞覆函先生,奉还前借各文件,并告前所托查找册页未得到明确回复。

守和先生道鉴:

手书奉悉,承赐有关留美学生史料索引多条,至所感激。承借宋史研究文件,刻已用毕,谨以奉还。嘱查"教育部"出版之小册作者中文姓名,仅函询"教育部",据复,均不知有此书。刻又托人函台"中央博物院"等机构查询,一有结果,当再函陈。肃此,祗颂道安。

---

① 杨联陞著《莲生书简》,北京:商务印书馆,2017 年,页 46—49。

后学宋晞谨上

七月十七日

〔University of Chicago Library, Yuan T'ung-li Papers, Box 2〕

七月十八日

先生致信 Delafield，感谢其参与编纂胡适西文著作目录，告知另有中文部分由台北编辑，并建议英文各部分以时间为序编排。

July 18, 1956

Dear Mr. Delafield:

I am so grateful to you for the excellent bibliography of Dr. Hu which you have so carefully prepared. I concur in your selection and judgment in every way. It will be a great contribution to the memorial volume which is now being edited.

I shall ask the managing editor to send you three additional copies of the Chinese edition and six additional copies of the English edition. Owing to the late delivery of some of the articles promised, I am afraid that there may be some delay in their publication. Dr. Li Chi, director of the Institute of History and Philology, is heading a small board of editors.

In addition to the bibliography of Dr. Hu's writings in English, there is another bibliography of his writings written in Chinese. This bibliography is being edited at Taipei and will no doubt include his latest book on the life of Dr. Ting. I should have informed you about this in my previous correspondence.

I wonder if you would like to see the chronological arrangement of Dr. Hu's writings. If so, I shall be glad to rearrange the titles and send the draft back to you for checking. It will be published under your name.

I recall that back in 1918 Dr. Hu wrote an article about Chinese language reform in the *China Weekly Review*, then known as *Millard's Review*. If I could locate it, I shall have it added to the bibliography.

Thanking you once more for your most kind cooperation.

Yours sincerely,

T. L. Yuan

〔University of Chicago Library, Yuan T'ung-li Papers, Box 9〕

按：his latest book on the life of Dr. Ting 即《丁文江的传记》,1956年 11 月初版。an article about Chinese language reform 似指 The Chinese Literary Revolution,刊于 *Millard's Review of the Far East*, Vol. 8, No. 8,(19 April, 1919)。该件为录副。

七月二十日

胡适覆函先生,感谢协助查实道光朝福建各处知府,并谈 Delafield 所编"西文著作目录"的遗漏和问题。

守和兄:

七月十七日的信,已收到了,十分感谢。

有个虚云和尚,有法汇两册,附年谱一册,颇有人崇信,甚至于有人写信来劝我参加翻译他的"著作"! 这个和尚的年谱里自称他生于道光二十年庚子(1840),据说今年还生存,是一百十七岁人了!

年谱说他俗姓萧,湖南湘乡人,"予父"名玉堂,以举人官福建:

戊戌、己亥间,任永春州知州。

道光 20—23,任泉州府知府。

道光 24—26,调任漳州府知府。

27—29,调任福宁府知府。

30,回任泉州府。冬月丁母忧回籍。

这都是可以覆勘证实的。所以我请你一查。承你查出福宁府知府在道光 27—29 是庄受祺。漳州府知府,道光 24—26 是王广业、赵镛、王用宾、徐耀。两府都没有湘乡举人萧玉堂之名! 这就可以证实年谱的作伪了。多谢,多谢!!

关于 Delafield 的胡适"西文著作目录",匆匆看过,十分失望! 他翻见了"*Eminent Chinese*"有我的序,他就没看见此书下册有我的长文"A Note……"举此一例,可见他的粗心。

他竟不知道(或忘了)他藏有我的整部的 Books! 如

1. *Development of Logical Method in Ancient China*.

2. *The Chinese Renaissance*

3. *China Too Is Fighting to Preserve a way of life*(精印,精装,—a

Collector's item！）

举此三例，可见此目的不完全。

我参加的 Symposium，当时成为 Best Sellers，有这些：

Charles A. Beard's(ed.) *Whither Mankind*.

Simon & Schuster(Pub.)：*Living Philosophies*

Fadiman's(Editor)：*I Believe*.

此目也没有收！他收的 145 目，绝大多数可删弃也。

我明早（廿一日）西行去 University of Wyoming（Laramie,Wy.）有七天勾留。又飞回东方，赴 University of Vermont（Burlington.Vt）作两天的勾留（七月30—31）。

我把此目带去，暇时修改了寄还你。但恐无此工夫耳。有何见教，乞寄 c/o Prof. Yale W. Mcyee, U.of Wyoming, Laramie,Wy.

匆匆，敬祝双安。

适之

七,廿

〔University of Chicago Library, Yuan T'ung-li Papers, Box 7〕

刘国蓁致函先生，转寄北京来信。

守和博士先生尊鉴：

敬启者，日前奉上芜笺，并代转北平来信，量邀尊览。顷得接另北平来信一函，特为奉上，敬希亮察为幸。新亚书院事，倘荷鼎力赞勤，感戴靡涯矣。如何之处，伏祈示知为祷。专此，敬请崇安。

愚晚国蓁顿首

一九五六年七月二十日

〔袁同礼家人提供〕

七月二十一日

李霖灿致函先生，就此前接待表示感谢，并告知将离耶鲁大学前往波士顿。

守和长者赐鉴：

乡下人进纽约，可以想见其迷乱，两个星期的停留，总算把这世界上最大的都市看了一些，最大的，最小的，最华丽的，最贫乏的，最热闹的，最寂寞的……都一一收入文集画囊。明日即离此赴耶尔大学转波士顿，谨于此向我此次美国之行的总导演三鞠躬致谢！

后学李霖灿敬上（演员）

七月廿一日

〔University of Chicago Library, Yuan T'ung-li Papers, Box 2〕

按：省略号为李霖灿原函中的标注。落款处李霖灿应用纳西文写了敬词。

七月二十三日

Delafield 覆函先生，告乐见先生在《密勒氏评论》中寻找胡适有关"文学革命"的文章，另外增补两种 1956 年新出版的书刊，并对《胡适先生著作目录》联合署名表示感谢。

Dear Mr. Yuan,

Thank you for your most kind letter of the 18th.

Yes, I think if you can locate a copy of *Millard's Review* with Dr. Hu's article on Chinese language reform, it would be an important item to add, considering Dr. Hu's connection with the subject.

I am enclosing two more items which have just come to hand from Doctor himself just before I left for a weeks' vacation at the tip of Long Island, at a little village called Orient. The first I have been waiting for from Paris. It is: "*Tchang Ta-Ts'ien, Peintre chinois*". Ville de Paris, Musée d'art Moderne, Juin-Juillet 1956, Paris. Introduction by Hu Shih. Pages (1 - 2). Chang Dai-Chien by Lin Yutang; Preface by Vadime Elisséeff; Note Biographique by Kuo Yu-Shou. 26 plates. Paris 1956.

The second title is: "The So-Called 'Shui-Ching-Chu' Text Collected by Three of Ch'uan Tsu Wang's Ancestors" by Hu Shih. This is a title given for a two pages abstract of the 18-page article in Chinese. It first appeared in the "*The Tsing Hua Journal*" New Series, Vol. I. No. 1., as an essay. It is really a pamphlet. It has just been published in Taiwan.

It is most kind of you to say that my contribution will be under my name, however there were several pieces that I was not familiar with. So, I think it only just that both our names should appear on the bibliography.

If you think I might help at all after you have arranged the chronology, I should be pleased to see it.

Most sincerely.

Eugene L. Delafield

July 23, 1956.

〔University of Chicago Library, Yuan T'ung-li Papers, Box 9〕

按：*Tchang Ta-Ts'ien, Peintre chinois* 实为张大千在巴黎近代美术馆所开画展的图册；"The So-Called 'Shui-Ching-Chu' Text Collected by Three of Ch'uan Tsu Wang's Ancestors" 即《所谓"全氏双韭山房三世校本"水经注》，刊于《清华学报》第 1 卷第 1 期。该函为其亲笔。

七月二十四日

徐家璧覆函先生，告知李霖灿在纽踪迹，并答复此前先生托其查找各节之结果。

守和先生尊鉴：

敬肃者，月之十七日接奉十五日手示，诵悉一是，欣慰无既。惟斯时正属工作紧张之际，又值李霖灿兄来馆参观，致无暇立即代查呈覆，无任歉仄。而十九日璧在馆中休假开始，又未如常到馆，嗣李君以纽约事繁且有数处私家所藏国画势在必看，于是展缓去纽海芬，行期共四日，最后之五六日中，璧曾朝夕相伴李君前往各处观摩国画，发现珍品颇不在少，获益匪浅。此外，李君并曾在白马社（纽约之国人文艺组织）公开讲演麽些文，迟迟于昨日（二十三日）下午三点始离纽北去，知注特陈。于是，璧于今日始得机去馆中代为查核所开问题。兹将结果奉报如次：

壹、胡适之先生托查人名：

一、福建泉州府知府——在道光二十年（至二十六七年）系黄德峻（高要县人），在道光二十七年（可能至三十年）系徐耀（宛平县人）。（按本馆入藏之《缙绅全书》缺道光 21、22、24、25、28 年各册）。

二、漳州府知府——赵镛（道光二十年任），王用宾（二十五年任），方宝庆（二十六年任）。

三、福宁府知府——庄受祺，阳湖人，道光二十七年任；徐正青，宿松人，接庄任，但年未详。

贰、尊嘱：Curtis, Florence Rising: *Translations from the Chinese* 一

书,并非排印本,而系普通打字本,书名页(似后加)下,并无出版处,亦无年份。不过该书系于一九五一年十一月廿六日赠送本馆,若能得睹其赠书原函(假定有信),则可知著者之所在地。其书之高度(尺寸)系 28cm。Soulie, Charles Georges 所著之 Les Lignes……一书,遍查无着,亦无编目片,惟有俟今后再为查找。德国 Franz Kuhn 所译作品,除尊单所列外,本馆尚有下列各种:

1. *Das Perlenhemd*.(即《今古奇观》之一段)

2. *Chinesische Staatsweisheit*.

3. *Der Traum der roten Kammer*.(即《红楼梦》)

4. *Die Jadelibelle*.(即 yü ch'ing t'ing,不知中文应如何写法?)

余不尽意,专乞恕罪,敬颂道安!

尊夫人前,并乞候安为感!

晚徐家璧鞠躬

七月廿四日夜半

〔袁同礼家人提供〕

按:Florence Rising Curtis(1873—1944),美国图书馆教育家,信中提及的 *Translations from the Chinese* 似确未正式出版。Charles Georges Soulié,生平及著作待考。Franz Kuhn(1884—1961),德国律师、翻译家,通译作"孔舫之",1909 年至 1912 年在德国驻清朝使馆服务,曾于 1912 年担任驻哈尔滨副领事,*Das Perlenhemd* 即《珍珠衫》,*Chinesische Staatsweisheit* 直译作《中国状况》,具体所指待考,*Die Jadelibelle* 则指《玉蜻蜓》,清代弹词。

七月二十五日

查良鉴(台北)致函先生,告其回台后工作情况及查询留法学生姓名进展。

守和先生赐鉴:

前以奉命赴美办理毛案,每于公暇得亲教益,至感欣幸。经数年之奋斗,客秋卒将最困难最繁杂之两瑞士银行存款百数十万元收回,藉裕国库,差堪告慰。事毕即奉准返国,以行色匆匆,未克拜别,良用歉然。数月以来,仍在原岗位服务,谬荷"总统"颁给勋章,徒增愧赧。平时在部则对于法令修改业务推进,略抒一得之见,未敢言何供献,风便当乞时惠教言,以匡不逮是荷。

月前承函嘱代查法国留学生著作者姓名,当经向谢副院长冠生先生询问,以皆系后起,不易识别,嗣向其他方面询问,颇久只查悉二人,难以报命,后多方设法,直至前日始得十二人,其中仅何任清在台湾"高等法院"任推事,其余散处各地或滞留大陆,则未可知。兹谨另纸附上,即希察核。

勉仲家兄在"考试院"任考试委员,此外对于教育事业,如师范教育、社会教育及侨生教育等事项亦常参加研讨,相当忙碌。月涵先生最近两度返台,对于原子能教育热心提倡。虽台湾地狭人少,经济拮据,但一般学者之研究兴趣则极浓厚。

先生时作海外旅行,得便至希能抽暇留台小住,学术界莫不欢迎宝贵之南针也。专此奉复,顺颂暑安,并候潭福。

后学弟查良鉴拜上

七,廿五

适之先生近晤面否? 乞代致意。

〔University of Chicago Library, Yuan T'ung-li Papers, Box 2〕

按:查良鉴(1904—1994),字方季,籍贯浙江海宁,法学家。"毛案"应为毛邦初侵吞巨额公款案,查良鉴被派往美国,依照法律途径,于美国、瑞士、墨西哥等三国法院提起诉讼,历时三载终将大部分公款追回。谢冠生(1897—1971),本名寿昌,字冠生,以字行,浙江绍兴人,法学家。何任清(1910—?)字伯澄,广东兴宁人,1936 年在法国图卢兹(Toulouse)获得法学博士学位。"勉仲"即查良钊,查良鉴胞兄。

七月二十九日

Delafield 致函先生,就先生所拟的草目增补两种书刊信息。

Dear Mr. Yuan,

Just returned to town to-day While away I kept turning over in my mind Dr. Hu's works to see if I had forgotten anything of importance. So, this haste note with two more titles is the result.

Under Books: "*Selected Articles on China Yesterday and Today*." Compiled by Julia E. Johnsen. Introduction by Dr. Ping Wen Kuo. New York. 1928. "Renaissance in China" by Dr. Hu Shih. Pages 133–145,

Note: from article in *Royal Institute of International Affairs*. November 1926 (China?).

Under <u>Newspapers</u>:

"Analysis of the Monarchical Restoration in China: by Suh Hu." In: *Columbia Spectator*. Page 7, January 14, 1916.

Note: This is very important, as it is one of Dr. Hu's first articles in English.

I trust I will not cause you any undue inconvenience by belatedly sending this on.

With kindest regards,

Eugene L. Delafield

July 29, 1956.

〔University of Chicago Library, Yuan T'ung-li Papers, Box 9〕

按：该函中提及的书籍、期刊文章，第一种、第三种没有收录在翌年刊印的 *Selected Bibliography of Dr. Hu Shih's Writings in Western Languages*（《胡适先生著作目录（二）西文》），极有可能是被胡适本人删掉，另 Analysis of the Monarchical Restoration in China 也不是胡适最早的英文文章。该函为其亲笔。

八月四日

先生致片李书华，感谢赠书，告国会图书馆无《书隐丛说》，已函询哈佛燕京图书馆。

润章吾兄：

承赐大著，拜读获益甚大，谢谢。<u>书隐丛说</u>此间未入藏，当日即函询哈佛，迄今一周尚未得复，恐劳远念，特先奉闻。该校办事甚慢，容得复再函达。顺颂著祺。

弟同礼

八，四

〔Columbia University Libraries Archival Collections, Shuhua Li Papers, 1926–1972, Volume II: Modern Eminent Chinese Leaders〕

按：《书隐丛说》清代袁栋撰，为其读书札记，全书十九卷，分音韵、诗文、戏剧、人物、风俗、物产、科举、衣食、神异等类，所叙内容征引自周秦汉魏至明季史籍。

先生覆信张君劢,询问其病症恢复情况并告知 Hummel 的中文姓名。

> 君劢先生著席:
>
> 　　两奉手教,欣悉出院后调养经过,今后注意饮食,数月后即可复原。去年内人亦患此病,现已康复。欣闻友忠夫妇即来波城相聚,同礼等亦愿前来,只惜道远耳。Hummel 汉文姓名为"恒慕义"。顺颂痊安。
>
> 　　　　　　　　　　　　　　　　　　同礼叩
> 　　　　　　　　　　　　　　　　　　八,四
>
> 内人附笔问安。

〔国家图书馆善本组手稿特藏〕

　　按:"友忠夫妇"应指施友忠(1902—2001),福州人,时在西雅图华盛顿大学任教。

八月五日

先生致信董作宾,请其为刘国蓁谋取新亚书院图书馆职务撰写推荐函,并谈拟购书画事宜。

> 彦堂吾兄著席:
>
> 　　友人刘国蓁先生前在冯平山图书馆服务多年,对于图书整理经验颇丰。在抗战期间,平馆及中央馆一部分图书寄存该馆,得刘君协助之处甚多。前以人事关系脱离港大,暂在报界服务,未能用其所长。近闻宾四先生主持之新亚书院正在发展,下学期将在新校址上课,需人必多,拟请吾兄作函介绍,俾能如愿。兹嘱刘君晋谒,即希赐予接见为感。此恳,顺颂教祺。
>
> 　　　　　　　　　　　　　　　　弟袁同礼顿首
> 　　　　　　　　　　　　　　　　八月五日
>
> 　　又,日本卷子纸业已购到,毋须麻烦贵友之令郎矣。其余之件,望交其带来,并附一清单。托其到美后□□寄下。弟之通讯处为:11 Eighth Street S. E. Washington 3. D. C. 赵少昂之画,弟愿得一小幅,吾兄能接洽否?润笔请暂垫并盼裱好,或迳交刘先生,由渠代裱、代寄亦可。

〔清风似友・台北古书拍卖会(2024)〕

按：贵友之令郎似指张迪善，待考。

八月九日

全汉昇（台北）致函先生，请尽快寄下胡适著作英文目录，并请在美代为催促他人稿件。

守和先生：

许久没有给先生问候，想近况安吉为慰！胡先生祝寿论文集，我们在这里已经先后收到论文十八篇，其中有八篇是从美国及意大利寄来的。因为希望能够赶于本年十二月胡先生生日以前出版，故我们现在决定先把已收到的稿子先行付印，以后如有论文寄到，则随到随印。先生负责编辑胡先生著作的英文目录，请早日寄下。关于此间编辑的中文目录及其他问题，李济之先生说不久即寄信给先生。兹有恳者：下列各先生，过去虽然已经去函征稿，但尚未接到寄来论文，晚和李济之先生等拟麻烦先生就近在美代为从旁婉转催促一下。这些先生名单如下：陈荣捷、陈观胜、何淬廉、何炳棣（最近有在剑桥）、李田意、柳无忌、梅贻宝、邓嗣禹（不知已自日返美否？）、蒋廷黻、王际真、陈源、洪业、陈受颐、W. Simon（与济之先生通信，已答允）、F. Lessing（已答应济之先生寄稿）、Paul Demieville（已函李方桂先生，愿寄稿），及Peter A. Boodberg等。费神种种，不胜感谢！专此，敬祝俪安。

晚全汉昇敬上。

一九五六年八月九日

〔University of Chicago Library, Yuan T'ung-li Papers, Box 2〕

八月十日

李济覆函先生，告"胡先生祝寿论文集"组稿进展，并请将英文著作目录早日寄送。

守和吾兄：

奉七月廿九日大函，敬悉适之先生祝寿文，海外寄来者共八篇，中有四篇是外国人的，D'Elia、Waley、Goodrich、Kennedy各一篇，我们送出的征文函件共三十余封，其中有回信不能参加的（两位），也有答应参加而文尚未收到的，一切详汉昇兄信。现在我们共收到文稿将近廿篇，约四十万字，再加将近完成的稿件，共有五十万字左右。昨日开了一次编辑会议，决定将已收到的稿件先付印，以后随收随印，希望能在胡公生日前印成。徐高阮君所编之中文著作目录,已将近完成,并已告其钞壹份送胡先生校订,英文著作目录并希早早赐寄。Max Loehr 的新著,弟已读了,并写了一章书评,此公对考古似甚外行,汉文阅读能力太不高明,若为一普通收藏目录,自是上品,但其所考问题,似对于现代考古学所知并不多也。余不尽。专此,并颂撰安。

方桂太太返美时,闻携有火锅,不识是否有兄件也。兄曷不就近一询。

弟济拜上

八,十日

〔University of Chicago Library, Yuan T'ung-li Papers, Box 2〕

按:"Max Loehr 的新著"即 *Chinese Bronze Age Weapons: the Werner Jannings Collection in the Chinese National Palace Museum, Peking*。"方桂太太"即徐樱女士(1910—1993),安徽萧县人,北洋政府要人徐树铮长女,徐道邻之妹。此函以航空信方式寄送,先生收到后曾致信李方桂。

八月十四日

噶邦福致函先生,略述在堪培拉从事研究的情况,并询问廖家珊、刘崇鋐的通信地址。

Aug. 14, 1956

Dear Mr. Yuan,

I am not sure that this letter will reach you, because only your address of 1954 is in my possession. But in the hope that, whatever maybe the case, my letter will be forwarded to you, I wish to write you and should like to hear from you, too.

During these three years, 1954–56, I have obtained some success in a new country. I mean my work at Canberra University College, first casual, but later more expanded. It is not exactly the same as I had at Tsing Hua, but anyhow, in a field of Russian studies congenial and known to me. This year, because of the absence of my chief, who is in London now, I am in good and responsible situation. The authorities and colleagues are amiable and friendly people, and life at Canberra is peaceful and serious, just to my liking. There are some people here, who have lived at Peking and know you—others than those I have mentioned earlier. Prof. Bielenstein is Head of Oriental Dept. in our College and van der Sprenkel coming soon.

Now I have a question, or even two, to you: my wife has lost the address of your sister-in-law, Tania, and wishes to have it as to send a letter to her from time to time now is easier or some parcels, when postal communications have been restored. She asked the Australian cultural delegation to inquire, but they had no time to do so. And I should like to know the address of Prof. Liu Chung-kung, who used to be my colleague and friend at Tsing Hua and with whom I should like to keep in touch when both of us are old and out of China.

If possible, tell my regards to President Mei and also news about my life and work at Canberra, I think he will be glad to hear them. In particular, regard of my wife to Mrs. Mei.

Now, with best wishes for your family,

J. J. Gapanovich

〔University of Chicago Library, Yuan T'ung-li Papers, Box 2〕

八月十八日

刘国棻覆函先生,告汇款及代转之信均已妥收妥办,并告冯秉华联系方式,另询罗原觉藏书是否有机构愿意购入,此外说明购书款余额。

守和博士尊鉴:

敬启者,十二日拜奉五日手教,敬悉。附汇单十美元并北平王先生信(经已□□票寄发),致董彦堂教授及钱宾四院长函,均已妥收。董、钱两信日间当分别趋谒,情形若何当再奉禀。此次叨蒙不遗在远,鼎力吹嘘,感荷恩慈,宪无既极。秉华东翁仍在歌城,惟已迁居,新地址是:18 North Second Street, Colorado Springs, Colo. 尚未返港。昨年拟定本年六月间回港,但因事不果行,闻现拟改为十二月见成行云。三月前由挂号邮奉上敝友罗原觉先生所藏《水浒传》及画屏等影印本与说明,量邀尊览,未悉尊意以为如何,便中敬希示知,俾得转覆罗君为幸。又《曾文正公书札》,美国可能购买否? 如再须样本,当可寄奉。汇票十元找得港银六十元(因运河事件,金钞皆涨),连前八元二角半,共六十八元二角半,上次航邮费贰元,八月份两小报费三元一角半,寄费七角半,续定《新闻天地》半年廿三元,共支廿八元九角,比对尚存卅九元三角半在晚处也。《新闻天地》已着其接续期数寄奉,两小报每十日奉上一次,想皆能到达无误也。今年暑假先生有无到别处旅游,想甚快乐渡假耳。港中天气颇为炎热,惟近来稍转凉快也。专此,敬请崇安!

愚晚国蓁顿首

一九五六年八月十八日

〔袁同礼家人提供〕

　　　　按:该函扫描件右下角有折叠。

八月二十二日

李方桂覆函先生,告所托求取之对联尚待裱好后寄台,并告因未知需要火锅未敢在台代购。

　　　　守和我兄:

　　　　　　手示奉悉。离台前,收到孔德成书对联,已付裱,但行期太促,不及俟裱好,只好嘱友(裱好后)寄美。黄君璧托毛子水兄代求(弟不识黄君)。乞径函子水以问究竟。前函未说明要火锅,故未敢代购。如急需,弟亦可函台北购好寄奉,如何? 匆此,即颂俪安。

弟李方桂

八月廿二日

〔University of Chicago Library, Yuan T'ung-li Papers, Box 2〕

　　　　按:孔德成(1920—2008),字玉汝,号达生,山东曲阜人,孔子第七十七代嫡长孙,袭封三十二代衍圣公兼第一代大成至圣先师奉祀官。黄君璧(1898—1991),原名允瑄,号君璧、君翁,广东南海人,画家。

八月二十七日

胡适致函先生,寄上拣选后的英文著作目录。

　　　　守和兄:

　　　　　　英文目录,今天匆匆挑出了一些,即作为一个选择的目录,似比不选择的较胜。送上乞吾兄审定后,即乞打字抄了,用航空寄去,何如?

劳贞一送来中文著作一目,是徐高阮君做的,我稍加增删,今日航空寄去,可惜不及请老兄一审定了。

我八月卅一日西行。匆匆,敬祝双安。

弟适之

一九五六,八,廿七

〔University of Chicago Library, Yuan T'ung-li Papers, Box 7〕

按:此函后附胡适著作英文目录22页,皆为其亲笔。

是年夏

邓嗣禹请先生物色合适人员前往印第安纳大学图书馆负责中日文图书编目工作,先生遂推荐蒲友书。〔彭靖《1956年周一良给邓嗣禹信札透漏的讯息》,《澎湃·私家历史》,2020年4月19日〕

按:邓嗣禹对蒲君虽甚满意,但后者以未习日文为由,婉言谢绝。Delafield覆函先生,附上校阅后的《胡适西文著作目录》,并谈该目的局限和问题,建议编纂更为全面的目录。

Dear Mr. Yuan,

Here is the check list bibliography of Dr. Hu Shih's works. First, I shall take up what, as I assume, will be the function of this particular bibliography. It is to inform the world where is to be found in a reasonable accessible form, the works of Dr. Hu Shih. In this premise I may be wrong. But in the short time given me and not having you in easy reach to consult. On questions not only of policy of this bibliography, but individual questions as well. I had to go ahead and use my own judgement. For example, you will see at the end I have listed only one newspaper contribution in English, and that because of its great importance. I have left out all others, because of the difficulty of the reader in procuring them. Also, on the same basis only his published works are included. You did not mention my supplying any Chinese language material, whether published in China, Taiwan, or here. So, I left all that in your hands. However, I shall mention, as possibly you may not have heard of it yet, a biography which the Doctor is just now publishing in Taipei, of his friend, V. K. Ting, who died in 1937. This should be out any day now, so someone there can get the title and details from whoever is publishing it there and add it to the Chinese section of the bibliography.

If I have committed any errors in my part of the bibliography, kindly publicly beg the reader to accept my humble apologies. I have tried to be as complete as possible within the limits it covers and only can hope no errors have crept in. And if they have, and you run across any, please accept my personal apologies. Perhaps someday you might consider doing a full bibliography of Dr. Hu with me. I personally would be honored by such a collaboration.

I keep wishing we had had more time and could profusely consult together; before rushing into print the way we are doing. The time element does not lend itself to a rush job.

If there are any entries which you feel need editing, or the entries need rearranging, please feel free to do what you feel is right. I shall leave such matters to your good judgment.

Trusting all goes well with the project, I remain

Most sincerely,

Eugene L. Delafield

P. S. I should like to get three copies of the Chinese language edition, and six copies of the English language edition. Over and above the complimentary copy which you said I would receive. Let me know how much the 9 copies will cost and I will send a check to cover them, and to whom should I send it.

〔University of Chicago Library, Yuan T'ung-li Papers, Box 9〕

按:此函为其亲笔,但无时间标注,暂系于此。

九月八日

先生致信加斯基尔,告知预计前往康乃尔大学的时间,并申请一间阅览室。

September 8, 1956

Dear Miss Gaskill:

I should like so much to consult your card catalog of western books on China and I expect to be in Ithaca next Thursday and Friday. I hope your Library is open in the evenings during the holiday.

If you could ask the Union to reserve a room for a day or two, I shall be grateful.

Looking forward with much pleasure to seeing you,

Yours sincerely,

T. L. Yuan

〔Cornell University Library, Wason Collection Records, 1918-1988,

Box 1, Folder Koo, T. K. Letters〕

按:先生预计前往的时间为 13、14 日两天。此件为打字稿,落款处为先生签名。

九月中旬

先生赴康乃尔大学查阅文献。〔Cornell University Library, Wason Collection Records, 1918-1988, Box 1, Folder Koo, T. K. Letters〕

九月二十四日

先生回到华盛顿。〔Library of Congress, Council on Library and Information Resources Records, Box 95〕

九月二十五日

先生致信克莱普,告知回抵华盛顿,并祝贺其担任美国图书馆资源委员会主席。

September 25, 1956

Dear Mr. Clapp:

Upon my return to Washington yesterday, I was delighted to learn your election as President of the Council on Library Resources, Inc. While I share keenly L. C.'s loss in your departure, I can see immense opportunities for service in your new assignment. May I offer you my heartiest and sincerest congratulations?

In view of your significant achievements in the past, I am sure that your new effort in solving the complex problems of modern library development will be crowned with success. All of us foreign librarians will continue to come to you for advice, guidance and inspiration.

With best wishes,

Yours sincerely,

T. L. Yuan

〔Library of Congress, Council on Library and Information Resources
Records, Box 95〕

按:此件为打字稿,落款处为先生签名。该件于 27 送达,10 月 2
日克莱普覆信表示收到。

九月二十九日

先生撰写 Memo on the supplement to Cordier's *Bibliotheca Sinica*, 1921 –
1955.〔袁同礼家人提供〕

九十月间

先生委托国会图书馆东方部为裴开明查阅《三才图会》中有关匈奴的图
片、章节。〔《裴开明年谱》,页 654〕

十月二日

董作宾致函先生,告知先生等人购买各文玩字画将托张迪善携至纽约转交。

守和吾兄:

上次奉书,已详开各物及价目,弟未存底本(请一查前单,除去信
笺),以其全部交张迪善君带纽约。张君闻人言不能带荣宝斋之物,故
所买之信纸廿余元,一包留下,以后再设法寄去。

兄八月五日函,托刘君转来者,此时张君各物已装箱,不便令其取
出。又磁器不能寄,只好仍烦张君。张君上次船未走,此次决于十月
六日上克里佛兰号航,七号启程。到纽约后,即照兄八月十三日函所
嘱一切送交徐家璧先生,当可转上。钱存训兄之画,夹在兄之字画内,
仍烦便中转与也。

刘君未来晤谈,新亚业已开学,人事早已满额,恐不便介绍矣。傅
尚霖君返港,闻已与兄及何义均兄晤及,知公等安吉,甚慰! 专此,即
颂近安!

弟董作宾拜上

十,二

〔University of Chicago Library, Yuan T'ung-li Papers, Box 2〕

按:张迪善所携带的文玩可参见是年 11 月 9 日徐家璧致先生函。
"刘君"应指刘国蓁。先生对瓷器颇有研究,甚喜收藏,故租住大

宅子,用以陈列、欣赏。①

十月十四日

刘国蓁覆函先生,已告其应创兴书院之聘,并告代购圣诞节卡片、购书款余额等事。

守和博士先生钧鉴:

敬启者,蒹葭秋水,倍切溯洄,恭维崇祉绥和,清祺畅适,定符私颂。上月拜奉手教敬悉,并附信二笺经已加邮付寄,又附致王书林教授函等日昨收到,代转吴维健先生信一函,兹特奉呈,敬希察收为幸。晚素蒙不遗在远,屡为吹嘘,感荷恩慈,寔无既极。上月前,港中银行家廖宝珊先生创办一中英文中学,名创兴书院渠为监督,于德辅道西。晚得敝戚之介,为其主理图书馆,而创设伊始,凡百待举,是以极为辛苦,更兼每日八时返校,五时返家,六时返报馆,十二时返家,一时许方能休息,只睡眠六小时而已,精神十分疲倦也。但为生活挣扎,亦无可如何耳。来示嘱代购圣诞节片二三百片付上,现港中新货尚未上市,而中号之中国艺术片,如昨年晚付上之一种亦要五角一片,五元一打,若购廿五打则须一百廿五元也,若稍为好些则要七八元一打矣。尊账前存卅九元三角半,现支九十月小报费六元三角,寄费一元五角,此次邮费二元,共九元八角,比对尚存廿九元五角半而已。港中双十节日之极不愉快事件,以至无可收拾,殊深惜痛,时至今日将可解决而渐复常态矣。专此,敬请钧安。

愚晚刘国蓁顿首
一九五六年十月十四日

再启者,创兴书院校长为曹炎申博士,渠与先生相熟,并有问及尊况与地址也。

〔袁同礼家人提供〕

按:廖宝珊(1903—1961),潮州富商,创兴书院初设于香港岛西区石塘咀屈地街,后迁往山道独立校舍,现校址位于新界荃湾绿杨新邨22-66号,1976年易名为廖宝珊纪念书院。"港中双十节日之极不愉快事件"即香港"双十暴动",此次骚乱造成数十人死

①《思忆录》,中文部分页108。

亡,数百人受伤,1000 余人被捕,14 日上午戒严方告解除。曹炎
申(1892—?),广东番禺人,曾任香港中华基督教青年会总干事、
上海青年会中学校长,编著《美国教育》等。

十月十八日

胡适致函先生,告知中基会给予美金三千元用以完成《西文汉学书目》的
编纂。

October 18, 1956

Dear Mr. Yuan:

I have the pleasure to inform you that at the 27th Annual Meeting of
the China Foundation held on October 6, 1956, it was decided to grant
you a special research fellowship of $ 3,000, in order to enable you to
complete the work on a supplement to Cordier's *Bibliotheca Sinica*.

The grant will be paid in 2 equal installments at the end of March
and September in 1957.

Yours sincerely,
Hu Shih
Director
〔袁同礼家人提供〕

　　按:此件为打字稿,落款处为胡适签名。

十一月五日

李济致函先生,请先生转让图书与史语所,并告其近况。

　　守和吾兄惠鉴:

　　　　前承见示徐森玉近年编刊《画苑掇英》与《沈石田卧游册》二书,
已在英购到,查本所对此二书亦颇需要,拟烦吾兄转让本所,书价当即
汇奉,可否并请示知。劳神至感! 弟月前因事忙,近又因足骨微伤,尚
未痊愈,致稽久未复,深以为歉! 专此,顺颂撰祺。

弟济敬启
十一月五日
〔University of Chicago Library, Yuan T'ung-li Papers, Box 2〕

　　按:《画苑掇英》共收历代古画一百二十四幅,1955 年上海人民美
术出版社初版,全三册,每部定价七十元。《沈石田卧游册》明代

沈周绘,荣宝斋新记木板水印十五张,1953 年 10 月刊行。

十一月九日

徐家璧致函先生,告知张迪善送来文玩各件情况。

守和先生尊鉴:

敬肃者,本日上午香港张迪善先生业经到馆送来董彦堂先生嘱转尊处之对联暨文具多件。兹将款目列下:

一、送交尊处者,计有:

条幅叁张,小对联壹对

宣纸贰卷,毛笔拾支

端砚附红木盒壹副

彩绘笔筒壹只,徽墨壹块

水盂壹只,笔洗壹只

花磁印盒(无印泥)壹只,花磁印盒(带印泥)壹只

二、送交何义均先生者,计有:

大小对联陆副,共十二件

三、送交钱存训兄者,计有:

黄君璧山水画壹幅

以上各物因件数过多,且有细磁伍件暨红木盒等,似未便邮寄,可否俟公再来纽约或有便人返华府时再行交运,未悉以为若何? 兹随函先将发票四张奉上。何义均先生处恳祈就便通知为感,至于存训兄处,璧或将去函告知,即祈释念为荷。又前承寄上散戚罗万森君俄文著作 L. C.卡片壹张,早经收讫,并此申谢。匆匆,敬请道安。

晚徐家璧鞠躬

十一月九日

尊夫人前并乞便中代为叩安为感。

致钱君函,业已书就寄出,乞毋念!

〔袁同礼家人提供〕

十一月十二日

先生致信加斯基尔,请其代为查询书目信息并申请复制胡适在康乃尔大学读书时的手稿。

November 12, 1956

Dear Miss Gaskill:

I was so happy to have consulted your growing collection on China and I wished very much to spend more time there. I do want to thank you for your courtesy and assistance.

There are several items on which I would like to have full bibliographical information. I shall be much obliged to you if you would check it for me.

During his student days Dr. Hu Shih wrote an essay on Browning, the manuscript of which is being kept either in your Library or in the Alumni collection. Will you kindly locate it and arrange to have it reproduced either by photostat (1 negative and 1 positive); or by typescript. I should like to have two copies of this essay and shall be glad to pay for the expenses thus occurred.

Thanking you for your valuable help,

Yours sincerely,

T. L. Yuan

〔Cornell University Library, Wason Collection Records, 1918-1988, Box 1, Folder Koo, T. K. Letters〕

按:请协助查询书目信息的纸张并未保存下来,Dr. Hu Shih wrote an essay on Browning 应为 A Defense of Browning's Optimism。此件为打字稿,落款处为先生签名。

十一月十四日

先生向国会图书馆人事部提交职位申请。〔袁同礼家人提供〕

按:11 月 8 日,国会图书馆发布公告,十进制分类部(Decimal Classification Section)有一个空缺职位。

十一月二十日

徐家璧覆函先生,告前由香港购入之文玩已托蓝乾章带至华盛顿,并谈邓衍林返国事。

守和先生尊鉴:

敬肃者,昨奉月之十四日手谕,敬悉一是。关于张迪善君带下尊处暨何义均先生各件,兹以蓝乾章兄来京之便,即请便程将全部物品托渠带上,以快先睹,至乞于送到后按前寄各单点收为荷。应转何先生之对联,即恳便中分神代转,无任感祷。钱君之画拟即按其意旨邮寄,诸乞毋念。承嘱转致张君函壹件,业经照转,渠之现址如下:Mr. Ti-shan Chang, 225 Sassafras Street Millville, N. J.

又九日渠来馆送物之际,璧曾邀其午餐以示略表谢意而已。据告,渠此次来美系按移民身份,故似将久居此间,下学期并拟入学继续攻读,今后来京晋谒机会当极易也。

邓衍林兄离纽而后,曾在夏威夷来片,又在菲律滨来函,沿途平安,惟对于促璧返国之意,至为坚决,殊属费解。至渠患病,颇有几分事实,但据知决非癌症,又渠之事业心仍甚炽烈,此番回国志在辅助建设,自不能纯以病体赴之。

余俟续呈,敬请秋安。

晚徐家璧鞠躬
十一月二十日

尊夫人前并乞代为叩安。

〔袁同礼家人提供〕

按:蓝乾章(1915—1991),湖北省武昌人,1938 年毕业于文华图书馆专科学校,时在哥伦比亚大学图书馆进修。

十二月一日

噶邦福覆函先生,谈诸事。

Canberra,
Dec. 1, 1956

Dear Mr. Yuan.

Excuse me, please, that I have not yet replied your letter of Sept. 8th, of course, received long ago. In fact, I had not information to communicate to you.

The easiest was the year of Prof. Brandt's death, which happened 1 year or two before my return to Peking. I asked Mrs. Karpinsky, who knows this date exactly, to inform you. I asked her twice, and it is easy to her, living America, to do so. But one cannot rely on ladies.

By the way, Mr. Karpinsky is released now, and is on his way to

Hong Kong already. I have had a lengthy letter from him. When he comes to America, as he seemingly and naturally intends, you might keep in touch with him and hear some recent news about China. His impressions, except of course his imprisonment, are generally good.

I asked Prof. Fitzgerald immediately to compile a list of publications wanted by you. But first he was busy, delivering lectures on his trip to China, then he was free, but outside of Canberra, now he takes care of Chinese opera artists coming to our place. When all this is over, he will send a desired bibliography to you. In advance, I can say that only a few works were published in Australia, the most important of them being *Empress Wu* by Fitzgerald, because Prof. Bielenstein's dissertation was published in Sweden. Indeed, there are some articles or lectures (particularly, Morrison's series) which may be found here. The reports by Fitzgerald and Prof. Partridge were printed in Voice, July-August this year. But as I say, you will receive a list.

People in China, as I hear from these visitors, are free and happy. Still, I cannot receive even a simple postcard from your brother. Nor have I heard anything from Winter, I think or is he afraid?

My greetings from Christmas and new year to your whole family.

Sincerely yours,

J. J. Gapanovich

〔University of Chicago Library, Yuan T'ung-li Papers, Box 2〕

按：Prof. Brandt 即 J. J. Brandt（1869–1944），俄国汉学家，中文名卜郎特，圣彼得堡大学毕业，20 世纪初来华，先后在哈尔滨、北京俄文学校任教，后任北洋政府外交部顾问，曾编著数本有关学习中文的教材、读物。*Empress Wu* 即费知乐的专著《武则天》，1955 年墨尔本初版。该函为其亲笔。

十二月六日

先生致信芒太尔，请其发来中瑞西北科学考查团所有出版物目录，并就附单中的瑞典学者填写其生年。

December 6, 1956

Dear Dr. Montell:

　　Although I have not written to you for some time, you are frequently in my thoughts. When I was in Europe, in the autumn of 1954, I wanted to come visit you in Stockholm, but because my longer stay in Germany, I simply could not make it. I hope that before very long we might meet again.

　　I am compiling a bibliography on China and I want to include all the works included in Sino-Swedish scientific expedition to the Northwest series. Will you kindly send me as complete a list of these publications as possible?

　　After each author, I usually insert the year of his birth. I now enclose a list of Swedish authors and I shall be most grateful to you if you could find out their years of birth for me. I know this request would give you too much trouble, but since most of them live in Stockholm, it might not be too difficult.

　　Thanking you for your valuable assistance and warmest regards,

Yours sincerely,

T. L. Yuan

〔University of Chicago Library, Yuan T'ung-li Papers, Box 7〕

十二月十二日

刘国蓁致函先生,已代为转寄往来书信并告书报账目及余额,另谈其生活近况。

守和博士先生钧鉴:

　　敬启者,许久未修书敬候,抱歉殊深,恭维著述宏丰、起居安乐,至以为颂。月前拜奉手教敬悉,并代转寄大陆函件两封,经已遵命办理,昨日得接北京及无锡来信各一封,兹特为转呈左右,敬悉察收为幸。逝水韶华,又届圣诞节,晚于月前由包裹邮奉上英国杂饼壹罐、贺简壹函,敬希哂纳,幸甚幸甚,区区微意,聊表寸心而已,想该包裹必能及时到达也。尊账前存廿九元五角半,代支付十一月份小报费三元一角半,寄费九角半,及十二月份报费三.五元、寄费七.五角,代购香港邮笺(航空)十张五元、寄费四角,及上次与今次邮费共六元,共支银十九元四角,比对尚存十元零壹角半在晚处也。《新闻天地》前订半年,至一九五七年一月尾便告截止,如欲再订,恳请早日示知,以资办理为幸。晚仍继续日夜工作,十分辛苦。月来体重减轻三磅耳,更兼学海书楼重新整顿,亦蒙委任负责整理,专员盛情难却,亦免为其难也。匆匆,余当续禀。专此,敬请崇安。

愚晚国蓁顿首

一九五六年十二月十二日

〔袁同礼家人提供〕

按:1923 年,赖际熙(1865—1937)在香港创立学海书楼,旨在宣扬国粹,时应在上环般含道。

十二月十三日

杨联陞覆函先生,告知*Reminiscences of a Chinese Official* 一书信息。

守和先生:

十二月五日大札及胶卷奉悉。

此书原本,似仅出于英文。原书名 *Reminiscences of a Chinese Official*(小题 revelations of official life under the Manchus),Tientsin Press, 1922. 其 Introduction 起首云 "*The Reminiscences of a Chinese Official* were first published in the columns of the now defunct *Peking Gazette*. They were the work of a young foreign educated Chinese, and were based upon various Chinese publications which were surreptitiously circulated during the Manchu regime. The Editor of the *China Illustrated Review* secured the permission of the Author to revise them with a view to their republication in book form⋯⋯"哈佛大图书馆有此书,编号 ch188.99.5,去年曾翻过,觉得尚有趣味,卷首官吏收贿时图像亦见原书,故寻检尚不为难也。胶卷已遵命转赠汉和图书馆矣。Li Chang 之名不详,似是法译者,非原作者也。(非查 *Peking Gazette* 不敢断言)。

内子曾住医院,已恢复百分之九十余,大约新年后再作最后一次复诊,便可功行圆满矣。敬请双安!

晚学联陞敬上

一九五六年,十二,十三

〔University of Chicago Library, Yuan T'ung-li Papers, Box 2〕

十二月十五日

先生致信克莱普,希望其能就《西文汉学书目》的出版与哈佛大学出版社沟通。

December 15, 1956

Dear Mr. Clapp:

I am indeed most grateful to you for your interest in the publication of the Supplement to Cordier's *Bibliotheca Sinica*. I am confident that through your influence we should be able to work out a satisfactory arrangement for its publication.

I enclose herewith the memo. Perhaps you may like to try the Harvard University Press first. I know that you would like to do what you can to expedite its early appearance.

With sincere greetings,

Yours sincerely,

T. L. Yuan

〔Library of Congress, Council on Library and Information Resources Records, Box 95〕

按:该信附两页备忘录。

先生致信 Gregg M. Sinclair,询问谭卓垣遗稿的保存情况,并建议该校申请福特基金会资助将其出版,以供学术界利用。

December 15, 1956

Dr. Gregg M. Sinclair

University of Hawaii

Honolulu, T. H.

Dear Dr. Sinclair:

With the premature death of the late Dr. Taam, I have been wondering whether his manuscripts for a bibliography on China are ready for publication and whether the University of Hawaii is ready to publish it. Knowing that you are keenly interested in Dr. Taam's work, I hope that you would see to it that it is to be published in the immediate future.

You may have learned that the Ford Foundation now has a program to support and stimulate the publication of scholarly books in the humanities and social sciences. I enclose a clipping which is self-explanatory.

Under the terms of the grant, individual scholars are not eligible for such a grant, but the program is being administered through grants to eligible university presses. If Dr. Taam's work needs further editing, I hope your colleagues will bring it into good shape and will get the University Press to apply for a grant. All inquiries should be addressed to Mr. W. McNeil Lowry at the Ford Foundation, 477 Madison Avenue, New York 22, N. Y.

As Western Literature on China has become enormous, it was my understanding that I devote my efforts on the monographs and pamphlets, while Dr. Taam on scholarly articles scattered in various journals. As he has spent much time in its completion, I hope you would do your very best to have it published—a matter which is very dear to Dr. Taam's heart.

With sincere greetings,

Yours sincerely,

T. L. Yuan

〔University of Chicago Library, Yuan T'ung-li Papers, Box 7〕

按：Gregg M. Sinclair(1890-1980)，长期执教于夏威夷大学，1935年至1940年担任该校东方研究所所长，1941年至1956年担任该校校长。此件为录副。

刘国蓁致函先生，转寄袁道冲致袁慧熙信。

守和博士先生钧鉴：

敬启者，昨日奉上芜函并附北京、无锡两信，量邀尊览。顷奉令岳丈大人手示，内有"十月初曾寄一函，并附致小女一笺奉托尊处转达，其时正值香港多事，不知尊处有无受惊，由不知前函有无因此延搁，甚为悬念"等语。晚想该函经已转呈，但先生尚未有回信也。兹又有一函嘱为转达，特此奉上，敬希察收为幸。令岳处晚已回信答覆矣。专此，敬请崇安。

愚晚刘国蓁顿首

一九五六年十二月十五日

〔袁同礼家人提供〕

按:"正值香港多事"即香港"双十暴动"。

十二月十七日

先生寄送胡适早年的一篇论文影照本,并写短片。

近在康奈尔大学发现尊著稿本,适值先生六五大庆,爰以影照本奉献,敬希晒纳。

同礼

一九五六年,十二,十七

〔台北胡适纪念馆,档案编号 HS-NK05-197-004〕

按:"尊著稿本"即 A Defense of Browning's Optimism,胡适写于1914 年,正文部分共 19 页。①

先生致信克莱普,告已向国会图书馆提交职位申请但无回覆,请其协助沟通,如十进制分类部的职位已有合适人选,则希望能够有其他的岗位可以应聘。

December 17, 1956

Dear Mr. Clapp:

My application for a position in the Decimal Classification Section was submitted on November 14, but I have had no news thus far one way or the other. At your suggestion, I am enclosing Posting 3703 dated November 8, 1956.

If this position has suddenly been abolished, I hope I may have the opportunity to serve in some other capacity. I shall be extremely grateful to you if you could make the necessary contact on my behalf.

Yours sincerely,

T. L. Yuan

〔Library of Congress, Council on Library and Information Resources Records, Box 95〕

按:此件为打字稿,落款处为先生签名。20 日克莱普覆函先生,

---

① 页码显示为 18 页,但页码数字 4 重复了一次。另有章节目录 1 页。

表示收悉 15、17 来信，将就职位事予以询问。

费知乐致函先生，告已按前请寄上访华见闻但请不要公开并引用，至于澳大利亚和新西兰所出有关中国的书目信息则请先生询问澳大利亚国立图书馆。

17th December, 1956

Dear Dr. Yuan:

Professor Gapanovich sent me your letter to him in which you refer to the visit I made to China in May last with the Cultural Delegation from Australia. After my return I did make a report on that visit to the University, and though, of course, it does not by any means cover the whole field of modern China but is mainly a record of things seen and people met, I would be glad to send you a copy for your own information. It is not, however, for publication, and I feel sure you will understand that I would not like it publicly cited.

As regards your second query about any new publications on China which have appeared in Australia and New Zealand before 1955, I am not quite sure what you mean by "New." There no doubt has been publications on China appearing in these two countries in earlier years, but I cannot recall anything published in this country or New Zealand. There has been works written by New Zealanders who have revisited China, but these have been published in London, and this, I think, has usually been the case as it was with my own book *Revolution in China* which, though written here, was published by the Cresset Press in London. I think that the most certain check on this could be to write to the National Library here in Canberra.

I am glad to hear from you and hope that you are flourishing. Van der Sprenkel has now come here to work at Canberra University College, so we have quite a little group of old Peking characters. Best wishes for the New Year.

Yours sincerely,

C. P. Fitzgerald

〔University of Chicago Library, Yuan T'ung-li Papers, Box 2〕

按：*Revolution in China*，1952 年初版。

十二月二十二日

先生撰写 Supplement to Cordier's *Bibliotheca Sinica*，Final Report。〔Library of Congress, Council on Library and Information Resources Records, Box 95〕

十二月二十三日

刘大钧覆函先生，谈其最近阅读之书及申请工作的进展。

> 守和兄：
>
> 　　奉手教、贺年片及经济书目，谢谢。书目包罗甚多，谅无复遗漏，如以后发见，当随时奉告也。该书目似以西文参考材料为限，然否？承询中国作者六人之中文姓名，愧无以应命，未知国会图书馆中有无历年出版之 *Who's Who in China*？唯如果有之，兄必经常翻查也。弟目前尚未进行研究工作，终日在阅读经济与统计书籍，颇获实益。在初完成 Comment for Economic & Industry Research 之工作后，则阅看科学（经济与统计除外）及哲学之书籍。因非本行，择其通俗者阅之。如 Durant, *The Story of Philosophy*；Dewey, *Reconstruction in Philosophy*；Barnett, *The Universe and Dr. Einstein*；Sullivan, *Limitation of Science* 之类，胸襟为之一畅，脑中尘埃亦得以洗净，奉闻以博一粲。申请公民事，手续已完成，闻证书日内可寄到。但此步虽经办好，能否得工作，尚不可知耳。幸小儿女辈在外工作，津贴家用，故弟之负担减轻不少。耑复，顺颂俪祉。
>
> 弟大钧鞠躬
十二，廿三
>
> 原名单奉还，备转询他人之用。

〔University of Chicago Library, Yuan T'ung-li Papers, Box 2〕

　　按：1947 年 10 月，刘大钧出任国民政府经济部驻美大使馆商务参事，1953 年退休，移居纽约市皇后区。"经济书目"应指 *Economic and Social Development of Modern China: A Bibliographical Guide*。

十二月二十七日

胡适致函先生，感谢寄赠文章副本，并告知最近行程安排。

> 守和兄：
>
> 　　谢谢你送我的寿礼！

这篇文章,我自己也忘记了,竟蒙老兄影印送我,又装订的如此精雅!

我今天(廿七日)飞回<u>加大</u>,把这学期赶完,一月尾仍回来一次,因为二月二日<u>中基会</u>要开一次执行委员会。

我大约二月中旬可以飞<u>台北</u>。

匆匆,敬祝新年双安。

弟适之
一九五六,十二,廿七晨六点
(通宵料理稿子,没有睡!)

〔University of Chicago Library, Yuan T'ung-li Papers, Box 7〕

Delafield 致函先生,感谢寄送 A Defense of Browning's Optimism 影本,附上费用支票,并告胡适行踪。

145 East 82 St.
New York City, N.Y.
Dec. 27, 1956

Dear Mr. Yuan,

Yes, I think your so-called friend is a rather expensive friend; at five dollars a volume. However, I am very glad to have the Browning Essay. And do appreciate greatly the trouble you took in having it photostated, and having it bound. Even though I think it rather high for binding, I want you to know that I think it came out really quite well in black and white.

The Doctor thought so too. He was quite amused and wondered how I had ever gotten it. The only other photostat is in Waco Univ. or College in Texas. Enclosed pleased to find my check for the binding. Don't I owe you for the photostating? You have been so kind to take all this trouble that the least I can do is see to it that you are not out of pocket in any way.

With my kindest regards and deepest thanks and the hope that all does & goes well with you in the coming years.

Eugene L. Delafield

P. S. Hope to see you when you next pay New York a visit. The Doctor came back for about 4 to 5 days only from California. He goes back today. Will be back the end of January for good.

〔University of Chicago Library, Yuan T'ung-li Papers, Box 2〕

按：该函为其亲笔。

十二月二十九日

先生致信克莱普，寄上报告以供参考并请转交国图图书馆参考部主任 Adkinson，另告《西文汉学书目》因收录一九五六年出版的书籍，拟于一九五七年二月完成书稿的编纂工作。

December 29, 1956

Dear Mr. Clapp:

In view of your valuable help in the publication of my Supplement to Cordier's *Bibliotheca Sinica*, I am enclosing copy of a report which I recently submitted to Dr. Poleman for transmission to Dr. Adkinson. I trust that you may like to have it for reference.

As I shall include all new publications on China published in the final months of 1956, my entire manuscript will not be ready for the printer until February 1957. I hope that by that time, you may hear definitely from the university presses with regard to the publication of the present work.

With Season's greetings,

Yours sincerely,

T. L. Yuan

〔Library of Congress, Council on Library and Information Resources Records, Box 95〕

按：此件为打字稿，落款处为先生签名。1 月 23 日，克莱普致信哈佛大学出版社，开始初步沟通，但因该社社长不在国内，导致进展缓慢。

是年

先生所编书目 *Economic and Social Development of Modern China: a bibliographical guide*（《中国经济社会发展史目录》）刊行，出版方为 Human Relations Area Files。

　　按:先生对本书目评价不高,应仅为完成 Human Relations Area Files 任务,参见 1962 年 11 月 16 日,先生致拉铁摩尔信。

梁在平根据先生《中国音乐书举要》增订成《中国音乐书谱目录》一书,台北中华国乐会刊行。

　　按:梁在平(1910—2000),河北高阳人,中国古琴、古筝演奏家,曾任平绥铁路站长,1949 年后在台任公共关系学会理事长等职务。《中国音乐书谱目录》较之先生在《中华图书馆协会会报》所登载的《中国音乐书举要》,各节均有增补。其中,西文部分增补最大,多由美人协助提供。①

---

① 本书附有梁在平中英文两份序言,前者提及西文书目"复承美国奥瑞岗大学图书馆莫莉丝女士(Miss True Morris)的协助,寄了她所找到的一份目录来";后者则没有感谢该女士,提到的只有 Mr. William Lichterwanger, Associate Director of NOTES, Music Library Association of the United States of America.

一九五七年　六十三岁

一月四日

克莱普致函先生,感谢寄赠《中国经济社会发展史目录》。〔Library of Congress, Council on Library and Information Resources Records, Box 95〕

一月七日　哈佛

先生访杨联陞。〔《杨联陞日记》(稿本)〕

　　按:所谈之事似与李田意欲影印在日本所见《三言》古本相关。

一月八日

芒太尔覆函先生,告前信所询瑞典学者信息已经代为收集,并告将前往墨西哥。

Stockholm January 8, 1957

Dear Professor Yuan,

　　I was really very happy to hear from you again. It is long ago since we met and the world has changed a lot.

　　It took some time before I could get together the information wanted by you as I was so occupied by preparations to go to Mexico for a short period. As I have no real assistant, I have to arrange everything myself. I expect to leave January 25th and return to Stockholm in end of April.

　　A new edition of *Vem är det* just has appeared.

　　I hope to hear from you soon again.

Yours sincerely

Gösta Montell

〔University of Chicago Library, Yuan T'ung-li Papers, Box 7〕

　　按:Vem är det 应为瑞典语版本的名人录。落款处为其签名。

一月十二日

董作宾(香港)致函先生,谈代购赵少昂画事及在港生活状况,并告知其回台打算。

守和吾兄：

　　承惠赠水笔，现在即用此笔写此信，甚合用。弟曾于十一月底，为"中研院"筹备开院士会议，飞回台北。在台北住了一月余，于本年一月六日返港。幸弟下人口平安，故未久留。

　　张迪善君为兄带去之物，曾有详目奉告。留下未带者为荣宝斋彩色套印信封笺一小包，因恐检查出大陆出品，不许入口也。留在此弟亦未用，将来设法寄上。兄前次所言购赵少昂画一事，弟与他不太熟，故托人找他的画十幅，弟曾亲见，但定价稍大者 600 元，小者 250 元，弟觉太贵，故未敢买之。且皆花鸟，弟亦不知何种能合兄之意见，故未能办，亦未奉告，乞谅之！

　　在此虽已住一年，但各方面仍生疏，每买一物，必烦朋友相伴，费时甚多。且托人带美，亦极不易，故视买物为畏途。弟已决定暑假满期即归。一位老人，孤身久居于外，甚非所宜，且弟患血压高症，虽常服药，亦不能保不出毛病也。年来稍清静，可一理旧稿，如此而已。专函道谢，并叩□□新年安好！

弟董作宾
一，十二，灯下

〔University of Chicago Library, Yuan T'ung-li Papers, Box 2〕

一月十九日

先生致信福梅龄，感谢寄赠亚洲基督教高等教育联合董事会报告，并请寄送该董事会出版物清单，另询问四位人士的信息。

January 19, 1957

Dear Miss Ferguson:

　　Thank you so much for your kindness in sending me your very interesting report which I read with a great interest and admiration. I feel keenly that your work is meeting a timely need and you certainly have my very best wishes for your success.

　　Will you please send me a list of the historical monographs which your Board has so far published? The only monograph which I do not happen to have seen is that on the University of Nanking. If it has been issued, could you send me a copy with your bill?

With thanks and kind regards,

Yours sincerely,

T. L. Yuan

P. S. In connection with my bibliography on China, I have included those on Cheeloo, Hangchow, St. Johns, Soochow, Fukien Christian, Ginling, and Hwa Nan, but I have not seen those on West China Union and Univ. of Nanking.

May I also request you to check the year (not the dates) of birth of the following authors: W. B. Nance, Matilda S. Thurston, and L. Ethel Wallace. Also, the year of death of Rev. John J. Heeren whom we all know very well. Many thanks for your valuable help.

〔Yale University Divinity School Library, United Board for Christian Higher Education in Asia Records, RG 11 Series Ⅱ, Box 79, Folder 2146〕

按：补语涉及的学校依次为齐鲁大学、之江大学、圣约翰大学、东吴大学、福建协和大学、金陵女子学院（大学）、华南女子文理学院，以及华西协和大学、金陵大学。W. B. Nance 即 Walter B. Nance（1868－1964），美国监理会（Methodist Episcopal Church, South）传教士，中文名文乃史，1896 年来华，在东吴大学执教，曾任副校长、校长；Matilda S. Thurston（1875－1958），中文名德本康夫人，1902 年随其夫来华，翌年归国，1906 年再次来华，在长沙雅礼学校任教，后曾任金陵女子学院首任院长；L. Ethel Wallace（1880-?），曾任华南女子文理学院教务长，中文名华惠德；John J. Heeren（1875-1941），美国长老会传教士，中文名奚尔恩，1911 年来华，长期担任齐鲁大学历史学教授。此件为打字稿，落款处为先生签名，于 1 月 24 日送达。

一月二十八日

福梅龄覆函先生，告东海大学近况及亚洲基督教高等教育联合董事会出版的有关中国基督教大学著作日期，并告前信所询四位人士的生年或卒年。

January 28, 1957

Dear Dr. Yuan:

Thank you for your letter of January 19th and for your kind comments on the recent reports of the work which the United Board is now doing in Asia. We are ourselves particularly happy about developments at Tunghai University in Taiwan where the institution seems to be making a very real place for itself on that beautiful island. Of course, we have only two classes of students so far but in another two years we will have a full four-year enrolment and there is certainly no lack of students who want to be admitted! Our only difficulty is in building up a faculty of the quality and strength which this eager group of young people deserve to have. Under the effective administration of President Tseng, however, with the devoted and hard-working group he has already gathered around him this too is on the way to accomplishment.

I list below the historical monographs on the China Colleges which have so far been issued, showing in each case the date of publication:

Cheeloo (Shantung Christian University)—August 1, 1955

Fukien Christian University—July 6, 1954

Ginling College—January 15, 1956

Hangchow University—January 15, 1956

Hangchow University—January 15, 1956

Hwa Nan College—September 21, 1956

St. John's University—August 1, 1955

Soochow University—March 23, 1956

The monographs on Yenching University, West China Union University and the University of Nanking are not yet ready. We hope that the one for Yenching will be out sometime before summer but I do not know yet what the publication dates for the other two will be.

You ask for the year of birth of the following authors: Dr. W. B. Nance, 1860; Mrs. Matilda S. Thurston, 1875; Miss L. Ethel Wallace, 1880. Dr. John J. Heeren died on February 7, 1941.

In connection with the date of birth of Mrs. Thurston and Miss

Wallace, may I remind that some women are sensitive about having their age known! I do not know whether this applies to either Mrs. Thurston or Miss Wallace but I think it is something to remember.

　　　With warm personal greetings to Mrs. Yuan and your good self,

Cordially yours,

Mary E. Ferguson

Associate Executive Secretary

　　　〔Yale University Divinity School Library, United Board for Christian Higher Education in Asia Records, RG 11 Series Ⅱ, Box 79, Folder 2146〕

　　　按:President Tseng 即曾约农(1893—1986),湖南湘乡人,曾国藩曾孙,祖父曾纪泽,谥号"惠敏",撰有《金轺筹笔》。1949 年曾约农赴台,1955 年至 1957 年任私立东海大学首任校长。

二月四日

克莱普致函先生,告知哈佛大学出版社主任 Thomas J. Wilson 不在国内,尚未获得实质性回复。〔Library of Congress, Council on Library and Information Resources Records, Box 95〕

二月八日

克莱普致函先生,告知其已与哈佛大学出版社副主任 Mark Carroll 取得联系,后者表示出极大兴趣,请先生与其直接联系,商洽出版事宜。

February 8, 1957

Dear Dr. Yuan:

　　　Further to my letter of February 4, 1957:

　　　Mr. Thomas J. Wilson, the Director of the Harvard University Press is still abroad but I have had an exchange of correspondence with his assistant, Mr. Mark Carroll. In his letter to me of February 6, 1957 Mr. Carroll tells me that "we are indeed interested in considering the possibility of publication here. Would you transmit our expression of interest to Dr. Yuan, as you have so kindly offered to do, and tell him that we look forward to hearing from him? I am especially interested to learn whether the possible subsidies for publication cover preparation of the manuscript, for the final report does not make this clear."

Accordingly, I now suggest that you write to Mr. Carroll; I think his interest has been whetted. But, if I can be of assistance, especially in making suggestions about reproduction from typewritten copies, I should be glad to do so. I told Mr. Carrol about the Bissainthe bibliography, but I very much doubt whether he has seen the volume.

In this connection, it would almost seem to me that, if your work were to be reproduced from typewritten copy (as was the Bissainthe work) it might promote efficiency if the typing were done under your supervision. In the case of the Bissainthe bibliography the author read proof on the same day that the sheets were typed.

Sincerely yours,

Verner W. Clapp

President

〔Library of Congress, Council on Library and Information Resources Records, Box 95〕

按:Thomas J. Wilson,1947 年至 1967 年担任哈佛大学出版社主任,Mark Carroll(1924－2010),1956 年加入该社。2 月 6 日,Mark Carroll 回覆克莱普的信中还有一句非常重要的评价:"His final report on the project is most informative, and I hasten to say that we are indeed interested in considering the possibility of publication here."Bissainthe 即 Max Bissainthe(1911－1978),历史学家、海地文学的档案学家,曾在 20 世纪 40 年代至 50 年代出任海地图书馆馆长。Bissainthe work 应指 *Dictionnaire de bibliographie Haitienne* ,1951 年华盛顿出版,海地文学的首个书目,信中提及此人此书,似与其中涉及多种语言文字有关,尤其是美国印刷厂中罕见的文字铅排,可以借鉴该书的方式。该件为录副。

徐家璧覆函先生,告知嘱办各事情况,并谈邓衍林归国后希望更多图书馆专业人才能够回国效力。

守和先生尊鉴:

敬肃者,昨奉月之三日手谕,诵悉一是。关于嘱办各事,奉覆于下：

一、唐盛镐君住址，似在 514 W.114th St.，但确否尚待查，又其所住 Apt.号数，亦不知悉。故尊函暂留，一俟查明，当即转去不误。

二、Ke Han 著作，经已再查，兹将整个著录列下：

Ke, Han（重庆新华日报记者）

The Shansi-Hopei-Honan border region; report for 1937－1939, pt.1. Chungking, New China information committee [1940], 34 p. fold. map. 18 cm. (New China information committee bulletin, no. 15) [又哥大无是书之 pt. 2]

三、陈鸿舜君生年，经查哥大圕校档案，知为一九〇五年十一月十一日，谅甚可靠。

四、Ryusaku Tsunoda 先生曾在哥大任教，并创办日文部，任 Custodian 之职，先后凡三十年，于 1954 年告老退休，是以并非富路特先生学生。其生年经查系在 1877 年，上月中已渡其八十生辰矣。

此外邓衍林兄返国后，近已来信，略谓一切情况良好，且圕近则甚受政府重视，大有可为，甚盼吾人亟早作归计，以便对于祖国建设，有所贡献耳。彼个人则已受北大圕学系之聘，当任教授，主讲圕机械化之种种设施！实亦大可惊异之事也。余容续呈，敬请道安！

晚徐家璧鞠躬

二月八日下午

尊夫人前并乞叱名叩安为感！

〔University of Chicago Library, Yuan T'ung-li Papers, Box 2〕

按：Ryusaku Tsunoda 即角田柳作（1877-1964），被哥伦比亚大学称为"日本学之父"。邓衍林于 1956 年 11 月返国。[1]

董作宾（香港）覆函先生，告知查访吕碧城生卒年结果，并已托唐君毅访美时带上所购笺纸。

守和吾兄：

前由台赴港接奉大示，林仰山一纸，当即转去，想彼必有函奉复也。承询吕碧城生卒年一事，曾托友人查访，兹据云仅访得吕女士卒

---

① 邓衍林《幸福的回忆，深切的怀念》，《图书馆工作》，1977 年第 1 期，页 20-22。

于民国三十一年阴历十二月十九日,其生年无人知之。又云其译出之佛经印本前曾刊有其小传,不知在华府能访得之否? 此间求之不得也。

近日新亚教务长友人唐君毅兄,应华府之聘,赴美讲学,乘此机会,托唐兄带去上次买到之信笺一包(此一批早已在购物单中,约二十元左右),至华府即可奉上。又兄曾托求赵少昂画,弟托人取阅数幅,皆已精裱,多为大件,润笔由六百至二百五十元,故未购求,因携带亦不甚便也。前函似已奉告。

唐兄初到美洲,拟参观国会图书馆,乞拨冗代为介绍吴光清兄招待之。专此,即颂旅安,新春百福!

弟董作宾拜上。

二,八

香港大学

〔University of Chicago Library, Yuan T'ung-li Papers, Box 2〕

按:吕碧城(1883—1943 年 1 月 24 日),其去世确为"卒于民国三十一年阴历十二月十九日"。

二月十二日

先生覆信克莱普,表示感谢并会立刻联系 Mark Carroll。

February 12, 1957

Dear Mr. Clapp:

I am most grateful to you for your letters of February 4 and 8 and for the fruitful contact you have made with the Harvard University Press. I shall write immediately to Mr. Mark Carroll as you suggest, giving him all the information he desires to know.

When I was in Cambridge last year, I noted that a copy of Bissainthe bibliography was on display in the reading room of the Widener Library. As I presume that it is still there, I shall ask Mr. Carroll to have a look of it.

I shall, of course, keep you informed as to further development of this project.

With renewed thanks,

Sincerely yours,

T. L. Yuan

〔Library of Congress, Council on Library and Information Resources
Records, Box 95〕

　　　按：此件为打字稿，落款处为先生签名。

二月十九日

刘国蓁致函先生，感谢寄赠各物，已遵嘱代转往来书信，并告已将代购火锅
交唐惜分带美，另谈书报账目余款等事。

　　守和博士先生尊鉴：

　　　　敬启者，时光不再，又报春□□□□著述宏富，清祺畅适，至以为
颂。未修书敬候，又已两月余，殊深抱歉，亦因贱务羁身，无时或已，知
我量我，其为先生乎！上年十二月时，拜奉手教，内附代转寄二信及美
金单十二元，上月拜奉赐赠衫料一件、领带夹一个、圣诞咭一函，及大
作英文 *Economic and Social Development of Modern China: a
bibliographical guide* 一册，感荷恩慈，寔无既极。日昨又拜奉手教，内
附代转寄三信，均已敬悉，代转信皆已发出。日昨收到北京外文出版
社覆函，现附呈左右，敬希亮察为幸。唐惜分先生已回信，答允代带火
锅一具，晚即为购买、包扎好送至珠海书院签收。因渠已定期本月廿
一日乘搭威尔逊总统轮来美，但只在三藩市居留，如抵步后，渠当直接
请示如何再转上也。

　　　　尊账前存十元〇一角五分，此次十二美元找得港银七十三元三角
（六一一算），总共八十三元四角五分，代支前次及今次邮费四元，一、
二月份小报费六元三角，寄费一元五角；《新闻天地》续定半年（由二
月至七月），银廿三元；火锅一具，银八元，共支四十二元八角，对比尚
存四十元〇六角五分在晚处也。秉华东翁仍在美国，惟已迁居，其地
址为 303 Alsace Way, Colorado Springs, Colo. 尚未悉何时方能返港一
行也。港中天气严寒，最低为卅二度六，亦为六十三年来所仅见者，想
尊处已大雪纷飞矣，伏祈珍重。专此，敬请崇安。

　　　　　　　　　　　　　　　　　　　　　　愚晚国蓁顿首
　　　　　　　　　　　　　　　　　　　　　一九五七年二月十九日

　　　　　　　　　　　　　　　　　　　　　　〔袁同礼家人提供〕

　　按："北京外文出版社覆函"上款为"袁重三先生"，应为先生化

名。该函右下角有折损。

二月二十日

叶良才覆函先生,告知胡适因胃溃疡入院手术的大致情况。

February 20, 1957

Dear Dr. Yuan:

Thank you for your letter of February 18, 1957. Dr. Hu was admitted to the New York Hospital in the evening of February 17 because of bleeding from peptic ulcer. He lost a great deal of blood that evening and was given 4 blood transfusions. The next day he rested very well. It was hoped then that an operation could be avoided. (The doctor did not want to have the operation because of his heart condition). However, he was bleeding again midnight of February 18th and an emergency operation was decided upon. The operation took 3.5 hours because the doctors had to go very slowly in applying anesthesia. The operation was very successful. We understood form the Hospital this morning that his condition up to now has been very satisfactory. His room number is 1209. No visitors are as yet permitted.

We will try to mail out the check to you before March 12.

Our warmest greetings to you and Mrs. Yuan,

Yours sincerely,

L. T. Yip

〔袁同礼家人提供〕

按:本年 2 月 13 日,胡适因检查身体被查出胃溃疡,17 日送往 New York Hospital,翌日手术,3 月 11 日方出院。① 此件为打字稿,落款处为其签名。

二月二十四日

Peter Townsend 覆函先生,答复询问各节并略谈其早年访华之目的。

9 Ripplevale Grove,

London N. 1

---

① 《胡适日记全集》第 9 册,页 271—274。

Feb. 24 1957

Dear Mr. Yuan

I am very sorry your first letter has reached me — & your mail took time. However, if it's not too late, here are the data:

1. No other books apart from the two you mention.

2. Born 1919 in London.

3. Other writings in '*New Statesman*' London; 'The Spectator', London, Newspapers.

4. I don't know whether there is anything else you want. From your letter I gather that is all. But in case—I went to China with the (Quaker) Friends Ambulance Unit; worked with the Chinese Industrial Co-operatives, and was a journalist & special correspondent for the BBC there.

Many apologies for this delay,

Sincerely,

Peter Townsend

〔University of Chicago Library, Yuan T'ung-li Papers, Box 2〕

按:Peter Townsend(1919-2006),其父母为贵格会(Quaker)会士,1939 年加入公谊救护队,1941 年作为志愿者经新加坡、仰光、滇缅公路来华服务,1949 年底离开中国。two you mention,应指 *China Monthly*(期刊)和 *China Phoenix: the revolution in China* (1955)。此函为其亲笔。

三月一日

叶良才致函先生,告知胡适术后恢复情况并寄上中基会支票。

March 1, 1957

Dear Mr. Yuan:

Thank you for your letter of February 18, 1957. Dr. Hu is resting well. He is now able to take in some food and also to do some reading but by doctor's order, visitors are still not permitted except by special permission.

Enclosed is Foundation's check, No. 57-2 for $1,500.00 in your favor and receipt for same in duplicate. Kindly sign both copies of the receipt and return.

With best greetings to you and Mrs. Yuan,

Yours sincerely,

L. T. Yip

〔袁同礼家人提供〕

按:此件为打字稿,落款处为其签名。

汪敬熙覆函先生,告知近况,并告所托查询各事的进展。

守和吾兄:

来示敬悉。适之先生因 gastric ulcer 入医院开刀,弟岂会不知。承示,谢谢! 周元松先生在何处实习,弟不知。一俟查到,即将信代寄。弟之实验工作进行顺利,但人事方面困难颇多。希望暑假后,可到 Mid-West 一大学工作。内人回台后,已愈,现在"监察院"任翻译。此地只有一 Professional Dinner Club,似无学生会。人名单有了,俟找到寄上。专此,顺颂俪安。

弟敬熙拜上

三月一日

〔University of Chicago Library, Yuan T'ung-li Papers, Box 2〕

三月二日

蒋彝覆函先生,告知其近况及打算,并向先生请教两问题。

守和先生:

二月廿一日手教敬奉悉,本拟早日修候,总以事冗未果。最近曾往西雅图一行,归后又是琐细,本年因兼代王际真兄课,故较忙。哥大六月底合约满期后,拟返英,因年薪一千元不够维持也。去年向 Bollingen 请补助事无所成,已奉闻,花旗总是花旗,可玩之花样实不少,但如何耍法需时耳。上述各节,常在不安状态中,很想再游华府,却不敢动也。拙作绝句多打油性质,承过誉,惭悚惭悚。瑞士出版之儿歌系由英国版本翻译者,英本作者萧淑芳乃萧淑娴之妹,弟所序乃为英本,并非瑞士版本,故对王君中文姓名毫无所知,盖萧淑娴女士(瑞士一德籍音乐家之妻)并未将瑞士版寄弟也,也许寄过但在战争期中失落。辱询之点,无从应命,歉甚歉甚。但弟现欲转请教者则是崔骥之生年死日,足下或有所知,可否赐示。又*L'Écriture chinoise et le geste humain: essai sur la formation de l'écriture chinoise* 作者 B. Tchang Tcheng Ming, S. J.之中文姓名,如能一并赐告,不胜感祷之至!

嫂夫人玉体,想早复原,健壮日增是颂是念。耑复,敬颂俪安。

弟蒋彝顿首

三月二日

〔University of Chicago Library, Yuan T'ung-li Papers, Box 2〕

按:萧淑娴(1905—1991),广东香山人,出生于天津,音乐教育家、作曲家,1924 年入北京女子高等师范音乐科,后与德国指挥家赫尔曼·舍尔兴(Hermann Scherchen)结婚并定居瑞士,她与袁同礼夫人袁慧熙应为校友;萧淑芳(1911—2005)为其妹,1926 年入北京国立艺术专门学校西洋画系,1949 年后在中央美术学院任教。崔骥,应指江西籍作家,1937 年由江西省政府派遣赴英考察,著有 *A Short History of Chinese Civilization*(《中国史纲》,1945 年伦敦),1948 年与蒋彝、熊式一同在英国牛津大学,1950 年因肺病去世,先生曾就此询问尤桐。B. Tchang Tcheng Ming, S. J.即张正明(1905—1951),字伯达,江苏嘉定人,后以字行,耶稣会神父,1937 年获得巴黎大学文字学博士,归国后历任徐汇中学校长、震旦大学文学院院长,信中提及之书的中文题名为《中国文字与人体姿势》。"嫂夫人玉体,想早复原"应指 1955 年秋袁慧熙因患胃溃疡入院治疗一事。

三月十四日

陈源覆函先生,告知家中近况、伦敦经济学院同学中文姓名,及先生托购刷子的不同价目。

守和吾兄:

大教敬悉。叔华在新加坡,无意继续任教,在辞职中,大约初夏可返英。弟去冬在新德里开会后,曾去星洲省亲,且同到曼谷一游。其画展目录,不知收在何处,恐须候其回英后方知有无存余也。鲠生到英曾晤及,谈话亦尚自由,惟见解不易相同耳。

伦敦经济学院同学中文姓名如下:

Chen Paky 陈伯骥 Ph. D 广东人,似在澳经商;

Tai Erh Ching 戴尔卿,东北人,前伦敦总领馆随习领事,似未
毕业。英撤销承认后,曾一度开香烟店,后回大陆。

陈尧圣日内陪同英方人士八九往台访问。

括胡须之刷子,曾到 Selfridge 探听。廉者仅数先令,贵者至五几
尼,寄去外国大约可免购买税。来函谓"要最上等的",不知系最高价
者,抑二镑左右即可用。弟不知其毛之好坏,仅觉其大小有别耳。兹
将较高价者列表于后,请示知再去买。顺颂著祺。

弟陈源顿首
三月十四

〔University of Chicago Library, Yuan T'ung-li Papers, Box 2〕

按:该函后确附胡须刷价目表,笔者认为价值不大,故略去。
Selfridge 即塞尔福里奇百货公司,伦敦家喻户晓的百年老店。此
时,陈源的通讯地址为 14a Adamson Road, London, N. W. 3。

三月十七日

尤桐覆函先生,告知其对崔骥的印象,并谈普林斯顿大学玉兰花期。

守和先生:

手示敬悉。关于崔骥的生平,我知道的不多。在师大我们不在一
系,似乎我比他高几班。见他有时和王重民往还,总想他是读国文系
的。因为乡谊的关系,而且他比我们年岁都小,弟常都叫他"小崔"。
他当时给我的印像是一个沉静寡言,很用功读书的好学生。他不喜欢
作激烈运动,但饭后往往跟同学在操场散步。毕业后的生活,毫不清
楚。他在英国时,我们因不在一处,没有什么接触,只听说他一面在熊
家教书,一面又作《中国文化史》,生活十分刻苦。

玉兰花约在五月十日前后盛开,至盼先生来此一游。我们搬到乡
下,很僻静,来时请住在舍下,至盼。此祝俪安。内子清旭附笔问好。

弟桐上
三,十七

〔袁同礼家人提供〕

按:崔骥非北京高等师范学校国文系毕业,实为英文系。① "清

---

① 《风光》(周报)第 22 期,1946 年 8 月,页 7。

旭"即戴清旭,尤桐夫人。

房兆楹覆函先生,告知嘱查人名信息,并谈其最近研究计划。

加省大木镇

三月十七

守和先生:

去年九月我们到华盛顿时,您正有事到纽约去了,没有见着,至今想起来还觉得何以那样不巧。今年我们不想到波士顿去。也许明年可以去,到时一定先跟您约会好了,免得再错过去。

承问著者四人中文姓名,其中只有继任泰助德效骞译《汉书》的潘洛基是旧交,其他三人并不认识,也许是在英国读书的,那么蒋彝先生处不妨问一问。同时我们在 U. C. 问问陈世骧等人。

我现在编高丽旧板书颇有心得,普通高丽活字本拿起来就可以猜得字体和年代。这是近两年来读书的成绩。现正写书目,还有《十七世纪高丽铸活字复兴记》一篇小文。联喆正在编《民国初年名人小传》。两人到整天各忙各的。

祝康乐,并请夫人安好。

兆楹

联喆附笔问候

胡先生已全愈否? 念念。

〔University of Chicago Library, Yuan T'ung-li Papers, Box 2〕

三月二十一日

李霖灿(台中)致函先生,告所嘱各事均已遵办,即将影印出版《麽些经典译本》,并请代问华盛顿诸先生安好。

守和长者赐鉴:

顷奉三月十三日来示,敬悉在美一切安吉,甚慰远慕。夫人座前先乞代为问安,久疏函覆问答之罪,亦望能海涵恕我。元肉一事,当即遵办,即日寄呈,唯平寄需时,恐在一二月后方能收到也。刘大悲先生函已遵嘱寄李玄伯先生矣,勿念。询及麽些发音人,名为和才(Ho Tsai),因思在字典前页有其中文名,故未即时裁答,乞谅。"中央博物馆"联合管理处自杭立武先生出任"大使"后,现由孔德成氏继任。霖之另一著作《麽些经典译本》(霖及张琨、和才合编者),共六种,在最近即可全部影印出版(《中华丛书》),届时当即邮寄一份呈教,唯恐不及入目矣,知注附闻。前日得曾培光先生函,知大家在华府甚好,远心甚慰,见面时望代谢谢一声,不另覆函曾公矣。Beal博士近况可好,见面望代致意,吴光清、徐亮、王恩保诸公座前都请便中代我问好。霖灿归来后可云大忙一阵,最近因岳父逝世,一两月来未得执笔,不久当接续将美国之行所得所感汇作整理,或将出一单行本,彼时自当呈来求指正,并博一粲也。匆匆先覆,草草勿罪。谨肃,问福安。

后学李霖灿拜呈

三月廿一日,台中

〔University of Chicago Library, Yuan T'ung-li Papers, Box 2〕

按:"元肉"即桂圆。《麽些经典译本》实于1978年以《麽些经典译注九种》(《中华丛书》)出版。曾培光,即曾琦的侄子,时与徐亮等人同在国会图书馆东方部中文组任编目。

三月二十五日

Hans H. Fränkel致函先生,询问滕固、崔骥生平信息。

March 25, 1957

Dear Dr. Yuan:

Thank you very much for your prompt reply to my enquiry about Sié Kang.

If I may trouble you further, I should like to find out whether Professor T'eng Ku 滕固 is still alive; if not, I'd like to have the year of his birth and death, if possible. Also I have been unable to find the year of the birth of Tsui Chi 崔骥, who died in 1950.

I have just seen Professor Maenchen and asked him about your query. He said he had already written to you about his "*Katalog der chinesischen Lackkunst*," which he says was published in Vienna.

With best regards to you and Mrs. Yuan,

Sincerely yours,

Hans H. Frankel

〔University of Chicago Library, Yuan T'ung-li Papers, Box 2〕

按:Hans H. Fränkel(1916-2003),德国汉学家,中文名傅汉思,娶

张充和为妻,时应在加州大学伯克利分校东亚研究所任教,1961年转耶鲁大学东亚语言文学系任教。Sié Kang 应指嵇康。1941年 5 月 20 日,滕固在重庆去世。Professor Maenchen 即 Otto J. Maenchen-Helfen(1894-1969),奥地利汉学家、历史学家,1938 年移民美国,时亦在加州大学伯克利分校任教。此件为打字稿,函中汉字及落款则均为其亲笔。

三月二十六日

陈源覆先生函,告知嘱购胡须刷价格并谈近况。

> 守和吾兄:
>
> 　　手教敬悉。今日又去 Selfridge 购买括须刷子,方知如须免税,必须由兄直接汇款至该公司。如由弟付款,则因弟为本地之 resident 仍不能免。如兄直接汇款,可购一个 75/- 及一 17/6,尚不到四镑。如由弟购只可购一 65/- 及一 12/6 也。故仍函请卓裁。
>
> 　　天放先生在伦住一周,每日陪同参观,昨日去巴黎。叔华经南大当局再三挽留,求去不得,已允再教一学期。回英之期当在八月左右矣。
>
> 　　端六去世之说,恐系传闻之误。去秋尚得其夫人一函,谓端六年老,已不教书,仅任研究工作。武大教授逝去者有刘南陔(秉麟)、邬保良。在平逝去者有杨今甫、李儒勉。弟后日去法,当有一月勾留。赐示可寄子杰兄转,或寄联教组织"中国代表处"。专此,顺颂著祺。
>
> 弟源顿首
三月廿六

〔袁同礼家人提供〕

按:"端六"即杨端六(1885—1966),其夫人为袁昌英。刘秉麟(1891—1956),曾任武汉大学法学院院长,经济学家;邬保良(1900—1955),武汉大学化学系主任;杨今甫即杨振声(1890—1956);李儒勉(1900—1956),江西鄱阳人,1920 年考入金陵大学,后赴英留学,曾任武汉大学外文系教授等职。

三月二十七日

Otto J. Maenchen-Helfen 覆函先生,告知展览图录信息。

March 27, 1957

Dear Mr. Yuan,

The insignificant catalogue has the title: '*Ausstellung Ostasiatische Malerei Chinesisches Lackgerat* .' Publisher: Krystall-Verlag, Wien, 1937. The first 12 pages are a catalogue of the paintings shown in this exhibition them follows on pages 13‒24 what I wrote, on pp. 13‒14 an introduction, on pp. 15‒25 a catalogue of the 103 pieces of lacquer, of which 13 are illustrated on plates X-XVI. My name appears only on p. 14, at the end of the introduction to the part of the catalogue which has to do with lacquer. So you see, it is one of those items which drive bibliographers to desperation.

Yes, I have known Arthur von Rosthorn. I saw him last in 1938. At that time, he was deeply depressed by the political events. If he had been younger, he undoubtedly would have left Austria and gone to England which he loved. I wonder what happened to his fine library.

With best regards.

Sincerely, yours,

Otto J. Maenchen-Helfen

〔University of Chicago Library, Yuan T'ung-li Papers, Box 2〕

　　按：*Ausstellung Ostasiatische Malerei Chinesisches Lackgerat* 直译作"东亚绘画和中国漆器展览"。

三月二十八日

朱文长致函先生,感谢寄来白寿彝简历。

　　守和世伯赐鉴：

　　　　承袁澄世兄交来白寿彝先生简历,至为感激！世侄因作一书评,需要此项材料而苦无觅处,得此一纸,幸何如之。白君所编之咸同滇变见闻录,耶鲁大学图书馆亦藏有一部,殊为难得。此书白君已扩充之,编为回民起义之首二册,想老伯早已见到。又白君尚有民国卅三年十一月由重庆商务印书馆出版之中国回教小史一小册,此间藏有一部,想尊处亦必已著录矣。闻老伯所著之中华书志即将出版,今后此类材料均可按图索骥矣,于学术界之贡献至大至巨,实可庆贺。世侄若干年前即已在北平图书馆中坐享"前人种树"之福,于老伯景仰至深,甚盼今后能多聆教益也。去夏来耶鲁后得与世兄朝夕聚首,彼聪明好学,前途无量。将门虎子,诚非偶然! 可喜可贺之至。甚盼老伯今后有便来此一游,不但可与世兄小聚,亦可容侄辈一倾多年景仰之忱! 肃此致谢,即颂撰安!

世侄朱文长敬上
三月廿八日

〔University of Chicago Library, Yuan T'ung-li Papers, Box 2〕

　　按:朱文长(Chu, Wen-djang),朱经农之子,时在耶鲁大学任教。

三月二十九日

先生致信福梅龄,询问两位旧友的生卒年及蒲爱德在纽约的住址。

March 29, 1957

Dear Miss Ferguson:

Thank you most heartily for your very kind letter of January 28 which gave me all the information I had been seeking. Your courtesy has been gratefully appreciated.

Now there are two old friends of ours about whose year of birth and death I should like to be informed:

Rev. James Henry Ingram

Prof. Malcolm F. Farley (of Fukien Christian University)

I shall be most grateful if you could help me in verifying the dates. I recall that Rev. Ingram passed away in 1947, but I do not remember exactly.

With many thanks.

Yours sincerely,
T. L. Yuan

Could you let me know the address of Miss Ida Pruitt in New York?

〔Yale University Divinity School Library, United Board for Christian
Higher Education in Asia Records, RG 11 Series Ⅱ, Box 79, Folder
2146〕

　　按:James Henry Ingram(1858-1934),中文名盈亨利,美国公理会传教士,19 世纪 70 年代末来华,1887 年在华北地区传教,热心医学和教育事业,北京通州潞河医院的创办人之一,还协助创立协和医学院,并任华北协和华语学校校董,对中国古钱币研究颇有兴趣。Malcolm F. Farley(1896-1941),中文名沙善德,美国传教士,1922年赴福建协和大学任教,担任西文系主任,对考古有十分浓厚的兴趣,长期在华南沿海各地文物点进行考古调查,后在该校建立沙氏博物馆,后被日军掠夺一空。Miss Ida Pruitt 即蒲爱德女士(1888-1985),美南浸信会传教士蒲其维和蒲安娜之女,出生在山东蓬莱,1920年洛克菲勒基金会派其来华筹建协和医院社会服务部,翌年开展医疗救助、生活服务等工作,抗战期间协助路易·艾黎(Rewi Alley,1897-1987)成立"工业合作社",并担任该组织国际组织美国总部干事。此件为打字稿,落款处为先生签名,于4月1日送达。

四月五日

先生致信赵元任、杨步伟夫妇问安,并请寄来所作英文曲谱目录。

　　元任先生、夫人:

　　　　上月金山地震,阖府想未受惊,金山的朋友谅亦未受任何损失,均在念中。尊处以英文作曲及乐谱限于英文,前后共有若干种,至盼赐一目录,注明出版年月以便著录。弟所编之书目有 Musical Compositions 一部分,将我国学者关于音乐方面之作品,拟一并列入。如承指示,无任感盼。适之先生近到大西洋城休息,恢复的很快,凡鱼类、鸡蛋等均能吃了,想不久可返纽约。内人去年亦患此病,幸未开刀,经过一年之调养始行复元,所以多日亦未能通讯,在此得病实不得了。今夏两位拟东来否?语言学会在何处开会,盼望不久能晤谈也。敬颂俪安。

　　　　　　　　　　　　　　　　　　同礼顿首

　　　　　　　　　　　　　　　　　内人附笔问安

　　　　　　　　　　　　　　　　　　四月五日

〔University of California, Berkeley, The Bancroft Library, Yuen Ren Chao papers, carton 10, folder 39, Yuan, Tongli and Yuan, Huixi〕

　　按:3月22日旧金山地震,赵元任夫妇均未受影响。"所编之书目"即 *China in Western Literature*,该书确有 Musical Compositions

一节(518 至 521 页)，其中收录有赵元任的作品。本年 4 月初，赵元任被诊断患有胆结石，5 月 21 日手术，后在家中调养，并未东行，亦未参加语言学会会议。①

四月十日

杜乃扬覆函先生，告知无法提供出版商那世宝的资料，建议先生联系法国外交部。

Le 10 avril 1957

Cher Monsieur,

Pardonnez-moi de n'avoir pu vous envoyer encore les références dont vous avez besoin. Je suis accablée de travail et tout travail supplémentaire est bien difficile à mener à bonne fin. J'ai transmis vos réclamations à Monsieur Josserand et j'avais eu communication de votre dossier dès réception de votre lettre. Je lui avais déjà fait remarquer que vous étiez désireux de payer pour les recherches faites. Le plus simple serait à l'avenir de vous adresser directement à l'Office de Documentation dont je vous joins les conditions. Vous obtiendrez satisfaction bien plus vite. Nous ne sommes malheureusement pas assez nombreux pour nous lancer dans des recherches bibliographiques toujours compliquées dans une aussi grande institution que la nôtre. Impossible d'obtenir du Ministère des Affaires étrangères quelque renseignement concernant Monsieur Nachbaur, mais si vous écriviez peut-être vous répondrait-on, alors que mes coups de téléphone se perdent de bureau en bureau. Monsieur Cain est revenu enthousiaste de son voyage en Chine. Il a fait une conférence au corps des bibliothécaires à la Bibliothèque de Peking et a été longtemps interrogé, mais il ne m'a pas parlé des périodiques ni ouvrages mis à la disposition des lecteurs. La découverte de la Chine est certainement une merveilleuse expérience pour qui n'en soupçonne qu'à peine la richesse.

Veuillez recevoir, cher Monsieur, mes excuses et mes sentiments bien

---

① 《赵元任年谱》，页 350-351。

fidèlement dévoués

M. R. Guignard

〔University of Chicago Library, Yuan T'ung-li Papers, Box 2〕

按:此函为其亲笔。

四月十七日

下午二时许,先生至华盛顿联合车站接梅贻琦,后者暂住先生家。晚饭后童季龄来,晤梅贻琦。〔《梅贻琦文集》第 1 册,页 185〕

四月十八日

上午十点半,梅贻琦从先生家出,到各处访问,下午三点半回此休息。〔《梅贻琦文集》第 1 册,页 185〕

四月二十四日

赵元任覆函先生,告其身体近况及英文作曲事。

> 守和我兄:——
>
> 对不起老没回信,我们又闹忙又闹病,韵卿有背腿神经痛,每星期上透热三次,我闹胃病,发现是胆石,打算暑假时□去刺掉,所以好些事都慢下来了。今天又在□□加大出版部的审查委员会,每月总有千把页的稿子得看,所以时间老是不够。
>
> 承问拙著英文作曲及乐谱,好像我□根□□没写过任何英文词儿,至于无词的乐曲,作过几个很短的小品的钢琴曲,另张开上备览。
>
> 适之想已回纽约,我上一次到纽开会,在他家里见了一面,那还是在他到大西洋城以前,看他精神气色倒还不错。匆此,即颂双祺。
>
> 弟赵元任上
>
> 韵卿附笔

〔University of California, Berkeley, The Bancroft Library, Yuen Ren Chao papers, carton 10, folder 39, Yuan, Tongli and Yuan, Huixi〕

按:此信右上角标注"APR 24 1957",应为发出日期,该件笔迹淡去,几无法辨识。

四月二十五日

先生致信洪业,请教两位中国作者的信息。

> 煨莲先生著席:
>
> 违教忽逾一载,时深企念! 闻所编字典又出二卷,引企贤劳,至为

佩仰！此间所编之书,至为迟缓,弟尚未拜读也。弟所编之书目大致完成,内中中国人著作共收二千人,其中文姓名均已查明,仅有另纸所列二人,一为我兄同学,一为燕大学生,想台端必知其名,即希赐示,不胜感谢！专此,顺颂教祺。

弟袁同礼顿首
四月廿五

〔Harvard-Yenching Library, Papers of William Hung (1893-1980) 1915-1996, From Yuan Tung-li to William Hung, Apr. 25, 1957〕

按:"字典"即哈佛燕京学社所主持的 Chinese-English Dictionary Project。信中所提"另纸"不存。

四月二十七日

洪业覆函先生,告所询一人姓名,另一人则建议询问傅泾波。

承询二人姓名,其一为徐声金,盖弟之同学;又其一则不知谁何也。司徒先生之秘书傅泾波,想或知之。原单谨奉缴。□□守和先生著祺

四月廿七日

〔Harvard-Yenching Library, Papers of William Hung (1893-1980) 1915-1996, From Yuan Tung-li to William Hung, Apr. 25, 1957〕

按:徐声金,字瑞釭,早年赴美留学,获哥伦比亚大学哲学博士学位,曾任厦门大学社会学教授并兼文学院院长。此件为底稿,写于先生 25 日来信背面,特此说明。

四月二十九日

金守拙致函先生,表示耶鲁大学出版社对《西文汉学书目》出版十分有兴趣,并询问细节问题。

April 29, 1957

Dear Dr. Yuan:

Mr. Davidson of Yale Press has given me copies of your correspondence with him, and has suggested that we explore the possibilities of publishing your book. I should be most happy to undertake this and am prepared to start work on it in June, with the hope that a manuscript might be completed early next year.

I have examined the copy of the Bibliographical Guide compiled by you and published by the Human Relations Area Files. I should prefer in the supplement to Cordier to do a much more professional job and to give it a form as nearly as possible similar to that work. I should therefore like to include Chinese characters in the text, rather than relegating them to an index.

From the cards which you have sent, I am not clear whether you wish to have reproduced all the cross references and catalogue numbers that appear. If this is so, it would be simplest to photograph the Library of Congress cards. Out of the group of cards which you sent, only two are not included in the Library of Congress cards. In undertaking to publish this material, I should have to request that the sequence of information was made entirely clear, so that the cards could be handled by an ordinary typist. I note that sometimes information has been put in above or below the printed matter and often struck off in corners. We should have to be quite clear as to where this fits in.

I am returning 3 cards to illustrate what I mean. Where I have encircled the following numbers, my question would be as follows:

1. Where are these dates supposed to go?
2. Does this information come in large or small type?
3. What is the significance of the brackets?
4. Are both names to be included and if so, is this to be done for all Chinese authors?

We are very much interested in seeing this work published and ready to cooperate to the fullest extent. If there is similar interest on your side, perhaps I should make the trip to Washington to see your material and discuss with you the form in which we could handle it.

Sincerely yours,

George A. Kennedy

〔Library of Congress, Council on Library and Information Resources Records, Box 95〕

按：此件为录副。

五月三日

先生致信克莱普，告知哈佛出版社久无回音，无奈之下自己联系了耶鲁大学出版社，并附上金守拙覆函，另谈国会图书馆职位申请变动事。

May 3, 1957

Dear Mr. Clapp:

Thank you ever so much for your letter of April 30.

I wrote to Harvard University Press soon after the receipt of your last letter. But for over two months I have had no reply. Then I requested Prof. Serge Elisséeff, Director of the Harvard-Yenching Institute, to see what he could do.

Failing to get any reply from him either, I wrote to another publishing agency, the Yale University Press. It was day before yesterday that something definite came out of the impasse. I now enclose copy of a letter from Professor George A. Kennedy. If he comes to Washington in June and if you are to be in town at that time, I hope we may solicit your advice in regard to its printing.

For my future work, I have been hoping to join the Reference Department at L. C., but no word has come from Dr. Adkinson. In the meantime, there was a vacancy in the Descriptive Cataloguing Division which I applied. As my application has been approved by the Librarian, I hope to join the staff after May 15. It is not the kind of work (GS 7) I like to have, but under the present circumstances, it is better than doing nothing.

With renewed thanks for your interest,

Yours sincerely,

T. L. Yuan

〔Library of Congress, Council on Library and Information Resources Records, Box 95〕

按：此件为打字稿，落款处为先生签名。4 月 30 日，克莱普致函先生，询问与哈佛大学出版社讨论出版《西文汉学书目》的进展。

五月十三日

先生致信 Burton W. Adkinson,告知已向著录编目部(Descriptive Cataloging Division)申请了一份临时职务,并请其在参考部内考虑有无合适的岗位。

13 May, 1957

Dear Dr. Adkinson:

It was very kind of you to promise to explore possibilities for my employment in the Library of Congress. I have been hoping that with your support some opening in the Reference Department might be available.

Having had no further word from you, I applied for a temporary position (GS7) as cataloger in the Descriptive Cataloging Division. As the recommendation for my appointment had been approved by the Librarian over a month ago, I expect to attend to my new duties beginning from the 16th of May.

This position is not the one I would like to have. But under the present circumstances, it seems better than doing nothing. If a suitable opening in the Reference Department should occur in the future, may I hope that you would bear me in mind?

You will be interested to know that Yale University Press has at last agreed to publish my comprehensive bibliography of modern China. Professor George A. Kennedy is coming to Washington in June and will have further discussions with Dr. Poleman, Dr. Beal and other sinological scholars interested in the early publication of this work.

Sincerely yours,

T. L. Yuan

〔袁同礼家人提供〕

　　按:此件为录副。

陈祚龙覆函先生,告知所询之事的结果,并告喜得一女。

　　守和先生赐鉴:

　　　　拜读来示(四月十日),计有日矣!

　　　　关于所经垂询各事,祚龙现只可以查明其中两点奉答;对于其余之问题,办理仍属毫无结果。怅甚,歉甚!

项闻此间国家图书馆当局亦曾对先生所询各节代为分头探究,至其收获如何,谅必已有专函奉告一切矣。

耑此拜复,敬颂潭安!

后学陈祚龙拜上

五月十三日

今后赐教尚祈写寄:CHEN Tsu lung, 21 Rue de Penthièvre, Sceaux, Seine, FRANCE

再者:客月二十三日内子在此举得一女,大小托庇,均称平好,并此奉闻。

陈祚龙再拜。

〔University of Chicago Library, Yuan T'ung-li Papers, Box 4〕

按:此函暂系于 1957 年。

五月十六日

Burton W. Adkinson 覆函先生,告知参考部暂时没有合适的岗位。〔袁同礼家人提供〕

五月中下旬

先生赴国会图书馆著录编目部工作。〔袁同礼家人提供〕

按:先生的职务为编目员(cataloger),级别为 GS-7。[①]

五月

《“中央研究院”历史语言研究所集刊》刊登先生和 Eugene L. Delafield 合编的 *Selected Bibliography of Dr. Hu Shih's Writings in Western Languages*(《胡适先生著作目录(二)西文》)。〔《历史语言研究所集刊》第 28 本(下),1957 年 5 月,页 909-914〕

按:该目共收录篇目 83 种,结尾处有一注释,标明以上著作、文章、册页、书评、序言等仅仅是一选目,更完整的目录将会在今后问世。

六月十二日

蒋彝致函先生,告知其将继续在美工作,并谈美国版税惯例。

---

① Library of Congress, *Information Bulletin*, Vol. 16, No. 20, 1957, P. 239.

守和先生：

屡承关注，铭感实深。弟最近决定再留美一年，暂仍哥大之旧，王际真兄归来兼代之课自无可能，然尚在另谋他法，一方面想将波士顿游记写成再说。至于 ACLS 之补助金，略有所闻，但请求不易，过去已成之局尚且失败，难为冯妇也。

先生原来在美求学，识人甚多，故对各方接洽比较容易。弟两年来经验，非美国大学毕业而欲进入美国文教界，非易事也。又若学工学其他科学，在美求生实非难耳。

大著已完成，可贺可贺。照美国书局与作家合约标准为始自10% 至 15%，弟所得为头一万本版税为 10%，过一万本则增至 15%，但弟书从无超过一万本希望也。谨此奉闻，顺颂俪安。

弟蒋彝顿首

六月十二日

联陞现想已抵东京，将于七月十六日飞台北。

〔University of Chicago Library, Yuan T'ung-li Papers, Box 2〕

七月十八日

先生致信胡适，告知在国会图书馆翻检各书所获林颐山的信息，并谈何炳棣曾辗转请平馆拍照馆藏文献胶卷。

适之先生：

奉赐书，欣悉先生正考林颐山的事迹，连日翻检各书，所获的资料不多，仅在民三重印光绪廿五年所修之《慈溪县志》内，发现林颐山是光绪十七年辛卯科举人，又是十八年壬辰科进士 知县，分发江苏，如此则在其未中举五年以前，他的《经述》已被王先谦收入《续经解》内，在《江阴续志》内又觅到掌教题名六人，林氏何年任掌教，则未查出。日内查到其他资料，再行奉闻。至于林颐山所提的"宗师"，大概指王先谦。又检《王祭酒年谱》，在光绪十八年壬辰五十一岁，主讲城南书院……《合校水经注》四十卷，序例内提到"林颐山斥为伪造……兹编一字不敢阑入"等语。顷接加拿大何炳棣君来信，谓北平图书馆可照 Microfilm，渠已收到若干，如先生需要任何资料，可由敝处函告，径寄何君收转较为妥当。余容再详，敬候痊安。

同礼拜上

七，十八

〔台北胡适纪念馆，档案编号 HS-NK05-062-001〕

按：林颐山，字晋霞，浙江慈溪人，清末学者，曾任南菁书院山长。王先谦(1842—1917)，字益吾，湖南长沙人，清末民初教育家、经学家、历史学家，《续经解》应指《皇清经解续编》，《王祭酒年谱》则指《葵园自订年谱》。该信附有抄录资料，如"重建江苏学政节略记"等。

七月十九日

先生邀唐君毅共进午餐。〔唐君毅著《日记》上，台北：学生书局，1988年，页290〕

按：唐君毅在美国停留七周，主要目的之一是为新亚书院谋取国会图书馆、芝加哥大学赠书。唐君毅在其日记中并未详细记录与先生往来，但本月9、16、17、20日皆往国会图书馆，似均与先生见面。

七月二十四日

先生致信胡适，告暂未找到缪荃孙生平资料，仅得林颐山小传之篇目信息，正在函询哈佛、斯坦福大学，目前尚无法判断林颐山与黄以周有无交往，并告浙江督学所在，及《西文汉学书目》将由耶鲁大学出版。

适之先生：

正拟寄奉若干资料，又奉赐书。承询《缪荃孙年谱》及《小传》，竟未觅得，仅在《国学论文索引》内觅到关于林颐山的小传之记载，原文为冯昭通作，载《华国月刊》二卷一号，馆中无有，已函询哈佛及斯丹福两校。又在《南菁文钞》(《南菁讲舍文集》第二集)黄以周序内有"主讲此席十二年矣"，此序是光绪二十年所写，则自光绪九年起即任掌教。至林颐山于光绪十八年中进士，以知县分发江苏。后任南菁书院掌教，似不会任黄以周之助教，二人交往的资料迄未觅到，如能觅到缪荃孙的小传或可找到若干资料。又纽永建为南菁书院学生，《南菁文钞》收其文章。如仍健在，可托台北友人就近一询关于黄、林两先生事迹也。

浙江督学行署确在宁波，光绪三年《鄞县志》记载较详见附件。如尊处需要其他资料，并盼指示，当再续查。同礼所编之书目，最近决定委托耶鲁大学为之印行，其工作报告拟八月杪再行奉上。承中基会支持数年，总算有一结束。近馆中拟编《全国中文书总目录》，约同礼协助,大约一俟国会正式通过豫算,方能组织起来。关于平馆照书事,拟委托何炳棣代办,将来寄到加拿大再转纽约。馆务近三年均由丁西林主持,但渠兼文化部副部长,恐无暇兼顾。仍由张某_{中共党员}任秘书长,主持一切也。专此,敬候暑祺。

同礼叩

七,廿四

〔台北胡适纪念馆,档案编号 HS-NK05-062-002〕

按:黄以周(1828—1899),字元同,号儆季,浙江定海人,清季学人,光绪八年(1882)江南学政黄体芳在江阴创建南菁书院,后聘黄以周任主讲。"纽永建"应即钮永健(1870—1965),字惕生,江苏松江人,民国时期政治人物,确曾在南菁书院学习,并与吴稚晖交好。"张某"应指张全新。"光绪九年"处,胡适批注"十"。该信附抄录资料数页。

八月一日

先生致信福梅龄,询问两位来华教授的信息。

August 1, 1957

Dear Miss Ferguson:

Some weeks ago, I requested your help in finding out the year of birth and death of the late Malcolm F. Farley of Fukien Christian University. I hope very much that I have not given you too much trouble.

Will you kindly locate my previous letter and try to ascertain the information for me?

Now I wish to know the year of birth of Dr. Paul H. Stevenson, of P. U. M. C. May I solicit your assistance in this matter also?

Thanking you for your help and with best wishes for a most pleasant summer,

Yours sincerely,

T. L. Yuan

〔Yale University Divinity School Library, United Board for Christian Higher Education in Asia Records, RG 11 Series Ⅱ, Box 79, Folder 2146〕

按:Fukien Christian University 即福建协和大学,1915 年 9 月,美以美会联合公理会、归正会以及圣公会宣布成立"福建协和大学"及其董事会,翌年该校正式成立,1951 年与华南女子文理学院合并成为福州大学。Paul H. Stevenson(1890-1971),中文名许文生,长期执教于北平协和医学院解剖学系。[1] 落款处为先生签名,该件于 8 月 3 日送达。

八月八日

先生致信胡适,告知所查各项信息,并言已函何炳棣设法影照北平所藏《水经注》。

> 适之先生:
>
> 晨间寄上林颐山的传志记,提到黄以周的传尚有下列三篇:
>
> (一)《清史列传》,第 69 册第七一页
>
> (二)《清史稿·儒林传》,黄式三名下
>
> (三)《续碑传集》,卷七五,第二叶
>
> 又林氏在《学古堂日记》内有一序文:昆山余宏淦《读尚书日记》序"……颐山……遂于日记工竣后弁数语于卷首云,光绪丙申仲冬慈溪林颐山谨序",证明该年林氏在学古堂。至冯文所提林氏为安徽巡抚陈□□所赏识,似有错误,按存古学堂设在湖北,当时总督兼巡抚似为陈夔龙,林氏卒于江苏,似未到武昌也。芝加哥大学藏有《学古堂日记》四十九卷,与此间所藏十六卷不同,已函钱存训君一查其内容矣。
>
> 尊款第一次之三十元尚未用完,第二次之三十元迄未动用。影照北平所藏《水经注》,已函何炳棣君设法,尚未接其复函。敬颂著祺。
>
> 　　　　　　　　　　　　同礼拜上
>
> 　　　　　　　　　　　　八月八日晚

〔台北胡适纪念馆,档案编号 HS-NK05-062-003〕

按:丙申处,胡适标注"廿二年(1896)"。"陈□□"照录,非无法识别。

八月九日

先生致信胡适,告所获黄以周的相关文献。

---

[1]《私立北平协和医学院简章》,1936 年 9 月,页 29。

适之先生：

项由斯丹福大学寄来《华国月刊》二卷一期，《林晋霞传》内中述及与黄元同的关系，并确定其生卒年，想尊处亦愿得此资料。又检孙雄、唐文治诸人文集，均无关于林君的记载。有下列两篇，不识已见到否，如需用，当再寄上：

《艺文堂文续集》卷一，《黄以周墓志》

《茹经堂唐文治文集》卷二，《黄元同先生学案》附著作概要约十余叶

又章太炎之《黄传》，亦需用否？并希赐示。专此，敬颂暑祺。

同礼拜上

八月九日

缪、闵两《碑传集》均无林君之传，不日函哈佛出版部寄上《清代传记引得》，此书颇有用，想未入藏。

〔台北胡适纪念馆，档案编号 HS-NK05-062-004〕

按："缪、闵两《碑传集》"应指缪荃孙、闵尔昌等人所编的《碑传集》《续碑传集》。

八月十九日

先生致信胡适，在国会图书馆尚未查到光绪初年宁波知府姓名，并告哥伦比亚大学图书馆所藏《大清缙绅全书》较为齐全，或可前往查阅，并盼赐一书法作品。

适之先生：

赐书敬悉。连日翻阅光绪三年《鄞县志》，在"书院""族塾""里塾"各栏内均未查到关于"辨志六斋"之记载，亦未查明光绪初年宁波知府的姓名，又查《大清缙绅全书》1889、1890、1893、1899 各年，均未查到宋源瀚之名及其到任之年，仅查到当时知府为绩溪胡元洁，又在光绪十二年《浙江同官录》内亦查到胡元洁之详细履历，谅为府上前察。惟前在哥伦比亚大学图书馆查书时，见其所藏《缙绅全书》较为齐全。先生到该校查书时，似可一查光绪初年各期，想能查到。此书甚有用，可惜此间所藏者极不全也。又《清代三十三种传记引得》现已绝版，只得另觅旧的。

先生得暇时，至盼写一小中堂或横批，以便悬挂并志景仰，有便人来此时托其携下为感。

著作中文本五册顷亦收到,谢谢。如能再寄五册,当分赠此间各图书馆及友人也。专此,敬祝俪安。

　　　　　　　　　　　　　　　　　　　同礼叩上

　　　　　　　　　　　　　　　　　　　八,十九

　　　　　〔台北胡适纪念馆,档案编号 HS-NK05-062-005〕

按:"著作中文本"或指《丁文江的传记》,待考。

八月二十六日

福梅龄覆函先生,为错置本年春天来信致歉,并告知本月所询各位医学教授的生卒年。

August 26, 1957

Dr. T. L. Yuan

1723 Webster Street N. W.

Washington 11. D.C.

Dear Dr. Yuan:

I am covered with confusion to find that somehow or other I mislaid your letter of last spring in which you asked for the date of birth and death of Dr. J. H. Ingram and Professor Malcolm F. Farley of Fukien Christian University. On my return from vacation, I find your letter of August 1st., reminding me of that letter and asking for the year of birth of Dr. Paul H. Stevenson. I hasten to send you such information as I have.

Dr. Ingram died in June 1934 when you will recall he was the victim of armed robbers in his summer cottage at Shih Ching Shan. He was then said to be 75 years of age which would put the year of his birth as 1859. You can confirm the exact date of his birth by inquiring at the American Board of Commissioners for Foreign Missions, 14 Beacon Street, Boston, Maas.

We have no dates on Professor Malcolm F. Farley but Mrs. Farley is still living and her address is Box 1781, Balboa, Canal Zone. I think that a letter to her would get the desired information.

I am interested to see from your letterhead that you have moved from Eighth Street where you lived so long in such convenient proximity to the Library of Congress. I am always hoping to spend a few days in

Washington to see some of my old friends and perhaps this autumn I may be fortunate enough to have the hope become a reality. In that case, I will certainly call you up and hope at least for a little talk on the telephone.

With warm personal regards,

Cordially yours,

Mary E. Ferguson

Associate executive Secretary

P. S. Dr. Paul H. Stevenson's birth date is December 22, 1890.

〔Yale University Divinity School Library, United Board for Christian Higher Education in Asia Records, RG 11 Series Ⅱ, Box 79, Folder 2146〕

九月五日

先生致信国会图书馆雇佣办公室,递交著录编目部高级编目员职位申请。

September 5, 1957

Dear Sir:

I beg to submit here with my application for the position of Senior Cataloger in Descriptive Cataloging Division described in Posting No. 4232.

It is my earnest hope that an outstanding American scholar with wide administrative experience will be selected as the Head of Far Eastern Section. If my application for the position of Senior Cataloger would be approved, I would be most happy to serve under him and to assist him in improving the quality of cataloging cards for Far Eastern materials.

However, I would withdraw my application in case a young Chinese or Japanese is appointed to that position. I wish very much to make this clear before my application is considered by Library authorities.

Thanking you for your attention,

I remain,

Yours sincerely,

T. L. Yuan

〔袁同礼家人提供〕

按:此件为录副。

九月六日

先生致信国会图书馆雇佣办公室,同时申请著录编目部远东组主管职务。

September 6, 1957

Dear Sir:

In my letter to you yesterday, I indicated that if my application for a Senior Cataloger would be approved, I would be most happy to work under an American scholar if he accepts the position as Head of the Far Eastern Section in the Descriptive Cataloging Division.

My friends in the Library feel keenly that as a Japanese had already applied for the above-mentioned position, it is only fair that a Chinese scholar of more administrative experience should also be considered. All of them have urged me to apply, though I feel that as I have not yet obtained my U. S. citizenship, it is a drawback which the authorities will have to consider.

I now enclose my application for the position as described in Posting No. 4221. It is my hope that my two applications will be duly considered by the authorities.

I remain,

Yours sincerely,

T. L. Yuan

〔袁同礼家人提供〕

按:此件为录副。

九月二十八日

先生撰写 *China in Western Literature : a continuation of Cordier's Bibliotheca Sinica* 最终报告。

Supplement to Cordier's *Bibliotheca Sinica*

Final Report

The second edition of Henri Cordier's *Bibliotheca Sinica*, published between 1904 and 1924 in six volumes, is a classified bibliography of Western works on China from the 16th century to the first two decades of the 20th century.

The Supplement, now completed, is a continuation of Cordier's work consisting of Western works on China published between the years 1921 and 1956. In its present form, it includes about 20,000 titles and will be made up in three volumes. At the end of the bibliography, there is a comprehensive index of authors, compilers, editors, translators and illustrators.

The title of the Supplement will be known as *China in Western Literature: a continuation of Cordier's Bibliotheca Sinica*. It will be published by the Yale University Press in the summer of 1958.

In reporting the completion of this work, the undersigned wishes to express his sincere gratitude to the Trustees of the China Foundation for the encouragement and support given to this project.

Respectfully submitted,

T. L. Yuan

September 28, 1957.

〔台北胡适纪念馆,档案编号 HS-US01-026-014〕
　　按:此件为打字稿,落款处为先生签名。

是年秋①

查良钊赴美,与先生多有往来,譬如至国会图书馆查阅资料,一起观看话剧《改变》。〔《思忆录》,中文部分页9〕

　　　　按:查良钊时任"考试委员",赴美参加"道德重整会"。先生对工作认真负责的态度和对文化事业的勤勉努力给查良钊留下极深印象,让后者想起 1917 年先生服务清华学校图书部的情形。

十月十四日

先生致信饶大卫,对空缺中的耶鲁大学东亚馆藏负责人职务表示兴趣,询问是否对外招聘等细节。

14 October 1957

---

① 《王云五先生年谱》,页 946。

Dear Professor Rowe:

I hear that the Curator of your Oriental Collection has resigned and is going to join the staff at the Library of Congress here. Since you have always taken a great interest in the development of your Oriental Collection, I wonder if you could advise me whether the position has been filled.

I am rather interested in a position of this kind especially in an institution such as Yale. Before submitting my application, I should like to know if Yale would prefer to promote a junior member to this position, or to get a well-trained librarian from outside. Also, I should like to know the amount of the annual salary which Yale offers.

As I have a heavy financial burden, I would not be able to accept a position under $ 6,000. As you were good enough to recommend me for the position at Stanford Research Institute in 1951, I hope you could find out the desired information for me. I shall be grateful if you could let me hear from you at your convenience.

Yours sincerely,

T. L. Yuan

〔袁同礼家人提供〕

按:此件为录副。

十月十五日

上午九时许,徐亮陪同王云五赴国会图书馆,与先生、吴光清晤谈。〔《王云五先生年谱》,页911〕

按:10月14日,王云五从纽约转至华盛顿,拟以两周时间在国会图书馆阅读有关胡佛委员会的书籍、期刊,并托徐亮预约研究室。

十月二十二日

饶大卫覆函先生,因耶鲁大学图书馆副馆长生病,暂时不能获得确切的信息,但东亚馆藏负责人职务应是开放招聘,并表示愿意推荐先生。

22 Oct. 1957

Dear Mr. Yuan:

I was happy to receive your letter of 14 October and to know of your interest in the position now open in our Library.

I cannot answer all your questions right now. But to answer in part, I believe that the University will have to go outside its own staff to fill the vacancy caused by Mr. Tsuneishi's going to Washington. I cannot be sure of this, however. The position seems to be that they will take the best fitted person from any source, depending upon availability.

I do not think there is any way in which to find out what will happen just now, in view of the illness of the Associate Librarian in charge of such matters. However, as soon as I can get to him, I will try to see what is planned.

In the meantime, it would be very helpful to me if you would send me as soon as possible a complete biographical sketch of yourself. I am sure that would be helpful.

I would certainly like to see you come here to fill our post, as I cannot imagine anyone more qualified in every way.

With best wishes,

Sincerely yours,

David N. Rowe

Professor of Political Science

〔袁同礼家人提供〕

按:Mr. Tsuneishi 即常石道雄(Warren M. Tsuneishi,1921-2011),日裔美国图书馆学者,生于加州蒙诺维亚,1953 年至 1957 年、1961 年至 1966 年两度担任耶鲁大学东亚图书馆馆长,1957 年至 1960 年赴华盛顿,负责组建国会图书馆编目部下属的远东处。

十月二十四日

先生覆信饶大卫,略述 1949 年后先生在美履历及著述,并评价耶鲁大学东亚馆藏的现状。

24 October 1957

Dear Professor Rowe:

Thank you for your letter and your compliments. Professor Kennedy was also good enough to call me up yesterday.

My biographical sketch may be found in the 1948 ed. of *World Biography* which is on the reference shelf at Yale. Since coming to the United States in 1949. I have served as Consultant in Chinese Literature at the Library of Congress, Chief Bibliographer at the Stanford Research Institute, Research Fellow of the Rockefeller Foundation, Consultant to Human Relations Area Files, etc.

I have been cataloging both Western and Oriental books for the Library of Congress. *The Annotated Catalog of Rare Chinese Books in the Library of Congress* which I edited in 1954 will shortly be published in two volumes by the Government Printing Office here.

As I told Prof. Kennedy on the phone, the Far Eastern collection at Yale is far behind that of Harvard, Columbia and Princeton. If Yale is to hold its present academic position, the Oriental collection must also be strengthened in the near future. You seem to need not only a well-trained cataloger, but also a person who could work out a development program for building up systematically a comprehensive collection for the use of scholars.

I have been working on a bibliography of Russian works on China which forms part 2 of my larger work entitled: *China in Western Literature*, *a continuation of Cordier's Bibliotheca Sinica*. In view of the excellent Russian collection in Washington, I wish very much to complete the work before I am transferred elsewhere.

Will you kindly show this note to Prof. Kennedy, so that I need not repeat it in another letter?

With many thanks,

Yours sincerely,

T. L. Yuan

〔袁同礼家人提供〕

按：此件为录副。

十一月初　纽约

先生、吴光清一同前往拜访胡适，后者嘱在国会图书馆中查找摄制平馆善

本书籍胶片的档案记录,并留二人晚餐。〔台北胡适纪念馆,档案编号 HS-NK05-037-010〕

> 按:11 月 19 日,吴光清致信胡适,告知已查实国会图书馆确实曾允诺赠送 3 份原始胶片与中国,1947 年王重民所带走者为其中 2 份,可据此向该馆函索余下的第 3 份。①

十一月三日

先生致信 John H. Ottemiller,告收到三十日函,期待本月中在华盛顿与之晤谈,并附呈申请。

November 3, 1957

Mr. John H. Ottemiller

Associate University Librarian

Yale University Library

New Haven, Connecticut

Dear Mr. Ottemiller:

Thank you so much for your letter of October 30. I am happy to learn that you expect to be in Washington the middle of this month. I am looking forward with much pleasure to meeting you.

I am interested in the position at Yale not so much for its present status, but more for the possibilities of rendering a useful service in building up a center for research in Far Eastern studies. I am therefore very anxious to know the amount of your annual budget for the acquisition of Oriental materials. Perhaps you could spare one evening and have dinner with me, so that we could talk over matters in a leisurely way.

I enclose herewith my application form which is self-explanatory.

Yours sincerely,
T. L. Yuan

〔袁同礼家人提供〕

按:此件为录副。

---

① 吴光清表述有误,1947 年王重民仅带走其中的 1 份,1948 年 7、8 月间国会图书馆应先生请求将 1 套胶片寄送国立中央图书馆,此时仅存 1 套本拟送给中国相关机构的原始胶片。

十一月六日

先生致信胡适,告知国会图书馆已找到平馆存美善本书胶卷,并建议其尝试运台。

适之先生:

近闻当局对于先生返台至为关切,想在最近数月内尚不致成行,最好候天暖再行动身。关于平馆善本胶卷一事,曾托负责人分别查明。在以往文件中,迄未查到任何证据。但近在地下储藏室内发现一批胶卷。经吴光清君断定,即是第二套尚未运华的。渠曾主张由"中研院"致函先生,请根据以前的了解,向此间接洽,予以运回。但近来馆中人事又有变动副馆长及参考部主任均已更动,恐新来的人,以胶卷价值关系不肯卖账,反成僵局。经一再考虑,拟建议改用外交方式进行此事,即由"中央研究院"致函"外交部",由部径向"美大使"接洽。公文内似可附一节略,说明先生与前任馆长接洽经过。此间当局接到国务院的公文,即不致予以否决矣。先生如认为可行,不妨代"中研院"拟一节略,并可声明院中愿以刊物永久交换,似此措辞必可如愿以偿,仍祈钧裁为感。此上,敬候著祺

同礼拜上

十一,六日

〔台北胡适纪念馆,档案编号 HS-NK05-062-006〕

按:翌年4月2日,胡适自纽约乘飞机出发,途经旧金山,于4月8日抵达台北。

十二月二日

先生致信加斯基尔,请其协助查询书籍信息。

December 2, 1957

Dear Miss Gaskill:

I trust that your Library has the following books. May I bother you once more as to their full bibliographical data?

My work on the Supplement to Cordier is about to be completed. It includes only monographs, but not periodical articles. My friend Dr. Taam had been working on periodical literature on China, but he passed away as a result of hard labor—a victim of bibliography.

I hope everything goes well with you. I note with particular satisfaction that books in your Library are cataloged much faster than any other Library—a real achievement!

With thanks and kind regards,

Yours sincerely,

T. L. Yuan

Hsi, Yung: *Buddhism and the Chan School of China*. Transl. by Chou Hsiang Kuang. Allahabad, 1956.

(Could the author be His-yun 希运 of the 9th century? What is the Chinese name of this author?)

Between Husband and Wife; a play in one act; written collectively by the Peking People's Art Theatre, tr. by Sidney Shapiro. Peking, 1953.?

(*Supplement to China Reconstructs*, No. 6, 1953)

〔Cornell University Library, Wason Collection Records, 1918–1988, Box 1, Folder Koo, T. K. Letters〕

按:1956 年 10 月 23 日,谭卓垣去世。[1] Yung Hsi 应指融熙法师（1888—1959）,1954 年曾在香港新亚书院讲授《佛教与禅宗》;Chou Hsiang Kuang 即周祥光（1919—1963）,浙江黄岩人,曾从杨仁山入室弟子龚云白学佛,后赴印度加尔各答及德里大学深造,获得博士学位,担任印度国际大学、阿拉哈巴大学等校教授。*Between Husband and Wife* 即《夫妻之间》,1952 年 12 月 8 日首演,导演为凌珀如、李醒。Sidney Shapiro 即沙博理（1915–2014）,中国籍犹太人,翻译家。

十二月六日

先生致信蒋复璁,请教留德学生姓名及"中华文化出版事业委员会"出版物名录等事。

慰堂吾兄左右：

前承惠寄留德同学名单及贵馆刊物,至为感谢。近蓝乾章君来

---

① Yao, Kuang-tien, Cheuk-woon Taam and the Chinese Collection at the University of Hawaii Library, *Journal of East Asian Libraries*, No. 156, p. 26. 先生在 *China in Western Literature* 序言中写作 10 月 20 日去世,暂依 Yao, Kuang-tien 之说。

此,欣悉近况,至慰远怀。前接西德图书馆 Seuberlich 博士来函,愿得台北刊物,曾告其与兄接洽交换,想已函达。弟在德时,一般民众对于我国旧文学之译本嗜好极深,对于大陆之新著莫不淡然置之。近接柏林友人来函,亦有同感。兹有留德同学数人之中文姓名,未能在留德同学名单内予以查明,用特奉上,请就所知者赐予填注,凡不知者并盼转询其他友人,早日赐覆,感荷无似。又"中华文化出版事业委员会"出版之英文小册为数颇多,兹需全部出版目录一份,亦盼代为函索,早日赐寄,至为感谢。前见"教部"出版关于中国艺术之小册,著者为 Hsin Kwau-chi,其中文姓名可否赐示。种种费神,敬谢敬谢。顺颂时祉。

弟袁同礼顿首
十二月六日

Chang, Pao-yuan:*Die Eisenbahnen in der Mandschurei*……Leipzig, 1930

Chen, Shu-chiung: *Die Strafzumessung im chinesischen und deutschen Recht*……Jena, 1937

Tchang, Pi-kai:*Die Bodenzersplitterung in China*. Freiburg, 1934

Ching, Liang (or, Liang Chiang):*Die chinesische Wirtschafts-und Sozial-verfassung zwischen Freiheit und Bindung, ein Überblick bis zum Jahre 1937*. Würzberg, 1938

Deng, Bao-sjang:*Das blutende China*, Berlin, 1928

Li, Huan-hsin, 1901 -: *Die Wurminfektionen des Menschen in China*, Hamburg, 1936

Liang, Ssu-mu:*Die Wirtschaftsstruktur Chinas und die Wirtschaftspolitik der Nanking-Regierung*. Frankfurt, 1934

Tung, Zeh-faah:*Das Zollwesen Chinas*. Berlin, 1935.

〔台北"中央图书馆"档案,档案编号 348-5 至 348-10〕

按:此信于 12 月 14 日送达台北。

十二月十二日

晚六点半,"教育部在美文教顾问委员会"郭秉文、曹文彦在华盛顿北宫饭店宴请梅贻琦,董显光、谭绍华、李幹、萧庆云、先生、黄中、高宗武、宋晞等人作陪。〔《梅贻琦文集》第 1 册,页 274;赵赓飏编著《梅贻琦传稿》,台北:邦迪文化

信息公司,1989 年,页 196〕

　　按:曹文彦(1908—?),字卧云,浙江温岭人,中央大学毕业,时应
任"教育部国际文化教育事业处"处长。谭绍华(1897—?),广东
台山人,外交官。"北宫饭店"又称北宫楼。

一九五八年　六十四岁

一月十八日

蒋复璁覆函先生，寄"中华文化出版委员会"出版之英文小册目录，留德同学人名则待查明。

> 守和先生大鉴：

> 　　前奉手教，敬悉一一。兹遵嘱附上"中华文化出版委员会"出版之英文小册全部目录一份，乞察收是幸。至留德同学数人之中文姓名，以弟久已不问留德同学会事，接触不多，容查明再行奉闻。尊著闻已由国会图书馆出版，谅必一纸风行、洛阳纸贵也。匆复，敬请旅安。

> 　　　　　　　　　　　　　　　　弟蒋复璁顿

> 　　　　　　　　　　　　　　　　　元，十八日

> 〔University of Chicago Library, Yuan T'ung-li Papers, Box 2〕

> 　　按："尊著"即《国会图书馆藏中国善本书录》。该函为文书代笔，落款处为其签名。

一月二十日

芮沃寿覆函先生，欢迎张贵永到斯坦福大学访问，但该校并不能为其提供福特基金会项目下的访问资助。

January 20, 1958

Dear Dr. Yuan:

　　Thank you for your letter of January 6, and your information concerning Professor Chang and his visit to the United States. I hope very much that he will pay us a visit here, and I think he would find the Hoover collections of considerable interest. We should be glad to show him hospitality here.

　　Under the terms of our new grant from the Ford Foundation I don't quite see how we could justify a three to six month period of research for Professor Chang at Stanford. Our grant provides in general for rather more long-term undertakings, particularly by members of our own faculty and staff. I do hope, however, that you will pass on our very warm invitation for him to pay us a visit here.

We shall look forward very much to receiving a copy of your new catalogue of Chinese rare books. I thank you very much for sending it to us.

With best wishes for us both.

Your sincerely,

Arthur F. Wright

〔University of Chicago Library, Yuan T'ung-li Papers, Box 4〕

按:张贵永(1908—1965),字致远,浙江鄞县人,1929 年毕业于清华大学历史系,1930 年去德国留学,入柏林大学,1933 年获博士学位,后再赴英国研究西洋史,时任"中央研究院"近代史所研究员,并在台湾大学兼课。

一月二十五日

先生覆信芮沃寿,已转达对张贵永的邀请,并寄送有关"俄文中国论著"研究备忘录,希望胡佛研究所考虑给予资助。

January 25, 1958

Dear Professor Wright:

Thank you for your letter of January 20. Professor Chang is now in Washington and I shall pass on your invitation to him.

I enclose herewith a memo re my work on Russian works on China and I shall be grateful if you could bring it to the attention of the authorities of the Hoover Institute.

As it is a small project, there are other institutions which are interested in giving aid towards its completion. But as I used mainly the materials of the Hoover Library, I would like to given priority to it.

Hoping to hear from you before long,

Yours sincerely,

T. L. Yuan

〔University of Chicago Library, Yuan T'ung-li Papers, Box 4〕

按:该件为录副,并附一张 Russian Works on China 1917-1957: a selected bibliography 备忘录,预计需要 2000 美金的资助。

一月三十一日

先生致信加斯基尔,请其帮助在华生特藏中查找有关新疆的近现代文献。

January 31, 1958

Dear Miss Gaskill:

I trust that you have a list of the pamphlets in the Wason collection. Would it be possible for you to check if you have any material relating to the history of Kashgar, the life of Yakub Beg, and Anglo-Russian rivalry in Central Asia between 1870-1890?

I recall that you Library has the collection of Eugene Schuyler. Perhaps you might find some material in this collection also.

Thanking you for your assistance,

Yours sincerely,

T. L. Yuan

〔Cornell University Library, Wason Collection Records, 1918-1988, Box 1, Folder Koo, T. K. Letters〕

按:Kashgar 即新疆喀什;Yakub Beg 即 Mohammad Yaqub Beg(1820-1877),汉名阿古柏,他在沙俄以及英国的支持下,于1865年至1877年成立"哲德沙尔汗国",后被陕甘总督左宗棠击败;Eugene Schuyler(1840-1890),美国外交官、探险家、作家。此件为打字稿,落款处为先生签名。

二月十三日

加斯基尔覆函先生,告知只找到一种相关书籍。

February 13, 1958

Dear Mr. Yuan:

The pamphlets in that big collection of pamphlet volumes that came with the Wason Collection are mostly cataloged only in the Wason catalog, with no subject headings, so it is impossible to get at them except by author and title.

I have searched in our catalogs for material on Kashgar, Yakub Beg and Anglo-Russian rivalry in Central Asia, but have found only one title which is not in LC or Cordier. It is:

Jerningham, Hubert Edward Henry. *Russia's Warnings: collected from official papers*, 2nd ed. London, 1885. vii, 56p.

I am sorry that I can be of so little help about this.

Sincerely yours,

Gussie E. Gaskill

Curator, Wason Collection

〔Cornell University Library, Wason Collection Records, 1918–1988, Box 1, Folder Koo, T. K. Letters〕

二月十七日

先生覆信加斯基尔,请查证相关册页,告《国会图书馆藏中国善本书录》出版并将寄赠康乃尔大学。

February 17, 1958

Dear Miss Gaskill:

Thank you so much for your letter of February 13 and for the information about the work by Hubert Edward Henry Jerningham.

I am glad to know that all the pamphlets in the Wason collection have been cataloged. I now enclose a list of authors and I shall be much obliged to you if you could check if there are any pamphlet material relating to Central Asia.

I trust that you would attend the meeting of the Association of Asian Studies in New York. If you could arrange to spend a few days in Washington, I do hope to have the pleasure of seeing you here.

The annotated catalog of Chinese rare books which I edited for the Library of Congress in 1954 has just been published by the Govt. Print. Office. I have already put your Library on the mailing list to receive a complimentary copy and I hope you will receive the two volumes within a week's time.

With many thanks for your help,

Yours sincerely,

T. L. Yuan

〔Cornell University Library, Wason Collection Records, 1918–1988, Box 1, Folder Koo, T. K. Letters〕

按:此件为打字稿,落款处为先生签名。先生所附书单一纸,因由铅笔所写,现已难以识别,特此说明。

二月二十四日

陈源覆函先生,告所托代购之事并未办妥,并谈联合国教科文组织翻译各国名著项目进展缓慢。

守和吾兄:

手教到此甚久,未早覆为罪。

承嘱购买小勺。因弟近年极少至他城旅行,平时亦不到旧货店观光,故牛满江君到英时尚未觅得。牛君曾晤谈,当告以此种情形。彼回美后但有信来,谓已转达,不知何以有误。

奉尊示后,曾将原款四镑存入尊户。银行经理覆函,谓该款是否可收,当视来源性质决定。此函附上。弟又去函说明此款原由尊款中提出,现在归还。迄今未再得其函件,想来已经存入矣。

Unesco 翻译中国名著,进展极迟缓,至今尚无数种。去年六月号之 Unesco *Courier*,为 Great Literature East & West 专号,中有译著目录,请一查即知目下情形。

弟自去年十一月底起即患 shingles,左腿长疮,至为痛苦,不能行动,至一月中方渐恢复。叔华因请假回英,现仍在此,拟至四五月间再回南大。

专此,顺颂俪祺。

弟源顿首

二月廿四

叔华附候

〔University of Chicago Library, Yuan T'ung-li Papers, Box 2〕

按:"小勺"似应作"小勺"。牛满江(1912—2007),河北博野人,生物学家,1932 年入北京大学生物系,后留校任教,1944 年留学美国,入斯坦福大学并获博士学位,时在美从事 mRNA 研究。*Courier*(《信使》)为联合国教科文组织发行的刊物,1948 年创刊,时在巴黎出版，Great Literature East & West 准确题名应为 *Great Litrature of East & West* ，1957 年第 10 卷第 6 号第 24、25 页确有目录表，为预备翻译成英文、法文的世界名著，其中法文项下有《红楼梦》以及戴密微、铎尔孟编译《中国诗选》。Shingles 即带状疱疹。"南大"应指新加坡南洋大学。

加斯基尔覆函先生，告知未在华生特藏中找到有关中亚的相关书籍，并期待获得赠书。

February 24, 1958

Dear Mr. Yuan:

I have checked the list of names you sent in the Wason catalog, but did not find any pamphlets relating to Central Asia by any of these authors. I am sorry to say. It must be that the Wason Collection is just weak in this area.

I do expect to be in New York for the AAS meetings, but I'm afraid I'll not get to Washington. Will you be in New York?

It is good news that the catalog of Chinese rare books is out, and I shall be looking for it eagerly.

Sincerely yours,

Gussie E. Gaskill

Curator, Wason Collection

〔Cornell University Library, Wason Collection Records, 1918—1988, Box 1, Folder Koo, T. K. Letters〕

二月二十八日

先生致信蒋复璁，赠《国会图书馆藏中国善本书录》，并请其在台代购图书。

慰堂吾兄著席：

此间图书馆所藏中文善本书录，近由弟编辑出版共二册，已告馆中径寄贵馆壹部，并寄"教部"、史语所、台大、师大、省立图书馆、台湾文献委员会、故宫博物院及编译馆各一份，此外台北、台中方面尚有何机关应赠送者，并盼函告。因仅印五百部，不久即绝版也。弟愿购下列各书，能否费神代购交邮寄下，共价若干，当即奉趋，特此拜托。顺颂道祺。

弟袁同礼顿首
二，廿八日

《民国学术论文索引》，"中央馆"编《出版总目》、《方志联合目录》、《宋元本联合目录》等，昌彼得《板本学略要》。

〔台北"中央图书馆"档案，档案编号299-0104至299-0105〕

按："昌彼得《板本学略要》"应为屈万里、昌彼得合著之《图书板本学要略》（"中华文化出版事业委员会"，1955年）。此信3月7日送达台北。某人在该信末尾处标注"送善目一部"。

二月

《国会图书馆藏中国善本书录》（*A Descriptive Catalog of Rare Chinese Books in the Library of Congress* ）由王重民编纂、先生校订，正式出版。该书以传统的经、史、子、集四部分类法，著录了国会图书馆所藏1777种善本书，著录项包括善本书的版式行款、撰著者、收藏序跋、题记，以及对于版本的考证等。

按：该书版权页则记作1957年，特此说明。

三月初

先生赴温哥华英属哥伦比亚大学（University of British Columbia）协助王伊同、何炳棣审查澳门姚氏代售古籍目录。〔《思忆录》，中文部分页11〕

按：王伊同在《哀守和丈》写道"方予之就馆加拿大也，何君炳棣怂恿当局，斥巨资，尽购姚君钧石①之蒲坂书楼。凡十五万卷。丈得讯憬然，自华府来，披书目指某卷曰……"。查王伊同约在1957年12月赴温哥华任教职，而1958年春何炳棣将严文郁寄来的售书目录转给英属哥伦比亚大学图书馆请其考虑；此外，3月22日胡适给先生的覆函中提及"明义士的甲骨，我也听Goodrich说过，大概都是碎片，很少有成句的文字。五千美金亦太贵，我怕济之对此一'藏'没有多大兴趣"，此时先生似已在加拿大询问过该批甲骨的去留意向及待售价格。基于以上种种，笔者认为先生此次前往温哥华约在是年三月初。

---

① "姚钧石"应作"姚钧石"。

三月六日

先生致信 John W. Cronin，告已经得知自己将赴主题编目部履职，感谢其给予的支持。

March 6, 1958

Dear Mr. Cronin:

　　Mr. Spalding told me yesterday that with the Librarian's approval, I am to be transferred to the Subject Cataloging Division. May I write to thank you for your recommendation and support? While I very much prefer to work on materials in European languages, I realize that you would like to see me placed in a strategic position where my services would be most useful to the Library.

　　As I foresee it at present, there are many delicate problems which have to be skillfully handled if cards for Far Eastern materials were to be printed for distribution to other libraries. Fully aware of the great responsibilities lying ahead, I wish to assure you that I shall do my best to contribute my share to further the development of this program, worthy of your confidence and support.

　　With sincere thanks and warm regards,

Your sincerely,
T. L. Yuan
〔袁同礼家人提供〕

　　按：此件为录副。

三月七日

莫余敏卿覆函先生，告知加州大学洛杉矶分校没有中国同学会，感谢先生寄赠《国会图书馆藏中国善本书录》，并谈愿与马鉴直接联系购买藏书。

March 7, 1958

Dear Dr. Yuan:

　　Thank you very much for your kind letter of Feb. 14th.

　　I have asked five or six Chinese students who came to study in this Library and they all told me that they do not have a Chinese students club on this campus because they have to study very hard and have no time to organize it. However, if I find or know of any list or directory later, I will send to you.

I am very grateful to you for asking L. C. to send us a copy of your Annotated Catalog of Chinese Rare Books. As soon as we receive it, I will write you again.

I want to thank you also for informing me about Prof. Ma Kien's collection. As I want to write to him direct, would you be kind enough to give me his address? It seems now money is no question for us. The only thing is whether they are what we need.

With warmest regards to you and Mrs. Yuan.

Sincerely yours,

Man-Hing Mok

〔袁同礼家人提供〕

按：该函为其亲笔。

三月十四日

先生致信蒋复璁，告知拟寄赠《国会图书馆藏中国善本书录》，询问《"中央图书馆"善本书目》编辑近况，并请屈万里撰写书评。

慰堂吾兄：

前寄一书，请将台湾较大之图书馆开单见示，以便将此间所藏《善本书目》由该馆径行寄出，谅荷台察。闻贵馆《善本书目》业已印出，拟请检寄壹部以快先睹，奉上美金伍元，即希查收。闻乙编亦在编辑中，如能附一"人名及书名索引"，检查较便，谅荷采纳。又尊处前购番禺沈氏及吴县许氏藏书，其姓名已不记忆，尤盼示知，至感。此间所印之善本录，仅印五百部，即将告罄。本拟赠屈万里兄一部，以格于规定不赠个人，如渠能写一介绍，则可用 Review Copy 名义由馆赠送，请为转达，并盼示复是荷。此上，顺颂时祉。

附美钞五元。

弟袁同礼顿首

三月十四晚

贵馆出版之各种书目，可否检寄全份，款如不敷，示知当再续缴。

〔台北"中央图书馆"档案，档案编号299-0106至299-0107〕

按:1957年,《"国立中央图书馆"善本书目》由中华丛书委员会印行,分为甲、乙两编,各十卷。蒋复璁在信中"番禺沈氏"处批注"太侔",即沈宗畸(1857—1926),字太侔,号南雅、孝耕、繁霜阁主,广东番禺人;"吴县许氏"处批注"许博明",即许厚基,字博明,祖籍浙江吴兴,生卒年不详。此二人旧藏皆在抗战时期归入中央图书馆(筹备处)。

三月十五日

汪季千致信先生,询问丁文江论文及中国自由职业史料。

> 守和先生惠鉴:
>
> 　　昨在费城晤及顾一樵先生,询以中国工程人才造诣。渠谓具体情形渠不愿谈,但中国人在美之科学论文,先生处有详表可查云云。此表似未发表,想经油印,能借阅否? 又□□□云丁文江最大成就(亦中国地质学中最好者)为 Sedimentation of the Yangtze River and the Extension of the Coastal line 之论著,顷检 *China in Western Literature* 中未见有关该题之文,不知何故,是否发表在1921前耶? 又晚拟查中国自由职业之发展,律师公会及会计师公会等最初成立之年,国会图书馆已查过,无会员录等书,《申报年鉴》中仅有律师公会少许数字,并无历史叙述。我公见广,亦知何处有相关记载否? 专此,即颂春祉。
>
> 晚汪季千上
> 星六
>
> 　　王宠佑去年初似尚健在,顷见尊著则渠已于去年作古矣,似未在 *N. Y. Times* 见其 Obituary,不知系何月事,能见示否?

〔University of Chicago Library, Yuan T'ung-li Papers, Box 2〕

按:汪季千,原名汪一驹,字季千,后以字行,曾在伪中央大学执教。[1] 该信首页右上以铅笔标注"3/15/58",查该日确为周六,另外注有"*Report on the geology of the Yangtze Valley*, Shanghai, 1919",此两处皆应为先生标识。王宠佑(1878—1958年8月31日),字佐臣,祖籍广东东莞,生于香港,矿冶专家,中国地质学会、

---

[1] 中央大学秘书处编《国立中央大学复校第一届毕业纪念刊》,1944年,"本校民国三十二年度下学期教授通讯录"页3。

中国矿冶工程师学会的创建者之一。

三月中旬

经国会图书馆馆长同意,先生调任至主题编目部(Subject Cataloging Division),主要负责远东文献。〔袁同礼家人提供〕

> 按:先生的级别调整至 GS-9,后在此职位上工作,直至 1965 年 1 月 15 日退休。[1]

三月二十一日

先生致信裘开明,请其在下月召开的美国图书馆协会编目和分类部特别会议上提议规范台湾地区的英文表述,以利书刊编目。

> 阐辉先生著席:
>
> 　　关于台湾各政府机关出版之西文书,各图书馆编目时有用 Formosa,或用 Taiwan 冠其首者,办法颇不一致。下月 ALA-CCS 委员会在纽约开会时,可否由兄提议一律改为台湾,以期一致,想荷赞同。遇必要时,可将弟名列入也。专此,顺颂大安。
>
> 弟袁同礼顿首
> 三月廿一
>
> 〔Harvard-Yenching Institute Archives, Letter of Yuan Tung-li to Alfred K'aiming Ch'iu, March 21〕
>
> 按:《裘开明年谱》将此信错系在 1956 年。[2] CCS 即编目和分类部(Cataloging and Classification Section),它隶属于美国图书馆协会下属的图书馆馆藏与技术服务协会(Association for Library Collections and Technical Services),"纽约开会"指 4 月 3 日在哥伦比亚大学东亚图书馆召开的远东资料专门委员会。Formosa 为台湾被日本占据时的称呼,先生认为沿用此词实在不妥,建议修改。落款处有标注,应为 3 月 24 日收悉此信。

蒋复璁覆函先生,所需各书均将寄赠一部,并告台湾其他各大型图书馆。

> 守和先生大鉴:
>
> 　　先后奉二月廿八日及三月十四日手教,均谨拜悉。蒙惠赠《美国图书馆所藏中文善本书录》,及嘱转各份均尚未收到,俟到时当代转送

---

[1] Library of Congress, *Information Bulletin*, Vol. 17, No. 10, 1958, p. 127;《思忆录》,英文部分 p. 36。

[2]《裘开明年谱》,页 639。

也,先乞释念。承示《民国学术论文索引》、《板本学要略》、《中华民国出版图书目录》等书,均系《民国基本知识丛书》之一种,其余如《宋元本联目》、《方志联目》、《善本书目》等,则皆敝馆编印者,以上各书均由馆付邮奉赠,即乞哂纳赐正。关于在《善本乙编》附印"人名及书名索引"一节,因该目日内即将出版,不及排入,惟尊意甚善,容当另行编印耳。台湾较大之图书馆,在台北者尚有"国立政治大学"图书馆、省立台北图书馆,在台中者如东海大学、省立台中图书馆,在台南者如成功大学图书馆等所。敝馆前购之番禺及吴县两家藏书为沈太侔及许博明两氏,惟拙文乃举例一提而已,其实尚不止此也,知注谨及。美金五元,以无需要,仅以璧奉。敬希察收为荷。敬颂撰安。

〔台北"中央图书馆"档案,档案编号299-0103〕

按:此件为底稿,该函于3月22日下午航挂寄出。

徐家璧覆函先生,告所询各节查询结果,并述邓衍林返国后力促其归国效力。

守和先生尊鉴:

敬肃者,三月十七日手谕业经诵悉。承询 Lu Ding 书一种,查本馆并无中文本,即在著者目录中亦未见"鲁汀"名字,其人似甚生疏也。

至于此间同学姓名,五人中已查得其四,其余一人经询耿忠之君办公处亦未获悉,至为抱歉。

邓君近又有信来托购大批书籍,并谓渠在北大担任之功课,系"中西文参考书暨圖参考工作"(前函内所报导者有误),于三月初开始授课,然即此亦颇难为渠矣。又四月间尚拟往南京讲课一周,不知听众将为何许人。邓太太或将加入北大圖工作,现任馆长、副馆长为向达、梁思庄二人,其他吾等旧识友好类均仍在圖界服务,惟物质生活清苦、政治观念严格,适应新环境当非一朝一夕之功,但渠仍极力促璧返国,横施压力,使璧几穷于应付,未悉如何解决。先生亦有以教导否? 匆匆不一,敬请春安。

晚徐家璧鞠躬

三月廿一日

尊夫人前乞叱名叩安为感。

〔University of Chicago Library, Yuan T'ung-li Papers, Box 2〕

三月二十二日

胡适致函先生,告赴台行期及此行计划,并谈《国会图书馆藏中国善本书录》之瑕疵。

March 22, 1958

守和兄:

梦溪笔谈收到了,多谢。

Giles 的敦煌经卷目录,仍可由弟购买,最好请将其书邮寄台北南港"中研院"交弟收。(寄 New York 寓亦可。)

明义士的甲骨,我也听 Goodrich 说过,大概都是碎片,很少有成句的文字。五千美金亦太贵,我怕济之对此一"藏"没有多大兴趣。回台时,当将恒先生的意见转告他。

我已定四月二日起飞,八日可到台北。此行不作久留计,拟看看①居住问题,②工作问题,③"中研院"的本身问题,拟五月底即回来,秋初才搬家回去。

王有三的善本书目两册已收到,乞兄代向 Beal 先生道谢。关于此书内容,有小意见,也请兄转告 Beal 与光清兄。

①P. 356 水经注笺

'李长庚序云,"忠臣李生克家佐有劳勘,一日持以见过。"'

此是有三误读李序。"忠臣"应属上文"遂成此书忠臣"。全句为"……又与四方博雅之士所得于退搜逖览者,互相参纠,斳归于是,遂成此书忠臣。"

故我盼望兄等能将此篇文字稍加删节,为有三掩此小失。此页(P. 356),第三行删"忠臣"二字,第四行"卷内引李克家云……"起,至第九行"窜乱也"止,共五整行,完全删去。如此则文理仍通顺可读了。

②P. 86 毛诗古音考

"焦竑序万历四十四年(一六一六)自序,又自跋万历四十四年(一六一六)"

查我的日记,及 Hummel's *Eminent Chinese* Vol. I. p. 423,陈第此书初印在 1606,而不是 1616。乞查馆藏此书,焦序的自跋的年月是万历三十四年(1606),还是四十四年(1616)?这个 date 关系重大,是值得一勘的。倘蒙比勘后见告,至感!

　　匆匆,敬祝双安。

　　匆匆不及来华府辞行了,乞告光清兄及诸友。

弟胡适敬上

〔潘光哲主编《胡适中文书信集》第 4 册,台北:"中央研究院"近
代史研究所,2018 年,页 421—422〕

　　按:"焦竑序万历四十四年(一六一六)自序,又自跋万历四十四
年(一六一六)",此处确如胡适所言有误,《毛诗古音考》初印应
在 1606 年(丙午),而非 1616 年。

三月二十九日

徐家璧覆函先生,告知其决定暂不回国,并谈贺昌群、汪长炳近况。

　　守和先生尊鉴:

　　　　敬肃者,日昨接奉二十五日手谕,诵悉一是。承对回国问题加以
指示,尤所心感。通讯一事于初回国者似尚能实行一时,稍久即亦不
复再能作书,证之过去回国友人类皆如此,未悉何故。邓君回国以后,
在纽未了之琐事尚多,最近几番来信,除催促璧从速归国外,则委托代
办各事,并托璧代为采购图书馆学书籍暨参考资料,故有时使璧思及
逗留此间仍可尽相当之义务,何必回国方能服务。据邓君来函,告贺
昌群先生现任中国科学院图副馆长,而南京图副馆长则为汪长炳先
生,两馆馆长皆另有人也。迄今邓君全家尚在候拨北大教职员宿舍,
故恐尚在公寓中暂住。先生如欲与彼通讯,请径寄北大图学系即可。

　　　　关于 Theodore M. Liu 之中文姓名,经查得其电话后与彼家中直
接通话,得悉彼之中文姓名系"刘孟治",彼本人现在新嘉坡工作也。
又前询之鲁汀著戏剧一种,Lu Ting 二字或系"绿汀",其全名或系"贺
绿汀",未悉有近似处否? 总之,本馆尚无所询之书,歉甚歉甚。余容
续呈,敬颂道安。

晚徐家璧鞠躬
三月廿九日下午

尊夫人前乞代为候安为感。

〔University of Chicago Library, Yuan T'ung-li Papers, Box 2〕

　　按:贺绿汀(1903—1999),湖南邵东人,作曲家,曾参加左翼歌

曲作者协会,作曲有《四季歌》《天涯歌女》等,1943 年前往延安,任中共中央党校文艺工作研究室音乐组组长,负责筹建中央管弦乐团,并任团长兼合唱队长,1949 年 9 月任上海音乐学院院长。

三月下旬

傅吾康赴国会图书馆拜会先生。〔《为中国着迷:一位汉学家的自传》,页 258〕

四月二日　纽约

American Library Resources for Research on Asia 会议假 Sheraton-McAlpin Hotel 的红厅召开, G. Raymond Nunn、钱存训、Horace I. Poleman、Cecil Hobbs、先生等人与会。晚,与会人员赴纽约公共图书参观。〔袁同礼家人提供〕

　　　　按:本次会议就美国各图书馆有关东亚的馆藏情况做了较为详细的统计和分析,譬如主要馆藏机构数量、卷数规模、语种涵盖和各自比例、东部和西部以及中部的比例。

四月三日

上午九时,美国图书馆协会编目和分类部远东资料专门委员会假哥伦比亚大学东亚图书馆召开会议,先生、钱存训、徐家璧、裴开明等人参加。上午讨论分类问题,下午则集中于有关描述编目的问题,晚六时结束。〔袁同礼家人提供〕

　　　　按:参会人员中有 7 位华人,其中 5 位曾在平馆服务,除徐家璧、钱存训外,童世纲、莫余敏卿、严文郁也极有可能与会。

四月四日

上午,美国图书馆协会编目和分类部远东资料专门委员会参会人员赴哥伦比亚大学参观,了解其东亚馆藏及编目情况。〔袁同礼家人提供〕

杨联陞致信先生,请赐《国会图书馆藏中国善本书录》一部,并谈身患高血压事。

　　守和先生:

　　　　四月初,AOS 与 AAS 在纽约年会,未见先生,殊觉怅怅。从胡适之先生处得见先生改定王重民旧作《善本书目》二册,甚有用,未知尊处是否尚有余书,能惠赠一部否?

　　　　正月末抄自华府归来后,医生发现晚学血压颇高,已服药两个月,并注意少吃盐,多休养,似尚有效。近来血压已降下不少,惟既有此病,即须事事留意,终身小心,殊可恼耳。敬请双安。

> 晚学联陞敬上
> 一九五八年四月四日

〔University of Chicago Library, Yuan T'ung-li Papers, Box 2〕

按:"AOS 与 AAS"分指美国东方学会(American Oriental Society)和美国亚洲学会(Association for Asian Studies),傅吾康在其回忆录中亦提及此次联合年会。[1] 该信落款日期有涂改,但应为四日,特此说明。

四月六日

谭伯羽致函先生,请协助查找同治朝陕西布政使人名。

> 守和我兄先生大鉴:
>
> 久不闻问,想起居佳胜为慰为颂。兹有请者,弟正欲知先祖文勤公同治十年辛未任陕西布政使之前任姓氏,不审兄能于图书馆清史记载中查得否? 是时翁同爵为陕西巡抚也。不情之请,幸乞恕之。专此相烦,容待面谢。即颂大安。

> 弟谭伯羽顿首
> 四月六日

〔University of Chicago Library, Yuan T'ung-li Papers, Box 2〕

按:"先祖文勤公"即谭钟麟(1822—1905),字文卿,谥文勤,湖南茶陵人,晚清官员,同治十年辛未(1871)由陕甘总督左宗棠奏准调入陕西,出任陕西布政使,其前任应为林寿图(1809—1885)。翁同爵(1814—1877),字侠君,号玉甫,江苏常熟人,清朝大臣,翁同龢的二哥。

四月上旬[2]

美国亚洲学会年会在纽约举行,先生前往旁听。〔《思忆录》,中文部分页 60〕

按:时,朱文长与会并宣读论文,因会场人员众多、声音嘈杂,颇为沮丧、失落,先生特意鼓励他,让其深受感动。

四月十一日

谭伯羽覆函先生,感谢惠示方志,并允为摘抄谭延闿事略。

---

[1]《为中国着迷:一位汉学家的自传》,页 259。

[2] 朱文长将此事错记为 1957 年,该年 The Association for Asian Studies 年会在波士顿举行,而非纽约。

守和吾兄先生道席：

　　奉教敬悉。承示《陕西通志》，知先祖布政使之前一任亦即翁同爵，至为感激不尽。先君年谱近始脱稿，尚有待修正，一时未能付印。至简单事略，当为兄一录之也。专此鸣谢，即请日安。

弟谭伯羽谨启
四月十一夜
〔伯羽用笺。袁同礼家人提供〕

四月十七日

Wolfgang Seuberlich 覆函先生，感谢告知书籍信息，并谈前普鲁士国家图书馆现状，此外其赴美访问各学术机构的计划难以实现。

April 17, 1958

Dear Mr. Yuan:

　　I am most grateful to you for your letter of April 4, 1958, and for the names of Chinese authors given in Chinese characters. The information received from you is of invaluable help for our current work as without it the respective books could not be cataloged in a proper way.

　　The former Prussian State Library in East Berlin from October 1, 1946, till November, 1954, was known as "Öffentliche Wissenschaftliche Bibliothek". Since November 29, 1954, the name of that library is "Deutsche Staatsbibliothek". In charge of the Ostasiatische Sammlung there still is Mr. Guido Auster, whom you probably know personally. Under this guidance the Oriental Department of that library has been fairly well restored and the "Orientalischer Lesesaal" could be reopened at its old place.

　　Thank you very much for sending me the program for the meeting of the Association for Asian Studies. I hope it will arrive soon as I am very much interested to see it.

　　As to my wish to visit the United States, it does not seem to be so easy anymore to be included in the "exchange of persons program" of the State Department as it used to be some time ago. At least there seems to be no possibility to finance a short term trip (for about 2 months) to the

United States with the purpose of visiting various learned institutions in different parts of the country. With the only exception of the German program of the United States Educational Commission in the Federal Republic of Germany (Fulbright Commission) all other exchange programs, according to the American Consulate General in Frankfurt am Main, have been reduced to such an extent that there is no hope for me left to be included in such a Program. The Fulbright Commission on the other hand nowadays is paying only the travelling expenses of persons who are invited to one single American learned institution with the obligation to stay there for at least three months. That would be too long for me anyhow as I cannot afford to be absent form here for more than, let us say, 6 or 8 weeks. Thus, my prospects of seeing you in Washington are not very promising.

　　With best wishes and warmest regards,

Yours sincerely,

W. Seuberlich

〔University of Chicago Library, Yuan T'ung-li Papers, Box 4〕

四月二十二日

先生向国会图书馆馆长 L. Quincy Mumford 和馆长助理 Rutherford D. Rogers 提交一份本月初赴纽约参会的简报。〔袁同礼家人提供〕

五月十五日

先生覆信张君劢,告知伍藻池来函内容,并称许吴康在台出版的新作。

　　君劢先生著席:

　　　　手片拜悉,陈、吴两君通讯处另纸录奉。前接伍藻池来信,谓《文化宣言》迄未收到,香港自由出版社复信则云业已售罄,可见洛阳纸贵。尊处如收到,望寄壹份。此颂道祺。

同礼拜上

五,十五

　　　　又老友吴康近印《宋明理学》,内容甚佳,尊处已见否(台北华国出版社出版)?

〔国家图书馆善本组手稿特藏〕

按：伍藻池（1903—？），广东台山人，1946 年当选制宪国民大会中国民主社会党代表，后移居美国。20 世纪 50 年代初，自由出版社在香港成立，该社为美国驻港新闻处资助的文化出版机构之一，主要负责人为谢澄平。"文化宣言"似直接与"中国自由民主战斗同盟"相关，张君劢、伍藻池均为该组织的成员，前者更是"同盟"驻美代表，该会中有毛以亨等先生故知。吴康（1895—1976），字敬轩，广东平远人，哲学家、教育家，1916 年入北京大学，后获文学学士学位，1925 年赴法留学，1932 年获巴黎大学文学博士学位，归国后曾任中山大学文学院院长等职，1951 年赴台。1955 年 10 月《宋明理学》初版，后再版多次。

五月二十三日

下午三时许，郭廷以赴国会图书馆，与先生晤谈。〔《郭量宇先生日记残稿》，页 67 〕

五月二十八日

莫余敏卿覆函先生，表示加州大学洛杉矶分校图书馆愿意买入先生购重的《说文解字引经考》，并谈马鉴寄来的第一批售书目录。

May 28, 1958

Dear Mr. Yuan:

Thank you very much for your letter of May 16th and for letting me know about the Chinese bookstore in N. Y. I hope I will have a chance to visit it in near future. I am looking forward to receiving the list which you so kindly arrange for us.

We shall be happy to purchase your 2nd copy of 马 's 说文解字引经考, Peking, 1958 at £ 4.0.0. Will you kindly send it to me at the Library's address and your invoice in triplicate copies addressed "Library, U. C. L. A." so that I can arrange for its payment? Thanks.

I heard from Prof. Ma last week, he was very kind to send us a list of Chinese works for sale by his friends in H. K. Unfortunately, out of the 300 titles on the list we have already had more than 200 in our Library. So, we did not have very much to choose from but I hope he will send us another list later.

I am very much excited to learn that your bibliography of China will soon be out by the Yale U. Press. I wish to congratulate you for this monumental and important work. I am sure it will receive a great welcome from scholars.

Our warmest regards to you and Mrs. Yuan.

Sincerely yours,

Man-hing Mok

〔袁同礼家人提供〕

按:《说文解字引经考》,马宗霍著,1958 年科学出版社初版,一函七册线装,限量 930 套。该函为其亲笔。

五月三十一日

晚,先生设宴招待郭廷以,张贵永夫妇、王伊同、何连玉、童季龄等人作陪。〔《郭量宇先生日记残稿》,页 69〕

按:本年春,张贵永及夫人纪凝娴赴国会图书馆拜访先生,后张贵永在该馆手稿部查阅詹森档案,先生协助给予各种便利。①

七月三日

郭廷以赴国会图书馆查阅资料,与先生晤谈,先生劝其设法将"驻法使馆"档案运回,郭廷以则建议"驻美使馆"档案可就近请人整理。〔《郭量宇先生日记残稿》,页 78〕

按:"驻法使馆"档案运回似有后续动作,可参见郭廷以 1959 年 12 月 4 日的日记。② 在与先生晤谈后,郭廷以旋即询问了张馨保,后者表示愿意从事整理"驻美使馆"档案。

七月八日

刘国蓁致函先生,寄送罗原觉所藏善本书目,请其在美各公藏机构物色买家,并询代订期刊是否展期。

守和博士先生尊鉴:

敬启者,许久未修书敬候,抱歉殊深,恭维著述丰宏,清祺畅适,至以为颂。五月时奉上令岳丈大人信壹封并芜笺壹纸,量邀尊览。晚仍日夜辛劳,依然如故,乏善可陈,所幸小儿钧源经已在香港大学文学院合格毕业,稍堪告慰,但仍在谋事中,如能获得枝栖,则可稍减晚之负

---

① 《思忆录》,中文部分页 51。

② 《郭量宇先生日记残稿》,页 153。

担也。敝友罗原觉君所藏善本书籍已编就书目两册,嘱晚寄奉,敬希亮察,并请鼎力赞勤,介绍与国会图书馆或其他大学圈,全部价银贰万七千美元,如不用全部购置,亦可分售,但至少亦要三份一,方有商量也。尊帐前余七元九角,现支六七两月小报费共七元八角,只余一角而已。《新闻天地》周报于本月尾满期,是否续订,恳请早示知,以资办理,至所厚幸。《春秋》半月刊须订阅否? 亦请示覆。匆匆,余当续陈。专此,敬请崇安。

愚晚国蓁顿首

一九五八年七月八日

〔University of Chicago Library, Yuan T'ung-li Papers, Box 2〕

七月十一日

先生致信蒋复璁,感谢寄来屈万里所撰《国会图书馆藏中国善本书录》书评,并告知美国学术刊物发表文章之惯例等事。

慰堂吾兄惠鉴:

两奉手教,并承惠寄万里先生所撰书评,钦佩无似,并将原件转交此间当局以供参考。美国学术性之刊物多属季刊性质,稿件积压甚多,不能在短期内予以发表。敝意除在学术季刊登载外,并可由尊处译成英文在《中国文化》发表,该两刊在美均畅销也。前承惠允将台北出版关于法律之书报开单见示,迄今尚未寄到,可否从旁一催,早日寄下至盼至感。大陆方面近将平馆旧藏之《五体清文鉴》及《宋会要》等予以翻印。上海古典文学会徐森老必在内所印之书,内容亦佳,想尊处业已购到。专此,顺颂时祉。

弟袁同礼顿首

七月十一日

〔台北“中央图书馆”档案,档案编号299-115至299-116〕

七月十八日

先生致信裘开明,询问哈佛燕京图书馆有无空闲职位,拟推荐 Kathryn Chang 前往。

July 18, 1958

Dear Dr. Chiu:

As you are about to move into new quarters soon, you would

probably need additional staff members.

Miss Kathryn Chang, a member of the staff in the Law Library here, is looking for a position in Cambridge and would be interested in library work there. She is a graduate student at Georgetown University specializing in American history. For the last few months, she has been doing preliminary cataloging work for the Law Library. Because of budget limitations, her work here will probably be terminated in September.

If there is any opening in your Library, I hope you could bear her in mind. May I hope to hear from you soon?

With best wishes,

Yours sincerely,

T. L. Yuan

〔Harvard-Yenching Institute Archives, Letter of Yuan Tung-li to Alfred K'aiming Ch'iu, July 18, 1958〕

按:此件为打字稿,落款处为先生签名。此信被《裘开明年谱》错记在 6 月 18 日,特此说明。

七月二十四日

裘开明覆函先生,告知暂时不能聘用 Kathryn Chang,但如果她能够在来年获得图书馆专业的相应学位,则可以给予优先考虑。

July 24, 1958

Dear Dr. Yuan:

Thank you very much for your letter of July 18, inquiring about the possibility of a position for Miss Kathryn Chang in our new library.

I am very sorry to report that all the regular positions were fixed and filled way back in April for the coming academic year 1958－59. As to casual workers and student assistants we have had more applicants than our budget provides. It is absolutely impossible to find any more money to engage additional help. As you know, there are always excellent talents among Chinese students and wives of Chinese personnel in the Boston area, who want to work. Therefore, it is seldom necessary for us to engage non-technical help from outside areas. But when Miss Chang graduates with a regular degree in library science from Georgetown University next fall, she will be a favorable candidate for consideration for our technical staff, that is, we shall need technically trained Chinese, Japanese, and Koreans (especially in cataloging and classification) to replace any of our present staff who may want to leave us next year.

It was a great pleasure for us to have your sweet daughter for dinner last Saturday. She lives so near both to our new library and our home.

With kindest regards to Mrs. Yuan and your two good sons.

Sincerely yours,

A. Kaiming Chiu

Librarian

〔Harvard-Yenching Institute Archives, Letter of Alfred K'aiming Ch'iu to Yuan Tung-li, July 24, 1958〕

七月二十八日

蒲立本致函先生,拟于八月初前往华盛顿,如有机会将与先生晤谈。

28 July, 1958

Dear Mr. Yuan:

Your letter to me about Huang Sung-k'ang 黄松康 was forwarded to me from England. As it happens I expect to be in Washington next week on Monday and Tuesday and I shall try to look you up.

Yours sincerely,

E. G. Pulleyblank

〔袁同礼家人提供〕

按:该件为其亲笔。

八月十九日

胡适致函先生,请在国会图书馆内代为查找《中国学报》刊载的文章。

守和吾兄:

中基会定于九月五日在美京"大使馆"开年会。我想知道老兄的书目大作付印的事现在已印成否? 何时可印成? 倘蒙便中见示几句,以便有人问起时可以答复,我就十分感激了。

又有一件小事,乞代为一查。

　　抗战期间，重庆出有一个"中国学报"，似只出了两三期。其中载有熊会贞的水经注疏"遗言"卅九条，我记得我曾抄有全文，不幸遗失了。国会馆似收有此报。如不难检查，我想请老兄替我 photostat 全文。十分感激！

　　杨守敬、熊会贞的水经注疏，大陆印本，赵元任兄买了一部送我，使我甚感激，故拟作一书评报之。匆匆，祝双安。

弟胡适敬上

一九五八，八，十九

〔University of Chicago Library, Yuan T'ung-li Papers, Box 7〕

　　按：1943 年 1 月，《中国学报》（重庆）创刊，翌年停刊，胡适知悉此刊或与刘修业有关，后者曾在该报第 1 卷第 2 期上刊登有《海外所藏中国小说戏曲记》一文。"《水经注疏》'遗言'卅九条"即《补疏水经注疏遗言》，载于该报第 1 卷第 2 期（页 106–109）。熊会贞（1859—1936），湖北枝江人，历史地理学家，杨守敬弟子，二人一同编纂有《历代舆地沿革图》。

八月二十九日

胡适致函先生，告知收到《中国学报》文章影印件并请再照它文，感谢协助"中央研究院"获取国会图书馆拍摄北平图书馆善本书的缩微胶片。

　　守和兄：

　　得手示，十分高兴！"中国学报"居然在字纸堆中找到，可算奇迹！

　　承照熊会贞"遗言"，至感！汪辟疆的杨守敬熊会贞传，倘不大费事，亦乞代为照印。熊会贞的传记资料甚少，如此传不是合传，则单照熊传已够了。如系合传，则乞全照。（我有邻苏老人手谱。）

　　尊纂书目付印，十月底可印成，闻之极欣慰，敬贺！

　　赠送"中研院"之 microfilm 一套，承示"一切已无问题"，至感。日内当备函致馆中。

　　孟邻先生九月三日夜飞抵华府，我大概四日下午到。匆匆，敬祝双安，并谢费神！

弟适上

一九五八，八，廿九夜

〔University of Chicago Library, Yuan T'ung-li Papers, Box 7〕

按:《邻苏老人手谱》即《杨守敬年谱》。

九月二十三日

何炳棣覆函先生,告加拿大英属哥伦比亚大学无力购买罗原觉藏书,并略述到纽约后的近况。

守和先生:

本月十二日惠书敬悉,罗氏善本书目两册亦经收到。翻阅之后,立即与王伊同函商,渠意(晚亦同意)散校目前正在尽最大努力洽购澳门姚氏蒲坂书楼典籍,无力再考虑罗氏善本。兹将书目两册邮上,刘国蓁先生处,素昧生平,散校既无能力考虑,晚亦不拟直接函覆。千乞鉴原为幸。

澳门书事最近进展为何,自离西岸后尚未得其详。大约胡家健先生未能直接在港取得洽售权,内中恐书主与严有契约关系,盖八月中严曾致函散校图书馆主任,并附有香港中文信,一切由严经手,不告让价,则严之辣练可以想见。

晚此番来哥大,全系东亚研究所新所长 Wilbur 先生之意,晚事前毫无所闻。无正常课务,除准备对 university seminar 及研究所仝人及研究生几度演讲外,可全部时间致力写撰。希望明春明清 social mobility 一专刊初稿可以完成。晚人口(1368—1953)一专刊,最近将送进哈佛出版社,计距初稿之成已逾四年矣。

胡先生曾三度晤谈,《水经注》复制胶片未成一事,业经面禀。蒙惠赠伟著书目,极感极感,惟晚离温前,似未曾在图书馆中见到,当再问伊同。请道安。

晚炳棣叩

1958,九月廿三

〔University of Chicago Library, Yuan T'ung-li Papers, Box 2〕

按:"澳门姚氏蒲坂书楼典籍"即姚钧石旧藏,由严文郁居间介绍,1959 年入藏加拿大英属哥伦比亚大学图书馆。[①] Wilbur 即 Clarence M. Wilbur(1908-1997),今译韦慕廷,美国历史学家。

---

① 郭明芳《严文郁与广东姚氏蒲坂书藏——记蒲坂书藏售书史料一则》,《东海大学图书馆馆刊》第 16 期,页 24-28。

九月二十四日

刘国蓁致函先生,请为其子刘钧源谋事,并告代购书刊的支出情况。

> 守和博士先生尊鉴:
>
> 　　敬启者,久疏敬候,抱歉殊深。恭维著述宏富,清祺畅适,至以为颂。昨日拜奉令岳丈大人手教,嘱将附函代转呈尊夫人,兹遵命奉上,敬希察收为幸。小儿钧源(英文名为 Lau Kwan Yuen)已于六月时毕业香港大学文学院经济系,获得文学士衔,本拟领取奖学金赴英伦深造,但至今尚未有消息,或者不获选,是以在港谋事,已有应考香港政府各职位又无结果。东亚银行则极欲聘任他,而所给薪水不多(只是中学毕业生待遇而已)。最近他闻港美国领事馆请聘人员,用是不揣冒昧,恳请鼎力赞勷介绍。现其驻港总领事为皮礼智先生(James Byrd Pilcher,前为台湾"大使馆"参事兼副馆长)及尚有其他副领事,未悉先生与渠等熟识否?倘蒙赐函介绍,当能获得枝栖,感荷恩慈,寔无既极耳。月前由航空包裹邮奉上罗氏书目两册,量邀尊览,未悉有无结果。据敝友罗原觉君云及得见马鉴先生,亦有谈及,渠谓先生亦有书信来往,并谈及购置书籍事云。七月时拜奉手示,并附美汇票十元等,已将其找换港银五十八元一角,连上存一角共五十八.二元,代支邮笺十张五元,邮票一元,"家常菜"书籍一册一.四五元,《新闻天地》半年二十三元,八九十月小报费共十一.七元,此次邮费二元,共支银四十四元一角五分,比对尚存壹十四元○五分在晚处也。关于嘱购入厨书籍,现只有该册购得,经已连同小报奉上,不日当可到达,其余各册若搜购得则续奉上。秉华东翁返港后公私事忙,晚大约隔一二日则见渠一次,渠体重日增,寔堪告慰。匆匆,余俟续陈。专此,敬请崇安。
>
> 　　　　　　　　　　　　　　　　　　愚晚国蓁顿首
> 　　　　　　　　　　　　　　　　　一九五八年九月廿四日
> 　　　　　　〔University of Chicago Library, Yuan T'ung-li Papers, Box 2〕

　　按:1962 年 3 月 18 日,刘钧源离港赴澳大利亚留学。[1] 该信左侧有先生亲笔批注"《模范英华双解新辞典》、《中西回史日历》、万

---

[1]《华侨日报》,1962 年 3 月 19 日,第 5 张页 2。

国鼎《中国历史纪年表》、刘敬恕《历史年代表》"。

九月二十九日

先生致信钱存训,请代为查询颜任光是否获得博士。

> 公垂吾兄:
>
> 　　开学以后,研究中文之学生想又增加,如有关于东方语言及史学系之*Bulletin*,望告注册部寄下壹份是荷。北大教授颜任光 Yen, Kia-lok 在芝大研究物理,不识已得博士学位否,1922 左右。前曾函芝大图书馆,迄无覆音,望到总目录代为一查,示复为感。专此,顺颂教祺。
>
> 弟同礼顿首
> 九,廿九
> 〔钱孝文藏札〕

按:颜任光(1888—1968),字耀秋,海南乐东人,物理学家、教育家,1918 年获得芝加哥大学物理学博士学位[1],历任北京大学、私立海南大学、光华大学教授。

九月三十日

刘麟生致函先生,感谢赠书,并就其对清词评价表达自己的意见。

> 守和尊兄著席:
>
> 　　临别宠荷盛馔,饫领教言,无任感戴。《彊邨语业》卷三谅蒙披阅,顷又荷赠书,所论清词裒集甚富,持论亦似平允,当再细读。惟篇末辑词与鄙见尚多出入也。专复并谢,敬请双安。
>
> 教小弟刘麟生顿首
> 九,卅
> 〔University of Chicago Library, Yuan T'ung-li Papers, Box 2〕

按:刘麟生(1894—1980),字宣阁,安徽无为人,上海圣约翰大学政治系毕业,曾任商务印书馆、中华书局编辑,1956 年随董显光调任华盛顿,任私人秘书。《彊邨语业》在朱孝臧(1857—1931)生前刻有二卷本(1924 年),第三卷应该是龙榆生等人在其身后代为辑录,信中所言赠书待考。

---

① University of Chicago. Alumni Council. (1920). *Alumni directory, the University of Chicago*, 1919. Chicago, Ill.: The University of Chicago press, p. 383.

十月三日

钱存训覆函先生,告知芝加哥大学远东图书馆已搬入新址。

> 守和先生:
>
> 顷奉九、廿九日大函,敬悉一一。芝大远东研究概况已嘱校中寄奉一份,以供参考。至颜任光之名在目录中并未查到,想未写论文也。远东图书馆现已迁移 Harper Library 楼下 E.Ⅱ,有阅览室一间,研究室一间,采访编目一大间,又办公室一间,并占楼下书库两层,较前地位大为宽畅同事亦加至十二人,将扩充日文及有关近代中国之资料也。专此,即请大安。
>
> 后学存训敬上
> 十,三
> 〔University of Chicago Library, Yuan T'ung-li Papers, Box 2〕
>
> 按:"远东图书馆现已迁移 Harper Library 楼下 E.Ⅱ",可参见钱存训"留美杂忆"中的记述。[1] 受此信影响,先生未将颜任光列入《中国留美同学博士论文目录》。

十月十二日

刘国蓁致函先生,代转北平来信,并请为其子刘钧源谋事。

> 守和博士先生钧鉴:
>
> 敬启者,九月廿四日奉上令岳丈大人函并芜笺一纸,量邀尊览。日昨又收到由北平来信一封,兹特为转呈,敬希察收为幸。小儿钧源谋事尚未成就,倘荷鼎力赞勷,当能收效。敝友罗君书籍事,如何之处尚望示覆,至所厚幸。尊账前存港银十四元〇五分,除此次邮费贰元外,尚存十贰元〇五分。匆匆,余当续陈。专此,敬请钧安。
>
> 愚晚国蓁顿首
> 一九五八年十月十二日
> 〔University of Chicago Library, Yuan T'ung-li Papers, Box 2〕

十二月二十二日

黄建中(台北)致函先生,请协助其女前往美国攻读图书馆学研究生。

---

① 钱存训著、国家图书馆编《钱存训文集》第 3 卷,北京:国家图书馆出版社,2012 年,页 355。

守和吾兄左右：

　　年初敬复一函，度蒙察及，比来起居如何，甚以为念。小女淑兰现肄业"国立台湾大学"四年级史学系，历年总平均成绩皆在八十分以上，本学年选习图书馆学，深感兴趣，尤喜研究中国七略、四部及杜威十类法，明夏毕业后颇欲留美深造半工半读。兄为斯学权威，对于美国设置此一学系或学科之大学及学院，必知之甚悉，其有奖学金名额与工读机会者烦预为介绍，俾便申请入学。若华盛顿可一面在大学上课，一面在图书馆作零工（如星期日），亦祈设法鼎荐，以遂其志愿。不情之请，且惭且感。专此，敬颂年祺。

弟黄建中再拜
十二，二二
〔University of Chicago Library, Yuan T'ung-li Papers, Box 2〕

按：黄建中（1889—1959），字离明，湖北随县人，民国初年毕业于湖北德安府中学，后升入北京私立明德大学和北京大学，1922年赴英留学，归国后曾任暨南大学教务长、湖北省政府委员兼教育厅厅长。

一九五九年　六十五岁

一月八日

先生致信钱存训,介绍友人赴芝加哥看书,并谈借书等事。

> 公垂吾兄:
>
> 　　友人陈启天君此次来美,颇愿搜集关于韩非子之资料,不日来芝城看书,请予照拂。兹需用《伊黎定约中俄谈话录》在《内乱外祸历史丛书》内,又该丛书内尚有曾纪泽《金轺筹笔》,已入藏否,请按馆际借书办法寄至此间之 Inter-library loan dept 转交弟收为荷。又吾兄前为考取硕士及博士时,写过计划书一份,曾寄弟审阅,兹愿暂借一用,亦盼便中寄下是荷。顺颂教祺。
>
> 弟同礼顿首
一月八日
>
> 〔钱孝文藏札〕
>
> 　　按:陈启天(1893—1984),字修平,湖北汉阳人,社会学家、政治活动家。《金轺筹笔》后为先生所编《新疆研究丛刊》第八种,1964年5月初版。

一月十五日

钱存训覆函先生,告陈启天在芝加哥大学停留经过,并谈顾立雅最近研究之兴趣,先生所需之书已交校图以馆际方式寄出,另有一篇合撰小文发表。

> 守和先生尊右:
>
> 　　奉到一月八日手教,敬悉一一。陈启天先生在此勾留数日,曾介绍与顾立雅君接谈甚欢。顾君近研究申不害,曾为其搜罗辑本,仅得玉函山房一种,尚有严可均及黄以周辑本两种,无法查到恐未印行,如有所知,并乞见示是幸。此间所藏《内乱外祸丛书》不全,其中《伊犁定约中俄谈话录》已交总馆奉上,至《金轺筹笔》则未入藏也。所要论文计划书两种,均已无存,甚以为歉。博士论文提要尚存有一份,如需用,可以寄奉。去春所作美国之中文藏书调查,曾加扩充,与 Nunn 所

写日文部分合并在 *Library Quarterly* 一月号发表,现已出版,俟单行本印就,当再奉呈指教。专此,即请近安。

> 后学存训拜上
>
> 一月十五日
>
> 〔袁同礼家人提供〕

按:G. Raymond Nunn(1918-2009),英国出生,后入美籍,图书馆学家,1951 年至 1961 年担任密歇根大学图书馆亚洲部负责人,1961 年应夏威夷大学之聘前往该校出任教授,并任该校 East-West Center 图书馆首任馆长。[1] 所写日文部分即 Far Eastern Resources in American Libraries,刊于 *The Library Quarterly: information, community, policy*(vol. 29, no. 1, 1959, pp. 27-42)。

二月初

China in Western Literature 正式出版发行。〔University of Chicago Library, Yuan T'ung-li Papers, Box 7〕

按:虽然该书的书名和版权页均记作 1958 年,但由先生在 1959 年 1 月下旬致富路德、金守拙等人的信中可知,实际出版日期为 1959 年 2 月。此书通译作《西文汉学书目》。

二月七日

张贵永致函先生,告溥心畬书画润格。

> 守和先生道席:
>
> 前上一函,谅邀尊鉴。顷溥心畬代理人章宗尧来此,并出示书画润格一纸,谓先生之事可照"美大使"旧例,以四尺屏画三千五百元计(原定四千),未知先生愿意出此高价否? 溥君为人骄傲,且为美女夫人绝对控制,生活习惯均甚怪僻。晚认为疏通已告失败,一切尚得先生决定。谨此,并颂道祺。
>
> 后学张贵永顿首
>
> 二月七日
>
> 夫人均候。
>
> 邮寄美钞危险,请勿再寄。

---

① 1960 年前后,该校似有意聘请先生出任该中心图书馆主任,参见《思忆录》中文部分页 27。

附溥君润格一纸。

〔University of Chicago Library, Yuan T'ung-li Papers, Box 2〕

按："美女夫人"应指李墨云。

二月十四日

胡适（台北）致函先生、吴光清，请与国会图书馆馆长洽商将四十年代拍摄平馆暂存国会图书馆的善本书缩微胶卷一套及目录装箱寄送台北。

守和、光清两兄：

现寄上我给 Dr. Mumford 的信的副本一份，乞两兄看了，转给 Mr. Beal 一份。

此信本该去年在<u>纽约</u>时写的，只因为那时我十分忙乱，总不得工夫写长信。又因为那时正当<u>共产党炮击金门各岛</u>，外国人总不免把<u>台湾</u>看作危险地带，所以我先回来看看，也可以使我们的朋友们知道这里并没有什么危险。

如蒙国会馆馆长同意。只好烦劳你们两位把这一大批 microfilms 连同目录点查一遍，装箱托<u>招商局</u>的朋友设法运来。如招商局一时无便船，可托他们（或托别位有经验的朋友）打听<u>麦司克轮船公司</u>（Maersk Co.）的"Maersk"船，这家公司的船有定期，又经过 New York——Mr. J. C. Sung, 42 Broadway, New York——替我寄五箱书，交"Luna Maersk"船运回，只四十五天就到了，——比<u>招商局</u>的船运的还快三十多天。一切装运等费，均乞两兄估计，用空邮示知，当即用空邮寄奉支票。

一切费两兄清神大力，万分感谢。

另寄近作"神会和尚遗著两种"单本两份，乞指正。

匆匆，敬祝两兄及府上平安，并问华府诸友平安。

弟胡适敬上
一九五九，二，十四

〔台北胡适纪念馆，档案编号 HS-NK01-164-006〕

按：国会图书馆赠送"中央研究院"史语所的平馆寄存善本缩微胶片，于 1959 年 12 月运抵台北。[1]　此函右下角标注"二，十四航

---

① 黄彰健《校印国立北平图书馆藏红格本明史录序》，页 14。

空发"。此件应为他人录稿。《胡适中文书信集》收录此信,但有错排。

二月十六日

先生致信富路德教授,请其为《西文汉学书目》撰写书评。〔University of Chicago Library, Yuan T'ung-li Papers, Box 7〕

二月二十日

先生致信蒋复璁,感谢赠书并询问台湾出版的学术论文有无索引。

慰堂先生左右:

前承惠寄贵馆《善本书目》上、中各一册,至为感谢,惟下册《乙编》及索引尚未收到,如承检寄,俾成完帙,尤所企盼。又台湾出版之学术杂志论文,有无索引之编制《民国学术论文索引》极不全,此间极感需要,大陆出版之《中国史学论文索引》及其他索引极便检查。尊处能否将近十余年来台湾出版之论文编一索引,至为企望。拙编 China in Western Literature 已于日前寄"教育部"四部,拟请转委总务司于收到后分配贵馆及台大、"中研院"、"教育部"图书馆各一部为感。专此,顺颂时社。

弟袁同礼顿首
二月二十日

《中华民国图书选目》英文本亦盼赐寄一部。

〔台北"中央图书馆"档案,档案编号 299-112 至 299-113〕

按:《中国史学论文索引》由中国科学院历史研究所第一、二所及北京大学历史系编辑,1957 年科学出版社初版。该信于 2 月 28 日送达台北。

先生致信法斯,寄上《西文汉学书目》,感谢洛克菲勒基金会给予的鼎力支持,并附上研究计划,希望该基金会予以考虑。

February 20, 1959

Dear Dr. Fahs:

With the generous assistance of your Foundation, I was able to complete a major portion of my bibliography on China. After much unnecessary delay, it has recently been published. A copy is being mailed to you from the publisher. A copy is being mailed to you from the publisher and I hope you would accept it with my best compliments.

Another piece of research, smaller in scope, is nearing completion and I am rather anxious to make it available to a wider circle of readers. I enclose herewith a short memorandum about this work and I hope your Foundation may find it possible to lend me the needed support.

Like my bibliography on China, the present work is also a labor of love as I have been continuing the research outside of my office hours. I hope, therefore, that your grant could be made to me as a mature scholar, not through an institution.

However, if your grant has to be made through an institution, may I suggest the name of the Institute of Modern History of "the Academia Sinica" which will be glad to sponsor such a project.

Thanking you once more for your valuable help.

Yours sincerely,

T. L. Yuan

〔University of Chicago Library, Yuan T'ung-li Papers, Box 4〕

按：该件为录副，并附一页 China in Russian Literature, 1917-1958，希望给予 2500 美金资助。

法斯致函先生，收到寄赠的《西文汉学书目》，对先生长时间辛苦研究表示敬佩。〔University of Chicago Library, Yuan T'ung-li Papers, Box 4〕

二月二十四日

克莱普致函先生，祝贺《西文汉学书目》的出版，尤其对克服多种语言所造成的困难表示称赞。〔Library of Congress, Council on Library and Information Resources Records, Box 95〕

三月十三日

费正清致函先生，邀请其出席亚洲学会年会，并祝贺《西文汉学书目》出版。

March 13, 1959

Dear Shou-ho:

It appears that I am president of the Association for Asian Studies this year and must make a speech at a luncheon. I should like to invite you to sit at the head table with me and other officers on Tuesday, March 24 at 12:15 in the West Burgundy Room of the Sheraton Park Hotel.

I am delighted to see your new volume out and admire very much your capacity to have produced it. It will be of the greatest value to us all.

With cordial regards,

J. K. Fairbank

〔University of Chicago Library, Yuan T'ung-li Papers, Box 3〕

按:此件为打字稿,落款处为其签名。

三月十八日

法斯覆函先生,告知洛克菲勒基金会不支持先生关于编纂《俄文中国论著书目》的资助申请。

March 18, 1959

Dear Dr. Yuan:

Following receipt of your letter of February 20 with regard to the question of help for work on a bibliography on China in Russian literature, I brought the matter up for discussion with my associates here. I regret now to have to reply that we see no possibility of obtaining here the help which you would need for this project.

I regret having to report this negative conclusion to you as I recall very vividly our earlier discussions in Peking about the need for Russian studies and so understand that this has been a long-time interest of yours.

With best personal regards and good wishes,

Sincerely yours,

Charles B. Fahs

〔University of Chicago Library, Yuan T'ung-li Papers, Box 4〕

三月下旬

先生受邀参加亚洲学会年会。

按:本次年会在华盛顿举行,会期为 23 日至 25 日,现可以确定先生聆听了 25 日上午的会议。①

---

① Mote, Frederick W. "The Association for Asian Studies: Summary for the Year 1958－59." *The Journal of Asian Studies*, vol. 18, no. 4, 1959, pp. 547－549.

四月四日

先生致函费正清,请向洛克菲勒基金会社会科学分部写信支持自己的资助申请,并拟由哈佛大学东亚研究中心作为该项目的管理方。

April 4, 1959

Dear Professor Fairbank:

Referring to my bibliography of Russian works on China, I applied sometime ago for a small grant from the Rockefeller Foundation. As I had expected, it was turned down by Dr. Fahs. But when he attended the Annual Meeting, he seemed to have been especially impressed with the papers by John Thompson and Martin Wilbur and the discussions which followed.

After that session last Wednesday, he did promise that he would refer my request to the Division of Social Sciences of the Foundation, as the bibliography chiefly consists of materials in the field of modern history and the social sciences.

In view of your interest in this project, I hope you would write to the Division of Social Sciences supporting my request for a grant. If it could be obtained from this source, I would include important articles on China which would make the bibliography more useful to scholars. For your information I enclose copy of the memo which I had submitted to the Foundation.

As the Foundation prefers to make grants to institutions, I hope your Center would supervise the project and to have it published under the auspices of the Center. If you would make it clear to the Foundation that your Center would be glad to administer the grant, it would meet the approval of the Foundation.

Although I have not talked with Prof. Kennedy about the printing, I am sure that he would be glad to do the offset printing after the manuscript has been typed and proof-read in Washington.

Yours sincerely,

T. L. Yuan

〔University of Chicago Library, Yuan T'ung-li Papers, Box 4〕

按:John M. Thompson(1926-2017),美国外交领域专家,专攻俄

国近现代史，时在印第安纳大学历史系执教。该件为录副。

四月七日

费正清覆函先生，建议等斯卡奇科夫《中国书目》第二版出版后再将先生申请计划递交洛克菲勒基金会。

April 7, 1959

Dear. T. L.:

　　We greatly enjoyed our evening with you and appreciated the chance to get together.

　　I have just received a letter from one of our students in Leningrad who says that a new edition of Skachkov's *Bibliografia Kitaya*, brought up-to-date, is now at the press and should be out in June or July. He also adds that the announced edition is rather small, but I do not know exactly how to order copies.

　　The publication of such a volume, since it will be in Russian and not in English, would by no means make the publication of your own bibliography undesirable. On the contrary, the latter would be of great help, but I imagine that it would be desirable to see Shachkov's volume before proceeding to the publication of your own. I hope we may keep in touch on this point and that whenever the Skachkov volume is seen by you, you will let me have your impressions.

With cordial regards,

John

P. S. I have just received your letter of April 4 and the copy of your statement for Rockefeller. It seems to me this bibliographical effort is important, and I will certainly stand ready to urge our Research Committee to give it the sponsorship of this Center. The one problem is to get hold of the new Skachkov volume, about which I know no more than is stated above. It looks as though everything will have to be held up until we can see it and your project can take account of it.

JKF

〔University of Chicago Library, Yuan T'ung-li Papers, Box 4〕

按：New edition of Skachkov's *Bibliografia Kitaya* 即 1960 年出版的《中国书目》第 2 版，该版补录了初版后 1930 年至 1957 年苏联出版的俄文中国论著。[①]

四月二十三日

戴密微致片先生，告知宝道生日且仍在世，另不建议先生现在为《通报》编纂索引。

Paris, 23/4/1959

Dear Dr. Yuan,

I hear from the son of Georges Padoux, who is working at the French Embassy at New Delhi, that his father was born at Alexandria (Egypt) on Feb. 21, 1867, and is still alive (92 years! At Artemare, Ain). He entered the Affaires Etrangères in 1890, the same year as Paul Claudel.

Yours sincerely,

P Demiéville

I think it is too early to compile an Index to *T'oung Pao* for only 15 years. Better wait at least 20 years. I have asked for an Index to *HJAS*, so far without success! Can you help to decide them?

〔袁同礼家人提供〕

按：此件为打字稿，落款和补语皆为戴密微亲笔，其寄出地址为 234 bd. Raspail, Paris 14.

五月二十日

先生致信克莱普，附美国图书馆藏有关中国俄文文献联合目录出版备忘录，请图书资源委员会考虑资助出版。

May 20, 1959

Dear Mr. Clapp:

As your Council is dedicated to the development of American library resources, I wish to submit herewith a memorandum regarding a <u>Union List of Russian Works on China</u> which I have been compiling for several years.

[①] 柳若梅《俄罗斯东方学和汉学史上的斯卡奇科夫》，《汉学研究通讯》第 100 期，2009 年，页 39-40。

As a labor of love, I have been doing this work outside of my office hours and without clerical assistance. Now, a number of scholars have urged me to publish it on the grounds that Russian sources contribute to a better understanding of China, particularly at this time. With a small grant from your Council, the materials thus collected could very soon be made available to libraries and research scholars.

With cordial regards,

Yours sincerely,

T. L. Yuan

〔Library of Congress, Council on Library and Information Resources Records, Box 95〕

按：此件为打字稿，落款处为先生签名。另附两页备忘录，题为 A Union List of Russian Works on China in American Libraries，该信于 5 月 22 日送达。

五月二十八日

克莱普覆函先生，表示图书资源委员会无力支持该出版计划。

May 28, 1959

Dear Dr. Yuan:

I acknowledge with much interest your letter of May 20, 1959, and return herewith, in accordance with your request, the bibliography on "Russian Works on China, 1918–1958", being a selection, in the field of history and culture, from the larger bibliography having the same title.

We are sympathetically much inclined to the assistance which you request and are very conscious of what this bibliography represents in terms of scholarship and expenditure of time. We are also impressed by the potential contribution which it might make.

Nevertheless, as I think you are to some degree aware, we have been compelled to abstain from the support of bibliographical work, for the very simple reason that there is so much work of potential usefulness which needs such support-unless these projects can promise either the widest general usefulness or the demonstration of improved techniques which can be carried to other work.

Much as I admire the accomplishment represented by *China in Western Literature*, and much as I would be very happy to assist in the publication of this supplement to that work, I must regretfully tell you that I do not believe this to be within the scope of the program of this Council.

I do not know whether there is other assistance which I might bring; but I would be very happy, were this the case.

Sincerely yours,

Verner W. Clapp

President

〔Library of Congress, Council on Library and Information Resources Records, Box 95〕

按：该件为录副。

六月十日

Giok Po Oey 覆函先生，就前询巴厘岛在印尼语中的发音及峇里源自何种中文文献予以答复。

June 10, 1959

Dear Mr. Yuan:

Thank you for your kind letter. Regarding your problem of transliteration, however, I do not feel qualified to be of any advice to you. The most I could do is to answer your question on the official pronunciation of the name Bali in the Indonesian language: It is pronounced just as it is written; b as in bad, a as in far, l as in land, I as in Chinese li.

I have no idea where the characters 峇里 have come from. It is possible that they have been derived from some early Chinese record. But so far I could check from secondary sources, they have not been derived from 二十四史, 星槎胜览, 瀛涯胜览, 海语, 佛国记, 本草纲目, 东西详考, 太平寰宇记。

The problem of identification of ancient geographical names have always interested me. However, due to my present exhausting job, I have not yet been able to do any research of my own.

I am sorry that I have not been able to be of any substantial help to you. I hope that in the meantime you have found the answer to your problem from other sources.

Please give my regards to your family.

Yours sincerely,

G. P. Oey

An Indonesian scholar

〔University of Chicago Library, Yuan T'ung-li Papers, Box 7〕

按:Giok Po Oey(1922-2010),出生于印度尼西亚爪哇岛的苏加武眉,华裔,1951 年入加州大学伯克利分校,1953 年获康奈大学文学硕士,后短暂回到印度尼西亚,1957 年返回康乃尔大学,受雇于该校图书馆,从此致力于构建东南亚馆藏,1985 年退休。此件为打字稿,中文和落款处均为其亲笔。

八月八日

先生致信 George E. Taylor,请其考虑资助《新疆研究文献目录》的编纂与出版。

August 8, 1959

Professor George E. Taylor, Director

Far Eastern and Russian Institute

University of Washington

Seattle, Washington

Dear Professor Taylor:

In view of your interest in Inner Asian studies, some of our common friends suggested that I should solicit your advice in regard to the support of my project on Sinkiang. During the past twelve months I have been engaged in compiling a comprehensive bibliography on Sinkiang the scope of which is set forth in the enclosed memorandum. Although it is a labor of love, I am now in need of clerical assistance in order to bring it to early completion.

Since the Russians have taken a lion's share in the exploration of

Sinkiang, Russian literature is of great scientific importance. Although I have collected over 1000 titles, there is still a long way to go. To analyze the serial publications volume by volume is a time-consuming task; but when the work is completed, it would be of great help to future scholars and policy makers.

I should like to obtain a small grant for $3000 for the first year and $2000 for the second year mainly for clerical assistance. Mr. Vetch in Hong Kong would like to publish it as it is cheaper to have it printed in Hong Kong than in this country.

As you are a great promoter to Russian and Inner Asian studies, I know you would be willing to render some assistance if circumstances permit. Would it be possible to include it as one of the research projects of your Institute? I shall be much honored if it could be published under its name.

Here at the Library of Congress, I have better facilities for a work of this kind. If I could have some financial support, the project could be completed in two years.

With cordial regards,

Yours sincerely,

T. L. Yuan

〔University of Chicago Library, Yuan T'ung-li Papers, Box 1〕

按:George E. Taylor(1905－2000),英国人,汉学家,中文名戴德华,1930 年在哈佛燕京学社的资助下前往北京学习,后曾在南京、北平等地执教,1939 年起出任华盛顿大学教授,1946 年担任该校远东和苏俄研究中心主任。Mr. Vetch 即出版商魏智,时在香港大学出版社任职。此件为录副。

八月十二日

胡昌度覆函先生,已与卫德明商妥并拟同访戴德华,愿竭尽所能协助先生申请补助。

守和先生尊右:

奉读九日大示,荷蒙奖掖,惭感交并。今夏在此尸位,获益良多,惟暑校结束在即,转眼即须束装东返,颇有依依之感耳。我公近作于新疆内亚研究,必多贡献。数日前已于无忌先生处获悉尊意,当即与卫德明先生商榷,曾允在泰勒及其余负责诸公前提出补助问题。今日又于接到手示后再度提及,并将我公致泰勒函出示,现拟约期同访泰勒先生,期能早作决定,料不久可得正式答复。度在此一日,凡力之所及当图报命。友忠先生数日前自台经欧洲返此,嘱代向我公致意。专复,祗请撰安。

后学胡昌度叩

八,十二

〔University of Chicago Library, Yuan T'ung-li Papers, Box 1〕

按:胡昌度(C. T. Hu,1920—2012),原名胡邦宪,教育家,1942 年获复旦大学英文文学士,后赴印度、缅甸担任盟军翻译,1954 年获华盛顿大学博士学位,其论文题目为 The Yellow River administration in the Ch'ing dynasty,时应在哥伦比亚大学教育学院任教,刻下参加华盛顿大学(西雅图)暑期研究班。“泰勒”即戴德华(George E. Taylor)。

八月十八日

张贵永覆函先生,请赐寄中美关系报告,并请先生在美为其夫人谋一图书馆职位,另告台北经售西文书籍的书店。

守和先生道席:

谨覆者,七月十三日手示前日始得拜读,迟覆为歉。原因由于暑期中除每星期必须去南港“中研院”三日外,大都在家阅读,极少至台大,而校工亦懒于送信,机关太大而生流弊。近维尊体清健,府上迪吉为慰为颂。国会图书馆曾寄来数种有关中国现代史书籍不甚有学术价值,颇感失望。《一九四二年之中美关系》以及陆续出版之资料,请设法由国会图书馆径寄南港“中央研究院”近代史研究所,作为海防档及以后出版之中苏档、越南档等交换品,则幸甚矣。《台湾大学概况》一书(英文)图片及说明颇佳,已嘱校长室直接寄奉,决不致误。内人在美(西雅图)继续攻读图书馆学,明年或可卒业,深欲得一枝栖,未悉尊处或其他各大学图书馆能有机会否?谨此拜托,并颂暑祺。

后学张贵永顿首

八月十八日

夫人均候。

《一九四二年中美关系档案》一册，如蒙惠赐，请先寄舍间亦可，地址：台湾台北云和街38号。义均兄嫂及元照兄嫂请代候为感。

台北经售西书较有经验与基础者如下：

文星书局 The Book World Co. 台北市衡阳路十五号

东南书报社 The SouthEast Bk. Co. 台北市博爱路 105 号

燉煌书店 The Care Book Store 台北市中山北路二段？号

虹桥书店 The Rainbow Bk. Co. 台北市衡阳路 46 号

〔University of Chicago Library, Yuan T'ung-li Papers, Box 2〕

按：《一九四二年之中美关系》应指 *Foreign Relations of the United States: diplomatic papers, 1942, China*，G. Bernard Noble、E. R. Perkins 合编，1956 年美国政府印刷局印行。

九月九日

刘国橐覆函先生，请就近询问刘钧源前往华盛顿服务之事有无进展，并告在港所购书刊及账目。

守和博士先生钧鉴：

敬启者，未修书敬候，瞬已数月，蒹葭秋水，倍切溯洄，恭维著述丰宏，清祺畅适，至以为颂。正拟申纸握管作函候安，忽奉手示，欣喜奚似，不遗在远，幸何如之。令岳丈大人许久未有来信，故无从转递，是以亦疏音候也。小儿钧源自服务美国新闻处后，又已八阅月，现仍继续工作。上二月前，他由 Kirby 教授介绍他到亚洲基金会香港办事处接洽，系前往尊处美京为国会议员服务，订期九个月，但至今未有若何消息，用是不揣冒昧，恳请先生就近调查该事如何进行，倘蒙鼎力赞勷得成事，寔感荷恩慈，寔无既极。晚仍依然故我，都是日夜工作，最近提出向学校辞职，但尚未批准。倘将来辞退，则可较多休息，此亦因日前晚患头痛之疾已月余之久，颇为辛苦也。月来接续奉上《天文台》及《新闻天地》，想皆得到达无误。尊账前存六十九.七五元，支《新闻天地》今年二月至明年一月两半年共四十六元，《天文台》与邮费由二月至九月共二十四元，寄字典邮费一.四五元，共七十一.四五元，比对支长一.六元也。关于中文古书在港发售皆由大陆运来，俱是由民间搜集，各公私及学校图书馆皆有，交集古斋出售。其最近目录，本月十五日发出,到时当寄奉一册。中外图书公司规模甚小,是家庭式而已,其书目亦当同奉上。匆匆,专此,敬请著安。

> 愚晚国棻顿首
> 一九五九年九月九日

〔University of Chicago Library, Yuan T'ung-li Papers, Box 2〕

十月二十九日

先生致信费正清,告知无法购得斯卡奇科夫新版《中国书目》,并告因受 John M. Thompson 的鼓励,已向美国社会科学研究委员会下属斯拉夫研究委员会申请资助编纂《俄文中国论著》,另告已请《华裔学志》寄送抽印本。

October 29, 1959

Dear Professor Fairbank:

After you had informed me that Skachkov's Bibliografia Kitaya is being brought up-to-date, I ordered four copies through four different channels. But so far none of them has turned up.

While I have been hoping to see the appearance of Skachkov's before proceeding to the publication of my own, I have recently had some encouragement from Professor John M. Thompson, now at Indiana University. He suggests that I should explore the possibilities of obtaining a small grant (about ＄2000) from the Joint Committee on Slavic Studies. He further indicated that the "Slavis series" at Indiana would be interested in publishing my bibliography when it is completed.

I am therefore sending my application to the Social Science Research Council as the closing date for applications under this program is November 2. Since you are very much interested in this work, may I ask you to serve as one of my references? Enclosed herewith is a "confidential report" form. Please mail it directly to the Council.

A selected bibliography in the field of history and culture by Russian authors has just been issued by the *Monumenta Serica*. I have asked the editor to send you a copy of the reprints and another copy for your Center.

Thanking you for your interest and help,

Your sincerely,

T. L. Yuan

〔University of Chicago Library, Yuan T'ung-li Papers, Box 4〕

十一月六日

先生致信戴德华,告知已向美国学术团体理事会递交资助申请。

November 6, 1959

Dear Professor Taylor:

I appreciate very much your letter of September 18, and your assurance that my request for research assistance in connection with my work on Sinkiang will meet sympathetic consideration from the Asian Grants Committee of the ACLS.

I have accordingly submitted my application for a subsidy of $ 3000. It is my hope that I may count on your continued interest and help.

With cordial regards,

Yours sincerely,

T. L. Yuan

〔University of Chicago Library, Yuan T'ung-li Papers, Box 1〕

按:此件为录副。

费正清致函先生,告知已致信社会科学研究委员会支持美国图书馆藏有关中国俄文文献联合目录编纂计划,并将于圣诞节假期前往华盛顿。

November 6, 1959

Dear T. L.:

I am glad you are going ahead with the Joint Committee on Slavic Studies. The counterpart on contemporary China is just getting underway and as yet has no program or funds. I have written to SSRC in the strongest support of your project.

Our own efforts here are still held up awaiting the prospect of some kind of financing. Even so, I am by no means certain how much we can put into bibliographical work. I am sorry not to have got this Center behind your current bibliography but it seems to me most appropriate for the Joint Committee on Slavic Studies to take it on. Please let me know how this comes out.

Thanks for the reprints you mention from *Monumenta Serica*. We are leaving January 1st on sabbatical leave but will be in Washington at Christmastime, when perhaps we can get together.

With cordial regards,

John

〔University of Chicago Library, Yuan T'ung-li Papers, Box 4〕

按:SSRC 即 Social Science Research Council,12 月 19 日该委员会下属斯拉夫研究联合委员会未批准先生的此项申请。

十一月八日

先生致信 Jaroslav Průšek,寄送《西文汉学书目》及《华裔学志》文章抽印本,并请撰写书评,另请协助获取捷克出版的有关马可波罗的书目。

November 8, 1959

Dear Professor Prusek:

It has been so long since I had the pleasure of seeing you last in Peking. I am therefore much flattered by your request for a copy of my bibliography on China. I am asking my publisher to send you a review copy and I hope it arrives safely. When your review is published, may I request for a copy?

I am also asking the Editor of *Monuments Serica* to send you direct from Japan a reprint of my article on Russia works on China which might be of interest to you.

As I am compiling a bibliography on Marco Polo, I would greatly appreciate your assistance if you could ask your librarian to send me titles of books and articles on Marco Polo published in Prague. The following two book are the only ones I have seen already.

I am also anxious to obtain bibliographies on China and Mongolia published in Prague and in the Soviet Union. If you could help me in obtaining these bibliographies, I shall be most grateful.

I have ordered Skachkov's, but so far it has not been received. Do you happen to have seen the revised edition?

No doubt you have built up a good collection of Chinese books in your Institute. I should like to visit your beautiful city once again.

With cordial regards,

yours sincerely,

T. L. Yuan

Polo, Marco:

Milion, dle jedin ého rukopisu spolu s přislu šným z ákladem latinským , Justin Václav Prášek, 1902, 305 p.

Marko Polo: *jeho cesty a dílo by Bohuslav Hor ák*, 1949. 72 p.

〔University of Chicago Library, Yuan T'ung-li Papers, Box 8〕

按:Jaroslav Průšek(1906-1980),通译作雅罗斯拉夫·普实克,捷克汉学家,汉学布拉格学派的创始人,1953 年被任命为捷克斯洛伐克科学院东方研究所所长。

卜德覆函先生,表示很高兴担任先生项目申请的推荐人,并期待《西文汉学书目》之期刊论文部分早日问世。

Nov. 8, 1959

Dear Dr. Yuan:

I am glad to act as one of your references for SSRC, and hope the project is approved. However, I must confess that I am even more anxious to see the appearance of your companion volume to *China in Western Literature*, that on periodical articles.

I return Dr. Thompson's letter to you, but not the copy of your articles, since you did not ask for it. If you want to have it back, please let me know.

I also enclose my review of another Russian book which may be of interest to you. Have you heard that *Sovetskoye Kitayevedenie* has gone out of existence, apparently after its third issue (1958)? See Edmund Clubb's article on Soviet oriental studies in *Pacific Affairs* , vol. 32, no. 3 (Sept. 1959), p. 306.

I did not know that you know Russian, but the MS of your

Monumenta Serica article looks like a fine piece of work. May I suggest that when your larger bibliography is completed, it would be useful to have it read by a Russian specialist. I wish you could make the bibliography really complete by visiting libraries in Russia, but the small grant you ask for obviously makes such a step impossible.

Sincerely yours,

Derk Bodde

〔University of Chicago Library, Yuan T'ung-li Papers, Box 9〕

按:先生申请的研究计划应为*Russian Works on China, 1918-1960 in American Libraries* 之雏形。《西文汉学书目》确未收录期刊论文,因此部分本由谭卓垣负责,但收录了曾出版单行本的期刊论文。my review 应指卜德 1958 年发表的一篇书评,对象为 Ocherki po Istorii Russkogo Vostokovedeniya[①],其意为"苏俄东方学简史"。*Sovetskoye Kitayevedenie* 即 Soviet Sinology,该刊由苏联科学院主办。Edmund Clubb's article 即 Oriental Studies Through Soviet Eyes;MS of your *Monumenta Serica* article 即 Russian Works on China, 1918-1958: a selected bibliography 之底稿。

十二月四日

罗家伦致函先生,略述"国史馆"、"党史会"近况,请在美访查日本外务省及陆海军档案缩微胶片目录,并复印《伦敦蒙难记》一书。

守和吾兄道鉴:

久疏音问,罪无可恕;但与此间老友见面时常谈及兄,不敢忘也。适之先生及月涵、勉仲(查)、子水诸兄均常相聚。弟任党史会(原名党史史料编纂委员会)主持人以来,收集中国近代史史料颇多,其中原始材料亦不少。所编《革命文献》已至二十辑,还要继续下去。凡此刊物所载之文件,无不字字存真,恪守"知识真诚"(Intellctual Honesty)之原则,可以告慰于老友者。弟曾陆续寄送国会图书馆,不知二十辑都收到否? 如没有,请开单来补。又弟处有合订本(精装),如要,弟可寄赠一套。前年起恢复"国史馆",弟又不得已而从事。现

① Bodde, Derk. *Journal of the American Oriental Society*, vol. 78, no. 4, 1958, pp. 304-305.

在又从积极征辑文献上做工作。"国史馆"有一特殊便利,即按法律规定,可以搜收或抄写各机关过期或现有之档案。现在弟所苦者即无大的史库,可以储藏,以致不敢放手做去。如最近"总统府"移送来百余箱档案,弟只得仍寄存在原来设备安全之处,虽可随用随调,亦不便也。弟颇知在美国各图书馆所藏的中文史料颇多,而西文中(无论文件或私人著述)有关中国近代和现代的史料亦不少。此二者皆弟所应当知道者。兄对此项史料,素来关心,不知有已经收辑之目录或记载可以指示否? 现在还有两件事要请兄先行指教的:

(1)日本外交军事各首脑部门之资料,当其战败后均就地或移美用 microfilm 照去,闻已照完并已印有目录,可以任友邦政府与学术机关出钱复印。我们正在编纂《抗战实录》,除本国材料外,更需要对方材料,可以互相考订。为此请兄将复印手续及其应付之代价,迅速示知。并就兄估计有关中日战争材料之数量_{战争之起因当然在内}(范围不妨广,凡可以知其内容及彼对我方情况之报告均所需要)及经费之约数,以便准备。(前曾托吴相湘君调查,但彼语焉不详,而且不甚知其内容。)

(2)孙中山先生所著"*Kidnapped in London*"一书之英文本(闻有几个 edition,不知有异同否),如国会图书馆能将所藏照一套复印本寄"国史馆",弟有用处,款当照寄。

一切拜托拜托!

兄与嫂夫人必安康,敬此问候潭福!

弟家伦敬启
十二月四日

〔University of Chicago Library, Yuan T'ung-li Papers, Box 1〕

按:吴相湘(1912—2007),湖南常德人,北京大学历史系毕业,时应在台湾大学历史系任教。该函为罗家伦亲笔,并注"台北市北平路二号"字样。

十二月八日

先生致信我妻荣,请赐寄其个人西文著述清单。

December 8, 1959

Dear Professor Wagatsuma:

As I have been compiling a bibliography on Japanese law and legal institutions, I have included the following articles which you contributed to various journals:

1.Democratization of the family relation in Japan

2.Guarantee of fundamental human rights under the Japanese Constitution

3.Chattel mortgages in Japanese law

4.Japanese legal system 1945－55……

As you have undoubtedly written other articles in Western languages, may I request you to send me a list, indicating in which journals they are to be found.

My bibliography consists of books and articles on the laws of Japan including literature in Russian, Italian, French and German, besides English. No works in Japanese are listed in view of your excellent bibliography in the *Japan Science Review-Law and Politics*.

At present I have no idea where it is to be published. I thought the Editor of *Monumenta Nipponica* may be interested in publishing it, but I shall greatly appreciate your advice.

There are about 1600 titles in this bibliography. If it could be published in Japan, it would be a useful tool to research scholars in the field of law.

Thanking you in advance for your help,

Yours sincerely,

Tung-li Yuan

〔University of Chicago Library, Yuan T'ung-li Papers, Box 2〕

按:我妻荣(Sakae Wagatsuma,1897－1973),日本民法学家,东京帝国大学法学部毕业。

十二月九日

陈祚龙致函先生,请在美为其谋求教职。

守和先生赐鉴:

久疏函候,罪甚! 兹敬恳者:龙自由英转此,倏忽已经三载,一面寄于法人之篱下,生活实已日趋于艰危与悬惶。按龙每日穷忙抄写,本只可籍此换求当日一家五口之温饱,至其有关之名位与实惠,故得概由法人所兼揽,即使如许佣书编目之事体,眼看亦将为法人宣告了结也！顷悉国人在美专任汉学教职者,为数固多,即连主任汉学研究者,据闻亦属不少。而是项机会,在此则永属空想耳。法人现在汉学教学研究方面,排除异己,其情其景实比英人惟有过之而无不及！今特函请先生,希望可以为龙在美介绍一份如许之工作。至于龙之心愿,只求家小生活之安定,并不问工作性质之高下与大小也。如说国人在美讲授汉学需要助理,美国汉学图书馆需要掌管以及当地大学专门研究汉学计划需要合作,只要任期较为久长,则属龙所乐就。有劳心神,容图后报。肃此,敬颂谭祺百福！

愚陈祚龙拜上
五九,十二,九,于巴黎。

复示尚祈写寄:

CHEN Tsu-lung, 21 Rue de Penthièvre, Sceaux, Seine, FRANCE

〔University of Chicago Library, Yuan T'ung-li Papers, Box 2〕

十二月十七日

先生致信罗家伦,谈其在美收集中国史料,愿任"国史馆"名誉采访。大意如下:

1.《伦敦蒙难记》1897 年英文本已照像寄来,另有伦敦 *Times* 的记载甚多,如果需要可照相寄来;

2.美国照好的日本军部及外交档案,与《抗战实录》关系最大,全套约两万美元,目录随信寄送;

3.编成一种西文《中山先生文献目录》,问台北能否为其出版。

〔罗久芳、罗久蓉编辑校注《罗家伦先生文存补遗》,台北:"中央研究院"近代史研究所,2009 年,页 626〕

　　按:罗家伦认为在美国对中国史料、图书情况的熟悉程度,无人可与先生相提并论,先生愿意帮助,"此真好消息"。

十二月十八日

刘国錞致函先生,询问刘钧源申请赴美之议有无进展,并询国会图书馆是否藏有同治朝《英语集全》,愿付费补抄。

　　守和博士先生钧鉴:

　　敬启者,引领慈云,倍深瞻仰,恭维著述丰宏,履躬清胜,定符私颂。日昨奉到惠赠圣诞珍物领带夹一个,袖口纽一对,感荷恩赐,寔无既极。十一月三十日奉上芜笺,量邀尊览。曾奉托代向亚洲基金会调查关于小儿钧源拟来美京事,未蒙示覆,时在念中。上月由包裹邮奉上荔枝、红茶两罐、贺简成函,另代购明前龙井茶壹斤二两,想当可到达也。兹有恳者,晚日前购得同治元年(一八六二)纬经堂版之《英语集全》一部六册(唐廷枢著),颇为古旧,并且第一册内卷一人体缺第四十八至五十一页(四页)及宫室缺第五十四页(一页)共五页,未悉国会图书馆有无此书,可否觅人代补抄,及酬劳费若干。如可能办理,敬希示知,至所感幸。至纸章方面,晚可邮寄奉,页内间格亦可间便,只抄字句而已。该书全港皆无,故特函奉托也。尊帐支长五十四元四角,或可不必付下以为酬劳费用。企待卓裁。匆匆,余当续陈。专此,敬请撰安。

愚晚国蓁顿首

一九五九年十二月十八日

〔University of Chicago Library, Yuan T'ung-li Papers, Box 7〕

按:唐廷枢(1832—1892),广东香山人,近代企业家、慈善家,《英语集全》为学术界公认中国较早的一部汉英词典。

十二月二十三日

刘国蓁覆函先生,前询香港大学毕业生姓名已查实,并转寄先生岳父袁道冲信函。

守和博士先生台鉴:

敬启者,十八日奉上芜笺,量邀尊览。日昨拜奉手教,敬悉内附汇单贰十美元一张,亦经妥收,代转司各脱函,已付邮去,嘱查港大毕业生中文名已查妥,原纸奉回,敬希亮察。此次,大函到港时已十分破烂,由邮局代为再加封,派字条着晚亲自往取回,并要当面拆开看内里有无缺少等情,原因该信封薄脆而内附颇重,是以搬运时破裂故也。昨奉到令岳丈来示嘱代转上两函,当时想渠忘记将信封入内便贴口矣,特为奉上,伏祈察收。汇单换得港银壹百十三元九角(五六九五算),前支长五十四元四角,现付邮费贰元,共五十六元四角,比对尚存五十七元五角。前函恳请费神代查有无《英语集全》一书,未悉如何,便中敬希示覆,至为感幸。专此,敬祝圣诞快乐,并贺新禧。

愚晚国蓁顿首

一九五九年十二月廿三日

〔University of Chicago Library, Yuan T'ung-li Papers, Box 7〕

十二月二十七日

陈祚龙覆函先生,感谢推荐往哈佛大学继续求学,但生活不易,恐不能前往。

守和先生赐鉴:

复示(廿二日)已经拜读。承告一切,感激不尽! 哈佛表格,谅必不日即可邮到,唯龙既已带家负小,转靠奖金求学,即使可以申请成功,事实恐亦极难解决合家生活之问题也。目前在美既无工作可就,尚祈将来机会呈现,先生可以为龙稍予留意,是所感祷! 肃此,敬颂谭祺百福!

愚陈祚龙拜上

五九,十二,廿七,于巴黎。

〔University of Chicago Library, Yuan T'ung-li Papers, Box 2〕

十二月二十八日

Bryce Wood 致函先生,告知社会科学研究委员会无法资助美国图书馆藏有关中国俄文文献联合目录编纂计划。

December 28, 1959

Dear Mr. Yuan:

I am sorry to have to report that the Subcommittee on Grants of the Joint Committee on Slavic Studies, at its meeting on December 19, did not vote to recommend that the Council award you the grant in the program for research in Slavic and East European Studies requested in your application dated October 28, 1959.

The Subcommittee, finding that the total amount requested by the substantial number of candidates was considerably in excess of the funds available to it, has been regretfully obliged to disappoint many well-recommended applicants.

Please forgive the formality of this communication. We are resorting to the use of a form letter in order to notify all applicants without delay.

Sincerely yours,

Bryce Wood

〔University of Chicago Library, Yuan T'ung-li Papers, Box 4〕

按:Bryce Wood(1909-1986),1933 年获哥伦比亚大学政治学博士学位,1949 年起担任社会科学研究委员会行政助理。

是年

《华裔学志》刊登先生文章,题为 Russian Works on China, 1918-1958: a selected bibliography。〔*Monumenta Serica*, vol. 18, 1959, pp. 388-430〕

一九六〇年　六十六岁

一月一日

任以都覆函先生,告知所查三位同学中文姓名,并告其家人近况。

> 袁伯伯:

> 久未上书请安,极为歉惭! 您和袁伯母近来想一切安好,念念。

> 您所嘱查的三位同学中文姓名,另单附上,请查收。本年宾州大学的中国同学会,并不曾印名单,以致不能寄上,很抱歉。除有教授四位外,另外有几位读学位的同学,此外则是 ICA 送来短期的台湾同学为多。

> 家父母都在上海,常有信来,偶尔亦有小照。家父兴致尚高,仍旧喜欢写写诗,侄等引以为慰。以安今年改到美地质调查所工作,时间很紧,节期也未能来一聚。侄处托福粗安,守全在校工作如常,研已经三岁又十个月,入了幼儿园,和小伴们玩。

> 静妹是否仍在剑桥? 各位弟弟近况如何? 敬请著安。

> 请袁伯母安。

侄以都谨上

一九六〇,元旦

守全附候

〔University of Chicago Library, Yuan T'ung-li Papers, Box 2〕

按:"研"即任以都和孙守全的大儿子孙研(Albert),1956 年出生。

张贵永覆函先生,感谢寄赠史料并谈诸事。

> 守和先生道席:

> 顷奉手示,得悉尊况,至为欣慰。承赐寄国务院《1942 年中美关系档案》一册,尤为感激。溥心畬画送来时当为精裱,托友人寄上。兹附奉台银存款空白印□一张,存款存入凭条及取款凭条二张,如尚需要其他单据,当陆续寄上。近代史所现正赶印中苏档第一册外蒙古,不久即可问世,出书后自当寄往国会图书馆。小儿张翀现在台大四年级,今

夏毕业,尚须军训一年,1961 年方能赴美深造。世兄想已早在哈佛研究院,其成就必甚卓绝。夫人及府上想均安好。谨此,并颂道祺。

晚张贵永顿首

1960 年元旦

〔University of Chicago Library, Yuan T'ung-li Papers, Box 2〕

按:"中苏档第一册外蒙古"即《中俄关系史料:外蒙古(1917–1919)》,版权页所注为 1959 年 10 月 30 日初版。

一月四日

先生致信卫德明,请其从旁协助《新疆研究文献目录》申请美国学术团体理事会资助的亚洲研究项目。

January 4, 1960

Dear Professor Wilhelm:

Dr. C. T. Hu now at Columbia told me recently that you were very much interested in my work on Sinkiang. I am very grateful for your interest and help.

Professor George Taylor wrote me in September and suggested that I should apply for one of Asian grants sponsored by the ACLS. Accordingly, I did submit my application, but as most members do not know my previous work, I am not sure whether I could get any favorable consideration. As Professor Taylor is a busy administrator, may I ask you to give him a reminder?

As there are fifteen languages included in this bibliography, I am hoping to get Mr. Vetch interested in publishing it. It could be done much cheaper than in the United States. Your German and Chinese Dictionary is a notable work and Vetch did a good job in publishing it.

Recently I sent you some reprints which represent a small portion of a larger work which I hope to publish in the not distant future.

With best wishes and sincere greetings of the season,

Yours sincerely,

T. L. Yuan

〔University of Chicago Library, Yuan T'ung-li Papers, Box 1〕

　　按：Your German and Chinese Dictionary 即 *Deutsch-Chinesisches Wörterbuch*（《德华大辞典》），1945 年上海璧恒图书公司（Max Nößler & Co.）刊行，非魏智出版，先生记忆有误。

罗家伦覆函先生，聘先生为"国史馆"名誉采访，并请注意代购与《中华民国开国实录》与《抗战实录》相关之史料、书籍。

　　守和吾兄道鉴：

　　　　奉去年十二月十七日手书，甚为快慰！承惠示在华盛顿有关中国史料情形，并允为经常协助与指导，尤为感激！兹遵示奉聘老兄为"国史馆"名誉采访，聘书另函奉上。每月致送象征性的办公费台币伍佰元，以此在台北为代购老兄所要买的书籍寄上。（以中美币值相合计，此款微细得可笑，但亦可买些书；弟月薪连配给为一千元台币，外人听到，将以为说大谎也。一笑！）承寄出之五包书和照片，尚未收到。兹托中大旧同事招商局经理唐心一兄赴美之便带上 US $ 200（请兄写一收据以便公家存案），请先拨还代垫之 $ 32.69，余款存尊处，为以后陆续购史料之用途。《伦敦蒙难记》到后，当为重行翻译，因原译本太坏，至于当时伦敦《太晤士报》记载，望设法印或打来。照像或打字两者何择，以便于阅读与不太费钱为衡量，请代为决定。（此处尚无放 mircofilm 的阅读机，不知较简便者要多少钱，望调查见告。）因弟前曾做过一番考订工作，有新材料当然继续的做去。兄之《国父文献目录》亦望继续，当为在国内出版。说到中国史料，弟以为当注重旧书店中的旧书。"国史馆"在最近期内，以编《中华民国开国实录》与《抗战实录》二种为重心。对此二项之史料，尤望代为注意。其余"美印日本军部文档"与"詹森文档"二事，弟亦极有兴趣，因其与《抗战实录》关系至切，容下次来信再谈。专此奉候鸣谢，并颂年喜，与嫂夫人曼福！

　　　　　　　　　　　　　　　　　　　　弟罗家伦敬启

　　　　　　　　　　　　　　　　　　　　元月四日，台北

　　　　　〔University of Chicago Library, Yuan T'ung-li Papers, Box 1;《罗家伦先生文存补遗》，页 626〕

　　按：唐心一（1904—?），江苏如皋人，中央大学毕业，曾任招商局轮船股份公司主任秘书。该函为其亲笔。

先生寄送书籍和文件给罗家伦，其中有 *Kidnapped in London*（《伦敦蒙难

记》）照片两套。〔《罗家伦先生文存补遗》，页 638〕

  按：时，罗家伦在考订《伦敦蒙难记》译本与原文之间的差异，并拟将此照片附在该书重译本内。

一月六日

莫余敏卿致函先生，感谢寄赠《中国音乐书谱目录》，并表示丈夫莫泮芹在学术休假期内不拟赴台，或可前往华盛顿等东部地区。

January 6, 1960

Dear Dr. Yuan:

  Thank you very much for the copy of *Bibliography on Chinese Music* edited by you and Mr. Liang. It will be an excellent reference tool to us and to our readers particularly students and professors of our music Dept. who are interested in Chinese music. Thanks again for sending it to us.

  Mr. Mok will be on sabbatical leave next semester (see the enclosure). Since he does not want to go to Taiwan to teach, we will stay here. If our plans go well, we might go East for a few weeks. Do not be surprised, if we come to see you sometime in the Spring or Summer.

  Our Library is still running. I have requested for a special fund to purchase books. Until the request is granted, there is nothing special to report.

  Mr. Mok joins me in wishing you and Mrs. Yuan a very happy and prosperous new year.

Sincerely yours,
Man-hing Mok
〔袁同礼家人提供〕

  按：Mr. Liang 即梁在平。该函为其亲笔。

一月十二日

先生致信克莱普，再次向图书资源委员会递交出版资助申请，并表示以格雷夫斯、卜德、费正清、富路德为代表的学术界对该书的出版表示兴趣。

January 12, 1960

Dear Mr. Clapp:

  In view of the forthcoming session of the International Congress of

Orientalists to be held in Moscow in the summer, a number of Sinological scholars have urged me to publish my bibliography of *Russian Works on China* which I have been preparing for the past few years.

Although the manuscript is ready for publication, further research is still necessary. I now submit a memo setting forth the scope of this bibliography. I hope that through your sympathetic support, this application will receive due consideration from your Council.

Dr. Mortimer Graves, Professor George B. Cressey of Syracuse, Professor Derk Bodde of Pennsylvania, Professor John K. Fairbank of Harvard, Professor L. Carrington Goodrich of Columbia, Professor Herrlee G. Creel of Chicago and Professor David N. Rowe of Yale are among those who are interested in the early publication of this work. Professor Fairbank is on his way to the Far East, but all others would be glad to serve as references.

Yours sincerely,

T. L. Yuan

〔Library of Congress, Council on Library and Information Resources Records, Box 95〕

按：此件为打字稿，落款处为先生签名。该信附一页说明，包括范围、申请资助金额，于 14 日送达。翌日克莱普覆信，表示将与格雷夫斯等人讨论后再答覆。

普实克覆函先生，欣悉先生近况并愿意发表有关《西文汉学书目》的书评，告 Mattušová 女士将为先生编制捷克语中有关马可波罗的文献目录，并告苏联出版社将出版论文集，其中附有捷克斯洛伐克东方研究的参考书目，另外愿意为先生获取一套斯卡奇科夫《中国书目》。

PRAGUE, January 12, 1960

Dear Professor Yuan,

I was very pleased to receive your kind letter of November 8, 1959 and I also have to thank you very much for your important bibliography of Western literature on China which reached my hands recently. We are going to publish a review of your book in our Archiv Orientální as early as possible and will not fail to send you offprints of same.

We are trying to compile for you a bibliography of scientific contributions on Marco Polo published in Czechoslovakia. *The Millione* has been newly translated into Czech recently by Dr. Mattušová who is a specialist in Italian literature. She also has found some interesting facts about the earliest Czech translation of *Millione* which are of value for the history of the text itself. At any rate, the compilation of the bibliography required by you will take some time.

In a few months the Soviet Izdatel'stvo vostotchnoy literatury is going to publish a volume of papers written by Czechoslovak orientalists to which will be appended a bibliography of Czechoslovak oriental studies. You will find therein probably anything you might be interested in.

The only bibliography on China published in the Soviet Union known to me and to yourself is the great work of Skachkov. However, we unfortunately do not possess either the first or the new edition which has just been published. We will try to obtain a copy of it for you.

In the meantime, wishing you a good health and success in your further work, I remain, Dear Professor Yuan,

With my best greetings and regards.

Yours very sincerely,

J. Průšek

〔University of Chicago Library, Yuan T'ung-li Papers, Box 8〕

按：*The Millione* 即指《马可波罗游记》(《世界奇迹之书》)，Million 源自马可波罗的昵称 Emilione。Dr. Mattušová 即 Miroslava Mattušová(1917-?)，捷克学者、目录学家，她的《马可波罗游记》于 1961 年问世。Soviet Izdatel'stvo vostotchnoy literatury 直译作"东方文学理事会出版社"。

一月十三日

卫德明覆函先生，告知美国学术团体理事会对亚洲研究类申请的审查已于日前完成，结果即将揭晓。

13 January, 1960

Dear Mr. Yuan:

Thank you very much for your letter. The ACLS committee on Asian grants has, as far as I know, met last week so you should know pretty soon now how your application fared, if you do not know already.

As all of us here are very highly interested in seeing your bibliography finished and in print, would you please let us know how you came out?

With all my best wishes.

Sincerely yours,

Hellmut Wilhelm

〔University of Chicago Library, Yuan T'ung-li Papers, Box 1〕

按：此件为打字稿，落款处为卫德明签名。

一月十四日

格雷夫斯致函先生，对先生申请研究资助项目表示支持，并表示自己有意翻译某些俄语文献。

906 Windsor Lane

Key West

January 14, 1960

Dear T. L.,

Of course, I shall be happy to support both your projects to the best of my ability, though I am not so sure that my influence is as important as you seem to think. Of course, what I should really like to see is the publication of your bibliography, and then a small library of translations of highly selected Russian works in the field which give us information not otherwise readily available. In fact, I'd like to do one of the translations myself.

Sincerely yours

Mortimer Graves

〔University of Chicago Library, Yuan T'ung-li Papers, Box 1〕

按：此件为打字稿，落款处为其签名。

一月十五日

罗家伦致函先生,寄上"国史馆"聘书并请留意旧书店中的近代史料书刊。

　　守和吾兄道鉴:

　　　　前上一函,并托唐心一君带上美金支票二百元,为"国史馆"及党
　　史委员会购买史料书籍之用,谅荷察阅。闻兄愿屈就"国史馆"名誉
　　采访,弟无任欣慰。兹奉上聘书一份,尚祈惠纳。另有两本书,请代
　　购。弟意许多史料书在一般读者认为过时,旧书店有的是,如能与若
　　干旧书店联络,经常得其书目或报告,所得必多而廉。兄对此非常熟
　　悉,无待弟言也。匆匆,敬颂俪祺!

　　　　　　　　　　　　　　　　　　　　　　弟家伦敬启
　　　　　　　　　　　　　　　　　　　　　　一,十五

　　　　　　　　〔University of Chicago Library, Yuan T'ung-li Papers, Box 1〕

　　按:此函为罗家伦亲笔。附聘书一份,自 1960 年 1 月起,聘期暂
　　定一年。

一月二十日

先生致信莫泮芹、莫余敏卿夫妇,对西方学院给予莫泮芹的肯定和称赞表
示祝贺,并请代为寻找岭南大学校友名录,另外问询加州大学洛杉矶分校
所藏俄文书刊情况。

January 20, 1960

Dear Professor and Mrs. Mok:

　　Hearty congratulations for the distinguished honor given to you by
Occidental College. You certainly deserve it, as it is long overdue.

　　We are most happy to learn that you plan to come to the East for a
part of your sabbatical leave. It would be wonderful if your book on Sino-
American cultural relations could be published soon. We are in urgent
need of such a good treatise.

　　When you come to Washington, be sure to give us a ring. We should
like so much to see you.

　　At present I am in need of a directory of the Alumni of Lingnan
University, or a directory of the Alumni now in the United States. Is there
any way in which you could obtain a copy for me?

When I was in Los Angeles, the UCLA Library had already a good collection of Russian works. As you have added many items in recent years, I wonder how large your collection of Russian works on China is. Will you check with your curator of Russian books how many such work which you have do not appear to have been acquired by L. C. (no L. C. cards have been printed). I am only interested in those works published after 1918. If you could ask him to send me a list of those works which he thinks are not available in Washington, I shall be most grateful.

Thank you so much for the delicious oranges which you sent us. All of us enjoy them so much.

Yours sincerely,

T. L. Yuan

〔袁同礼家人提供〕

按：Occidental College 即位于洛杉矶的私立西方学院，1887 年成立，是美国西海岸历史最悠久的文理学院，莫泮芹在此执教，并曾担任历史系主任。此件为录副。

张捷迁覆函先生，告知其或将前往华盛顿，届时可以面晤，此前询问之人或为陈迪。

20 January 1960

Dear Mr. Yuan:

I have heard a lot about you during my early days and your contribution in China, and I appreciate your kind words about me and your story about our mutual friends Mr. and Mrs. Hsiung Shie-I.

I will not be in Washington D. C. for the next few months. In case I am there I will get in touch with you. I will be glad of the opportunity to meet you.

As far as the directory of Chinese students is concerned, I have requested the officials to send you a copy directly.

I am not sure when you ask about Mr. and Mrs. Chen Ling. I wonder whether you mean Mr. and Mrs. Dick Chen. They went to California, Stanford University, to finish his degree and he just came back to

Minnesota again and is appointed as assistant professor in Electrical Engineering. If you do mean then you can write directly to him.

With my best regards,

Yours sincerely,

Chieh-Chien Chang

〔University of Chicago Library, Yuan T'ung-li Papers, Box 9〕

按:张捷迁(1908—2004),辽宁开原人,气象物理学家,1927年考入东北大学预科,九一八事变后在北平工学院借读,1934年担任清华大学工程学系助教,1940年赴美留学,师从冯·卡门(Theodore von Kármán,1881–1963),1952年获得古根涵基金会资助(Guggenheim fellowship),赴英国大学讲学,1966年入选"中央研究院"院士。Dick Chen似指陈迪,1959年获得斯坦福大学博士学位,其论文题目为A study of the linear emitting-role magnetron amplifier。

一月二十四日

Frederick W. Mote覆函先生,感谢寄赠《华裔学志》所载文章抽印本。

January 24, 1960

Dear Dr. Yuan:

I note with embarrassment that I have failed to reply to your letter of 11 December, & to acknowledge the receipt of two copies of your recent article on Russian language works on China. I have found the article very useful, for although I do not read Russian, some of my students of Chinese do read Russian, & your articles is a great aid to their research, I am most grateful to you for sending it to me.

I shall pass the second copy on to Prof. Cyril Black, who teaches Russian history & who is much interested in Asian Studies.

As for the International Congress of Orientalists in Moscow, I still do not know whether I shall be going, but in any event, your article is of great interest to me, with many thanks,

Sincerely,

Fritz Mote

〔University of Chicago Library, Yuan T'ung-li Papers, Box 3〕

按：Frederick W. Mote(1922-2005)，美国汉学家，中文名牟复礼，长期执教于普林斯顿大学，专攻元、明两代历史。your recent article 即《华裔学志》第18卷所刊文章——Russian Works on China, 1918-1958 a selected bibliography。Prof. Cyril Black(1915-1989)，1939年至1986年在普林斯顿大学执教，历史和国际关系专业教授。该函为其亲笔。

一月二十六日

宋晞覆函先生，寄赠《中国文化季刊》，并告另付邮寄上新疆史料四种。

守和先生道鉴：

前奉手书，敬悉种切。陈受颐先生为尊著所撰书评已刊《中国文化季刊》二卷三期，该刊已奉赠乙册。又该刊一卷一、二两期亦于元月十三日付邮，谅二月间亦可收到。新疆书目之编撰必大助留心我国边疆问题者。兹另付印寄上此间出版之书籍四种(张大军：《新疆民族变迁及现状》；《新疆近四十年变乱纪略》。许崇灏：《新疆志略》。洪涤尘：《新疆史地大纲》。)，其余当陆续留意搜购。专此奉复，为颂撰安。

后学宋晞敬上

元，廿六

〔University of Chicago Library, Yuan T'ung-li Papers, Box 7〕

按：《中国文化季刊》即 Chinese Culture: a quarterly review，张其昀主编，1957年7月在台北创刊。《新疆民族变迁及现状》《新疆近四十年变乱纪略》1954年"中央文物供应社"初版；《新疆志略》1944年正中书局初版，《新疆史地大纲》1935正中书局初版。

一月二十八日

傅吾康覆函先生，告知其已为《西文汉学书目》撰写书评，刊登在《东亚自然和人类文化学协会简报》而非《远东》。

28 January 1960

Dear Dr. Yuan:

Many thanks for your letter dated January 8, 1960. I wrote a review of your book "*China in Western Literature*" which is going to be published in the 1959 issue of the "*Nachrichten der Gesellschaft für Natur-und Völkerkunde Ostasiens*". This issue's publication is due since a long time, but has been rather belated. I hope it will be out during the next month, and we will not fail to send you a copy.

I hope you agree that the review is published in the *"Nachrichten"* and not in the *"Oriens Extremus"* since the *Oriens Extremus* only reviews on publications in East Asian languages published in one of the East Asian countries. Volume VI, No. 2 of the *Oriens Extremus* is to come out in these days. The first number for 1960 (volume VII) is due in May or June this year.

With best wishes,

Yours sincerely,

Wolfgang Franke

P. S. Many thanks also for the bibliographies offprint of *Monumenta Serica*.

〔University of Chicago Library, Yuan T'ung-li Papers, Box 4〕

按:落款和补语皆为其亲笔。

一月二十九日

永积昭覆函先生,告知东洋文库无法寄赠前信所需书籍,并感谢赠书目。

January 29, 1960

Dear Mr. Yuan:

Thank you very much for your letter of January 16. We sought the book which you wanted to have, till I found only a copy which had been preserved for the purpose of preservation. Please excuse me that we cannot forward you three copies instead of one. But I could not help it on account of its scarcity. Though I asked some book-shops if they still keep a copy, I always got a negative answer.

I am very much delighted to know that you are sending us a copy of your bibliography which will be quite indispensable in the field of Sinology and such others.

Thank you very much again.

Yours sincerely

Akira Nagazumi

Librarian

〔University of Chicago Library, Yuan T'ung-li Papers, Box 2〕

按：永积昭（Akira Nagazumi，1929—1987），日本历史学家，专攻东南亚历史，1954 年东京大学东洋史专业毕业，时任东洋文库（Toyo Bunko）馆员。the book which you wanted to have 应指《敦煌文献研究论文目录》，1959 年东洋文库敦煌文献研究连络委员会出版，该书实应为劳榦所需，并拜托先生代为寻找，参见本年 5 月先生致劳榦信。此件为打字稿，落款处为其签名。

一月三十日

先生致信卫德明，询问有无可能将《新疆研究文献目录》作为华盛顿大学中亚研究所的项目，以利向洛克菲勒基金会等处申请资助。

January 30, 1960

Dear Professor Wilhelm:

Thank you so much for your recent letter. The ACLS has written to say that it was not possible to make a grant for my bibliography on Sinkiang. This is, of course, not unexpected, in view of its limited interest.

I believe that if the project is supported by an institute, I might try the Rockefeller Foundation, as the Foundation prefers to deal with institutions rather than with individuals. In view of the interest of your Institute in Inner Asian studies, I wonder if Professor Taylor and your other colleagues would be interested in the completion of my project. If so, I should like to say when writing to the Rockefeller Foundation that this project is to be carried on under your Institute auspices and the grant should be made to your Institute direct. I shall be obliged if you could ascertain the views of Professor Taylor and let me hear from you.

If this is not possible, I shall try other possible channels, as I hate to give up the entire project after having spent so much time and money on it.

With hearty thanks,

Yours sincerely,

T. L. Yuan

〔University of Chicago Library, Yuan T'ung-li Papers, Box 1〕

按：此件为录副。

Wolfgang Seuberlich 致函先生，感谢寄赠《华裔学志》文章抽印本，并询问一位中国学者的中文姓名。

January 30, 1960

Dear Dr. Yuan:

I thank you and Mrs. Yuan very much for your kind seasonal greetings. Moreover, I am most grateful to you for kindly sending me a copy of your very important bibliography of Russian works on China, 1918－1958. As your big bibliography *"China in Western Literature"* already is, this article, too, will become a permanent adviser and reliable friend of mine.

At this opportunity I would like to ask you for a Chinese author's name who is not included neither in *"China in Western Literature"* nor in your recent article. It is

Dapen Liang, Ph. D., the author of:

The Development of Philippine Political Parties . Printed by South China Morning Post, Hongkong, 1939.

If this author's name is included in your collection, please, be so kind as to tell me how his name is written in Chinese. Thank you.

With best wishes and kind regards, I remain,

Sincerely yours,

Wolfgang Seuberlich

〔University of Chicago Library, Yuan T'ung-li Papers, Box 4〕

按：Dapen Liang 即梁大鹏，海南乐会人，*The Development of Philippine Political Parties* 为英文本。

二月一日

先生致信格雷夫斯，寄上阿理克教授作品，并告知学术团体理事会不愿意支持此前自己递交的新疆研究计划。

February 1, 1960

Dear Dr. Graves:

Thank you so much for your recent letter and for your support of my projects.

I sent you the other day a copy of Prof. Vasily M. Alekseyev's
□□□□□□. The first illustration showing his study must be quite
familiar to you. It was in this study that I had many hours of interesting
discussion with him. As this book reminds me of my long association with
him, I trust that it would be of interest to you and that you would enjoy
reading it.

I have had word from the ACLS to the effect that it was not possible
to make the grant. This is, of course, not unexpected in view of the
limited interest in Inner Asian studies.

With all good wishes,

Yours sincerely,

T. L. Yuan

〔University of Chicago Library, Yuan T'ung-li Papers, Box 1〕

按:该件为录副,其书名处有涂抹。

范一侯覆函先生,告知所托书信已转寄凌济东。

守和先生惠鉴:

前奉元月三日手示,附下致凌济东先生之函,当即转去,尚祈释
念。凌先生已去西岸,闻约两月之后始返纽约,惟其住处(501. W.
123rd St., Apt. 10B, New York 27, N. Y. Tel M02-9012)之花草及信件,
则请同楼之李润章先生每日照料耳。

《南开校友录》拟近修订,一俟印就,当立即奉上。袁静同学住址
为:50 Mt. Vernon St. Cambridge, Mass.不识最近有无更动? 敬颂道安!

后学范一侯谨复

二,一

〔University of Chicago Library, Yuan T'ung-li Papers, Box 2〕

按:凌济东,20 世纪 20 年代在南开大学服务,后曾任驻古巴
公使。

齐如山致函先生,感谢代为影照书目并寄赠其最近著述。

守和兄鉴:

代影两种书目均接到,邮差适于除夕八点钟送到,快慰已极,谢
谢。照的非常清晰,一定要再在杂志中重行披露,并要抽印若干份,届

时定当奉上不误。惟当年《季刊》中所登《百舍斋所藏通俗小说书录》一项,文与题为两事。当时曾把小说及戏曲两种目录交与王重民君,请其改正,戏曲共四百来种,小说尚多几十种,可惜只把戏曲改正且登《季刊》,而小说登出与否,尚未得消息。此次所登者乃鄙撰《小说勾陈》,原共四十余种,北平《新民报》登了三十余种,此则只登了二十几种,盖因有几种颇为猥亵,故未登录也。然在台湾能得此,于我也有大益处了。

所云肉松一节,因适在元旦前后各物卖的很多,所存者亦是剩残之货,只好多候六七天,俟有新制成者,再寄不迟,口味比剩者总好的多。兹有影印家存《三字经》一本,特寄上二本,其余一本可送图书馆或朋友,前有序文,请一看便知其经过了,润章及元任处亦均寄去。又前者出版之《回忆录》所存无多,亦寄上一本,现又写了一本《国剧艺术汇考》,约三十万字,行将出版。现已颇觉颓唐,写东西已远不如前,且所有原料及可参考的书籍纪录都在北平,一本未能带出,真也无法写了。新年忙碌之中,却拉杂写了这么许多,书及肉松都须过几日才能付邮。先此奉闻,即颂春祺。

弟齐如山敬上
二月一日

〔University of Chicago Library, Yuan T'ung-li Papers, Box 2〕

按:"当年《季刊》"指《图书季刊》新第 8 卷第 3-4 期(1947 年 12 月),刊登《百舍斋所藏通俗小说书录》,其中"百舍斋"即齐如山藏书斋号。《国剧艺术汇考》,1962 年 1 月台北重光文艺出版社初版;《齐如山回忆录》,1956 年 4 月"中央文物供应社"初版。

二月二日

郭廷以致函先生,谈近代史研究所出版史料、申请资助等事。

守和尊兄道席:

华府拜别,瞬已年余,无时不在念中。去岁杪惠教,以辗转投递,上月中旬始行奉到,惟承赐之日本外务省及陆海军档案缩片目录,则迄未获睹。日前曾与志希先生商谈,一俟收到,再共同斟酌,分别径购。但近史所财力有限,申请结汇复极不易,恐须待至下年度矣(七月以后)。闻国会图书馆所摄是项资料,可以相当之书刊交换。如属可行,敝所愿将新近出版中俄关系史料及以后续印之其他各书寄呈,敢希便中一询,见示为祷。近史所人手不足,加之待遇菲薄,工作进行,未克尽如理想。就资料整理而言,除已刊行之海防档外,最近两年所完成者,计有一、《中法越南交涉史料(一八七五——一九一一)》,约三百余万字,今夏准备付印。二、《清季矿务档(一八六五——一九一一)》,约四百余万字,本月内付印(经费由亚洲基金会担负)。三、《中美关系史料(一七八四——一八七四)》,约一百五十余万字。四、《中俄关系史料(一九一七——一九一九)》,约五百余万字,分为六编(共九册),即俄国革命、外蒙古、中东路、东北边防、新疆边防、出兵西伯利亚,其中"外蒙古"编已于去冬印就,兹先邮奉一册就正,"中东路"编正在排版,其余四编之印刷经费,尚待设法。在进行中之工作,有《近代中国之西方认识(一八二一——一九二七)》,分为八辑,本年七月,可望完成第一辑(一八二一——一八六一);有《清季教务及教案(一八六〇——一九一一)》,本年七月,可望完成同治朝前期之部;有民国史口述,系分别访问军政元老,预计五十余人,已接洽及开始谈话者,有何成濬、莫德惠、赵恒惕、秦德纯、傅秉常等十余位。目前之最大困难,为同人之生活问题,上月曾函商福特及洛氏基金会并提具计划,请予协助,恐亦不易获得满意结果,甚望能得长者一言为重,便中代向该两基金会吹嘘,成与不成,均所感激。吾人所求,极为有限,每年如能有一万元以上之补助,裨益已屡不鲜。过去华盛顿大学每年资助近史所仅四千元,今年起,已告中止矣。郭鸿声先生乃弟之恩师,想常晤及,可否代为致意,亦请从旁为助之处,尚希卓裁。谨此,祗颂福绥!

弟廷以拜启

二、二

府上均好。

　　《俄人研究中国文献》一书前日邮到,谢谢。又及。

〔University of Chicago Library, Yuan T'ung-li Papers, Box 2〕

　　按:郭鸿声即郭秉文(1880—1969),江苏江浦人,1947年留居美国,后在美组织"中美文化协会",时任会长。

二月三日

格雷夫斯覆函先生,感谢寄赠书籍,并愿意就先生的研究计划向福特基金会询问有无资助可能。

February 3, 1960

Dear T. L.

What a gracious, thoughtful thing to do! I received the book yesterday—before your letter—and read the introduction and the first couple of pages as well as scanning through the whole thing. I am sure that I shall enjoy it, save that it will recall happy days that can never return.

I wonder if we couldn't give your bibliography more appeal to the foundation if we thought of it as the first step in getting some of the translation of the Russian contribution to study of the Far East made. This is what I have said in the couple of letters that I have written about it. Do you have any very definite ideas about any items—perhaps especially with respect to Western China and Central Asia—which are so important that they simply demand translation into one of the western languages? The Ford Foundation is sending a man down here to Key West on February 24 to discuss several matters with me, and I should not have the slightest objection to bringing up a question in this area if that seems to have any promise. Of course, I cannot promise anything; it may only be that some character in the Ford Foundation wants an excuse for spending a few days down here in the midst of the New York's worse winter. But I'd be glad to try.

Sincerely

Mortimer Graves

〔University of Chicago Library, Yuan T'ung-li Papers, Box 1〕

　　按:此件为打字稿,落款处为其签名。

二月六日

张贵永致函先生,请为夫人纪凝娴在美谋职。

守和先生道席:

　　久未奉候,想尊体清健,阖府迪吉,为慰为颂。兹有恳者,内子在西雅图攻读图书馆学多年,将于今夏卒业,无意返台,拟在美找寻职业,苦无门径,未识尊处尚有一枝可栖否? 素仰先生道德学问,为世

□□，必能启发后学，□□提携则感德无涯矣。谨此，并颂著祺。

后学张贵永顿首

二月六日

夫人均此道候。

〔University of Chicago Library, Yuan T'ung-li Papers, Box 2〕

　　按：本年夏天，先生多方致信为纪凝娴谋求图书馆职位。我妻荣覆函先生，就此前寄来的书目加以补充并作订正，此外不建议在日本出版这类目录，或可考虑联系美国高校的日本研究中心。

February 6, 1960

Dear Mr. Yuan:

Thank you very much for your letter of December 8, 1959.

Other than those mentioned in your letter, I have written an article in English:

Post-War Agricultural Land Reform in Japan (Atti del Primo Convegno Internazionale di Diritto Agrario vol. 1, 1954)

I suppose that "materials for seminar on the law of Japan for the third summer workshops for international legal studies" mentioned in your letter are those which were published not in Tokyo but in Berkeley, California as the "Part II" and Part IIA" of the whole materials for that summer workshops.

I have not published materials for the fourth or fifth summer workshops.

As for publishing the bibliography you are compiling, I am afraid it would not be easy to do it in Japan, unless you find some fund for publication. As you would certainly know, this type of publication, though academically invaluable, does not pay on commercial basis. And moreover, it would almost be impossible in Japan to get some fund to supplement publication costs. Would it not be advisable to publish it in the States? For instance, Center for Japanese Studies at University of Michigan or at University of California, Berkeley, might be interested.

With warmest regards,

Sincerely,

Sakae Wagatsuma

〔University of Chicago Library, Yuan T'ung-li Papers, Box 6〕

二月九日

先生覆信郭廷以,请寄上近代史研究所申请书副本,以便在美从旁鼓吹。

　　廷以先生大鉴:

　　　　奉到手教,欣悉所务进行顺利,只以限于经费,未能积极发展。弟
　　极愿从旁协助,已请此间学术界闻人 Dr. Mortimer Graves 力为吹嘘,
　　以期早日实现。渠愿得贵所申请书复本,以便进言时更为具体,即希
　　于日内航邮寄下。因下月两基金会均在纽约开会,必须于开会前提出
　　也。余俟再陈,顺颂时祉。

　　　　　　　　　　　　　　　　　　　　　　　　弟袁同礼顿首
　　　　　　　　　　　　　　　　　　　　　　　　　二月九日

　　　　日本海陆空军档案缩印本目录已由杨觉勇先生赠送贵所一份,于
　　上月交邮寄上。

　　　　　　　　〔台北"中央研究院"近代史研究所档案馆,〈郭廷以〉,馆藏号
　　　　　　　　069-01-02-089〕

　　　　按:杨觉勇(John Young,1920—2013),生于天津,日本问题专家,
　　　　早年赴日留学,1946 年担任赴联合国中国代表团远东委员会委
　　　　员,负责研究日本战后重建设计,1956 年获约翰·霍普金斯大学
　　　　博士,时在夏威夷大学任教。郭廷以在信封正面标注"2,16 已
　　　　复"。

二月十二日

先生致信格雷夫斯,建议其翻译一本关于新疆的俄文著作,并请从旁推动
台北近代史研究所向福特基金会和洛克菲勒基金会申请资助用以出版近
代档案史料。

February 12, 1960

Dear Dr. Graves:

　　So delighted to have your recent letter. One of the Russian works on
Sinkiang which should be translated is the following:

　　Babkov, Ivan Fedorovich: *Vospominaniia omoei sluzhbie v Zapadnoi*
　　Sibiri, 1859-1875. St. Petersburg, 1912. x, 579.

It contains all essential information how thousands of miles of Chinese territory were ceded to Russia in those years. It coincides with the Chinese records printed in the series of diplomatic documents.

Your effort in reprinting Skachkov's bibliography and in translating Romanov's *Russia in Manchuria* had won the gratitude of all scholars. If this effort could be continued, my two bibliographies could serve as useful guides.

You probably know that three years ago, the archives in " the Chinese Ministry of Foreign Affairs" were transferred to the Institute of Modern History, "Academia Sinica", at Taipei, Taiwan. The Institute has published two series, (1) Coastal defense and (2) Sino-Russian relations. The other series to be printed are Sino-French negotiations regarding Indo-China, Sino-American relations, 1784 – 1874, Sino-British relations, etc.

The opening of the archives and the subsequent publication of source materials are great events. In order to hasten the early publication of these sources, the Institute has applied for a grant from the Ford Foundation and the Rockefeller Foundation. If you see their representatives, may I request that you urge favorable consideration of this request?

I think you would agree with me that in view of the uncertainties of the international situation, early publication is most desirable. You may recall that if we did not publish the I-Wu-Shih-Mo before the Japanese invasion in 1931, it could remain in manuscript even by this time.

Shall send you more titles from time to time.

Yours sincerely,

〔University of Chicago Library, Yuan T'ung-li Papers, Box 1〕

按：Babkov, Ivan Fedorovich 即 Бабков, Иван Фёдорович（1827-1905），即本谱先生与郭廷以等人通信中的"巴布阔福"，俄罗斯步兵上将，外交家和地理学家，1864 年代表沙俄和清政府签订了《中俄勘分西北界约记》，割占了中国西北边疆大片领土；*Vospominaniia amoei sluzhbie v Zapadnoi Sibiri* 即本谱下文中的

《巴布阔福回忆录》，但此处转写似有错误。Romanov 即 Романов, Борис Александрович（Boris Aleksandrovich Romanov, 1889-1957），苏俄历史学家；*Russia in Manchuria*：1892-1906，今一般译为《俄国在满洲》。此件为底稿。

二月十三日

先生致信罗家伦，告收到友人携带购书款，并请将办公费送交张贵永。大意如下：

> 承聘名誉采访，至感厚意。收到一月四日及十五日二函及唐心一携来二百元。一月至六月收据，先随函附上，请以一千五百元径送张桂永。余款、伦敦《泰晤士报》及《国父信札》另交邮寄上，可与《伦敦蒙难记》同时印出。新法 Xerox，Microfilm 阅览机 500 左右，可暂缓。

〔University of Chicago Library, Yuan T'ung-li Papers, Box 1〕

按："张桂永"即张贵永。此件非底稿，实为摘要性质。

二月十五日

卫德明覆函先生，已将申请意向函转交该校中亚研究计划主管。

15 February 1960

Dear Dr. Yuan:

Thank you very much for your letter of January 30. As I wrote you before, we are very much interested in having your bibliography finished and published. I have handed on your letter to Robert Ekvall who at present chairs out Inner Asia Project. He will contact you directly on this matter.

Sincerely yours,

Hellmut Wilhelm

〔University of Chicago Library, Yuan T'ung-li Papers, Box 1〕

按：Rober Ekvall 即 Robert B. Ekvall（1898-1983），美国传教士、人种学家，出生于甘肃岷县，父母为美国基督教宣道会（Christian and Missionary Alliance）传教士，曾在西藏地区传教，后随母亲回美国，进入惠顿高中（Wheaton Academy）、惠顿学院（Wheaton College），此后长期在中国阿坝地区传教并从事人类学研究，1944年回到美国在军队服务，时任西雅图华盛顿大学中亚研究项目主席。此件为打字稿，落款处为其签名。

二月十六日

郭廷以覆函先生，谈近代史研究所申请洛克菲勒、福特基金事。

> 守和先生道席：
>
> 　　二月九日大教奉悉，至感厚谊。福特及洛氏基金会已均有覆信，反应尚佳，惟尚无具体表示。洛氏代表 Compton 及福特代表 Everton 等，将分于四月及九月再度来台访问。兹将近史所上月提交两基金会计划复本邮呈就正，并请转 Graves 先生等一阅。如能于两基金会下月会议期间获得批准，当即积极准备。谨再谢。
>
> 　　又承赐日本海陆军档案缩片目录，亦已收到，请释念，并代向杨觉勇先生致意。《中俄关系史料》第二册（中东路）下月内出版，容续呈。第三、四册正在排印中。谨此，敬颂道安！
>
> 弟廷以拜上
二月十六日
>
> 〔University of Chicago Library, Yuan T'ung-li Papers, Box 2〕

按：Compton 即 Boyd R. Compton，1946 年毕业于普林斯顿大学，后在洛克菲勒基金会人文和社科部任职，曾任法斯的助手。[1] Everton 应指 John S. Everton（1908-2003），美国学者、外交官，后曾担任美国驻缅甸大使。

二月十八日

先生致信斯坦福大学图书馆参考部，为"国史馆"申请复制该馆所藏《国父信札》。

February 18, 1960

Reference Librarian

Stanford University Library

Stanford, Calif.

Dear Sir:

　　The late Dr. van Patten published in 1943-44 *The TEN LETTERS FROM SUN YAT-SUN*. Two or more copies are on file in your Library.

---

[1] *The Rockefeller Foundation Annual Report for 1964*, p. xi；《夏志清夏济安书信集》卷 4，页 86。

As I have not been able to obtain a copy for the Academia Historica at Taipei, may I request you to make duplicate copy by the xerox process (cheaper than photostat)?

Please mail it to the following address:

Academia Historica

Attention: Dr. C. L. Lo

2 Peking Road

Taipei, Taiwan

The bill is to be made out in the name of the academy and sent to me for payment.

Yours sincerely,

T. L. Yuan

〔University of Chicago Library, Yuan T'ung-li Papers, Box 1〕

按：*The Ten Letters of Sun Yat-Sen*，1942 年影印，限量一百册。先生致信克莱普，递交*Russian Works on China* 出版资助预算。

February 18, 1960

Dear Mr. Clapp:

Referring to my request for a grant from your Council, I am now able to submit an estimate for the printing of my bibliography *Russian Works on China, 1917-1959.*

In comparing the estimates from various publishers, the one from Far Eastern Publications of Yale University seem to be most reasonable. A subsidy of $650 is required for the printing of 500 copies (paper cover) plus $50 for Chinese characters, provided the manuscript is typed and proof-read in Washington. The following is an approximate cost of the project:

Subsidy to publisher	$ 650
Chinese characters	50
Typing	350- 400
Research and clerical assistance including proofreading and	

indexing	750- 700
Travel	200
Total	$ 2000

I trust that before making any decision, your Council may like to have these figures. In view of the need for such a bibliography, I hope I may hear from you before very long.

Yours sincerely,

T. L. Yuan

〔Library of Congress, Council on Library and Information Resources Records, Box 95〕

按:2 月 24 日,克莱普覆函先生表示会尽快将结果告知先生。Heinrich Busch 致函先生,附上额外 25 份抽印本及相关邮费的账单,并告知接受先生稿件 Russian works on Japan,拟于《华裔学志》第 19 卷刊发。

February 18, 1960

Dear Mr. Yuan:

Enclosed in this letter please find the bill for excess (over 25) offprints and postage of your bibliography of Russian works on China. For the shipment to America, we have charged the cost of ordinary mail. The cost of air mail by which it was actually sent amounted to Yen 29, 250. The printing company was kind enough to share the difference with us.

I am glad you are satisfied with the way your bibliography was published. As I wrote you at the time offprints which you wanted to be sent to addresses in East Asia were mailed from here. We are sending you, by ordinary mail, acknowledgments of receipts sent to us. Some more may have been sent to you directly.

With regard to your new bibliography of Russian works on Japan I first had some misgivings whether we should accept your offer to publish it in our journal. Out of consideration for the *Monumenta Nipponica* of the Jesuit Fathers in Tokyo we do not, as a rule, publish papers on Japan

unless China or Chinese sources are involved. Since, however, your
bibliography is a counterpart to the one already published in *Monumenta
Serica* we are willing to accept it for publication. We plan to go to press
with the next issue sometime during summer.

Sincerely yours,

H. Busch, S. V. D.

〔University of Chicago Library, Yuan T'ung-li Papers, Box 7〕

按:Heinrich Busch(1912-2002),德国圣言会神父,1939 年来华,
在山东地区传教,1954 年起任 *Monumenta Serica*(《华裔学志》)
主编。[①] your new bibliography of Russian works 即 Russian Works
on Japan: a selected bibliography,共收录书目词条 221 项,分为 15
类,另附索引。*Monumenta Nipponica* 其汉文名称为《日本文化志
丛》,由上智大学出版发行,应于 1938 年创刊。

二月十九日

先生致信李书华,请其协助查明两位哥伦比亚大学物理博士的中文姓名。

润章先生著席:

年杪在纽匆匆一晤,次日本拟走访,适因印书事赴新港接洽,以致
未果,下次再来当再趋教。兹因拙编之《留美博士论文目录》即将付
印共收四千余人,查出姓名者将及四千人,内中尚有哥大研究物理者二人之中
文姓名尚未查出,因念 1953 年左右台端适在哥大研究,想能记忆,如
承指示,至为感幸。顺颂著祺。

尊夫人同此问好。

弟同礼顿首

二,十九

内人附笔致意

〔Columbia University Libraries Archival Collections, Shuhua Li
Papers, 1926-1972, Volume II: Modern Eminent Chinese Leaders〕

按:"共收四千余人",《中国留美同学博士论文目录》实际收录的

---

① Malek, Roman. "In Memoriam: Heinrich Busch (1912-2002) Und Eugen Feifel (1902-1999)."
Monumenta Serica, vol. 54, 2006, pp. 491-508.

人数只有 2799。[①]

Robert B. Ekvall 覆函先生,告知美国学术团体理事会不支持新疆研究文献目录的编纂计划,该校远东和苏俄研究中心愿意提供必要的支持。

February 19, 1960

Dear Dr. Yuan:

As has been previously indicated, we here of the Inner Asia Research Project of the Far Eastern Institute consider your bibliography project a most important one with particular bearing on the area of our primary interest. We regret to hear that the ACLS did not see fit to give you the necessary grant and wish you all success as you take your request elsewhere.

Dr. Taylor, Director of the Institute, has seen your letter and has authorized me to assure you that we will be glad to give you whatever backing is necessary, and, if so desired, act as sponsors and provide whatever supervision is needed.

Please keep us informed of developments and be assured of our best wishes for success.

Sincerely yours,

Robert B. Ekvall, Chairman

Inner Asia Research Project

〔University of Chicago Library, Yuan T'ung-li Papers, Box 1〕

按:此件为打字稿,落款处为其签名。

图齐致函先生,感谢寄赠《西文汉学书目》,表示有兴趣出版《马可波罗书目》,请寄来说明或书稿。

19 Feb. 1960

Dear Professor Yuan,

I have learned with great pleasure, from Prof. Lanciotti, that you will be so good as to send me your valuable *"China in Western Literature"*. The work has real interest for me, and from this moment I thank you for

---

① 此数目不包括获得名誉博士之人,特此说明。

your kindness.

I am also aware that, during my absence due to our archaeological campaigns in Asia, you have kindly written to the Institute, informing them that you had completed your *"Polian bibliography"*. We would be interested in the publication, so that I would request you to supply me with precise indications of the work, or perhaps you would prefer kindly sending me text. I shall be awaiting for your courteous reply, thanking you in advance for your much appreciated co-operation in the field of Polian studies, to which we attach great importance, owing to their deep significance in the frame of cultural exchanges between East and West.

With beat regards, and all good wishes for your activities, I remain,

Yours sincerely,

Giuseppe Tucci

〔袁同礼家人提供〕

按：Lanciotti 即 Lionello Lanciotti（1925-2015），意大利汉学家。

二月二十日

何炳棣覆函先生，告加拿大不列颠哥伦比亚大学东亚馆藏筹备迟缓亟待聘请专业人员负责，并谈哥伦比亚大学（纽约）欲请其回校执教。

守和先生赐鉴：

惠书今晨敬悉。拙著人口多蒙过奖，至感且愧。年前曾由 L. C. 转呈明清 *Social Mobility* 单行本请正，想亦邀尊教，现后者专书初稿甫毕，正在重新修正打字中。

敝校中日文图书方面专任负责人之聘，实已达无可再拖阶段，惟目前尚无法决定。盖年前香港大学圕主任 Mrs. Dorothea Scott 曾推荐伊之左右手广东小姐 Ng（中文姓氏不详）者，系冯平山馆主持人，二年前曾得加拿机补助来美深造考察。此位小姐坚持携母同来，据云已为此邦移民部所拒，但敝校圕主任 Neal Harlow 先生最近已托本省大有力者某公向移民部长亲自疏通，如再被拒，晚拟与王伊同兄正式向校方提出立即聘请专家一位（两位似目前决无可能），最好能稍通日文，至于地位及待遇一层，此刻颇难预料，惟资历相当想可能博——部主任，薪水当不难在 6000 与 6500 之间。另外有其他种种福利条款（本校一向每年扣教职员薪水 5%，另由校方出 10% 作为强迫养老金，另由校方津贴医药人寿保险，再另加本省之 free hospitalization，似亦不为过薄）。一俟鄂大瓦具体回示达到，即飞函请代为推荐。

魏尔博氏彬彬君子，对先生素所敬仰，与晚和交亦笃，五月间晚将东行，在纽约小住两月，或过华府翻明版，届时当与面谈。如先生欲早日得一谅解，乞示，晚当即专函代洽。尊目之学术价值，自尽人皆知，无待赘述者也。

哥大下年远东语系将有剧变，何、魏两公似将尽力拉晚返哥大，惟晚一向以西史标准治史，克己克人是否能为该系所容，殊不容过分乐观。好在最终决定操诸副校长、研院长及若干资历最深之教授，皆深知客观世界治史标准者，虽然如此，晚亦非以退为进不可。拙著人口既出，在美师友辈或因精力衰退，或因种种原因，尚无意撰评。而 *London Times* 于本月十二日 Leading editorial 已根据拙作之第十章有所发扬，相形之下不无感慨，其他若干远东界外文一等学术期刊似皆在物色书评人选中，知晚者其西洋史学家乎，一叹。以上乞勿示人为祷。肃此，敬请撰安。

袁太太乞代致候。

晚炳棣敬叩

1960 年二月廿日

〔University of Chicago Library, Yuan T'ung-li Papers, Box 2〕

按："拙著人口"即 *Studies on the Population of China 1368-1953*，1959 年哈佛大学出版社初版；"明清 Social Mobility 单行本"即 Aspects of Social Mobility in China, 1368-1911（论文），刊于 *Comparative Studies in Society and History* 第 1 卷第 4 期，"后者专书初稿"则指 *The Ladder of Success in Imperial China: aspects of social mobility, 1368-1911*（《明清社会史论》）。"广东小姐 Ng"即伍冬琼（1919—2014, Tung King Ng），香港大学中文系毕业，1956 年接替陈君葆担任冯平山图书馆馆长，刘国蓁亦在其下任职，1960 年底被聘为加拿大不列颠哥伦比亚大学东亚图书馆馆长。"鄂大瓦"即渥太华（Ottawa）。"魏尔博"应指韦慕庭；"何公"即何廉。"*London Times* 于本月十二日 Leading editorial 已根据拙

作之第十章有所发扬”, 应为何炳棣好友郝桑寄来。^① 事实上, 何炳棣并未前往纽约执教, 而是 1962 年应芝加哥大学之聘。

二月二十三日

先生致信法斯, 向洛克菲勒基金会申请资助《新疆研究文献目录》的编纂计划, 并拟将该计划隶属于华盛顿大学远东和苏俄研究中心。

February 23, 1960

Dear Dr. Fahs:

　　In view of the Foundation's interest in the promotion of studies on neglected areas, I beg to apply for a grant-in-aid of $5000 for completion of a comprehensive bibliography on Sinkiang. For your reference, I enclose herewith a memorandum setting forth the scope and significance of this project.

　　In the course of one year, I have already collected much material buried in journals and scientific publications. Although immense amount of labor is involved, the completion of the task would greatly stimulate further studies on a sensitive area which, as you realize, is destined to play an important role in the geopolitics of Asia.

　　As my work is closely related to the teaching and research program at the University of Washington, Dr. George E. Taylor has authorized me to state that all members of his Inner Asia Research Project consider my bibliography a most important one with particular bearing on the area of their primary interest. The Far Eastern Institute stands ready to sponsor this project and to provide necessary supervision. If it would be possible for you to recommend favorable action, may I suggest that the grant be made to the Institute to which I shall submit periodically reports of the progress of my editorial work.

　　There does not seem to have any difficulty in publishing this bibliography. Both the Far Eastern Publications at Yale and the University of Hong Kong Press would be interested in sponsoring its publication. It is my hope that through your encouragement, an apparatus for advanced

---

① 何炳棣著《读史阅世六十年》, 商务印书馆(香港)有限公司, 2019 年, 页 314。

study will be made available to a wider circle of scholars.

Sincerely yours,

T. L. Yuan

〔University of Chicago Library, Yuan T'ung-li Papers, Box 1〕

按:3 月 3 日,该基金会人文部副主任 Boyd R. Compton 致函先生,告知收到申请书,并将妥善考虑。此件为录副。

二月二十四日

先生致信 Robert B. Ekvall,告知已向洛克菲勒基金会递交了正式申请,并将《新疆研究文献目录》的范围扩大到中文和日文,希望戴德华能够写推荐信给洛克菲勒基金会。

February 24, 1960

Dear Dr. Ekvall:

I am much obliged to you for your letter of February 19 informing me that your Institute is now ready to sponsor my project on bibliographical guide to the literature on Sinkiang. With your assurance, I have submitted an application to the Rockefeller Foundation. A copy of my letter is enclosed herewith for your file.

When I applied for ACLS grant, my project was limited to Russian and Western literature on Sinkiang. Now I have included Chinese and Japanese literature on the subject and have enlarged the scope to a considerable extent. My bibliography on Chinese literature will be annotated for the convenience of western scholars. To those who have not gone through this difficult task, the compilation of bibliographies is an easy task. If it is intended to be a standard work of reference, high quality of work requires time, energy, and scholarship.

Before I receive another negative answer like the one I received from the ACLS, I would strongly urge Dr. Taylor to follow up a letter to the Rockefeller Foundation if he sees fit. Please thank him for me for his interest and valuable help.

I have read your works on the Kansu-Tibetan border while in China, I recall that when they were published during the War, I ordered some twenty copies for distribution to Chinese libraries. I should like so much to meet you if I come to Seattle after the grant is made.

Yours sincerely,

T. L. Yuan

〔University of Chicago Library, Yuan T'ung-li Papers, Box 1〕

按：此件为录副。

普实克致函先生，寄上波希米亚地区出版的有关马可波罗书目，并告将刊登有关《西文汉学书目》的书评。

PRAGUE, February 24, 1960

Dear Professor Yuan,

Referring to my letter of January 12, 1960, I am very pleased to be able to send you enclosed the promised bibliography on Marco Polo in Bohemia.

The list was compiled by Dr. Miroslava Mattušová, of the Cabinet for Modern Philology, Czechoslovak Academy of Sciences, Prague I., Liliov 13. As you see, the same is very detailed and you will probably not be interested in all the items, but it will surely be best if you make your choice personally.

We have translated the titles of the books mentioned in the list in order to make them more accessible for you, but should you need more explanations, please do not hesitate to let me know your enquiries and we will try to do our best in the matter. Your valuable bibliography will be reviewed in our journal *Archiv Orientální*.

We have not yet obtained the bibliography of Skachkov, but we shall not fail to mail it to you as soon as we shall secure a copy.

In the meantime, I remain, Dear Professor Yuan,

Yours very sincerely,

J. Průšek

〔University of Chicago Library, Yuan T'ung-li Papers, Box 8〕

二月二十七日

先生致信格雷夫斯，请其支持郭廷以（近代史研究所）向福特基金会、洛克菲勒基金会申请资助。

February 27, 1960

Dear Dr. Graves:

When I learned that the Institute of Modern History, "Academia Sinica", at Taipei, is applying for a research grant from the Ford Foundation and the Rockefeller Foundation, I wrote to Mr. Ting-Yee Kuo to the effect that although you have retired, you still take great interest in the promotion of historical studies. I told him that if he would send you a copy of his letter to this foundation, he could count on your moral support.

I am enclosing herewith copies of these letters for your information. After you have seen them, you would be in a better position to judge the merit of the application. If you could lend your support, I am sure all sinological scholars will feel grateful.

Yours sincerely,

T. L. Yuan

〔University of Chicago Library, Yuan T'ung-li Papers, Box 1〕

二月二十九日

先生致信赖肖尔,向哈佛燕京学社申请资助用以出版日本法律及司法机构书目。

February 29, 1960

Professor Edwin O. Reischauer, Director

Harvard-Yenching Institute

Cambridge 38, Massachusetts

Dear Professor Reischauer:

When my bibliography on Japanese law and legal institutions was ready for publication, Professor David N. Rowe and Professor Earl Swisher, former representatives in the Orient of the Asia Foundation, suggested that I should request that Foundation for a grant for its publication. Dr. Rabinowitz of the Harvard Law School asked me to approach the Center for Japanese Studies at Michigan.

Having failed to get a favorable response, I wrote to Professor

Wagatsuma asking him to ascertain the views of the editor of *Monumenta Nipponica*. His reply together with others are enclosed herewith for your information.

The bibliography, compiled primarily for my own use, was a labor of love. Those who have seen the manuscript and those with whom I corresponded feel that it would be an indispensable tool of reference not only to students of comparative law, but also to scholars engaged in East Asiatic studies.

Consisting more than 2000 items (mostly articles buried in journals) in the major languages of the West, it is an exhaustive piece of research. As much material is not found in Professor Hugh Borton's Selected List, it would serve as a useful supplement if it could be published.

In view of your interest in the development of Japanese institutions, I wonder if it would be possible for you to recommend for a grant from your Trustees. Any of the following agencies would be glad to publish it, provided a subsidy of $ 750 is given:

1.Far Eastern Publications, Yale University

2.Parker School of Comparative Law, Columbia University

3.American Journal of Comparative Law, University of Michigan.

I shall be grateful if I could count on your support. Aside from the question of a possible grant, may I request you to be good enough to honor me with a Foreword. I shall be glad to send you the manuscript if you would let me know.

With cordial regards,

Yours sincerely,

T. L. Yuan

〔University of Chicago Library, Yuan T'ung-li Papers, Box 6〕

按：Edwin O. Reischauer(1910-1990)，生于东京，美国历史学家、日本问题专家，通译作"赖肖尔"，时任哈佛燕京学社第二任社长。Earl Swisher，1956 年至 1958 年担任亚洲基金会驻台代表。Hugh Borton(1903-1995)，美国历史学家，专攻日本史，Selected

List 应指 *A Selected List of Books and Articles on Japan* , 1954 年出版。

Robert B. Ekvall 覆函先生, 告知戴德华已经授权该研究中心致信法斯, 表示支持先生编纂《新疆研究文献目录》计划。

Feb. 29, 1960

Dear Dr. Yuan:

Thank you for your letter of Feb. 24th with the copy of your letter and proposal which you sent to the Rockefeller Foundation.

Upon authorization from Dr. Taylor, I have just written Dr. Fahs to assure him that we heartily endorse your request for a grant and will be glad to assume responsibility for any help and supervision that may be deemed desirable. Late, should it prove necessary, Dr. Taylor himself will back this up.

I look forward with keen anticipation to meeting you for I have heard much about your work.

I do hope that this attempt to find financial support for your project will be successful.

With very best wishes,

Yours sincerely,

Robert B. Ekvall, Chairman

Inner Asia Research Project

〔University of Chicago Library, Yuan T'ung-li Papers, Box 1〕

按: 此件为打字稿, 落款处为其签名。

三月三日

柳无忌致函先生, 请为胡昌度主编的新书撰写书评文章。

3 March 1960

Dear Dr. Yuan:

A few days ago, I asked our office to send you a complimentary copy of *China: its people, its society, its culture* , the newest volume in the Survey of World Cultures series published by HRAF. As you will see, this is the final result of HRAF's program directed by C. T. Hu. At present we are not doing anything on this area but hope to return to it if the plan to compile an outline of the peoples and cultures of Eurasia will come through.

In regard to the China volume, both C. T. and I sincerely hope that you will find time to read it and to write a review for the Library of Congress publications or any other scholarly journal. Any comment or criticism by such an outstanding scholar as you will be greatly appreciated here.

With warm personal greetings to you and Mrs. Yuan.

Sincerely yours,

Wu-chi Liu

〔University of Chicago Library, Yuan T'ung-li Papers, Box 3〕

按：HRAF 即 Human Relations Area Files，由耶鲁大学倡议成立，并由芝加哥大学、哈佛大学、科罗拉多大学、普林斯顿大学、华盛顿大学等十五所大学加盟的人文社科研究机构。*China: its people, its society, its culture* 一般译作《中国之人民、社会、文化》，1960 年 HRAF 初版。

Julius P. Barclay 覆函先生，告知斯坦福大学将寄赠"国史馆"、先生各一册《国父信札》复印本。

March 3, 1960

Dear Mr. Yuan:

Thank you for your letter of February 18. A Xerox copy of our polished volume *The Ten Letters of Sun Yat-Sen* will be mailed to Dr. Lo in the near future. Please accept the copy as a gift from the Stanford University Libraries. Please let us know if we can be of any further help.

Sincerely yours,

Julius P. Barclay

Librarian, Division of Special Collections.

〔University of Chicago Library, Yuan T'ung-li Papers, Box 1〕

三月七日

先生致信北达科他州大学图书馆参考馆员 Evelyn Swenson，询问前信中提到博士论文的页码。

March 7, 1960

Dear Miss Swenson:

Thank you so much for your letter of March 2 giving me the desired information.

May I trouble you once more to check the number of typewritten leaves of each of the dissertations listed in your letter. If you could drop me a card, I shall be most grateful.

Yours sincerely,

T. L. Yuan

〔袁同礼家人提供〕

按：此件为打字稿，落款处为先生签名。该片右下方有两处铅笔标记，分别为 J1951/C36 124p，J1952/C45，115p。

三月八日

先生致信卜德，请其联系赖肖尔支持自己向哈佛燕京学社申请出版资助。

March 8, 1960

Dear Professor Bodde:

Last November you were kind enough to give support to my bibliography of "Russian Works on China". The SSRC had notified me that it was not possible to make a grant. This is, of course, not unexpected in view of the keen competition among the applicants.

While it would mean a considerable delay in its publication, I am still continuing the work by keeping it current. I hope that when there is a sufficient interest in the future, other sources of support may be explored.

Another small project of mine—a Bibliography on Japanese Law and Legal Institutions—is ready for publication. Although the work is academically important as stated by Professor Wagatsuma, no publisher would like to publish it without a subsidy. I enclose herewith copy of my recent letter to Professor Edwin O. Reischauer which is self-explanatory.

Although it involves only a small sum and although he may be interested in its publication, some of the Trustees may not agree with him.

I thought that if a distinguished scholar like yourself would write to him to support it, it would strengthen his position. May I therefore count on your moral support?

Professor Hugh Borton's Selected List of Books and Articles on Japan lists 50 items in the field of law, to keep proper balance with other sections of the List. In my bibliography there are over 2000 entries in western languages (English, French, German, Russian and Italian) published between the years 1879 and 1959. If it could be published, it would be a useful tool to all students of Oriental studies.

With many thanks,

Yours sincerely,

T. L. Yuan

P. S. You are the only person I am asking to write such a letter.

〔University of Chicago Library, Yuan T'ung-li Papers, Box 6〕

按:此件为录副。

三月十日

先生致信 George L. Anderson,推荐张贵永到堪萨斯大学历史系执教。

March 10, 1960

Dear Professor Anderson:

My friend Dr. Hsin-pao Chang told me that you have been looking for one who is qualified to give courses on Far Eastern history. I hope that by this time you might have found the right person.

In case you have not obtained the services of a trained historian, I would like to suggest that you contact Professor Chang Kuei-yung, Department of History, Taiwan University, Taipei, Taiwan, who would be interested in helping to build up your Far Eastern Department. I enclose a card showing his thesis submitted at Berlin in 1934. Since then he has been teaching both European and Far Eastern history in various Chinese universities.

If you wish to have more information about him, you may write to Professor Earl Swisher, Department of History, University of Colorado, and to Professor David N. Rowe, Department of Political Science, Yale University.

I studied history under Professor Carlton Hayes at Columbia in 1920-22. While in China, I read with much interest your book:*Issues and Conflicts; studies in twentieth century American diplomacy*. Although I have not had the pleasure of meeting you, I feel that we already have much common interest. I visited your University some years ago and I feel certain that under your direction, your History department is already well staffed.

Yours sincerely,

T. L. Yuan

〔University of Chicago Library, Yuan T'ung-li Papers, Box 6〕

按:George L. Anderson(1905-1971),美国历史学家,1945 年执教堪萨斯大学历史系,1949 年至 1968 年担任该系主任。Dr. Hsin-pao Chang 即张馨保(1922—1965),天津人,1946 年毕业于燕京大学新闻学专业,后在《大公报》编辑部工作,1958 年获哈佛大学博士学位,导师为费正清,时应在爱荷华州立大学执教。Carlton J. H. Hayes(1882-1964),美国历史学家,外交官,曾担任美国历史学会会长。

三月十六日

先生覆信普实克,感谢 Mattušová 编制捷克有关马可波罗的文献,并请协助订购斯卡奇科夫《中国书目》。

March 16, 1960

Dear Professor Prusek:

I am most grateful to you for your letters of January 12 and February 24, and for the bibliography of Czech works on Marco Polo which Dr. Mattušová has so kindly prepared for me. It is a scholarly piece of research and I owe her a deep debt of gratitude for her valuable help. Will you kindly convey my hearty thanks?

Thank you also for your help in trying to obtain a copy of the new revised edition of Skachkov's *Bibliography of China*. I hope you would be able to get it for me, as I have failed to do so, although I placed the order for it in London and in New York. If you need any books published in this country, I hope you will let me know. It would give me much pleasure to be of possible help to you in your very important work.

　　With renewed thanks and cordial regards,

Yours sincerely,
T. L. Yuan

〔University of Chicago Library, Yuan T'ung-li Papers, Box 8〕

　　按:此件为录副。

三月十七日

Wolfgang Seuberlich 覆函先生,寄上德国期刊中有关孙中山的文章目录五十条,并告知其将会向奥地利国家图书馆参考部询问该国期刊中的相关文献。

March 17, 1960

Dear Dr. Yuan:

　　I am most obliged to you for your letter of February 3, 1960, and the Chinese name of the author Dapen Liang.

　　Enclosed I am sending you 50 odd titles of articles in German on Sun Yat-sen. That is all we could find. Titles marked with a red mark + could not be checked in the original as these publications are not extant in our library. However, the source wherefrom the information given is derived has been indicated in each case.

　　Unfortunately, the exact dates of birth and death of authors in many cases could not be ascertained. I think that most of the authors born in the nineteen-seventies are no more alive as well as, for instance, Zenker, born in 1865, already died. But our reference books and other available sources do not mention their death years.

　　You will notice, that all titles sent to you now belong to articles published in Germany. In the index to German periodicals (Dietrich) we could not find a single article on Sun Yat-sen published in Austria. However, it is improbable that there actually has been none in Austrian journals. To be sure, I am now going to send an inquiry on this subject to the Reference Department of the Österreichische Nationalbibliothek at Vienna, Austria.

I hope that this information will be of some use for you. If you have additional questions, please, don't hesitate to let me know. I gladly shall do all I can for you.

Please, excuse the delay of this answer. Since about one month I have two younger assistants (one Sinologue and one Japanlogue) to help me in my work. The scope of the work to be done in this department, however, has been so considerably augmented during the last few years, that my own burden of work still seems to have not changed too much.

With cordial regards,

Yours sincerely,

Wolfgang Seuberlich

〔University of Chicago Library, Yuan T'ung-li Papers, Box 4〕

三月十九日

罗家伦覆函先生,告知办公费已按照要求方式支付,并附上待购书籍清单两份。

守和吾兄道鉴:

前接二月十三日手书,至感热心协助,并以事冗稽复为歉! 承惠赠及代购之西书五包,业已收到。本月初又接寄来代购西书一册(一九二九——一九五四中国与各国外交文件汇编),惟未附发票,尚祈补下。新台币壹仟元,业经送交张贵永先生代收,闻彼已购溥心畬画一小帧,在装裱中。三月至六月份之款,当俟兄指定用途后,再行遵办。本馆现又需西书一批,敬附上清单两份,恳为代购,惟第一单二十四种并不急用,故如能买到旧书更佳。又蒙兄欣赏拙书,甚感愧幸,稍暇当写就裱好托人带上。专此,即颂撰祺!

弟家伦敬启

三,十九

〔University of Chicago Library, Yuan T'ung-li Papers, Box 1〕

按:此函为文书代笔,落款处为其签名。

三月二十五日

先生致信钱存训,询问谭卓垣所编汉学论文索引下落,并请教芝加哥留学生姓名。

公垂吾兄：

去夏大驾赴檀岛之前，曾函告拟询谭卓垣君所编汉学论文索引之下落，不识结果如何？近有人来此询问，亟盼示知。下月在纽约举行之十二次年会，不识能抽暇前来否？兹奉上芝大同学名单一纸，内中如有不识者，可否转询留芝较久之人，见示为盼。此上，顺颂俪安。

弟袁同礼顿首

三月廿五

又芝城中国同学录亦盼代觅一份寄下为感。

〔钱孝文藏札〕

按：据先生与他人信函可知，一直未能找到谭卓垣遗稿（即《西文汉学书目》最初拟定之期刊论文部分），故又专托钱存训代为寻找。"十二次年会"应指美国亚洲学会第 12 届年会，4 月 11 日至 13 日举行。

三月下旬

先生向罗家伦寄送伦敦《泰晤士报》关于孙中山蒙难的报道。〔《罗家伦先生文存补遗》，页 650〕

按：4 月 5 日，罗家伦收到此批文献资料。

四月二日

先生致信李济，有意推动在美寄存的居延汉简运台，并谈台北故宫文物赴美展览计划。

济之吾兄：

近见北平所印《居延汉简甲编》封面内有"最多的一批已为美帝国主义掠去"等语。不知吾兄在哈佛图书馆中见到否？敝意此批汉简似宜早日取回，不识夏间有无研究人员搭轮返台者，并盼注意。又《思永考古论文集》近由夏鼐君编印出版，所列其著作竟遗漏 New stone age pottery 一文，可见大陆材料仍感缺乏。关于故宫文物明夏在美展览壹事，三月三、四两日，纽约《华侨日报》登载抗议，想已见到。此事原由立武发动，弟曾劝其停止进行。此次雪艇先生复来接洽，内中不无政治作用，似非局外人所知。下星期一，弟到纽约十一至十三参加年会，星期五、六十五、十六来康桥查书，极盼一谈。如大驾亦来纽约，则更方便。恐彼此相左,特先函达。余俟面谈。顺颂旅安。

嫂夫人同此问好。

弟袁同礼顿首
四月二日
〔西泠印社 2015 年秋季拍卖会〕

按:《思永考古论文集》即《梁思永考古论文集》,1959 年科学出版社初版,考古学专刊甲种第五号。1926 年李济在山西夏县发掘西阴村遗址,发现和仰韶相同的文化遗存,梁思永将其部分陶面加以分析,写成硕士论文《山西西阴村史前遗址之新石器时代的陶器》(New Stone Age Pottery from the Prehistoric Site at Hsi-Yin Tsun, Shansi, China)。

四月六日

先生致信宋晞,感谢赠书,并向《中国文化季刊》推荐袁清论文。

旭轩先生著席:

前奉手教并承惠寄《新疆史地大纲》等书,厚意隆情,至感至感。近晤鸿声先生,承告《中国文化季刊》需稿颇亟,兹奉上小儿近著关于阿古柏论文一篇,业经 Hummel 诸人看过,认为不无价值,即希尊酌是荷。如能刊载,并盼赐赠单行本,以便分赠友人。专此,顺候著祺。

弟袁同礼顿首
四月六日

又《国会图书馆藏中国善本书录》,贵馆已入藏否? 如未入藏,望示知,当即奉赠也。

〔袁同礼家人提供〕

按:此件为底稿。

四月十一日

戴德华致函先生,邀请参加"中美文化合作会议"。

April 11, 1960

Dear Dr. Yuan:

The Steering committee of the co-sponsoring universities cordially invites you to participate in a "Sino-American Conference on Intellectual Cooperation", to be held in Seattle July 11 – 15 of this year. The co-sponsoring universities, besides the University of Washington, are Harvard, Princeton, Cornell, Chicago, Michigan, Indiana, and California.

The thirty Americans who are being invited are divided more or less equally between the natural sciences, the humanities, and the social sciences. While there are many technical problems on the disciplinary level that can be discussed at the conference, it is our expectation that at least two major proposals, one relating to scientific and the other to cultural development on Taiwan, will be discussed. We shall be concerned with the problems of intellectual cooperation in general as well as with problems of Sino-American intellectual cooperation in particular.

We are assured of a first-rate delegation from Taiwan, chosen by "the Academia Sinica" and Taiwan University. It includes several very able native-born Taiwanese. There will be several scholars from Hongkong invited by the steering committee on our side.

The American delegation includes representatives of all the sponsoring universities as well as distinguished scholars from other institutions.

I might emphasize that this is a working conference to which newsmen are not invited, and there will be little, if any, publicity. In addition to normal contribution of discussion, we would expect most of the participants to take some part in the proceedings in a manner to be suggested later.

The committee feels that you would make a valuable contribution and hopes that you will be able to accept our invitation. Travel and hospitality will, of course, be taken care of by the conference.

Sincerely yours,

George E. Taylor

Chairman, Steering Committee

〔University of Chicago Library, Yuan T'ung-li Papers, Box 1〕

按:此件为打字稿,落款处为其签名。

四月十二日　纽约

美国亚洲学会下属美国图书馆远东资源委员会在哥伦比亚大学东亚图书

馆举行第四次会议,毕尔、G. Raymond Nunn(主席)、加斯基尔、裴开明、钱存训、童世纲、夏道泰、吴文津、先生等二十二人出席。〔Harvard-Yenching Institute Archives〕

> 按:会议讨论了包括敦煌资料、民国前中国出版的西文报纸、中共文献缩微胶卷等 21 个议题。4 月 20 日,Nunn 撰写了本次会议纪要。夏道泰(Hsia Tao-tai),江苏泰州人,其父为民国法学家夏勤(1892—1950),时在国会图书馆服务①,后曾任远东法律组主任。

四月十四日

罗家伦致函先生,感谢先生向美国陆军部索取赠书,并请代购三种书籍。

> 守和吾兄道鉴:
>
> 三月十九日寄上一函,谅早递达。顷接"美国驻华大使馆"陆军武官处 Col. Paul Godbey 来书,以吾兄函请该处赠送本馆书籍四种,特检送现有两种,并告知其余两种出版处所及售价,弟已复函致谢。兹抄奉来函复本,敬祈察阅,至于 *Stilwell's Mission to China*,*Stilwell's Command Problems* 两书及 *Time Runs Out in the CBI* 一书(按此书阅最近美国书评,为系美国军方出版战史之第三册……缅甸 I 系印度,但不知第一、二两册为何……)拟一并烦请惠予设法代为征集或购买,以资参考,是所感荷。再者,日昨收到惠寄影印 1896 年《泰晤士报》三张,甚为感谢,此项影印倘非征而系自印或价购者,尚祈将费用收据或发票掷下为荷。肃此,即颂撰祺。
>
> 弟罗家伦敬启
> 四,一四
>
> 〔University of Chicago Library, Yuan T'ung-li Papers, Box 1〕
>
> 按:*Stilwell's Mission to China*、*Stilwell's Command Problems* 和 *Time Runs Out in the CBI* 均属于 United States Army in World War II, China-Burma-India Theater 丛书,由华盛顿 Office of the Chief of Military History 出版,依次于 1953 年、1956 年、1955 年问世。"1896 年《泰晤士报》"应指孙中山在伦敦蒙难报道。该函为文书代笔,第二页右上部分破损,落款处为其签名。另附 1960 年 3 月

---

① 《夏志清夏济安书信集》卷 4,页 288。

31 日 Paul Godbey 致罗家伦信副本一页。

四月中旬　马萨诸塞州剑桥

先生赴哈佛大学看书。

四月十九日

先生覆信戴德华,接受"中美文化合作会议"的参会邀请。

April 19, 1960

Dear Professor Taylor:

I wish to acknowledge the receipt of your letter of April 11, inviting me to participate in a "Sino-American Conference on Intellectual Cooperation" to be held in Seattle July 11－15. I appreciate very much your invitation which I accept with much pleasure.

The various topics for discussion listed on the agenda have my hearty approval. I am sure that the meeting of minds at such a gathering will bring about closer cultural cooperation between our two peoples.

With cordial regards,

Yours sincerely,

T. L. Yuan

〔University of Chicago Library, Yuan T'ung-li Papers, Box 1〕

按:此件为录副。

四月二十日

任以都覆函先生,告知收到袁清论文,并谈其研究计划和所需史料类型。

袁伯伯:

前周奉到手示,谢谢!知道清弟现在已经精于研究工作,真是喜愉。侄能得他相助,也是幸运。夏天如能请他开车来 State College 一聚,则更妥当。清弟的论文也收到,日内读毕当即奉还。近东史是现在极被人重视的一门专科学问,他将来发展机会将无限量。

谢谢您提议给侄大陆近年出版关于经济史的资料。侄所着重的是矿业发展与中国经济全面进展的关系,如能得关于此类的资料,将给我不少资助,先谢谢。

侄补助金在七月起始,所以从七月以后,清弟任何时愿开始都很合适。应查的书籍,侄处略有大概,届时和他细谈。侄意是先找历史材料,如地方志,各朝会典、会要、实录等等。如他可以有时代搜查资料,则更是一助。

　　静妹去英国深造,十分可佩,您们想来也很欣慰。余容后禀,敬请尊安。

侄以都谨上

一九六〇,四月二十日

请袁伯母安。守全附候。

〔University of Chicago Library, Yuan T'ung-li Papers, Box 2〕

四月二十三日

先生致信耶鲁大学档案馆,请求协助查找该校博士毕业生论文页面信息。

April 23, 1960

Curator

The Archives

Yale University

New Haven, Conn.

Dear Sir:

　　At the request of "the Sino-American Cultural Committee", I am compiling a Guide to doctoral dissertations by Chinese students in this country. Although I have checked your published lists of dissertations, 1861－1927, 1928－1930, and the manuscript lists covering the years 1931－1959, I could not find the number of typewritten leaves or pages of each thesis. Nor could I find the information from your catalog, nor from the cards which your Library had sent to the National Union Catalog.

　　I am therefore enclosing a list of authors who have submitted their dissertations to Yale. I shall be most grateful if you could check the number of leaves or pages of each thesis. As I have already had the titles, there is no need for you to list them. I fully realize the trouble I am giving you, but in order to make the record complete, full bibliographical information is necessary.

　　With sincere thanks,

Yours sincerely,

T. L. Yuan

〔袁同礼家人提供〕

四月二十九日

洛克菲勒基金会人文部批准代号 HUM6042 的资助,给予先生(西雅图华盛顿大学)五千美金用以编纂《新疆研究文献目录》(*Bibliography on Sinkiang*),其中四千美金用于研究和事务性支出,余下部分则用于支付差旅费用,自本年五月一日开始生效,为期两年。〔Rockefeller Foundation. "Rockefeller Foundation Records, Projects, Rg 1.2." Series 200: United States; Subseries 200. R: United States-Humanities and Arts. Box 463. Folder 3955;University of Chicago Library, Yuan T'ung-li Papers, Box 1〕

> 按:5 月 1 日,洛克菲勒基金会致信华盛顿大学校长 Charles Odegaard,通知批准先生的申请。此外,先生申请的该项资助是在西雅图华盛顿大学远东和苏俄研究中心的监督下展开。7 月 13 日该校研究经费办公室负责人致信先生,告知寄送 1000 美金支票到 National Captial Bank 先生账户。

五月初

先生致信劳榦,告知《敦煌文献研究论文目录》无法购到,并托香港书店寄上《贩书偶记》。

> 贞一先生著席:

> 前东洋文库编印《燉煌文献目录》,曾请其以两部径寄尊处。近接该文库复函,谓印的有限,业已绝版,想系实情,因美国各图书馆仅存两部也。兹托香港书店寄上《贩书偶记》,著录《四库》未收之书,亦尚有用,收到后请以壹部转送适之先生是荷。

〔袁同礼家人提供〕

> 按:《贩书偶记》,孙殿起著,中华书局(上海)1959 年 8 月 1 版 1 刷,翌年 4 月第 2 次印刷。此件为底稿。

五月十二日

金问泗致函先生,寄赠图书,并告有两处被退回,另谈相关史料搜集。

> 守和吾兄惠鉴:

> 此次分送拙作小册子,诸承指导,铭感良深。分送单本拟当面奉还,并再领教,以一时不拟往图书馆,特先寄请察收,多谢多谢。内中

退还者只 Prof. Russell H. Fifield 与 *World Politics* 两处,均注明无法递送,尚乞吾兄吉便时查示为盼为荷。Fifield 所著之书 *Woodrow Wilson & the Far East*,弟于图书馆中见及,但是 Stephen Pichon 之书却未查到。闻兄前次说起书中提及与顾公晤谈一节,他日欲当面请益,何如?又 Arthur Walworth 君,弟已得与晤谈一次,所撰《威而逊传》两巨册,亦已约略翻阅过,但未详读。新旧书籍越看越多,"吾生也有涯,而知也无涯",良然良然。至老祖宗正希公之著作,前曾读到吾兄大作评论一段,深佩中肯,晤时亦当领教,辄先函陈,并布谢意。敬候俪福。

弟泗谨启

5-12-60

〔University of Chicago Library, Yuan T'ung-li Papers, Box 2〕

按:"小册子"或指《金问泗诗词稿》,1960 年远基印刷厂刊行,但由信文内容看,似不应指文学作品,待考。Russell H. Fifield(1914-2003),美国政治学家,尤其对东南亚区域颇有研究。*World Politics* 似指普林斯顿大学出版的期刊。Stephen Pichon 即 Stephen Jean Marie Pichon(1857-1933),法国外交官、政治家,曾担任驻清朝公使、法国外交部长。Arthur Walworth 即 Arthur C. Walworth(1903-2005),美国作家、传记作者,1958 年出版传记 *Woodrow Wilson*。

Robert B. Ekvall 致函先生,告知洛克菲勒基金会批准《新疆研究文献目录》的资助申请,并表示卫德明将作为该项目的监督者。

May 12, 1960

Dear Dr. Yuan:

The enclosed copies of correspondence are for your information. We are gratified that the grant, for which you made a request, has been granted. It is an acknowledgement both of the importance and worthwhileness of the project and of your special and very great competence.

By the terms of the grant Professor Hellmut Wilhelm, Far Eastern Department, University of Washington, has been assigned the responsibility of being Project Investigator. So now the full round of reference and correspondence, initiated by your letter of January 30, 1960, has been completed and you are again in contact with him.

　　With very best wishes,

Sincerely yours,

Robert B. Ekvall, Chairman

Inner Asia Research Project

〔University of Chicago Library, Yuan T'ung-li Papers, Box 1〕

　　按:此件为打字稿,落款处为 Robert B. Ekvall 签名。

五月十三日　马里兰州公园市

第六届"中美文化关系圆桌会议"在马里兰大学举办,先生出席并发言。

〔University of Chicago Library, Yuan T'ung-li Papers〕

罗家伦致函先生,告知汇来美金用以购书,但为"国史馆"购买者应在六月底前寄送发票以便报销,并问办公费作何用途。

　　守和吾兄道鉴:

　　　　三月中寄上一函及购书清单二份,谅早承察及。兹于五月十日由台湾银行汇奉美金贰百元,此款仍系"国史馆"及党史委员会购买书籍之用者,即馆与会各有二百元存兄处也。惟馆方之款须于本会计年度终了时(六月底),凭实际购到资料之发票办理报销,故请吾兄惠照前所开上之书单即予赐购,新旧均可,并请将发票先行寄下,以便如期办理报销,是至企感。再"国史馆"应致送三至六月份公费,计新台币贰千元,作何用途,亦祈惠示,俾即遵办。专此,祇颂俪祺。

弟罗家伦敬启

五,一三

〔University of Chicago Library, Yuan T'ung-li Papers, Box 1〕

　　按:此信为文书代笔,落款处为其签名。

五月十四日[①]

郭廷以致函先生,告知近代史研究所近况及与洛克菲勒基金会代表 Boyd R. Compton、费正清交涉资助情形。

[①]《郭廷以先生书信选》(页54)将信错记为1964年,实际上该信落款处并未注明年份,其纪年字样应为主编或整理人员誊录时擅自加入的。《郭量宇先生日记残稿》不仅记录了1960年5月14日"分函公权、淬廉及袁守和、包华德(Boorman)",也在4月27日提及 Compton 的拜访。

守和先生有道：

　　二月十六日曾肃一笺，谅早邀鉴。近史所事备承爱护，公私均感。洛氏基金代表康君（Compton）上月来台，对于"近代中国之西方认识"及"口述民国史"两计画，颇感兴趣，六月间将再度前来，容续奉陈。长者得便，仍希鼎力相助。

　　费正清先生到此已四周，晤谈之下，赞许有加，愧不敢承，以近史所实少成就可言。渠除撰文送交《亚洲学报》介绍外，并力劝将拙编《近代中国史事日志》出版（全书约二百余万字），已函哥大包华德（Boorman）先生商洽。《中俄关系史料》、《中东铁路》编两册已成书，另行邮奉就正。其《俄国革命》及《东北边防》两编四册，亦可望于下月内印就，当续呈。今夏七月在西雅图召开之"中美学术合作会议"，弟或将前往参加，如情势许可，甚望能重去东部一游，俾获面聆明教。

　　公余之暇，务希时锡箴言为幸。匆此，祗颂道绥！

弟廷以拜上
五、十四

府上均好。

〔University of Chicago Library, Yuan T'ung-li Papers, Box 2〕

　　按：《郭量宇先生日记残稿》第 181 页将（Boyd R.）Compton 错排为 Campton，笔者自行订正，特此说明。

五月十七日

先生致信 Robert B. Ekvall，感谢西雅图华盛顿大学协助向洛克菲勒基金会申请资助《新疆研究文献目录》编纂。

May 17, 1960

Dear Dr. Ekvall:

　　Thank you so much for your letter of May 12 informing me that the Rockefeller Foundation has made the grant to enable me to complete a comprehensive bibliography of Sinkiang.

　　It was entirely due to the support of your Institute that this project can be materialized. May I express to you and to Professor Taylor my hearty thanks for your interest and support?

　　I am particularly happy that Professor Hellmut Wilhelm has been designated as Project Investigator. In a day or two I shall write to him and solicit his further advice.

　　With sincere thanks,

Yours sincerely,

T. L. Yuan

〔University of Chicago Library, Yuan T'ung-li Papers, Box 1〕

　　按：该件为录副。

戴德华致函先生，寄送"中美文化合作会议"新的日程安排，并对与会人员的发言主题、提交论文长短给予建议。〔University of Chicago Library, Yuan T'ung-li Papers, Box 1〕

五月十八日

先生致信罗家伦，告知收悉书信、汇款，并将购书及发票、收据寄上。

　　志希馆长吾兄著席：

　　　　连奉四、十四及五、十三赐书，拜悉种切。美国军方出版战史内容不佳，而书价甚昂，故前请其赠送或交换，凡不肯赠送者始行自购。至于三月间寄下书单，内中各书多已绝版，曾到旧书店搜访不获，至近日始行配就，已分四批邮寄，均在途中，谅不日可以收到。兹奉上发票，以便报销。第一次汇款贰百元尚余104.21元，兹又奉到第二批汇款贰百元，已将收据径寄纽约中国银行矣。日前寄上。

五，十八

〔University of Chicago Library, Yuan T'ung-li Papers, Box 1〕

　　按：此件为底稿。

五月十九日

先生致信卫德明，感谢给予的支持并将仔细检阅德国的学术期刊，拟将赴加拿大查找匈牙利文期刊。

May 19, 1960

Dear Professor Wilhelm:

　　Dr. Ekvall informed me that the Rockefeller Foundation had made a grant to enable me to complete my bibliography on Sinkiang. It was entirely due to the support of your Institute that my request was granted. May I write to thank you and your colleagues for your interest and support?

I am delighted that you have been designated as Project Investigator and I shall look forward to your advice and guidance from time to time.

Among German contributions to the literature of Sinkiang, the *Petermanns Mitteilungen* occupies a unique place. Although I have collected a considerable number of articles from this journal, I shall examine it more systematically, so that no articles of scientific importance will be omitted.

One or two Hungarian journals are found only in Canada. During the summer I hope to make trips to Canada and other centers. For this reason, I hope the ＄1,000 for travel suggested by the RF may be made immediately available. I now enclose a schedule of payments which your Comptroller may like to have. Please let me have your approval before transmitting it to him.

With hearty thanks,

Yours sincerely,

T. L. Yuan

〔University of Chicago Library, Yuan T'ung-li Papers, Box 1〕

按：*Petermanns Mitteilungen* 应指*Petermanns Geographische Mitteilungen*，1855 年创刊，德文地理学期刊。

五月二十三日

劳榦覆函先生，告收到《贩书偶记》并依嘱转赠胡适一部，另谈胡适身体、台湾物价等近况。

守和先生赐鉴：

前奉手书，月前承惠赐《贩书偶记》均已收到，惟此书由港寄来，颇费时日，幸已收到无误。其中一部已经转呈适之先生，想适之先生亦已有函达左右矣。适之先生今年身体稍差，四月间曾因心脏不甚正常（轻微的不正常），住台大医院检查，现在已渐次痊可，惟总以多休息为是。最近又因盥洗时右手中指受伤，并不严重，惟一时不便写信耳。

台湾近况一切如常，上月物价稍有波动，约涨百分之十左右，幸今已平息。今年雨水甚多，本月以来几无日不雨，现在将到阴历端阳，过去端阳时已服单衣，今年此时尚需穿毛衣，已略有美国西部之况味矣。专此，敬颂俪安。

后学劳榦谨上
五月二十三日

〔University of Chicago Library, Yuan T'ung-li Papers, Box 2〕

按：是年 5 月 29 日为端阳节。

五月二十五日

程其保致函先生，请将发言早日寄下以便汇编，并询未经付印之留美博士论文是否会收录到先生所辑《中国留美同学博士论文目录》中。

守和先生道右：

上周之"中美文化会议"，承费神宣读论文，贡献至大，特函伸谢。上项论文如荷早日赐下，以便汇编报告，尤所感激。关于《留美学生论文集》，不识进行到何程度？据弟所知，颇有几位同学，论文已经完成并经学校认可，而以种种关系，未能付印成册，不知亦一并列入否？如何杰才先生（一九一八）之《中国外交关系》，邱椿之《王阳明教育思想》（一九二四）及弟之 Financial ability to support an adequate public education in China（一九二三），即其例也。弟之论文本经 Dr. Kandel of Columbia 通过，但当弟返国时发还将内容（尤其数目字）修正、补充，再行付印，嗣以种种关系始终未办，复以此种论文已失时效，即完全置之矣。祇颂道安。

弟程其保拜启
五，廿五

〔University of Chicago Library, Yuan T'ung-li Papers〕

按：何杰才（1895—1969），字其伟，上海人，清华学校毕业后赴美留学，先后入哈佛大学、哥伦比亚大学学习，归国后在北洋政府任职。Dr. Kandel of Columbia 应指 Isaac Leon Kandel（1881－1965），美国教育学家，出生于罗马尼亚，1910 年起执教于哥伦比亚大学，程其保论文题目为 Financial ability to support an adequate public education in China，《中国留美同学博士论文目录》编号为 145。

五月二十九日

先生致信李书华,请其家人协助查明留美博士学生的中文姓名。

> 润章吾兄:

> 　　两周前"中美文化圆桌会议",晤纽约来此诸友,询问起居,惜未得一聆教言为怅耳。兹有前在圣路易大学同学数人,亟愿知其中文姓名,拟请转托令郎或令媛在该城同学录内代为一查,径行寄下,不胜感盼,并乞代达谢意。顺颂俪安。

> 弟袁同礼顿首
> 五,廿九

> 〔Columbia University Libraries Archival Collections, Shuhua Li Papers, 1926—1972, Volume II: Modern Eminent Chinese Leaders〕

五月三十日

先生致信胡适,询问其健康情况并请协助申请"教育部"资助。

> 适之先生:

> 　　上月闻贵体不适,入院检查,至为企念。在纽拜谒尊夫人,欣悉出院后曾有电来,渐次痊可,并悉大驾将与子水兄等于夏间来美,欢慰无似,惟望特别保重,多加休息,讲演等事最好谢绝为宜。同礼近来亦感精力不如以前,春间郭鸿声先生委托编印《留美同学博士论文目录》,已得三千余人,其中最大困难为(一)使其完备无遗漏,(二)查明每人之中文姓名,且须到各校详查目录,费用较大。鸿声先生拨来五百元,早已用罄。因念此项工作于"教部"职责不无关系,如该部或中基会略予资助约二千元,颇愿在一年以内将留美、留加、留欧之博士论文汇为一编,结一总账约五千人,想先生亦必赞同。可否在离台以前,与有关人士一商,如有可能,再将申请书寄奉,统希尊裁是感。近购大陆出版史料数种,拟俟大驾返美后,再行面呈。先此,敬候道祺。

> 同礼拜上
> 五,三十日

> 〔台北胡适纪念馆,档案编号 HS-NK01-164-007〕

　　按:该信6月6日送达台北。

六月六日

任以都覆函先生,告知近况并归还袁清学士论文,另就先生所询两位留学生的中文姓名予以答复。

袁伯伯：

前些日奉到您的来示,承寄下国内近年出版有关经济史书籍的卡片,十分感谢。侄已进行托人订购,希望能买到。

清弟的论文稿子,读过奉还。见他加注等等都十分精细,可见是认真读历史的,侄得此同志,不胜欣喜！需要他帮忙查抄的书目,不日就写一部份寄去,以期他在有便暇时开始。侄因六月内须赶出几项文稿,所以至今不能在新的题目上多下工夫,但是预计七月初可以开始。

您所问 Penny State 以前两位毕业生的中文姓名,其中 Li Lai-yung 不知是谁(此地论文原本都没注中文名),年久无人可问。另一位 Kuo Ping 实是 Ping, Kuo,中文是宾果,守全与他相识。(数年前在台湾不幸失事去世。)

近得国内信,知陶孟和伯伯四月中逝世了,十分惋惜,不悉您们是否已知道。敬请尊安。请袁伯母安。守全附候。

侄任以都谨上

一九六〇,六月六日

〔University of Chicago Library, Yuan T'ung-li Papers, Box 5〕

按:袁清学士论文题目为 Yakub Beg and the Moslem Rebellion in Chinese Turkestan, 1862 – 1876,后发表于 *Central Asiatic Journal*, Vol. 6, No. 2 (June 1961), pp. 134-167。本年 4 月 17 日,陶孟和于上海去世。

六月十日

先生致信加斯基尔,询问可否寄送新馆开幕仪式邀请函以便告假外出。

June 10, 1960

Dear Miss Gaskill:

I recall that you told me in New York the probable date of the formal opening of your new library. I presume that you and your staff must be quite busy in preparing to move your collections to the new quarters.

Although I am anxious to consult your catalog, I have followed your advice to postpone my trip until the formal opening of the new building. If you could send me an invitation with a note to the effect that you would like me to examine your Chinese collection, I might be able to get official leave here.

    With all good wishes,

Yours sincerely,

T. L. Yuan

〔Cornell University Library, Wason Collection Records, 1918–1988, Box 1, Folder Koo, T. K. Letters〕

    按:此件为打字稿,落款处为先生签名。

六月十三日

先生致信钱存训,请协助查找六位留学生的中文姓名并检寄芝加哥地区中国同学录一份。

    公垂吾兄:

        承寄大著,业已拜读,至为佩慰。暑中多暇,想可从事著述,仍担任暑校教席否,为念。兹需用芝城中国同学录,可否代觅一份,交邮寄下。又下列六人之中文姓名,亦盼示知。专此,顺颂教祺。

弟袁同礼顿首

六,十三

〔钱孝文藏札〕

A. G. Morkill 致函先生,告知已寄送英国大学中国委员会往期年报,并谈中英两国学术交流现状,另告自己已担任肯辛顿自治委员会公共图书馆委员会主席且正在营造新馆。

13 June, 1960

Dear Dr. Yuan:

    Thank you for your letter of May 7th. I have posted under separate cover some back numbers of U. C. C.'s Annual Reports and when this year's is printed, I will send you a copy. It is good to hear from you again and your continuing interest is much appreciated.

    As no students come direct from the mainland of China and the only visitors lectures which the two countries exchange are likely to be propagandists or fellow travelers, those interesting and at one time useful activities of U. C. C. are in abeyance.

I have been chairman of the Kensington Borough Council Public Libraries Committee and we have been building a new Central Library at the cost of £ 600,000. I am reminded of the very interesting day I spent when you showed me over that marvelous and beautiful building—the National Central Library of Peking. We too have built in a traditional style. If you have time, I should be very grateful if you would tell me when the National Central Library was built－I believe not very long ago.

With best wishes,

Yours sincerely,

A. G. Morkill

〔University of Chicago Library, Yuan T'ung-li Papers, Box 5〕

按:A. G. Morkill,英国学者,长期担任英国大学中国委员会秘书,与中国学术界有相当往来,本谱中译作"马克尔",曾在 1948 年夏访华。①

六月十四日

莫余敏卿覆函先生,告东行计划及所询两位博士中文姓名的查询结果。

June 14, 1960

Dear Dr. Yuan,

Thank you for your letter of June 5th and for your kind invitation to visit you when we go to Washington. Our plans are not very definite because we do not know how long we will stay in Cambridge. We certainly will call on you and Mrs. Yuan while we are there, as we are very anxious to see you all.

I have checked the two names for you. The first one (Lew, Joon) is a Korean, although the second one is a Chinese, but I am unable to find his name in Chinese at all. I can find is that he was born in "Wusih" and received his B. A. in Chiao-Tung university in 1949.

We are leaving here on July 6th and will visit Michigan, Yale and Princeton on the way. We hope you will have a pleasant trip too.

---

① 《竺可桢全集》第 11 卷,页 103。

Best regards,

　　　　　　　　　　　　　　　　　　Yours sincerely

　　　　　　　　　　　　　　　　　　M. Mok

　　　〔University of Chicago Library, Yuan T'ung-li Papers, Box 4〕

按：该函为其亲笔。

六月十五日

加斯基尔覆函先生，告知该校图书馆新馆开幕被推迟到一九六一年秋。

　　　　　　　　　　　　　　　　　　June 15, 1960

Dear Mr. Yuan:

　　The formal opening of the new library is not to be until the fall of 1961, and that seems a long time for you to wait to come up. We hope to begin moving in November, and I hope that the Wason Collection will be reassembled and pretty well in order by next spring.

　　I don't know anything at all about plans for the formal opening, but I should be very glad to have you come up as soon after we are settled in the new quarters as you can to examine the collection.

　　　　　　　　　　　　　　　　　　Sincerely yours,

　　　　　　　　　　　　　　　　　　Gussie E. Gaskill

　　　　　　Curator, Wason Collection on China and the Chinese

　　　〔Cornell University Library, Wason Collection Records, 1918-1988,

　　　Box 1, Folder Koo, T. K. Letters〕

六月十六日

蒋复璁致函先生，告知将来美参加西雅图"中美学术合作会议"。

　　守和先生赐鉴：

　　　　久疏奉候，至以为歉。惟诸大吉羊为无量颂。弟以应西雅图"中美学术合作会议"邀请，当随同适之师及其他诸君子飞美，约在一月停留，下月底可至华府观光与毛子水兄偕来，当趋承教益。余容面罄，即请著安。

　　　　　　　　　　　　　　　　　　弟蒋复璁顿首

　　　　　　　　　　　　　　　　　　六，十六

　　吴光清先生、徐亮先生、陶维勋兄，敬呈代候，恕不另缄。

　　　〔University of Chicago Library, Yuan T'ung-li Papers, Box 7〕

六月十九日

李济致函先生,请代台北购买国会图书馆所摄日本外交档案缩微胶卷。

> 守和吾兄:
>
> 　　芮逸夫兄来信,有一条:"分期购买美国会圕小型胶卷日本外交档案事,已于上月由蓝乾章先生函托袁守和先生代为接洽,惟尚无回示,敬希就便与袁先生一谈。兹暂决定购买之档案如下:
>
> > 1.Papers recovered in October 1950 by "the ministry of foreign affairs" (PVM) 76 reels　798.00
> >
> > 2.Telegrams 164 reels　1722.00
> >
> > 3.Selected archives of Japanese Army, Navy of other government agencies　1467.00
> >
> > 　　　　　　　　　　　　　3987.00"
>
> 以上信是六月九日自台北发的,弟已覆信给他们,告诉他们胶卷涨了价,并说涨价一样买,并已托了老兄。他们似乎盼望您有一回信,是否可以烦兄一纸与他们说明,可以即时把钱汇,由兄就钱买货,这笔钱必须在八月内化完,否则就要缴回洛氏基金。弟因这两个月到处跑路,函件来往不便。所以直接把此事拜托老兄了。请函告他们把钱寄出,由此处办理,弟当面写信给他们。余不尽,明日赴加。此次多承厚待,曷胜铭感。即颂双安。
>
> 　　　　　　　　　　　　　　　　　　　　弟济谨启
>
> 　　　　　　　　　　　　　　　　　　　　六,十九
>
> 　　　　　　　〔University of Chicago Library, Yuan T'ung-li Papers, Box 7〕

　　　　按:本年夏,李济确在美国访问。

六月二十日

先生撰写与会论文底稿,题为 Some Reference Work Needed for Sinology。
〔袁同礼家人提供〕

　　　　　　按:该篇后改称 Sinological Reference *Desiderata*,7月在西雅图华盛顿大学举行的"中美文化合作会议"上提交。

钱存训覆函先生,告前信所询人名仅查实其中三人,并告今年暑期将修改论文,另询问有无合适的出版社可代印论文。

守和先生尊鉴：

奉到六月十三日手教，敬悉一一。嘱查名单六人，仅知其三，奉告如后，

　　　Chen, Lucy M. C.　　　赵萝蕤（陈梦家夫人）

　　　Hsieh, Yi-ping　　　谢义炳

　　　Sun, Siao-fang　　　孙孝芳

其余三人无法查到。又原纸因托人查询遗失，未能寄回为歉。中国同学录已嘱同学会负责人检寄，惟未知是否有存耳。今夏不拟他往，希望利用暑假修改论文。去年曾请 L. C. Goodrich 先生审查，颇蒙嘉许，并怂恿出版，但 AAS monograph 无款代印，未知先生有可介绍之出版家否？其中有关"书刀"一节曾抽出改写中文，将印入史语所集刊庆祝董彦堂六十五生日论文专集，俟收到抽印本再奉呈指正。今日接蒋慰堂函告，伊将于下月中来美参加西雅图"中美文化合作会议"，约十六、七到芝云云。伊谓曾嘱其学生两人合译训与 Nunn 合作之一文刊入大陆什志，但误译甚多也。专此，即请暑安，合府均候。

　　　　　　　　　　　　　　　　　后学存训拜上

　　　　　　　　　　　　　　　　　六月廿日

　　　〔University of Chicago Library, Yuan T'ung-li Papers, Box 2〕

　　按：赵萝蕤（Chen, Lucy M. Chao）、谢义炳、孙孝芳三人均在芝加哥大学获得博士学位，《中国留美同学博士论文目录》中依次记在第 110、1468、2211 号，惟"孙孝芳"应为孙宵舫，钱存训书写有误，先生在目录中记述则是正确的。"'书刀'一节"即《汉代书刀考》，收录在《庆祝董作宾先生六十五岁论文集》下册，1961 年 6 月台北初版。"Nunn 合作之一文"即指 Far Eastern Resources in American Libraries。

六月二十六日

先生覆信钱存训，推荐纽约出版商并告知最近行程安排。

公垂吾兄著席：

手教拜悉，大著修正后极盼早日出版。闻纽约 Ronald Press 对于学术刊物颇愿印行，吾兄如与该店经理不甚相识，弟可请陈受颐先生写一推荐信以利进行。弟参加西雅图会议后，将在斯丹佛与

之晤面也。弟大约下星期日(三日)来芝城,下午拟到 Madison 等处一游,再到西雅图。到后约上午九时左右当再电闻,余俟面叙。顺颂暑安。

弟同礼顿首

六,廿六

〔钱孝文藏札〕

六月二十七日

先生致信 Ernst Wolff,告知萧一山将以观察者身份与会,并谈自己的行程安排,请协助订购返程机票。

June 27, 1960

Dear Dr. Wolff:

Thank you very much indeed for your letter of June 15. As my plans have been rather uncertain, I have not been able to write to you earlier. Will you excuse me for the delay?

Mr. Hsiao I-shan(　), the author of the History of the Ch'ing Dynasty, had asked me to inform the Conference Secretariat that he would like very much to attend the Conference as an observer. As he is a guest of the Department of State, he has had the necessary permission from that Department which will be responsible for his expenses while he stays at Seattle. All you have to do is to book him a room at Lander Hall. I shall be most grateful to you if you would convey this message to Professor Taylor.

On my way to Seattle, I shall spend two days at Minneapolis and shall arrive by air on Thursday, July. As the time of arrival is uncertain, please do not bother sending any one to the airport. I shall then leave for Vancouver and return to Seattle Saturday afternoon. I shall take a taxi to Lander Hall, as you directed.

For my return trip, will you book an air ticket from Seattle to San Francisco on Friday afternoon immediately after the Conference, and also an air ticket from San Francisco to Chicago on the morning of Thursday, July 21? I expect to remain at Chicago for two days before returning to Washington by train.

Looking forward to the pleasure of meeting you,

> Yours sincerely,
>
> T. L. Yuan

〔University of Chicago Library, Yuan T'ung-li Papers, Box 1〕

按：该件为录副。

六月二十九日

先生致信钱存训,告知行程有变并请借用西北大学、伊利诺伊理工学院中国同学录。

公垂吾兄:

日前奉上一缄,计达左右。兹因此间事务较繁,延期西行,拟由此径赴西雅图,一俟返芝再行晤谈(大约在七月廿二、廿三)。兹需用西北大学及 Illinois Institute of Technology 中国同学名单,如有熟人,盼与之一商,暂借数日为感。顺颂暑祺。

> 弟同礼顿首
>
> 六月廿九

〔钱孝文藏札〕

六月三十日

戴德华致函先生,告知纪凝娴已获得图书馆学文凭,并欲留在美国工作。

June 30, 1960

Dear Dr. Yuan:

Mrs. Lucy Chang has asked me to write you about her wish to secure employment in this country. Mrs. Chang secured her diploma from the School of Librarianship here at the University, doing her field work in the Far Eastern Institute Library. I think that she would be a conscientious worker in a well-run Library working with people she liked and trusted, and I very much hope that she can find such a position.

We are all looking forward to seeing you here soon.

> Sincerely yours,
>
> George E. Taylor
>
> Director

〔袁同礼家人提供〕

按：Lucy Chang 和下文出现的 Lucy G. Chang 均指张贵永夫人纪凝娴。

六月

先生致信罗家伦，婉拒此前推荐主持台北故宫博物院古物来美展览一事。

> 志希馆长吾兄著席：

> 连奉五月廿八日及六月二日手教，拜悉一一。贵馆需要之资料，近又奉上四包，共十五种，附上发票两纸，即希点收。故宫书画在美展览一事，为一重大事件，自应指定大员主持一切。弟摆脱故宫职务业已多年，对于艺术更属门外汉，兼之目前为美机关服务，事实上亦无法分身。承兄推荐，益觉汗颜，务乞转恳雪艇先生另简贤能。敝意郑茀廷"大使"前曾主持英伦艺展，成绩卓著，此次似可请渠帮忙，必能胜任愉快。

> 〔University of Chicago Library, Yuan T'ung-li Papers, Box 1〕

> 按："故宫书画在美展览"即翌年"中国古艺术品展览会"。"郑茀廷"即郑天锡（1884—1970，Cheng Tien-hsi），字云程，号茀庭，广东香山县人，法学家、外交官。1935 至 1936 年，以国民政府特派委员名义前往英国主持"伦敦中国艺术品国际展览会"。此件为底稿。

七月初

先生与杨联陞晤谈。

> 按：5 日至 9 日，杨联陞前往加州拜谒赵元任。

七月五日

李霖灿致函先生，请在西雅图会议期间借机为其谋划赴美访学机会。

> 守和长者赐鉴：

> 在西雅图接到这封信时，想会吃惊一下。我是在报上见到长者要来西岸参加"中美学术合作会议"，于是想到请张次瑶兄代转此信，一为问候，一为此次既是学术合作会议，很可能有什么"机缘"发生。国会图、哈佛大学、西雅图华大都有麽些经典，若能请得一笔研究经费，再来美国住三年，把英文逼好，未始不是一条妙计。因为今年没有请到哈佛燕京的补助金，一忙于生活杂务，大好研究时光都被促去，痛心之至，所以才出此"洋"策，请长者代为留意策划一下，——当然，是要

机缘顺手也,不必勉强争求。毕尔 Beal 博士亦与会,见面时望代我问候,或许他有力为国会圕一提,是亦一术也。长者以为如何? 专此奉托,肃叩旅安,合府百吉。

晚李霖灿鞠躬
七月五日

〔University of Chicago Library, Yuan T'ung-li Papers, Box 2〕

七月上旬

先生前往加拿大温哥华(Vancouver)。

> 按:此次行程十分短暂,似在 7 月 7 日至 9 日之间,或与先生 5 月 19 日致卫德明信中提及赴加拿大检阅匈牙利文期刊(Hungarian journals)有关。

七月十日　西雅图

"中美文化合作会议"("The Sino-American Conference on Intellectual Cooperation")在西雅图华盛顿大学(University of Washington)召开,先生以国会图书馆馆员身份与会并提交两篇论文,分别为 Some Problems and Possibilities in Bibliography and Library Resources 和 Sinological Reference *Desiderata* ,其中前者是与毕尔共同署名提交。〔*"Sino-American Conference on Intellectual Cooperation": Report and Proceedings* , held at University of Washington, July 10-15, 1960. Seattle: University of Washington〕

> 按:本次会议自 7 月 10 日始,至 7 月 15 日止,发起及参与机构众多,如"中央研究院"、台湾大学、加州大学、芝加哥大学、康乃尔大学、哈佛大学、印第安纳大学、密歇根大学、普林斯顿大学、华盛顿大学等。Desiderata 为拉丁语,意思为"亟需之物"。这两篇英文论文均失收于《袁同礼文集》。

七月十一日

先生致信赵元任、杨步伟夫妇,敬贺赵小中与丘宏义的婚礼。

> 元任先生、夫人:
>
> 上月四小姐婚礼,未能前往参加,听说新郎才貌俱佳,可称佳耦,敬贺敬贺。此次开会本想在此聆教,顷晤联陞兄,知担任教席,不克分身。兹拟于闭会后在金山小留,届时当趋前拜访一聆教言。先此,敬候俪安。

同礼顿首

七,十一

〔University of California, Berkeley, The Bancroft Library, Yuen Ren Chao papers, carton 10, folder 39, Yuan, Tongli and Yuan, Huixi〕

　　按:"四小姐"即赵小中,6月25日,她与丘宏义的婚礼在波士顿举行。丘宏义(1932—),上海出生,高能天体物理学家,父亲丘汉平为民国时期经济学家、律师,曾任福建省财政厅长。赵元任在加州大学开设暑期课程,故不能前往西雅图。

七月十八日　斯坦福

郭廷以赴胡佛研究所图书馆(Hoover Institution Library),与先生晤谈。

〔《郭量宇先生日记残稿》,页197〕

　　按:今日,郭廷以从西雅图乘飞机至加州,抵达后至该馆访曾宪琳、吴文津等人,先生恰在此处等候。

徐家璧覆函先生,表示无意申请冯平山图书馆空缺,而哥伦比亚大学图书馆亦无空闲位置可聘张贵永夫人纪凝娴。

　　守和先生尊鉴:

　　　　接奉七月十二日手示,诵悉一是! 先生参加中美学术合作会议,想多新猷贡献,俾益于中美学术者至深且钜,甚望能贯澈实施耳。伍冬琼女士(曾于前年来馆参观)所遗冯平山圕主任一缺,璧颇无意申请,仍觉以株守哥大之为宜也。渥蒙德爱提携,非常心感! 至于张桂永夫人,业已到馆接洽,曾分别与 Linton 暨璧详谈数次,无奈本馆(中文部份)目前已有 Professional 三人,clerical 一人,实无扩充余地。璧已建议伊往公立圕接洽,未悉其结果若何? 方命之处,至觉愧歉,伏乞宽恕是幸! 余容续奉,敬请福安!

　　　　　　　　　　　　　　　　　　　　　　晚徐家璧鞠躬
　　　　　　　　　　　　　　　　　　　　　　七月十八日

　　尊夫人前,乞代叱名问安!

　　　　　〔University of Chicago Library, Yuan T'ung-li Papers, Box 7〕

Wolfgang Seuberlich 覆函先生,告知得到奥地利国家东亚图书馆的消息,未能查找到有关孙中山的文章,另告即将前往莫斯科参加国际东方学者大会。

　　　　　　　　　　　　　　　　　　　　　　July 18, 1960

Dear Dr. Yuan:

Thank you very much for your kind letter of July 5, 1960, as well as for the Program of the Twelfth Annual meeting of the Association for Asian Studies sent to me in April. I was sorry to learn that you have been so sick during last spring. It is my sincere hope that your health has been restored by now.

Regarding possible additional data on German language articles, as Sun Yat-sen from Austria mentioned in my letter of March 17, 1960, I received from the Ostasiatische National Bibliothek a quite unsatisfactorily reply. They simply stated that beyond the index of German periodicals (Dietrich) these is no other source of information on Austrian periodicals available.

As to the International Congress of Orientalists in Moscow, I am to start for the Soviet capital from Berlin on August 6th, by train.

With very very best wishes for your health and the success of yours. I remain, with kind regards,

Yours sincerely

Wolfgang Seuberlich

〔University of Chicago Library, Yuan T'ung-li Papers, Box 4〕

　　按:该函为其亲笔。

七月十九日

上午,郭倞闿开车送其父郭廷以、先生、阎振兴至加州大学伯克利分校,会房兆楹、赵元任、Irwin 等人。〔《郭量宇先生日记残稿》,页 197〕

　　　　按:阎振兴(1912—2005),字光夏,河南汝阳人,清华大学土木系
　　　　毕业,后赴美留学,入爱荷华州立大学,获博士学位,归国后曾任
　　　　西南联合大学教授、河南大学工程学院院长。Irwin,《郭量宇先
　　　　生日记残稿》记为 Irving,应为误识。

金问泗覆函先生,请协助查找巴黎和会时中国代表团信息,以利书稿修改。

　　守和吾兄赐览:

　　　　多时未晤教为念。兹以薛光前兄主编英文《亚洲丛书》欲以拙作
　　"山东问题"一篇,重印于内,为求适合全书体例,拟稍稍充实、删改,

并更欲乞吾兄惠予帮查两点如下,即(一)记得吾兄前次说起 Stephen
Pichon 之 Memoires 一书内提及巴黎和会时曾与少公晤谈请参阅拙篇 p. 26,
foot note no. 11,倘书内道及谈话大旨以及会晤日期,鄙意拟欲补叙,可否请
将书名、页数,以及发行之年暨承印书店名称等等查示,俾便补入注脚;
(二)此外拟补入五代表(陆、王、顾、施、魏)之洋文名姓及其官衔,但须
完全依照官文书以期拼法一样,弟曾托友人代查未得,亦请吾兄代为一
查。种种费神,容当面谢。至拙稿尚须加以修改之处,无论在实质在
文字各方面,吾兄倘有指教,务乞详示,勿要客气。拙作诗词稿已印
成,外表尚不太坏。俟面晤时当奉赠吾兄嫂一本。专托,敬候著祺。

弟金问泗谨启

7-19-60

〔袁同礼家人提供〕

按:函中所指书稿,后题为 *China at the Paris Peace Conference in
1919*,1961 年由圣若望大学(St. John's University)出版社初版。
薛光前(1910—1978),原名贵生,江苏青浦人,1930 年入私立东
吴大学,1935 年赴意大利留学,1936 年 9 月返国,曾任铁道部翻
译处处长,抗战胜利后担任中华民国驻意大利使馆公使,1948 年
皈依天主教,1949 年赴美,时在圣若望大学任历史系教授并担任
亚洲研究学院院长。Stephen Pichon(1857-1933),法国政治家,
曾任法国驻清朝公使、外交部长。

七月二十三日

侯服五致函先生,转上嘱查中国留学生中文姓名,并告现状及联系地址。

July 23, 1960

同礼先生道席:

顷接苏君伟先生由 Michigan State U.来函称,前后学托渠代查中
国名学姓,已部份完成使命。按苏君覆函虽稍迟缓,先生或仍乐知渠
之调查结果也。

后学已被留此执教,以后□再□差使,请即径函此间政治系,当尽
棉薄也。余不赘,敬颂夏安。

后学侯服五顿首

〔University of Chicago Library, Yuan T'ung-li Papers, Box 2〕

按:侯服五(Houn, Franklin W.,1920—2014),1953 年获得威斯康星大学博士学位,时应在内布拉斯加大学(The University of Nebraska)政治系执教。"苏君伟"似指苏均炜(So, Kwan-wai, 1919—2005),1951 年获威斯康星大学博士学位。

七月二十八日　华盛顿

郭廷以赴国会图书馆,与先生、吴光清晤谈。〔《郭量宇先生日记残稿》,页 199〕

七月二十九日

中午,先生设宴款待郭廷以,席间谈中美学术界情形。〔《郭量宇先生日记残稿》,页 199〕

七月三十一日

毛准由纽约至华盛顿,先生负责招待,并邀其赴国会图书馆看书。〔《传记文学》,第 52 卷第 1 期,页 76〕

八月三日

王季高覆函先生,告张贵永夫人纪凝娴已获某图书馆职位,并告与郭廷以晤谈事。

> 守和先生惠鉴:
>
> 　奉阅手示,至感关注。张致远兄之夫人近已获得一图书馆方面之妥适工作,不日即将上班,其待遇亦甚优厚,详细情形想彼本人不久即将陈报。郭廷以兄来,已晤谈一切,极感快慰。季高自去秋已在南方一小大学任教,耶节及暑假仍返纽约与家人团聚,所提 Ducksen Chang 实不知为何许人,无法复命,敬祈原谅。专此函复,即请近安。
>
> 　　　　　　　　　　　　　　　王季高谨上
> 　　　　　　　　　　　　　　　八月三日
>
> 〔University of Chicago Library, Yuan T'ung-li Papers, Box 2〕

　　按:8 月 1 日,郭廷以访王季高。[1]

八月四日

先生致信李书华问安,并告知李麟玉近况。

> 润章先生著席:
>
> 　近月以来,想贵体业已复原,时在念中。弟以琐事相缠,久未来

---

[1]《郭量宇先生日记残稿》,页 200。

纽。上周适之夫人来京,弟等探询近状,据云电话不通,或已更换号码亦未可知,弟下次来纽,当再趋候。弟在中共刊物上久不见圣章大名,近在日本刊物上忽然见到,附上一纸,想吾兄亦愿闻也。专此,顺颂俪安。

弟同礼顿首

八月四日

〔Columbia University Libraries Archival Collections, Shuhua Li Papers, 1926-1972, Volume II: Modern Eminent Chinese Leaders〕

按:后附一纸,上有"北京工业学院"、"清华大学"两校校(院)长名单。

八月五日

陈祚龙覆函先生,告知无意申请牛津东方学院图书馆职位,并请告知王世杰论文的详细信息以便查找。

守和先生大鉴:

拜读手教(七、廿五),至以先生关怀下情可感! 承告牛津东方学院拟予扩充,Hawkes 氏曾函 Beal 氏愿以年薪£1300 求代罗致一人前往担任采访及编目等等,如此讯息,实属难得! 唯以 H 氏既已存心在美求才访贤,即使龙愿前往效劳,亦恐难于成事! 同时,就龙所知,国人现在英伦者为数并亦不少,如说 H 氏乐得国人前往合作,谅必牛津吴、熊诸位,早已别有保举;此外,龙与 H 氏过去固属同学、同事与同航,然而彼此绝少过从。基于上述种种,故龙仍无申请是职之意,尚望先生惠予谅之。

嘱查王世杰之博士论文事,顷因 Sorlome 已经放假,而龙今在国家图书馆之目录部中仅见其收有王氏之"Education in China, Shanghai, China United Press, 1935, in-8^0-45 p. 8^0 R. 42149(3)",尚希先生能将是项论文稍予描述,以便在此继续查考其有关详要者。肃此,敬颂合府大安!

愚陈祚龙合十

六〇,八,五,于巴黎

今后赐教,可请写寄: CHEN Tsu-lung, 35 Rue Montéza, Paris 12e, FRANCE.

〔University of Chicago Library, Yuan T'ung-li Papers, Box 2〕

按:Hawkes 应指 David Hawkes(1923-2009),英国汉学家,通译
作霍克思;Beal 即毕尔,"吴"似指吴世昌,"熊"应指熊式一。

八月八日

李书华覆函先生,告知左臂复原情况并谈家人近况,另寄送《筹算与珠算》
抽印本。

> 守和先生惠鉴:

> 八、四手书敬悉。弟左臂受伤,骨早已接上,然动作尚未复原;每
日仍继续作各种 exercises,但进步甚慢,或再需六个月的时间方能复
原,亦未可知。敝寓电话仍为 M06-9719,并未更换号码,大约适之夫
人打电话时,或将号码叫错,致有此误会耳。弟已十年无圣章消息,承
抄示日本刊物上的消息,甚慰,谢谢。小女□□正在预备博士学位(生
物化学),尚未完成;其丈夫为□□□。兹由邮寄上拙著《筹算与珠
算》抽印本一册,希指正。该文详载适之在台代查书的结果,对于算盘
的起源,似可作为定案。匆匆,敬请双安。

> 弟李书华敬启
> 八月八日

> 大著《博士论文目录》,闻正在印刷中,实为有用的一部参考书。

〔University of Chicago Library, Yuan T'ung-li Papers, Box 7〕

按:《筹算与珠算》收录于《庆祝董作宾先生六十五岁论文集》上
册,1960 年 7 月《"中央研究院"历史语言研究所集刊》外篇第
4 种。

八月十四日

晚,先生在家设宴款待叶公超、罗家伦。〔《罗家伦先生文存补遗》,页 656〕

八月十五日

上午,先生陪罗家伦在国会图书馆看中文馆藏,后至国家美术馆(National
Gallery)参观。晚,叶公超设宴,先生、罗家伦、王季高、谭伯羽等人与席。
〔《罗家伦先生文存补遗》,页 656〕

八月十六日

上午,先生与罗家伦至国家档案馆(National Archives)参观各部门。〔《罗家
伦先生文存补遗》,页 656〕

先生致信陈受颐,请寄下关于钱存训博士论文出版的推荐函。

受颐先生著席：

上月在波城晤教，并承款待，厚意隆情，心感无似。前介绍钱存训先生拟印论文，请作函推荐于 Ronald Press，荷蒙惠允，望便中掷下，无任企盼。暑期学校即将结束，想贤伉俪下月即将南返，仍希随时珍摄是幸。专此，敬颂暑祺。

弟袁同礼顿首

八，十六

嫂夫人同此致意。

钱君论文题目：Tsien, Tsuen-Hsuin, The Pre-printing records of China: a study of the development of early Chinese inscriptions and books. 302 l. Thesis Chicago, 1957

〔台北"中央研究院"台湾史研究所，陈受颐文书（副本）〕

八月十七日

郭廷以致函先生。〔《郭量宇先生日记残稿》，页205〕

八月十九日

何炳棣致函先生，告知其访问苏联经过及当地所藏中亚古物、文献概况。

守和先生：

所需俄文中国书目，已托 Iona College（New Rochelle, N. Y.）之 Prof. Ernst Winter（渠能说俄语）在 Moscow 代索，如一时无货，渠将代订。书款已交渠，想不致有误。

在俄一周，连天阴雨，行动不自由，如自旅舍进城，须请 Intourist Service 代雇 taxi，手续麻烦，被敲竹杠尚系次焉者也。

两俄京中文古籍相当缺乏，惟有关中共资料较北美为富。Leningrad 之 Hermitage 有敦煌壁画，Turkestan Collection 极富，铁木耳寝陵 mosaic 大块陈列，玲琅满目。其余中国方面，绘画及陶瓷均远不如英伦也。

书事一有所闻，当自西岸飞函奉告。二三日内即飞返温市。请撰安。

晚炳棣拜

八月十九日

〔University of Chicago Library, Yuan T'ung-li Papers, Box 2〕

按:1960 年,加拿大学术基金会派出一个小型代表团赴莫斯科参加第 25 届国际东方学者大会,William A. C. H. Dobson 和何炳棣等六人前往与会。①

八月二十日

先生致信中基会理事会,申请资助编写《中国留美同学博士论文目录》。

August 20, 1960

Dear Sirs:

In view of the lack of a complete record of doctoral dissertations by Chinese students in the United States and Canada, I have been compiling a check list of these dissertations. A memorandum setting forth the scope and objective of this undertaking is herewith submitted for your reference.

As most of these dissertations are in typescript and housed in the archives of different universities, personal checking is necessary in order to make the record as complete and definite as possible. For travel and research assistance, a sum of $ 1200.00 is needed in order to bring the work to completion.

Serving as a permanent record of China's contribution to science and learning, this bibliographical guide is a tool of reference. In view of its significance, I hope the project will have the necessary support from the Trustees of the Foundation.

Yours Sincerely
T. L. Yuan

〔台北"中央研究院"近代史研究所档案馆,〈中华教育文化基金董事会〉,馆藏号 502-01-09-006,页 119〕

八月二十七日

先生致信钱存训,商借《亚洲学术杂志》《边政公论》两刊,并告知最新影照图书的仪器 Xerox 914 极为便利。

公垂吾兄:

手教拜悉。《亚洲学术杂志》内中多王静庵之著作,购到后望暂

---

① 何炳棣著《读史阅世六十年》,页 315。

借一用,或将每期之目录钞示亦可。重庆《边政公论》V.1-4愿借一用,盼交馆际互借处寄下是盼。敝处有 Xerox 914 Copies,影照之速较 Photostat 方便多多,芝大如尚未添置,可建议租一架(概不出卖),学者需用之资料可用此法录副也。顺候教祺。

弟袁同礼顿首
八,廿七

芝加哥区中国同学及职业同人通讯录,望代觅一份。

〔钱孝文藏札〕

按:《亚洲学术杂志》(*The Journal of The Asiatic Learning Society*)由亚洲学术研究会出版发行,撰稿人多为流寓上海的清末学人,自 1921 年 8 月至 1922 年 8 月共刊发四期,其中王国维署名文章五篇,分别为《西胡考》(第 1 期)、《摩尼教流入中国考》(第 2 期)、《高昌宁朔将军麴斌造寺碑跋》(第 3 期)、《罗君楚传》、《罗君楚妻汪孺人墓碣铭》(第 4 期)。《边政公论》由中国边政学会边政公论社于 1941 年在重庆发行,从第 5 卷第 1 期开始迁至南京出版,改为半年刊,第 6、7 卷为季刊,1949 年停刊,共发行 7 卷。Xerox 914 Copies 即施乐复印机,1959 年 9 月中旬该款机型问世。

八月三十一日

钱存训覆函先生,告知所托诸事办理情况。

守和先生:

奉到八、廿七手教,敬悉一一。重庆《边政公论》四册已交馆际借书部奉上应用,不日想可到达。另有金陵大学出版之《边政研究论丛》二册 1941-4 成都出版,内有边疆问题选目,不知见到否?《亚洲学术什志》如购到,当再奉闻。此间同学通讯录,最近未有新印。专覆,即颂暑祺。

后学存训拜上
八月卅一

〔University of Chicago Library, Yuan T'ung-li Papers, Box 2〕

九月六日

Toshio Kono 覆函先生,商讨有关 *Russian Works on China in American Libraries* 出版费用分担问题。

September 6, 1960

Dear Mr. Yuan:

We received your letter of September 4, 1960, with further reference to your forthcoming bibliography, *Russian Works on China.*

In view of the fact that you are unable to raise the proposed subsidy of $ 650, we would like to suggest that you and the Far Eastern Publications share the publication cost with an equal basis. Although the printing cost has risen slightly since last winter, we are sure that each share will not exceed $ 450.

We would prepare the financial report semi-annually and you would be receiving 50 per cent of NET proceed after deducting 10 per cent shipping charge and 20 per cent trade discount to the bookstores. We had the same arrangement with the Far Eastern Association, and it seems to us the most simple and fair agreement to both parties concerned.

If the above arrangement is satisfactory to you, we would be glad to undertake this project jointly. For typing the final copies for reproduction, we recommend IBM typewriter with carbon paper ribbon to give an even density. We ask you to send us a couple of pages typed in an area of 6×9 so that we can agree on the actual final size before you start typing the whole manuscript.

Sincerely yours,

Toshio Kono

P. S. Despite Mr. Kennedy's unfortunate death, we are carrying on his well-established tradition.

〔Library of Congress, Council on Library and Information Resources Records, Box 95〕

按：Toshio Kono 日名应为高野俊郎，8 月 15 日金守拙在从日本回美国的船上突发心脏病去世，此后 Toshio Kono 接替其负责远东出版中心事务。此为抄件。

九月十二日

先生致信克莱普，告知收到耶鲁大学远东出版中心的回复，此前向图书资源委员会申请出版补助可减为一千美金。

September 12, 1960

Dear Mr. Clapp:

　　With reference to my application for a grant of $ 2000 from your Council, I wish to report that the editorial work on my bibliography of *Russian works on China, 1917-1959* is now completed. In view of its wide scope, it would meet a timely need when it is published.

　　Publication of this work by the Far Eastern Publications of Yale University (which you prefer to the Indiana University Press) is now assured. After having asked the publisher to quote me the lowest cost possible, I received a favorable reply, a copy of which is enclosed herewith for your information.

　　For the cost of the Cyrillic typing and proofreading, an amount of $ 450 will be required. The insertion of Chinese characters will cost another $ 100. It now appears that with a grant of $ 1000 from your Council, this reference tool could be published expeditiously.

　　As this survey is a union catalog of *Russian works on China in American libraries* and as it serves as a useful guide for Russian sources on China, I earnestly hope that this humble request for support may have your early favorable consideration.

Yours sincerely,

T. L. Yuan

　　〔Library of Congress, Council on Library and Information Resources Records, Box 95〕

　　按:*Russian Works on China in American Libraries* 出版时,其涵盖范围为 1918 年至 1960 年,非信中所注 1917 年至 1959 年。Cyrillic 即西里尔字母,又称斯拉夫字母。此件为打字稿,落款处为先生签名,该信于 14 日送达。

胡适致函先生,告知中基会已经批准 1200 美金用以资助先生编纂《中国留美同学博士论文目录》。

Sept. 12, 1960

Dear Mr. Yuan:

I have the pleasure to inform you that the China Foundation at the 31st Annual Meeting held on Sept. 2, 1960 has considered your application of August 20, 1960 and has decided to grant you a sum of $ 1,200 for the compilation of a record and a check list of doctoral dissertations by Chinese students in the United States and Canada from 1905 to 1960.

The grant will be paid in April 1961.

Yours sincerely,

Hu Shih

Director

〔University of Chicago Library, Yuan T'ung-li Papers, Box 1〕

按:此件为打字稿,落款处为其签名。

九月十三日

先生致信叶良才,请其提供曾受中基会帮助获博士学位的人员名单。

September 13, 1960

Dear Mr. Yip:

I am fully aware of the heavy responsibilities in my compilation of the GUIDE TO DOCTORAL DISSERTATIONS. In order to avoid any possible omission, I should like to have a list of CF fellows who received their doctor's degree with the aid of the foundation. There is no need for rush for such a list which will be needed in final checking. Please put down Chinese characters, if possible.

As I expect to visit a number of libraries soon, I wonder if I may expect to receive a part of the grant.

I enclose herewith a photostat for Dr. Hu. When you see him, will you do me the favor of asking him if he happens to know the Chinese name of Dr. Yen Chin-yung, the first Chinese who received his doctor's degree from Columbia. Will you ask Dr. Chiang if you see him one of these days?

Yours sincerely,

T. L. Yuan

〔台北胡适纪念馆，档案编号 HS-NK05-062-008〕

按：Dr. Yen Chin-yung 即严锦荣，广东人，1905 年获哥伦比亚大学博士学位，论文题为 Rights of Citizens and Persons under the Fourteenth Amendment。此件为打字稿，落款处为先生签名，该信于翌日送达。

九月十七日

胡适致函先生，谈其留在北平的旧藏《水经注》版本。

守和兄：

谢谢你寄示 photostat 一页。此页上没有我的藏本。我的三柜水经注可能仍在北大图书馆，或仍在有三家。

此页上有：

①沅叔家的残宋本　残存十一卷（此目作十二卷）

②沅叔家的孙潜校录赵琦美与柳佥校本（但此目上没有指出柳佥校本）　残存十六卷（袁廷梼校）

这都是我校过的。

但此页又有四个"明抄本"，似值得注意：

①明抄本　何焯、顾广圻校，袁廷梼跋，此即袁氏用来校孙潜本的明钞本。

②明抄本　王国维、章炳麟跋，此本可能是王静庵校过的朱逖先家藏本？我曾校过，并写了长跋。（逖先的儿子伯商未出来。他的女儿曾说此本在她手里，不在大陆。）

③明抄本　"周捐"（一良之父）。

④明抄本。

你问的 Yen Chin-yung，我不知道。我到美国已是 1910 年，故不认得此人。可试问郭秉文先生。

敬祝双安。

适之

一九六○，九，十七夜

（乙二）永乐大典影印本

（辛四）王梓材重录本（张约园藏）

（辛六）薛刻"全校本"（初刻校改本）

（壬二）戴震自定水经一卷

（壬三）戴震自定水经一卷（北大圕藏）

此目中之（乙二）有过录宋本,似应保存。若能邮寄来,最好。（只寄有过录宋本的各卷,以减重量。）此目可否寄二三十册? 北大展览水经各本之中,

（辛四）似尚在思杜手中,可取出交还上海张芝联先生。

（辛六）原十二册,其上有过录"五校本"全文,其中 2-11 册,臧晖带出了。尚余①⑫两册,因在展览,未取出,似尚在思杜处。可付邮寄,或协和医生带来。

（壬二）如在北大馆,可否寄来?（薄薄一小册）

（壬三）能否影钞一本寄来?（同上）

东潜诗稿钞本四册,可否寄来?

〔University of Chicago Library, Yuan T'ung-li Papers, Box 7〕

按:该档胡适信片均为散页,且亦未标注页码顺序,信末补语布排谨参据《胡适中文书信集》。

九月十九日

梅贻宝覆函先生,告知在爱荷华州立大学询问华人有关留学生中文姓名的结果。

September 19,1960

Dear T. L.

Thank you for your kind note of September 12 and the assuring news concerning Y. C. 五嫂不断有信。

I had an opportunity to consult Chu-tsing Li, who is the oldest resident member on the SUI campus, about your list. Even he could help out only with the Chinese name of one of the people on the list. I did not know what to do about the rest of them.

I know that President Yen 阎 of the Cheng Ku Engineering University at Taiwan was a Ph. D. graduate of SUI of some years back. Possibly he might be able to supply the Chinese names of some of the other people.

I remember very warmly the evening spent with you and Mrs. Yuan at the delicious dinner and with such fine company in your home in Washington.

With best wishes,

Sincerely yours,

Y. P. Mei

〔University of Chicago Library, Yuan T'ung-li Papers, Box 5〕

按:"五嫂"即梅贻琦夫人韩咏华;President Yen 即阎振兴(1912—2005),1957 年 8 月担任台湾省立成功大学校长。SUI 即 State University of Iowa,Cheng Ku Engineering University 即成功大学。此件为打字稿,落款和信中汉字均为其亲笔。

九月二十日

柳无忌致函先生,告知匹兹堡大学图书馆中文馆藏近况,并请先生寄送国会图书馆分类表中有关中国语言与文学部分以利编目。

September 20, 1960

Dear Dr. Yuan:

It has been quite a few months since I had the pleasure of visiting you and enjoying your hospitality. It was certainly a most delightful evening that I had at your house.

Since then, we have been busily engaged in selling the house in New Haven, packing, moving, and getting adjusted to the new environment in Pittsburgh. I have gone back to teaching and my wife is also working at the library here. Very soon, she will start cataloguing the Chinese books that we have been buying for the University Library. We hope to build up a modest collection for undergraduate use and for faculty research.

As the Chinese collection will start from scratch, we feel we should be able to do a good job with some planning and to learn from past experiences. One thing we have decided to do is to follow the LC system. By thus availing ourselves of the facilities offered by LC, it is figured we could save considerable time, effort, and money. Even then, some cataloguing would have to be done here and my wife is very anxious to get a copy of the "PL" Schedule of Classification for Chinese Language and Literature. We would be grateful if you could kindly locate one and send it to me. If it is for sale, please also let me have the bill so that the University will pay for it. Thanks a lot.

The Pitt Library, as of now, is very much crammed up in three stories in the Cathedral of Learning. The space and facilities are not adequate and the working conditions poor. But we are looking forward to the time when a new 10 million dollar library—now in the blueprint stage—will be built and the Chinese collection properly housed.

This year we have a fairly good Far Eastern Program on the undergraduate level. At present, there are 12 courses connected with the Chinese Language and Area Center with a total enrollment of 101 students in these courses and 17 of them studying the Chinese Language. I enclose here a brochure just put out for publicity by the University.

My wife joins me in sending our best regards to you and Mrs. Yuan.

Sincerely yours,

Wu-chi Liu

〔University of Chicago Library, Yuan T'ung-li Papers, Box 3〕

按："PL" Schedule of Classification for Chinese Language and Literature 指国会图书馆分类表中针对中文语言与文学的部分,其具体编号范围为 PL1001-PL3208。此件为打字稿,落款处为其签名。

九月二十五日

先生致信胡适,告知正努力获取平馆所藏《水经注》版本目录,并请其寄下所获名誉博士清单。

适之先生:

赐书敬悉。尊藏水经注多种,既未列入馆目,想仍在有三处,前向渠索取水经注展览目录,迄未寄到。近又托吴世昌君以牛津名义代索一份,不识能如愿否? 大驾即将返台,未能到纽送行,至以为怅。此次赖各董事赞助,拙编可以早日出版,感谢无似。书后有一附录,注明我国学者名誉博士之授与大学及年月,因念先生所得学位,在我国史上为第一人,拟请列表赐下包括香港、牛津,以便汇编,如不记得年月,则仅列大学名称,当再向其函询,至盼早日寄下,不胜企盼。敬候双安!

　　　　　　　　　　　　　　　　　　　同礼顿首

　　　　　　　　　　　　　　　　　　　九,廿五

〔台北胡适纪念馆,档案编号 HS-NK05-062-009〕

按:吴世昌(1908—1986),字子臧,浙江海宁人,历史学家、《红楼梦》研究者,时在英国牛津大学等处任博士学位考试委员。

九月二十八日

叶良才覆函先生,已将十三日信录副并转寄胡适、蒋梦麟,请寄下《西文汉学书目》,另请留意中国政治学会的章程、细则等册页。

Sept. 28, 1960

Dear Dr. Yuan:

　　With reference to your letter of Sept. 13, 1960, I have made copies and sent them to Dr. Hu Shih and Dr. Chiang Monlin. I have asked them to inform you directly if they know of the Chinese name of Dr. Yen Chin-yung. I have not seen Dr. Chiang Monlin lately. He has been very busy with the UN meetings.

　　The Foundation should like to have on file 2 to 3 copies of your work on the *Supplement to Bibliotheca Sinica*. If you do not have that many copies, please send us at least one.

　　Will you be able to find in any place the constitution and by-laws of the Chinese Social & Political Science Association and other material relating to the Association's institution or organization? Please let us know. We are still interested to find out the possibility of its reactivation. Thank you.

　　　　　　　　　　　　　　　　　　Yours sincerely,

　　　　　　　　　　　　　　　　　　L. T. Yip

〔University of Chicago Library, Yuan T'ung-li Papers, Box 1〕

按:此件为打字稿,落款处为其签名。

九月二十九日

郑德坤覆函先生,告索取中国学者获剑桥大学名誉博士信息的方法。

守和先生赐鉴：

　　九月廿六日大教敬悉。剑桥大学赠予名誉博士与我国学者人数、姓名，据云须番查旧档，倘能正式直接函 Mr. R. M. Rattenbury, Registry, The Old Schools, Cambridge, England 询查，当可照办。我国留英同学会，久无来往，手中亦无历年留学名录，不克应命，至为抱歉。令媛来牛津研究化学，假期中如得来剑桥一游，务请约其光临舍下一叙为快。敝舍小名"木扉"，是以拙藏名 Mu-Fei Collection。拙作承过誉，不胜惭愧，厚爱鼓励，感激万分，尤冀时与指教为盼为荷。专此奉覆，并颂撰祺。

弟德坤再拜

九月廿九日

　　　　〔University of Chicago Library, Yuan T'ung-li Papers, Box 5〕

　　按："番查"似当作"翻查"。"拙作"应为 *Archæology in China*，此处似指 1959 年剑桥 W. Heffer & Sons Ltd. 印行的第一卷 Prehistoric China（史前中国）。

是年秋

先生将胡适在西雅图华盛顿大学召开的"中美文化合作会议"上所作"中国的传统与将来"（The Chinese Tradition and the Future）演讲的单行本送给恒慕义。〔台北胡适纪念馆，HS-NK05-152-044〕

　　按：10 月 10 日，恒慕义致信胡适表示感谢。

十月四日

吴世昌覆函先生，告其已联系赵万里索要《北京大学五十周年纪念展览目录》，并谈可以查得牛津大学授予名誉博士学位的相关资料书籍。

守和先生有道：

　　从学院转到九月廿五日来教，敬悉。承嘱向国内索寄《北大五十周年纪念展览目录》，晚因与王友三先生素不相识，故已函托斐云兄代觅，俟得复即行奉告。此间图书馆常与北京图书馆交换出版物，原无困难，惟过去经验，只能换到新出版书籍，绝版书较为困难，实因国内一般文化及社会教育大量提高，书籍供不应求，又各地遍设图书馆，即寻常视为冷僻书籍，亦被庋藏。前年北大副校长周培源兄来此，据谈一九五六年北京一地投考中文系者二万余人，只能每百人中取一人，

以视过去青年视中文系为"老古董"者大不相同。关于牛津历来赠与学者博士学位之名单,可在下列书中查得:

1. The Historical Register of the University of Oxford up to 1900

2. idem supplement 1901-1930

3. idem supplement 1931-1950

以上三书均由大学注册课编,Oxford University Press, at the Clarendon Press 出版,想美国大图书馆中均有,如欲问询,可向注册主任函询。至于中国留英学生名单,晚素无所知,大概即学生本人亦只知同时同学且未必有全单。前四年有台湾学生二人在曼彻斯城,但其来英前经五家铺保,不许与在英其他中国学生接触,否则五家连坐,去年此间亦有一研究生(闻已在台湾任医学教授),亦避不与华人接触,其他学生多为香港及新加坡马来籍,多在伦敦,故亦不常见面。

女公子来牛津,深为欢迎,想不日可到。澄兄近况如何,至念。

尚此,即颂祺。

晚吴世昌上

十月四日

〔University of Chicago Library, Yuan T'ung-li Papers, Box 6〕

按:《北大五十周年纪念展览目录》似指《北京大学五十周年纪念:水经注版本展览目录》,此册应为胡适代索。时吴世昌通讯地址为 16 Banbury Road, Oxford, U. K.。

十月七日

朱文长致函先生,请代为在国会图书馆搜集其父朱经农的专著和文章。

守和老伯:

自年前在纽约匆匆拜见后,忽又数年。遥想起居顺遂,为颂为祝!

明年三月九日将为先君经农先生逝世十周年纪念。世侄有意将先君遗著及传记材料搜集成书,即使一时无力出版,亦可免于继续散失。然手头材料不多,故不能不向各方搜集。国会图书馆方面,自必有不少材料,然世侄职务羁身,无法前来,不知可否烦渎老伯,代为留意?目前世侄特别需要者,有下列诸件,可否乞代查,国会图书馆有否?

1.民国三十一年左右,湖南耒阳出版,湖南省教育厅编:朱经农先生主持《湖南省教育十周年纪念刊》。（书名或少有出入。）

2.湖南教育厅自民二十一年至三十二年间各种出版物。

3.先父各项遗著之成书者。（此间已有①《教育大辞书》，②《明日之学校》，③《教育思想》三书，其他则尚缺。）

4.尊处不知有何种报纸杂志索引，可以用以寻觅散处于各杂志中之论文者。（尤其需要关于①《教育杂志》已有；②《东方杂志》民十以后；③《独立评论》；④民十三至十六年间之《申报》；⑤民廿年至廿六年之《大公报》；⑥民十七至十九年，民三十二至三十八年间之《中央日报》；⑦民十六年至十九年，民三十四至三十七年间之《教育部公报》，不知国会图书馆均有否？）

此事不急，老伯如无暇，不妨搁置，因此种事殊为琐细，只因无他人可托，故来烦渎老伯，尚乞宥之。肃此，即颂教安！

世侄朱文长敬上
十月七日

〔University of Chicago Library, Yuan T'ung-li Papers, Box 2〕

十月十日

格雷夫斯致函先生，告知此前在医院接受腹部手术，已向 Fred Burkhardt 写信推荐出版*Russian Works on China, 1918-1960 in American Libraries*。

760 Main St.

W. Newbury-Mass

October 10, 1960

Dear Dr. Yuan

You have not heard from me because I have been ill. The illness culminated in a serious abdominal operation three weeks ago. I returned from the hospital yesterday, and recuperating very rapidly and well, but I am still terribly weak and confined to my room and immediately contiguous areas (happily including my study) for some time to come.

I have written a recommendation to Fred Burkhardt, expressing the hope that their bibliography can be published and then made the basis for program of translating some of the major works.

Mortimer Graves

〔University of Chicago Library, Yuan T'ung-li Papers, Box 1〕

按：Fred Burkhardt 即 Frederick H. Burkhardt（1913–2007），美国学者，1933 年获得哥伦比亚大学哲学学士，1940 年获得博士学位，1955 年担任美国学术团体理事会主席，1974 年退休，对该理事会人文组研究项目颇多支持。该函为格雷夫斯亲笔。

十月十一日

胡适致函先生，告所获名誉博士，并述博士学位因何晚十年获得。

守和兄：

我本月十四日起飞了。十六日到台北。

承问及我的名誉学位，匆匆不及细答了，请你查"*Who's Who in America*" Vol.27（1952–53）, p. 1218, under "Hu-shih"，那似是我依据大使馆时代保留的材料，稍加补充，故有 1935 至 1950 的名誉学位。此表是依学位性质为次序，如"文学博士 LiH. D."下，分记 Harvard (1936); McGill (1941); Dartmouth College (1942), Denison U. (1942), University of the State of New York (1942), Bucknell (1943), Colgate (1949)，共七校。"人文学博士 L. H. D."下，分记二校。"法律博士 L. L. D"下，分记廿一校。"民法博士 D. C. L."下，分记二校。以上共三十二。应加 Litt.D. Univ. of Hawaii 1959，总共三十三。大致似没有遗漏了。

又我的 Ph. D.论文考试是 1917 年完毕的，故我列在 1917；但当时规矩需要一百本印本论文，故我在 1917 年回国时没有拿 Ph. D 文凭。我的论文是 1922 年在上海印行的，我没有工夫送一百本给哥大，直到五年后，一九二七年我在哥大讲学，他们催我补缴论文印本百册，我才电告亚东图书馆寄百册去。我的文凭是 1927 年发的。

我多年没有留意名誉学位问题，偶有人问我，我总记不清。承你一问，我才检 *Who's Who*，才知道清楚。谢谢你的一问。

别了，敬祝珍重！并祝府上都平安！

弟适之

一九六十，十，十一

〔University of Chicago Library, Yuan T'ung-li Papers, Box 7〕

十月二十一日

先生致信胡适,就国会图书馆赠送平馆善本缩微胶片与"中央研究院",请致谢函。

适之先生:

前奉赐书,承示名誉学位之接受与前此搜集之资料,多出Claremont及Hawaii两处,感谢感谢。返台以后,诸事待理,尚希节劳保重为祷。国会图书馆前赠之平馆善本书胶片全套,迄未接到先生谢信。在馆方以价值关系约九千美元颇盼早得谢函,以资结束,尚希提前办理,不胜企荷(谢函可径寄Dr. L. Quincy Mumford, Librarian of Congress)。上海近印《丛书综录》共三册,其第一册业已出版,与《地方志综录》于两旬以前交邮径寄南港,即希惠存。二、三两册一俟出版,当再续寄。专此,敬候道祺。

同礼拜上

十月廿一日

〔台北胡适纪念馆,档案编号HS-NK05-062-010〕

按:该信于10月27日送抵台北。

十一月初

先生与傅冠雄晤谈。

十一月四日

先生致信钱存训,谈其论文出版事宜,并请查询留学生中文姓名。

公垂吾兄:

关于论文印行事,前请陈受颐先生写一介绍信,迄未寄到。想托其他学者写信亦可发生效力,敝意不如请Creel写信,出版家亦必接受也。如愿在英出版更觉容易,因排印人工费较廉且印刷亦精,可先从芝大出版部入手,如不肯印行,则托Prof. Simon在伦敦进行,亦是一法。又许卓云先生之兄是否为许织云,St. Louis华大毕业。兹有该校同学数人之中文姓名,除许君外恐无他人知之者,奉上一单,请托许先生向其老兄一询,示复为感。弟数日以后将到Mich. Ill.各校搜查资料,路过芝城当再趋谈。顺颂俪安。

弟同礼顿首

十一,四日

〔钱孝文藏札〕

按：许织云（1915—2014），浙江温州人，非许卓云之兄，燕京大学
主修生物，后于 1948 年毕业于圣路易斯华盛顿大学，其博士论文
题目为 Influence of Temperature on Developments of Rat Embryos，
参见《中国留美同学博士论文目录》第 120 页。

十一月五日

徐家璧覆函先生，告熊叔隆、庄竹林二人履历。

> 守和先生尊鉴：
>
> 敬肃者，昨奉月之一日手谕，诵悉一是。南洋大学图书馆主任熊
> 叔隆先生确已在哥大圕院研究，前仅于该院学员团体参观时晤过一
> 面，并未得机会长谈。嗣因我公嘱托，乃于日昨约彼便餐，除谈叙一般
> 情形外，并询得彼系于一九三八年在康奈尔大学（Cornell）得哲学博士
> （科目化学），毕业回国后曾在岭南大学教学，一九四九年后曾协助庄
> 泽宣先生在槟榔屿办中学，庄离后彼接任校长，继于一九五六年就南
> 大化学教授职，前年改任圕主任，现已不授化学矣。彼此来为期一年，
> 因时间限制关系恐不克攻学位，拟除上课听讲外，多注重实习与参观
> 工作。华府方面定于圣诞节假期中前来观摩，届时自当面谒先生，请
> 示种切。至于庄竹林先生，据告则系密西根哲学博士，年份及科目暂
> 时未能详询，至希本此消息能将各人之论文题目查获也。哥大举办之
> 中央亚细亚文物展览，俟其开幕后，当觅其展览目录寄上不误。余容
> 续奉。敬叩崇安！
>
> 晚徐家璧鞠躬
> 十一月五日夜
>
> 尊夫人暨阖府统乞叱名代为候安为感！

[University of Chicago Library, Yuan T'ung-li Papers, Box 7]

按：熊叔隆，广东人，1958 年专任南洋大学图书馆主任。[1] 庄泽宣
（1895—1976），浙江嘉兴人，1917 年清华学校毕业，旋以庚款留
学生身份赴美专攻教育学及心理学，获哥伦比亚大学教育学硕
士、哲学博士学位。庄竹林（1900—1973），福建惠安人，1925 年
福州协和大学毕业，后赴美留学，1933 年获密歇根大学博士，其

---

① 《南洋大学创校十周年纪念特刊》，1966 年，页 135。

论文题名为 Municipal home rule in Michigan。

十一月六日

刘国蒏致函先生,告知其身体近来两次患病,并谈最近代购大陆书刊之困难。

守和博士先生尊鉴:

敬启者,未修书敬候,又已月余,引领慈云,倍深瞻仰,恭维著述丰宏,履躬清胜,至以为颂。上月时,小儿媳拜领惠赠银器两事,高谊隆情,殊深感铭。经已着其修函敬谢,量邀尊览。月前曾奉上芜笺,想能奉达,惟许久未蒙赐示,时在念中。令岳父大人亦许久未有来信代转,系念殊深。晚近月来时运不齐,左脚生一血疮,颇为痛苦,待其好得七八时,左眼尾又一火钉疮,更为辛苦,延医诊治,现已渐全愈矣。日前曾到万有图书公司坐谈,闻先生嘱托其代购书籍,想当可办妥。现时在港购大陆出版各书籍颇为艰难,因到港数量少不足分配,尤以各杂志为甚,多种不发海外,十分难做也。奉上《新闻天地》及《天文台》等,想邀尊鉴。前函曾奉闻支长港银十五元,连九月十月及十一月份《天文台》共九元,即共支长廿四元也,时乎不再!圣诞节快来临,晚由包裹邮敬奉上龙井青茶两罐、贺简成函,敬希笑纳,区区微意,礼不成敬意。港中各样如常,工商业仍甚兴盛,尊处已届大选时期,情形当热闹紧张也。专此,敬请大安。

愚晚国蒏顿首

一九六〇年十一月六日早

〔University of Chicago Library, Yuan T'ung-li Papers, Box 7〕

十一月七日

先生致信 Heinrich Busch,寄上 Russian Works on Japan: a selected bibliography 人名索引,并告此前稿件的两处错误请其协助订正,另表示愿意承担额外抽印本的费用。

November 7, 1960

Father H. Busch, Editor

MONUMENTA SERICA

Nanzan University

Nagoya, Japan.

Dear Father Busch:

Sometime ago you were very kind to promise my article on Russian Works on Japan. I should have submitted it to you much earlier, but owing to heavy pressure of other duties, I was not able to send the manuscript to you until a week ago. Dr. Loewenthal was kind enough to look it over and made constructive suggestions.

In view of the late delivery of the manuscript, I hope I have not caused you any inconvenience. It would be quite agreeable to me if you could print it in smaller type and make the lines closer together. In this way, it would not take too much of your space for the forthcoming issue.

I am sending you herewith the Index. On the main text there are two corrections to be made. I list them below:

Item no. 4, Bellesort, Andre, line 3

"S. P. Burg" should be changed to S. -Peterburg.

Item no. 112, Ishii, Kikujiro, line 1

The date of his death －1945－should be inserted.

I hope I may have an opportunity to read the last proof. I should be glad to pay for extra copies of the offprints. In this case, only 40 copies extra will be needed.

Thank you once more for your kindness,

Yours sincerely,

Yuan Tung-li

〔University of Chicago Library, Yuan T'ung-li Papers, Box 7〕

按：该信提及的两处错误均得以订正。

十一月二十一日

罗家伦致函先生,告已向先生在台亲戚转交"国史馆"办公费,并谈在台代购故宫博物院出版品等事。

守和吾兄道鉴:

在美聆教,至深欣感！返台以来,因较忙碌,致稽函候,无任歉仄！承嘱办之事:(一)派人送交袁仲默夫人新台币伍佰元,已于昨日送到,附上名片收据一张;(二)《故宫名画三百种》此间售价为新台币陆仟元，经商洽照批发价九折计算，另加包装及邮费叁佰元，共计伍仟柒佰元，吾兄如决定照购，即请见示，以便遵办。书款可不必寄来，即在吾兄征集费项下代付可也。兹附奉本年七月至十二月空白收据六张，请加盖印章后寄下为感。专此，敬颂道祺！

弟罗家伦敬启
十一，二一

嫂夫人前候安致谢！

　　再者 National Archives 所影印之外交人员报告，即前次参观时彼方负责人指以告我们者，尚请随时注意。因我们正从事"开国实录"及"开国五十年纪念册"（后者于明年双十出版），其中或有材料可参考引用也。其他见闻亦乞惠告。

弟伦再拜

〔University of Chicago Library, Yuan T'ung-li Papers, Box 1〕

　　按：袁仲默，浙江桐庐人，袁昶之子，与先生岳父袁道冲为昆仲，其夫人名待考。《故宫名画三百种》由"国立故宫博物院"、"国立中央博物院"编印，1959 年 5 月初版，日本大塚巧艺社珂罗版印刷，限量 1500 部。该函为文书代笔，落款、补语则为罗家伦亲笔。

十一月二十五日

先生致信钱存训，告知行踪，并奉还美金拾元。

公垂吾兄大鉴：

　　在芝城匆匆一聚，未能多留，至以为怅，别后在 Lansing、Ann Arbor、Detroit 诸城获到不少资料。今日在 Rochester 访晤蒋硕杰诸兄，日内即返华京。承借拾元，兹随函奉上，即乞察收，至谢至谢。匆匆，顺颂俪安。

弟同礼顿首
十一，廿五

〔钱孝文藏札〕

十一月二十六日

傅冠雄致函先生，转顾维钧支票一纸，并代达谢意。

守和吾兄学长左右：

　　月初叙谈为快，谈后曾由纯孺兄函告顾少公。日前接少公来函，对吾兄慨允协助编辑资料,深为欣感。寄来支票一纸(一百元),嘱转上,作雇员打字及应用纸张、文具等费。原票奉转,请查收备用为荷。纯使处亦已告之。专此,诸容晤谈,敬颂著安,并祝嫂夫人安好。

弟冠雄拜上

十一,廿六

少公并命即购大著一部,已由弟径函耶鲁订购矣。

〔University of Chicago Library, Yuan T'ung-li Papers, Box 1〕

按:"大著"应指 *China in Western Literature*。

十一月三十日

先生撰写《新疆研究文献目录》研究计划的阶段报告,涵盖八月一日至本日的工作内容,分为检查已有书目和索引、查阅十二家图书馆所藏相关专著、对俄文专著的题名转译三部分。〔University of Chicago Library, Yuan T'ung-li Papers, Box 1〕

十二月二日

先生致信卫德明,寄上《新疆研究文献目录》研究计划的阶段报告,并请 Ekvall 寄送有关新疆的书目卡片。

December 2, 1960

Dear Professor Wilhelm:

When I was in Seattle, I proposed that in order to keep you informed about the progress of my work on Sinkiang, I should send you a report every four months.

Herewith please find the report ending November 30. Mr. Ekvall may like to see it also.

Mr. Ekvall told me that there is a file of cards on Sinkiang left by a member of your staff. Although he thought I have had most of the titles, it might be useful to check it once more. He promised to mail these cards to me, but I have not yet received them. When you see him, will you be good enough to remind him again?

With cordial regards,

Yours sincerely,

T. L. Yuan

〔University of Chicago Library, Yuan T'ung-li Papers, Box 1〕

按：此件为副本，附一页英文报告。

十二月五日

刘国蓁覆函先生，告知收到汇款单，并谈代购中文书刊及莲子等事。

守和博士先生尊鉴：

敬启者，未修书敬候又已一月，晦明风雨，企念时殷。恭维撰祉延鸿，文祺纳燕，至以为颂。上月廿六日，拜奉廿二日手教敬悉，附汇单十五美元一张，亦已收妥。贱体经已恢复健康，请释锦注，不遗在远，殊深感幸。晚依然故我，乏善可陈，仍是一样工作，并无半点懒惰。虽然娶媳妇及各子侄皆有事做，但帮助家计甚少，他等亦要动用及储蓄也。晚为芝大购藏中文书籍经有十年之久，但无如现在之困难情形者，因大陆所到港书籍数量不多，货到即抢购，续到要候许久时日，颇为难做也。尊款找得港银八十五元〇五分（五六七算），除支长廿四元及遵嘱代购新上市莲子一斤十二两（本拟购一斤，但包裹邮最低限度是三磅计，故凑足重量）四元二角（二元四角一斤），邮费六元半（不足三磅亦须此数），共支卅四元七角，比对尚存五十元〇三角五分。本月份《天文台》周报已如命停寄，《新闻天地》周报则待明年一月尾交款续订。晚寄莲子包裹时，报关纸系填明该名，并注明是圣诞礼物，不写价值，未知美国海关准许入口否？想在圣诞节及新年当可放宽也。晚前寄过糯米粉与纽约友人，亦不准入口，检查后将该件退回，并要付邮费，颇为麻烦也。如得收后，请示知以慰远望为幸。专此，敬请台安。

愚晚国蓁顿首

一九六〇十二月五日

〔University of Chicago Library, Yuan T'ung-li Papers, Box 7〕

十二月十二日

先生致信加斯基尔，请给予更长的馆际互借时间，并询问可否受邀前往其新馆开馆仪式。

December 12, 1960

Dear Miss Gaskell:

In September I borrowed, through inter-library loan arrangements, a copy of your "*Manuscripts and Printed Editions of Marco Polo's Travels*" by Shinobu Iwamura. I need this brochure in connection with my bibliography on Marco Polo.

Owing to the pressure of official duties, I have not had much time to study this book in detail. May I therefore request for the privilege of keeping it a few weeks longer. But if there is a call for it among your readers, I shall send it on right away.

I presume that you must be very busy in preparing to move into the new building. Be sure to send me an invitation with a covering letter, so that I could attend the opening and obtain "official leave".

With Season's greetings,

Yours sincerely,

T. L. Yuan

〔Cornell University Library, Wason Collection Records, 1918-1988, Box 1, Folder Koo, T. K. Letters〕

按：信中*Manuscripts and Printed Editions of Marco Polo's Travels*旁有标注"Wason 28703 I93"，应为加斯基尔注明，即华生特藏的目录编号；Shinobu Iwamura 即岩村忍（1905-1988），日本历史学家，1949 年日本国会图书馆（National Diet Library）出版*Manuscripts and Printed Editions of Marco Polo's Travels*。此件为打字稿，落款处为先生签名。

十二月十五日

李济（台北）致函先生，请为重刊《明实录》撰写题跋。

守和我兄有道：

暑中别后，弟即兼程返国，已于九月初抵台，一切称顺，请释锦注。兹有请者，孟真先生长本所时，即开始校勘《明实录》，所用底本系假北平图书馆所藏钞本晒蓝者，去岁本所收到适之先生转来国会图书馆赠送院方影印北平图书馆运存该馆善本书胶片全部，至足珍贵，其中《明实录》部份，尤有助于本所进行有年之校勘工作。按本所研究计划中，原列有重刊《明实录》一项，兹以该书校勘竣事，拟即据上述胶片照相制版，重为刊行，末并附有本所编订之校勘记，以广流传。吾兄对于图书之流传，素极热心，此事谅荷赞助，如蒙惠赐题跋，俾光篇幅，尤所企幸。专此,敬请旅安。

弟李济敬启
十二月十五日

〔University of Chicago Library, Yuan T'ung-li Papers, Box 2〕

按:此函为他人代笔,落款处钤李济名章。

十二月十六日

卫德明覆函先生,告所需卡片须与研究中心李方桂、Nicholas Poppe 等教授商洽后才能决定是否给予。

16 December 1960

Dear Mr. Yuan:

Thank you very much for your note and your report of December 2. All of us here appreciate very much your courtesy in keeping us informed on the progress of your work. Your question concerning a bibliographic file on Sinkiang done by the Inner Asia Project I have referred to Professors Li and Poppe who now jointly chair the Inner Asia Project.

Very sincerely yours,
Hellmut Wilhelm

〔University of Chicago Library, Yuan T'ung-li Papers, Box 1〕

按:Professors Li and Poppe 分别指李方桂和 Nicholas Poppe (1897-1991),后者通译为尼古拉斯·鲍培,在烟台出生,德裔苏联东方学家,1949 年移居美国,美国蒙古学研究奠基人之一,也是阿尔泰语系的研究专家。此件为打字稿,落款处为其签名。

十二月十七日

先生致信钱存训,请在该校图书馆检出《留德学生年报》交馆际互借寄送,并询问芝加哥地区留美学生同学录是否刊行。

公垂吾兄:

前在芝加哥大学图书馆卡片上见有《留德学生年报》,主编人似为魏宸组,以限于时间未能提出一观,拟请便中在 Wei, Tsen-tzu 或 Chen-tzu 名下将该刊提出,交馆际互借部径寄国会馆住址见后转交,以快先睹,此刊未在他馆见到也。此托,顺颂时祉。

弟袁同礼顿首

十二,十七

本年油印之芝城同学录如已出版,亦望代索一份,上年者甚有用也。

〔钱孝文藏札〕

按:魏宸组(1885—1942),字注东,湖北江夏人,清末革命人士、外交家,1903年赴比利时留学,后参加同盟会,民国后历任南京临时政府内阁外交部次长,唐绍仪内阁的国务院秘书长,驻荷兰、比利时公使等职务。

十二月二十一日

先生致信顾维钧,告知将寄送当代中国史料的影照件,并询问其所获荣誉博士学位情况。

December 21, 1960

My dear Dr. Koo:

Mr. K. H. Fu recently forwarded to me a check for $100 in connection with the reproduction of documents relating to your work in China in the twenties. I have already made a number of photostats and shall show them to "Ambassador King" and Mr. Fu before forwarding them to you. I shall send them to you in one shipment with a table of contents—an arrangement which would meet with your approval.

In my bibliography of doctoral dissertations, I shall include an appendix indicating the number of honorary degrees conferred upon Chinese scholars by Chinese and foreign universities. Although I know roughly the honorary degrees which you have received, I should like to insert the exact year in which these degrees were conferred upon you. I shall therefore greatly appreciate any information which you may give to me.

With sincere greetings of the season,

Yours sincerely,

T. L. Yuan

〔University of Chicago Library, Yuan T'ung-li Papers, Box 1〕

按：此件为录副。

十二月二十八日

顾维钧覆函先生，表示其在北洋政府时期担任驻外公使的文件，因存放天津故居恐已不存，并列其所获名誉博士学位。

150 Cremerweg

The Hague, Holland.

Dec. 28, 1960

Dear Dr. Yuan:

Thank you for your Christmas card and your letter & the 21st list. I am looking forward to seeing the photostat of the documents relating to my work in China.

Speaking of the documents and data about my work, I regret very much that those relating to my tenure as Chinese Minister 1915－20 in Washington and my personal interviews during the Paris conference were left in my Tientsin house in China. According to some reports, they have been burned by my guest tenant. I still hope these reports are not true.

As to the years during which I was conferred honorary degrees, I have filled them in the list you sent me. I have put a question mark after St. John's 1922, since there is a strong possibility that the honorary degree was actually conferred on me in <u>absentia</u> after the Paris Peace Conference in 1919－20 along with Dr. Alfred Sze, another St. John's alumnus and a plenipotentiary at the same conference, though I recall clearly, that upon my return to Shanghai after the Washington conference, I was given a special welcome at St. John's.

L. L. D. Yale, 1916

.. Columbia, 1917

.. St. John's, 1922(?)

.. Aberdeen, 1943

.. Birmingham, 1944

.. Manchester, 1944

L. H. D. Rollins, 1947

〔University of Chicago Library, Yuan T'ung-li Papers, Box 1〕

按:1919 年 11 月 15 日,圣约翰大学举行 40 年校庆纪念活动,顾维钧和施肇基均被授予名誉博士学位。① 该函为顾维钧亲笔,信尾所附获得名誉博士学位的时间与实际情况略有出入,如 Birmingham 应为 1942 年,Manchester 应为 1946 年。

十二月底

先生致信郭廷以,嘱代为查询华盛顿会议文件。〔《郭量宇先生日记残稿》,页 237〕

按:此信于翌年 1 月 4 日送达。

是年冬

《华裔学志》刊登先生文章,题为 Russian Works on Japan: a selected bibliography。〔*Monumenta Serica*, vol. 19, 1960, pp. 403-436〕

按:该卷实际印行时间似在 1961 年春,暂依其标注系在 1960 年。

---

① "Anniversary of St. John's University: fortieth birthday." *The North-China Herald and Supreme Court & Consular Gazette* (1870-1941), Nov. 22, 1919, p. 497.